TEXTBOOK ON

CONSUMER LAW

David Oughton,
Professor of Commercial Law,
De Montfort University, Leicester

and

John Lowry,
Associate Director, Centre for Consumer and
Commercial Law Research, Brunel University

BLACKSTONE
PRESS LIMITED

First published in Great Britain 1997 by Blackstone Press Limited,
9-15 Aldine Street, London W12 8AW. Telephone 0181-740 2277

© D. Oughton, J. Lowry, 1997

ISBN: 1 85431 538 2

British Library Cataloguing in Publication Data
A CIP catalogue record for this book is available from the British Library.

Typeset by Style Photosetting Ltd, Mayfield, East Sussex
Printed by Ashford Colour Press, Gosport, Hampshire

Contents

1 PERSPECTIVES 1

1.1 Who is a consumer? 1.1.1 Individual not acting in a business capacity 1.1.2 Supplier acting in the course of a business 1.1.3 Non-business and private use or consumption 1.1.4 Non-contractual consumers 1.2 The context of consumer protection 1.2.1 Historical context 1.2.2 Why protect the consumer? 1.2.3 Rationales for consumer protection 1.2.3.1 Information problems 1.2.3.2 Other factors

2 INSTITUTIONS AND POLICIES OF CONSUMER PROTECTION 18

2.1 Central government and government agencies 2.1.1 Development of consumer protection policy 2.1.1.1 The Department of Trade and Industry 2.1.1.2 The Fair Trading Act 1973 and the Office of Fair Trading 2.1.2 Protection of consumer economic interests 2.1.3 Protection of consumer health and safety interests 2.1.4 A general duty to trade fairly 2.1.4.1 Current aspects of the duty to trade fairly 2.1.4.2 The need for a general duty to trade fairly 2.2 Local government 2.2.1 Enforcement 2.2.2 Consumer advice 2.3 Government-sponsored bodies 2.4 Public services and utilities 2.5 Voluntary organisations 2.6 Trade associations and codes of practice 2.6.1 Features of codes of practice 2.6.2 Advantages and disadvantages of codes of practice 2.7 Ombudsmen

3   CONSUMER REDRESS   68

4   THE LAW OF CONTRACT AS A MEANS OF   81
CONSUMER PROTECTION: GENERAL ISSUES

5   TORT LAW AND PRINCIPLES OF THE LAW OF   134
RESTITUTION AS MEANS OF CONSUMER PROTECTION

6 PRODUCT QUALITY   145

7 PRODUCT SAFETY AND THE CIVIL LAW   183

8 DEFECTIVE CONSUMER SERVICES   206

9 HOLIDAY LAW   238

10 CONSUMER INSURANCE   257

11 CONSUMER FINANCE   302

14   PRODUCT QUALITY AND SAFETY UNDER   383
THE CRIMINAL LAW

15   FOOD LAW   405

19 MISLEADING PRICE INDICATIONS   486

20 SALES PROMOTION   507

Preface

Since the first edition of this book was published in 1991, there have been a number of changes — not just those of law. In particular the format for the present edition has changed to that of text only, with the removal of extracts from cases and statutory and other materials. It is to be hoped that the extension of the text will allow students to consider in more depth the critique and exposition of consumer protection law issues.

The other principal change is one of authorship, heralding the welcome contributions of John Lowry on matters concerning consumer services and insurance law.

We have attempted to set out the principal legal issues concerning English consumer protection law and the context in which they are to be found, concentrating particularly on the main consumer concerns of deficiencies in goods acquired and services provided. It has also been possible to make reference to some comparative material, to highlight possible deficiencies in English consumer protection law. The Europeanisation of many aspects of consumer law continues, particularly in the areas of consumer safety law, food law, product liability law, advertising law and holiday law, and is reflected in this book at appropriate points. This trend can also be detected in the teams turned out by Middlesbrough and West Ham, from whom much inspiration has been derived.

What should be covered in a book on consumer law is always open to debate. We have chosen to include materials on institutions of consumer protection, consumer redress, product quality, product safety, defective services, unfair contract terms and advertising and sales promotion law. For the sake of convenience, the traditional distinction between private and public law has been maintained in the greater part of the book, with the result that there are separate chapters concerned with the role played by the law of contract, the law of tort and the criminal law as instruments of consumer protection. The issue of administrative control of trading activities is also addressed when considering the various institutions which play a part in protecting consumers.

While this is intended primarily as a student text, it is hoped that some use might be made of it by practitioners, retailers, consumer advisers and trading standards departments and others concerned with consumer protection and trading law. In preparing the manuscript for publication, we have incurred numerous debts of gratitude. We would like to thank all at Blackstone Press, especially Heather Saward, for their patience and kind assistance in bringing this work to fruition. Thanks also go to Martin Davis, Katharine Thompson, John Birds, Rob Merkin, Philip Rawlings and Geoffrey Woodroffe for help and encouragement in relation to various aspects of this book. Special thanks must be accorded to Rod Edmonds at Sussex University for his continued vigil against the split infinitive.

Needless to say, the views expressed are our own and all responsibility for mistakes and infelicities rests with the authors. We are especially grateful for the help provided by Sue Oughton in assisting with the boring task of proofreading. Special thanks also go to our wives Sue and Yasmin and our children Gareth, Alastair, Karen and Alexander (in order of seniority) for their patience and good humour in the time it has taken to write this book and for their willingness to ignore the hunched appendages to the computer upstairs in Dad's study!

The much appreciated assistance of Heather Saward and especially Paula Doolan at Blackstone Press is recorded. Without their help this book would have contained many more infelicities than may now be found!

So far as possible, we have tried to base the text on materials available to us on 1 January 1997, although we have managed to insert some later material at proof stage.

David Oughton
John Lowry
Hailsham and Scaynes Hill, Sussex
April 1997

Table of Cases

Table of Statutes

Table of Statutory Instruments

ONE

Perspectives

1.1 WHO IS A CONSUMER?

In a book on consumer protection law, it is appropriate to consider at the outset who it is the law purports to protect. In a literal sense, a consumer is 'one who purchases goods or services' (*Longman Dictionary of the English Language*, 2nd ed. (Harlow: Longman, 1991)). This would include any user of goods or services supplied by another, with the result that a construction company purchasing building materials for use in the construction of a housing estate would be acting as a consumer. However, for the purposes of consumer protection law, the term 'consumer' has a narrower meaning which is based on the capacity in which the consumer and the supplier of the goods or services supplied have acted.

The traditional view of a consumer, or at least that given by the thrust of modern consumer protection legislation, is of an individual dealing with a commercial enterprise. However, the term 'consumer' can also be used to describe a person who makes use of the services provided by public-sector bodies or privatised monopolies subject to public control or scrutiny. On this basis, consumer protection law would also cover complaints by individuals about the services provided by railways, water authorities, electricity companies and gas suppliers. Furthermore, in what remains of the public sector, the consumer might also have reason to complain about the way in which he or she has been dealt with by the Department of Social Security or may have a legitimate complaint about service received in hospital. It may also be argued that a tenant's complaint about the way in which he or she has been treated by a landlord should be regarded as an aspect of consumer protection law. Indeed, the American guru of consumerism, Ralph Nader, has taken the view that the term 'consumer' should be equated with the word 'citizen' and that consumer protection law should be regarded as an aspect of the protection of civic rights.

Various statutes which purport to protect consumer interests contain relevant, but limited definitions. For the most part, a direct definition of the term 'consumer' is not provided. Instead, Parliament has chosen to define phrases such as 'acting in the course of a business' or 'dealing as a consumer'. The effect of these definitions is that a person who acts in the course of a business must act or refrain from acting in a particular manner detrimental to consumer interests. Likewise, if a person deals as a consumer, the supplier of goods or services may be subject to obligations which would not otherwise be imposed or the consumer may have entitlements not conferred on others. The European dimension must not be forgotten since there is now an increasing number of regulatory requirements which have resulted from European Union attempts at harmonisation of laws in favour of consumers. As will be seen below, legislation based upon European initiatives tends to concentrate on the protection of individual, natural persons rather than the wider range of protected species covered by purely domestic legislation.

A difficulty presented by some of the domestic statutory definitions of the word 'consumer' is that they emanate from statutes which impose criminal liability. In contrast, others are to be found in Acts concerned with civil law liability. It may be that civil and criminal law provide different emphases. In particular, despite the fact that consumer protection legislation creates what can be described as merely 'regulatory offences', the imposition of criminal liability is not lightly undertaken, and it may be that the law adopts a more generous attitude towards the defendant in cases which involve the imposition of criminal liability. If this is so, a single test may not be appropriate, since different standards could be expected of statutory provisions which create civil rights and obligations. However, the judicial approach to the definition of the terms 'dealing as a consumer' and 'acting in the course of a business' appear to bear remarkable similarities, regardless of the context in which the particular statutory provision operates.

In general, a consumer transaction involves three elements. First, the consumer must be an individual or other protected person who does not act in a business capacity. Secondly the supplier must act in a business capacity and finally the goods or services supplied must be intended for private, not business use.

1.1.1 Individual not acting in a business capacity

The standard perception of a consumer is of an individual purchaser of goods or services and in most instances this will be the case. Indeed, most of the provisions of the Consumer Credit Act, 1974 (CCA) only apply where the debtor is an individual. But the definition of an individual in s. 189(1) of that Act is drafted widely, with the result that a business debtor may still be protected by the Act. In particular, while a company is not an individual, a partnership or other unincorporated body of persons is regarded as an individual for the purposes of that Act. In contrast, there are some provisions which apply only to individuals. For example, the Unfair Terms in Consumer Contracts Regulations 1994 (SI 1994/3159) only apply in favour of a 'natural person' who acts for purposes which are outside his business (reg. 2(1)).

Generally, a consumer is regarded as a non-business purchaser of goods or services, but the difficulty is to decide when a purchaser acts in a business capacity. It is clear that a person who purchases at an auction sale is not to be regarded as a consumer (Unfair Contract Terms Act 1977, s. 12(2)). The Unfair Contract Terms Act 1977, s. 12(1)(a) provides that a person deals as a consumer if the other party to the contract is unable to prove (s. 12(3)) that he neither makes the contract in the course of a business nor holds himself out as doing so. The difficulty here is to determine when a person purchases in the course of a business or holds himself out as doing so.

In a broad sense, every time a company enters into a contract, it does so in the course of its business because if this were not the case, the transaction would be *ultra vires* (*R & B Customs Brokers Co. Ltd* v *United Dominions Trust Ltd* [1988] 1 All ER 847, 853 per Dillon LJ). Thus, it could be argued that where a company which runs a grocer's shop buys a new delivery van, it acts in the course of a business (ibid.).

An alternative view is that a company can be a 'consumer' purchaser where the purchase is not for some definite business purpose and is one which is not regularly made by that company. In *R & B Customs Brokers Co. Ltd* v *United Dominions Trust Ltd* [1988] 1 All ER 847 (see Brown 1988 JBL 386; Price (1989) 52 MLR 245) the plaintiff, a company carrying on the business of a freight forwarding agent, purchased a car for both business use and for the private use of its directors. It was alleged that, as the roof leaked, the defendant was in breach of the implied term in the Sale of Goods Act 1979, s. 14(3), that the car would be fit for the purpose for which it was intended, namely, driving in English weather conditions. The defendant finance company sought to rely on an exclusion clause in the contract, which would only protect it if the buyer did not deal as a consumer, since liability for breach of the implied terms in s. 14 cannot be excluded when dealing with a consumer (Unfair Contract Terms Act 1977, s. 6(2) and see chapter 12). The Court of Appeal held that since the purchase of the car was only incidental to the business of a freight forwarding agent, the particular transaction could not be said to have been entered into as an integral part of the business carried on by the plaintiff as there was no degree of regularity in the type of purchase concerned. It therefore followed that the company had purchased as a consumer and the Unfair Contract Terms Act 1977, s. 6(2), prevented the exclusion clause from taking effect (see also *Rasbora Ltd* v *JCL Marine Ltd* [1977] 1 Lloyd's Rep 645 and *Peter Symmons & Co.* v *Cook* (1981) 131 NLJ 758.) The view expressed by Dillon LJ was that:

> . . . there are some transactions which are clearly integral parts of the businesses concerned, and these should be held to have been carried out in the course of those businesses; this would cover apart from much else, the instance of a one-off adventure in the nature of trade where the transaction itself would constitute a trade or business. There are other transactions, however such as the purchase of the car in the present case, which are at the highest only incidental to the carrying on of the relevant business; here a degree of regularity is required before it can be said that they are an integral part of the business carried on and so entered into in the course of a business ([1988] 1 All ER 847 at 854).

The decision of the Court of Appeal may be criticised on a number of grounds. First, the interpretation of the Unfair Contract Terms Act 1977, s. 12(1)(a), may not give effect to the intention of Parliament. If s. 12(1)(a) is interpreted literally, it distinguishes between a business purchaser and a consumer purchaser and does not require the court to consider the purpose for which the goods are required. The distinction between the two approaches is one which was referred to by the Law Commission in its report which led to the enactment of the Unfair Contract Terms Act 1977 (Law Com. No. 24 (1969) paras 90–5). The Commission concluded that legislation should impose an absolute prohibition on exclusions of liability for breach of the terms implied by what is now the Sale of Goods Act 1979 in consumer sales in the strict sense and that exclusions in contracts entered into by 'business consumers' should be subject to a reasonableness test.

The second ground for criticism is that the reason for the ban on the use of exclusion clauses in consumer contracts is that the consumer is weak in terms of bargaining power, however, the same cannot be said of 'business consumers'. Dillon LJ in *R & B Customs Brokers Co. Ltd* v *United Dominions Trust Ltd* considered, *obiter*, that had the purchase been in the course of a business, the exclusion clause would have satisfied the reasonableness test because the company was '*ex hypothesi* dealing in the course of a business' ([1988] 1 All ER 847 at 855) and one of the directors was not devoid of commercial experience (ibid.). It seems strange that where two business contractors are of broadly similar bargaining strength, one of them is entitled to the protection of a blanket prohibition on the use of exclusion clauses.

Even if the plaintiff in *R & B Customs Brokers* did not contract in the course of a business, there is a strong argument that it held itself out as acting in the course of a business (see Brown [1988] JBL 386, 394). The company made the contract in its corporate name and in a section of the contractual document headed 'Business Details' the nature of the company's business, the number of years trading and the number of company employees had been stated. It is suggested that these matters taken together point to a purchase in the course of a business or at least one made by an organisation holding itself out as a business rather than one made by a consumer devoid of commercial experience.

1.1.2 Supplier acting in the course of a business

The second distinguishing feature of a consumer transaction is that the supplier of the goods or services contracted for acts in the course of a business. This requirement is to be found in both legislation imposing criminal sanctions (for example, the Trade Descriptions Act 1968, s. 1(1); Unsolicited Goods and Services Act 1971, s. 2; Business Advertisements (Disclosure) Order 1977 (SI 1977/1918), art. 2(1)) and provisions relating to civil redress in consumer transactions (Unfair Contract Terms Act 1977, s. 12(1)(b); Sale of Goods Act 1979, s. 14(2) and (3)).

The interpretation of the phrase 'in the course of a business' in this context is not consistent. In particular, there would appear to be a difference of approach in relation to the Sale of Goods Act 1979 and the Trade Descriptions Act 1968.

So far as the Sale of Goods Act 1979 is concerned, the implied terms of fitness and quality in s. 14(2) and (3) apply only where the seller sells the goods in the course of a business. It is clear that for these purposes a person who sells by way of trade can be regarded as a business seller despite not habitually trading in goods of the type in question (*Ashington Piggeries Ltd* v *Christopher Hill Ltd* [1972] AC 441, 494 per Lord Wilberforce; see also *Final Report* of the Committee on Consumer Protection (Molony Committee) (Cmnd 1781, 1962), para. 443). Accordingly, for the purposes of this Act, the sale of stock-in-trade or other irregular sales by a trade seller will be regarded as sales in the course of a business and the implied terms in s. 14 will apply to the transaction. Thus in *Ashington Piggeries Ltd* v *Christopher Hill Ltd*, Lord Wilberforce observed of the Sale of Goods Act 1893, s. 14(1) (which is now the Sale of Goods Act 1979, s. 14(3)) and s. 14(2), that:

> . . . it is in the course of the seller's business to supply goods if he agrees either generally, or in a particular case, to supply the goods when ordered, and . . . a seller deals in goods of that description if his business is such that he is willing to accept orders for them. I cannot comprehend the rationale of holding that the subsections do not apply if the seller is dealing in the goods for the first time. ([1972] AC 441 at 494)

In contrast with this approach, it has been held, in the precise circumstances set out by Lord Wilberforce, that a person charged with the commission of an offence under the Trade Descriptions Act 1968, s. 1, cannot be said to have acted in the course of a business on the first occasion on which he disposes of stock-in-trade. In *Devlin* v *Hall* [1990] RTR 320 a taxi proprietor had been operating in business for some months and subsequently sold one of his cars, subject to an incorrect mileage recording. Despite the fact that there was evidence that he had also sold other cars on two or three occasions in the subsequent two years, it was considered that the defendant had not acted in the course of a business on the first occasion, since at the time that transaction was entered into there was no regularity in the number of sales made. The unfortunate effect of this decision is that if the same approach were to be applied to the Sale of Goods Act 1979, the consumer purchaser would have no remedy in respect of a breach of the implied terms of satisfactory quality and fitness for purpose, since these terms are only implied where the seller sells in the course of a business.

The approach in *Devlin* v *Hall* is identical to that adopted in *R & B Customs Brokers Co. Ltd* v *United Dominions Trust Ltd* [1988] 1 All ER 847 in relation to 'business consumers'. In *Davies* v *Sumner* [1984] 1 WLR 1301 the defendant, a professional courier, sold the car he used in his work. Contrary to the provisions of the Trade Descriptions Act 1968, s. 1(1)(a), he sold the car subject to a false statement of the mileage it had covered. It was held by the House of Lords that the defendant had not sold the car in the course of a business since such a sale must be an integral part of the business carried on by the defendant. While the defendant did operate a business, the business was that of delivering parcels etc., not selling cars. Furthermore, it was held that in order to achieve the status of a sale in the course of a business, the transactions concerned must have been entered into with some degree of regularity. Thus the renewal of hire cars every two years by a car-hire firm can constitute a sale in the course of a business since the required degree of regularity is established (*Havering London Borough Council* v *Stevenson* [1970] 1 WLR 1375), but it would appear that the occasional sale of a car used by a doctor for both private and professional purposes does not possess the necessary element of regularity to allow for a conviction under the Trade Descriptions Act 1968 (*Davies* v *Sumner* [1984] 1 WLR 405, 410 per Robert Goff LJ; see also *Devlin* v *Hall* [1990] RTR 320). It has even been held that a postman who renovates, regularly advertises and resells cars does not sell in the course of a business, if the work is performed by way of a hobby (*Blakemore* v *Bellamy* [1983] RTR 303). The one exception to this approach arises where an isolated transaction is carried out with a view to profit (*Davies* v *Sumner* [1984] 1 WLR 1301, 1305 per Lord Keith of Kinkel). Thus a person who arranges for the publication of a book of poems, supplies copies of the book to public libraries and subsequently demands payment can be said to have demanded payment in the course of a trade or business for the purposes of the Unsolicited Goods and Services Act 1971, s. 2(1) (*Eiman* v *Waltham Forest London Borough Council* (1982) 90 ITSA Monthly Review 204). Similarly in *Corfield* v *Sevenways Garage Ltd* [1985] RTR 109 the defendants regularly sold petrol from a filling station, but on the occasion under consideration had purchased a second-hand car at an auction. The car had been lent to someone else and while it was under that person's control, the speedometer was broken and subsequently replaced. The defendants were not told of this. The defendants checked the car, carried out some repairs and decided to display it for sale, not realising that the mileage reading displayed was inaccurate, thereby exposing them to liability for a breach of the Trade Descriptions Act 1968, s. 1. Despite the fact that selling cars was not regarded as a normal part of the defendants' day-to-day business, this sale was regarded as part of that business since it was clearly entered into with a view to making a profit.

The approach adopted in relation to the Trade Descriptions Act 1968 and other penal legislation favours the seller to a greater extent than the approach adopted in relation to the Sale of Goods Act 1979. This may be justified on the ground that in cases of doubt a penal provision should be construed in favour of the defendant. However, there may be a danger that, in the interests of consistency, the same approach may be adopted in relation to the Sale of Goods Act 1979. This danger may already be real following the application of the *Davies* v *Sumner* test to the Unfair Contract Terms Act 1977 in *R & B Customs Brokers Co. Ltd* v *United Dominions Trust Ltd.* It would be undesirable in the extreme if the implied terms in the Sale of Goods Act 1979, s. 14, were held not to apply to one-off sales by trade sellers. In any case, there are other reasons why total consistency in relation to all of the statutory provisions that contain the phrase 'selling in the course of a business' is impossible to achieve. In particular, the Unfair Contract Terms Act 1977 has a further requirement that the goods purchased by the consumer should be of a type ordinarily supplied for private use or consumption, whereas no such restriction applies to the Sale of Goods Act 1979. Accordingly, it is suggested that there should continue to be a difference between the definition of a sale in the course of a business and a purchase in the course of a business.

Paradoxically, while the penal legislation referred to above adopts an opening stance which is highly favourable to the supplier of goods in requiring a degree of regularity before it can be said that there has been a supply in the course of a business, there have been occasions when individual employees have been successfully prosecuted under, for example, the Trade Descriptions Act 1968. The way in which this strange result may obtain is a consequence of the wording of what may be referred to as a bypass procedure which comes into play when the statutory defences are pleaded in order to avoid conviction of a strict-liability criminal offence (see further chapter 13). The general effect of these provisions is that if a company is charged with the commission of an offence under the 1968 Act, it may plead that the commission of the offence is due to the act or default of another person and that the body charged with the offence has acted with due diligence and has taken reasonable precautions to avoid the commission of such offence (Trade Descriptions Act 1968 s. 24(1)). The Trade Descriptions Act 1968, s. 23, provides that the person whose act or default is alleged to be responsible for the commission of the offence may be proceeded against whether or not proceedings against the other person are brought. For the purposes of section 23, it is clear that the 'other person' does not need to be someone who acts in the course of a business. Thus in *Olgiersson* v *Kitching* [1986] 1 All ER 746 the private owner of a car was responsible for turning back the mileage reading on a car which he subsequently sold to a car dealer. In proceedings under the Trade Descriptions Act 1968, s. 1, the dealer pleaded the act or default of the private owner, who was subsequently successfully prosecuted under s. 23. Similarly, it would be possible for a corporate employer to point to the default of a junior employee in order to escape liability, with the result that the individual employee might face the prospect of a fine under the Trade Descriptions Act 1968 (see, e.g., *Whitehead* v *Collett* [1975] Crim LR 53).

In terms of general policy, it would seem to be highly undesirable that a penal statutory provision should be used in this way to make scapegoats of private individuals when the purpose of such legislation is to improve trading standards. In this regard, it is interesting to note that some more recent legislation contains language which would deny the liability of the employee or the private individual in *Olgiersson* v *Kitching*. The Consumer Protection Act 1987, s. 39(1), provides a defence similar to that in the Trade Descriptions Act 1968, s. 24(1), but in the corresponding bypass provision in s. 40(1) of the 1987 Act, it is provided that the person proceeded against must be guilty of an act or default done 'in the course of any business of his'. In *Warwickshire County Council* v *Johnson* [1993] 1 All ER 299 the defendant was the branch manager of a Dixons electrical store who had displayed a notice to the effect that Dixons would beat any price for televisions, hi-fi and video recorders by £20 'on the spot' but failed to honour the pledge, thereby committing an offence under the Consumer Protection Act 1987, s. 20. It was accepted that Dixons were able to rely on the statutory due diligence defence under s. 40(1) of the 1987 Act, but the enforcement authority decided to prosecute the manager under the bypass procedure. In reaching the conclusion that the prosecution should fail, the House of Lords held that the intention of Parliament was clearly that individuals should not be prosecuted since the view had been expressed in Parliamentary debate that the inclusion of the words 'in the course of any business of his' should be taken to mean 'any business of which the defendant is either the owner, or in which he has a controlling interest' (at p. 304 per Lord Roskill).

In terms of policy, this would appear to be a more sensible position to adopt, in relation to junior employees, since there seems to be little purpose in prosecuting such persons with little or no interest in the advancement of the employer's business and who have little or no control over the manner in which that business is run. However, it may be questionable not to allow the prosecution of more senior employees such as the defendant in *Warwickshire County Council* v *Johnson* since they have a greater interest in the way the business is being run and have more control over the trading policy adopted in the branch for which they are responsible. However, it will be seen that the decision in *Warwickshire County Council* v *Johnson* is consistent with the approach adopted by the House of Lords in *Tesco Supermarkets Ltd* v *Nattrass* [1972] AC 153 in which a distinction was drawn between the 'directing mind and will' of a company, identifiable with the company itself, and lesser employees such as branch managers who are regarded as being separate from the company (see further chapter 13).

1.1.3 · Non-business and private use or consumption
Some statutory provisions impose a further requirement on the definition of a consumer transaction, namely, that the goods or services acquired should be intended for non-business or consumer use (Unfair Contract Terms Act 1977, s. 12(1)(c); Consumer Protection Act 1987, ss. 10(7) and 20(6)) or that the transaction is entered into by a person acting for purposes which are outside his business (Unfair Terms in Consumer Contracts Regulations 1994, reg. 2(1)). It is clear that in order to satisfy this requirement, goods do not need to be exclusively used by consumers (the Unfair Contract Terms Act 1977, s. 12(1)(c), refers to goods of a type *ordinarily* supplied for private use or consumption). For example, it is possible that some goods could be used for both business and consumer purposes, such as a car used by a doctor for his own domestic use and for the purposes of his medical practice. Difficulties may arise where goods are of a type ordinarily purchased for private use or consumption but are in fact put to business use. In such a case, s. 12(1)(c) may indicate that the buyer deals as a consumer, but it is also the case that if the buyer deals in such goods in the course of a business, the provisions of the Unfair Contract Terms Act 1977 in relation to consumer sales will not apply. Thus, if a business purchases raw materials which might also be purchased by a consumer, but uses them in its manufacturing process, clearly the purchase is not one made otherwise than in the course of a business.

Lesser problems arise in this respect under the Unfair Terms in Consumer Contracts Regulations 1994 since reg. 2(1) requires a consumer not to act for business purposes when entering the regulated transaction. Given the apparent subjectivity of this test, it should be easier to look at the particular purpose for which goods or services have been acquired without having to ascertain whether the goods etc. are ordinarily supplied for business purposes or for consumption purposes.

The problem created by the Unfair Contract Terms Act 1977, s. 12(1)(c), can also be considered in reverse. Suppose a consumer purchases material ordinarily put to a business use, such as a cement mixer. It may be that the consumer does not act in the course of a business, but if s. 12(1)(c) is not complied with, the buyer does not deal as a consumer. It may be that what is ordinarily supplied for private use will need to be considered on a case-by-case basis as consumer purchases change over a period of time. For example, the growth of the 'do it yourself' market may mean that articles which have been regarded, in the past, as the subject of trade purchases may come to be regarded as items ordinarily supplied for private use.

The word 'type' may also create difficulties if it requires the court to consider merely the nature of the thing sold. For example, the purchase of a bale of peat from a garden centre would be a consumer purchase, but could the same be said of a bulk purchase of, say, 500 bales? The thing sold in each case is the same, but the quantity sold may indicate that the subject matter of the contract is being put to something other than a purely consumer use.

Similar, but not identical provisions are contained in the Consumer Protection Act 1987, s. 20(6), in relation to the definition of a consumer for the purposes of the penal provisions of the Act concerned with misleading pricing. For these purposes a consumer of goods is one who 'might wish to be supplied with goods for his own private use or consumption' (Consumer Protection Act 1987, s. 20(6)(a)). This formulation avoids the objectivity of the Unfair Contract Terms Act 1977 s. 12(1)(c), by concentrating on the use to which the consumer might wish to put the goods. This may mean that the provisions of s. 20 apply to cases where the subject matter is capable of being put to private use, although this is not in fact the case. A better formulation would have been 'might reasonably wish' (see R. M. Merkin, *Guide to the Consumer Protection Act 1987* (London: Financial Training, 1987), para. 14.2).

In relation to misleading statements concerning the charge made for services, facilities or accommodation, the essence of the definition of a consumer is that the service etc. is not required for the purposes of a business (Consumer Protection Act 1987, s. 20(6)(b) and (c)). Whether there is a difference between purchasing goods for private use and acquiring a service for non-business use is not clear. However, it is likely that the two provisions will be construed in a similar manner.

1.1.4 Non-contractual consumers
The foregoing discussion assumes that there is a consumer purchaser and a supplier who contracts in the course of a business. While a consumer is often

a person who has entered into a contractual relationship with a supplier, it is also true that there are many non-contractual consumers.

Until recently, the protection of such consumers was left largely to the tort of negligence in the form of the narrow rule in *Donoghue* v *Stevenson* [1932] AC 562 (see chapter 5), but in recent years, the position of the non-contractual consumer has been recognised. In particular, the provisions of part I of the Consumer Protection Act 1987 seek to give such a person a remedy in damages against the producer of a defective product. Other developments in the field of civil redress might have taken the position of the non-contractual consumer to even greater heights, had the government been prepared to lend a more sympathetic ear. In particular, a recent attempt by the National Consumer Council (*The Consumer Guarantee* (PD29/89) (1989)) to secure the enactment of legislation in respect of consumer guarantees commanded considerable public support, but was ultimately defeated by government intervention. This may not be the end of the matter so far as consumer guarantees are concerned, since there is now a European initiative aimed at introducing a Union-wide producers' guarantee of the quality of goods put on to the consumer market (*Green Paper on Guarantees for Consumer Goods and After-Sales Service* (COM (93) 509) and see further chapter 6). The premise which underlies this proposed intervention is that cross-border shopping within the European Union can only flourish if consumers can be assured that they will enjoy the same guarantee and after-sales service wherever they happen to purchase a particular product. Sadly, there appears to be no corresponding intention in relation to consumer services, apparently on the basis that services are so dissimilar in nature as to be incapable of being subject to a common form of guarantee across the whole of the European Union.

Many statutory provisions creating criminal offences on the part of traders or providing for means of administrative control do not require the formation of a contractual relationship. For example, some of the offences created by the Food Safety Act 1990, the Consumer Protection Act 1987 and the Trade Descriptions Act 1968 may be committed where there is no consumer purchase at all or where the person harmed by an unsafe product is not the person who bought it from the retailer. The Director General of Fair Trading is required by the Fair Trading Act 1973, s. 14(1), to review consumer trade practices and may recommend legislation, and it is clear from the definition of a consumer trade practice in the Fair Trading Act 1973, s. 13(1), that certain practices will affect both contractual and non-contractual consumers. In particular s. 13(1)(c), (d) and (e) refer to methods of sales promotion, salesmanship and packaging which may affect more than just the immediate purchaser.

1.2 THE CONTEXT OF CONSUMER PROTECTION

1.2.1 Historical context
While consumer protection law is often regarded as a modern phenomenon, typical of the twentieth century, it is in fact the case that many of what we now regard as statutes with an emphasis on consumer protection had their

origins in a much earlier age. For example, there has long been regulation in respect of essential items such as bread, meat, ale and fuel, and there was early regulation in relation to prices and the provision of short measures. Whether these statutes should be properly regarded as consumer protection measures is doubtful, as much of the motivation for their enactment probably stemmed from a desire to protect honest traders from their dishonest competitors. As such, much of the earlier legislation can be regarded as being directed towards fair trading rather than consumer protection. For instance the Trade Descriptions Act 1968, which is regarded as one of the earliest examples of modern regulation in the consumer interest is based, in part, on the provisions of the Merchandise Marks Acts 1887 to 1953, the avowed intent of which was to protect honest traders against unscrupulous competitors who sought to create a trading advantage by means of misdescribing the products they sold.

As trade in basic consumer commodities increased pressure for legal controls increased. Business self-regulation by trade guilds had been employed in order to control the adulteration of food by unscrupulous traders but this did not effectively control the abuses. The excesses of some traders were such as to involve a danger to life as well as giving them a trading advantage over their honest counterparts. Reported practices included the failure to remove impurities from bread, sugar and pepper, the addition of grease to coffee and the addition of sulphuric acid to vinegar (*Butterworths Law of Food and Drugs*, para. 2). Modern food law can be traced to the Adulteration of Food and Drink Act 1860, which, amongst other provisions, prohibited the sale of food containing injurious material or ingredients. Subsequent legislation also rendered it unlawful to sell food not of the nature, substance or quality demanded by the purchaser.

Early attempts at legislating for uniform weights and measures can be found as far back as the thirteenth century. It was a criminal offence under the Assize of Bread and Ale of 1266 (51 Hen 3) to supply these commodities in short weight. Particularly frowned upon was the deliberate use of unjust balances. Various methods of enforcement were employed, but one which proved to be effective in this particular respect was that of excommunication. In relation to bread and coal, legislation dating back to the seventeenth and eighteenth centuries allowed local justices to fix the price of the product according to its weight and other relevant market conditions. Necessary in the process of regulating the supply of consumer commodities was the establishment of a set of measuring norms. Clearly, it would be intolerable to the trader to have a movable standard with which compliance was difficult or impossible. In early years, royal decrees sought to establish basic standards of measurement. For example, in 1305, Edward I enacted that '3 grains of barley, dry and round, make an inch, 12 inches make a foot and 3 feet make an ulna' (later to become a yard). It was common practice for monarchs to keep standard measuring rods in their treasury. Many of these early measures, particularly those relating to capacity, were crude, to say the least, often being based on the weight of materials which were likely to alter in terms of volume in different temperatures or in differing conditions.

The civil law of consumer protection was most markedly affected by developments in the nineteenth century, in particular the principles of freedom of contract and *caveat emptor*. The period was characterised by a general unwillingness to interfere in business affairs (see *Printing & Numerical Registering Co.* v *Sampson* (1875) LR 19 Eq 462, 465 per Sir George Jessel). As a general rule, the parties to a contract were not obliged to volunteer information with the result that if a person wanted a warranty that the goods or services he purchased were of sound quality he could contract for this result and pay accordingly (see *Parkinson* v *Lee* (1802) 2 East 314). The principle of *caveat emptor* was consistent with the principles of freedom of contract and self-reliance which were features of the nineteenth century. This approach may well have been justified at the time since few goods would have cost enough to warrant common law protection (Atiyah, *The Rise and Fall of Freedom of Contract* (Oxford: Clarendon Press, 1979), p. 179), but later developments in mass production techniques led to the eventual downfall of the *caveat emptor* principle and the development of consumer protection measures. However, at the time, it was still possible to argue that the buyer could afford to learn from his mistakes and that legislative intervention in favour of the consumer was unnecessary.

Even in the ninteenth century, *caveat emptor* was not always blindly adhered to. Some members of the judiciary were prepared to imply warranties of fitness and quality on the part of the seller of goods (*Jones* v *Bright* (1829) 5 Bing 533), which ultimately appeared in statutory form in the Sale of Goods Act 1893. The implication of such terms in contracts can be explained by the substantial increase in the number of manufactured goods which began to appear in the middle to late nineteenth century, heralding the age of the consumer which was to develop in the twentieth century. If a buyer paid a sound price, he could expect his purchase to be of like quality.

1.2.2 Why protect the consumer?

Many of the assumptions which underlie common law rules, especially those concerned with the law of contract, may be seen to be fundamentally at odds with the idea of consumer protection. Much of the law of contract is premised upon the freedom of the individual to make whatever contract he likes, on the assumption that all contracting parties have roughly equal bargaining strength. In many respects, this position is understandable, since common law rules relating to contracts can do little more than lay down a general framework within which all contracting parties must work. Thus the common law has to deal with both contracts between business or commercial enterprises and those in which one of the parties is a consumer. The general framework of the common law cannot stray too far in favour of disadvantaged parties such as consumers, since the establishment of a general rule will apply across the board to all types of contract.

The background against which common law rules operate consists of a mixed economy in which many transactions are left subject to market forces operating according to the laws of supply and demand, but at the same time there are aspects of government planning which are geared towards subduing some of the greater excesses of the market. It is within this area of State planning that consumer protection legislation finds its place.

In general terms, economic theory divides the participants in economic behaviour into 'households,' 'firms' and 'central authorities', all of whom operate within the rules created by the market. From our present perspective, consumers fall within the first group, since a household will consist of a number of consumers of goods and services. The traders with whom they deal are the firms, and central authorities are concerned with matters such as regulation of the market and the parties who deal with each other according to the rules of the market.

The central assumption of the laws of supply and demand is that households (and therefore consumers making up a household) act rationally when they make a particular decision and in so acting, they will seek to maximise their wealth or 'happiness'. But this assumption may be regarded as questionable as a means of analysing legal rules designed for the protection of consumers, since the consumers who make up a 'household' may differ in the way they react to different situations, with the result that the assumption of rationality in decision making may not always hold good. Moreover, it will be seen below that the making of a rational choice requires a consumer to be as fully informed as possible before any decision is made and it is apparent that in many situations a consumer may not have all relevant facts at his fingertips at the time of making an important purchasing decision.

What underlies the laws of supply and demand in the context of a market economy is that, provided the economy is competitive, no single producer or supplier will be able to dominate the market, since consumers will choose to purchase products which offer the best value in terms of price, quality and suitability. Accordingly, no producer will be able to charge excessive prices or get away with the constant supply of poor quality materials, since consumers will simply switch to the product of another producer. Demand for the defective or expensive product will fall to such an extent that the producer will then have to make changes in order to attract other customers. Much as markets are affected by consumer behaviour, it is clear that the control of prices and product quality cannot be left solely to market pressures. Most modern Western economies can be described as mixed in the sense that there is a mixture of free-market policies coupled with central regulation of trading practices. Thus, for example, even though there have been a number of high-profile 'privatisations' of quasi-monopoly suppliers of public utility services such as telecommunications, air travel, water, gas and electricity, these organisations still remain partially under State control in the form of regulators who have been appointed to ensure that consumers get a satisfactory deal in terms of prices and quality assurance. Moreover, the whole tenor of what may be described as consumer protection laws is a form of centralised control of businesses in the interests of consumers by protecting the latter from unsafe and poor quality products and services and from misleading descriptions and price comparisons.

Laws intended to protect consumers, as opposed to other traders, are seen as a comparatively recent development. But it needs to be asked why such laws are necessary. The early attempts at regulation could be said to be based on discouraging fraudulent or dangerous practices and protection against such practices is clearly desirable. However, many modern consumer protection measures no longer require proof of fraud. Indeed, a feature of statutes such as the Trade Descriptions Act 1968, the Consumer Credit Act 1974, the Consumer Protection Act 1987 and the Food Safety Act 1990 is that, subject to the availability of statutory defences, a trader can be found guilty of a criminal offence without proof of criminal intention. It would appear to follow from this that there is some other justification for intervention in favour of the consumer.

A number of factors may be regarded as reasons for intervention in favour of consumers. Many trade practices may result in a general lack of information on the part of consumers with the result that the ability of the consumer to make a prudent shopping decision is diminished (see Trebilcock, 'Consumer protection and the affluent society' (1971) 16 McGill LJ 263).

First, there were substantial changes in the nature of the consumer market after the Second World War. Articles such as televisions, synthetic fibres, processed and pre-packed foods, records, magnetic tapes and more recently products based on microchip technology have come on to the market. The rate of change has been so fast that the consumer could hardly be expected to appreciate fully the operation of many of the sophisticated products available for purchase. Such knowledge as the consumer might have had soon became dated. In many cases, even the retailer had little more understanding of the complexity of the product sold than the consumer. The same can also be said of the market for consumer services with the result that the consumer is often in no position to make a proper evaluation of the service he receives. For example, few consumers can be said to appreciate fully the nature of work carried out by a mechanic on a motor vehicle.

Other relevant factors in the growth of the consumer market included the general increase in consumers' income and the more ready availability of credit in the form of hire purchase. The increase in spending power led to a corresponding increase in the number of complex products purchased.

Businesses became much better organised and operated on a very large scale. The post-war years have seen a decline in the number of corner shops and a substantial increase in the number of supermarket chains. The organisation of business is a natural consequence of traders devoting their whole working day to the business and ensuring that it is profitable. By contrast, the consumer has a number of other interests to attend to. The consumer does not spend the whole day making purchases but must also consider the demands of his work, other members of his family etc.

It can be argued that modern advertising methods tend to disinform rather than to inform the consumer. In particular, it can be said that advertisements do not provide information on an objective basis. The advertiser only tells the consumer what he wants the consumer to hear, and other facts which might be relevant to a prudent shopping decision tend to be omitted. A further objection to advertising techniques is that they may encourage irrational purchases, for example, it has been argued that consumer 'wants' are artificially created by advertising (Galbraith, *The Affluent Society*, 4th ed. (London: Deutsch, 1984)). Conversely, sometimes a product fails despite being the subject of a heavy advertising campaign, which some would argue points to the continued power of consumers in the market place. Certainly, there are instances in which consumer confidence in a particular product is so heavily damaged that it may take a long time for that confidence to return and for demand for that particular product to increase. Recent examples can be found in the lost consumer confidence in beef products following the BSE scare and its relationship to Creutzfeldt–Jakob disease in the middle 1990s. Where there is an increased consumer demand for a particular type of product, there is a corresponding increase in production, which creates an expanding economy which in the long run is good for the consumer.

1.2.3 Rationales for consumer protection

Much modern consumer law can be said to be based on an attempt to rectify the inequality of bargaining power which is said to exist between the individual consumer and the more powerful supplier of goods or services with whom he deals (Law Com. No. 69 (1975); *Consumer Credit: Report of the Committee* (Crowther Committee) (Cmnd 4596, 1971)). It is necessary to consider how this imbalance of power has come about, how the use of common law rules and legislation has sought to combat it and whether regulation of trade practices is truly in the consumer interest. To say that regulation in the consumer interest is justified in order to counteract inequalities of bargaining power is not helpful unless the reasons for this alleged inequality are articulated. A consumer is not in a position of equal bargaining power principally because of difficulties in obtaining information. The consumer does not have the ability to acquire the necessary information to be on the same level as the supplier with whom he deals. However, inequality of bargaining power may also arise for another reason, namely, that the cost of seeking redress is too great (see chapter 3).

1.2.3.1 Information problems If the market is to function in an efficient manner, consumers need to be supplied with adequate information about the price and quality of products and services available from competing traders and about the terms on which those traders are prepared to do business. Armed with this information, the consumer can make a prudent shopping decision. If the consumer is adequately informed, he can indicate his preferences which will lead to competition between traders to satisfy those preferences. However, if the necessary information on price, quality and terms is not available, little competition, if any, will follow.

If, for some reason, adequate information is not available, intervention in the market in favour of the consumer may be justified. It is important to stress that adequate, rather than perfect information is all that is required. It might be possible to stipulate that consumers should be armed with all possible information, but to do so would prove to be inefficient since the cost of intervention would outweigh any benefits derived therefrom.

A straightforward cost-benefit analysis does not provide the full answer as it is also important to consider the distributional effects of intervention or non-intervention. It may be that intervention in a particular way has the effect of benefiting one particular group of consumers to the detriment of another group. In such a case, it is important to consider whether this distribution of resources is justified. For example, the provisions of the Unfair Contract Terms Act 1977 in relation to purported exclusions of liability in respect of a breach of the implied terms of quality and fitness in a contract for the supply of goods could be said to benefit anyone who purchases goods. Since this covers the entire consumer community, the intervention is of benefit to everyone. The same might not be true of a proposal to compel manufacturers to give a five-year parts and labour warranty on new cars as this would only benefit those who were able to afford a new car. Intervention of the latter type might clearly benefit the better off, but the cost of complying with the compulsory guarantee provisions would make new cars more expensive, which in turn would make second-hand cars more expensive without necessarily conferring any benefits on the purchasers of second-hand cars.

Where there is a lack of relevant information, the greatest danger is that the consumer will make a purchase for the wrong reasons. For example, but for the provisions of the Trade Descriptions Act 1968 in relation to misdescriptions of goods or the Consumer Credit Act 1974 requirements in relation to truth in lending, a consumer might make a purchase he would not otherwise make because of misleading claims about performance or rates of interest.

In determining whether legislation is required in order to ensure the availability of information, it is necessary to consider if intervention is justified. It may be that the cost of intervention is too great in comparison with the benefits it confers. Sometimes, the necessary information is readily available without the need for a detailed and costly search. In such a case, intervention to ensure the availability of the information is not needed. For example, where food is bought frequently, there is no need to provide information on taste, as this is a matter which can be assessed by experience. In contrast, there might be greater justification for intervention in order to warn of risks to health or potentially large financial losses, particularly where the commodity is infrequently purchased and experienced. For example, control of the excesses of doorstep double glazing salesmen may be justified on the ground that this is the sort of purchase which consumers infrequently make. In these circumstances there is little market pressure on the salesman to tell the truth as the consumer is unlikely to return in order to make other purchases at a later date. Similar arguments appear to lie behind the unsuccessful proposals for legislation in respect of a statutory consumer guarantee to cover new cars and expensive, infrequently purchased domestic appliances (National Consumer Council, *The Consumer Guarantee* (1989), paras 3.2.1–3.2.4). Despite the lack of success on the issue of producer guarantees at a purely domestic level, the argument has not gone away and there is now mounting pressure at a European level to impose on producers of consumer goods a Europe-wide obligation to offer a guarantee of their products (see *Green Paper on Guarantees for Consumer Goods and After-Sales Services* (COM (93) 509)).

A particular problem with many consumer purchases is that since the consumer does not buy these products on a regular basis, there is no incentive on the part of the producer to give full information. However, if a producer can give a worthwhile guarantee with his product, this may be seen as giving him a competitive advantage over others who cannot provide the same sort of guarantee. In these circumstances, it is suggested that the consumer will be supplied with product information to a greater extent than would otherwise have been the case. The possible problem with involvement at a European level is that the need for a Europe-wide guarantee may be unnecessary, given that there is no widespread consumer practice of cross-border shopping (see Cranston, 'The Green Paper on Guarantees' (1995) Consum LJ 110). Even where there is a competitive market, there are some types of information which may not be made available. Manufacturers of a product which contains an inherent defect are unlikely to make that information widely known, unless they are required to do so. For example, what cigarette manufacturer would voluntarily print a health warning on his product or his advertising copy? Furthermore, there is some information which is not always made available for fear of disadvantageous competition. For example, some manufacturers may decline to engage in comparative advertising on the ground that competitors may unfavourably compare a rival product with their own. The end result may be a general agreement in that sector of the market not to engage in comparative advertising.

It is sometimes argued that information will be passed to consumers by 'information brokers' such as retailers or doctors prescribing medicines. These brokers are said to have an interest in keeping the consumer properly informed as their own reputation depends on them supplying good quality products, but retailers may be just as ignorant of the performance of complex products as is the consumer, in which case the information is not passed on.

1.2.3.2 Other factors Apart from the problem of consumer information, other rationales may be put forward for protecting the consumer. It may be argued that consumer protection laws are based on the notion of paternalism. In some instances, there may be a distrust of the consumer's ability to protect himself. In particular, it would be reasonable to assume that where legislation has been passed in order to protect consumers against physical injury, there is a paternalist motive behind the enactment. It is not just where there is a risk of physical injury that paternalist arguments prevail. Where there is a high risk of considerable financial loss, intervention on paternalist grounds may be justified. For example, the enactment of the Unfair Contract Terms Act 1977 and many of the provisions of the Consumer Credit Act 1974 appears to be based on the assumption that the consumer is not always in a position to protect himself (see *Consumer Credit: Report of the Committee* (Cmnd 4596, 1971)). An alternative argument in favour of consumer protection legislation is that it preserves community values, such as fair dealing and honesty. Also, some commentators claim there is a consumer right to protection, particularly where physical injury caused by unsafe products is concerned.

TWO

Institutions and policies of consumer protection

2.1 CENTRAL GOVERNMENT AND GOVERNMENT AGENCIES

A wide range of central government departments have a role in relation to consumer protection. Some would argue that the range of departments concerned is too great and that, due to the large number involved, the consumer interest is sometimes prejudiced at the hands of another interest. It might be argued that the consumer interest would be best protected by the creation of a specific department of government devoted to consumer affairs, although a proposal to this effect was dismissed by the Molony Committee on Consumer Protection (Cmnd 1781, 1962, para. 886) as a grandiose notion. In 1974 the Labour government set up a Department of Prices and Consumer Protection, but following the Conservative victory in the general election of 1979, the department was disbanded and its functions were transferred to the Department of Trade and Industry. At the present time, that Department has an Under-Secretary of State for Industry and Consumer Affairs. Other consumer protection functions are performed by the Department of Health, the Office of Fair Trading, the Home Office and the Ministry of Agriculture, Fisheries and Food (MAFF).

It might be objected that the absence of a department of government devoted to consumer protection is disadvantageous, particularly where competing interests are dealt with by the same department. Moreover, to have an Under-Secretary with responsibility for both industry and consumer affairs is likely to give rise to cause for concern, since the interests of both are bound to conflict from time to time. The same can also be said of the dual role of MAFF in representing the interests of consumers of food and the agricultural community. For example, in recent years public concern has been shown over the safety of certain foods including eggs, cheese and beef. In each case, MAFF was torn between the interests of the consumer and the interests of the agricultural community, resulting in general public confusion over what was safe to eat.

Broadly speaking, the role of central government in relation to consumer protection can be described as the initiation and furtherance of legislative policy and supervising the enforcement of consumer protection measures designed to protect the economic and safety interests of consumers within the general constraints of the market.

2.1.1   Development of consumer protection policy
The two government departments most closely associated with the development of consumer policy are the Department of Trade and Industry and its satellite, the Office of Fair Trading. Other departments have a specific policy role in specialised areas which are considered below in respect of consumer economic interests and consumer health and safety.

2.1.1.1   The Department of Trade and Industry   Amongst other things, the Department of Trade and Industry (DTI) is responsible for the development of policy in the fields of trading standards and fair trading, weights and measures, consumer credit and consumer safety. The DTI also has important functions in relation to monopolies, mergers and restrictive practices. Much of this work devolves to agencies under the general control of the DTI and so is not actually performed by the department itself.

2.1.1.2   The Fair Trading Act 1973 and the Office of Fair Trading
The Office of Fair Trading (OFT) was set up under the provisions of the Fair Trading Act 1973. Broadly speaking, the OFT serves a dual role, namely, to protect the consumer against unfair trading practices and secondly to promote economic efficiency. The operation of an administrative agency such as the OFT provides a useful alternative to the employment of the criminal and civil law as a means of consumer protection. In particular, this agency has an important role to play in monitoring and controlling trade practices and also has responsibility for the licensing of traders in those areas where the added protection of a licensing system is regarded as desirable.

The attraction of administrative control is that it appears to keep certain consumer protection matters out of the courts, except in the most extreme cases. In many instances, the actions of an administrative agency may achieve the desired effect of dissuading a trader from engaging in unfair practices. Moreover, if the licensing of, for example, credit businesses, is effective, it will prevent traders who might act against the best interests of consumers from entering the consumer market in the first place.

In contrast to these claimed advantages, the cost of setting up an administrative agency is substantial, and it is always possible that this cost may outweigh the benefits derived from having this back-up to existing civil and criminal laws.

2.1.1.2.1   Consumer trade practices   The consumer protection role of the Director General of Fair Trading which most directly relates to the development of consumer policy consists of the review of commercial activities in the UK which relate to the supply of goods and services to consumers (Fair

Trading Act 1973, s. 2(1)(a)). The Director is required to identify practices which may adversely affect the economic interests of consumers. The Director also has an information collection function in respect of trading practices which affect consumer interests, whether they relate to economic, health and safety or other matters (s. 2(1)(b)). This information may be passed to the Consumer Protection Advisory Committee (CPAC), in so far as it relates to consumer economic interests, (s. 14). Following such a reference, CPAC may recommend that the DTI should legislate in respect of the practice, or it can modify or reject the Director General's proposals (s. 21).

The theory behind the creation of CPAC was that it should act as a jury to assess the merits of proposed regulations and help determine whether or not a particular practice was detrimental to consumer economic interests. In the event, four references were made to CPAC. In each case, CPAC chose to modify the Director's proposals and out of those four references, only three resulted in an order being made. No references have been made since 1976 and membership of CPAC is currently suspended.

For the purposes of the reference procedure, a consumer trade practice is defined in s. 13 as a practice carried on in relation to the supply of goods or services to consumers and which relates to the terms on which they are supplied, the way in which contract terms are communicated, sales promotion and methods of salesmanship, packaging of goods or methods of seeking payment for goods or services supplied. It is evident from this that s. 13 covers practices such as purporting to exclude the consumer's inalienable rights, excessively complicated or ambiguous language used in standard-form documents, misleading advertising campaigns and doorstep selling, amongst others. However, certain practices appear not to fall within the scope of s. 13. Since s. 13 is concerned with the supply of goods to consumers, transactions involving a purchase from a consumer are not within the scope of the provision. Section 13 makes no mention of the quality of goods, which is left to be dealt with by the civil law. Since s. 13 is concerned only with practices, it would be reasonable to assume that it has no application to isolated incidents which may subsequently grow into a practice. Section 13 requires the Director to wait until a continuing and significant state of affairs has come into existence.

Under s. 17(2), where it appears to the Director that a particular practice is misleading in relation to consumer rights and obligations or is apt to put consumers under pressure to enter transactions or causes contract terms to be inequitable to consumers, he may make a reference which includes a proposal that the practice should be controlled by Order made by the Secretary of State. The Director's reference under s. 17 should state the effect the trade practice has and CPAC must then report on the reference, having taken into account representations from interested bodies. The mere fact that a practice has one or more of the effects listed in s. 17(2) does not automatically mean that it is detrimental to consumers' interests. It must also be considered what beneficial effects it has and the benefits and detriments have to be weighed against each other.

Unfortunately, the procedure created by the 1973 Act is subject to a number of criticisms. It is cumbersome and depends on the use of criminal sanctions as a means of implementing proposals for changes in the law. In some instances, it may be difficult and expensive to prove the necessary detriment to consumer economic interests in order to make a reference in the first place. Sometimes, it may be as easy for the OFT to secure a change in business attitudes by seeking to inform the public rather than to coerce them through the use of regulations.

An illustration of the defects of the s. 17 procedure can be found in comparing two methods of dealing with cases of non-compliance with statutory controls on the use of exclusion clauses. One of the references to CPAC under s. 17 concerned purported exclusion of inalienable consumer rights and resulted in the Consumer Transactions (Restriction on Statements) Order 1976 (SI 1976/1813). The reference was made to CPAC in 1974, when it was discovered that following the enactment of the Supply of Goods (Implied Terms) Act 1973 some retailers were still displaying notices to the effect that no refunds were available should the goods purchased prove to be defective. The effect of this was that some consumers wrongly believed that they had no redress in such circumstances. CPAC received the Director's recommendations and submitted their report to the Secretary of State in July 1974, but the Order was not made until the end of July 1976. Quite apart from the delay in implementing the Director's proposals, which were in any event modified by CPAC, the Director's own report would have been costly to compile and, in the end, the Director admitted that the publicity which surrounded the s. 17 reference procedure had resulted in more people becoming aware of inalienable rights with the result that the number of 'no refund' notices had markedly decreased before the Order was laid before Parliament (Director General of Fair Trading, *Annual Report* 1975, p. 9).

In contrast to this, when the Unfair Contract Terms Act 1977 was enacted, it provided that a contract term or notice could not be used to exclude or limit liability for negligently caused death or bodily injury. It subsequently appeared that some businesses continued to display notices to the effect that they accepted no liability for injury and damage, howsoever caused. Instead of invoking the reference procedure, the Director General of Fair Trading conducted an informal information campaign through the use of press releases, articles in legal periodicals and direct communication to trade associations and individual businesses. This proved to be as effective as the drawn-out and expensive s. 17 reference procedure, and regulations to ensure compliance with the requirements of the 1977 Act never proved to be necessary.

2.1.1.2.2 Codes of practice A second important role played by the Office of Fair Trading in relation to the development of consumer policy is to encourage trade associations to publish codes of practice for adherence by their members (Fair Trading Act 1973, s. 124). This has become one of the most important weapons in the field of consumer protection. A wide range of codes have been disseminated in a number of areas of trade including the supply of motor vehicles, caravan lettings, travel facilities, credit facilities, domestic electrical appliances, antiques, furniture, footwear, funeral services, some home improvement services and mail order trading services.

The areas of trade in which codes of practice have emerged have tended to be those from which the greatest number of consumer complaints have been heard. Where there is widespread consumer dissatisfaction, the role of the OFT is to initiate discussions with interested parties representing both consumers and the trade itself in order to identify deficiencies in the way in which the trade operates. Once the problems have been identified, the primary responsibility for preparing the code of practice lies with the trade association itself which will submit a draft code to the OFT for approval. Modifications to the code may follow suggestions for improvement given by the OFT in order to ensure effective protection of the consumer. Following dissemination of the code, the trade association's responsibilities continue, in that it is important that the code is kept up to date in the light of changing circumstances and the identification of new consumer problems.

In some instances, it is the trade itself that initiates the procedure without initial suggestions having been made by the OFT. For reasons to be considered below, codes of practice have a number of important advantages over laws and these advantages are clearly appreciated by the trade associations which choose to prepare their own codes independently. This may be because during the period when most codes of practice were prepared (1973–9) there was always a threat of regulation if a trade association did not get its own house in order. Since 1979 the government has been less prepared to regulate trade practices. If the threat of regulation is removed, there is less incentive on the part of trade associations to impose further controls upon their members (see Borrie (1984) 7 J Consum Policy 197).

The supervisory role played by the OFT is important since, unless there is pressure from a body which has the consumer interest in mind, there is a danger that self-regulation on the part of the trade itself might address only the interests of traders. It was observed by Adam Smith that where people of the same trade meet together there is likely to be a conspiracy against the public or some contrivance to raise prices (*The Wealth of Nations*, ed. R. H. Campbell and A. S. Skinner (Oxford: Clarendon Press, 1976), vol. 1, p. 145).

2.1.1.2.3 Licensing of traders The mere identification of conduct detrimental to the consumer interest is of no use if there is not also in place a system whereby that abuse may be eliminated or, at least, reduced to a bare minimum. Clearly, the criminal law has an important role to play in eradicating unscrupulous trading practices, but the criminal law is only effective if it covers all forms of known trading abuse. Given that over a period of time new misleading trade practices may be developed, there is always the possibility that existing laws will prove to be inadequate. One method by which high standards can be maintained is through the operation of a licensing system under which a trader wishing to engage in a particular business must be licensed to do so. If it later comes to light that the trader is engaging in practices which are detrimental to the consumer interest his licence may be withdrawn.

The most well-known licensing system operating in the United Kingdom is the one set up by the Consumer Credit Act 1974, under which any person wishing to engage in a credit business or an ancillary credit business must be licensed to do so (s. 145(1)). Any person, acting in a business capacity, who wishes to provide consumer credit, hire goods to consumers, engage in credit brokerage, debt-counselling, debt-adjusting or debt-collecting, or operate a credit reference agency must be licensed to do so. Even those who indirectly engage in a credit business must be licensed to trade, otherwise they will commit an offence under s. 39(1). For example, in *Hicks* v *Walker* (1984) 148 JP 636 it was held that for the purposes of s. 39(1) an unlicensed car dealer who sold cars to a licensed dealer in order to facilitate finance arrangements committed a criminal offence because he was considered to be indirectly engaged in the business of credit brokerage.

The licensing requirement of the Consumer Credit Act 1974 extends only to those who act in a business capacity. For these purposes, the fact that a person carries on a business only occasionally means that he will not be treated as acting in the course of a business (s. 189(2)). As a result, if the number of occasions on which a television dealer supplies goods on credit is minimal (for example, two or three transactions in a four-year period), a licence would not be required (see *R* v *Marshall* (1989) 90 Cr App R 73; *Hare* v *Schurek* [1993] CCLR 47), although other provisions of the 1974 Act, for example, those relating to contract formalities, would still apply.

Licences under the Consumer Credit Act 1974 may be either standard licences or group licences. A standard licence may be issued to an individual, a company or a partnership and lasts for 10 years unless revoked at an earlier stage. A group licence may be issued to an organisation which represents the interests of a specified group of businesses. For example, the Law Society has been issued with a group licence which covers all solicitors who hold a current practising certificate. An important feature of all licences is that they specify the credit businesses they cover. Accordingly, a solicitor who wishes to engage in a credit business which is not covered by the Law Society group licence must obtain a standard licence to cover the activity in question.

While it is a criminal offence for a business to operate a credit business without a licence, perhaps the most important sanction is that any contract entered into by an unlicensed trader is unenforceable against the consumer unless the Director General issues a validating order (s. 40) or the consumer consents to the transaction (s. 173(3)). Some responsibility for ensuring that a trader is licensed also falls on the principal creditor by virtue of s. 149. Accordingly, there is a strong incentive on creditors to ensure that the credit brokers with whom they deal are appropriately licensed. The reason for this is that the principal agreement is only enforceable against the consumer if the Director General issues a validating order once it has been discovered that the credit broker is not licensed.

The obvious sanction associated with a licensing system is that if a licence is refused or revoked, the trader goes out of business. For this reason, the administrative authority must have very good grounds for declining to grant or renew a licence to trade.

Under s. 25(1), the Director General of Fair Trading (DGFT) must consider whether an applicant for a licence is a fit person. The burden of proving fitness is placed on the applicant and the Director is entitled to consider a number of factors in determining whether an applicant for a licence is a fit person. These include whether the applicant has been found guilty of fraud or dishonesty; whether he has contravened any statutory requirement in relation to the provision of credit; whether he has committed any act amounting to sex or race discrimination and whether he has engaged in oppressive or deceitful business practices (s. 25(2)). Where appropriate, the Director may indicate that an application is subject to a 'minded to refuse' notice (s. 27(1)(a)) or he may invite the applicant to make representations in support of his application (s. 27(1)(b)). If the Director does issue a minded to refuse notice, it will refer to any of the matters listed in s. 25(2), but other factors may also be relevant. In determining whether a licence should be refused, regard must be had to the nature of the business in respect of which a licence has been applied for. For example, a conviction for the commission of an offence involving personal violence will be particularly relevant to an application for the licensing of a debt-collection service, whereas a similar conviction might not be as relevant if the applicant intends to set up a credit reference agency where there is less likelihood of face-to-face contact with members of the public. Similarly, a conviction for an offence of dishonesty would be particularly relevant wherever the applicant is likely to come into contact with money.

While previous convictions are a relevant consideration, it is clear from the wording of s. 25(2) that other matters may also be considered. In particular, the Director will have to take account of any complaints which might have been received from members of the public and local authority trading standards or consumer protection agencies, even where these may not have resulted in a prosecution. The problem with taking such matters into account is that such complaints only give one side of the story and, since the matter has not been tested in court, the applicant will not have had the opportunity to explain his actions. In these circumstances the Director will have to tread carefully and it is likely that a licence will be granted even if there is some cause for concern (see Borrie, 'Licensing practice under the Consumer Credit Act 1974' [1982] JBL 91). Alternatively, s. 27(1)(b) might be of use in these circumstances, since the applicant could be called upon to make representations in support of his application.

As a further alternative to refusing to grant a licence, the Director may also limit a licence to specified activities (s. 23(2)). Thus a licence could be granted merely for the purposes of carrying on a consumer credit brokerage business, but not for the purposes of the supply of credit.

At first sight, a licensing system would appear to be a very powerful means of controlling trade practices since it serves to deny the opportunity to engage in business and therefore spreads a very much wider net than is possible with specific controls concerned with individual transactions (see *Consumer Credit: Report of the Committee* (Cmnd 4596, 1971), vol. 1, p. 255). Moreover, the administrative body responsible for the licensing programme has a flexible tool with which it can act in relation to activities which are not strictly controlled by law and can dissuade businesses from engaging in undesirable, but lawful practices. Licensing as a means of control of business practices also appears to allow for consistency of approach to the standards of conduct required of licensees.

The licensing system also has other useful side-effects. In particular, it will provide a considerable amount of information on the area of business subject to the licensing requirement. The licensing authority will be able to identify emerging practices which may require legislative action in the interests of consumers.

The advantages of a licensing system have to be set against its disadvantages, perhaps the most important of which is cost. In order to set up a licensing system on the scale of that envisaged by the Consumer Credit Act 1974, it has become necessary to create a huge administrative machine. This cost can be borne by the public purse, but it is also possible to make a licensing system self-financing by charging a fee for the grant of a licence.

Where the scale of the licensing system is substantial, it is more likely to give rise to problems of cost. For example, the scheme set up under the Consumer Credit Act 1974 involves a system of positive licensing under which anyone wishing to engage in a credit business must be granted approval prior to setting up in business. Some would argue that this system goes too far, particularly since it also requires dealers, credit-brokers and other ancillary credit businesses to be licensed. By the end of 1987, the number of licences granted totalled 217,378, of which the largest category was that of credit brokerage (*Annual Report of the Director General of Fair Trading* 1987, app. 1, s. 6). Initially, licences were granted for a period of 15 years, with the result that the first round of renewals were effected in 1991. Since that date in excess of 300,000 applications for standard licences have been received in the OFT (OFT Press Release, 10 April 1991). Since 1991, the period of validity of licences has been reduced to five years (Consumer Credit (Period of Standard Licence) Regulations 1991 (SI 1991/817)).

The general cost of the licensing system has caused concern to the DTI. A consultative document (*Deregulation of UK Consumer Credit Legislation* (1995) concluded that the requirement that licensed traders should automatically report changes in business management to the DGFT under the 1974 Act, s. 36, is too onerous on credit businesses and serves little useful purpose. In its place, at the suggestion of the DGFT, it has been proposed that all that should be disclosed is the fact that a person involved in the management of a licensed credit business has been convicted of an offence of dishonesty, has contravened anti-discrimination legislation or has contravened provisions of the Consumer Credit Act 1974 itself.

In contrast with the elaborate system employed under the Consumer Credit Act 1974, other licensing schemes have fallen short of a system of positive licensing. For example, the scheme employed under the Estate Agents Act 1979, ss. 22 and 23, can be better described as a negative system under which any person may operate as an estate agent until it is shown that he is unfit to do so.

Apart from problems of size and cost, a licensing system can also lead to unfair refusals to grant or renew a licence. In this respect, it is important that any challenge procedure works properly and that appropriate administrative law measures exist in order to deal with possible abuses of the system.

2.1.1.2.4 Unfair trading conduct   Under the Fair Trading Act 1973, s. 34, the Director General of Fair Trading may intervene in order to prevent a person from acting in a manner which is detrimental to the economic, health or safety interests of consumers and in a manner which is unfair to consumers. Unlike some of the other functions of the OFT, this particular role involves direct dealings with members of the trading community and is not merely a general monitoring or policy role.

In order for the Director General to be able to seek a written assurance, there must have been a persistent course of trading conduct which is detrimental to consumer interests (whether they be economic, health or safety interests) (s. 34(1)). For a practice to be regarded as unfair, the trader must have committed a breach of an existing requirement of the criminal law (s. 34(2)) or, alternatively, there must have been a persistent course of conduct which amounts to the breach of an obligation enforceable by civil proceedings (s. 34(3)). However, in neither case is it necessary for civil or criminal proceedings to have been commenced or concluded, since the Director General may also take into account complaints which have been received from individuals, from consumer advice agencies and from local authority trading standards or consumer protection departments (s. 34(4)).

Since unfair trading conduct is not confined to matters of safety but also covers the economic interests of consumers, the breach of any civil or criminal law provision which is geared towards the protection of consumers will suffice, provided there is sufficient evidence of a 'course of conduct'. Examples of what amounts to unfair trading conduct include persistent breaches of safety regulations (see *R* v *Director General of Fair Trading, ex parte F. H. Taylor & Co. Ltd* [1981] ICR 292), breaches of the penal provisions of the Trade Descriptions Act 1968, failures to comply with the requirements of the Unfair Contract Terms Act 1977 in relation to the exclusion of liability for negligently caused death or bodily injury and repeated supplies of food which fails to comply with the requirements of the Food Safety Act 1990 (see *Director General of Fair Trading* v *Smiths Bakeries (Westfield) Ltd* (1978) *The Times*, 12 May 1978). The repeated supply of services not in accordance with contract specifications would also amount to unfair trading conduct. However, since the definition of unfair trading conduct is tied to evidence of breach of existing criminal or civil law requirements, failure to comply with the requirements of a trading association code of practice which does not also amount to contravention of existing legal requirements would not be classified as unfair trading conduct. Whether this position should change is a matter considered below in relation to the question whether there should be a general duty to trade fairly.

One of the most serious difficulties presented by the wording of s. 34(1) is that the trader must have 'persisted' in a particular course of conduct. On numerous occasions, annual reports of the Director General of Fair Trading have emphasised how difficult it is to prove persistence. Removal of this requirement would make the written assurance procedure a far more potent weapon against trading malpractice. It seems likely that the wording of s. 34 may be amended to take on board this particular issue, if a recent announcement emanating from the DTI is implemented. In the consultation paper *Reform of Part III of the Fair Trading Act 1973* (DTI, 1994) it was suggested that the reference to 'persisted in' should be removed and that the Director General should be able to seek an assurance where a trader has 'carried on a course of conduct which is detrimental to the interests of consumers'.

Although the power conferred on the Director General under s. 34 is capable of protecting consumer interests, there is, in fact, no requirement in s. 34(2) to the effect that particular trading conduct should specifically relate to consumers. Accordingly, trading conduct which amounts to a public or private nuisance affecting only the interests of other businesses could still be regarded as unfair trading conduct. However, s. 34(1)(a) does make it clear that what the Director General should consider is whether a particular course of conduct is detrimental to the interests of United Kingdom consumers. Accordingly, for practical purposes, it is likely that this part of the 1973 Act is effectively confined to consumer protection issues.

There is a two-tier procedure for dealing with unfair trading conduct, once it has been identified. In the first place, the Director General, once he has identified a course of trading conduct which is unfair, may seek a written assurance from the trader that the conduct and any similar conduct will not be repeated (s. 34(1)). This may be sufficient to dissuade the trader from any further transgressions, in which case no further action will be necessary. Since many offenders will be companies which may go out of business, there is also provision for seeking an assurance from senior company officers or persons with a controlling interest in a company (ss. 38 and 39). It follows that if a person promotes a company which engages in a course of unfair trading conduct but subsequently ceases trading, the person against whom an assurance has been sought will continue to be subject to that assurance in the event that he may later set up business under a new trading name.

If a trader gives a written assurance, but subsequently breaks it, or if a person refuses to give a written assurance when requested to do so, the matter can be taken further by the Director General under the second-tier procedure permitted under the 1973 Act. It is open to the Director General to seek an order in the Restrictive Practices Court to the effect that a trader should refrain from engaging in a particular course of conduct. Alternatively, the court can seek a binding assurance from the trader. In either event, if the trader fails to comply with the court order, he may be held to be in contempt of court and punished accordingly (s. 35).

An important consideration is that the unfair trading conduct procedure operates in addition to existing criminal and civil law rules. Accordingly, there is the possibility that a particular trader may have been proceeded against in the criminal or civil courts and may have been required to pay a fine or damages in the event of judgment being entered against him. If, in addition to this, a written assurance is sought or the Director General chooses to bring proceedings in the Restrictive Practices Court, the impression may be given that the trader is being further penalised. However, in *R* v *Director General of Fair Trading, ex parte F. H. Taylor & Co. Ltd* [1981] ICR 292, Donaldson LJ, at p. 296 considered this not to be the case, expressing the view that the purpose of part III of the Fair Trading Act 1973 is not to drive rogue traders out of business, but to provide additional deterrence in the hope that the offending trader will rehabilitate himself and reform his ways.

While the part III procedure may operate in a deterrent fashion, the Director General must also be careful not to take matters too far when publicising the fact that assurances have been given, since this could easily create the impression that the administrative authority is attempting to penalise the rogue trader for having stepped out of line. So far as publicity is concerned, s. 124 confers on the Director General the power to publish information and advice, but it is clear from s. 124(2) that any publication which is specific to an individual or a body of persons should avoid any material which might be regarded as prejudicial to that person or persons. It is clear that publicity regarding part III undertakings is capable of falling within this requirement, with the result that the Director General should exercise extreme caution before he goes to press. In *R* v *Director General of Fair Trading, ex parte F. H. Taylor & Co. Ltd* [1981] ICR 292 a company had been convicted on 13 occasions of offences contrary to safety regulations made under the Consumer Protection Act 1961. The Director General sought a written assurance which was given, but the Director also prepared and published details of the assurance, making it clear that the assurance had only been given after the trader had been warned that legal proceedings would be commenced in the Restrictive Practices Court. The press release also set out the number of convictions recorded against the company and the amount in fines it had been ordered to pay. The company sought a declaration that this course of action was beyond the Director's powers and that it should have been warned by the Director General that a consequence of non-compliance with a request to supply an assurance was that adverse publicity might follow. The Divisional Court decided that the application should fail on the ground that if adverse publicity was justifiable, there was no need for a warning to be given. However, the court was also of the opinion that some of the actions of the Director General were very close to the line between that which was acceptable and that which was not. In particular, Donaldson LJ expressed the view that since the purpose of the part III procedure is to give a trader a chance to mend his ways, what was done in this case in setting out in full all the details of the applicant's past wrongdoing might have exceeded the limit of what was fair. Conversely, this had to be set against the fact that the Director General must be able to get his message across by communicating to all bodies and persons who may be expected to let the Director General know if there has been a breach of the assurance given by the particular trader.

The powers conferred under part III of the 1973 Act all refer to the Director General, but the question has arisen whether anybody other than the Director may bring proceedings in respect of a failure to comply with a written assurance. In *Mid Kent Holdings plc* v *General Utilities plc* [1996] 3 All

ER 132 the question arose whether a company adversely affected by a person's failure to comply with an assurance given to the Secretary of State for Trade and Industry under the monopoly provisions of the Fair Trading Act 1973 could bring proceedings in respect of that failure to comply. It was held that the matter of non-compliance with a written assurance was enforceable only by an officer of the Crown, by virtue of the specific wording of the Fair Trading Act 1973, s. 93. Similarly, under s. 35 it is clear that the only person able to bring Restrictive Practices Court proceedings in respect of an unfair trading conduct written assurance is the Director General of Fair Trading.

2.1.1.2.5 Injunctive relief The Director General of Fair Trading has import-ant monitoring powers in relation to unfair terms in consumer contracts and in respect of misleading advertising generally. Both these powers arise by virtue of two European Community Directives, namely the Misleading and Unfair Advertising Directive (84/450 EEC, OJ L250, 19.9.1984, p. 17) and the Unfair Terms in Consumer Contracts Directive (93/13/EEC, OJ L95/29, 5.4.1993).

Under the Unfair Terms in Consumer Contracts Regulations 1994 (SI 1994/3159), the Director General of Fair Trading is under a duty to consider all complaints made to him to the effect that a particular variety of term employed for general use in consumer contracts is unfair (reg. 8(1)) and if he considers the term in question to be unfair, an application may be made for an injunction to prevent the use of that variety of term (reg. 8(2)). If an injunction is granted it may relate not just to the particular term in respect of which the application for an injunction is made, but it may also be applied to any similar term and any term having a like effect to that in respect of which the application is made (reg. 8(6)).

The Control of Misleading Advertisements Regulations 1988 (SI 1988/915) also allow the Director General of Fair Trading to seek an injunction to restrain the publication of advertisements to which the Regulations apply and which are considered to be misleading under the definition given in the Regulations. For the purposes of the Regulations, an advertisement is any form of representation which is made in connection with a trade, business, craft or profession in order to promote the supply or transfer of goods, services, immovable property, rights or obligations (reg. 2). From this definition, it is clear that advertisements in relation to goods and services are covered, but so also are advertisements relating to the transfer of an interest in real property, provided the representation is made in the course of a trade or business etc. Accordingly, misleading statements made by a private seller of a house would not be covered, but misleading statements made by an estate agent could be the subject of the DGFT's powers if all other avenues of redress have been exhausted.

A representation is misleading, for the purposes of the Regulations, if, *inter alia*, it deceives or is likely to deceive persons to whom it is addressed or whom it reaches and is likely to affect the economic behaviour of such persons or be likely to injure a competitor (reg. 1(2)).

What is meant by the word 'misleading' was considered in *Director General of Fair Trading v Tobyward Ltd* [1989] 2 All ER 266, in which Tobyward Ltd had advertised a product under the name 'Speedslim' making claims to the effect that it could result in permanent weight loss with 100 per cent safety by preventing fat from entering the bloodstream; that success was guaranteed; that the product contained an ingredient which represented a unique medical advance and that a user could lose a specific amount of weight in a specified period of time. At the time, no specific legal control could prevent the making of such claims and, despite the fact that the Advertising Standards Authority regarded the claims to be unacceptable under the British Code of Advertising Practice, the defendants appeared to have no intention of accepting their advice. Complaints had been received from trading standards departments and the Advertising Standards Authority, with the result that the DGFT applied for an interlocutory injunction to restrain publication of these claims and any advertisement in similar terms which might convey a similar impression.

Hoffmann J considered that the advertisement was deceptive simply because it contained statements which were false in relation to the product advertised ([1989] 2 All ER 266, 270). The advertisement was likely to affect the economic behaviour of persons to whom it was addressed because it was 'more likely that they would buy the product' after seeing it (loc. cit.). Accordingly, an injunction was granted to restrain the further use of this and any similar advertisement by the defendants.

The Regulations are designed to apply to the majority of advertisements, although there is a specific exception in reg. 3 for investment advertisements and advertisements in respect of certain matters dealt with under the Financial Services Act 1986, part V, since these are dealt with separately by rules made under the 1986 Act.

That the Control of Misleading Advertisements Regulations 1988 are a 'safety net' is clear from the provisions of reg. 4, which specifies that in the event of a complaint to the Director General of Fair Trading, the complainant may be required to establish that all other means of dealing with the complaint have been employed and have failed to deal adequately with it (reg. 4(3)). If the matter can be dealt with by means of action under a code of practice, such action should be allowed to take its course.

Where it is clear to the Director that all other avenues have been exhausted and that the advertisement is misleading, he may bring proceedings for an injunction, including an interlocutory injunction, against any person who appears to be concerned with the publication of the advertisement (reg. 5). Where such proceedings are brought, the High Court may grant an injunction on such terms as may appear appropriate to the circumstances of the case, provided the advertisement appears to the court to be misleading.

Where an injunction is granted, it may relate not only to the advertisement in respect of which the complaint has been received, but also to any advertisement in similar terms or one which is likely to convey a similar impression (reg. 6(2)). An injunction may be granted even though no evidence has been called to the effect that loss has been caused to anyone (reg. 6(5)(a)) or that the publisher intended the advertisement to mislead (reg. 6(5)(b)).

Generally, the onus lies on the publisher to adduce evidence which will justify a refusal to grant an injunction. Thus, if the publisher can prove that his advertisement is factually accurate (reg. 6(3)), or if he calls evidence of the matters referred to in reg. 6(5), the inference is that an injunction will not be granted.

2.1.2 Protection of consumer economic interests
The DTI is probably the most influential government department so far as consumer economic interests are concerned. It funds the Office of Fair Trading and has general responsibility for consumer affairs, trading standards, weights and measures, and consumer credit. Because of these general functions, the DTI is responsible for, *inter alia*, the enforcement of the Consumer Credit Act 1974, the Trade Descriptions Act 1968, the Consumer Protection Act 1987, in so far as it concerns misleading pricing, and Orders made under the Fair Trading Act 1973.

The DTI also has general responsibility for monopolies and mergers and other restrictive practices. Many of these functions are delegated to the Office of Fair Trading. In particular, this satellite of the DTI, in addition to its consumer policy role, has powers to control persistent unfair trading conduct under part III of the Fair Trading Act 1973. Other functions served by the Office of Fair Trading which further the economic interests of consumers include the overseeing of monopolies and mergers, the licensing of credit businesses and the publication of consumer education materials.

The DTI is also responsible for the work of other agencies whose work is related to both economic and health and safety interests of consumers. The department sponsors the work of the British Standards Institution and oversees the work of the National Consumer Council amongst other agencies.

Other central government departments which concern themselves with consumer economic interests include the Home Office, which is responsible for legislation concerning shops, and the Department of Social Security in so far as it is concerned with matters such as welfare benefits etc.

2.1.3 Protection of consumer health and safety interests
In the field of health and safety, a wide range of government departments have a role to play. Which department is responsible depends on how the threat to the consumer's health or safety comes about.

Some of the responsibilities of the DTI feature in this respect since it is responsible for general consumer safety and therefore oversees the enforcement of the Consumer Protection Act 1987 in relation to general product safety.

The Home Office has a supervisory role in relation to the control of firearms and explosives, dangerous drugs and poisons and is also responsible for the licensing of premises used for the supply of alcoholic drinks etc.

Where food is concerned, the Department of Health and the Ministry of Agriculture, Fisheries and Food (MAFF) both share the role of consumer protection watchdog. The two are responsible for the enforcement of the Food Safety Act 1990 and the Medicines Act 1968 and any regulations made under those statutes. Both the Department of Health and MAFF are partly responsible for matters of food hygiene and safety. The Department of Health will offer medical advice on possible contamination of consumer goods. MAFF has particular responsibility for laying down standards in respect of the composition of food and the labelling and advertising of products intended for human consumption. Relevant government departments (namely the Department of Health, MAFF, the Department of Social Security and relevant departments for the purposes of food policy in Scotland, Wales and Northern Ireland) are advised by the Food Advisory Committee on the composition, labelling and advertising of food and additives, contaminants and other substances which may be present in food.

2.1.4 A general duty to trade fairly

It has been observed already that the range of devices employed as a means of protecting consumers is broad, including the use of the criminal law, the civil law, administrative control under the guidance of the Office of Fair Trading and other central government departments and business self-regulation under voluntary codes of practice. Despite this broad range of controls on trading abuse, at various stages, it has been considered whether English law should adopt a general duty to trade fairly. The effect of such a duty would be to impose on traders generally a duty not to engage in any practice which is deceptive, misleading or unconscionable, such as can be found in the Australian Trade Practices Act 1974, s. 52, or the United States Federal Trade Commission Act 1970, s. 45(a)(1), both of which use such general language. This contrasts with the subject-specific approach which has been the hallmark of the English Parliamentary draftsman in many consumer protection initiatives.

In drafting a general duty of this kind, a number of factors must be taken into consideration. In the first place, there is no point in bringing about wholesale change unless the ultimate effect of the changes is to raise trading standards and, at the same time, provide cheaper and more readily accessible means by which consumers may obtain redress (*A General Duty to Trade Fairly* (OFT, 1986), para. 5.13). A general duty should reduce reliance on the criminal law in as many respects as possible, while still providing suitable sanctions and appropriate means of enforcement and preserving, where possible, the certainty created by the present use of the criminal law (loc. cit.)

2.1.4.1 Current aspects of the duty to trade fairly It is arguable that in certain respects, there is already a partial duty to trade fairly, in so far as the Director General of Fair Trading has powers under the Fair Trading Act 1973, ss. 34 and 35 (considered in 2.1.1.2.4), to seek assurances from traders to the effect that they will not engage in practices detrimental to the consumer interest. However, it has been seen already that the power to seek assurances is currently confined to trading conduct which amounts to a breach of existing civil and criminal law obligations.

In addition to the Director General of Fair Trading's powers, there are specific areas in which fair trading is required as a matter of law. For example, the licensing provisions of the Consumer Credit Act 1974 mean that if a credit business engages in conduct which is detrimental to consumers, there is the possibility that its licence to deal may be revoked.

In recent years, there has also been a general move away from specifically drafted criminal offences in consumer protection legislation. At one stage, the Parliamentary draftsman would seek to define in very specific language the constituent elements of a statutory criminal offence. For example, the Trade Descriptions Act 1968, s. 2, contains a very long list of types of statement which are capable of amounting to trade descriptions, and the now repealed provisions of the Trade Descriptions Act 1968, s. 11, in respect of misleading price comparisons, was very specific in defining the types of comparison which were prohibited. Unfortunately, the effect of such specific legislation is that over a period of time, traders may develop practices which comply with the letter of the law but not necessarily its spirit (see *A Duty to Trade Fairly* (OFT, 1986), para 2.5). In relation to price comparisons, it is interesting to compare the regime introduced by the Consumer Protection Act 1987, s. 20(1), which makes it an offence to give, by whatever means, a misleading indication as to the price at which goods, services, accommodation and facilities are available (see further chapter 19). Of course one of the problems with such a generally worded provision is that, without qualification, it would be difficult to know when a particular price comparison is lawful or not. In order to meet this problem, a statutory code of practice has been issued under s. 25 of the 1987 Act, which gives general guidance on what is to be regarded as misleading and what is acceptable. If this can be done for price comparisons, presumably there would be no great difficulty in doing the same for other potentially misleading statements. The same preference for generality as opposed to specificity can also be found in the General Product Safety Regulations 1994 (SI 1994/2328), which lay down a general duty on producers to produce only safe products (reg. 7). Similarly, in the field of advertising law, the Control of Misleading Advertisements Regulations 1988 (SI 1988/915) introduce a general restriction on misleading statements in advertisements, supported by a power on the part of the Director General of Fair Trading to seek injunctive relief in respect of contraventions of the Regulations. A similar monitoring role can be found in the Unfair Terms in Consumer Contracts Regulations 1994 (SI 1994/3159).

In the field of food safety law, there has also been a move towards more generally worded legislation in the form of a requirement that food should not be sold if it fails to satisfy statutory food safety requirements (Food Safety Act 1990, s. 8(1) and (2)) . For these purposes, it is an offence for a person to supply, offer to supply or possess for the purposes of supply any food which is injurious to health, unfit for human consumption or is so contaminated that it would not be reasonable to expect it to be used for human consumption (see further chapter 15). In similarly general terms is the requirement in the Consumer Protection Act 1987, s. 10, to the effect that it is an offence for a person to supply, offer to supply, agree to supply, expose for supply or possess for the purposes of supply any consumer goods which are not reasonably safe. It appears that this particular provision, although of comparatively recent origin, is likely to have a very short shelf-life, since it will now be of use only in circumstances in which the more recent General Product Safety Regulations 1994 (SI 1994/2328) are inapplicable. Under reg. 7 there is a general requirement to the effect that no producer shall place a product on the market unless that product is a safe product (see further chapter 14).

In addition to the use of the criminal law and administrative action as a means of securing basic standards of fair trading, aspects of the civil law may be seen in the same light. For example, a consumer who has been persuaded to enter a credit bargain as a result of doorstep salesmanship may, in certain circumstances, cancel the agreement during a cooling-off period provided by statute (Consumer Credit Act 1974, ss. 67 and 68; see chapter 11). The effect of including an unfair term in a consumer contract is that the relevant term may be struck out and is not to be regarded as binding on the consumer (Unfair Terms in Consumer Contracts Regulations 1994 (SI 1994/3159), reg. 5; see also chapter 12).

· At one stage, it appeared that certain members of the judiciary were prepared to allow the development of a general principle of inequality of bargaining power which would permit a party in an unequal bargaining position to escape the consequences of the contract he had entered into. According to *Lloyd's Bank Ltd* v *Bundy* [1975] QB 326 this general principle is based on four essential requirements, namely, lack of advice, disparity of consideration, exploitability and pressure or influence by the stronger party. The fortunes of this general principle appear to have been short-lived, since the House of Lords has subsequently taken the view that the task of providing a general principle against inequality of bargaining power is a matter for Parliament, not the courts (*National Westminster Bank plc* v *Morgan* [1985] AC 686, 708 per Lord Scarman). It was also the view of the House of Lords that such a task had been partly undertaken in the form of modern consumer protection legislation, in particular the power conferred on courts to reopen extortionate credit bargains under the Consumer Credit Act 1974, ss. 137–139 (see further chapters 4 and 11).

Despite the failure of a general principle of inequality of bargaining power to take hold in the courts, there are periodic judicial statements which may be taken as support for a general duty to trade fairly. For example, in *Interfoto Picture Library Ltd* v *Stiletto Visual Programmes Ltd* [1988] 1 All ER 348 Bingham LJ recognised that common law systems were unusual in that they do not recognise and enforce the overriding principle that in making and carrying out contracts, parties should act in good faith or should act in accordance with the principle of open and fair dealing. Having asserted that this is not a general principle in English law, his lordship went on to observe that English law has developed piecemeal solutions to demonstrated problems of unfairness, such as rules on unconscionable bargains in equity, common law and statutory rules on sufficiency of notice and other controls on the use of exemption clauses, statutory rules on the form of consumer credit agreements, the principle of utmost good faith in insurance law and rules on disguised penalty clauses in the form of agreed estimates of loss arising from a breach of contract. Perhaps the reason why English law has developed along the lines of piecemeal solutions rather than general principles is that the development of a principle of good faith or inequality of bargaining power would strike at the fundamental general principle of contract law that, within limits, the parties to a contract are free to make whatever contract they like, which is of particular importance in the context of commercial contracting, but which is capable of giving rise to serious problems in the context of consumer contracts.

2.1.4.2 The need for a general duty to trade fairly Given the range of current provisions which may be described as aspects of a duty to trade fairly, the question arises whether it is necessary to go any further. One feature of the changes which have occurred to date is that they have been introduced on a piecemeal basis, dealing with particular issues when the need has arisen. No attempt has been made to overhaul the basis of consumer protection law by imposing on traders a general duty to refrain from all forms of deceptive and misleading trade practices.

Whether there is a need for such a general duty depends on whether there are trade practices which remain unregulated. The view of the Office of Fair Trading, at one stage, was that there were areas of doubt, evidenced by consumer dissatisfaction at the way in which consumer protection laws were being implemented which could be taken to justify the imposition of a general duty to trade fairly (see *A General Duty to Trade Fairly* (OFT, 1986), paras 1.13 to 1.17; *Consumer Dissatisfaction* (OFT, 1986)). At the time, it was proposed that there should be introduced a horizontal duty applicable generally to each sector of trade and a range of vertical duties, applicable to specified trade practices. The principal advantage of such a general duty is that it tends to avoid a case-by-case approach to trading malpractice and concentrates, instead, on general patterns of trading practice, providing a flexible tool to counteract trading abuse. However, the principal disadvantage is the lack of certainty it can create. The United States experience of a general duty not to engage in any form of deceptive, misleading or unconscionable conduct under the Federal Trade Commission Act 1970, s. 45(a)(1), is that the more open-ended the definition of the duty, the more likely it is that it will generate endless litigation aimed at ascertaining what conduct is misleading, deceptive or unconscionable. From the point of view of traders, their representatives, enforcement agencies and consumer advisers, if there is no definitive list of what practices are acceptable, the whole process of compliance with the law becomes very difficult. To counteract this problem, it might be possible to do what has been done under the Consumer Protection Act 1987, ss. 20, 21 and 25, namely to produce a list of guidelines, setting out which practices are acceptable and which are not.

Despite the potential advantages of a general duty to trade fairly, it was accepted by the Office of Fair Trading that the proposal to introduce such a duty was excessively complex, and in the end, it was decided not to pursue the idea of a general duty any further (see *Trading Malpractices* (OFT, 1990), pp. 20–2). What was considered a more appropriate direction was to concentrate on those deceptive or objectionable practices which are not subject to control or cannot be effectively controlled by existing means (*Trading Malpractices*, para. 1.6). In this regard, current thinking appears to be that the most effective means of controlling trading malpractice is an appropriately amended form of the procedure under part III of the Fair Trading Act 1973 (see 2.1.1.2.4). However, the necessary amendments to s. 34 of that Act would involve the removal of the need to show that there is a 'persistent' course of trading conduct before a written assurance can be sought. Furthermore, it is also considered necessary to redefine the word 'unfair'.

It will be recalled that, at present, unfair trading conduct is confined to breaches of existing duties imposed by law, including breaches of duty enforceable by way of civil proceedings. However, as presently worded, the Fair Trading Act 1973, s. 34, does not apply to a failure to comply with the requirements of a trade association code of practice or to deceptive conduct which is not currently controlled by law.

The provisional view of the Office of Fair Trading was that 'unfair' should be redefined to include 'deceptive or misleading' practices and 'unconscionable' practices (*Trading Malpractices*, paras 5.18–5.28). It was further suggested that there should be a list of illustrative acts or practices which could be regarded as unfair, which could be added to as and when new misleading practices should be developed (loc. cit.). However, later proposals emanating from the DTI suggest that the term 'unfair' should be extended in meaning to include 'deceptive, misleading or oppressive' conduct and that there should be no illustrative blacklist of such practices (*Reform of Part III of the Fair Trading Act 1973* (DTI, 1994)). It seems that the phrase 'unconscionable' contained in *Trading Malpractices* is regarded as being too wide and subjective a concept to be capable of enforcement (*Reform of Part III of the Fair Trading Act 1973*, para. 6.3).

2.2   LOCAL GOVERNMENT

Local authorities have two important roles to play in respect of consumer protection. One is to enforce the provisions of regulatory measures concerned with the conduct of trade and the other is to provide consumer advice and information.

2.2.1 Enforcement

Local government departments bear the day-to-day responsibility of enforcing many statutory provisions which seek to protect the consumer and the honest trader. Most local authorities have created consumer protection, trading standards and environmental health departments which bear responsibility, at a local level, for the enforcement of the provisions of statutory provisions such as the Trade Descriptions Act 1968, the Consumer Credit Act 1974, the Weights and Measures Act 1985, the Consumer Protection Act 1987, the Food Safety Act 1990 and the Property Misdescriptions Act 1991, amongst others, and the various orders made under consumer protection legislation generally. In addition to bringing prosecutions for breaches of the penal provisions of these Acts of Parliament, local authorities also have responsibility for testing equipment used by traders, sampling products put on the consumer market by manufacturers and retailers and for the inspection of premises, particularly those at which food for human consumption is present, with a view to the maintenance of high standards of hygiene and safety.

Under the provisions of the Local Government Act 1972, there was a dramatic reduction in the number of enforcement authorities from 241 to 88, resulting from the creation of a middle tier of local government in the form of metropolitan authorities. A consequence of this was that the smaller number of metropolitan authorities and county councils became responsible for the enforcement of consumer protection legislation. This in turn led to a more uniform policy of enforcement and reduced the unevenness of interpretation of the law by the much larger number of authorities which previously existed. Subsequently, the Local Government Act 1985 abolished the metropolitan authorities with the result that much of the uniformity of approach was potentially lost. The 1985 Act did insist on the creation of coordinating committees to be set up by the metropolitan districts which inherited the role of enforcement authority, but these committees have not proved to be effective. The 1985 Act also allows the Secretary of State to create a single enforcement body in metropolitan areas, but it appears that no attempt has been made to create any such body.

A major difficulty which arises from local, as opposed to national enforcement of consumer protection legislation is that local authorities may differ in their interpretation of the law, with the result that there is no uniform policy of enforcement. Clearly it would be undesirable for a trader to discover that he had been prosecuted by one authority for an infringement in respect of which another authority might not take exception. Similarly, with the growth of multiple-outlet retail stores, it would be unhelpful in the formulation of a general policy on compliance with statutory standards if it were to be discovered that what was regarded as unlawful in one area could be carried on without comment in another. From a consumer perspective too, uneven enforcement patterns are equally undesirable, since a consumer seeking advice on what can be done to remedy a particular infringement might receive conflicting advice according to the part of the country in which he or she happened to live.

Mindful of the potential problems of uneven enforcement patterns, the Association of County Councils and the Association of Metropolitan Authorities reached an agreement in 1976 under which they set up a body known as the Local Authorities Coordinating Body on Trading Standards (LACOTS), which was authorised to consult and negotiate with central government and trade and industry bodies with a view to establishing standards of quality. Uniformity of enforcement is achieved by asking one authority to conduct a test case in areas where the law is in doubt. Following the test case, other authorities can be advised of the outcome.

To avoid the problem of conflicting advice given by local authorities to manufacturers and retailers, LACOTS has approved the principle of the 'home authority'. If a manufacturing or retailing concern with more than one place of business requires advice on how to comply with new regulations, it is advised to approach the authority in which its principal place of business is to be found. This authority is known as the 'home authority' which will act as a coordinator in determining what advice should be given to the trader or manufacturer. In particular, the home authority will consult with other authorities in which the trader has a trading base before giving any significant advice. Also, should a complaint be received by an enforcement authority, that authority should, first, consult the relevant home authority to determine what advice has been given. The fact that the home authority has advised a trader that a particular practice is lawful does not prevent the enforcement authority from taking action, but in most cases, the trader will be aware of what should be done to comply with legal requirements.

The fact that local government has gone to so much trouble to set up a coordinating body like LACOTS would seem to suggest that central government enforcement of consumer protection legislation might be more appropriate. Certainly, the United Kingdom seems to be the only European Union member State which charges the responsibility of consumer protection to local authorities instead of operating a more centralised system. Whether or not centralisation would be an advantage or not is a moot point. From the point of view of large-scale businesses with multiple outlets, centralised enforcement of legislation such as the Trade Descriptions Act 1968 would make sense, but the same view may not necessarily be held by small-scale businesses (see *Review of the Trade Descriptions Act 1968* (Cmnd 6620, 1976), p. 80). Certainly in relation to food production, there is probably a strong case for centralised administration of the law, since it has been shown that 10 of the largest food manufacturers and processors are responsible for producing more than one third of the annual turnover of food (Audit Commission, *Safe Food — Local Authorities and the Food Safety Act 1990* (HMSO, 1990)).

In the case of larger businesses, advice to the head office or a single successful test case will usually produce swift results on a national level, whereas if the matter is left to local enforcement, there could be several actions before a trader decides to alter his practices. Conversely, although larger businesses do operate on a national level, it must always be recognised that there may be specific local issues which can only be taken account of by local enforcers.

Local authority enforcement would appear to be more appropriate where a trader operates on a smaller scale, especially since local enforcement is likely to be more responsive to the needs of local consumers and businesses.

A factor which may be relevant in determining whether local or national enforcement is preferable is the question whether central or local authorities are more prone to 'capture' by the trade or representatives of the trade they are supposed to regulate. It has been argued that regulatory bodies may start off life enthusiastically pursuing wrongful conduct, but in time, due to familiarity with the bodies with which they deal, regulators are prone to become an arm of the trade sector they were originally intended to police. In the end, the regulator begins to serve the interests of the trade to the detriment of the consumers he was intended to protect (Galbraith, *The Great Crash* (Houghton Mifflin, 1955), p. 171).

Whether or not the 'capture theory' is accurate in practice is not entirely clear, as there are some regulatory bodies which have remained active in pursuit of the traders they were set up to police. One suggestion is that capture is more likely to occur where a bargaining process exists such as in cases where a regulator must obtain information from the body or bodies he is required to regulate (Commission of the European Communities, *Symposium on the Enforcement of Food Laws* (Waters, 1980)). If this is true, it would seem to be the case that a simple enforcement authority which is not dependent on information supplied by regulated businesses is not very likely to be captured. On the other hand if a local authority department is required to obtain information in order to carry out its enforcement functions, this role is very likely to result in capture, especially in the light of the continuing trend towards the reduction of local authority spending. Moreover, although this is not presently the case, if a system of compulsory competitive tendering were to be introduced into the enforcement arena, it would become more likely that an enforcement authority with information-gathering responsibilities would become subject to possible capture by the regulated trade.

Capture theory is much less likely to be applicable where a regulatory body has a wide range of different types of business to police and does not become excessively familiar with the practices of one specific type of business. In particular, it is likely that the wider the range of businesses regulated, the more likely it is that there will be competing interests, all of which the regulatory body must consider (see Posner, 'Theories of economic regulation' (1976) 5 Bell Journal of Economics 335). Accordingly, given the range of competing interests, the regulator is likely to adopt an objective and open stance, which is unlikely to favour one particular interest over another. It would appear that the majority of local consumer agencies have a fairly wide range of businesses with which they must deal, which might lead to the conclusion that this form of regulation is not particularly prone to capture. On the other hand, the same can also be said of centralised organisations such as the Office of Fair Trading, which also have a wide range of trade sectors with which to deal.

A possible reason for doubting the correctness of the capture theory is that where it is shown to explain regulatory failure, it is that a trade body has captured a regulator. However, there is frequent contact between regulators and consumer agencies, which often requires the supply of information by the consumer agency, yet there has never been any suggestion that a consumer agency has ever effectively captured a body responsible for regulating an industry in which there is a distinct consumer interest (Posner, op. cit.).

2.2.2 Consumer advice
Local authorities have an important role to play in providing advice facilities for consumers, by virtue of the requirements of the Local Government Act 1972, ss. 137 and 142. In particular, it was seen as a priority to extend the availability of advice to as wide a range of consumers as possible. While the 'middle classes' who tended to be the main subscribers to the Consumers' Association publication *Which?* were able to avail themselves, at a price, of

the services provided by that association, a large proportion of the consumer population had no ready source of advice when things went wrong. It is true that such bodies as the Citizens' Advice Bureaux and some local authority weights and measures departments were prepared to advise in respect of certain matters, but there was no coordinated approach to the giving of advice generally.

Local authorities have assisted in the provision of consumer advice in two ways. They have set up consumer advice centres which may serve a preventative role by giving pre-shopping advice or a remedial role by advising on consumer problems in the event of a consumer complaint. The other important respect in which local authorities have advised consumers has been through support for or the setting up of neighbourhood law centres in relatively deprived areas.

The role of consumer advice centres has declined since 1979 when the government decided to withdraw all funding from these bodies on the grounds of inefficiency. It was perceived that the role of advice giver could be best served by bodies such as Citizens' Advice Bureaux, the central support for which was doubled. As a result of the withdrawal of funding from consumer advice centres, it was reported that in 1986 there were only 29 such centres and that the local authority role in providing advice had fallen upon trading standards departments instead, who responded by employing a small number of 'consumer advisers' who had no responsibility for enforcement of the law against traders and producers (National Consumer Council, *Ordinary Justice* (1989), pp. 52–3).

2.3 GOVERNMENT-SPONSORED BODIES

Two bodies, namely, the Consumer Protection Advisory Committee (CPAC) and the National Consumer Council (NCC) are directly sponsored by the government. The role of the former in respect of consumer protection has been considered already, although it should be observed that the role of this body is now non-existent in the light of the fact that its membership has been suspended. The NCC was set up in 1975 with a view to representing consumer interests in dealings with the government, local authorities, the OFT and trade bodies. It also advises on consumer protection policy through the publication of reports on matters concerning consumers and through making representations to relevant bodies.

The range of issues taken on by the NCC is substantial, as is evidenced in the reports it has published or had commissioned. These include representations made concerning incomprehensible language in consumer contracts and official publications (*Gobbledegook*, 1980), public services (*Consumer Concerns*, 1990), legal services (*Ordinary Justice*, 1989; *Legal Services*, 1990), whether and how the law in respect of the quality of goods and services should be reformed (*Service Please?*, 1981; *The Consumer Guarantee*, 1989), consumer credit and debt (*Consumers and Credit*, 1980; *Consumers and Debt*, 1989) and disadvantaged consumers (*Why the Poor Pay More*, 1977). The Council also issues on a regular basis policy statements on perceived consumer problems and developments in the law over a very wide range, including not just matters related to the supply of goods and services, but also issues such as the environment, electricity and water pricing, disconnections by privatised utility companies, drug testing, National Health Service complaints, personal investments, competition in the State education sector, international trade, consumer education, housing, social security and health care. Some of these initiatives it takes up on its own account, but the NCC is also frequently asked to respond on topics referred to it by the government.

In one sense, it is perhaps surprising that the NCC still exists, as it was created in the era of corporatism of the middle 1970s which was so despised by the Conservative government of 1979. When in opposition, the Conservatives argued against the establishment of the Council, but there has been no subsequent attempt to disband it.

2.4 PUBLIC SERVICES AND UTILITIES

Nationalised industries and privatised large-scale suppliers of goods and services (such as British Gas, British Telecommunications and National Power) often find themselves in a position whereby they have a monopoly or a near-monopoly in the supply of a particular product or service. Because of this potential monopoly power, it is generally regarded as necessary to oversee their operation and to subject their activities to close scrutiny.

As an example, the Telecommunications Act 1984 provides for the appointment of a Director General of Telecommunications (DGT), who is empowered to review the provision of telecommunications facilities. Furthermore, the DGT or the Secretary of State is required to license bodies wishing to provide such services. The DGT heads the Office of Telecommunications (OFTEL) and has powers to ensure that, so far as is practicable, there is an adequate supply of telecommunications facilities to meet all reasonable demands (Telecommunications Act 1984, s. 3). Particular emphasis is placed on the need for emergency services, call-box facilities, maritime services and user information services. The DGT's duty is to act on behalf of the consumer.

The extent to which regulatory controls have an effect on the performance of these large utility companies may sometimes be doubted because of the monopoly position occupied by the company. However, in recent years, there has been a marked trend towards opening up markets once occupied by nationalised industries. For example, in the telecommunications sector, British Telecommunications has not been the sole provider of such services for some time. If this trend continues and true competition is introduced into the consumer market place, what ought to follow is an increased standard of service for consumers at competitive price levels. However, if true competition does not develop, there is always a danger that complacency will set in. For example, in 1985 OFTEL received 10,000 complaints on consumer matters, particularly in relation to tariffs, charges, quality of service and disputed accounts. By 1990, the standard of service appeared to have improved substantially, since a NCC survey showed that overall, 72 per cent of the population were satisfied with telecommunications services (NCC, *Consumer Concerns* (1990), p. 3).

2.5 VOLUNTARY ORGANISATIONS

A number of voluntary bodies offer advice, provide information or in some other way provide services of assistance to consumers. The most important of these are the Citizens' Advice Bureaux, the Consumers' Association, the National Federation of Consumer Groups and the British Standards Institution.

Citizens' Advice Bureaux (CABx) can be found across the country and deal with a wide range of consumer problems, although it should be observed that not all of the work of the CABx is consumer-protection-related. For example, other matters dealt with include matrimonial advice, social security claims, debt and problems with the police.

CABx are funded by both central government which makes a grant to the National Association of Citizens' Advice Bureaux, and by local authorities which provide funds on a local basis. Although the CABx do employ staff on a full-time basis, they are also heavily dependent on voluntary workers (some with legal professional skills) who offer their services on a rota basis.

The Consumers' Association is a company limited by guarantee which provides consumer information on competing products and services in its magazine *Which?* It may be objected that the Consumers' Association is unrepresentative of the consumer population as a whole since it appears that the majority of subscriptions to *Which?* come from social groups A and B (upper-middle and middle class) with very few subscriptions coming from the lower social classes and that *Which?* magazine therefore attends closely to the needs of groups A and B (Smith, *The Consumer Interest* (John Martin Publishing, 1982), p. 284).

Some would argue that the approach of the Consumers' Association to sampling the goods and services it tests is subject to criticism on the ground that its samples are small and therefore unrepresentative. Moreover, given the rate at which new products and models appear on the market, it is evident that *Which?* reports soon become dated.

The National Federation of Consumer Groups (NFCG) coordinates the activities of the growing number of local consumer groups. The aim of these groups is to encourage local interest in consumer affairs. The NFCG is partly funded from grants from the Consumers' Association and the DTI.

The British Standards Institution (BSI) was set up, in its present form, in 1929 and sets standards, dimensions and specifications for manufactured goods. A 'British Standard' is a document which stipulates the specifications, requirements for testing or measurements with which a product must comply in order to be suited to its intended purpose and work efficiently. Before a standard is set, there will have been lengthy consultation with interested parties and organisations.

Compliance with BSI standards is generally a matter of choice rather than compulsion so far as producers and manufacturers are concerned. However, in some cases, where there is a potential for serious personal injury, compliance with a British Standard is made compulsory. This is the case with products such as motorcycle crash helmets and car seat belts. A producer who does choose to comply with a BSI standard may apply for certification of his product and may then display the BSI 'Kitemark' on it, though he must be prepared for subsequent inspections by the BSI to ensure that standards are being properly maintained. These standards are minimum requirements. Merely because a product reaches BSI standards and can display the well-known 'Kitemark' it does not follow that legal requirements have been satisfied since the regulatory regime may require a standard higher than that set by the BSI (see *Balding* v *Lew-Ways Ltd* (1995) 159 JP Rep 541).

2.6 TRADE ASSOCIATIONS AND CODES OF PRACTICE

A significant feature of many aspects of consumer protection law is the extent to which laws are supplemented with or even, in some cases, replaced by codes of practice drawn up by trade associations after consultation with the Office of Fair Trading and other interested bodies. These non-statutory codes take the form of voluntary controls and guidance prepared by trade associations for the benefit of their members and which are intended to promote acceptable trading standards across the business sector to which they relate. Such codes may be prepared entirely voluntarily by particular areas of business, such as the Code of Advertising Practice prepared by the advertising industry, but other areas of trade may require prompting. In this last respect, it has been observed already that one of the functions of the Office of Fair Trading is to encourage trade associations to prepare codes of practice to be sent to their members with a view to safeguarding and promoting the interests of consumers (Fair Trading Act 1973, s. 124(3)).

In addition to voluntary codes of practice prepared by trade associations, there is also an increasing number of statutory codes of practice and notes of guidance which are intended to supplement parent legislation for the purpose of providing assistance in ensuring compliance with a particular Act of Parliament and regulations made thereunder. Codes are, for example, issued under the Food Safety Act 1990 to assist local authorities in the enforcement of the parent Act and to provide the food industry with guidance on how to ensure compliance with the regulatory framework set up by it (see further chapter 15). Similarly, the Consumer Protection Act 1987, part III, which regulates the use of price indications and comparisons, is supported by a code of practice, made under s. 25, which indicates whether a particular price comparison is acceptable or not (see further chapter 19).

It has been observed that despite some of the disadvantages of codes of practice considered below, it would be unwise to dismiss them as a means of protecting consumers since the Parliamentary timetable is very tight and if a code of practice can protect the consumer interest in the absence of relevant laws, this is to be appreciated (see Borrie, 'Consumer protection laws for the 1990s' [1988] JBL 116, 121). Some of the means of consumer redress provided by voluntary codes of practice have the effect of reducing the cost of obtaining a remedy by cutting out the need for litigation (ibid.). Also codes of practice are particularly important in helping to structure standard contract terms used by traders, since it is common for trade associations to formulate a standard-form contract for use by their members. The effect of such standard terms is often to invalidate certain types of term which may operate against the consumer interest and to make the resulting contractual terms used by members of the association less one-sided than they might otherwise have been (ibid.). This particular feature of standard-form contracts is most easily identifiable in the terms prepared by ABTA for use by travel agents and tour operators, under which code, the contractual rights of consumers have been, for some years, better than those demanded by the law (see chapter 15).

2.6.1   Features of codes of practice

Codes of practice may be particularly useful in dealing with cases of possible trading abuse which may not be susceptible to legal controls, but the advantages of codes of practice need to be weighed against their disadvantages, which, in some instances, may be substantial. In formulating a code of practice, it is important that the duties of traders and the rights of consumers are clearly outlined. Mere expressions of goodwill towards consumers are insufficient and it is important that codes of practice are kept up to date in the light of changing circumstances (Director General of Fair Trading, *Annual Report* 1976, p. 9). A code of practice should be designed to encourage higher trading standards, remove trading abuses and provide a suitable means of handling consumer complaints (ibid.).

The essence of a trade association code is that it is designed specifically to meet the problems encountered in a particular area of trade. Because of this the content of one code of practice may differ substantially from that of another trade association. However, there are certain features which appear to be common to most of the codes developed in recent years. For example, there may be statements concerning the standard of service to be expected of members of the association, restrictions on advertising and promotion techniques, provisions in respect of the exclusion or limitation of liability to consumers, provision for a customer complaint service, including in some cases an arbitration scheme, provision for full price information and provision for refunds to be given to dissatisfied customers.

For the most part, the codes of practice which have been developed in conjunction with the Office of Fair Trading have been concentrated in the areas of trade which have given rise to the greatest number of consumer complaints. Thus codes regulating the trade practices of suppliers of motor vehicles (Joint Code of the Society of Motor Manufacturers and Traders (SMMT), the Motor Agents Association (MAA) and the Scottish Motor Trade Association (SMTA)), domestic electrical appliances (Codes produced by the Association of Manufacturers of Domestic Electrical Appliances (AMDEA), the Electricity Council and the Electrical and Television Retailers Association (RETRA)), footwear (Code of the Footwear Distributors Association), furniture and holiday caravans.

Codes of practice have also appeared in service sectors most closely associated with consumer dissatisfaction. In particular, codes have been developed to deal with the practices of funeral directors (Code of the National Association of Funeral Directors) and the suppliers of home improvement services, particularly double glazing contractors (Code of Ethical Practice of the Glass and Glazing Federation). Codes also cover the servicing of motor vehicles (Joint Code of SMMT, MAA and SMTA; Vehicle Builders and Repairers Association Code of Practice) and domestic electrical appliance repairs (AMDEA, RETRA and Electricity Council codes), postal services (Post Office Code of Practice for Postal Services), photographic processing services, domestic laundry and cleaning services (Code of the Association of British Laundry, Cleaning and Rental Services) and package holiday services (Association of British Travel Agents Codes of Conduct and see also chapter 9).

2.6.2 Advantages and disadvantages of codes of practice

Provided a code of practice does deal adequately with the causes of consumer dissatisfaction and is kept up to date in the light of changing practices, it can be argued that such codes are capable of dealing with matters not regulated by the law. For example, some codes of practice are well ahead of the law in that they allow for the cancellation of contracts where no similar legal remedy exists. Moreover, codes of practice are particularly useful in controlling practices which would be difficult to regulate by law. For example, the code of practice of the National Association of Funeral Directors provides for what should happen if two funeral directors arrive at the home of a bereaved consumer — a matter which is hardly conducive to legislative regulation.

In general, it can be argued in favour of codes of practice that they are more flexible than laws in that they can be tailored to the needs of a particular trade or industry. Furthermore, since responsibility for drafting and enforcement rests with those who have a close knowledge of the trade, it can be said that codes are often more successful in dealing with likely consumer problems.

While codes of practice can claim to have advantages when compared with legislation, it is also true that they have a number of deficiencies. In particular, it can be said that there are problems of implementation, structural deficiencies, motivation and enforcement. There is also some evidence to the effect that whether a code of practice does provide adequate provision for consumer protection depends entirely on the vigilance of the trade association which promotes the code. For example, a report by the Consumers' Association has highlighted laxity on the part of a large number of trade associations in checking the credentials of persons applying to become members, monitoring the quality of services provided by members and providing an effective consumer complaints procedure (see *Which?*, August 1996, pp. 24–7).

So far as implementation is concerned, one of the features of almost all trade association codes of practice is that they apply only to members of the association. It follows from this that traders who have chosen not to belong to a relevant trade association will not be subject to the sanctions the trade association may wish to impose in the event of a breach of a requirement of the code. Moreover, since non-members are more likely to engage in conduct detrimental to consumer interests, the only constraints on the activities of such traders would appear to emanate from legislative or judicial controls. The problem of unfair practices amongst non-members of a trade association is also likely to lead to resentment amongst traders who have voluntarily submitted themselves to the rules of the association, particularly if the non-member is seen to derive a competitive advantage from engaging in such practices without being punished.

A further problem of implementation is that trade associations can sometimes appear to be slow to enforce the terms of the code against their members. Against this it should be observed that codes of practice are not like rules of law and that a process of encouragement rather than compulsion is sometimes beneficial. Having said this, it remains the case that trade associations are dependent for their survival on members' subscriptions and there may be some substance to the view that there is a tendency not to look at possible cases of abuse from a truly independent position. It is arguable that so far as this particular issue is concerned, wider use of Parliamentary codes of practice, such as those attached to the Food Safety Act 1990 and part III of the Consumer Protection Act 1987 regarding price comparisons may be the route to adopt in the future, especially if the administrative provisions of the Fair Trading Act 1973, part III, are to be expanded (see above). The major advantage of codes of practice attached to specific pieces of legislation is that they apply to all traders alike, whether members of a trade association or not, but are more flexible in that amendments can be made to codes more easily than is possible in the case of Acts of Parliament or even delegated legislation.

A further argument against codes of practice is that consumer views are not always considered prior to their formulation and they tend to be based on current business practice. However, in the case of codes of practice drawn up in consultation with the Office of Fair Trading, there is ample evidence that appropriate consumer organisations and other interested parties will have been consulted. Moreover, in the case of the British Code of Advertising Practice, there is also a process of full consultation with representatives of consumer groups (see Thompson, 'Self-regulation in advertising' in *Consumer Law in the EEC*, ed. Woodroffe (1984), pp. 53–68).

The problem of motivation is based on the argument that codes of practice generally tend to come into existence as a means of averting a threat of legal control. Furthermore, some would argue that the provisions of some codes of practice provide a form of insulation from competitive forces. However, there are good examples of code of practice provisions which provide useful means of consumer redress in excess of that which can be provided by the law, which would seem to suggest that it is not just business which benefits from their provisions.

Some codes of practice suffer from problems of enforcement in the sense that they appear to possess few real sanctions. Some trade associations are prepared to impose fines in the event of an infringement, but others may provide merely for a reprimand or the publication of adverse reports in a trade journal. Ultimately, there is the sanction of dismissal from membership of the association, but this is only an effective measure if the trade association claims a very high proportion of traders of the type under consideration as members. If there is a high proportion of 'fringe' operators who are not members of the trade association concerned, the threat of dismissal would appear not to be an effective sanction. In the end, the extent to which trade association sanctions are effective will depend on the vigilance of the trade association itself and it would appear that some are more vigilant than others.

A possibility which has been canvassed is whether consumers could enforce the terms of a trade association code of practice on the basis that there is an implied term in any contract with a participating trader to the effect that he will comply with the requirements of the relevant code of practice. However, in order to arrive at this conclusion, it would be necessary for the judicial tests on the implication of contractual terms to be complied with (see chapter 4). It would have to be shown that any term which is sought to be implied is reasonably necessary under the test in *Liverpool City Council* v *Irwin* [1977] AC 239, or required in the interests of business efficacy in order to make sense of the contract (see *The Moorcock* (1889) 14 PD 64) or can be implied under the 'officious bystander' test as representing the presumed intention of both parties at the time the contract was entered into (see *Shirlaw* v *Southern Foundries (1926) Ltd* [1939] 2 KB 206). Whether or not the courts would be prepared to imply such a term into a consumer contract is doubtful. Certainly, it would require an omitted matter to be of paramount importance to the contract before it could be regarded as the subject of a term implied out of necessity. Moreover, since the other tests for implying terms into a contract appear to be based, at least in part, on the presumed intentions of the parties, it might be difficult to discern a common intention that compliance with the requirements of a code of practice should form part of the contract.

Probably the most that consumers can expect of the contractual effect of codes of practice is that, in rare cases, the trade association may be taken to have contracted with the consumer by promising something of substance which may be regarded as the subject matter of a collateral contract (see chapter 4 and *Bowerman* v *ABTA Ltd* (1995) 145 NLJ 1815). Alternatively, as has been observed above, a number of contractual terms may appear as express terms of a standard-form contract at the insistence of a trade association, giving rise simply to an issue of normal contractual interpretation.

Some of the problems of enforcement have been addressed by a former Director General of Fair Trading (Borrie, *The Development of Consumer Law and Policy* (1984), chapter 4), who suggests that the requirements laid down by codes of practice could be enforced by means of the procedure in the Fair Trading Act 1973, part III, in respect of unfair trading conduct (see above). This suggestion would necessitate a change in the law since, at present, part III of the 1973 Act applies only to a breach of existing requirements of the criminal or civil law. If failure to comply with a trade association code of practice were to be subject to the written assurance provisions of ss. 34 and 35 of the 1973 Act, a powerful means of enforcement would lie in the hands of an agency with consumer interests in mind. Whether or not progress is to take place on this matter is in some doubt, since the DTI Consultation Paper, *Reform of Part III of the Fair Trading Act 1973* (DTI, 1994), makes no reference to this as an area of development.

Even if the proposal were to be taken up, it is not without its difficulties since there are many requirements laid down by trade associations which might prove difficult to enforce by such means and it might become necessary to review the wording of many codes of practice if such a power were to be introduced. Furthermore, the proposal, as it stands, would not address the problem of unfair practices engaged in by non-members of a trade association. To meet this problem, it would be necessary to introduce a mandatory requirement of membership of a relevant trade association.

2.7 OMBUDSMEN

It has been noted above that one of the defects with some trade association codes of practice is that they can appear to represent the interests of members of the association rather than the interests of consumers. This criticism is particularly apt in the case of codes of practice which do not provide for truly independent reference of disputes to binding arbitration. As an alternative, in certain trade sectors an apparently more impartial means of resolving consumer problems is through an ombudsman scheme.

If a particular ombudsman scheme has been approved by the British and Irish Ombudsman Association, consumers can be sure that the scheme is entirely independent and that any adjudication on a particular dispute will be completely impartial. This is because in order to be approved by this Association, the scheme must satisfy four basic criteria of independence, effectiveness, fairness and public accountability.

The ombudsman schemes so far adopted cover a broad range of trading sectors including banking, insurance, building societies, investment services, legal services, pensions, corporate estate agents, funeral services and police complaints amongst others. What the schemes cover is dependent upon the terms of reference under which each scheme was set up. But in general terms, an ombudsman will not step in to resolve a consumer complaint until he is satisfied that the business in respect of which a complaint has been made has exhausted its own internal complaints procedures. Moreover, there is also a general provision in most schemes that the ombudsman will not consider a complaint if legal proceedings have already been instituted.

Where an ombudsman finds in favour of a consumer, his powers are not merely concerned with securing a proper remedy in respect of the specific complaint which has been made to him. Instead, part of the general role of an ombudsman is to attempt to improve the service sector over which he has jurisdiction. Thus, part of an ombudsman's determination may involve a recommendation that certain steps be taken to improve the business practice which resulted in the complaint in the first place. Whether or not compensation can be ordered will depend upon the terms of the particular scheme under which a complaint has been made. As an example, the Insurance Ombudsman has a power to award compensation up to a maximum figure of £100,000.

Sadly, not all ombudsman schemes make provision for the enforcement of an award against a trader in the event of adjudication in favour of the consumer, since an ombudsman does not possess the same status as an arbitrator, whose awards are binding upon the parties who submit themselves voluntarily to arbitration as an alternative to litigation. However, in practice, it would appear that the majority of businesses subject to an ombudsman scheme will comply with the decision, usually in order to avoid the adverse publicity which would follow from non-compliance, given the ability of ombudsmen in their annual reports to name businesses which fail to comply with a ruling against them.

2.8 EUROPEAN INSTITUTIONS AND POLICIES

Many modern consumer protection initiatives now emanate from the institutions of the European Community. UK membership of the EC has continued since our late entry in 1973, some 25 years after its initial foundation. But the impact of membership has been great especially in consumer protection. For example, it has been estimated that by 1990, 80 per cent of legislation regarding food was based upon EC initiatives (Painter (ed.) *Butterworths Law of Food and Drugs*, 1(A9)). Similarly, there has been a substantial increase in domestic legislation based upon harmonisation Directives in the field of consumer safety generally, and more recent initiatives on the part of the Commission have moved in the direction of consumer economic interests (see, e.g., the *Green Paper on Guarantees for Consumer Goods and After-Sales Service* (COM (93) 509)). Also of relevance particularly in the context of advertising law is the role of the European Court of Human Rights and its interpretation of the freedom of expression provisions of the European Convention for the Protection of Human Rights and Fundamental Freedoms 1953, to which all member States of the European Community are now signatories.

2.8.1 European institutions
The four main EC institutions are the Council of Ministers, the Commission, the European Parliament and the Court of Justice of the European Communities.

2.8.1.1 Council of Ministers This body is probably the most important Community institution consisting of one representative delegated by each of the 15 member States, who will always be a government minister. The delegate is not fixed, with the result that a different person may be sent according to the nature of the issue under consideration. The Council is seen as the principal decision-making body.

The role of the Council is to see to the implementation of the EC Treaty objectives (EC Treaty, art. 145). In many cases the Council can only act after a proposal has been made by the Commission and, following the provisions of art. 100A, the Council must also consult Parliament and the Economic and Social Committee before taking action in some cases.

Decisions of the Council may be taken by a simple majority (art. 148(1)) a qualified majority (art. 148(2)) or by a unanimous vote, depending on the nature of the vote taken. Where only a simple majority is required, eight votes in favour of a particular measure will suffice to see it through, but this system appears to be rarely used in practice.

The majority of decisions of Council are now subject to the qualified majority voting procedure set out in art. 148(2) under which the larger member States, namely France, Germany, Italy and the UK have 10 votes each and other States have a smaller number of votes according to their size descending to just 2 votes in the case of the smallest of States, namely Luxembourg. According to the voting system (as amended), in order for a measure to be adopted it must have 64 votes in its favour out of the total of 87 available. Accordingly, under this system, it is no longer possible for one member State to drag its feet in order to prevent the progress of a measure which commands the support of the majority of member States. This is particularly important since harmonisation measures, which tend to predominate in the field of consumer protection law, used to be subject to a requirement of unanimity under the old art. 100, but following the new provisions on harmonisation in art. 100A, a qualified majority vote in favour of a particular Directive is normally sufficient to see it through to the final stage.

In some instances, a requirement of unanimity remains, in which case one vote against a particular policy or measure will suffice to block its progress. Areas where unanimity is still required include proposals to harmonise the law on indirect taxation, decisions whether to admit a new member State and the granting of Community aid to a member State in financial difficulty.

2.8.1.2 Commission The Commission acts as the executive arm of the Community and consists of some 20 Commissioners appointed by all member States. Not more than two Commissioners may come from any single State, but all member States must be represented. In practice, the larger States are allowed to appoint two commissioners, this privilege being accorded to France, Germany, Italy, Spain and the UK.

Once a person is appointed as a Commissioner he must renounce political and national loyalties so as to be able to act completely independently. Moreover a Commissioner must not take instructions from a national government (Merger Treaty, arts 10 and 11) and member States undertake not to attempt to influence a Commissioner. Since independence is seen to be an essential requirement of members of the Commission, they are fully salaried and are not permitted to hold any other office during their period of tenure, whether paid or unpaid.

Although the Commission has only very limited powers to make legislation, it is nonetheless the initiator of Community action and, in important cases, the Council cannot act until it has received a proposal from the Commission. However, the Council has the power to request a proposal from the Commission in order that Community objectives may be achieved (EC Treaty, art. 152). Where legislative powers do rest with the Commission they have usually been delegated by the Council under art. 155. For example, such powers have been delegated in relation to the Common Agricultural Policy.

The Commission also has the power to act under art. 5 to ensure that Treaty obligations are complied with. Accordingly, it is the function of the Commission to bring proceedings against a member State in the case of an identified infringement (art. 169). In order to facilitate this investigative function, the Commission is conferred with powers to obtain necessary information from member States and other relevant sources.

2.8.1.3   European Parliament   The predecessor of the present Parliament was not an elected assembly, with the result that, originally, it was given very few powers. However, the present Parliament has now become a much more powerful body and is no longer the 'talking shop' it once used to be.

Since 1979 the European Parliament has consisted of elected members, MEPs, who are elected according to the voting system chosen by each member State and in numbers roughly corresponding to the size of each member State.

The Parliament has an advisory role and may object to proposals for new measures, albeit not indefinitely. If Parliament makes suggestions for the amendment of a measure, the Council may reject those amendments and implement the measure, but only by way of a unanimous vote. Parliament also has a supervisory role in that it may ask members of the Commission to explain their actions and answer questions regarding a proposed measure.

2.8.1.4   Court of Justice of the European Communities   The Court of Justice (ECJ) consists of 15 judges, one appointed from each of the member States. Although the appointees may have been judges in their home States, there is no such requirement for appointment to the ECJ, provided they would have been eligible for appointment as judges in their own country. Judges of the Court are assisted by Advocates General who prepare impartial submissions which cover the facts of the case being heard and the relevant legal arguments. The Advocate General will also recommend what judgment should be returned by the Court, although the Court is under no obligation to follow that recommendation.

The principal terms of reference of the ECJ include the hearing of actions to determine the legality of binding acts of the Commission and the Council. Such actions may be initiated under the EC Treaty, art. 173, by the Council, the Commission, a member State or by an affected individual or corporation. Under art. 177, a national court may also refer a matter to the ECJ for a preliminary ruling on any question of Community law. Where such a ruling is made, the decision of the ECJ is binding on questions of Community law, but it still remains the task of the national court to apply that ruling to the facts of the case and to decide other issues in the light of the ECJ ruling.

2.8.2   Community legislation
Legislation which emanates from the EC consists of primary legislation, such as treaty obligations, and secondary legislation such as Regulations, Directives, decisions, recommendations and opinions (EC Treaty, art. 189). Primary legislation is said to take direct effect as part of the domestic law of

each member State and therefore will confer direct rights upon individuals within a member State which may be enforced in the domestic courts of the member State concerned. Accordingly it was observed in *Van Gend en Loos* v *Nederlandse Administratie der Belastingen* (case 26/62) [1963] ECR 1 that art. 12 of the EC Treaty concerning the introduction of new customs duties on imports and exports 'is more than an agreement creating only mutual obligations between the contracting parties. . . . Community law . . . not only imposes obligations on individuals but also confers on them legal rights.' However, for a treaty provision to be directly applicable, it had to either make some explicit grant or impose obligations in a clearly defined manner so as to confer on individuals some specific legal right.

The effect of *Van Gend en Loos* was to confer on an individual a right of action against a State which had failed to comply with Treaty obligations, thereby giving rise to what may be called 'vertical' direct effects. But subsequently, the ECJ has also recognised that some treaty provisions can also confer 'horizontal' direct effects, thereby conferring on an individual a right of action against another individual. Accordingly in *Defrenne* v *Sabena (No. 2)* (case 43/75) [1976] ECR 455 it was possible for the plaintiff to enforce against her employer rights conferred under art. 119 concerning sex discrimination in employment. So far as secondary legislation is concerned, art. 189 provides that Regulations are of general application and will be directly applicable in all member States. In contrast, the same treaty provision declares a Directive to be binding only as to the result to be achieved, so such legislation cannot be directly applicable since it is for member States to select the means by which the result to be achieved by the Directive is to be given effect as part of domestic law. A Council or Commission decision is declared to be binding in its entirety upon those to whom it is addressed, but a recommendation is stated to have no binding force at all.

Perhaps of greatest importance in the context of consumer law is the legislative effect of Directives, since it has been through the EC harmonisation programme that most EC-initiated legislation has come to be implemented as part of English law. What is clear from the comments above is that Directives are not directly applicable as part of English law since Directives are addressed to member States and it is the responsibility of each member State to arrange for an appropriate means of implementation. Accordingly, the EC Directives on Product Liability, General Product Safety, Unfair Terms in Consumer Contracts and the Advertising Directive, have all had to be given effect to in English law either by way of an Act of Parliament or by way of statutory instrument.

In addition to legislative enactments which are directly applicable, the ECJ has also developed a doctrine of 'direct effect' under which certain obligations imposed by way of secondary legislation may take direct effect as part of domestic law under certain conditions. Initially the doctrine of direct effect as it applied to Directives was confined to 'vertical' direct effects with the result that in *Van Duyn* v *Home Office* (case 41/74) [1974] ECR 1337 it was possible for the plaintiff to invoke the provisions of an EC Directive so as to challenge a decision made by the Home Office to exclude her from entry and residence in the UK to take up work with the Church of Scientology. However, the provisions of the Directive must be sufficiently precise in order to take direct effect and in all events, there is no question of enforcing a Directive until the time period permitted for implementation has expired (*Pubblico Ministero* v *Ratti* (case 148/78) [1980] 1 CMLR 96).

What is much less clear is whether a Directive can create 'horizontal' direct effects so as to confer on an individual the right of action against another individual. *Van Duyn* and *Ratti* both concerned an action by an individual against an arm of the State and therefore did not raise the question of horizontal direct effect. The problem with Directives is that they are addressed to the governments of member States with the result that non-implementation ought not to be used as a defence by the government so as to prevent an individual from enforcing the Directive against the State. But the same argument does not necessarily hold good where an individual or a company, unconnected with the State seeks to hide behind the fact of non-implementation by the State.

Eventually, the question whether a Directive could create 'horizontal' direct effects arose for decision in *Marshall* v *Southampton & South West Hampshire Area Health Authority (Teaching)* (case 152/84) [1986] 1 CMLR 688 in which the question arose whether the Sex Discrimination Act 1975 contravened the requirements of the Equal Treatment Directive (76/207) so as to forbid the authority from discriminating between males and females by compelling Mrs Marshall to retire at the age of 60 when men could continue to work to the age of 65.

The Court concluded that so far as 'horizontal' effects were concerned, it was clear that since under art. 189 Directives were addressed only to member States, a Directive could not confer rights on an individual as against another individual. But in the event, it was also decided that as a public body, the Area Health Authority could be regarded as an arm of the State, in which case, the Directive could be enforced vertically.

What the decision in *Marshall* left undecided was how to define a 'public body' or an 'agency of the state'. *Marshall* itself makes it clear that an area health authority can be so regarded. So also is a police authority (*Johnson* v *Royal Ulster Constabulary* (case 222/84) [1986] 3 CMLR 240). But it was unclear whether a nationalised industry or a privatised monopoly subject to State control could be similarly regarded. In *Foster* v *British Gas plc* (case C-188/89) [1991] 2 CMLR 217 it was eventually decided that in order to be a public body, a particular organisation had to be subject to the authority or control of the State or have special powers beyond those which result from the normal rules applicable to relations between individuals. It followed from this that on the facts, British Gas, being a privatised company, was not a public body, but the interjection of the reference to special powers would mean that a nationalised industry could be regarded as an arm of the State, in which case, a Directive, if sufficiently precise, may be enforced against such a body.

The significance of this approach is that if the UK government fails to implement a harmonising Directive within the implementation period, it will be possible for a consumer to maintain an action against a public body within the definition applied in *Foster*, but at the same time, no action will lie against a company which is not conferred with any special powers over and above those conferred on other organisations. However, in *Doughty* v *Rolls-Royce plc* [1992] IRLR 126, even the presence of some State control over Rolls-Royce plc was not sufficient to allow the organisation to be regarded as an arm of the State since it had not been made responsible pursuant to a measure adopted by the State for providing a public service. What was important was that Rolls-Royce plc provided defence services to the State as opposed to services to the public for the benefit of the State.

What should be appreciated about *Doughty* v *Rolls-Royce plc* is that it was not a decision of the ECJ, but merely an interpretation given by a UK domestic court. Subsequently, attempts have been made to interest the ECJ in relaxing the approach adopted in *Marshall* specifically in the context of a consumer protection measure, namely the Directive on Cancellation of Consumer Contracts Negotiated away from Business Premises (EEC 85/577). In *Dori* v *Recreb srl* (case C91/92) [1994] I-ECR 3325 there was an attempt by a consumer to invoke the provisions of the Directive against a company at a time when it had not been implemented by the Italian government. The Advocate General's opinion invited the court to reconsider the position adopted in *Marshall* and suggested that enforcement should be permitted as against all parties, whether public or private, so as to allow for an effective and uniform application of Community law in order to bring about the completion of the internal market. It was accepted that the wording of the Directive was sufficiently precise in its terms to be enforceable, but the action failed on the ground that art. 189 of the EC Treaty, read literally, meant that Directives could only be enforced against the State and did not apply as between individuals. Instead, it was considered that the appropriate remedy was to bring an action for damages against the State for non-implementation, once it had been shown that damage had been suffered.

The decision in *Dori* is consistent with existing jurisprudence adopted by the ECJ, but it has been subjected to cogent criticism by more than one Advocate General. For example, it should be noted that since the defendants in *Marshall* were considered to be an arm of the State, what was said in that case about horizontal direct effect was strictly unnecessary. Moreover, there is nothing in art. 189 which specifically excludes the possibility of horizontal effects. Also, the decision in *Marshall* to regard a health authority as an arm of the State seems inappropriate where such bodies have little policy influence. Furthermore, it has been objected that it should be no objection to the creation of horizontal effects that a democratically elected body has failed to implement a Directive since there is an obligation to implement (see generally Jacobs AG in *Vaneetveld* v *SA Le Foyer* (case C-316/93) [1994] I-ECR 763).

In some instances, it has been held that a Directive may have indirect effects, especially where the Directive asserts that States must take 'all appropriate measures' to ensure fulfilment of Community obligations. Accordingly, it was held in *Von Colson* v *Land Nordrhein-Westfalen* (case 14/83) [1986] 2 CMLR 430 that the obligation imposed by EC Treaty, art. 5, to ensure that all appropriate measures are taken falls upon all authorities of a member State, including its courts. From this it follows that the courts of a member State must interpret national law in such a way as to ensure that the objectives of a Directive have been achieved. In this way Community law became indirectly effective through a process of interpretation of domestic law.

However, the extent to which the *Von Colson* principle can assist individuals depends entirely on the extent to which domestic courts regard themselves as having a discretion under domestic law to interpret domestic law in the light of Community law.

Subsequently, the *Von Colson* principle has been the subject of a rigorous review in *Marleasing SA* v *La Comercial Internacional de Alimentación SA* (case C-106/89) [1992] 1 CMLR 305 in which the plaintiff company sought a declaration that the defendants, their debtors, had set up contracts with a view to defrauding creditors contrary to Directive 68/151, the purpose of which was to protect members of a company and third parties from the doctrine of nullity of contracts. The Directive should have been in force in Spain at the time, but the Spanish government had not, at that stage, implemented it. Reiterating the *Marshall* principle, the ECJ asserted that a Directive of itself cannot impose obligations on private parties, but the Court also reiterated the *Von Colson* principle that national courts must, as far as possible, interpret national law in the light of the wording and purpose of a Community Directive in order to achieve the result desired by the Directive, whether or not the national provisions in question were adopted before or after the Directive. As a result, according to the ECJ, national courts are required to interpret national laws in such a way as to give effect to the desired objectives of a Community Directive. Later decisions suggest that National courts will not readily accept the ruling in *Marleasing*, especially in cases where it is considered not possible to marry Community and domestic laws (see *Webb* v *Emo Air Cargo (UK) Ltd* [1992] 4 All ER 929), for example, because domestic law is not open to an interpretation consistent with the Community Directive.

Given the defects in the doctrines of direct and indirect effect as means of providing a remedy for individuals, the ECJ decision in *Francovich* v *Italy* (cases C-6 & 9/90) [1993] 2 CMLR 66 may provide a useful alternative. In *Francovich* a group of employees sued the Italian government for its failure to implement a Directive which would have guaranteed them payment of arrears of wages in the event of their employer's insolvency. The Directive had been considered insufficiently clear and precise to be directly effective, but the ECJ nonetheless held the State to be liable in damages provided three conditions were satisfied. These were that the Directive had to confer rights on individuals; the content of those rights had to be clear from the provisions of the Directive and there must be a causal link between the breach of the State's obligations and the damage suffered.

The problems which flow from this decision are numerous. For example, while the ECJ accepted that there was an action for damages, it was also recognised that the circumstances in which *Francovich* could apply would involve an absence of Community legislation, so that the basis for assessment of damages would have to be relevant national law. But in English law, there appears to be no available action for damages for failure to legislate! However, it has been held subsequently that the ECJ, as guardian of the EC Treaty, has the power to make rules on the assessment of damages, where none exist at Community level (*Brasserie du Pêcheur SA* v *Germany* (cases C-46 & 48/93) [1996] 2 WLR 506). Accordingly, it was considered that the basis of State liability would depend upon whether required legislative action was intended to confer rights on individuals; whether there was a sufficiently serious breach on the part of the State and whether that breach can be shown to have caused damage to the individual (ibid.). For these purposes, it seems that if the state's legislative choice is strictly limited, as is the case with compliance with Directives, the mere infringement of Community law is to be regarded as a sufficiently serious breach to justify an award of damages (see *R* v *Ministry of Agriculture, Fisheries and Food, ex parte Hedley Lomas (Ireland) Ltd* (case C5/94) [1996] 3 WLR 787).

It is suggested that the ECJ in *Dori* has missed an important chance to develop the law on the issue of direct effect. The position of consumers would be far better in the face of an unimplemented Directive, if its provisions were to take direct effect as part of national law, both in relation to arms of the State and in relation to other individuals. Given that the present remedy seems to lie in an action for *Francovich* damages, should the conditions attached to that action be satisfied, it would appear that consumers may not be satisfactorily protected. If we take as an example *Dori* itself, in order for the plaintiff to recover damages against the State for non-implementation, it would first have to be proved that damage has been suffered. Accordingly, in *Dori*, the plaintiff would have to wait until a municipal court ordered her to fulfil the terms of her contract at the request of the company with whom she had contracted. Subsequently, Miss Dori would then have to institute proceedings against the State, the outcome of which would be highly uncertain since she would have to establish that she had suffered damage and that that damage was caused by the failure of the state to implement the Directive (see generally Tridimas (1994) 19 EL Rev 621). Following *Brasserie du Pêcheur SA* v *Germany*, it would also be necessary to show that there had been a sufficiently serious breach of Community law to justify making an award of damages. Life would be much simpler if the adversely affected consumer could directly enforce the identified rights which the State was under an obligation to implement at a stage prior to the alleged complaint on the part of the consumer.

2.8.3   Community policies

2.8.3.1   Background to a Community consumer protection policy
The EC consumer protection policy has had a somewhat chequered history. When the European Economic Community first came into existence, it would be fair to say that the consumer movement, albeit just about conceived, was not highly developed, with the result that there was very little in the original EEC Treaty which could pass as a justification for a consumer protection policy.

The EC Treaty, as it now stands after amendment by the Treaty on European Union (TEU), lays down a number of broad principles, setting out the purposes for which the Community was created. These are, *inter alia*, the establishment of a common market and an economic and monetary union; the development of harmonious and balanced economic activities, sustainable and non-inflationary growth; a high degree of economic convergence of economic performance and a high level of employment and of social protection (EC Treaty, art. 2). It is perhaps noteworthy that the specific purposes for which the EC was set up did not include the protection of consumers, yet from a relatively early stage, the EC Commission did propose the setting up of a Consumers' Consultative Committee (see OJ L283, 10.10.73, p. 18) which was required to advise on the development of consumer policy and to represent consumer interests.

Initially, the absence of any specific reference to a consumer protection policy in the Treaty of Rome led to some difficulty in justifying the development of such a policy, though it was, nonetheless, still promoted. More recent developments have served to place EC initiatives in favour of consumers on much more secure foundations, since the provisions of the new art. 100A of the EC Treaty, which, by way of derogation from the provisions of the old art. 100, gives a high priority to proposals which concern health, safety, environmental protection and consumer protection in seeking to implement the objectives stated in art. 8a in relation to the establishment of the internal market. Other aspects of the EC Treaty have been added following the enactment of the TEU, all of which make specific reference to consumer protection. For example, art. 3(s) (as amended by TEU, art. G(3)) provides that in seeking to achieve the purposes set out in art. 2, the activities of the Community shall include 'a contribution to the strengthening of consumer protection' and a new art. 129a (inserted by TEU, art. G(38)) introduces Title XI on Consumer Protection Policy to the EC Treaty. In particular, the new Title XI requires the Community to contribute to a high level of consumer protection through measures adopted pursuant to art. 100A in the context of the completion of the internal market and requires specific action to support policies intended to protect the health, safety and economic interests of consumers and to provide consumers with adequate information.

Prior to the effects of the TEU, the basis for the development of a consumer policy rested on one of two Treaty provisions. The majority of consumer protection measures found their justification under art. 100 concerning the approximation of laws for the purposes of establishing the common market or for facilitating its functioning. For these purposes, a number of Community measures concerning the health and safety interests of consumers were brought forward (see, e.g., the Directives on packaging and labelling of dangerous substances (OJ L196, 16.8.67, p. 1); low-voltage electrical equipment (OJ L77 26.3.73, p. 29); packaging and labelling of solvents (OJ L189, 11.7.73); cosmetic products (OJ L262, 29.7.76, p. 169) and products which come into contact with food (OJ L277, 20.10.84)). Article 100 was also used as the basis for protecting consumer economic interests (see the Product Liability Directive (OJ L210, 7.8.85, p. 29); the

Misleading Advertising Directive (OJ L250, 19.9.84, p. 17); the Directive on Contracts Negotiated away from Business Premises (OJ L372, 31.12.85, p. 31) and the Consumer Credit Directive (OJ L042, 12.2.87, p. 48, 87/102/EEC). More rarely, art. 235, which permitted otherwise unsanctioned action by the Community to achieve its stated objectives, might also be relied upon to justify consumer protection measures (see Directive on the Indication of Prices of Foodstuffs (OJ 1979 L158, 26.6.79, p. 19)).

The main difficulties which flowed from this somewhat flimsy basis for the development of a consumer policy were that it could be argued that any consumer protection measures introduced pursuant to arts 100 and 235 were *ultra vires* the powers of the Community institutions, since there was no specific mention of the Community aim to enhance the economic, health and safety interests of consumers, and furthermore it might not always have been possible to claim that some measures made under art. 100 were required in order to allow for the proper functioning of the internal market (see Close, 'The legal basis for the consumer protection programmes of the EEC' (1983) 8 EL Rev 221).

Quite apart from questions concerning the legality of a Community consumer protection programme, there were other important obstacles in the way of a coherent programme in favour of consumers. Perhaps the most important of these was that art. 100 required unanimity on the part of member States before a harmonisation measure could take effect. Accordingly, it was possible for a single member State to delay the implementation of harmonisation measures by using its power of veto. For example, it was possible for the Product Liability Directive to be delayed in its implementation for some considerable time due to its perceived effects by some member States on insurance premiums and industries at the forefront of technology (see further chapter 7).

It has been observed already that one of the effects of the TEU has been to introduce a more clearly worded basis for the development of a consumer protection policy based on the combined effects of art. 100A and Title XI (art. 129a). Furthermore, the problems associated with unanimity and the old art. 100 have been disposed of since agreement under art. 100A may be reached on the basis of a qualified majority vote, as described above. Measures based on the new provisions of the EC Treaty (as amended) include the Directives on Toy Safety (OJ L187, 16.7.88, p. 1), General Product Safety (92/59/EEC, OJ L228/24), Packaging and Labelling of Dangerous Preparations (OJ L187, 16.7.88, p. 14), Price Indications on Goods other than Food (OJ L142, 9.6.88, p. 19), Unfair Terms in Consumer Contracts (93/13/EEC OJ L95/29), Holidays and Package Tours (OJ L158 23.6.90, p. 59) and amendments to the Consumer Credit Directive (OJ L61, 10.3.90, p. 4).

2.8.3.2 Content of the Community consumer protection programme
The First Consumer Protection Programme (annexe to Council Resolution of 14 April 1975; OJ 1975, C92/1) had as its broad objectives the right to safety, the right to choose, the right to be heard and the right to be informed.

It addressed issues such as consumer information, education, redress and representation, consumer health and safety and the legal and economic interests of consumers. Of these issues, the health and safety of consumers was the subject of the greatest number of Directives and Regulations. The object of many of these was to secure the safety of basic foodstuffs such as fruit and vegetables. Other consumer goods affected by the early programme included solvents, food packaging, cosmetics and motor vehicles.

In relation to consumer information and education, Community policy was to ensure that the consumer was provided with sufficient information to enable him to assess the basic features of goods or services available to him and to be able to make a rational choice between competing products and services. It was the expressed policy of the Community to ensure satisfactory redress for the consumer in respect of any injury or damage caused by defective goods or services.

Laudable though these policies were, little was done during the currency of the First Programme to implement them. One Directive on the labelling of the energy consumption of domestic appliances was adopted by the Council in 1979, but little else can be said of the rest of the programme.

With a view to the protection of consumer economic interests, draft Directives on doorstep selling and producers' liability for defective products were submitted to the Council by the Commission, but it took some time before finalised legislation on these matters was eventually adopted. Directives on misleading advertising and consumer credit were also developed.

In 1981, the Council approved a Second Consumer Protection Policy (OJ 1981 C133) which reiterated the objectives stated in the First Programme and added a new direction, namely the field of consumer services.

In 1985, the Commission published a critique of the First and Second Programmes (*A New Impetus for Consumer Policy* (COM (85) 314 Final 23.07.85)), which pointed out the dilatory pace at which reform had been achieved and recommended action in respect of health and safety, consumer economic interests and the coordination of consumer policy with other Community policies. One of the principal reasons for the slow pace of change was seen to be the requirement of unanimity which applied to harmonisation provisions under art. 100, under which the majority of consumer protection measures had been promoted. The importance of art. 100A in this respect is that it allows the Council to act by way of a qualified majority on a proposal from the Commission in cooperation with the European Parliament. Other reasons for the slow pace of change cited by the Commission in *A New Impetus* included the effects of the deep economic recession of the late 1970s and the early 1980s and that member States may have regarded consumer protection as a matter for domestic legislation.

Subsequently a Council resolution on Future Priorities for the Development of Consumer Protection Policy (Resolution 92/C 186/01 of 13.7.92, OJ C186, 23.7.92, p. 1) identifies the anticipated consumer protection programme for the 1990s which was later followed by Commission communications setting out three-year consumer policy programmes for the periods 1993 to 1995 (OJ 28.7.93) and 1996 to 1998 (COM (95) 519). Some of the rhetoric of these two documents has a certain ring of familiarity, many of the previously stated objectives of Community policy being reiterated. For example, the 1992 Council resolution identifies matters such as the integration of consumer policy into other common Community policies as a matter of priority, recommending an impact assessment of proposals sensitive to consumers and urging new measures regarding food, financial services and payment systems (Resolution 92/C 186/01 of 13.7.92, annex (1)). The resolution also emphasises the need to improve consumer education and information particularly through the development of trans-frontier information centres (ibid., annex (2)) presumably in the belief that there will be a future increase in trans-border shopping, which also seems to underlie the Commission *Green Paper on Guarantees for Consumer Goods and After-Sales Service* (COM (93) 509, as to which see further chapter 6). Also recommended is future action on improving the transparency of price indications for professional and financial services and an increase in the provision of consumer information regarding recycling and the rational use of resources (Resolution 92/C 186/01 of 13.7.92, annex (2)).

The action plans for the periods 1993–5 and 1996–8 are significant for their increased politicisation of consumer protection issues in the light of the TEU. The action plan for 1993–5, in particular, assesses the successes of previous action plans, noting what progress in the form of the implementation of new measures was achieved in earlier years. But it also addresses the problem of ineffective implementation of Community measures by member States. It notes that at the beginning of 1993 a total of 42 Directives concerned with consumer policy had been adopted and had reached the date by which they should have been transposed into national law, yet the actual transposition rate averaged out at 94 per cent. Concern was expressed at this rate of failure to transpose and the Commission took the view that particular attention had to be paid to the process of implementation of Community measures if the consumer protection programme was to succeed.

The Commission communication concerning consumer policy for the period 1996–8 (COM (95) 519) emphasises a particular need to address the protection of consumer interests in the financial services sector. It also takes the view that more needs to be done to increase consumer confidence in food marketing, safety, quality and labelling, placing particular emphasis on the need to make food labels more usable by consumers. Also emphasised is the responsibility of all contributors to the food chain, with the result that the Commission considers it necessary to reconsider the application of the Product Liability Directive (85/374/EEC) to primary agricultural produce in the light of the fact that all but four member States have chosen to exempt farmers from liability in this respect. The 1996–8 programme also recognises the impact of new technology in the so-called 'information society' expressing an intention to examine what laws are necessary in this area.

Some of the early developments at Community level have been criticised. In particular a former Director General of Fair Trading has described the early Directives as falling within three broad categories, namely, irritating and irrelevant, retrograde, and well-intentioned but damaging to national interests. (Borrie, *The Development of Consumer Law and Policy* (1984), p. 106 et seq.)

Measures regarded as irritating and irrelevant included the Consumer Credit Directive (OJ L042, 12.8.87, p. 48) on the basis that it was based almost wholly on the provisions of the UK Consumer Credit Act 1974 and was therefore irrelevant at a domestic level. However, it is also the case that legislation similar to the Consumer Credit Act 1974 did not exist in some member States. Accordingly, with a view to harmonisation on a Community level, the Directive is to be welcomed.

In its original form, the Misleading Advertising Directive was regarded as retrograde in that it did not allow for implementation of its provisions by means of self-regulating codes of practice. However, this defect was remedied in the finalised legislation (OJ L250, 19.9.84, p. 17) with the result that the successful control of advertising practices under the British codes of advertising and sales promotion was allowed to continue.

Some Community initiatives were regarded as damaging to proposed domestic reforms. In particular, it was said that the Product Liability Directive (OJ L210, 7.8.85, p. 29) may have acted as a barrier to the implementation of what is now part I of the Consumer Protection Act 1987. However, it may also be argued that proposals for reform of the law in this area had been around for a long time and that it was only concerted effort on the part of the Community that found an element of consensus sufficient to justify legislation. Had the matter been left to individual member States, no change would necessarily have been forthcoming.

2.8.3.3 Specific application of European Community law Community legislation and proposals for change affect a wide range of issues relevant to consumer protection law. In particular, Community policy has a high regard for the consumer's health, safety and economic interests. However, consumer policy has to exist alongside other Community policies, and policy documents have repeatedly emphasised that consumer protection matters should be integrated into other Community policies as far as possible.

Particularly important for member States wishing to legislate for certain trading activities at a domestic level are Community policies which relate to the completion and maintenance of the internal market. For many years, Community policy has been geared towards the removal of barriers to free trade in goods and services. Accordingly, domestic measures, such as restrictions on imports and exports, which tend to stifle trade may be seen as not just relevant to trading interests, but also to consumer interests, since a restricted market offers less choice to consumers, with the result that there could be adverse effects on prices and the range of products available.

In relation to the importation of goods, the EC Treaty, art. 30, provides that quantitative restrictions on imports and all measures having equivalent effect shall be prohibited between member States. Article 34 makes similar provision for exports of goods. Both these provisions are subject to art. 36, which permits some potentially restrictive provisions, *inter alia*, on the grounds of public morality, public policy, public security, the protection of human, animal and plant health and life, and the protection of industrial or commercial property.

In relation to the supply of services, art. 59 provides that restrictions on the freedom to supply services shall be progressively abolished, although, as with the provisions concerning quantitative restrictions on goods, there are provisions in arts 56 and 66 which sanction certain restrictions on grounds similar to those set out in art. 36.

2.8.3.3.1   Quantitative restrictions on the import of goods and measures having equivalent effect   Technical barriers to free trade are a matter with which Community policies have generally taken a hard line. If left to their own devices, member States might be inclined to impose domestic restrictions on product standards which might adversely affect trade within the European Community. Clearly, if these standards were to differ widely amongst member States there would be a considerable barrier to free trade in that manufacturers would have to produce products to different standards in order to be able to export to different States. However, conditions and traditions may differ from one country to another, in which case the imposition of unusual standards may sometimes be justified.

Article 30 is concerned with quantitative restrictions on imports, by which is meant a total or partial restriction on the movement of particular goods. Thus a blanket ban on the import of a particular type of goods will be prohibited under art. 30, unless there is some justification for it. Thus in *Commission* v *United Kingdom* (case 261/85) [1988] 2 CMLR 11, a blanket ban on imports of pasteurised milk and unfrozen pasteurised cream from other member States was considered to contravene art. 30. A claimed justification on public health grounds under art. 36 was also rejected on the ground that a complete ban was not proportionate. Other measures, such as a system of monitoring milk imported into the country could have been adopted without producing such a disruptive effect on inter-State trade.

While it is clear that an outright ban will contravene art. 30, less extreme, but equally disruptive measures will also be treated similarly. Thus it has been held that the imposition of a licensing system upon those who wish to deal in a particular type of product may also amount to a quantitative restriction on trade. (*International Fruit Co. NV* v *Produktschap voor Groenten en Fruit (No. 2)* (cases 51–4/71) [1971] ECR 1107).

Even if a particular measure does not amount to a quantitative restriction on trade, it may be regarded as a measure having equivalent effect, which equally falls within the ban imposed by art. 30. Measures having equivalent effect are subdivided into those which are overtly protective or 'distinctly applicable' measures and those which are 'indistinctly applicable'. Included within the latter category are provisions which insist that goods conform to requirements of size or weight or any other requirement that goods should conform to nationally imposed standards.

The meaning of a measure having equivalent effect is amplified in Directive 70/50 (see also *Procureur du Roi* v *Dassonville* (case 8/74) [1974] ECR 837), which provides that such measures shall include those which hinder imports or make importation more difficult or costly than the disposal of a domestic product. Also included are those indistinctly applicable measures which fail to satisfy the principle of proportionality in *Internationale Handelsgesellschaft mbH* (case 11/70) [1970] ECR 1125. Thus an absolute ban on additives in beer will contravene art. 30 if the objective of protecting public health can be achieved by less restrictive means (*Commission* v *Germany* (case 178/84) [1988] 1 CMLR 780).

If a measure is to contravene art. 30 it is not necessary for it to be shown that there is actually an effect on trade — it is sufficient that the measure is capable of having that effect. Accordingly in *Procureur du Roi* v *Dassonville* a Belgian requirement that goods should carry a certificate of origin issued by the State in which the goods were produced was held to contravene art. 30 where a French supplier of Scotch whisky was unable to provide such a certificate. The Belgian importer attached a home-made certificate and was prosecuted for forgery, but successfully pleaded the illegality of the certification requirement. The provision was held to be capable of hindering inter-State trade because it was equivalent to a quantitative restriction. But what remained unclear from the *Dassonville* test was whether the only derogations from art. 30 were to be found in art. 36.

If a measure is of purely domestic application, it will not contravene art. 30 even if it is restrictive in relation to the sale of goods within that member State. What is important for the purposes of art. 30 is that there should be no restriction on trade between member States. In *Jongeneel Kaas BV* v *Netherlands* (case 237/82) [1982] ECR 483 regulations concerning permitted ingredients in Dutch cheese which applied only to Dutch producers were held to be lawful even though other member States might choose to apply less stringent measures.

As has been observed above, the *Dassonville* test was thought to mean that the only circumstances in which a hindrance to trade would be allowed could be found in art. 36. However, a restriction on the *Dassonville* test was laid down in *Rewe Zentrale AG* v *Bundesmonopolverwaltung für Branntwein* (case 120/78) [1979] ECR 649 (the *Cassis de Dijon* case), in which the Court took account of the proportionality principle and sought to make a clearer distinction between distinctly and indistinctly applicable measures. On the facts, the result of the *Cassis de Dijon* case was that there had been a breach of art. 30, but it was also stated that hindrances to the free movement of goods had to be tolerated if they resulted from disparities between national laws relating to the marketing of goods and those laws were necessary to satisfy the mandatory requirements relating to the effectiveness of fiscal supervision, the protection of public health, the fairness of commercial transactions and the defence of the consumer. This 'rule of reason' applies to indistinctly applicable measures, but not to distinctly applicable measures which will fall foul of art. 30, unless they are justified under art. 36.

The decision in *Cassis de Dijon* is important since the range of permitted restrictions under that rule is wider than the range of lawful restrictions under art. 36. Moreover, art. 36 contains an exhaustive list of permitted derogations from art. 30, whereas the rule of reason contains a non-exhaustive list of reasons for permitting restrictions on the free movement of goods. However, in the light of the actual result in *Cassis de Dijon* it is essential that the restriction is necessary to protect the interest concerned. Thus in *Cassis de Dijon* a German law which laid down a minimum alcohol content of 25 per cent for certain types of drink operated as a ban on the importation of the French liqueur cassis, which had an alcohol content of only 15–20 per cent. In the event, it was held that the German provision contravened art. 30, but the restriction was defended on the ground that it was intended to protect public health and was also intended to ensure the fairness of commercial transactions. The court considered that the ends used to justify the law could be achieved by means other than those adopted by the legislature. For example, it would have been possible to protect public health and commercial contracting parties by insisting upon clear labelling of the alcohol content which would not hinder trade in the same way as the insistence upon a minimum alcohol content.

The court also laid down a second principle to the effect that it can be presumed that where goods have been lawfully produced and sold in one member State, they may also be sold in another member State without having to satisfy additional requirements. The presumption is rebuttable where it can be shown that additional requirements are necessary in order to protect an interest covered by the rule of reason.

The presumption arising from the second principle in *Cassis de Dijon* is particularly difficult to rebut with the result that very strong evidence will need to be called to justify a restriction on trade in one member State where another member State does not impose a similar restriction. (*Criminal Proceedings against Karl Prantl* (case 16/83) [1984] ECR 1299).

While the way in which art. 30 has been interpreted suggests that a restriction on the free movement of goods will be permitted only where necessary, there is recent evidence that the ECJ is prepared to allow certain restrictions and to recognise the interests of individual member States. For example the *Cassis de Dijon* principle has been used to justify a restriction on the free movement of goods on the ground that it served to protect the environment (*Commission v Denmark* (case 302/86) [1988] ECR 4607) and on the ground that Sunday trading laws applicable to England and Wales were intended to protect national or regional socio-cultural characteristics (*Torfaen Borough Council v B & Q plc* (case 145/88) [1990] 1 All ER 129).

A possible reason for the recognition of a greater number of exceptions to art. 30 is that traders may have seen the basic principle in art. 30 as a means of challenging any rule which served to restrict their commercial freedom, even in circumstances in which there was no effect upon the products of other member States (see *Keck* (cases C-267 and 268/91) [1993] I-ECR I-6097). Thus it has been held that a prohibition of the resale of goods at prices lower than their actual purchase price (loss leading) does not necessarily infringe art. 30. The reason for this is that if the ban applies to all relevant traders operating in the area to which the restriction applies, then the same restriction, in law and in fact, is applied to the marketing of both domestic products and to products emanating from other member States in equal fashion (*Keck* and see also *Groupement National des Négociants en Pommes de Terre de Belgique v ITM Belgium SA* (case C-63/94) [1996] ECR I-2467). This different approach may be limited in its effect, perhaps only to sales promotion techniques, since other national laws which affect, for example, the physical make-up of goods or the packaging in which they are supplied could be regarded as a restriction which discriminates between the products of different member States. For example, suppose a national law forbids the use of packaging of a certain shape or colour, producers of goods of the kind in question might be forced to package goods differently for the purposes of exporting to the State which imposes the ban in question.

2.8.3.3.2 Other permitted derogation from art. 30 Apart from the 'rule of reason' which applies to indistinctly applicable measures, directly applicable measures which constitute a quantitative restriction on trade may still be permitted under art. 36. This permits such restrictions on the grounds of public morality, public policy, public security, the protection of the health and life of humans, animals and plants, the protection of national treasures and the protection of industrial and commercial property. Of these, the most relevant to the issue of consumer protection would appear to be the protection of the health and life of consumers, animals and plants, in so far as the last two of these may provide human food sources.

To succeed under art. 36, it will be necessary to establish that there is a real risk to health. Accordingly, if other member States have adopted methods of assuring the safety and quality of certain types of food, additional restrictions limiting those who can supply that type of food, purportedly on the ground that such controls ensure freedom from contamination, will not be justified under art. 36. (*Commission* v *United Kingdom* (case 124/81) [1983] ECR 203). However, if there is a risk to consumer health from imported produce which does not affect similar domestic produce, restrictions on imports may be justified under art. 36 (*Rewe-Zentralfinanze Gmbh* v *Landwirtschaftskammer* (case 4/75) [1975] ECR 843).

It is clear that the court will pay regard to the proportionality test in determining whether an art. 36 justification is made out. Thus if the objective sought to be achieved can be achieved by less restrictive means, it is unlikely that an art. 36 justification will be made out.

Following the provisions of art. 100A(4) regarding the common organisation of the market, if a harmonisation measure has been adopted at Community level, it seems unlikely that a single member State may adopt measures which are more strict than those sanctioned by the harmonisation measure, if the effect of those stricter measures is to operate as a restriction on trade. In any case, if such measures are contemplated, art. 100A(4) requires the member State concerned to notify the Commission which may bring proceedings if the measure is considered to constitute an improper use of power.

2.8.4 Advertising law and freedom of expression
General principles of international law are often invoked by the European Court of Justice as the basis for principles of Community law. Of particular importance in this respect are the principles contained in the European Convention for the Protection of Human Rights and Fundamental Freedoms

1953. All member States of the Community are signatories to this Convention and are bound by the principles it lays down.

In the context of consumer protection law, one of the most important principles established by the Human Rights Convention is that of freedom of expression contained in art. 10, which provides that the right shall include the freedom to hold opinions *and to receive and impart information and ideas without interference by public authority and regardless of frontiers*. It seems that this right to impart information also extends to 'commercial speech' (*Markt Intern Verlag GmbH* v *Germany* (1990) 12 EHRR 161). It follows from this that a number of restrictions on advertising, apparently imposed for the protection of consumers and honest traders, may infringe art. 10 and may be declared unlawful on the ground that they unnecessarily restrict an advertiser's freedom to put across his message.

Although the right to freedom of expression is stated in broad terms, it is subject to a number of restrictions under which a public authority may impose controls. In particular art. 10(2) provides that legal restrictions may be allowed if they are prescribed by law and necessary in a democratic society, in the interests of national security, territorial integrity or public safety, for the prevention of disorder or crime, for the protection of health or morals, for the protection of the reputation or rights of others, for preventing the disclosure of information received in confidence or for maintaining the authority or impartiality of the judiciary. It follows from this that there are two general preconditions to the validity of a restriction, namely that the restriction is prescribed by law and that it is necessary in a democratic society. On top of these two general requirements, there are the more specific reasons listed in art. 10(2) which may justify a restriction.

Since the restriction imposed upon the freedom of the advertiser must be prescribed by law, it appears that one of the preconditions of art. 10(2) may not have been satisfied under the regime which operates in England. The reason for this is that many of the controls placed upon advertisers take the form of voluntary constraints based upon the provisions of the British Codes of Advertising and Sales Promotion (see further chapter 16) and are therefore not controls prescribed by law. It would appear that such controls would not fall within art. 10(2) with the result that advertisers will still be considered to have their right of freedom of expression, since any limitation on advertising freedom will have been voluntarily undertaken.

Article 10(2) also lists a number of legitimate aims which may be pursued by the State with the result that a person's freedom of expression may be limited. In the case of advertising, competing interests have to be taken into account, with the result that although an advertiser is entitled to promote his product, he should not also be allowed to denigrate the reputation and rights of others, with the result that laws designed to protect those competing interests may be justified under art. 10(2). (*Markt Intern Verlag GmbH* v *Germany* (1990) 12 EHRR 161, 173). However, it may be argued that by giving precedence to one particular interest, the law may unfairly restrict the right to communicate information to others. Accordingly, a heavy burden should fall on the government wishing to impose a restriction upon advertising freedom to show that it is not just reasonable, but also relevant and sufficient (ibid., 176). If the necessity for the restriction is not convincingly established, then the restriction should be regarded as an infringement of art. 10.

The final consideration is whether the restriction is necessary in a democratic society, which appears to involve a cost-benefit analysis. The court must weigh the requirements of the protection of the reputation and rights of others against the right of the publisher to impart information. While it is the case that consumers deserve protection against misleading and less than objective advertising, the advertiser also has to be given the opportunity to put across his message. In seeking to balance these competing interests, the court will have to take account of the principle of proportionality. In *Markt Intern Verlag GmbH* v *Germany* a restraining order was placed upon the publication of an article in a trade journal which described a consumer complaint against a mail order company and requested evidence of other such complaints. The granting of the order was considered to be justified on the basis that the content of the article was contrary to honest practices. A bare majority of the European Court of Human Rights held that the restriction was justified and that there was no infringement of art. 10 since the restriction served to protect the reputation of others. However, it may be argued that the principle of proportionality was not adhered to. While regard should be had to the rights of others, an outright ban on publication might be said to go too far and that a more appropriate control might have been to allow the institution of criminal or civil proceedings.

THREE

Consumer redress

The fact that the consumer has legal rights in respect of defective goods and services is little compensation if there is not a suitable and inexpensive means of enforcing those rights. This chapter seeks to examine sources of consumer advice and assistance and the various avenues of consumer redress in both civil and criminal proceedings and those arising out of trade association codes of practice. Apart from the matters dealt with at this stage, the consumer may be able to obtain redress under one of the ombudsman schemes considered in chapter 2.

3.1 CONSUMER ADVICE AND ASSISTANCE

3.1.1 Consumer advice

Even where a consumer does have grounds for complaining about goods or services supplied to him, it does not always follow that he will be aware of his grounds for redress. Accordingly, there is a strong argument in favour of national publicity campaigns to ensure that the necessary information is made available to consumers to allow complaints to be taken further. Organisations such as the National Consumer Council and the Consumers' Association have played their part in publicising matters of consumer concern, seeking to explain in simple terms the rights of the consumer when things go wrong. Moreover, recent years have seen the codification of a number of common law rules affecting consumers, based on the generally held view that if matters related to consumer redress are conveniently stated in an Act of Parliament, people are more likely to be aware of those rights than if they are hidden in obscure common law rules. Clearly a campaign to increase consumer awareness of rights is essential, for without this basic information, there is no prospect of matters being taken further. In addition to the information provided by specific consumer organisations, consumer advice is also made available through local authority consumer advice centres and trading standards departments and Citizens' Advice Bureaux (see chapter 2). The advice given by these organisations may sometimes result in the settlement of a dispute, but frequently the matter may go further with the result that the complaint is referred to a solicitor with the possibility of legal action in mind. However, it is often the case that matters go no further since the prospect of pursuing a complaint through the court system may deter the consumer for a number of reasons. For example, the complexity of litigation or the simple value of the claim may be such that all but the most hardy of consumers quails at the thought of legal proceedings. In any case, there is evidence that the present system fails the consumer since lawyers generally show little interest in consumer complaints on the grounds of cost, and advice centres are hard pressed to deal with the social welfare problems that come their way. Accordingly, the consumer may find himself in a position where informed advice is only available from Citizens' Advice Bureaux, consumer organisations and the national and local media (Cranston, *Consumers and the Law*, 2nd ed. (1984), pp. 83–5).

It has been argued that a national consumer agency might be in the best position to provide the necessary 'competent and accessible national network of generalist advice agencies' (Royal Commission on Legal Services, *Final Report* (Cmnd 7648, 1979)). However, it has subsequently been observed that while progress has been made, the aim of the Royal Commission has been nowhere near achieved (National Consumer Council, *Good Advice for All* (1986), para. 1.3). The particular problems identified in the field of consumer advice appear to be a lack of any sort of centralised government policy; disparities in advice provision at a local level, in particular the availability of advice services in rural areas was very poor; and inadequate provision for funding of advice services (National Consumer Council, *Information and Advice Services in the UK* (1983)).

In order to improve provision for consumer advice, it has been suggested that there should be a comprehensive network of local advice centres capable of dealing with a wide range of matters such as social security, housing, fuel, money, employment, immigration and family matters, geared to the particular needs of the local area (ibid., para. 1.12). In addition to this basic provision, it is also recommended that there should be access to a wider specialist service which is capable of providing, *inter alia*, representation services, debt advice services, research and legal casework services (ibid., para. 1.13).

3.1.2 Legal aid and advice

Where the consumer considers taking matters further a means of obtaining legal advice and some means of financial support for the less well-off is necessary. It has been observed that the principle that everyone should have access to the law is meaningless if those who are unable to afford the services of a lawyer cannot use the legal system (National Consumer Council, *Ordinary Justice* (1989), p. 73).

The present legal aid and advice system for the purposes of civil matters manifests itself in three main forms, namely full legal aid, the 'green form' scheme and advice by way of representation, although the latter tends to be used mainly for matrimonial matters rather than consumer disputes.

3.1.2.1 Full civil legal aid The Legal Aid Act 1988, s. 2(4), provides that civil legal aid is available for any non-criminal litigation, including personal injury cases, contract disputes, negligence, matrimonial and debt matters. Where full civil legal aid is given, it will provide financial assistance in respect of the consumer's own legal costs and will cushion the recipient against the full financial consequences of an unsuccessful action since he is only required to pay the other party's costs so far as is reasonable, having regard to the means available to the parties.

The consumer may be turned down for legal aid on the ground that his means are sufficient to allow him to fund the action himself. The means test covers both the disposable income and capital of the applicant and his or her spouse. If the applicant's income is considered to fall within the specified upper and lower income levels, he will be required to make a contribution, which may be paid in instalments. Only those with very low incomes are entitled to free legal aid.

For the purposes of the means test, a litigant will be required to disclose his disposable income, assessed in accordance with the Civil Legal Aid (Assessment of Resources) Regulations 1989, which regard a person who is in receipt of either income support or family credit as having no disposable income. The means test will also take account of income which has already been disposed of, if there was no good reason for its disposal. (*R* v *Legal Aid Assessment Officer, ex parte Saunders* (1989) *The Independent,* 16 November 1989). However, no account will be taken of the value of the consumer's home and the tools of his trade.

In one sense, only unsuccessful litigants are legally aided since if the consumer is successful, the cost to the legal aid fund is recoverable from the costs awarded to the legally aided party on the basis of a statutory charge over any money or property recovered or preserved for the assisted party in the proceedings (Legal Aid Act 1988, s. 16(6)). This charge is particularly important in cases in which the successful consumer does not recover the full amount of his costs against the defendant. Moreover, matters will be even worse for the consumer if there has been a payment into court which is in excess of the amount awarded by way of judgment. In this case, the defendant's costs will have to be paid by the consumer, in which case, the statutory charge will apply to the consumer's own costs and the defendant's costs will also be recoverable from the amount awarded in the consumer's favour.

Not every applicant for legal aid will be successful since both a merit test and a means test will have to be endured before a legal aid certificate is granted. Thus, the consumer may fail at the first hurdle, if the legal aid area office decides that there are not reasonable grounds for taking or defending the action. Matters considered in determining whether there is merit in the action in respect of which civil legal aid is applied for include whether the applicant would gain only a trivial advantage by bringing proceedings or if the claim is one for which a solicitor would not normally be employed (e.g., small claims) or if the client could finance the claim from another source, for example, where there is insurance cover against legal expenses or where a trade union or motoring organisation will take up the claim (Civil Legal Aid (General) Regulations 1989, regs 29 and 30).

Unless a proposed action is particularly important, full civil legal aid is not normally granted in small claims proceedings. Since the majority of consumer complaints will fall within this category, the availability of legal aid is severely restricted.

3.1.2.2 The green form scheme The green form scheme is one whereby the consumer can obtain initial legal advice on any question of English law, which includes European Community law so far as it has been incorporated into English law (Legal Aid Act 1988, s. 2(2)). The range of advice which may be given is broad and covers not just matters of substantive law but also procedural issues. Thus it will cover cases in which the consumer wishes to present his case in person with the assistance of a 'McKenzie adviser' (*McKenzie* v *McKenzie* [1971] P 33).

In order to qualify for green form advice, certain tests of financial eligibility must be satisfied and in determining whether a person qualifies, the financial means of a cohabitee will also be taken into account (Legal Advice and Assistance Regulations 1989, reg. 13). However, if the applicant is in receipt of income support or family credit, full civil legal aid will be provided free of charge.

At one stage the amount of green form advice was limited to a fixed sum of £50, but now the scheme will cover two hours' work at the prescribed cost for that amount of work applicable to the preparation of a criminal case.

3.1.2.3 Critique of the legal aid and advice system One of the earliest criticisms of the system was that few people were aware of its existence. There is evidence that many litigants in personal injury actions had consulted a solicitor but were still unaware that financial assistance was available to them (Harris et al., *Compensation and Support for Illness and Injury* (1984)). Attempts have been made in more recent years to give greater publicity to the scheme by circulating an explanatory booklet to advice centres, libraries and the courts. In order to reach a wider audience, the booklet has also been translated into a number of different languages.

Other criticisms include the administrative delays in approving applications for legal aid and the inadequate payments made to solicitors participating in the scheme. One consequence of insufficient remuneration is that the number of solicitors now carrying out legal aid work is falling significantly.

Perhaps most importantly, the number of people eligible for legal aid has also fallen in recent years due to the fact that means test limits have not been kept in line with rises in the value of State benefits and average earnings, with the result that possibly 25 per cent of the population was ineligible for legal aid by 1986 and since then matters appear to have deteriorated (Glasser (1988) 85 (10) LS Gaz 11).

In the light of these criticisms, the Lord Chancellor's Department carried out a survey of the legal aid system, which recommended a closer relationship between solicitors in private practice and organisations such as advice centres.

The other principal recommendations of the survey were that green form advice should only be available for a limited range of legal problems, including the normal range of consumer complaints. There was a general recommendation that all initial advice should be given by advice centres and cases should only be referred to a solicitor when it becomes clear that legal action should be taken, thereby releasing public money for generalist advice centres.

The survey and a White Paper which followed it (*Legal Aid in England and Wales* (Cm 118, 1987)) resulted in the Legal Aid Act 1988, which creates a Legal Aid Board conferred with powers to administer the legal aid scheme and advise on possible improvements, still leaving overall control of the scheme in the hands of the Lord Chancellor's Department.

3.2   CONSUMER REDRESS IN CIVIL PROCEEDINGS

Where the legal advice given to the consumer is that he stands a reasonable chance of success in legal proceedings, he may decide to take the matter further. Where the consumer decides to sue, it is likely to be in contract or tort and, dependant on the value of the action, will be heard in the High Court or a county court, although the latter is now the more likely venue, for reasons to be considered below.

Formerly, the jurisdiction of county courts was limited by the value of the claim under consideration. Thus under the County Courts Act 1984 a ceiling of £15,000 was generally imposed upon their jurisdiction. However, since the High Court and County Courts Jurisdiction Order 1991 (made under the Courts and Legal Services Act 1990) county courts have an unlimited jurisdiction in respect of general list cases. Whether or not a case is heard in the High Court or a county court will now depend on matters such as the complexity of the case, its substance and whether or not it involves an important question of law (Courts and Legal Services Act 1990, s. 1(3)). Generally, the more complex the case, the more likely it is to be heard at High Court level, but if the claim involves an amount of £25,000 or less, it will normally be heard in a county court. Claims in excess of £50,000 will normally be heard in the High Court and those falling between the two figures may be heard in either court, depending on the criteria set out above.

In the context of actions by consumers, perhaps the most important development is that where the sum claimed does not exceed £1,000 it will be referred for arbitration by a district judge, unless a defence is filed, in which case the matter may be referred to a circuit judge. This so-called 'small claims' procedure will apply to the majority of consumer actions, which by their nature will generally not involve large amounts. The practical effect of this is that the majority of consumer claims will operate on a 'do-it-yourself' basis, since legal aid is not normally available in such cases, although the litigant in person may be able to obtain legal advice under the green form scheme considered above.

3.2.1   The problems of civil litigation
There are a number of considerations which may deter the consumer from instituting civil proceedings. A general feature of civil law rights is that the

consumer must take the initiative in commencing proceedings — no-one is going to do this for him. The opening assumption, therefore, is that the consumer knows his rights and is prepared to take action to enforce them, but this is frequently not the case since adequate consumer advice is not always available. There also appear to be other reasons why consumers do not take the initiative, for example, they may lack the motivation to take the matter further; the cost may appear too great; the formality and remoteness of the courts may appear too daunting and the amount the consumer stands to recover, if successful, may not make litigation worthwhile (see generally Cranston, *Consumers and the Law*, 2nd ed. (1984), pp. 81–3).

The response to many of these problems has been the introduction of a small claims procedure in the county courts designed to reduce the cost of litigation and cut out much of the formality associated with court proceedings.

3.2.2 County court litigation

More than 90 per cent of all civil proceedings commence in the county courts so virtually all claims by or against consumers of goods and services will be subject to the rules of procedure which apply to county courts.

Very few consumers who have a complaint actually use the county court. Indeed on one assessment it would appear that only 2 per cent of consumers who believed that they had grounds for complaint actually took the step of threatening action in the county court (Office of Fair Trading, *Consumer Dissatisfaction* (1986)).

3.2.2.1 Full county court procedure Assuming a consumer dispute is set down for trial in the county court, the action will normally be heard in a court in the district in which the defendant carries on business or lives or, in a contract action, the district in which the contract was made. The plaintiff will have to obtain a document called a 'request' which requires details of the parties to the action and the nature and amount of the claim together with payment of the appropriate fee. As well as the request, the plaintiff must also file 'particulars of claim', a document intended to set out briefly the key facts on which the plaintiff intends to rely. On receipt of the request and the particulars of claim, court staff will prepare a summons which is then sent to the defendant together with a form of admission and details of how to enter a defence or counter-claim. If the defendant admits liability, he will be required to pay into court in full or in part the amount claimed, together with costs in accordance with a scale set out in the summons. Where less than the amount claimed is paid into court, the plaintiff must decide whether or not to accept that amount. Here the danger is that if the lesser amount is rejected and the court subsequently decides to award damages in an amount less than that paid in by the defendant, the plaintiff may be held responsible for the defendant's costs.

If the defendant makes no response to the summons within 14 days of receipt, the court will normally enter judgment for the plaintiff.

Assuming the defendant does enter a defence or a counter-claim, there will be a pre-trial review under which the parties will meet before a district judge who will give appropriate directions on how best to proceed. Alternatively, at this stage the parties may reach a settlement by agreement or admission, in which case the matter will go no further.

3.2.2.2 Small claims arbitration procedure
In order to simplify matters and in an attempt to provide an accessible cheap and easy procedure for resolving the likes of consumer disputes, an automatic small claims arbitration procedure was introduced in 1973. The basis for the procedure is contained in the County Court Rules 1981, ord. 19, part I, which provides for defended claims of not less than £1,000 to go to arbitration before a district judge, or exceptionally a circuit judge or outside arbitrator. Under the scheme one of the parties can apply to the district judge to have the case heard in full court. However, this will only be allowed where a difficult point of law or fact is in issue, where a charge of fraud has been made or where it would be unreasonable for the matter to be heard by the arbitrator.

Exceptionally, cases involving an amount of £1,000 or less may be heard in full court on the grounds of complexity (County Court Rules 1981, ord. 19, r. 3(2)). For these purposes, however, it has been noted that the principal reason for the introduction of the small claims procedure is to improve access to justice (*Afzal* v *Ford Motor Co. Ltd* [1994] 4 All ER 720, 734 per Beldam LJ) and that a court should not rescind an automatic reference to arbitration merely because a question of law is involved or because the facts are complex. Instead, the complexity of the case has to be extreme before the matter is referred to the more formal procedure applicable to full county court trial.

Claims start off in a similar manner to that outlined above for full court hearings in that the plaintiff will make an initial request, after which the court will issue a summons. If the defendant enters a defence, the matter will normally be dealt with by a district judge, who has a discretion to either fix a date for a preliminary hearing or to proceed directly to arbitration. Although one of the purposes of the preliminary hearing was supposed to be to allow the district judge to encourage a settlement between the parties, research evidence has shown that this did not happen on a frequent basis (*Report of the Review Body on Civil Justice* (Cm 394, 1981), para. 520). Because of the criticisms of the use of preliminary hearings, the position is now that district judges must keep in mind the desirability of minimising the number of times the parties must appear in court, with the result that the County Court (Amendment No. 2) Rules 1992 provide that such hearings will only be held if the district judge considers them necessary to give special directions about the conduct of the case or to dispose of a case where a claim is ill-founded or there is no viable defence.

In theory, the principal advantages of the arbitration scheme are that strict rules of the law of evidence are inapplicable and that proceedings are much less formal than full court proceedings (County Court Rules 1981, ord. 19, r. 7(3)). Order 19, r. 7 makes it clear that a number of other procedural rules will be relaxed in order to dispose of some of the fears a litigant in person might have in proceeding with his claim. For example, there is no requirement that the case be heard in a court house, since any premises convenient to the parties may be used. The arbitrator is allowed to adopt any method of procedure he considers fair and which gives each party the opportunity to present his case. In doing so, the arbitrator may also assist a party by putting questions to a witness or to the other party to the proceedings. The specific rules applicable to arbitrations under the Arbitration Act 1996 do not apply to county court arbitrations (Arbitration Act 1996, s. 92).

The County Court Rules 1981 provide that there should be a preliminary hearing before a registrar to consider the dispute and try to find a way of resolving it (ord. 19, r. 5(2)). Should this not be possible, a date is fixed for the hearing at which the arbitrator may adopt such procedure as he considers appropriate to allow each party to present his case. Legal representation is permitted, but is generally not encouraged since there is a rule to the effect that costs of representation are only recoverable where incurred through the unreasonable conduct of the other party (County Court Rules 1981, ord. 19, part I). As a result of the Lay Representatives (Rights of Audience) Order 1992, it is now permissible for the parties to small claims actions to be represented by someone other than a solicitor, such as a trade union representative or a friend.

3.2.2.3 Critique of the small claims system

A number of deficiencies in the small claims arbitration scheme have been identified since it has been in operation. In particular, while the scheme was intended to open up the courts to the likes of consumers, statistics show that only a small proportion of plaintiffs bringing actions in the county courts are consumers whereas a substantial number of defendants are consumers. In other words the small claims procedure is being used to a substantial extent by businesses to recover debts from consumers. Statistics show that private citizens represented 38 per cent of plaintiffs and 58 per cent of defendants whereas the percentage of business plaintiffs was 52 per cent and business defendants 40 per cent (*Report of the Review Body on Civil Justice* (Cm 394, 1988) p. 89, table 12).

The fact that so few consumers use the small claims procedure also seems to suggest that there may be a publicity problem. While there is useful information published by the Lord Chancellor's Department which explains the nature of the arbitration scheme on a national level, the same level of information is not always available on a local level. For example, it has been suggested by the National Consumer Council that information provided by local courts is frequently not understandable because it is written in legal jargon and in some cases important information is omitted such as how long proceedings will take and what papers ought to be brought to court (*Ordinary Justice* (1989), p. 288). While information on procedure is available, little is said about how to enforce a judgment. While it may be fairly easy to secure judgment against a trader, it is not so easy to make him pay.

A further matter of concern was the old £500 limit on cases subject to automatic referral to arbitration. This limit has now been raised to £1,000 on the suggestion of the Civil Justice Review, which will substantially improve matters, by including a large number of consumer complaints in respect of relatively expensive items such as holidays, home improvement work, furniture, carpets, domestic appliances and motor vehicles.

While the small claims proceedure is supposed to be informal, much depends on the attitude of the district judge hearing the dispute. There is evidence that some judges have found it difficult to break away from their formal legal training and still adhere to the ordinary rules of evidence (National Consumer Council, *Ordinary Justice* (1989), p. 295). For example, the informal procedure has not prevented an unrepresented consumer plaintiff from being cross-examined by a solicitor acting on behalf of the defendants (*Chilton* v *Saga Holidays plc* [1986] 1 All ER 841). Since the rule-making body has decided that legal representation is not forbidden, it follows that the district judge cannot prevent a party from making proper use of the services of his solicitor (ibid., 843 per Donaldson MR).

3.2.3 Alternative arbitration schemes

Because of deficiencies in the county court arbitration scheme when it was first introduced, a number of alternative schemes have grown up, particularly those operated by trade associations. Many codes of practice contain provisions to the effect that consumer disputes should be referred to arbitration, should an initial conciliation process instigated by the trade association itself fail to achieve results. For the most part, such arbitrations are based on documentary evidence, with the result that costs are substantially reduced and the consumer avoids the problem of having to take time off work in order to attend a hearing.

One of the main difficulties with such schemes is that the way in which arbitration clauses in consumer contracts have been worded in the past suggests that they are a method of ousting the jurisdiction of the courts. However, the answer to this complaint is that arbitration clauses of this kind also tend to provide that where the matter is agreed to be referred to an arbitrator his decision on the matter is to be treated as final. As such, there is an agreement to go to arbitration and the arbitration clause cannot be treated as a unilateral attempt by one of the parties to the contract to oust the jurisdiction of the courts (*Ford* v *Clarksons Holidays Ltd* [1971] 3 All ER 454). While the reduction in costs brought about by arbitration provisions is often an advantage to the consumer, it cannot always be said that arbitration is an ideal solution to consumer disputes. Often, the complaint may be sufficiently serious for the consumer to wish to consider litigation. Unfortunately, the effect of an agreement to go to arbitration is to prevent the consumer from asserting his right to use the courts. In order to meet this criticism, the Consumer Arbitration Agreements Act 1988 (repealed by the Arbitration Act 1996) provided that where a person dealt as a consumer, an agreement that a dispute between the parties was to be referred to arbitration could not be enforced against that person, subject to three exceptions (Consumer Arbitration Agreements Act 1988, s. 1(1)). The three instances in which the consumer became bound by an agreement to go to arbitration were where there was a written agreement to go to arbitration after a dispute had arisen (s. 1(1)(a)); where there was a submission to arbitration in pursuance of the agreement (s. 1(1)(b)) and where a court order was made to the effect that the dispute should be referred to arbitration (s. 1(1)(c)).

The provisions of the 1988 Act gave rise to a number of difficulties of interpretation, but these apart, it is clear that an arbitration clause in consumer contracts may also amount to an unfair contract term in that it can have the effect of excluding or hindering the consumer's ability to pursue a legal remedy. It has now been decided that the best way of regulating the potential unfair effects of an arbitration agreement, whether contractual or not, is to subject such provisions to the Unfair Terms in Consumer Contracts Regulations 1994 (see Arbitration Act 1996, s. 89(1) and chapter 12). For these purposes, a term which constitutes an arbitration agreement may be regarded as unfair if it relates to a claim for a pecuniary remedy which does not exceed an amount which may be specified by any order made under the Arbitration Act 1996, s. 91(1).

Since an arbitration clause may be regarded as a provision in a consumer agreement which excludes or hinders the consumer's right to take legal action or exercise a legal remedy (Unfair Terms in Consumer Contracts Regulations 1994, sch. 3 para. 1(q)), such clauses may be regarded as unfair terms. However, this conclusion will not follow as a matter of course, since the list of potentially unfair terms in sch. 3 to the Regulations is merely an indicative list. Accordingly, what the Arbitration Act 1996 has done is to introduce a substantial element of uncertainty into the question whether a consumer arbitration agreement is to be regarded as unfair or not, whereas under the Consumer Arbitration Agreements Act 1988 an arbitration clause was automatically ineffective unless there was a written agreement to submit to arbitration after a dispute had arisen and a court order to that effect had been made.

Under the 1994 Regulations, it will be neccessary to consider whether the arbitration clause is capable of causing a significant imbalance in the rights and obligations of the parties to the contract (Unfair Terms in Consumer Contracts Regulations 1994, reg. 4(1)), having regard to the strength of the bargaining position of the parties, whether the consumer has received any inducement to agree to the term and the extent to which the other party to the contract has dealt fairly and equitably with the consumer (ibid. sch. 2). The matter of dealing fairly and equitably with the consumer is perhaps the most important of these considerations, especially where there has been a failure to bring to the notice of the consumer the effects of a clause which compels the parties to submit to arbitration in the event of a dispute rather than to allow the consumer to pursue his ordinary legal remedies, should he decide to do so. Accordingly, consistent with the general requirement that all terms in standard-form consumer contracts must be written in plain and intelligible language, it must be clear to the consumer, from the outset, that disputes arising under the contract will be subject to arbitration and it must be fair in all the circumstances to compel the consumer to abide by that agreement.

3.2.4 Class actions

It has been observed that one of the difficulties of the civil justice system is that, for the most part, it is left to the individual consumer to pursue the trader who has caused the damage of which the consumer complains. In many instances, the consumer may be deterred from taking matters further because of the cost and difficulty involved in doing so. However, in some instances, particularly in product liability cases involving design defects, a wide range of consumers may be affected by a single act on the part of a manufacturer. For example, in recent years the manufacture of the drugs thalidomide and Opren has resulted in widespread harm to consumers and the actions of the South Western Water Authority in allowing harmful chemicals to be deposited in domestic water supplies thereby resulting in extensive harm. In such cases, there is clearly some merit in pursuing consumer complaints on a class basis, whereby representatives of the consumer group sue on behalf of the rest.

If a number of different plaintiffs have been injured in the same accident as a result of a single defendant's alleged negligence, there is nothing to stop the actions of all plaintiffs from being joined. However, where there is no common accident, joinder of actions is not possible, but the use of a test case may be an alternative. For example, an individual plaintiff may be singled out as representing the whole class of plaintiffs affected by the defendant's action (Rules of the Supreme Court, ord. 15. r. 12). However, there is a major obstacle to such actions in that it has been held that damages cannot be recovered on the part of the class in a representative action because the merits of each individual plaintiff's case might differ (*Markt & Co. Ltd* v *Knight Steamship Co. Ltd* [1910] 2 KB 1021). Furthermore, it has been observed judicially that the concept of the class action is, as yet, unknown to the English courts (*Davies* v *Eli Lilly & Co.* [1987] 3 All ER 94, 96 per Donaldson MR). However, it was also stated that the desirability of such actions is something that ought to be considered and that in the meantime, courts must be flexible and adaptable in applying existing procedures with a view to reaching a decision quickly and economically where large numbers of plaintiffs are involved (ibid.).

In some instances, the courts have appeared to be more lenient. For example, it has been held that where a representative action is brought, it is open to a member of that class to treat the decision in the representative action as *res iudicata*, but it will still be necessary for him to prove damage in a separate action (*Prudential Assurance Co. Ltd* v *Newman Industries Ltd* [1979] 3 All ER 507, 521 per Vinelott J).

As an alternative to individual actions brought on behalf of a representative group of potential plaintiffs, it might also be possible to allow an action to be brought on behalf of consumers generally by a representative agency (see Tur (1982) 2 J Legal Stud 135, 162–3). Clearly, such actions would be public interest based rather than being geared towards the needs of individual consumers who may have suffered specific harm at the hands of a particular defendant. For example, action might be taken in respect of a particular practice which is potentially harmful to consumer interests generally. To a certain extent this power already exists in other areas of English law. For example, action may be brought by the Commission for Racial Equality or the Equal Opportunities Commission to eradicate persistent discriminatory practices. Similarly, the Director General of Fair Trading has powers under the Restrictive Trade Practices Act 1976 in respect of registrable restrictive trading agreements.

In cases involving the consumer interest, bodies such as the Consumers' Association appear to have some role to play. The Association's magazine *Which?* regularly runs a consumer advice column, requesting consumers to submit their legal problems and on occasions, the Association is prepared to commit resources to assisting a particular consumer if the case has a significant bearing on consumer interests generally. For example, in *Woodman v Photo Trade Processing Ltd* (7 May 1981 Exeter County Court, unreported, see *Which?* July 1981) the Association's chief legal officer appeared in the county court to argue one of the first cases to be heard under the Unfair Contract Terms Act 1977. But this is a long way from the type of representative action which may be brought in some other jurisdictions (cf. British Columbia Trade Practices Act 1979, ss. 18 and 24).

3.3 CONSUMER REDRESS UNDER TRADE ASSOCIATION CODES OF PRACTICE

It has already been observed that many trade association codes of practice operate an arbitration service which may be substantially to the benefit of consumers if it cuts the costs of obtaining redress (see chapter 2). A further beneficial effect of some codes of practice is that they provide for bonding schemes which may provide a useful source of recompense where a member of the association becomes insolvent owing substantial amounts of money to consumers with whom he has contracted. A good example of bonding arrangements can be found in the Association of British Travel Agents' Travel Agents Fund, under which travel agent members of ABTA are required to contribute an amount up to half the annual subscription to membership of the Association. The purpose of such payments is to form part of a fund which can be used to indemnify members of the travelling public against losses resulting from the insolvency of an ABTA travel agent. Similar schemes are operated by the Tour Operators' Study Group (TOSG) and the Civil Aviation Authority. Outside the travel trade, bonding arrangements are also to be found in the Mail Order Protection Scheme and the Glass and Glaziers' Federation Code of Ethical Practice. For an illustration of the working of such bonding arrangements see *Barclays Bank Ltd* v *TOSG Trust Fund Ltd* [1984] AC 626.

3.4 CONSUMER REDRESS IN CRIMINAL PROCEEDINGS

A significant part of consumer protection law is to be found in the form of statutory provisions imposing criminal liability on the part of traders (see chapters 13–19). While some of these statutes confer a right of civil action for damages in tort for a breach of statutory duty, others do not. The main purpose of the criminal law is not to provide compensation for individuals who may suffer at the hands of a wrongdoer, but to encourage improved trading standards.

Despite these general observations on the role of the criminal law as a means of consumer protection, ss. 35 to 38 of the Powers of Criminal Courts Act 1973 now give a criminal court the power to award compensation to the victim of a crime provided civil proceedings have not been concluded before the date of conviction of the offender (*Hammertons Cars Ltd* v *Redbridge London Borough Council* [1974] 2 All ER 216). If civil proceedings are subsequently successful, the amount of compensation awarded under the 1973 Act must be deducted from the subsequent award of damages (s. 38).

In order for the compensation provisions to apply there must be a conviction and the victim must be able to show that he has suffered loss in the form of 'personal injury, loss or damage' (s. 35(1)); *R* v *Horsham Justices, ex parte Richards* [1985] 2 All ER 1114). However, in some cases proof of the value of the harm suffered may be very difficult to provide, for example where the victim suffers distress or anxiety. In such cases, it would appear that such proof is unnecessary where the court is able to assume that the victim must have been terrified or frightened (*Bond* v *Chief Constable of Kent* [1983] 1 All ER 456).

While there must be a conviction, it is no longer the case that there must be a punishment in the form of a fine or imprisonment, since it is now provided that a compensation order may be made instead of punishment (s. 35(4A)). Furthermore, general encouragement in favour of making compensation orders is given by the requirement that if a court decides not to make an order for compensation, it should give its reasons for doing so (Criminal Justice Act 1988, s. 104(1)).

Certain matters limit the court's decision on the matter of compensation. In particular, regard must be had to the defendant's ability to pay (Powers of Criminal Courts Act 1973, s. 35(1A)) and the court is able to give the offender time in which to pay the compensation or order payment by instalments (s. 34).

FOUR

The law of contract as a means of consumer protection: general issues

4.1 CONSUMERS AND FREEDOM OF CONTRACT

The common law has been responsible for a number of important rules which have been adapted as consumer protection measures. Foremost amongst these are the implied terms in supply of goods contracts which require all goods supplied under a contract to be of satisfactory quality and fit for the purpose for which the buyer requires them (see further chapter 6). In contracts for the supply of services there is an implied term to the effect that the service provider will exercise reasonable care and skill in the performance of the service (see further chapter 8).

It has been observed already that an important consideration in respect of the use of general principles of the law of contract as a means of protecting consumers is that the desire to protect the weaker party may find itself in conflict with the general principle of freedom of contract (see chapter 1). It is also important to emphasise that the nature of the common law is such that principles of contract law which are developed apply not only to consumer contracts, but also to purely commercial transactions, with the result that the application of a particular rule in a consumer context may produce intolerable strains when applied to commercial dealings between business people. For example, one of the techniques adopted by the courts to deal with the issue of oppressive exemption clauses in standard-form contracts was the doctrine of fundamental breach of contract. Under this doctrine, a contract was considered to fail altogether where there was a breach which went to the root of the contract, with the result that the party in breach became unable to enforce the terms of that contract against the other party. When applied in a consumer context, the doctrine did serve to prevent reliance on exemption clauses which might otherwise operate unfairly against consumers. Thus it became possible to invalidate a purported exclusion of liability for breach of the implied terms relating to the supply of consumer goods where the goods delivered were not in accordance with the contract description. In *Karsales*

(Harrow) Ltd v *Wallis* [1956] 1 WLR 936 the supplier of a motor vehicle under a contract of hire purchase delivered a vehicle which was so badly damaged that it was incapable of independent movement. The contract contained a provision to the effect that there was no condition relating to, or warranty of, the condition or fitness of the goods supplied. It was considered that a motor vehicle which will not move cannot be described as a car with the result that there was a serious breach of condition relating to the description of the goods supplied. Applying the doctrine of fundamental breach, it was considered that no matter how extensive the exemption clause might be, it has no application if there has been a breach of a fundamental term.

Useful though this doctrine might have been in consumer contracts, when applied to purely commercial contracts, it was capable of undoing a perfectly valid allocation of risks agreed between two business contracting parties of roughly equal bargaining strength. Eventually, it was recognised that the doctrine of fundamental breach could operate only as a rule of construction and that it was necessary to consider what the parties intended when they agreed to a particular term of the contract. Thus if the parties have made their intentions clear, the relevant term has to be construed so as to give effect to those intentions, no matter how unpalatable the result might be (see, e.g., *Photo Production Ltd* v *Securicor Transport Ltd* [1980] AC 827). The inadequacy of the common law as a means of controlling these devices was eventually recognised by Parliament, which was able to provide for special protection in consumer contracts, in particular, in the form of the Unfair Contract Terms Act 1977. Moreover, since that date the European Community has participated in the drive towards the greater protection of consumers in the form of the Directive on Unfair Terms in Consumer Contracts (93/13/EEC, OJ L95/29), which was given effect in the UK by the Unfair Terms in Consumer Contracts Regulations 1994 (SI 1994/3159). What must be recognised is that the generality of common law rules, applying as they do to all contracts, may prove to be singularly ineffective as a means of protecting consumers from the bargaining strength of the businesses with which they deal on a day-to-day basis. Since common law contract rules are theoretically dominated by the principle of freedom of contract, the only way the consumer can be adequately protected is by means of legally imposed obligations such as statutory controls on exemption clauses in contracts for the supply of goods and services.

What is clear is that very often the more appropriate vehicle of consumer protection will be legislative action, which allows for specific rules designed to protect identified classes of contracting parties such as consumers, while applying a different approach to others. These general observations apart, there are nonetheless a number of common law developments which to some degree do serve as consumer protection measures.

4.2 RULES OF CONTRACT FORMATION AND CONSUMER PROTECTION

The general law of contract provides that a contract is formed when the parties, intending to create legal relations, have reached agreement and the respective promises of the parties to the contract are supported by a legally recognisable consideration. At the outset, it should be recognised that when the classical rules of the law of contract were developed in the nineteenth century, the modern phenomenon of the consumer society did not exist. The rules of contract formation had in mind as the paradigm contract, one between two business contracting parties of roughly equal bargaining strength who would haggle with each other and agreement would be reached on terms which were mutually advantageous to both parties. The classical law did not countenance the possibility that contracting parties might include informationally deprived consumers of mass-produced factory goods. Accordingly, it has been observed in *New Zealand Shipping Co. Ltd* v *A. M. Satterthwaite & Co. Ltd* [1975] AC 154, 167 (per Lord Wilberforce) that:

> It is only the precise analysis of this complex of relations into the classical offer and acceptance, with identifiable consideration, that seems to present difficulty, but this same difficulty exists in many situations of daily life, e.g. sales at auction; supermarket purchases; boarding an omnibus; purchasing a train ticket; tenders for the supply of goods; offers of rewards; acceptance by post; warranties of authority by agents; manufacturers' guarantees; gratuitous bailments; bankers' commercial credits. These are all examples which show that English law, having committed itself to a rather technical and schematic doctrine of contract, in its application takes a practical approach, often at the cost of forcing the facts uneasily to fit into the marked slots of offer, acceptance and consideration.

What this shows is that there are a substantial number of what may be called consumer contracts which set a challenge for the courts when it comes to analysing the relationship between the parties. The typical consumer transaction does not generally involve a drawn-out process of haggling at the end of which an agreement is reached. Instead, in the typical supermarket purchase, the consumer enters into an almost immediate exchange of goods for money, with little being said between the consumer and the check-out assistant. Yet we are told that this contract has to fit within the classical model of definite offer met by unconditional and communicated acceptance. Other improbable variants may also be considered. For example, we are told that when a consumer enters a multi-storey car park and is presented by a machine with a ticket, the consumer has accepted an offer to take parking space and time on the terms made known to him by the owner of the car park at the time the ticket was thrust at him by the machine (*Thornton* v *Shoe Lane Parking Ltd* [1971] 2 QB 163).

4.2.1 Offer and acceptance

Although the rules of offer and acceptance represent the core of the classical, freedom of contract based approach to contract formation, it is nonetheless possible to discern the use of these rules as an instrument of consumer protection. In classical terms, in order for there to be an agreement, there must be a definite offer, setting out with utmost clarity the terms on which the offeror is prepared to do business, an absolute and unconditional acceptance of that offer by the offeree which is communicated to the offeror by the offeree.

4.2.1.1 Who offers what to whom? Despite the fact that the majority of consumer transactions will not involve any sort of negotiation in the classical sense of that word, the law continues to employ the language of the classical model, including the rules of offer and acceptance, in analysing transactions entered into by consumers. It has been observed above that the classical rules of offer and acceptance work on the basis that contracts are concluded by a process of negotiation between the parties in which one person makes an offer which the other may choose to accept as it stands or he may modify the offer with his own counter-proposal. If this counter-proposal is acceptable to the other party, he may then choose to accept and a contract is consummated as a result of the agreement which is reached. The problem with consumer transactions is that it is rare that a consumer ever engages in the process of haggling envisaged by the classical rules of contract law.

The basic rule which applies to consumer transactions in retail outlets is that when goods are displayed for sale, the retailer merely invites offers from members of the public. Generally, despite the fact that a retail display of goods may be accompanied by words such as 'special offer', the display of goods is regarded as no more than an invitation to treat or an invitation to the consumer to make him an offer. Thus in *Pharmaceutical Society of Great Britain* v *Boots Cash Chemists (Southern) Ltd* [1953] 1 QB 401 the question arose whether the sale of certain pharmaceutical products had been entered into under the supervision of a registered pharmacist. In order to answer this question, it was necessary to decide whether the retailer offered to sell the pharmaceutical products or not. For these purposes, it was held that the retailer merely invites his customers to make an offer to purchase goods with the result that the contract of sale was entered into at the cash desk at which there was present a registered pharmacist. A number of reasons were given for arriving at this conclusion, which included the view that if the retailer was taken to have offered to sell the goods, that offer would have been accepted when the customer selected an item from the shelf and placed it in his shopping basket. Accordingly, the customer would have been denied the opportunity to change his mind and purchase another item he might see in another part of the store. Other arguments which also support the conclusion arrived at in the *Boots* case are that a retailer must be regarded as merely inviting offers, since if the opposite were the case, there might be circumstances in which the number of orders received was in excess of the stocks held by the retailer with the result that the retailer would be unavoidably in breach of contract every time an order is received and there are insufficient stocks to meet the order (see *Grainger & Son* v *Gough* [1898] AC 325).

A number of problems flow from the *Boots* analysis. First, suppose a consumer picks up a bottle of bleach, places it in his wire basket and subsequently the bleach leaks from the bottle, damaging the consumer's expensive designer training shoes. On the *Boots* analysis, if this occurs before the consumer has reached the check-out desk, there is no action in contract, and, assuming the retailer is not guilty of any fault, there is no action arising under the rule in *Donoghue* v *Stevenson* [1932] AC 562 (see chapter 7). Moreover, assuming the training shoes to be valued at less than £275, there would be no action against the producer of the bleach under the Consumer Protection Act 1987 (see chapter 7 and Consumer Protection Act 1987 s. 5(4)). Similar considerations will also apply where, for example, the consumer is injured by a defective container in which goods are packaged before reaching the check-out desk (see *Lasky* v *Economy Grocery Stores* (1946) 65 NE 2d 235), although in this case, there is a much greater chance of bringing a successful action against the producer of the defective product under the Consumer Protection Act 1987, since the defective product has caused personal injury (see chapter 7).

In the context of misleading advertisements, a supplier could make various tempting 'offers' with a view to attracting custom only to turn round later to say that he has offered nothing. For example, in *Lefkowitz* v *Great Minneapolis Surplus Stores* (1957) 86 NW 2d 689 the owner of a store placed a newspaper advertisement in two successive weeks which stated:

> Saturday 9 a.m. sharp; 3 brand new fur coats, worth $100. First come first served, $1 each.

On two occasions, the plaintiff, a man, attempted to purchase one of the advertised fur coats, but on each occasion, the defendants refused to sell to him. On the first occasion, the reason given was that under shop rules, the offer was only open to women and on the second occasion the reason given was that he was aware of the rules applicable to the special offer. The Supreme Court of Minnesota held that the defendants had offered to sell the coats at the price advertised, and accordingly the plaintiff was entitled to damages for breach of contract. This was an American decision, but there is no English authority which directly suggests that this would be regarded as anything more than an invitation to treat. This is particularly so since the general rule in English law is that a retailer does not make an offer when he displays an advertisement indicating that particular goods are for sale (see *Partridge* v *Crittenden* [1968] 1 WLR 1204).

The no-offer rule is particularly unhelpful in the context of consumer protection law, with the result that when Parliament has been faced with the task of drafting legislation aimed at misleading advertisements, it has had to introduce a statutory definition of the word 'offer', which includes the act of having possession of goods on retail premises with a view to sale (see Trade Descriptions Act 1968, s. 6 and see chapter 17).

Occasionally, there are circumstances in which the general law of contract will treat an advertisement as amounting to an offer, provided it is clear from the wording of the advertisement that there is a specific something available if the consumer acts in a particular way. For example, in *Carlill* v *Carbolic Smokeball Co.* [1893] 1 QB 256 the defendants published an advertisement extolling the virtues of the carbolic smokeball which claimed that the product would cure a wide range of common ailments and offered £100 to any person who contracted influenza after using the preparation in accordance with the manufacturer's instructions. Mrs Carlill sought to recover the promised £100 when she suffered from influenza despite using the smokeball. The Court of Appeal treated the advertisement as an express promise to pay £100 on condition that the offeree performed what was required of her under the terms of the advertisement. The important question, according to Bowen LJ (at p. 266) was to ask:

> How would an ordinary person reading this document construe it? It was intended unquestionably to have some effect and I think the effect which it was intended to have was to make people use the smokeball, because the suggestions and allegations which it contains are directed immediately to the use of the smokeball as distinct from the purchase of it. . . . The intention was that the circulation of the smokeball should be promoted, and that the use of it should be increased.

What is clear from *Carlill* v *Carbolic Smokeball Co.* is that where an advertisement specifies that something specific is available if certain conditions are fulfilled, it may be treated as an offer rather than the less specific advertisements which merely indicate that goods are available for purchase at a stated price, assuming agreement is subsequently reached. While the principle in *Carlill* is most likely to apply to specific advertisements, it can also be applied in other contexts. For example, displays in Association of British Travel Agents' (ABTA) shops to the effect that customers who purchase a holiday from an ABTA agent will be protected by a full money-back guarantee organised by ABTA have been held to amount to an offer on the part of ABTA, since ordinary persons reading such displays would understand that they were being given a guarantee of full reimbursement should their ABTA tour operator go into liquidation (*Bowerman* v *ABTA Ltd* (1995) 145 NLJ 1815, discussed further below).

Subject-specific advertisements apart, the question remains whether the no-offer rule which generally applies in English law is defensible. The principal reason given in the *Boots* case for treating a display of goods as an invitation to treat was that to decide otherwise would prevent the consumer from changing his mind if he saw a more tempting offer at a later stage. But other variants on this approach are possible. For example, the consumer might be considered not to accept the retailer's offer until he presents the goods at the check-out. Alternatively, it has been held in the United States that a consumer accepts an offer to sell before the goods are presented at the check-out, but has a power to cancel that acceptance before presentation of the goods. (*Sheeskin* v *Giant Food Inc.* (1974) 318 A 2d 874). Moreover, even in English law, the display of goods for hire has been considered to amount to an offer, particularly where the display invites personal selection by the consumer (*Chapelton* v *Barry Urban District Council* [1940] 1 KB 532) and a display of the terms on which parking space in a car park is available has been considered to amount to an offer (*Thornton* v *Shoe Lane Parking Ltd* [1971] 2

QB 163. Why then is a display of goods on a supermarket shelf to be treated differently? Certainly it would be difficult to distinguish the supply of vehicle fuel at a self-service forecourt from the selection of the deckchairs in *Chapelton* v *Barry Urban District Council.*

The other argument which is tendered in support of the no-offer rule is that retailers would be in breach of contract should they sell all their stocks and be unable to meet orders as they were placed. However, this problem is unlikely to arise where the retailer is one of the giants of the consumer market place, who operate very sophisticated stock control systems. Moreover, there should be little difficulty in implying in any offer deemed to be made by a retailer a condition to the effect that the offer should last only so long as there are stocks sufficient to meet orders as they are placed.

4.2.1.2 Communication of offers The requirement that there should be a clear and definite offer setting out the offeror's terms may be manipulated in favour of consumers. For example, it may be that the language used by one of the parties is not sufficiently clear to amount to an offer.

Even where the language used by one of the parties is capable of amounting to an offer, it is clear from *Thornton* v *Shoe Lane Parking Ltd* [1971] 2 QB 163 (see also chapter 12) that if an offeror is to be able to rely upon terms which exempt him from liability for breach of contract, he must have adequately communicated those terms to the consumer otherwise they will not be regarded as part of his offer. Accordingly, if the party dealing with a consumer wishes to limit or exclude his liability for breach of contract in some material respect, the exemption clause must be brought to the consumer's attention at or before the time when the contract is entered into. Thus in *Olley* v *Marlborough Court* [1949] 1 KB 532 an attempt to exclude the liability of a hotelier for loss of the personal effects of a guest was held to be ineffective where the notice drawing the guest's attention to the exclusion clause was displayed in hotel bedrooms. Since the contract was made at the time of registering as a guest at the hotel reception, any attempt to communicate the terms of the contract at a later stage was ineffective.

In some instances, awareness of an exemption clause can be implied from the fact that the parties have dealt with each other on the same terms on a consistent basis in previous transactions. This implication of awareness is much more likely to arise in business contracts where business contracting parties have dealt with each other on a consistent and regular basis. In the case of consumer contracts, the regularity of dealing which the law requires is much less likely to be present. It may be that a day-to-day rail or bus commuter does satisfy the requirement of regularity of dealing, (see *Mendelssohn* v *Normand* [1970] 1 QB 177) but generally most consumer contracts are entered into on such an infrequent basis that it would be difficult to say that the consumer has become impliedly aware of the terms used by the business with which he deals. For example, in *Hollier* v *Rambler Motors (AMC) Ltd* [1972] 2 QB 71, although the *ratio* of the decision is based on rules of construction of exemption clauses, it is clear that the consumer who had placed his car for repair with the defendants on only three or four occasions in five years could not be taken to be impliedly aware of a term in the contract to the effect that the defendants accepted no responsibility for fire damage.

4.2.1.3 Certainty of the language of an offer

Even where there is an offer which is capable of acceptance, it may be that the circumstances of the case are such that the parties need to be given more time in which to assess their respective positions. This will be particularly so where one or other of the parties is about to take on obligations of a serious nature or where the subject matter of the contract is particularly valuable. For example, perhaps the most serious obligation ever likely to be undertaken by a consumer is the purchase of a house, and in this area it is noticeable that the courts have developed a number of rules which give the parties time to reflect upon the seriousness of the obligations about to be undertaken. While the conventional rules of offer and acceptance indicate that an offer to purchase which is provisionally accepted by the vendor may amount to a binding contract of sale, the parties may use the device of declaring their agreement to be 'subject to contract' with the result that there will be no binding obligation to sell or to purchase until contracts have been formally exchanged (*Winn* v *Bull* (1877) 7 ChD 29; *Chillingworth* v *Esche* [1924] 1 Ch 97). The reason for this position appears to be for the protection of both parties. For example, the vendor of land would be unwise to enter into an open contract for the sale of his estate without the protection of more detailed terms but at the same time, the 'subject to contract' device gives the purchaser more time to investigate the property he provisionally intends to purchase and may arrange for a survey to be carried out before he finally commits himself to the contract.

Of course, unless the rule is qualified, the problem is that either party may withdraw from the contract before the date on which formal exchange is due to occur, which may itself give rise to cause for concern. This is particularly the case in times of steeply rising property prices when the 'subject to contract' rule may allow the vendor to 'gazump' the buyer by choosing to sell to another person who has offered a higher price. Given the problems of 'gazumping' the courts have sought to get round it where possible. For example, it has been held that technical slips in the process of exchange may be disregarded (*Domb* v *Isoz* [1980] Ch 548) and that where both vendor and purchaser use the same solicitor, there is no requirement of exchange of contracts (*Smith* v *Mansi* [1963] 1 WLR 26). Even where there is an agreement 'subject to contract' the parties may make it clear from their subsequent agreement or conduct that there is an intention to be bound, in which case they will have negatived the effect of the original agreement subject to contract (*Law* v *Jones* [1974] Ch 112).

Furthermore, a subsequent collateral contract may also restrict the effect of an agreement 'subject to contract' provided it is sufficiently tightly worded. For example, in *Walford* v *Miles* [1992] 2 AC 128 the defendants had been negotiating with a third party for the sale of a business, but were dissatisfied with the price offered. Subsequently they entered into negotiations with the plaintiffs who provided a letter of comfort from their bankers to the effect that credit of £2 million was available should the plaintiffs decide to purchase the business. In return, the defendants agreed not to give further consideration to any alternative proposal and that they would cease to deal with the third party with whom they had been negotiating. In fact, the defendants remained in contact with the third party throughout and subsequently sold the business to him after he raised his offer to £2 million. The House of Lords held that the defendants could be liable in damages to the plaintiff if it could be shown that they had agreed to lock themselves out of negotiations with persons other than the plaintiff for a specified period of time. It was considered that such lock-out agreements were not the same as an agreement to agree, which is generally regarded as void for uncertainty (see *Courtney & Fairbairn Ltd* v *Tolaini Brothers (Hotels) Ltd* [1975] 1 WLR 297) and would amount to little more than an unspecific agreement to negotiate in good faith. Instead, if there is an agreement specifically to lock the defendants out of negotiations with a particular person for a particular period of time, it could be regarded as binding. However, in *Walford* v *Miles*, it was concluded that the agreement was not sufficiently certain in the language used to have that effect. Conversely, if the criteria set out in *Walford* v *Miles* are satisfied in that there is an agreement not to deal with a specific person for an agreed period of time, that agreement may give rise to a collateral contract (see *Pitt* v *PHH Asset Management Ltd* [1994] 1 WLR 327).

4.2.2 Consideration

Generally, common law rules on consideration are unlikely to raise many important issues for consumer transactions. Since the majority of consumer transactions will involve the payment or promise of payment of money, there is unlikely to be any issue of sufficiency of consideration.

It might be argued that since consumers are often in a weak bargaining position in relation to the business contracting parties with whom they deal, there is the possibility that consumers are more likely than most contracting parties to enter into a bad bargain. However, it is clear that as a general rule, English law does not take account of the adequacy of consideration so as to relieve a weaker party from the consequences of an imprudent bargain. Accordingly, it has been held that a promise to give a person an option to purchase a valuable house in consideration of the payment of £1 is enforceable through an order for specific performance even where the promisor later finds it difficult to purchase an alternative property with the proceeds of sale (*Mountford* v *Scott* [1975] Ch 258). It follows from the general rule on adequacy of consideration that a court is unlikely to interfere where a consumer later discovers that he has agreed to pay more for goods or services than could have been obtained elsewhere. Thus if a house owner is faced with a burst water pipe at 10.00 p.m. on Christmas Eve, calls out a plumber and agrees to pay an exorbitant sum for, say, 45 minutes' work, there appears to be little that can be done (see further chapter 8).

It should not be thought that English courts wholly ignore the adequacy of consideration in all circumstances, but where the issue of adequacy is taken into account, it is often disguised in the form of other rules. The most open recognition that consideration of the issue of unfairness may be taken into account can be found in equitable principles. For example, in determining whether a contract may be set aside on the grounds of undue influence, it is clear from the decision of the Court of Appeal in *Lloyds Bank Ltd* v *Bundy* [1975] QB 326 that regard will be had to the adequacy of the consideration (ibid. 347 per Sir Eric Sachs).

In determining whether goods sold to a consumer are of satisfactory quality or not, regard must be had to the price paid (Sale of Goods Act 1979, s. 14(2) and see chapter 6). Accordingly, the higher the price paid for goods, the higher may be the consumer's expectations of quality.

In limited circumstances, a court will have the power to reopen an agreement entered into by a consumer. This is particularly the case where there is shown to have been an extortionate credit bargain under the provisions of the Consumer Credit Act 1974, ss. 137–9 (see further chapter 11).

4.2.3 Contractual intention

In addition to the general requirements imposed by the rules on contract formation, it is clear that unless there is evidence that the parties had an intention to create a contractual relationship, no legal consequences will follow from the fact of certain relationships. In a consumer context, there is little doubt that such an intention will exist as between retail suppliers and their customers, but it is possible that in less direct relationships a contractual intention may also be discerned.

In the course of dealing with point-of-sale suppliers, consumers are likely to be confronted with a large number of statements and advertising material which is intended to induce them to enter into a contractual relationship with the retailer. But it is quite possible that the source of this material is not necessarily the retailer himself, but some other body such as a manufacturer or other interested party. Whether or not such inducements to purchase give rise to a contractual relationship would appear to depend upon whether the consumer can reasonably construe the statement as offering him something of value.

In *Bowerman* v *ABTA Ltd* (1995) 145 NLJ 1815, the earlier decision of Mitchell J ((1994) 14 TrLR 246) which had gone against the consumer was reversed. The Court of Appeal, by a majority (Hirst LJ dissenting), held that a notice describing the ABTA scheme to protect consumers against the financial failure of ABTA members created a contractual relationship between the consumer and the trade association. The implications of this decision are very important for all trade associations, since direct contractual relations are normally considered to exist between the customer and the retailer, but hitherto there has been no suggestion that a trade association to which the retailer belongs also incurs contractual liability. The basis upon which the decision was reached (Waite and Hobhouse LJJ) was that the notice describing the ABTA scheme would be regarded by an ordinary member of the public as intended to create legal relations with customers of ABTA members and was therefore contractually binding.

In *Bowerman* v *ABTA Ltd* the first plaintiff was a 15-year-old schoolgirl who booked a skiing trip organised by the second plaintiff, a teacher at her school. The trip, which was organised by an ABTA member, was cancelled when the tour operator ceased trading. Arrangements for the holiday were taken over by another ABTA member, but a holiday insurance premium, estimated by ABTA to be £10 per person on the trip was not returned to the plaintiff. The question arose whether ABTA was contractually bound to make a full refund. In the present case, the amount in dispute was relatively small, but the point of principle at stake was important since it would substantially increase the liability of ABTA when the number of holidaymakers taking package holidays with ABTA members was taken into consideration.

Hobhouse LJ placed considerable emphasis upon the decision in *Carlill* v *Carbolic Smokeball Co.* [1893] 1 QB 256 where Bowen LJ (at 266) said of an advertisement which offered a reward of £100 to any person who used the carbolic smokeball according to the manufacturer's instructions and still contracted influenza, 'It was intended to be issued to the public and to be read by the public. How would an ordinary person reading this document construe it?'

In similar vein, Hobhouse LJ in *Bowerman* v *ABTA Ltd* considered that the various public statements made about the ABTA scheme were a cornerstone of the promotion of ABTA members, showing how ABTA protects the travelling and holidaymaking public from the risks of financial collapse. Understood objectively, these statements were clearly intended to have an effect on the reader and to lead him to believe that he is getting something of value. Although the ABTA scheme was set up between ABTA and its members, everybody knew that it was for the protection of the public since the various notices displayed in travel agents' shops made claims such as, 'ABTA seeks to arrange for you to continue with the booked arrangement' and 'ABTA ensures that you will be able to return to the UK' and 'The scheme is for your protection. . . . ABTA still protects you.' It is clear that these statements were all directed towards the public. As a result, Hobhouse LJ concluded that a member of the public could reasonably infer that he was being offered something by ABTA whenever choosing to do business with an ABTA member.

Waite LJ, the other member of the Court of Appeal to agree in the result that ABTA had contracted with Miss Bowerman, was less convinced of the utility of the *Carlill* v *Carbolic Smokeball Co.* principle, although, like Hobhouse LJ, Waite LJ also emphasised the objectivity of the approach to determining when there is an agreement which creates binding legal relations. Waite LJ concluded that it was necessary to construe the relevant documents in which words capable of having a promissory meaning appeared alongside other words representing a lesser commitment. Waite LJ was of the opinion that the notice displayed in ABTA members' shops could be construed as demonstrating an intention to create legal relations with customers of an ABTA member. The crucial words in Waite LJ's view were:

Where holidays or other travel arrangements have not yet commenced at the time of failure, ABTA *arranges for you to be reimbursed* the money you have paid in respect of your holiday arrangements.

That this decision is controversial may be seen from the fact that the Court of Appeal was not unanimous and that the trial judge had taken a different view in the Queen's Bench Division. Hirst LJ (dissenting) preferred to regard the statements about the ABTA protection scheme as being descriptive rather than promissory. He was unable to find any specific words of promise or binding commitment. He thought that *Carlill* v *Carbolic Smokeball Co.* was distinguishable on the basis that in that case there was a clear and crisp statement in the advertisement that '£100 reward will be paid'. On similar lines, Mitchell J in the Divisional Court was also not convinced of the promissory nature of the ABTA documentation. Merely by informing the public of the existence of a particular scheme did not amount to making a promise, especially given the equivocal nature of some of the statements contained in the notice displayed in ABTA members' shops. Mitchell J's preferred analogy was the Court of Appeal decision in *Kleinwort Benson Ltd* v *Malaysia Mining Corporation Bhd* [1989] 1 WLR 379, in which it was held that a letter of comfort which stated, 'It is our policy to ensure that the business of MMC Metals Ltd is at all times in a position to meet its liabilities to you' was merely a representation of present intention and not a binding contractual promise to guarantee the debts of MMC. On similar lines, Mitchell J opined that the ABTA notice consisted of a representation of fact as to the existence of the protection scheme, but did not contain any contractual promise.

The majority decision in *Bowerman* v *ABTA Ltd* does give rise to a number of difficulties. In the first place there is much to support the approach adopted by Hirst LJ in the Court of Appeal and Mitchell J in the Divisional Court, given the equivocal nature of many of the statements contained in the ABTA notice. Moreover, the analogy with *Carlill* v *Carbolic Smokeball Co.* is not as direct as it might, at first sight, appear. What should be remembered is that the Carbolic Smokeball Co. was the manufacturer of the product in respect of which the offer of a reward was made and that the reward notice was an unsophisticated and, in places, highly misleading advertisement for its product which was intended to increase sales. As a result, the company would have hoped to see an increase in sales as a result of advertising the availability of a reward. Given these circumstances, holding the company contractually liable for the loss incurred by the plaintiff seems to be justified if only because of the likely profit which would have been made. In terms of legal principle, the benefit to the company in the form of increased trade induced by the offer of the reward can be seen as the consideration for the defendant's promise to pay the reward, even though the actual purchase may be made from a high street retailer. Whether the same reasoning can apply to an organisation such as a trade association which has been set up as a quasi-regulatory body must be called into doubt. The consequences for trade associations generally appear to be quite alarming, though the fact that the particular trade association involved in this case was ABTA may be important. What should be appreciated is that ABTA commands almost 100 per cent membership in the travel trade for one reason in particular. This is that under the terms of a clause, known as 'stabiliser' in ABTA's articles of association, only ABTA members may sell ABTA products, and ABTA tour operators must sell their holidays only through ABTA travel agents. The effect of this has been to create a legalised cartel with the result that it would be commercial suicide for a travel agent or a tour operator not to be a member of ABTA. Given this position, it is not surprising that the provisions of the ABTA protection scheme are given widespread publicity, with the result that they are more likely to be read by members of the public and acted upon. Moreover, the ABTA bonding scheme is something most holidaymakers are aware of given the increasing numbers of financial failures in the travel trade and it would be an unwise traveller who did not book through an ABTA outlet.

What is also clear from *Bowerman* v *ABTA Ltd* is that the decision turns very much on the fact that customers booking a holiday at an ABTA travel agent did appear to have been promised something by ABTA rather than by the travel agent. In the light of this, it will not be every provision in a trade association code of practice which gives rise to contractual liability. There needs to be some code provision which offers something of value to the consumer before the decision in *Bowerman* v *ABTA Ltd* will bite.

4.2.4 Privity of contract
The doctrine of privity of contract dictates that only a party to a contract can claim rights under that contract and be subject to obligations arising from the contract. The doctrine is capable of being a major restriction on the availability of consumer remedies for breach of contract. The doctrine of privity can have both horizontal and vertical effects. For example, in the context of a product liability action (see further chapter 7) vertical privity is that which exists between one person and his immediate predecessor or successor in a descending chain of distribution from the producer to the retailer. In the same context, horizontal privity is that which exists between the consumer and the retailer who buys from him.

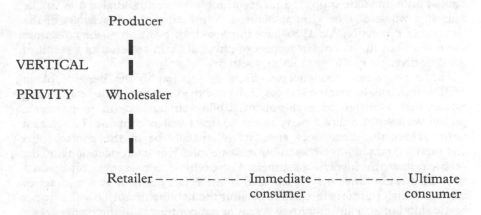

Frequently, a consumer purchase is made by one person on behalf of someone else. For example, a purchase of food may be made by one member of a family on behalf of other members of the same family or a person may buy an article as a present for a friend. In each case, the doctrine of privity of contract provides that the immediate purchaser may pursue a remedy in his own favour against the retailer, but cannot recover anything in respect of the harm suffered by the person for whom the purchase was made. In *Preist v Last* [1903] 2 KB 148 the plaintiff bought a hot-water bottle from the defendant, asking, at the time of purchase, whether it would hold boiling water. The plaintiff was advised that while the product would not withstand boiling water, it was suitable for holding hot water. Complying with these instructions, the plaintiff filled the bottle and gave it to his wife to relieve stomach cramps.

Subsequently, the bottle burst, depositing its harmful contents on the plaintiff's wife. In an action for damages for breach of the implied contractual term that goods supplied will be fit for the purpose required by the purchaser, it was held that the plaintiff was entitled to damages representing his own loss, but he was entitled to nothing in respect of the pain and suffering undeniably suffered by his wife.

The doctrine of privity is one of a number of nineteenth century rules which have served to hinder the development of the law of contract to meet new conditions. On occasions, judicial ingenuity has found ways of avoiding the harsher effects of the doctrine, but it has still operated in a manner which prevents the recognition of third-party contractual rights, given that there are repeated statements to the effect that English law generally does not recognise a *jus quaesitum tertio* (*Dunlop Pneumatic Tyre Co. Ltd* v *Selfridge & Co. Ltd* [1915] AC 847, 853 per Viscount Haldane LC). This is particularly important in relation to an action for economic loss suffered as a result of the purchase of a defective product. Generally, the purchaser of such a product will be able to maintain an action against the retailer for a breach of one of the implied terms of the contract of supply, but the non-purchaser will not be in the same position. Furthermore, the purchaser is confined to an action against his immediate supplier and, accordingly, no contractual action will lie against a wholesaler or a manufacturer. Admittedly, the provisions of the Consumer Protection Act 1987 have improved the position of the consumer somewhat, but this is only in respect of physical harm suffered as a result of the defectiveness of the product in question.

The doctrine also has adverse effects in relation to the benefits of an exclusion clause. In many instances, it may be the intention of the contracting parties that a purported exclusion of liability should extend to protect a person who is not a direct party to the contract which contains the relevant term. Where this issue does arise, it will usually be in the context of a commercial transaction between business people. However, occasionally, the problem may also involve consumers. For example, a passenger on board a ferry or a cruise liner may discover that there is a term in the contract of carriage which purports to exclude or limit the liability of not only the owner of the ship but also any employee, agent or subcontractor of the owner (*Adler v Dickson* [1955] 1 QB 158) or a bus pass issued to a concessionary passenger may seek to exclude the liability of the bus operator and individual bus drivers (*Gore* v *Van der Lann* [1967] 2 QB 31). The general common law response, in these circumstances, has been that the attempt to extend the protection of the exemption clause to others should fail, especially where the other contracting party is a consumer. This can be achieved readily through an application of the doctrine of privity by saying that the employee or subcontractor is not a party to the contract between the owner and the consumer. Moreover, so far as exemption clauses in consumer contracts are concerned, there is now extensive statutory protection of the consumer in the form of the Unfair Contract Terms Act 1977 and the Unfair Terms in Consumer Contracts Regulations 1994 (SI 1994/3159), which are discussed in detail in chapter 12.

A number of other methods of avoiding the harsher effects of the doctrine of privity of contract have also been developed. These include expanding the definition of who is a party to the contract, allowing the promisee to sue on behalf of a third party and permitting an action under some branch of the law of obligations other than the law of contract.

4.2.4.1 Extending the definition of a party to the contract   In some instances, it may be possible to regard one person as contracting as an agent for a third party. Ordinarily, this method of circumventing the effects of the doctrine of privity will not be available to a consumer, since principles of the law of agency require a principal to have expressly authorised the agent to act on his behalf. In most consumer transactions, it is unlikely that the purchaser of goods or services will state that he is purchasing on behalf of another with the consent of that other, in which case the agency route will not be available. However, on occasions the converse is the case and courts have been prepared to regard one person as making a contract on behalf of another. For example in *Lockett* v *A. & M. Charles Ltd* [1938] 4 All ER 170 the plaintiff's husband placed an order for a meal at the defendant's restaurant. Mrs Lockett ordered a dish of whitebait, which was contaminated, and as a result she suffered from food poisoning. It was accepted by Tucker J that it was the duty of the restaurant owner to ensure that the food he supplied was fit for human consumption and that this duty was strict in the same way as a retail supplier of goods in a shop guarantees the fitness of the goods sold for the purpose required by the consumer. He also considered that it made no difference that the restaurant booking was made in the name of one person and that the food was ordered by the plaintiff's husband. The reason given for this was that where two or more people go into a restaurant, each diner makes himself personally responsible to pay for the food which has been ordered. Since the restaurant owner would be able to sue each diner individually for the price, it had to follow that the restaurant owner was also responsible to each individual diner for the quality and fitness of the food supplied. It is implicit in Tucker J's conclusion that the person ordering the food is acting as an agent in the sense that he is the host and incurs responsibility to pay for the food for and on behalf of the other members of his party. Accordingly, it was observed (at pp. 172–3) that:

> . . . where there is no evidence to indicate to the proprietor . . . what the relationship between the parties is, and where there is no evidence that one

or the other is in charge of the proceedings, and yet one or the other takes on himself the position of a host entertaining his guests, the proper inference of law is that the person who orders and consumes the food is liable to pay for it as between himself and the proprietor of the restaurant. If that is so, it follows . . . that there is an implied warranty that the food supplied is reasonably fit for human consumption.

Whether the agency device can be widely used to extend the range of contractual plaintiffs is unclear. For example, it is relatively easy to make such an assumption in a restaurant booking case, since it is likely that the booking will have been made for a number of seats at a table with the result that the restaurateur will know that several people will be eating his food. Moreover, in order to be able to eat the food, the guests also have to be present at the restaurant, in which case they are then known to the owner. But it does not necessarily follow from this that a person shopping on behalf of his or her family contracts as an agent on behalf of those who eat the food purchased. However, there are dicta which suggest this is a possibility (see *Heil* v *Hedges* [1951] 1 TLR 512, 513 per McNair J).

Beyond purchases of food on behalf of another, there are also other commonly encountered consumer contracts in which it is possible to draw an inference that one person has contracted on behalf of others. This is commonly the case where a family holiday is booked in the name of one person, but since the booking form will always list all parties taking the holiday, it should not be difficult to infer that all members of the travelling group should be able to sue, should the holiday be a disaster. For example, in *Jackson* v *Horizon Holidays Ltd* [1975] 1 WLR 1468, the plaintiff was able to sue for damages representing the distress suffered by himself, his wife and children. Although the basis of the decision in this case has been subject to some criticism (considered below), it would have been relatively easy to treat this as a simple agency case, since Mr Jackson had signed the booking form, which contained a clause to the effect that, 'I have read and understand these booking conditions and accept them for and on behalf of myself and all the persons named on the booking form'.

4.2.4.2 Collateral warranties   If it can be shown that a manufacturer has given to a consumer a guarantee that his product is suitable for a particular use, it may be possible to infer a collateral contract between the consumer and the manufacturer, thereby circumventing the normal application of the vertical privity rule. In *Wells (Merstham) Ltd* v *Buckland Sand & Silica Ltd* [1965] 2 QB 170 the plaintiff purchased one load of a particular type of sand directly from the producer and a number of further loads of the same variety of sand from a retail supplier in reliance upon an express assertion given by the producer of the sand that it was fit for the purchaser's required purpose, namely propagating chrysanthemum plants. In fact the sand had a very high iron oxide content which rendered the sand useless in serving the plaintiff's intended purpose. It was held that the purchaser could succeed in an action against the producer, based upon a collateral warranty of fitness for purpose.

Although there was a direct contractual relationship with the retailer, it was not necessary for the retailer to be joined in the action since there was a collateral contractual promise by the producer, the consideration for which was entering into the contract with the retailer (see also *Shanklin Pier Ltd* v *Detel Products Ltd* [1951] 2 KB 854).

It is important to appreciate that the decision in *Wells (Merstham) Ltd* v *Buckland Sand & Silica Ltd* is based upon an express warranty that the sand supplied by the retailer would be fit for the buyer's intended use. Accordingly, the decision, as it stands, may not be particularly useful to consumers unless they have had direct contact with a manufacturer.

It would be far more useful in a consumer context if a similar approach could be adopted in relation to the implied warranties of satisfactory quality and fitness for purpose, so as to create a manufacturer's warranty or guarantee of the quality and suitability of the goods he puts on the market. (Such a guarantee is currently the subject of consideration at a European level; see further chapter 6.) Whether the common law could ever take the bold step of creating such a guarantee on the part of the manufacturer, based upon his promotional advertising, is unlikely, albeit theoretically possible. The problem in this regard seems to be that where there has been an express warranty of suitability as in *Wells (Merstham) Ltd* v *Buckland Sand & Silica Ltd* and the earlier decision in *Shanklin Pier Ltd* v *Detel Products Ltd*, the manufacturer is aware that the buyer intends to purchase the product from another supplier. However, in the case of implied warranties of fitness, the manufacturer is unlikely to be aware of any subsequent contract between the consumer and a retail supplier. In these circumstances, it would be difficult to say that the contract between the retailer and the consumer was induced by the manufacturer's claims about the product in question (*Lambert* v *Lewis* [1982] AC 225, 262–4 per Stephenson LJ).

In the present state of English law, the most frequent use of the collateral contract is to be found in relation to extravagant product claims whereby a consumer may have been misled into believing that he is being offered something of value by, for example, a manufacturer or producer. For example, in *Wood* v *Letrik Ltd* (1932) *The Times*, 12 January 1932, the defendant had advertised an electric comb for sale, stating that it was guaranteed to dispose of the problem of grey hair within 10 days. Further, the advertisement also guaranteed a payment of £500 if the device did not work. The plaintiff purchased one of the combs, used it as directed but instead of remedying his problem, it scratched the plaintiff's scalp and caused him discomfort. Rowlatt J held that the use of the word 'guarantee' was about as emphatic as could be imagined and that any ordinary, sensible person would take this to mean that the advertiser had offered to bind himself according to the terms of the advertisement (see also *Carlill* v *Carbolic Smokeball Co.* [1893] 1 QB 256 and *Bowerman* v *ABTA* (1995) 145 NLJ 1815).

While the collateral contract device may prove useful in relation to express assertions concerning consumer goods and services, traditional contract theory insists that there must be consideration to support the promised guarantee (*Heilbut Symons & Co.* v *Buckleton* [1913] AC 30; *Lambert* v *Lewis* [1982] AC 225). Usually, the fact that the consumer has contracted with a retail supplier on the strength of the manufacturer's claims will normally suffice to satisfy the consideration requirement. However, where there are no such dealings, the consideration requirement is a potential barrier to success. Conversely, there are examples of cases in which the court appears not to have searched too diligently for consideration supporting a collateral promise (see, e.g., *De Lassalle* v *Guildford* [1901] 2 KB 215; *Dick Bentley Productions Ltd* v *Harold Smith Motors Ltd* [1965] 1 WLR 623).

In other parts of the common law world the position of the advertiser is much clearer. For example, in the USA, there is a general refusal to be bound by a strict application of the doctrine of privity of contract, thereby allowing the consumer to proceed directly against the producer of goods in the event of a misleading statement about his product. In *Randy Knitwear Inc.* v *American Cynamid Co.* (1962) 181 NE 2d 399, the New York Court of Appeals held that a producer of material used to manufacture children's clothing could be held liable for the loss suffered by the plaintiff when the manufacturer claimed that the material was waterproof. It was clear that there was no direct relationship of privity between the parties, but that was held not to matter since the warranty given by the manufacturer was one effected by means of mass advertising and was ultimately responsible for inducing consumer purchases (see also Australian Trade Practices Act 1974, s. 74G).

4.2.4.3 Promisee sues on behalf of the third party

The person to whom a promise has been made may be able to sue for damages for breach of that promise and recover on behalf of a third party for whose benefit the promise was made. However, an award of damages is intended, in theory, to compensate the person who brings the action. If the promise is intended to benefit a third party, the promisee is likely to have suffered no loss with the result that any award of damages will be nominal only. In some instances this problem may be circumvented by regarding the loss suffered by the third party as part of the loss suffered by the promisee. In *Jackson* v *Horizon Holidays Ltd* [1975] 1 WLR 1468, the plaintiff booked a package holiday in his own name, but the booking form also required him to state the names of the other members of his party. These included his wife and twin children. As a result of breaches of contract on the part of the tour operator, the holiday was a disaster and all members of the Jackson family suffered distress and disappointment. The question arose whether the plaintiff could recover damages in respect of the disappointment suffered by the rest of his family. The Court of Appeal was unanimous in allowing the plaintiff's action to succeed, although the reasoning employed by the members of the court differed. According to James LJ, the loss suffered by Mrs Jackson and the three-year-old twins could be regarded as loss suffered by Mr Jackson, with the result that there was an overall award of damages of £1,100. However, Lord Denning MR approached the case on a different level, displaying his well-known contempt for the doctrine of privity of contract. In his view, the guiding principle could be found in the judgment of Lush LJ in *Lloyd's* v *Harper* (1880) 16 ChD 290 at p. 321 that:

. . . where a contract is made with A for the benefit of B, A can sue on the contract for the benefit of B, and recover all that B could have recovered if the contract had been made with B himself.

The effect of applying this dictum was that it did not matter that Mrs Jackson and the twins were not parties to the contract. Mr Jackson could recover on their behalf since the contract was made for their benefit. To emphasise the import of his judgment, Lord Denning MR also observed that in his view £1,100 was an excessive sum to award Mr Jackson on his own in respect of his personal distress and disappointment, but that that amount adequately reflected the combined disappointment of all members of the family. If taken to its logical conclusion this judgment of Lord Denning would have gone some way to driving a coach and horses through the doctrine of privity of contract, since every time it appeared that one person had entered into a contract for the benefit of others, it would be possible for that person to sue for substantial damages on behalf of the person for whose benefit the contract was made. Lord Denning cited other examples which in his view would also fall within the principle in *Lloyd's* v *Harper*, such as the vicar who books a return coach trip for his church choir only to discover that the driver has left them stranded at their destination with the result that they must hire cars in order to return, or a party booking at a restaurant which is overbooked so that the dinner party are left hungry and angry at the letdown.

Lord Denning was of the opinion that the principle enunciated by Lush LJ in *Lloyd's* v *Harper* was a statement by a common lawyer, speaking of the common law. However, this view has been strongly criticised by the House of Lords in *Woodar Investment Development Ltd* v *Wimpey Construction UK Ltd* [1980] 1 WLR 277 on the ground that *Lloyd's* v *Harper* was concerned with a trustee or an agent (an insurance broker), who may sue on a contract made by him on behalf of a beneficiary or his principal (the insured) if the contract provides for such a right, thereby giving rise to a fiduciary relationship. The view of *Jackson* v *Horizon Holidays Ltd* preferred by the House of Lords in *Woodar* was that expressed by James LJ [1975] 1 WLR 1468 at p. 147 that this was a 'contract . . . made by Mr Jackson for a family holiday' and that 'he did not get a family holiday'.

In the light of the reasoning of the House of Lords in *Woodar* it must be asked if the damages awarded only covered Mr Jackson's distress or that of the whole family? If it was the latter, it might be asked whether the same reasoning be applied to all consumer purchases obviously intended to be consumed by the whole family?

4.3 EFFECT OF STATEMENTS MADE TO THE CONSUMER

When a consumer deals with others, a number of statements may be made to him. Some of these may be made to the consumer directly by a retail trader, whereas others may be directed towards consumers through the advertising media. The remedies available to a consumer will depend on the classification of such statements. Some of these statements may become terms of the contract, amounting to a guarantee that a certain result will obtain. However, others may amount to no more than a pre-contractual representation which will not give rise to remedies for breach of contract, but may allow for an action for damages for misrepresentation. Alternatively, the statement may be regarded as so devoid of content as to amount to no more than a commendatory puff, thereby giving rise to no liability at all.

4.3.1 Commendatory puffs
Generally, advertising puffery, amounting to no more than commendatory praise of a product put on the market by a manufacturer, is unobjectionable. Most people will not regard such statements as having any meaningful content on which it is reasonable to rely. Thus a claim to the efect that a certain beer refreshes the parts of the body not reached by rival brands is merely intended to amuse and in so doing bring to the attention of consumers a particular brand name. Accordingly, it has been held that to describe land as 'fertile and improvable' is no more than puffery giving rise to no liability (*Dimmock* v *Hallett* (1866) LR 2 Ch App 21; *Scott* v *Hansen* (1829) 1 Russ & M 128). However, the advertiser needs to be careful not to cross the line between puffery and misrepresentation. If an advertisement is more credible and contains statements which may be construed as being factual, liability for misrepresentation may be imposed. There appears to be a general reluctance to allow a commercial promoter to escape liability on the ground that his advertisements amount to nothing more than trade puffery. In such a case, the courts will try to discover an intention to create legal relations on the part of the advertiser (*Esso Petroleum Co. Ltd* v *Commissioners of Customs & Excise* [1976] 1 WLR 1, 6 per Lord Simon). Thus where there is a very precise claim, for example that a proprietary medicine can cure influenza, the statement is likely to be treated as a contractual term, thereby giving rise to a possible action for damages for breach of contract (*Carlill* v *Carbolic Smokeball Co. Ltd* [1893] 1 QB 256).

4.3.2 Distinction between contractual terms and mere representations
The classification of a particular statement as a term or a representation may affect the consumer's remedies against the person with whom he deals. If a term of the contract is broken, depending on the seriousness of the breach, the consumer will be able to terminate his own performance obligations or pursue an action for damages. In contrast, if the statement is classified as a misrepresentation, the standard remedy is that of rescission of the contract, but damages may also be awarded in the tort of deceit or under the Misrepresentation Act 1967, s. 2(1), where the misrepresentation is made negligently. In theory, at least, where damages are awarded, the measures payable will differ since the objective of an award of damages for breach of a contractual term should put the plaintiff into the position he would have been in had the promise been fulfilled, whereas an award of damages for misrepresentation is intended to return the plaintiff to the position he was in before the false statement was made to him. In practice, however, it is likely that there will be little difference between the two measures in most cases.

Whether or not a statement is a term of the contract or a representation is often difficult to ascertain. It has been argued that if the maker of the relevant statement is not at fault, the statement will be a representation rather than a term of the contract (*Dick Bentley Productions Ltd* v *Harold Smith Motors Ltd* [1965] 1 WLR 623). In this context, fault may be considered established if the maker of the statement ought to have known better, or is possessed of such skill in relation to the transaction entered into with the consumer that his utterances may be reasonably relied upon. Accordingly in *Dick Bentley Productions Ltd* v *Harold Smith Motors Ltd*, a car dealer wrongly asserted that a second-hand car had travelled only 20,000 miles when it had, in fact, been fitted with a replacement engine and gearbox and had travelled in the region of 100,000 miles. What was considered to be important was whether the dealer made the statement with a view to inducing the other party to enter into the contract and that the other party did act upon the statement. If this intention could be ascertained, it then fell upon the maker of the statement to show that the representation was made innocently, in which case it would be actionable only as a representation rather than as a contractual warranty (ibid. 627 per Lord Denning MR).

However, this is not a universally applicable test, since there are circumstances in which a statement may not have been intended to induce a person to enter into a contract but is treated by the court as a term of the contract. Where this has happened, policy considerations may have been relevant. For example, in *Beale* v *Taylor* [1967] 1 WLR 1193 a consumer bought from a private seller a second-hand car which was unroadworthy by virtue of the fact that it consisted of parts of two different cars welded together. Normally, an unsafe product of this kind would be dealt with under the provisions of the Sale of Goods Act 1979, s. 14(2), on the basis that the car was not of satisfactory quality. However, since s. 14(2) only applies where there has been a sale in the course of a business, that provision could have no application to a person who sold in a purely private capacity. Moreover, the timing of the events under consideration was such that the Misrepresentation Act 1967 had no application. In the event, it was held that a combination of an advertisement which described the car as a 1961 Herald Convertible taken in conjunction with a badge which referred to the car as a 'Herald' and a registration document which referred to the vehicle as a 1961 model were sufficient to identify the car as a 1961 Herald Convertible. Since this was only true of parts of the car, it was considered that there was a breach of the implied term in the Sale of Goods Act 1979, s. 13, that goods should correspond with their description. However, it is suggested that this decision intolerably stretches the distinction between terms and representations and that the statements about the car should have been regarded as no more than mere representations, especially since the seller was not responsible for what had been done to the car and probably had no idea that the car was not as described and could not, therefore, be said to have been at fault. What seems to have driven the decision was a desire to compensate the buyer in circumstances where no other avenue of redress would have been available. It is probably better to regard this decision as an aberration which is not in line with the more acceptable approach to s. 13 which requires a descriptive statement to identify the thing contracted for. In cases like *Beale* v *Taylor* it is better to regard the contract as one for the sale of the specific article seen and purchased by the buyer, to which s. 13 is inapplicable.

A further test applied by the courts in determining whether a particular statement is a term or a representation turns upon the expertise of the person making the statement. Generally, a tradesman dealing with a consumer will be treated as having the greater expertise. In such a case, it is more likely that a statement made by a trader to a consumer will be treated as a term of the contract than is the case if the statement is made by the consumer to the trader (see *Dick Bentley Productions Ltd* v *Harold Smith Motors Ltd* [1965] 1 WLR 623; cf. *Oscar Chess Ltd* v *Williams* [1957] 1 WLR 370). If this approach is correct, it makes it all the more difficult to accept as correct the decision in *Beale* v *Taylor* since both parties could be regarded as equally unskilled in relation to the roadworthiness of motor vehicles, so it would seem to be unfair to place the risk of loss on the private seller by regarding his statement as forming the basis of a term of the contract.

Other factors relevant in determining whether a particular statement is a term of the contract or merely a representation are whether the subject matter of the statement is patently a matter of crucial importance to the consumer, whether the statement was made at a crucial stage of negotiations between the parties and whether the consumer has been advised by the trader to verify the truth of the statement or otherwise obtain a second opinion. Accordingly, if the consumer makes it clear from the outset that he only wishes to purchase a product if it meets certain specific requirements, it would be reasonable to regard an assurance of compliance with those requirements as a term of the contract (see *Bannerman* v *White* (1861) 10 CB NS 844). Apart from anything else, failure to comply with express requirements set out by the consumer should also involve a breach of the implied term in the Sale of Goods Act 1979, s. 14(3) (see further chapter 6). In some instances, the timing of a particular statement may become relevant. This is particularly so where there has been a delay between making the statement and entering into the contract. Generally, the greater the time between the statement under consideration and the date on which the contract is made, the more likely it is that the statement will be regarded as a mere representation (see *Routledge* v *McKay* [1954] 1 WLR 615). This would appear to be explicable on the basis that the longer the time lapse the less likely it is that the statement will influence the decision to enter into the contract. Similarly, if the supplier of goods warns the consumer to test them or to obtain an expert opinion before making a purchase, it is unlikely that the supplier's statement will be regarded as a term of the contract. Thus in *Ecay* v *Godfrey* (1947) 80 Ll L Rep 286 the seller of a boat warranted it to be sound, but also warned that the buyer should have it checked out by a marine surveyor. In the circumstances the warranty of soundness was regarded as nothing more than a representation.

4.3.3 Representations as statements of fact
A representation is generally regarded as a statement of fact which induces a person to enter into a contract, but does not amount to a term of the contract.

It has been observed already that factual statements need to be distinguished from mere commendatory puffs, which generally do not give rise to any liability at all, though their use may be controlled by the British Codes of Advertising and Sales Promotion Practice, where appropriate (see further chapter 16).

Factual statements also have to be distinguised from statements of opinion and statements of intention. An opinion, if honestly expressed, does not give rise to liability, but this does not mean that a person can escape responsibility by prefacing every statement he makes with the words 'I think' or 'I believe'. For example, if it can be shown that the maker of the statement could not possibly have held the opinion he expressed because his state of factual knowledge at the time of making the statement was such that he must have been aware that what he said was untrue, there will be an actionable misrepresentation. Accordingly, it is a misrepresentation for the owner of land to describe a sitting tenant as 'desirable' when he has a poor rent payment record (see *Smith* v *Land & House Property Corporation* (1884) 28 ChD 7). Moreover, if the opinion is expressed by a person with a known skill relevant to the matter on which the opinion is expressed, the expression of opinion may give rise to liability if it is reasonable for the addressee to rely upon the statement which has been made to him. Accordingly in *Esso Petroleum Co. Ltd* v *Mardon* [1976] QB 801, it was reasonable for the tenant of a petrol filling station to rely upon an estimate of likely sales made by an expert employed by Esso. Although the estimate could be regarded as a variety of opinion, the skill of the expert was something on which reasonable reliance could be placed.

A representation should also be distinguished from a statement of intention. Generally, the position in English law is that a promissory statement is only enforceable if it is supported by consideration and is therefore a contractual promise. However, in some instances what appears to be a statement of intention may give rise to liability for misrepresentation, if it is clear from the outset that there are circumstances in which that intention cannot be carried out or where the evidence shows that the maker of the statement has no such intention (*Edgington* v *Fitzmaurice* (1885) 29 ChD 459). For example, if an airline confirms the availability of a seat on a specified scheduled flight, but due to a deliberate policy of overbooking flights, a passenger with a valid ticket is denied boarding access, it may be said that there is an actionable misrepresentation. This is so because, at the time of confirming the seat, the airline must know there may be circumstances in which a passenger will be denied access to a flight (see *British Airways Board* v *Taylor* [1976] 1 WLR 13, a case decided under the Trade Descriptions Act 1968, s. 14 , as to which see chapter 18).

4.3.4 Contractual terms
The terms of a contract may be express or implied. From a consumer perspective, the latter variety is probably of the greatest importance since a large percentage of consumer transactions will be entered into without any detailed specification of what should be supplied. To avoid the possibility of

a consumer being left without redress, the law implies a number of terms into consumer contracts. Many of these are dealt with in later parts of this book (see particularly chapters 6 and 8).

Whether the terms of the contract are express or implied, the classification of those terms is important since this classification impinges on the issue of consumer remedies considered below. Traditionally, English law distinguishes between a condition, the breach of which allows the consumer to terminate his primary contractual obligations, and a warranty, breach of which allows only an action for damages. In recent years, the courts have developed the notion of the innominate term whereby a term is classified by reference to the seriousness of the consequences of breach (see *Hong Kong Fir Shipping Co. Ltd* v *Kawasaki Kisen Kaisha Ltd* [1962] 2 QB 26). Under this doctrine, an express term may be a condition in name, but its breach may not give rise to sufficiently serious consequences to justify termination of contractual performance obligations, when viewed in the light of the events surrounding the breach.

It is clear that the innominate terms doctrine is not applicable in all circumstances, since it may be clear from the intentions of the parties that the breach of a particular term is to be regarded in all events as giving rise to a right on the part of the innocent party to treat his obligation to perform the contract as being at an end. In particular, there are certain terms in commercial contracts which, through past practice, have come to be regarded as conditions of the contract. The innominate terms doctrine is particularly destructive of the element of certainty which goes with strict classification of terms according to the traditional distinction between conditions and warranties. For this reason, the House of Lords has expressed some reservations over the use of the doctrine, especially in relation to terms of the contract which relate to the time of performance (see *Bunge Corporation New York* v *Tradax Export SA, Panama* [1981] 1 WLR 711), which are normally regarded as being of the essence of the contract except where they relate to the time of payment.

The innominate terms doctrine has no application to statutory implied terms which have been designated either conditions or warranties by Parliament. The new s. 15A of the Sale of Goods Act 1979 (which was inserted by the Sale and Supply of Goods Act 1994) allows the court to refuse to allow a non-consumer buyer to reject goods on the ground that there has been an 'insignificant' breach of any of the conditions implied by the Sale of Goods Act 1979, ss. 13 to 15, but this does not apply to consumer purchases.

The Supply of Goods (Implied Terms) Act 1973, which applies to hire purchase and credit sale ageements, and the Supply of Goods and Services Act 1982, which applies to contracts for the supply of goods which do not amount to sale of goods contracts, use the terminology of conditions and warranties, but fail to give any statutory definition of the words 'condition' and 'warranty' (contrast ss. 61(1) and 11(3) of the Sale of Goods Act 1979, which stipulate the effects of a breach of warranty and a breach of condition). Given this lack of definition, it is possible that a court might feel able to apply the innominate terms doctrine to these terms in other types of supply contract. In relation to contracts for the supply of services, Parliament has chosen to use the nondescript word 'term' to describe the implied obligations arising from ss. 13 to 15 of the Supply of Goods and Services Act 1982. In these circumstances, there should be little difficulty in applying the *Hong Kong Fir* test, should it be considered appropriate.

4.4 REMEDIES FOR BREACH OF CONTRACT

The consumer's principal remedies for a breach of contract are those of repudiation of the contract in the case of a breach of condition, with a right to claim damages in respect of any additional loss suffered as a result of the breach or an action for damages only in respect of a breach of warranty. In very rare circumstances, it may also be possible to obtain an order for specific performance of a contract, which requires the other party to the contract to perform his side of the contract.

In the case of a contract for the supply of goods, repudiation will involve rejection of the goods and recovery of the price paid, whereas in the case of a contract for the supply of services, repudiation will mean that the consumer does not have to pay for the service and the supplier will be expected to cease provision of the service.

4.4.1 Compulsory performance
In some instances, the consumer might wish to compel a supplier of goods or services to perform his contractual obligations, for example, where the supplier of goods has failed to deliver or where a double glazing contractor has failed to turn up to start the job contracted for. Apart from the legal difficulties associated with obtaining an order for specific performance, the cost of taking such proceedings may also be a dissuading factor so far as consumers are concerned. In most instances, the consumer is more likely to find someone else to do the work or supply a replacement article and, if necessary, sue the contractor in breach for damages, if loss can be established. It is clear from the provisions of the Sale of Goods Act 1979, s. 52, that an order for specific performance of a contract for the sale of specific or ascertained goods is a possibility. However, as a general rule, it is said that specific performance will only be granted as a remedy in circumstances in which an award of damages would be inadequate. Since the majority of consumer contracts are for the supply of goods or services, it will normally be possible to obtain a replacement product or service from another supplier, in which case an award of damages based on the difference between the original contract price and the replacement contract price will normally provide a satisfactory remedy. Likewise, specific performance of a contract to sell shares is unlikely to be awarded, since market substitutes will usually be available (see *Re Schwabacher* (1908) 98 LT 127). The most likely event in which an order for specific performance will be granted is where the goods contracted for have some unique quality which would be difficult to replace by purchasing on the market. For example, there have been cases in which a contract for the sale of antique furniture (*Phillips* v *Lamdin* [1949] 2 KB 33

— Adam-style door) or a particular painting by a specific artist (*Falcke* v *Gray* (1859) 4 Drew 651) have been specifically enforced, although apparently 'Hepplewhite chairs' were regarded as 'ordinary articles of commerce' in the early part of the twentieth century (see *Cohen* v *Roche* [1927] 1 KB 169). Specific peformance is regularly awarded in contracts to dispose of an interest in land on the basis that the subject matter of the contract has no substitute, no matter how ordinary the house might be.

Although the general rule is couched in terms of refusing to grant specific performance, in the case of a contract for the sale of goods which are not 'unique', it might be better to consider not so much whether an award of damages is an adequate remedy, but rather whether it would be fair to confine the buyer to his remedy in damages (see *Sky Petroleum Ltd* v *VIP Petroleum Ltd* [1974] 1 WLR 576). For example, it may be possible to obtain an order for specific performance of a contract for the sale of goods which in normal circumstances are readily available but, because of unusual market conditions are not readily available, for example, where there is a spiralling market price resulting from an excess of demand over supply. To refuse to grant specific performance in such a case might allow the seller to decline to fulfil a contract of sale in order to be able to sell to someone else at a higher market price.

A further important restriction on the availability of the remedy of specific performance in sale of goods contracts is that the Sale of Goods Act 1979, s. 52 only applies where the goods sold are 'specific' or 'ascertained'. This means that the goods must either have been identified at the time of contracting or have become identified before the date for performance of the contract. Accordingly, a contract for the sale of purely generic goods or those identifiable only by their description would appear not to fall within the scope of s. 52. Thus it would appear that a contract for the sale of a television selected from a catalogue description would not be capable of specific performance if it is left to the supplier to choose which television to deliver, since the television is sold solely by reference to its description. However, s. 52 does not state that only contracts for the sale of specific and ascertained goods are capable of specific enforcement. Accordingly, there may be circumstances apart from those covered by s. 52 in which the remedy is available in relation to a contract for the sale of unascertained goods. This may be the case where there is a contract for the sale of unascertained goods which cannot be readily acquired on the market (see *Sky Petroleum Ltd* v *VIP Petroleum Ltd* [1974] 1 WLR 576).

4.4.2 Repudiation
If the supplier of goods or services is in breach of a condition of the contract, the consumer may treat his own contractual performance obligations as being at an end, thereby allowing him to decline to pay or to recover the price and sue for damages in respect of any proved, foreseeable loss suffered by him as a result of the breach of contract. Equally, if the consumer is considered to be in breach of a condition of the contract, it may follow from this that the other party seeks to terminate his contractual obligations. This last event is particularly relevant in the context of long-term consumer contracts, such as

credit transactions, as opposed to the paradigm consumer contract which is a form of instantaneous transaction, completed on the spot.

4.4.2.1 Events permitting repudiation Repudiation will be allowed in one of two circumstances. Either there has been repudiatory conduct on the part of the other party to the contract, indicating the unwillingness of that other person to fulfil his contractual obligations or there has been a breach of a condition of the contract.

In determining whether a person may treat his contractual performance obligations as being at an end, whether by virtue of an indication of unwillingness to perform or by virtue of a breach of condition, it will be important to determine in what order the respective performance obligations of the parties should be performed. For example, some performance obligations are regarded as independent, in which case the failure by one party to perform a contractual obligation will not allow the other party to perform his side of the contract. A typical example of this type of obligation may be found in a tenancy agreement under which the duty of the tenant to pay rent is independent of the landlord's obligation to keep the rented property in a fit and habitable condition. Accordingly, it will not be open to a tenant to stage a rent strike, merely because the landlord has failed to keep the property in a reasonable state of repair.

Alternatively, there are simultaneous performance conditions. In these circumstances the duty of one party to perform does not become enforceable until the other party to the contract is ready to perform what is required of him. For the purposes of sale of goods contracts, it is provided that the duty of the buyer to pay for the goods purchased is dependent on the seller being able to deliver the goods contracted for (Sale of Goods Act 1979, s. 28). Accordingly, a consumer buyer cannot be expected to pay for goods unless the seller is also ready to make the goods available for delivery. Thirdly, there are dependent conditions. In such a case, one party is not required to perform his side of the contract until the other party has performed.

Where necessary the rules on the order of performance may be manipulated so as to achieve a common sense result or to protect a weaker party such as a consumer. For example, in *Bentworth Finance Ltd v Lubert* [1968] 1 QB 680, a consumer debtor was apparently in breach of contract when he failed to make payments as agreed under his agreement with the finance company. Ordinarily this would have allowed the creditor to terminate the contract. However, the contract also required the creditor to have delivered to the consumer documents which indicated that there had been a change of ownership in the goods subject to the agreement. These documents had not been served, and it was held that the debtor's duty to pay did not arise until the creditor had fulfilled his obligations under the agreement in relation to service of documents. It followed from this that the consumer had not committed a breach of contract which allowed the creditor to invoke his termination rights under the contract.

4.4.2.2 Loss of the right to repudiate Although the rules on repudiation may work against the consumer where he is in breach of his contract with a trader, perhaps the most troublesome area, from a consumer perspective, arises where goods prove to be defective some time after the date of purchase. Where goods are defective, the supplier may be in breach of one of the implied terms of the contract of sale relating to description, quality or fitness (see chapter 6). If the term broken is a condition, the consumer will have a right to reject the goods, unless it can be shown that he has accepted the goods, thereby affirming the contract and waiving the supplier's breach to the extent that the buyer is confined to an action for damages for breach of warranty only.

The principal reason for this state of affairs is that the Sale of Goods Act 1979, s. 11(4), provides that:

> Subject to section 35A below where a contract of sale is not severable and the buyer has accepted the goods or part of them, the breach of a condition to be fulfilled by the seller can only be treated as a breach of warranty, and not as a ground for rejecting the goods and treating the contract as repudiated, unless there is an express or implied term of the contract to that effect.

4.4.2.2.1 *Entire and severable obligations*   Due to the wording of s. 11(4) it is necessary to consider what is meant by a non-severable contract, since severable contracts do not fall within the rule. The simple answer is that it is a contract which is not severable or, more specifically, a contract in which the parties' performance obligations cannot be subdivided into constituent elements.

Instances in which a contract may be considered to be severable will most frequently involve commercial transactions. For example, where an instalment contract requires each delivery to be separately paid for or where the contract provides for deliveries 'as required' it may be regarded as severable (see *Jackson* v *Rotax Motors Ltd* [1910] 2 KB 937). However, some consumer contracts may be regarded as severable, such as a contract to purchase a series of gold ornaments, to be delivered over a period of time, each to be paid for on delivery. In these circumstances, s. 11(4) has no application and it becomes necessary to ask what test is to be applied in order to determine whether the consumer may reject all future instalments. For these purposes, the Sale of Goods Act 1979, s. 31(2), provides that it is a question of fact, in each case, which depends upon the terms of the contract and the circumstances of the case. The test applied in commercial contracts is similar to the innominate terms approach to the question of termination of contractual performance obligations (considered above). For these purposes, it is necessary to consider the 'ratio quantitatively which the breach bears to the contract as a whole' and whether there is a substantial likelihood that the breach will be repeated (*Maple Flock Co. Ltd* v *Universal Furniture Products (Wembley) Ltd* [1934] 1 KB 148). Suppose a consumer contracts to purchase a 'collector's set' of 25 gold trinkets, to be delivered at the rate of one per month and the first 23 are delivered in perfect condition. If the seller then delivers one defective item, it seems unlikely that the consumer would be able to reject due to the insignificance of the single breach in relation to the whole contract. Moreover, if the last trinket is delivered in perfect condition, there is also no likelihood of a repeat breach, in which case the consumer will be confined to an action for damages.

However, the majority of consumer contracts will consist of entire obligations, to which s. 11(4) will apply, with the result that it becomes necessary to consider what is meant by 'acceptance'.

4.4.2.2.2 Inspection and acceptance   Prior to changes to the Sale of Goods Act 1979 which were introduced by the Sale and Supply of Goods Act 1994, the law was somewhat confused due to the fact that ss. 34 and 35 of the 1979 Act mixed the concepts of 'the right to inspect' and the notion of 'acceptance'. After the 1994 changes, the buyer's right of inspection is identified in s. 34, which now provides simply that, in the absence of an agreement to the contrary, where the seller tenders delivery of the goods and the buyer asks for a reasonable opportunity to examine the goods, the seller must give the buyer that opportunity. All references to the effect of acceptance are now contained in a substantially lengthened s. 35. The provisions of s. 35 have been considerably extended in order to spell out the circumstances in which a buyer is taken to have accepted goods supplied to him under a contract of sale. The principal reason for these amendments was to counteract the confusion created by the combined effect of the previous provisions of ss. 34 and 35. Between them it was possible for a consumer buyer to be deemed to have accepted goods despite the fact that he had not adequately inspected the goods delivered for the purposes of ascertaining whether they were in conformity with the express and implied terms of the contract. This possibility was graphically illustrated in *Bernstein* v *Pamson Motors (Golders Green) Ltd* [1987] 2 All ER 220, in which a consumer purchased a new motor vehicle which he was unable to use immediately because of illness. When the car had travelled only 140 miles, it came to a grinding halt because a piece of sealant had entered the lubrication system and had cut off the supply of oil to the camshaft. Despite the fact that the vehicle had been repaired under a manufacturers' warranty at no cost to the plaintiff, he had lost faith in the type of car he had purchased and wished to reject it on the ground that it was not of merchantable quality. Unfortunately for the plaintiff, a period of just short of a month had passed from the date on which the car had been delivered. In the circumstances Rougier J held that the buyer had had a reasonable time in which to inspect the car and had accordingly lost his right to reject. In determining whether a reasonable time had elapsed from the date of delivery, it was held not to be relevant to consider the nature of the defect in the goods or the speed with which the defect might have been discovered. All that had to be considered was what was a reasonably practical interval between delivery and his ability to return the goods to the seller. It followed from this that the plaintiff was entitled to damages only, which, in the event, proved to be minimal. For reasons considered below, facts similar to this might now give rise to a different result since the amended law allows consideration of relevant background circumstances which might include the fact of Mr Bernstein's illness.

4.4.2.2.3 Acceptance, waiver and estoppel   Where the acceptance rule operates, it serves to prevent the buyer from rejecting the goods he has purchased, but unlike in some other legal systems, it does not deny the buyer a remedy altogether, since he will still be able to claim damages where he can prove that he has suffered a quantifiable loss. What appears to be the rationale behind the denial of the remedy of repudiation is that, in line with common law rules on affirmation of voidable contracts, waiver and estoppel, the buyer has led the seller to believe that he intends to continue with the contract in the light of actual or presumed knowledge of the defect or vitiating factor. However, there are differences in the way in which rules on acceptance, affirmation, waiver and estoppel operate. For example, generally, a person will not be taken to have affirmed a contract induced by a misrepresentation unless he is aware of the conduct of the other party which permits rescission of the contract and is aware of his right to terminate the contract (see *Peyman* v *Lanjani* [1985] Ch 457). However, a buyer may be deemed to have accepted goods under s. 35 without the same state of knowledge. Where rules on waiver operate, the buyer will usually have made clear representations to the effect that he will not reject goods or services on the grounds of late performance, whereas it is clear that for the purposes of rules on acceptance, a clear representation is not always necessary. Likewise for the purposes of rules on estoppel, it appears that there must be a clear representation that contractual rights will not be insisted upon and reliance by the other party on that representation by altering his position.

For the purposes of consumer contracts, it is necessary to consider when a buyer will be deemed to have accepted goods which have been delivered to him. The general rule in s. 35(1) is that a buyer is to be deemed to have accepted the goods if:

(a)   he intimates to the seller that he has accepted them; or

(b)   he does some act inconsistent with the ownership of the seller after the goods have been delivered to him.

4.4.2.2.4 Express intimation of acceptance   So far as express intimation under s. 35(1)(a) is concerned, if a buyer signs a delivery note, this may be taken as an indication of acceptance. However, in consumer transactions, signing such a document often occurs without the content of the document being read. In order to meet this problem, s. 35(2) provides that if the buyer has not previously examined the goods, he is not to be deemed to have accepted them under s. 35(1)(a) until he has been given a reasonable opportunity to examine the goods. Accordingly, where a delivery note is signed by another member of the family or where the purchaser signs such a note but time is required in order to discover whether the goods are in conformity with the contract, there will be no acceptance until a reasonable time has elapsed from the date of delivery.

Although the problem of not reading contractual documents is more likely to apply to consumer transactions, s. 35(2) applies to all contracts for the sale of goods. However, there is a difference in the approach to consumer and non-consumer transactions in that s. 35(3) provides that a consumer buyer cannot lose *any* of his rights under s. 35(2) by agreement, waiver or otherwise. Accordingly, the common law rules on waiver and estoppel adverted to above cannot be invoked by the seller to deny the consumer buyer his right of rejection. However, by implication, a non-consumer buyer can lose the right of rejection, for example, by virtue of an exemption clause in the contract with the seller (subject to the requirement of reasonableness set out in the Unfair Contract Terms Act 1977, if it applies).

4.4.2.2.5 Act inconsistent with the ownership of the seller The second form of deemed acceptance identified in s. 35(1)(b) consists of the buyer doing some act inconsistent with the seller's ownership, after the goods have been delivered to him. In the old case law on commercial sales there are examples such as altering the goods, pledging them to another or selling them on to someone else (see *Hardy* v *Hillerns & Fowler* [1923] 2 KB 490; *Ruben* v *Faire Bros & Co. Ltd* [1949] 1 KB 254). A consumer buyer who takes delivery of a car and subsequently places an advertisement in the local press indicating that the car is for sale might be regarded as having accepted the goods through doing an act inconsistent with the ownership of the seller.

What seems to underlie the rule is that once the buyer has done something to the goods which prevents precise restitution of the goods to the seller, he must be considered to have accepted them. Accordingly, if food is delivered to the consumer, which is subsequently partially eaten or if a piece of glass is delivered for fitment in a window frame and the consumer cuts it to size, it may be said that something has been done which is inconsistent with the ownership of the seller.

The same may also be said of disposing of the goods to another person. Thus if flowers are purchased with a direction that they should be delivered to a third party, prima facie this is an act inconsistent with the ownership of the florist, but for reasons considered below, this will not automatically deny the buyer the opportunity to reject the flowers if they are subsequently discovered to be defective.

One matter which is not clear, even from the revised wording of s. 35 is whether negligent damage caused by the consumer is capable of amounting to acceptance under s. 35(1)(b). Arguably, it might be said that if the consumer buys a silk blouse, wears it immediately and stains the garment by spilling beetroot juice on it, an act has been done which is inconsistent with the ownership of the seller, since the garment cannot be returned to the seller in its original form. Moreover, it might be asked whether simply removing a garment from its wrapping has the same effect? The answer to this last point is to be found in s. 35(2) which makes it clear that this form of deemed acceptance is subject to the buyer's reasonable opportunity to inspect the goods. A buyer who has merely removed clothing from its protective wrapping cannot be said to have had any sort of opportunity to examine. However, the same cannot be said of the stained garment, if the irreparable damage is done on the third occasion it is worn.

While a direction to the seller that goods should be sent to someone else is capable of amounting to an act inconsistent with the seller's ownership, it is now clear that such action does not, by itself, constitute acceptance. Under s. 35(6)(b), it is now provided that the buyer is not deemed to accept goods merely because the goods are delivered to another person. In these circumstances, the proper place of inspection will be deemed to be the place where the goods are delivered. This provision means that the old decision in *Molling v Dean* (1901) 18 TLR 217 is now to be regarded as representative of the law. In this case, a consignment of books was delivered to an American sub-buyer, who rejected them on the ground that they were not fit for their intended use. The sub-buyer's rejection was regarded as rejection on behalf of the first buyer, so that repudiation was still possible.

A difficulty created by s. 35(6)(b) is that it does not say what happens if the person to whom the goods are delivered decides to reject. Since there is nothing in s. 35(6) which requires the first buyer to arrange for the return of the goods to the seller, this leaves a number of unanswered questions. For example, suppose the consumer buyer arranges for an expensive oil painting to be shipped to a relative in Australia under temperature-controlled conditions, and on arrival it is discovered to be damaged, with the result that the consumer wishes to reject the painting. While it would be undesirable for the law to require the consumer buyer to arrange for return of the painting, it might also cause difficulties for a small-scale supplier of the painting to bear the cost of returning the painting, and, given his distance from Australia, he might encounter some difficulties in disposing of the article *in situ*. Alternatively, suppose the consumer buyer does arrange for re-delivery to the seller, s. 35 does not say whether he can charge the re-delivery costs to the seller.

4.4.2.2.6   Retention for more than a reasonable time   Under s. 35(4), a further means by which a buyer may be taken to have accepted the goods is if he retains them for longer than a reasonable time after delivery without intimating to the seller that he has rejected the goods. Before the 1994 changes to s. 35 this issue merged with that of an 'act inconsistent with the ownership of the seller' in consumer transactions. Thus if a consumer spent time trying to arrange for minor defects to be attended to, there was the possibility that he might be seen to have accepted the goods through continued use. However, even before the 1994 changes, if the consumer made persistent complaints to the seller and demonstrated his lack of satisfaction with his purchase, even continued use did not always deny the right to reject, since the persistent complaints might be regarded as evidence that the goods had not been accepted (see *Rogers* v *Parish (Scarborough) Ltd* [1987] QB 933).

This particular form of acceptance is perhaps the most controversial from the position of a consumer. For example, the pages of *Which?* magazine, the Consumers' Association publication, are littered with examples of washing machines which break down after six months' use, diesel-engined cars which are bought for high-mileage purposes but require a replacement engine after only 80,000 miles and beds which collapse after only a few months' use. Although many of these examples may now be caught by the express inclusion of durability as an aspect of the condition of satisfactory quality in the Sale of Goods Act 1979, s. 14(2) (see chapter 6), it seems unlikely that the normal consequences of a breach of condition will apply due to s. 35(4). As was observed by Rougier J in *Bernstein* v *Pamson Motors (Golders Green) Ltd* [1987] 2 All ER 220, 230, the seller must be able to close his ledger on a transaction as soon as is reasonably possible after it is complete.

Consumer groups lobbied for a change in the law so as to allow consumer buyers a continuing right of rejection. However, the difficulty with such a right is that it allows the buyer to make full use of the goods he has purchased up to the time he chooses to reject but still be able recover in full the price he has paid.

Following the 1994 amendments to the Sale of Goods Act 1979, s. 35(5) now provides that in determining whether, for the purposes of s. 35(4), a reasonable time has elapsed, it is necessary to consider whether the buyer has had a reasonable opportunity to examine the goods within the meaning of s. 35(2).

Taken at face value this may suggest that the law has not changed, a view which is supported by the Law Commission (Law Com. No. 160 (1987), *Sale and Supply of Goods*, paras 5.14–5.19). However, it is arguable that the language of the new provisions differs from that of the old s. 35. As interpreted in *Bernstein* v *Pamson Motors (Golders Green) Ltd*, the old s. 35 merely required a consideration of the time between the date of delivery and the date of purported rejection. Accordingly, Rougier J considered that 'reasonable time means reasonable time to examine and try out the goods in general terms' (at p. 230). However, the new provisions of ss. 35(5) and (2) require the court to consider whether the buyer has had a reasonable opportunity to examine. It is suggested that there is room in this more subjective test for the court to take into account whether, in the particular circumstances of the case, the buyer has had a reasonable opportunity to examine the goods for the purposes of ascertaining whether they are in conformity with the contract. On this view, matters such as the illness of the buyer and whether the goods are subject to a latent defect which may take time to discover or manifest itself ought to be regarded as relevant considerations. The courts should not simply measure the time between delivery and purported rejection and ask whether a reasonable buyer would have been able to inspect in that period. Perhaps what should have been done was to distinguish between patent and latent defects. Clearly, in the case of an obvious defect, the buyer can be expected to complain relatively quickly. But more time may be required in order to identify a latent defect and take the appropriate action, in which case it might make sense, in consumer transactions, to allow time to run from the date on which the consumer could reasonably have been aware that there was a significant defect in the goods he has purchased which would allow him to reject (see Brown, [1988] JBL 56, 63). This particular view appears to have been adopted by the Court of Session in Scotland, which held in *Charles Henshaw & Sons Ltd* v *Antlerport Ltd* [1995] CLC 1312 that a relevant consideration in determining whether goods have been accepted (for the purposes of the old s. 35) is the complexity of the goods, since the more complex the product, the more likely it is that a longer period of time will be required in order to determine whether they conform with the contract. In contrast, relatively simple products which may be inspected visually may be deemed to have been accepted fairly soon after delivery. However, even complex products may be considered to have been accepted once they become incorporated in a larger structure. Thus in *Charles Henshaw & Sons Ltd* v *Antlerport Ltd*, building panels which were used by the builder in the construction of a building were considered to have been accepted under s. 35.

A further common consumer problem is that the goods purchased may suffer from a number of minor defects which he asks the seller to repair. On a literal interpretation of the *Bernstein* v *Pamson Motors (Golders Green) Ltd* interpretation of s. 35, it might be possible to conclude that waiting for defects to be repaired may cause the clock to start ticking, so that the buyer is deemed to have accepted the goods through the passage of a reasonable period of time from the date of delivery. However, it is clear from the new s. 35(6) that, by asking for repair, the buyer is not deemed to have accepted the goods. However, it does not follow from this that just because the consumer asks the seller (or the manufacturer) to repair a defective product, he will always have the right to reject. In *Rogers* v *Parish (Scarborough) Ltd* [1987] QB 933 the buyer was able to reject a new Range Rover car some months after the date of purchase, but the facts of the case reveal that the buyer had expressed his dissatisfaction with the vehicle on a regular basis and had constantly pestered the supplier to ensure that defects were put right. Only when it became apparent that the defects would not be remedied did the buyer successfully seek to reject.

One wholly unacceptable solution might be for the consumer to refrain from using the goods he has purchased pending the outcome of future litigation, but this would be impossible in most cases where the thing purchased is particularly expensive, such as a car, since few consumers would have the resources to purchase or hire an alternative vehicle, so as to be able to show that they have no intention of accepting the goods in question.

To be absolutely sure of preserving the right of rejection, it would be sensible for the buyer to make it clear from the start that unless the defects are successfully remedied, he will reserve the right to reject the defective article (see *Farnworth Finance Facilities Ltd* v *Attryde* [1970] 1 WLR 1053). Certainly if the buyer delays excessively from the last date on which repairs were effected, this would seem to point to implied acceptance of the goods. Accordingly, a delay of six months after the last date on which repairs were carried out has been held sufficient to destroy the right of rejection (see *Lee* v *York Coach & Marine Ltd* [1977] RTR 35).

4.4.2.2.7 Contracts of sale and other types of supply contract contrasted   In contracts for the supply of goods to which the Sale of Goods Act 1979 does not apply, such as those which are covered by the Supply of Goods and Services Act 1982 and the Supply of Goods (Implied Terms) Act 1973, the amendments to s. 35 of the 1979 Act have no application. Accordingly, the position is governed by the common law rules on affirmation of the contract, which appear to operate in a more favourable manner so far as consumers are concerned, although this may be a reflection of the different types of transaction concerned.

In hire purchase transactions, it is possible for the periodic payments due under the contract to be taken into account in order to recognise the fact that the consumer has had use of the goods during the period of hire. In these circumstances, the right to reject appears to last for some weeks or even months after the contract was first entered into and delivery is taken by the consumer. Since the contract is one of bailment, the supplier (finance company) will continue to have a proprietary interest in the goods up to the time when the consumer elects to exercise his option to purchase by paying the final instalment. Because of this, it can be said that the supplier does not have the same interest as the seller of goods in 'closing his ledger on the transaction'. Furthermore, since the relationship between creditor and debtor is continuing in nature, the courts appear to have concluded that the goods supplied should be of satisfactory quality during the continuance of the agreement.

In the light of the foregoing, the courts have been prepared to adopt a more flexible approach in determining whether the debtor can reject the goods. In particular, factors such as the conduct of the parties, attempts to repair, negotiations for a settlement, depreciation in value between the date of agreement and the date of purported rejection and the discovery of hidden defects have been taken into account. Thus in *Yeoman Credit Ltd* v *Apps* [1962] 2 QB 508 some five months after a second-hand Ford car was delivered to the defendant and after four instalments had been paid while the defendant was waiting for the car to be repaired, the defendant stopped paying the instalments as they became due. In deciding whether the defendant was entitled to reject the car, Holroyd Pearce LJ observed that had the transaction been one for the sale of goods, rejection would not have been permitted, but since the contract was akin to one of simple hire, in which there was a continuing breach by the hirer, rejection was allowed. However, in order to reflect the defendant's use of the car while the contract was in force, the defendant was unable to recover any of the instalments already paid, since there had been no total failure of consideration.

Where there have been attempts at repair by the supplier, these too may be taken into account when considering the debtor's rejection and claim to be entitled to recover instalments he has paid. For example in *Farnworth Finance Facilities Ltd* v *Attryde* [1970] 1 WLR 1053, the debtor was held to be entitled to reject a motorcycle which proved to be faulty right from the start. The debtor pressed for repairs to be effected, but these repairs made no difference. Eventually after four months' use and 4,000 miles of driving, the debtor realised that the motorcycle could not be relied upon and sought to reject. It was considered that he had not elected to go on with the contract merely by using the motorcycle, since in order to make an election, a person must be aware of all material facts. The debtor could not be said to be so aware until he realised the motor cycle could not be relied upon, with the result that he could not be said to have affirmed the contract (ibid., 1059 per Lord Denning MR). So far as the debtor's use of the vehicle was concerned, it was considered that the value of such use had to be offset against the inconvenience and trouble caused to the debtor in seeking to have the defects rectified (ibid., 1060 per Lord Denning MR). Further considerations are the nature of the negotiations which have taken place and that the longer the continuing relationship lasts, the greater will be the degree of depreciation in the value of the goods which are the subject matter of the contract. In *Porter* v *General Guarantee Corporation Ltd* [1982] RTR 384, it was considered relevant to use the requirement of the contract to pay monthly instalments to achieve a fair result. Thus although the car which was the subject matter of the contract was found to be defective on delivery, repairs, negotiations and inspections continued over a period of two months, during which time the debtor was aware of the defectiveness of the vehicle. It was held that the debtor could still reject the vehicle since it was in his interest to continue negotiations to see if the other party would pay for the necessary repairs, but it was also relevant to take account of the debtor's use of the vehicle in the interim period. In the event, it was thought possible to ask the debtor to pay instalments up to the value of the benefit he had derived from the use of the car. Accordingly, the debtor was required to pay an outstanding instalment due under the agreement at a time when the debtor was aware that he was in a position to repudiate the contract.

The nature of the defects in the goods may also have an impact on the remedy allowed. Where the defects are hidden, it is clear that the debtor will not be immediately aware of them and they may reveal themselves over a period of time. For these purposes, it was held in *Laurelgates Ltd* v *Lombard North Central Ltd* (1983) 133 NLJ 720 that in hire purchase contracts, the relevant time for the purposes of the right of rejection is the time when it becomes apparent that the goods are of unsatisfactory quality, rather than the date of delivery which applies to contracts of sale.

4.4.3 Damages

It has been seen above that in certain circumstances, a consumer will be compelled to treat a breach of condition as giving rise to an action for damages only. Moreover, there may also be circumstances in which it is not of any interest to the consumer to seek to terminate his contractual performance obligations. For example, this may be the case where specific expenditure has been incurred and the only interest of the consumer is to recover damages in respect of that identified loss where there has been a breach of contract by the other party. Typical examples arise where a consumer's annual holiday has been ruined by virtue of the fact that it has not lived up to the expectations engendered by statements made in the tour operator's brochure or where a consumer has purchased a house on the recommendation of a surveyor, only to discover that remedial work costing several thousands of pounds must be arranged in order to make the property habitable. Even where there has been a breach of condition, there is no obligation on the part of the consumer to treat this as a ground for termination, since he has a right of election. A serious breach may be waived, but the consumer still has the right to claim damages in respect of any provable, proximate loss resulting from the breach of the other party (see Sale of Goods Act 1979, s. 11(2)).

Where the consumer sues for damages, the purpose of an award should be to put him in the position he would have been in had the contract been performed (*Robinson* v *Harman* (1848) 1 Ex 850) although, for reasons of policy, not every expectation loss will be recoverable due to the operation of rules on factual causation, remoteness of damage and mitigation of loss.

4.4.3.1 Factual causation and contributory negligence Although normally factual causation issues tend to arise more frequently in tortious actions where it is necessary to determine whether the loss suffered by the plaintiff would have occurred but for the defendant's breach, there are occasions on which rules on factual causation may prevent a consumer from recovering damages in respect of that part of his loss which was caused by his own actions. In certain respects the rules on factual causation operate in a manner similar to the defence of contributory negligence, commonly pleaded in negligence actions. However, there are differences between the two. In particular, where the defence of contributory negligence applies, the court must apportion damages in accordance with the degree of fault attributable to the plaintiff and the defendant, whereas rules on factual causation tend to produce an all-or-nothing result — either the plaintiff recovers in full because his actions are not regarded as a factual cause of the loss suffered or he recovers nothing because his actions are regarded as the dominant cause of the loss in respect of which damages are claimed.

Generally, the defence of contributory negligence will not be available in a consumer contract, for the reason that in order for the defence to be available, there must be fault on both the part of the trader and the consumer (Law Reform (Contributory Negligence) Act 1945, s. 1(1) and s. 4). Accordingly, in consumer contracts for the supply of goods, where the supplier's obligations under the implied terms about description, quality and fitness are strict, there can be no fault on the part of the supplier (*Barclays Bank plc* v *Fairclough Building Ltd* [1995] QB 214). In contrast, there are some instances in which a defendant may be in breach of a contractual obligation which involves fault on his part. Most typically, this will arise where there is a contract for the supply of a service under which the service supplier will only be liable for a breach of contract if it can be shown that he has failed to take reasonable care in the provision of the service contracted for (see further chapter 8 and Supply of Goods and Services Act 1982, s. 13). For these purposes, if the contractual duty of care owed by the supplier is co-extensive with his common law, tortious duty to take reasonable care, it can be said that there is fault on the part of the defendant, with the result that if the plaintiff is partly to blame for the harm suffered, damages may be reduced accordingly. In *Sayers* v *Harlow Urban District Council* [1958] 1 WLR 623 the plaintiff entered a public toilet, having inserted a coin in the lock in order to gain entry. As such she was a contractual visitor to the premises and was owed a duty of care under what is now the Occupiers' Liability Act 1957, s. 2(1). The plaintiff subsequently discovered that the lock was jammed and that she was unable to leave the premises. Having discovered that her cries for help had not been heard, she decided to scale the wall of the cubicle, using the toilet-roll holder as a platform for climbing out. Unfortunately, the toilet roll, which had not been removed by the plaintiff, rotated with the result that she suffered injury in a fall to the ground. The Court of Appeal took the view that it made no difference whether the plaintiff's claim for damages was framed in contract or in tort and reduced her damages. To reach any other decision would be perverse in the sense that in cases of concurrent contractual and tortious liability a plaintiff could avoid having damages reduced by pleading the action as one for breach of contract unless the court was of the opinion that the plaintiff's fault was the sole cause of the harm suffered, in which case, the claim for damages would be wiped out altogether. This last approach appears to be the only option where a consumer enters into a contract under which the obligations of the trader are not fault based. Thus if in a contract for the sale of goods the buyer fails to follow comprehensible instructions on how to use a product he has purchased or fails to cook food in a manner which has come to be expected of members of the public, any illness subsequently suffered may not be actionable on the basis that the consumer's fault is the dominant cause of the loss suffered. Thus in *Heil* v *Hedges* [1951] 1 TLR 512 the plaintiff was unable to recover damages in respect of food poisoning suffered as a result of not having cooked pork sufficiently to kill off *Trichinella* infection. A similar result may also obtain where a consumer becomes aware of a defect in goods he has purchased, but continues to use the goods, having taken no steps to have the defect repaired. Thus in *Lambert* v *Lewis* [1982] AC 225 a retailer sold a defective towing hitch for use on a farmer's vehicle. After becoming aware of a defect in the hitch, the farmer continued to use it and was subsequently involved in a traffic accident in which the plaintiff was injured. It was considered by the House of Lords that the farmer's continued use of the defective hitch was a *novus actus interveniens* which severed the chain of causation between the retailer's breach of contract in supplying goods which were not fit for their intended use and the injury suffered. Accordingly, the retailer's breach was not the dominant cause of the harm suffered and so the farmer's action for an indemnity failed.

4.4.3.2 Remoteness of damage Where the consumer sues for damages, the loss he suffers as a result of the breach of contract must not be too remote. For these purposes, the general rules are those set out in *Hadley* v *Baxendale* (1854) 9 Ex 341 where a distinction was drawn between normal and abnormal losses. For the purposes of the former, any loss which arises naturally in the usual course of events from the defendant's breach of contract will be recoverable. In the case of abnormal losses, the law requires the parties to take advantage of the fact that they have the opportunity to negotiate with each other and to make known to the other party that there is a probability that a loss of the kind suffered might result from the defendant's breach.

The first rule in *Hadley* v *Baxendale* can also be found in statutory form in sale of goods contracts by virtue of the Sale of Goods Act 1979, s. 53(2) (see also the Sale of Goods Act 1979, s. 51(2), regarding damages for non-delivery), which provides that:

> The measure of damages for breach of warranty is the estimated loss directly and naturally resulting, in the ordinary course of events, from the breach of warranty.

It follows from this that in the case of normal or natural losses, there is no need for the consumer to communicate to the trader the possibility that such loss may ensue from the trader's breach, since such losses are considered to be within the contemplation of both parties at the time the contract was entered into. Accordingly, it has been held that in an action against a retailer for damages for defective products, consequential losses such as personal injury or property damage are regarded as natural losses. Thus it is readily foreseeable that if a smokeless fuel supplied for consumer use is mixed with a detonator it may cause damage to the buyer's house (*Wilson* v *Rickett Cockrell & Co. Ltd* [1954] 1 QB 598) or that if a hot-water bottle bursts, it may cause burns to the person who is using it (*Preist* v *Last* [1903] 2 KB 148). Similarly, the physical inconvenience and distress resulting from the purchase of a car which breaks down shortly after purchase and the cost of hiring a replacement while the car is being repaired may all be regarded as losses which arise naturally from the retailer's breach of the implied condition of satisfactory quality (see *Bernstein* v *Pamson Motors (Golders Green) Ltd* [1987] 2 All ER 220). Similarly, in holiday contracts, it is reasonably foreseeable that if the holiday is ruined by virtue of a breach of contract on the part of the tour operator, damages may be recovered in respect of the distress, disappointment and inconvenience suffered by the holidaymakers. Thus in *Jarvis* v *Swan's Tours Ltd* [1973] 1 QB 233 the plaintiff booked a 15-day 'house-party' holiday in Switzerland during the skiing season. Numerous claims had been made in the tour operator's brochure, which described the welcome the plaintiff might expect and set out the terms on which skiing equipment could be hired. The holiday proved to be a disaster for a number of reasons, not the least of which was that he was left to 'party' alone for the second week of his holiday and that the skiing equipment available was very limited, being confined to 'mini-skis'.

Although the value of the holiday, in market terms, was £63.45, and it was considered that the plaintiff had had half a holiday, the award of damages of £125 took on board the disappointment suffered by the plaintiff at having his annual holiday ruined. In particular, it was observed that it would be natural to expect a person to look forward to the enjoyment provided by a holiday when it has been booked far ahead. Although an award of damages for breach of contract is intended to protect a person against expectation loss, this expectation is normally confined to market losses, which in *Jarvis* v *Swans Tours Ltd* would amount to half the cost of the holiday. However, it should be appreciated that in holiday cases, the expectation which has been damaged is an expectation of enjoyment which can be regarded as a value placed upon a particular commodity which exceeds its market value, otherwise known as the 'consumer surplus value' (see Harris, Ogus and Phillips, 'Contract remedies and the consumer surplus' (1979) 95 LQR 581 and see also chapter 9).

Where the loss resulting from the breach of contract is regarded as unusual, the second rule in *Hadley* v *Baxendale* requires communication on the part of the consumer. It is not sufficient for the consumer to rely upon the expertise of the trader and hope that he can foresee unusual losses. The rationale underlying the second rule in *Hadley* v *Baxendale* may be said to be based on the dual grounds of fairness and efficiency (Posner, *Economic Analysis of Law*, 2nd ed. ((1977) pp. 94–5). On the one hand, the rule is said to be fair because it prevents the party in breach of contract (and his insurers) from being liable for unexpected amounts. Moreover, it is efficient since it facilitates negotiation between the parties who are known to each other and allows a contracting party to raise his price to take account of a known or foreseeable risk or to maintain his normal price and attempt to limit his liability through the use of an exemption clause. Furthermore, it would be economically inefficient to hold a contracting party responsible for unlikely losses unless the party likely to suffer such losses has disclosed relevant information. This reasoning may well be appropriate in relation to commercial dealings between business people, but it is somewhat less attractive when applied to consumer transactions, especially since consumers are not generally used to negotiating in business transactions. Moreover, it may be the case that a consumer does not immediately realise the importance of making known to the other party all of his hopes and fears in relation to the proposed transaction. For example, in *Kemp* v *Intasun Holidays Ltd* (1988) 7 TrLR 161 a holiday was booked by the plaintiff's wife on behalf of herself and the plaintiff, who suffered from asthma. In the course of making the booking, the plaintiff's wife made a passing remark about the plaintiff's condition, but it was considered not sufficiently forceful to bring it home to the travel agent that special facilities were required in order to make the plaintiff comfortable while on holiday. In an action for damages for general distress and inconvenience and for exacerbation of the plaintiff's condition, it was held that the defendants could not reasonably have contemplated the special circumstances relating to the plaintiff merely because of the casual remark.

What *Kemp* v *Intasun Holidays Ltd* illustrates is that there is a substantial threshold to be overcome before special losses can be said to be reasonably foreseeable. This follows from the interpretation of the second limb of *Hadley* v *Baxendale* in *Koufos* v *C. Czarnikow Ltd* [1969] 1 AC 350, where it was considered that the degree of foresight of harm in an action for damages for breach of contract is considerably higher than the requirement of reasonable foresight of harm which applies in a negligence action following the opinion of the Privy Council in *Overseas Tankship (UK) Ltd* v *Morts Dock and Engineering Co. Ltd* [1961] AC 388. The latter test, which applies predominantly to actions for damages for negligently caused physical harm to the person or to property can be satisfied by showing that the plaintiff has suffered damage of the kind which might reasonably be foreseen as a result of the defendant's breach of duty. Accordingly, it will not matter for these purposes that the extent of harm suffered by the plaintiff is greater than could have been foreseen so long as the kind of damage suffered is foreseeable. It was observed by Lord Reid in *Koufos* v *C. Czarnikow Ltd* (at pp. 385–6) that:

> The modern rule of tort is quite different and it imposes a much wider liability. The defendant will be liable for any type of damage which is reasonably foreseeable as liable to happen even in the most unusual case, unless the risk is so small that a reasonable man would in the whole circumstances feel justified in neglecting it.

In contrast, the degree of foresight of damage in a contract action is much higher. For example, Lord Reid considered that the degree of foresight required could be best summed up by asking whether the defendant realised that it was 'reasonably certain' that the harm suffered by the plaintiff might result from his breach of contract. Lord Hodson expressed approval of the use by the Court of Appeal of the phrase 'liable to result'. While different phrases were used by members of the House of Lords to identify the high degree of foresight required, they were unanimous in taking the view that it was not sufficient to ask whether the loss was foreseen by the defendant as being 'on the cards' as this degree of foresight was much lower and more likely to be equated with the test applied in tort actions.

Applying these principles to *Kemp* v *Intasun Holidays Ltd,* it is clear that the Court of Appeal in that case came to the conclusion that the tour operator could not be said to be reasonably certain that provision of inadequate holiday accommodation might affect the asthmatic plaintiff in the way it did since the company was unaware of his physical condition at the time the contract was entered into.

One particular difficulty which arises in determining what is the most appropriate remoteness test in consumer contracts is that in many instances the damage complained of will be of a physical nature. This is especially the case where a consumer buys defective goods which either damage other property belonging to the consumer or which cause physical injury. *Hadley* v *Baxendale* and the cases which have interpreted it have generally been concerned with the problem of economic loss in the form of lost profits suffered by business contracting parties. With the exception of *Kemp* v *Intasun Holidays Ltd,* there has been no direct consideration of the appropriate test to apply in consumer transactions.

Where the consumer complains that he has suffered physical harm as a result of the defendant's breach of contract, it is arguable that a test which is primarily concerned with economic loss in the form of lost profit is hardly appropriate. Moreover, it is quite possible that where physical consequences flow from a breach of contract, the defendant will be concurrently liable in tort for a failure to take reasonable care.

Despite the problem of concurrent contractual and tortious liability, the courts have continued to apply *Hadley* v *Baxendale* principles to actions for damages for breach of contract, with the result that there must be a very high degree of foresight of harm even where the loss complained of consists of physical harm to the person or to property. Thus in *H. Parsons (Livestock) Ltd* v *Uttley Ingham & Co. Ltd* [1978] QB 791 a farmer complained that his pigs had died as a result of the negligent installation by the defendant of a food hopper. A consequence of this negligent installation was that food stored in the hopper was insufficiently ventilated with the result that the food became mouldy and the plaintiff's pigs developed *E. coli*, a rare intestinal infection. In an action for damages representing the value of the lost pigs and lost sales and turnover, the majority of the Court of Appeal (Scarman and Orr LJJ) applied the *Koufos* v *C. Czarnikow Ltd* interpretation of *Hadley* v *Baxendale* taking the view that what mattered was whether the parties would have contemplated as a serious possibility the death of the pigs as a natural result of the breach of contract. In reaching this conclusion, Scarman LJ chose to ignore the fact that death as a result of the *E. coli* infection had been ruled out as something which could not have been foreseen as a serious possibility.

The problem which this analysis creates is that in the economic loss cases from which the contract remoteness test has been derived, the particular type of loss suffered must be foreseen, whereas in *H. Parsons (Livestock) Ltd* v *Uttley Ingham & Co. Ltd* this appeared not to be a requirement. In recognition of the fact that his decision might cause some difficulties, Scarman LJ's explanation was that in loss of profit cases, the factual analysis of what is foreseeable might take a different form from that applicable to physical damage cases. Accordingly, in physical damage cases all that has to be foreseen as a serious possibility is the type of consequence which follows from the breach, rather than the specific consequence. The decision of the majority does appear to distinguish between physical harm and economic harm and it was this distinction which underpinned the minority judgment of Lord Denning MR, who reached the same conclusion as the majority that the death of the pigs was a foreseeable consequence of the defendant's breach of contract, but by a different route. Lord Denning's preferred analysis was that a distinction should be drawn between economic loss cases, to which the stricter *Koufos* v *C. Czarnikow Ltd* formula should apply, and physical harm cases, to which the tort remoteness test in *Overseas Tankship (UK) Ltd* v *Morts Dock and Engineering Co. Ltd* should apply. On this analyis, all that would be required would be reasonable foresight of the kind of damage suffered by the plaintiff. Accordingly, it would be necessary only that death be foreseen as a possible consequence of the breach, regardless of how remote the precise cause of death might be.

4.4.3.3 Quantification of loss   The purpose of an award of damages for breach of contract is, so far as a money payment can do this, to place the plaintiff in the position he would have been in had the contract been performed according to his expectations. How this task is performed will differ according to the nature of the defendant's breach of contract.

4.4.3.3.1 Consumer damages for non-delivery and breach of warranty   In contracts for the sale of goods, there are two principal varieties of breach on the part of the seller which will give rise to the possibility of an award of damages in favour of the consumer. In the first place, the seller may fail to deliver the goods contracted for. Alternatively, there may be a breach of warranty or condition (Sale of Goods Act 1979, s. 11(2) and (4)), which gives rise only to an action for damages.

In the case of non-delivery, the Sale of Goods Act 1979, s. 51(2), provides, in accordance with *Hadley* v *Baxendale* (1854) 9 Ex 341, that the measure of damages is to be assessed as the loss directly and naturally arising, in the ordinary course of events, from the seller's breach of contract. As an example of the loss directly and naturally arising from the seller's failure to deliver, s. 51(3) provides that:

> Where there is an available market for the goods in question the measure of damages is prima facie to be ascertained by the difference between the contract price and the market or current price of the goods at the time or times when they ought to have been delivered or (if no time was fixed) at the time of refusal to deliver.

Thus if the consumer agrees to purchase a new car, to be delivered on 1 August for a price of £13,000 and the seller fails to deliver, with the result that the consumer has to buy a similar car elsewhere only to discover that the price of that type of car has risen by £800 in the light of unexpectedly high demand for the type of car in question, s. 51(3) confines the consumer's damages to the £800 difference between the original contract price and the replacement contract price. However, suppose the consumer in question is someone who likes to engage in 'one-upmanship' and feels aggrieved that he has not been the first person in Acacia Avenue to appear on the streets in a car which bears the new car registration prefix letter applicable to cars sold on or after 1 August each year. This he may regard as a variety of loss suffered as a result of the non-delivery, but it is clear from s. 51(3) that such 'damage' will not be recoverable.

As a variant on the example above, suppose the subject matter of the contract was not a new car, but one which was 12 months old. In these circumstances, it is arguable that s. 51(3) would have no application, since it has been accepted in the context of an action by a seller for damages for non-acceptance, that second-hand cars are unique chattels in respect of which there can be no available market (*Lazenby Garages Ltd* v *Wright* [1976] 1 WLR 459). Accordingly, it will be necessary to assess the actual loss directly and naturally arising from the seller's breach under s. 51(2). But if there is considered to be no market for goods of that kind, the court will face difficulties in assessing the loss suffered by the consumer.

In some instances, there will be an anticipatory breach on the part of the seller. For instance, in the example above in relation to the new car, suppose the seller indicates on 1 July that no car of the description given will be available on 1 August. Here there has been an anticipatory breach of contract, which the consumer has the option to accept or to waive. If the consumer accepts the repudiation, it has been seen already that he may treat the contract as terminated, but suppose he has to pay more than he would have done under the original contract for a replacement car. The difficulty which arises here is to determine on what date the consumer's damages are to be assessed, especially if there is a volatile market price. The general rule in cases of anticipatory breach of contract, where no time for delivery is fixed by the contract, is that the time of refusal to perform is ignored and that damages will be assessed on the basis of the market price at the date of assumed performance. In *Tai Hing Cotton Mill Ltd* v *Kamsing Knitting Factory* [1979] AC 91, sellers repudiated a commercial contract for the sale of bales of yarn in July 1973. Initially, the buyer did not accept the repudiation, but realised in November 1973 that no delivery would be forthcoming, and accordingly issued a writ for damages. The Privy Council (approving *Millett* v *Van Heeck* [1921] 2 KB 369) held that damages should be assessed on the basis of the difference between the contract price and the market price for similar goods on a date representing the expiry of a period of reasonable notice demanding performance. That period of notice was considered to be one month from the date on which the writ for damages was issued and the date of assumed performance was considered to have arrived at the expiry of that period of notice in December 1973.

The problem this decision raises for consumer damages is that suppose in July 1973 the market price of the goods contracted for is £12,000 compared with a contract price of £11,500, but the market price on the assumed date of performance has fallen back to £11,600. On the *Tai Hing* principle damages will be assessed at £100. But suppose that in November 1973, when the writ is issued and when the market price is still £12,000, the consumer buys a replacement. The consumer suffers an actual loss of £500. In this type of case, if the consumer needs a replacement car as soon as possible, the reasonable notice rule may work against him. Perhaps the answer, in consumer cases, is to reduce the length of the period of reasonable notice so that the assumed date of performance is much closer to the date on which the writ is first issued. Alternatively, the solution adopted in the United States Uniform Commercial Code, s. 2–712, that the substitute purchase price should be used as the basis for assessment of damages would make more sense.

In *Tai Hing Cotton Mill Ltd* v *Kamsing Knitting Factory*, the buyer did not immediately accept the repudiation, but it is clear that immediate acceptance is an option, in which case, damages will still be based upon the relevant market price at the date of assumed performance, but once the decision has been taken to accept the repudiation, the consumer must take all reasonable steps to mitigate his loss. However, in the absence of an agreed date for performance, where the buyer chooses not to accept the repudiation, it would appear to be possible for the buyer to keep open the seller's obligation to deliver for an extensive period of time (see *White & Carter (Councils) Ltd* v *McGregor* [1962] AC 413), unless the court was prepared to infer that the contract required delivery within a reasonable time of the contract being entered into.

The consideration of s. 51(3) above is premised upon the assumption that there is a market price for the goods contracted for. However, s. 51(3) is of no use where there is no market price and the goods are purchased for use or consumption. In this last event, damages will have to be assessed under s. 51(2), but it would make no sense to apply commercial considerations such as to ask what loss of profit has been suffered by the consumer. Instead, the buyer ought to receive damages representing the additional cost of buying a reasonable alternative, even if this alternative proves to be of better quality than the article originally contracted for (*Hinde* v *Liddell* (1875) LR 10 QB 265).

Where there has been a breach of condition or a breach of warranty on the part of the seller, the consumer may sue for damages in respect of that breach. Such a breach may arise if there has been a late delivery or a breach of contract relating to the quality of the goods contracted for.

In the case of a late delivery, the breach may not be sufficiently serious to allow rejection, but if the goods contracted for have to be replaced temporarily, pending their eventual arrival, an award of damages is the most appropriate remedy. Since consumers buy goods for use rather than for the purposes of resale, an award of damages must reflect the consequences of this prevention of use. In the first place, the consumer may set up the breach of warranty in diminution or extinction of the price (Sale of Goods Act 1979, s. 53(1)). Moreover, an award of damages under s. 53(2) must accurately represent the loss directly and naturally flowing from the defendant's breach. If the consumer has had to hire a replacement while he is awaiting delivery, the reasonable costs associated with that replacement may be recovered as damages. However, it is important to relate the action for damages to the requirement that the consumer should mitigate his loss. Thus, it will not be possible for the consumer to hire a markedly more expensive replacement, as this might be regarded as unreasonably increasing the loss suffered as a result of the seller's breach of contract.

Where the seller is in breach of a warranty of quality, the Sale of Goods Act 1979, s. 53(3), provides that the loss suffered by the buyer is prima facie based on the difference between the value of the goods as they were at the date of delivery and their value had they fulfilled the terms of the contract.

Ascertaining this diminished value may be difficult and may involve guesswork on the part of the court, unless there is an available expert who can advise on the likely diminution in value in the light of the defect. It is necessary to consider what the market value of the goods would have been had the consumer and the seller been aware of the defects at the time of delivery (*Jackson* v *Chrysler Acceptances Ltd* [1978] RTR 474, 481). Since it is the date of delivery which is instrumental in the process of assessment of damages, it follows that the consumer may lose out in times of inflation, since the award of damages will not be based on the enhanced market value of the subject matter of the contract in the light of inflationary pressures.

A particular problem which arises in consumer transactions is that the consumer ordinarily purchases goods for use or consumption and not for resale. Unfortunately, the Sale of Goods Act 1979, s. 53(3), does not distinguish between the two alternative reasons for buying goods.

Since the consumer purchaser requires goods for use or consumption, it may be possible to have the goods repaired so as to render them fit for the buyer's intended use. In such a case, the obvious measure of damages will be the cost of repair rather than the difference between the contract value and the diminished value in the light of the defects in the goods, although in practice, the two alternative amounts may not differ substantially. However, it is possible that the cost of repair proves to be uneconomic. This may be so in relation to contracts for the sale of goods, but the same problem equally applies to other consumer contracts, such as those for the services of a builder in effecting home improvement work (see further chapter 9). For example, in *Ruxley Electronics & Construction Ltd* v *Forsyth* [1996] AC 344 (a case which did not involve the sale of goods, but in which it was said that the same principles would apply whether the contract was one for the sale of goods or one for the supply of a service) the respondent contracted with the appellant for the construction of a swimming pool to be built to a depth of 6 feet 6 inches. Subsequently, the appellant agreed, for no extra reward, to construct the pool to a depth of 7 feet 6 inches at the respondent's request. In fact the finished product was shallower than had been contracted for and the respondent declined to pay the outstanding balance owed by him to the appellant. When sued by the appellant for damages, the respondent counter-claimed damages for breach of contract.

The Court of Appeal allowed the counter-claim, assessing the respondent's loss as the cost of rebuilding the pool to the depth contracted for, which, in this case, came to £21,560.

On appeal to the House of Lords, the loss suffered was assessed as no more than loss of amenity, amounting to £2,500, it being considered that to award the full cost of repair would be uneconomic, given that there had been no reduction in the value of the respondent's land.

Generally, there are two methods of assessing damages in cases of this kind, the first of which is to base damages on the cost of repair or reinstatement. Alternatively, damages may be based upon the diminution in value of the thing contracted for. Generally, the former applies where the subject matter of the contract has been acquired for use, such as where a house is purchased to be lived in (see *Murray* v *Lloyd* [1989] 1 WLR 1060) or where goods are purchased for consumption. In contrast, the diminution in value measure will be more appropriate in commercial contracts, where, for example, land has been acquired for investment purposes or goods acquired for the purposes of resale.

In *Ruxley Electronics & Construction Ltd* v *Forsyth*, it was considered that the swimming pool was not diminished in value as a result of the breach of contract, with the result that unless there was some other appropriate measure of damages, the owner had to be compensated on the basis of the cost of reinstatement in accordance with the terms of the contract. Generally, the difference in value measure will be most appropriate in cases where the thing contracted for is damaged or is not up to specification, but clearly, this will not compensate the plaintiff where there has been no diminution in value. However, the House of Lords also considered that it would be uneconomic to base damages on the cost of reinstatement, since the respondent, in that case, had a valuable swimming pool, albeit not constructed to the depth contracted for. Instead of awarding damages on the basis of the cost of reinstatement, the amount awarded was based on the respondent's loss of amenity, which was valued at £2,500.

The problem which this award raises is that of identifying what interest of the respondent's was protected. Clearly, it was not his full expectation interest, since to protect that would have involved reinstating the swimming pool to the depth contracted for. In reaching their conclusion that the full reinstatement measure was not appropriate, the House of Lords relied heavily upon the concept of reasonableness. In particular, it was accepted that the reinstatement measure would not be appropriate where the expenditure involved would be out of all proportion to the good to be obtained (Lord Lloyd of Berwick at 366–7 applying *Jacob & Youngs Inc.* v *Kent* (1921) 230 NY 239). Conversely, it was accepted that there are occasions on which the value of a promise to the promisee 'exceeds the financial enhancement of his position which full performance will secure' (per Lord Mustill at 360). For example, if an employer insists upon the use, in a house conversion, of lurid wall tiles which would not appeal to the taste of most people, but which are curiously appreciated by the employer, it is not for the builder or the court to substitute something which might be regarded as sensible by an ordinary person (per Lord Mustill at 361).

What is clear is that the £2,500 damages for loss of amenity represent what is described as the 'consumer surplus value', that is, a subjective value placed upon the thing contacted for by the consumer which exceeds its simple market value. Another example considered elsewhere in this book is the 'pleasurable amenity' afforded by a holiday and which is denied if the holiday proves to be a disaster.

The decision in *Ruxley Electronics & Construction Ltd* v *Forsyth* appears to leave the consumer in a somewhat vulnerable position. What it appears to say is that a builder can promise a whole range of additional features in his proposed work in order to secure the contract and then subsequently cut corners in order to reduce his costs, not incorporating all that has been promised. If it later appears that to rectify all of these defects would involve demolition and subsequent rebuilding, this might not be regarded as an economic solution, in which case, the consumer is then left to the uncertainty involved in placing a value upon his subjective expectations of performance. In this regard, it is clear from the views expressed by Lord Lloyd that judicial opinions may differ widely on how much those expectations are worth.

In addition to the cost of repair and the diminished market value, an action for damages for breach of warranty may also take account of consequential losses, such as personal injury, the cost of hiring a replacement, inconvenience costs, distress and minor expenses. For example, in *Bernstein* v *Pamson Motors (Golders Green) Ltd* [1987] 2 All ER 220, the court, having denied the right of the buyer of an unsafe car to reject it on the ground that the car had been accepted within the meaning of the Sale of Goods Act 1979, s. 35, allowed a claim for damages which took account of the cost of returning home by taxi after the car had broken down, the loss of a full tank of petrol, distress damages based on a spoilt day out and damages representing five days' loss of use of the car. In the event, the cost of repair was immaterial since this had been carried out under the terms of a manufacturer's warranty at no cost to the consumer, and there was considered to be no diminution in the value of the car since it had been restored to its original condition by the warranty repairs.

The sums involved in consequential losses can be quite substantial, and possibly out of all proportion to the initial cost of the consumer purchase. This is especially the case where a defective product causes personal injury, since the value of those injuries will be assessed on the same principles as apply to an award of damages in tort for negligently inflicted personal injury. In *Godley* v *Perry* [1960] 1 WLR 9, the seller of a toy catapult was liable for the loss of sight suffered by the child purchaser and in *Wilson* v *Rickett Cockrell & Co. Ltd* [1954] 1 QB 598 a coal merchant was liable for the extensive property damage caused by the presence of a detonator in the smokeless fuel he supplied to the plaintiff.

4.4.3.3.2   Consumer's liability for the price and for non-acceptance If the consumer wrongfully declines to accept goods which he has contracted for, this breach may expose him to either an action for the price under the Sale of Goods Act 1979, s. 49, or to an action for damages under the 1979 Act, s. 50.

If the consumer is to be liable for the price, it is essential that property in the goods should have passed under the terms of the contract, which will occur, in the absence of an agreement to the contrary, at the time the contract is made, if the goods contracted for are identified and agreed upon (Sale of Goods Act 1979, s. 18, rule 1). Despite this general rule, the courts appear to have little difficulty in consumer contracts in inferring that the time at which property is to pass should be delayed until the time of delivery or payment (*Ward R. V. Ltd* v *Bignall* [1967] 1 QB 534).

Alternatively, the seller may sue for the price under s. 49 if there is an agreement to the effect that the price is to be paid on a specific date stated in the contract, and that date has arrived, regardless of whether property in the goods has passed to the buyer. Generally, the right of the seller to sue for the price is very limited because of the narrow terms in which s. 49 is drafted, with the result that it is more likely that the consumer will be faced with an action for damages for non-acceptance where he declines to take the goods.

In the case of non-acceptance on the part of the consumer, the principles of assessment which apply are identical to those which operate in the consumer's favour in the event of non-delivery on the part of the trader with whom he has contracted. If there is a market for the goods in question, the seller will be confined to the difference between the contract price and the market price at the time when the contract should have been performed (Sale of Goods Act 1979, s. 50(3)). If there is no available market, the seller will be able to recover such loss as is considered to have arisen directly and naturally as a result of the consumer's failure to accept the goods in accordance with the terms of the contract (Sale of Goods Act 1979, s. 50(2)).

4.5 REMEDIES FOR MISREPRESENTATION

There are two principal remedies for misrepresentation, namely, rescission of the contract and damages. Although the traditional remedy for misrepresentation is that of rescission, simply returning the parties to the position they were in before the contract was entered into will not always provide adequate compensation, especially if there has been consequential reliance loss in the form of expenditure incurred.

4.5.1 Rescission of the contract

The object of an order for rescission of a contract is to restore the parties to the positions they occupied before the contract was made. The manner in which this restoration or restitution is achieved will differ according to the subject matter of the contract. This matter is pursued in more detail elsewhere in this book when considering the issue of consumer protection through restitutionary principles (see chapter 5).

4.5.2 Damages for misrepresentation

Where a consumer has been induced to enter a contract in reliance on the defendant's misrepresentation or has incurred detrimental reliance loss as a result of a misstatement or deceit, the measure of damages is assessed by restoring the status quo. Although a misrepresentation induces a contractual relationship, the action for damages is one which is based upon tortious principles — the tort being either that of deceit if the misrepresentation is fraudulent or the statutory tort created by the Misrepresentation Act 1967. For these purposes, a fraudulent misrepresentation is one made knowingly, or without belief in its truth or recklessly, careless whether it be true or false (*Derry* v *Peek* (1889) 14 App Cas 337). The award of damages is designed to place the plaintiff in the same position he would have been in if the statement had not been made rather than to put him into the position he would have been in had it been true.

In cases of fraudulent misrepresentation, the defendant is also liable for all the damage to the plaintiff which flows directly from the fraudulent statement (*Doyle* v *Olby (Ironmongers) Ltd* [1969] QB 158).

Until 1967 if the misrepresentation was not made fraudulently, there was no obvious basis for an award of damages, unless the statement fell within the common law rule in *Hedley Byrne & Co. Ltd* v *Heller & Partners Ltd* [1964] AC 465 relating to tortious liability for negligent misstatement (see chapter 5) or if the court was able to treat the statement as forming the basis of a collateral contract. However, since the enactment of the Misrepresentation Act 1967, s. 2(1), there is now available an action for damages for a negligent misrepresentation which has the added advantage of placing on the misrepresentor the duty of disproving negligence, while at the same time conferring on the plaintiff the advantages of the rules on remoteness and assessment of damages for the tort of deceit.

Under the Misrepresentation Act 1967, s. 2(1), the appropriate measure of damages is designed to put the plaintiff in the position he would have been in if the statement had not been made (*Royscot Trust Ltd* v *Rogerson* [1991] 2 QB 297). This clearly involves the application of tortious principles of assessment and remoteness of loss. The relevant tort rules to apply are not those employed in relation to a negligence action, but instead, those applicable to fraud actions. In *Royscot Trust Ltd* v *Rogerson* a consumer wished to acquire on hire purchase a car supplied by the defendant, but did not have the 20 per cent deposit required by the plaintiff, a finance company. In order to circumvent this the defendant deliberately misrepresented certain figures on a form returned by him to the plaintiff with the result that the plaintiff advanced to the consumer a greater amount than it would have done had it known what deposit had been paid. The consumer failed to keep up payments due under the hire purchase contract. Although the misrepresentation was fraudulent, the plaintiff chose to bring its action for damages under s. 2(1) of the 1967 Act with the result that the defendant bore the burden of proving that he had reasonable grounds for believing in the truth of the statement he had made to the plaintiffs. This he was unable to do. Damages of £3,625 were awarded, based on all the loss which flowed directly from the misrepresentation. £1,600 represented the additional amount the plaintiff advanced to the consumer and the balance was the amount owed to the plaintiff at the time of the consumer's default under the hire purchase agreement. This amount was considered to be justified on the basis that the appropriate rules for assessment of damages were not those which applied to common law negligence actions, but rather those which applied to an action for fraud or deceit since s. 2(1) of the 1967 Act refers to the person making the misrepresentation being liable 'had the misrepresentation been made fraudulently'. According to *Royscot Trust Ltd* v *Rogerson* the effect of s. 2(1) is to treat someone who has acted negligently as if he were fraudulent. However, it is arguable that this result might not have been intended by Parliament. When the history of misrepresentation law is considered, it must be appreciated that in 1967, the law was not, at that time, settled on what remoteness test was to be applied to fraud actions, since the leading decision in *Doyle* v *Olby (Ironmongers) Ltd* was not reached until almost two years later. Moreover, before the 1967 Act the only way in which a plaintiff could recover damages for misrepresentation was if fraud could be established. In 1967, there was no decision which suggested that the rule in *Hedley Byrne & Co. Ltd* v *Heller & Partners Ltd* could apply to parties who had entered into contractual negotiations, as was eventually established in *Esso Petroleum Co. Ltd* v *Mardon* [1976] QB 801 some eight years after the Act was passed. In the light of this brief history, it is perhaps unsurprising that the draftsman adopted the fiction of fraud, but it does not follow automatically from this that all the rules on actions for fraud should be applied blindly to someone who is merely careless.

A further controversial aspect of the decision in *Royscot Trust Ltd* v *Rogerson* is that although the basic principle of assessment of damages in these cases is that the defendant should be liable for losses which flow directly from the misrepresentation, it is arguable that the plaintiffs in this case recovered indirect losses as well, in the sense that the consumer's breach of the hire purchase contract could not be said to have flowed directly from the misrepresentation. However, the view expressed by Balcombe LJ was that both default by the consumer and a wrongful disposition of the subject matter of the contract could be regarded as foreseeable events, with the result that neither could be regarded as a *novus actus interveniens*.

Where a misrepresentation is made neither fraudulently nor negligently, there is no automatic right to recover damages, but the court has a discretion under the Misrepresentation Act 1967, s. 2(2), to award damages in lieu of rescission. This discretionary remedy is important because of the harsh effects previous remedial rules for innocent misrepresentation had. Before 1967, if a statement was regarded as a minor term of the contract, breach of that term would give rise to an action for damages for breach of warranty only, yet if the statement were to be regarded as a misrepresentation, the misrepresentee would be in a position to rescind the contract even though the financial effects of the statement might be regarded as inconsequential. In order to meet the problems thrown up by the pre-1967 rules on remedies for a purely innocent misrepresentation, it was recommended that a more elastic remedy based on discretionary damages should be introduced so as to cater for the situation in which the financial effects of rescission were out of all proportion to the damage caused by the innocent misrepresentation. For example, in *William Sindall plc* v *Cambridgeshire County Council* [1994] 3 All ER 932 it was considered *obiter* (on the facts it had been decided that there was no actionable misrepresentation with the result that what was said about s. 2(2) was unnecessary for the decision) that a discretionary award of damages would be appropriate where there was an innocent representation about the presence of a foul sewer buried below land purchased by the plaintiffs from the defendants. The cost of rectifying the damage caused by the presence of the sewer was approximately £18,000, which was disproportionately less than the financial effects of rescission which would require the council to repay the purchase price of £5 million at a time when the effects of a recession in the property market had reduced the value of the land to £2 million. It was considered that in deciding whether to award damages under s. 2(2), account should be taken of the nature of the misrepresentation in relation to the subject matter of the transaction. Other relevant considerations were considered to be the cost to the misrepresentee should the contract be upheld and the cost to the misrepresentor should rescission be allowed (see Law Reform Committee, *Tenth Report, Innocent Misrepresentation* (Cmnd 1782), paras 11 and 12). Since the cost of rectifying the damage caused by the misrepresentation only came to £18,000 compared with the loss which would have been caused to the misrepresentor by allowing rescission, the nature of the misrepresentation was considered to be relatively minor, with the result that this would have been an appropriate case for an award of discretionary damages, had there been a misrepresentation in the first place ((1994) 3 All ER 932, 953–4 per Hoffmann LJ). A further matter addressed in *William Sindall plc* v *Cambridgeshire County Council* is the appropriate measure of damages to apply in cases arising under s. 2(2). It has been seen that for the purposes of negligent misrepresentations under s. 2(1), the relevant measure of damages to apply is the fraud measure which contemplates all the loss flowing directly from the misrepresentation, including consequential losses. For the purposes of s. 2(2) where the misrepresentation is wholly innocent, the measure applicable to s. 2(1) would appear to be inappropriate, especially in the light of the language used in s. 2(3) which indicates that where damages are awarded under both s. 2(1) and s. 2(2), the award made under the latter should be taken into account in awarding damages under s. 2(1). This would seem to suggest that an award under s. 2(2) will ordinarily be less than that made under s. 2(1) (see also *Witter Ltd v TBP Industries Ltd* [1996] 2 All ER 573, 591 per Jacob J). In *William Sindall plc v Cambridgeshire County Council* it was observed that the purpose of an award of damages under s. 2(2) is to compensate the misrepresentee in respect of the damage caused by the subject matter of the contract not being what it was represented to be ((1994) 3 All ER 932, 954 per Hoffmann LJ), which, in any event, should not exceed the amount the plaintiff would have received had he been able to sue for damages for breach of warranty, had the statement been incorporated into the contract as a term (ibid. 955 per Hoffmann LJ). The principal reason for applying the contractual measure of damages in these circumstances is that the remedy under s. 2(2) is one which stands in place of the remedy of rescission, in which case the purpose of the award is to compensate the plaintiff where an order for rescission of the contract is refused. The damages should also reflect the loss suffered by the plaintiff *as a result of the misrepresentation*. In *William Sindall plc v Cambridgeshire County Council* the loss which would have resulted from the misrepresentation, had it been decided that there was a misrepresentation, was the cost of removing the foul sewer. The 'loss' suffered by the representee resulting from the decreased market value of the property would have been attributable to the recession rather than to the representation. This conclusion is particularly likely to be arrived at if the evidence shows that, but for the misrepresentation, the plaintiff would not have bought the property which is the subject matter of the representation, since then damages will be based upon the difference between the contract price and the market value of the property in the light of the misrepresentation *at the time when the contract was made* (see *Cemp Properties (UK) Ltd v Dentsply Research & Development Corporation* [1991] 2 EGLR 197, 199–201). This analysis makes it plain that it is essential to identify what has been represented, since there may be circumstances in which the diminution in value does result from the misrepresentation rather than from other causes.

A further issue under s. 2(2) is to identify the circumstances in which the discretion to award damages may be exercised. At one stage, it was believed that since an award of damages could only be given *in lieu of rescission*, if rescission would not have been available for some reason, there would be no justification for an award of damages under s. 2(2) (see Atiyah and Treitel, 'Misrepresentation Act 1967' (1967) 30 MLR 369 and *Atlantic Lines & Navigation Co. Inc. v Hallam Ltd* [1983] 1 Lloyd's Rep 188). However, this is not so, since the words 'has been rescinded' in s. 2(2) mean that the court can exercise its discretion if the agreement was 'rescissionable' (*Witter Ltd v TBP Industries Ltd* [1996] 2 All ER 573, 590 per Jacob J). In *Witter Ltd v TBP*

Industries Ltd it was said, *obiter*, that what matters is whether, at some earlier stage, the remedy of rescission was available. If the remedy of rescission might have been available, it may still be equitable to award damages in place of rescinding the contract. The mere fact that through lapse of time the right to rescind has been lost or it has become impossible to arrange for substantial restitution of the subject matter of the contract does not mean that the court is disentitled to award damages under s. 2(2) if it would be equitable to do so.

FIVE

Tort law and principles of the law of restitution as means of consumer protection

5.1 TORT LAW

Rules of the law of tort have been adapted in a number of ways as a consumer protection technique. The immediately obvious example is the adaptation of the tort of negligence in relation to the liability of manufacturers and producers for defective products and the liability of the supplier of a service, but tortious principles are also relevant in other respects. In particular, the law of tort may be of some limited use in the field of advertising law and in relation to the misuse of property belonging to another by both the consumer and the trader with whom he deals.

5.1.1 Product safety

The decision of the House of Lords in *Donoghue* v *Stevenson* [1932] AC 562 represents a landmark in the field of consumer protection law in providing that a manufacturer owes a duty of care to consumers in respect of the safety of his product. Difficulties have arisen in determining how far the duty extends. *Donoghue* v *Stevenson* was concerned with a negligent act (the act of manufacture) which caused physical harm to the person. Later cases have raised the question whether a manufacturer owes any tortious duty to a consumer who suffers economic loss, such as diminution in the value of the defective product itself. This is particularly relevant in the context of defective buildings, which may be regarded as no more than a large-scale and expensive product, which are capable of falling within the principles established in *Donoghue* v *Stevenson*. The position adopted in English law on this issue seems to be that, except in the most extreme cases, a producer will not owe a duty of care in respect of pure economic loss such as diminution in value, and that the consumer of such a product will be confined to an action for breach of contract, if one exists (see *D & F Estates Ltd* v *Church Commissioners for England* [1989] AC 177; *Murphy* v *Brentwood District Council* [1991] 1 AC 398). Moreover, defective building cases may also give rise to the question whether a 'producer' or builder can be held responsible for a negligent omission to act as opposed to a positive act which results in harm. Again the general response in this area, after some initial confusion, is that the tort of negligence is concerned with rectifying the effect of negligent acts rather than with omissions, since there is no general duty in English law that a man must act so as to improve the position of the plaintiff.

Apart from the problem of economic loss, the difficulties of establishing causation and proving fault on the part of the manufacturer have led to calls for reform of the law, culminating in the enactment of the Consumer Protection Act 1987, part I, which purportedly introduces a regime of strict liability into the field of product liability law. However, there are serious doubts about whether this harmonisation provision, based upon a European Community Directive, has resulted in any substantial change in the position of a consumer harmed as a result of a defective product, save in so far as there is no longer any need to prove fault on the part of the producer. However, at least one of the defences provided for in the 1987 Act and the definition of defectiveness may serve to do little more than reintroduce through the back door a fault-based standard of care on the part of a producer (see further chapter 7). In certain circumstances, manufacturers and retailers are under a statutory duty to comply with basic safety standards. For example, the Food Safety Act 1990 imposes a duty not to prepare food which is injurious to health or which does not comply with safety requirements and the General Product Safety Regulations 1994 (SI 1994/2328) impose a duty to comply with the general safety requirement. Although these broad statutory standards impose criminal liability on traders who fail to comply with their requirements, there is sometimes an available action in tort for damages for breach of a statutory duty. However, the requirements for the tort are demanding and it will be seen later that very few statutory standards will give rise to an action for damages in favour of consumers, usually on the ground that consumers as a class constitute too large a group of potential plaintiffs to warrant the protection of tortious principles (see chapter 7).

5.1.2 Defective services

Although the supply of services will very often involve a contractual relationship between a consumer and the service supplier, the tort of negligence can provide some assistance in circumstances in which services are supplied outside of contractual dealings. Doctors, lawyers, architects and surveyors are all required to exercise reasonable care in their dealings with both clients and others whom they may reasonably foresee as likely to be affected by their acts or omissions. It will be seen elsewhere that service suppliers, unlike suppliers of goods, are subject only to a fault-based regime (see chapter 8). However, some consumer representatives would argue that service industries should be exposed to greater liability in the form of a guarantee of the quality of the service provided. Such an obligation would go well beyond the present requirement that service providers should exercise reasonable care by reaching the standard expected of an ordinary supplier of services of the kind supplied. The introduction of such a guarantee was considered at one stage by the European Commission and resulted in the preparation of a draft Directive. However, in the face of widespread criticism, the proposal was dropped and seems unlikely to resurface for the time being.

The principal difficulty encountered in applying negligence principles to non-contractual suppliers of services is that the proximity of relationship between the consumer and the service supplier may not be sufficiently great. It is clear now that the neighbour principle established in *Donoghue* v *Stevenson* [1932] AC 562 requires consideration of more than just the foreseeability of harm suffered by the plaintiff. In determining whether a duty of care is owed by the service supplier to the consumer, it will be necessary to consider, in addition to the issue of foresight of harm, the proximity of relationship between the parties and whether it is just and reasonable to impose a duty of care in the particular circumstances of the case. It does not necessarily follow from this that the consumer must be known to the service supplier, but the consumer must fall into a group of people who could have been foreseen as likely to be affected by the negligent provision of the service. Thus a building society customer who relies upon a valuation carried out by a surveyor will be owed a duty of care since the surveyor ought to realise that such a person might rely upon the advice he gives in the form of the valuation survey report (*Smith* v *Eric S. Bush* [1990] 1 AC 831). However, it seems that whether or not a duty of care is owed in these circumstances will depend upon the part of the housing market in which the purchase is made. A purchaser who has substantial independent means may be expected to employ his own surveyor, whereas the plaintiff in *Smith* v *Eric S. Bush* purchased at the lower end of the market and could reasonably expect to rely on no more than the valuation survey (ibid. 859 per Lord Griffiths). Similarly, where an auditor, acting in accordance with the statutory requirements of the Companies Act 1985 conducts a company audit and advises as to the financial standing of that company, he owes a duty of care to the company, but no similar duty is owed to a potential investor in that company, since the advice given by the auditor was not intended to be read by or communicated to such persons (see *Caparo Industries plc* v *Dickman* [1990] 2 AC 605). Using the modern language employed in dealing with the issue of duty of care, it would not be just and reasonable to impose liability in these circumstances (see further chapter 8).

The tort of conversion may also play a limited role in respect of the misuse of consumer goods. For example, if a consumer leaves his property with another for the purposes of repair or safe-keeping and the repairer wrongly disposes of the goods to another, the consumer may have an action for conversion (see chapter 8). The same also applies where a consumer has temporary possession of goods belonging to the supplier, such as where a consumer hires a television set or where a consumer acquires goods on hire purchase, which during the currency of the agreement remain the property of the finance company. In either event, a wrongful disposition of the goods subject to the contract of hire or hire purchase by the consumer might expose the consumer to liability for conversion (see further chapter 11).

5.1.3   Advertising law

The principal controls on misleading advertising in favour of the consumer lie in the criminal law and in self-regulating codes of practice (see chapters 16–20). However, principles of the law of tort may have some minor significance.

Where there is no contractual relationship between the advertiser and the consumer, but the consumer has incurred expense through purchasing a product from a retail supplier, there may be the possibility of a negligence action arising out of an alleged negligent misstatement. Liability for such statements lies under the rule in *Hedley Byrne & Co. Ltd* v *Heller & Partners Ltd* [1964] AC 465, but recent explanations of the rule restrict the liability of the maker of the statement. Following the decision of the House of Lords in *Caparo Industries plc* v *Dickman* [1990] 2 AC 605, a duty of care will only be owed by the maker of a statement where three conditions are satisfied. First, it must be foreseeable that the plaintiff will suffer damage as a result of relying on the statement. Secondly, there must be a close relationship of proximity between the maker of the statement and the person to whom it is communicated and thirdly, it must be just and reasonable to impose liability on the maker of the statement ([1990] 2 AC 605, 617–18 per Lord Bridge of Harwich). Generally, advertising material is communicated to the world at large and there are strong reasons for doubting whether a misleading advertisement will give rise to a successful action for damages for negligent misstatement. While it may be foreseeable that a consumer will suffer damage as a result of relying on a statement contained in advertising material, it does not necessarily follow that there will be a sufficiently close relationship of proximity between the consumer and the advertiser or that it will be just and reasonable to impose liability.

It would appear that in deciding whether the maker of a statement is to be liable in negligence for the consequences of the plaintiff's reliance on that statement, six criteria must be considered (*James McNaughton Paper Group Ltd* v *Hicks Anderson & Co.* [1991] 2 QB 113, 125–7 per Neill LJ). These are (1) the purpose for which the statement was made; (2) the purpose for which the statement was communicated; (3) the relationship between the maker of the statement, the recipient of the information and any relevant third party; (4) the size of any class to which the recipient of the information belongs; (5) the state of knowledge of the maker of the statement; and (6) reliance by the recipient of the information.

The few cases in which a misstatement has been held to reveal the existence of a duty of care have involved statements directed towards a particular individual, made with the intention that that person should rely on the statement in question. In *Morgan Crucible Co. plc* v *Hill Samuel & Co. Ltd* [1991] Ch 295 statements made in the course of negotiations for the takeover of a company with the specific aim of inducing a person to become interested in the takeover were considered to be sufficiently directed towards the plaintiff to disclose the existence of a duty of care.

The problem with advertisements is that they are so general in their exposure that it would be difficult to say that they were sufficiently directed towards a specific individual to give rise to a duty to exercise reasonable care on the part of the advertiser. However, if an advertisement contains sufficient specifically misleading material, it may sometimes give rise to contractual liability on the basis of a collateral contract (see chapter 4).

Because advertisements are directed to a large class of people it is likely that the courts will be reluctant to impose a duty of care on advertisers for fear of opening the floodgates of litigation. Moreover, it might be difficult to argue that the advertiser is always aware of the particular manner in which the consumer will rely on the information given to him. However, it is to be hoped that this does not result in a general rule to the effect that manufacturers' promotional material can never give rise to liability, particularly since advertisements are specifically intended to induce consumer purchases (see Borrie, *Development of Consumer Law and Policy*, p. 31; cf. *Lambert* v *Lewis* [1982] AC 225, 262–4 per Stephenson LJ).

A major difficulty in this area is that, in its present form, the law of contract is badly equipped to deal with complaints about misleading advertising where the courts continue to adhere to the doctrine of privity of contract. At the same time, while developments in the tort of negligence in the 1970s and the early 1980s, for example, the 'two-stage' test in *Anns* v *Merton London Borough Council* [1978] AC 728 and *Junior Books Ltd* v *Veitchi Co. Ltd* [1983] 1 AC 520 were a judicial response to deficiencies in the law of contract, recent authorities suggest a return to the traditional role of the tort of negligence. In particular, the use of negligence as a means of compensating for economic losses is now subject to considerable restrictions on policy grounds and it is doubtful how far the consumer will be able to seek recompense in respect of expenditure incurred in reliance on a misleading manufacturers' advertisement in the absence of statutory intervention in favour of the consumer.

5.2 RESTITUTIONARY PRINCIPLES

Restitutionary remedies are based on the reversal of an unjust enrichment by the defendant at the expense of the plaintiff. As the law of restitution and the law of contract are quite distinct (*Lipkin Gorman* v *Karpnale Ltd* [1991] 2 AC 548), the availability of a restitutionary remedy is not dependent upon there being a breach of contract, but there is an overlap between the two branches of the law, for example, where a breach of contract results in an unjust enrichment. Most typically the consumer will encounter the possibility of a restitutionary remedy where he has contracted for the supply of a service (such as building work) and has paid in advance, only to discover at a later stage that the builder is unable to complete the work. However a restitutionary remedy may arise quite independently of any contract. For example, under the notion of autonomous unjust enrichment, the gain made by a defendant is the mirror image of the loss suffered by the plaintiff. Typically such a situation may arise where there has been an induced mistake of fact caused by, for example, a deliberate misrepresentation which results in a transfer of wealth by the plaintiff to the misrepresentor. In these circumstances, the enrichment of the defendant can be reversed through a court order for rescission of the contract entered into by the consumer as a result of the misrepresentation.

5.2.1 Enrichment

Enrichment may consist of either making a profit or saving on expenditure which might otherwise have been incurred. In both cases, to be recoverable, the breach of contract must have been the factual cause of the enrichment. Identification of an enrichment is relatively easy when it is in monetary form, as the defendant's gain will normally mirror the plaintiff's loss. Where the enrichment is in the form of a benefit conferred on the defendant, the tests of free acceptance, incontrovertible benefit or objective valuation may be employed.

The test of free acceptance is not universally regarded as an adequate basis for explaining when a restitutionary remedy may become available. But those who do defend the notion of free acceptance explain its operation by asking whether the defendant, as a reasonable man, should have known that a person in the position of the plaintiff would expect to be paid for a benefit which has been freely accepted by the defendant in circumstances in which the defendant has declined to take a reasonable opportunity to reject the benefit. This principle will be especially relevant where there has been a request from the defendant that the benefit be conferred. For example, suppose a consumer requests that building work on his house should proceed, but subsequently the consumer and the builder cannot reach agreement over the price. Technically, the failure to agree a price could mean that the contract fails for lack of agreement on a fundamental matter. However, the Supply of Goods and Services Act 1982, s. 15(1) provides that the consumer will pay a reasonable price for the service rendered. However, s. 15(1) only applies where there is no agreement on price with the result that if the parties provide in their contract that they will reach a future agreement on the price payable, the statutory provision will not be of assistance. In these circumstances, the consumer might be left in the position where he has had a valuable benefit conferred upon him in the form of the building work, for which it is only reasonable to expect him to make some payment since it was he who requested the work in the first place.

The test of incontrovertible benefit justifies a restutitionary remedy if no reasonable man could say that the defendant was not enriched. Such will be the case where the work done by the plaintiff would have had to be paid for by the defendant had it been carried out by someone else (*Craven-Ellis* v *Canons Ltd* [1936] 2 KB 403).

The test of objective valuation requires the court to consider what value would have been placed on the benefit conferred by a reasonable man. This particular test of enrichment is most likely to apply in cases where it is difficult to say whether the work performed has any particular value at the time when the remedy is sought.

5.2.2 Unjustness

When deciding if an enrichment is unjust two relevant tests may be applied. The first is that of non-voluntary transfer under which the court will consider the reasons why an enrichment has been conferred on the defendant by the plaintiff. Alternatively, a test of free acceptance may be applied, although it may be argued that the fact of a free acceptance does not reveal unjustness at all since the free acceptance of a benefit (for example, a gift) does not automatically indicate that the enrichment itself is unjust. Conversely, if the benefit is expected to be paid for, it can be said that there is a total failure of consideration, which would then reveal unjustness (see Burrows (1988) 104 LQR 576, 577).

In the context of restitution within contract the main reasons why an enrichment may be regarded as unjust are that the benefit has been conferred by mistake or, due to a misrepresentation or by compulsion. Moreover, subsequent events, such as a breach of contract or a frustrating event, may unfold in such a way that a benefit is conferred in circumstances which suggest that to allow it to be retained would create injustice.

5.2.2.1 Mistake   Where there is an operative mistake of fact, a remedy available to the mistaken party is that of rescission of the contract. This remedy cuts across both the law of contract and the law of restitution. In the case of contract law, the effect of rescission is to render the contract void if the mistake is fundamental, but it also serves to reverse an enrichment made by the defendant at the plaintiff's expense if a consequence of the mistake is that a payment has been made by the plaintiff to the defendant. Suppose a consumer makes a proposal for property insurance, but the contract fails because, unknown to the parties, the subject matter of the contract has already been written off. The consumer will be able to recover back any premium he has paid under the mistaken belief that the contract was valid, on the basis that either the consideration has wholly failed (*Strickland* v *Turner* (1852) 7 Ex 208) or that money has been paid and received under a mistake of fact (*Pritchard* v *Merchant's and Tradesman's Mutual Life Assurance Society* (1858) 3 CB NS 622).

5.2.2.2 Misrepresentation   A misrepresentation can cause a person to enter into a contract he would not otherwise have made. The standard remedy for misrepresentation is that of rescission of the contract, at the instance of the party misled, so as to restore the parties to the positions they occupied before the misrepresentation was made. This restoration differs according to the subject matter of the contract. Where the benefit conferred by the representee is in monetary form, the plaintiff's restitution measure is the value received. The plaintiff need not identify the money held by the defendant in order to obtain restitution. Thus if a consumer is misled into purchasing a car as a result of a misrepresentation about its roadworthiness and he subsequently decides that the car is in such a state that he does not wish to keep it, he will be able to rescind the contract and recover the price he has paid. Where the subject matter of the contract is not money, the effect of rescission is to ignore the contract and leave a right *in rem* in favour of the property transferred.

Sometimes rescission will not be allowed where one of the so-called bars to rescission applies. These are affirmation, lapse of time, the existence of third-party rights and impossibility of *restitutio in integrum*.

Affirmation means that the party seeking relief is aware of the facts which give rise to the right to rescind but, by words or conduct, has decided not to exercise that right. For example, suppose a consumer has been misled into purchasing a car due to a misrepresentation about its mechanical condition, but chooses to do nothing immediately. The longer the consumer drives the car while aware of its condition, the more likely it is that he will lose his right to rescind. Similarly lapse of time may be taken as evidence of affirmation as may an agreement to accept a cure of defects in the subject matter of the contract. In *Leaf* v *International Galleries* [1950] 1 All ER 693, the plaintiff purchased from the defendants a painting entitled 'Salisbury Cathedral' for £85. The defendants had innocently, but falsely, represented that the painting was by John Constable, but five years after the purchase it was discovered that this was not the case. The plaintiff sought to return the picture to the defendants and to recover the price he had paid. The Court of Appeal refused to grant rescission of the contract on the ground that the buyer, due to the lapse of time, was taken to have accepted the goods sold under the contract. In reaching his conclusion, Denning LJ equated the question of the availability of the remedy of rescission with the position arising under a contract for the sale of goods where the buyer is considered to have accepted the goods and is thereby prevented from rejecting the goods contracted for (Sale of Goods Act 1979, s. 35, and see chapter 4). Accordingly the buyer could be in no better position suing for misrepresentation than he would have been in had he sued for a breach of condition, with the result that the lapse of five years barred the remedy of rescission.

The approach adopted in *Leaf* v *International Galleries* does not appear to be universally accepted, especially in cases of 'rescission for breach of contract', where it has been held that before the remedy is barred, the plaintiff must have knowledge of his legal right to rescind. In *Payman* v *Lanjani* [1985] Ch 457 the plaintiff's legal adviser, who also acted for the defendant, urged him to perform a contract after he became aware of the fact that the defendant was guilty of impersonation amounting to fraud. Continuing with the contract was held not to amount to affirmation since the plaintiff was not aware of his legal right to rescind the contract, since at the time of continuing with it, the plaintiff had not been made aware of the legal consequences of the impersonation.

The second of the bars to rescission is concerned with third-party rights. If a contract is made as a result of a misrepresentation, the contract is voidable rather than void and the party misled can only seek rescission of the contract if this does not infringe a vested right in favour of a third party. Thus in the case of a contract for the sale of goods it is possible for a rogue to obtain possession of goods under a voidable title (Sale of Goods Act 1979, s. 23) and sell those goods to a third party. If the third party buys in good faith and without notice of any defect in title before the plaintiff has communicated his intention to rescind the contract, or has done the next best thing such as to inform the police that the goods have been stolen (*Car & Universal Finance Co. Ltd* v *Caldwell* [1965] 1 QB 525), it will then be too late to allow rescission, because the bona fide purchaser for value will have acquired property rights in the goods (see *Lewis* v *Averay* [1972] 1 QB 198).

The remaining bar to rescission is that the remedy will not be granted where *restitutio in integrum* is no longer possible. From the point of view of restitutionary principles, if the parties are to be restored to the positions they were in before the commission of the wrong which gives rise to the remedy of rescission, the plaintiff must be able to give back to the defendant any benefits conferred on him under the contract. Without this return to the pre-contract position, the plaintiff himself would be unjustly enriched if rescission were to be granted.

The most likely event preventing *restitutio in integrum* is consumption or disposal of the subject matter of the contract. If the thing which the plaintiff seeks to restore is radically different from the thing contracted for, rescission will not be allowed. In *Clarke* v *Dickson* (1858) El Bl & El 147, the plaintiff purchased shares in a company from the defendants. Subsequently, with the consent of the plaintiff, the company was reorganised as a limited liability company. At an even later stage that limited liability company was wound up, whereupon it was discovered that the defendants had been guilty of a misrepresentation. The plaintiff sought to rescind his contract with the defendant in order to recover the purchase price of the shares, but what he proposed to return to the defendant would have been different in kind to that which was contracted for. Accordingly, rescission was not granted.

Strict application of this particular bar to rescission is not always insisted upon since in some cases it is possible to value a non-monetary benefit and thereby allow rescission subject to an allowance in respect of any benefit conferred on the plaintiff by the defendant. If it is possible to quantify the value of the plaintiff's use of goods or property, rescission may be allowed if the goods are returned and the plaintiff makes a payment in respect of the value of his use (*Erlanger* v *New Sombrero Phosphate Co.* (1878) 3 App Cas 1218).

The remedy of indemnity is equally concerned with giving back to the plaintiff that amount which constitutes an advantage to or enrichment of the defendant. It is this feature which distinguishes this remedy from that of discretionary damages for innocent misrepresentation under the Misrepresentation Act 1967, s. 2(2) (see also chapter 4). It is clear that all the plaintiff is entitled to recover is the amount paid over to the defendant as a result of entering into the contract induced by the misrepresentation. Accordingly, there is no room for damages for consequential losses since these are a matter of compensation which must fit within existing rules of contract or tort, as the case might be.

5.2.2.3 Qualification by later events   The principal subsequent events which are likely to give rise to restitutionary problems are, first, a breach of contract which gives rise to a total failure of consideration; secondly, a contract may fail, for example, where it is void for uncertainty or where some element essential to its validity is absent and thirdly there may be an event external to the contract which serves to frustrate the contract.

Generally, where there is a breach of a valid contract, the appropriate monetary remedy is an award of damages to protect the plaintiff's expectation or status quo interest. Accordingly, what will matter is the loss suffered by the plaintiff. However, in the case of a serious breach of contract, one of the options open to the plaintiff is to terminate his performance obligations. In these circumstances the plaintiff may seek to recover any payment he has made on the ground that there has been a total failure of consideration. This remedy is restitutionary in nature since the contract has come to an end with the result that the plaintiff's expectation interest is no longer protected.

Sometimes, the problem may arise that a defendant is deliberately in breach of contract because this appears to be economically sensible to him. Here the question may arise whether the defendant can be required to disgorge the benefit of not performing his contract as agreed. In these circumstances, it is possible that the gain to the defendant resulting from his deliberate breach of contract exceeds the loss suffered by the plaintiff. However, the position adopted in English law is that these cases are to be treated as ones in which contractual damages, based on the plaintiff's loss, should be awarded, rather than restitutionary damages, based on the defendant's gain (*Tito* v *Wadell (No. 2)* [1977] Ch 106; *Surrey County Council* v *Bredero Homes Ltd* [1993] 1 WLR 1361).

Where the plaintiff has made a payment under his contract with the defendant and a condition precedent to his liability to make that payment has failed, there is a total failure of consideration. Such a failure most commonly arises where the defendant is in breach of his primary contractual obligations, thereby allowing the plaintiff to treat his own performance obligations as being at an end. In such cases, an action will lie for contractual damages or for restitution.

The main obstacle to a restitutionary award is the insistence that the plaintiff must have received nothing under the contract. Accordingly, a mere partial failure of consideration does not give rise to a restitutionary remedy (*Whincup* v *Hughes* (1871) LR 6 CP 78), unless the contract is severable or easily apportionable. Thus in *Ebrahim Dawood Ltd* v *Heath (Est 1927) Ltd* [1961] 2 Lloyd's Rep 512 a buyer was held to have justifiably rejected part of a consignment of steel sheets for which he had paid in advance. The court allowed him to recover a proportionate part of the price on the basis that he had received and accepted the consignments that were in accordance with the contract, but could reject those which did not conform, provided, as in this case, it was possible to sever the non-conforming goods from the remainder of the goods contracted for (see also Sale of Goods Act 1979, s. 35A, which permits a right of partial rejection).

It may be the case that a person who is in breach of contract himself subsequently seeks restitution in respect of that part of the work he has done up to the date of breach. For example, suppose a builder is engaged to carry out construction work on behalf of a consumer and only 50 per cent of the work is complete at the time when the builder 'downs tools' and leaves the consumer to arrange for the work to be completed by someone else. In these circumstances, the question may arise whether the builder who is in breach of contract is entitled to restitution in respect of the work he has done up to the date of breach. Although there is no rule against restitution in such cases, it is rare that a remedy will be given. In *Sumpter v Hedges* [1898] 1 QB 673 a builder who abandoned a contract for the construction of a house because he became insolvent was unable to claim for the *work* he had performed, as there was no free acceptance of the partial performance. However, a claim was allowed in respect of the cost of the materials supplied and used in the course of construction. What was important was that the contractual obligation of the builder was regarded as entire in the sense that he was required to complete all the work contracted for, in which case he would receive a lump-sum payment at the end (see also chapter 8).

SIX

Product quality

6.1 THE ROLES OF CONTRACTUAL AND TORTIOUS PRINCIPLES

The issue of product quality is regarded as largely a matter falling within the province of the law of contract. If a product is not qualitatively up to standard, it is not worth as much as the consumer expected when he bought it. In other words, the type of loss suffered is economic loss and is not to be confused with personal injury to the consumer or damage to property other than the defective product itself. This does not mean that physical damage, such as personal injury suffered as a result of eating defective food or damage to property other than the defective product itself, are not recoverable heads of loss in an action for breach of contract. It has long been accepted that such physical losses are actionable since they may be regarded as consequential upon the defectiveness of the product itself, provided the damage is foreseeable. Accordingly, the retailer of goods becomes a guarantor of the quality and safety of the goods he sells. Thus in *Godley* v *Perry* [1960] 1 WLR 9, the retailer was liable for eye injuries caused to the child purchaser of a defective toy catapult. Similarly in *Wilson* v *Rickett Cockrell & Co. Ltd* [1954] 1 QB 598 the seller of a brand-name domestic fuel was liable for the damage caused to the plaintiff's house when the fuel was inadvertently mixed with an explosive detonator. Where a product suffers from defective quality, the consumer's principal remedies will lie against the retailer from whom he has bought the goods rather than against the manufacturer or producer of those goods. The reason for this is that, generally, there is unlikely to be a relationship of privity of contract between the consumer and the manufacturer, by virtue of the length of the chain of supply under which the producer supplies goods to a wholesaler who in turn supplies to the retailer (see chapter 4).

Exceptionally, the law of tort, in the form of the tort of negligence, may assist the consumer by allowing an action for economic loss. However, it would appear that there are very few circumstances in which the proximity required between the parties for the purposes of a successful negligence action will be found. Moreover, there appears to be a general policy at House of Lords level that the issue of consumer protection is a matter best dealt with by Parliament rather than by the courts (*D & F Estates Ltd* v *Church Commissioners for England* [1989] AC 177, 208 per Lord Bridge of Harwich; *Murphy* v *Brentwood District Council* [1991] 1 AC 398, 472 per Lord Keith of Kinkel and see chapter 5). Accordingly, any consumer right to a quality guarantee from producers is more likely to come from legislative intervention, either at a domestic level or on a pan-European scale, than through developments in the courts (see European Commission, *Green Paper on Guarantees for Consumer Goods and After-Sales Service* (COM (93) 509) discussed below).

6.2 CONTRACTS OF SALE AND RELATED TRANSACTIONS

Given that the principal means by which a consumer may obtain redress for defects in the quality of the goods he or she acquires will be under the law of contract, it is necessary to consider the different varieties of contract under which goods are supplied. In many instances, the contract will be one of sale within the meaning of the Sale of Goods Act 1979, s. 2. However, there are a number of other types of contract which involve the ultimate transfer of ownership or possession in goods which also require the goods supplied to reach acceptable levels of quality.

The Sale of Goods Act 1979 implies terms into a contract for the sale of goods, which favour the purchaser. However, until 1973 it was not entirely clear whether these terms, relating to title to sell (s. 12), description (s. 13), satisfactory quality (s. 14(2)) and fitness for purpose (s. 14(3)), also applied to analogous contracts in which property in, or possession of goods passed to a consumer. Clearly some of these implied terms would not translate directly to all contracts for the supply of goods, since not all such contracts involve the transfer of ownership. But a consumer of goods supplied under a contract of hire or a contract for work and materials is just as likely to expect the goods supplied to reach reasonable standards of quality as the consumer who purchases the goods outright.

6.2.1 Transfer of property

The Sale of Goods Act 1979, s. 2(1), defines a contract for the sale of goods as one under which 'the seller transfers or agrees to transfer property in goods to the buyer for a money consideration called the price'. Because of this definition, any contract for the supply of goods which does not have as its principal object the transfer of ownership in goods will not fall within the 1979 Act.

If a contract involves the transfer of possession, but not ownership in goods, as in the case of contracts of bailment, the contract falls outside the scope of the Sale of Goods Act. Thus contracts of hire clearly fall outside the scope of the Sale of Goods Act.

Since the primary purpose of a contract for the sale of goods is the facilitation of the transfer of property in those goods, if the contract serves some other predominant purpose, it is likely that the contract falls outside the scope of the Sale of Goods Act. A contract of hire purchase which confers on the consumer an *option* to purchase as opposed to an *obligation* to purchase, is not a contract for the sale of goods.

Contracts for work and materials or skill and labour are not sale of goods contracts for the reason that the substance of the contract is the exercise of skill rather than the ancillary transfer of ownership in a material article. The relevant test to apply in order to distinguish between these two types of contract was established in *Robinson* v *Graves* [1935] 1 KB 579 in which Greer LJ said (at p. 587):

> If you find . . . that the substance of the contract was the production of something to be sold . . . then that is a sale of goods. But if the substance of the contract, on the other hand, is that skill and labour have to be exercised for the production of the article and that it is only ancillary to that that there will pass from the artist to his client or customer some materials in addition to the skill involved in the production of the portrait, that does not make any difference to the result, because the substance of the contract is the skill and experience of the artist in producing the picture.

The difficulty with the distinction between contracts of sale and contracts for work and materials lies in identifying the 'substance of the contract'. While this test is easy to state, it is much more difficult to apply in practice, especially at the borderline. On the one hand, there are contracts in which the substance is plainly the skill of the performer, such as a contract for the painting of a portrait (ibid.). However, it should be observed that in this particular example, property passes in the finished product, that is, the painting, rather than the materials used in composing it. At the other end of the scale, it has been held in *Lee* v *Griffin* (1861) 1 B & S 272 that a contract to manufacture, supply and fit a set of dentures was a contract for the sale of goods. The reasoning by which this conclusion was reached, however, is difficult to reconcile with the later decision in *Robinson* v *Graves*, since the view was expressed that virtually any contract can be classified as one of sale if its result is the transfer of ownership in a chattel. Moreover, it was observed that it would only be in cases where the thing transferred cannot be regarded as the subject of a sale that the contract would be one for skill and labour (*Lee* v *Griffin* (1861) 1 B & S 272, 278). Thus a contract under which a lawyer was engaged to prepare a deed would be one for the skill of the lawyer rather than one for the sale of goods, since the paper on which the deed was written would be difficult to regard as the proper subject of a contract of sale.

Applying these tests to a typical consumer contract, under which a plumber agrees to supply and fit a bathroom suite, it can be seen that there are two elements to the contract, namely a supply of goods and a supply of services in the form of the skill of the plumber. Under the *Robinson* v *Graves* test, if the value of the service exceeds the value of the goods supplied, it might be said that the contract was substantially one for the supply of a service. However under the test in *Lee* v *Griffin* it is likely that the contract would be regarded as one for the sale of goods. What this illustrates is that the substance of the contract test assumes that it is possible to distinguish between the supply of goods element and the exercise of skill — a distinction which is not always easy to make. Nonetheless the substance of the contract test operates on the basis that the contract is either one or the other, not a combination of both. Where the distinction becomes particularly relevant is when it comes to decide whether the contract is one for the supply of goods under which the supplier is strictly liable for the quality of the goods he supplies or whether the contract is one for the supply of a service, under which, generally, the supplier is liable only on proof that he has failed to exercise reasonable care in the performance of the service contracted for (see further chapter 8).

6.2.2   Money consideration

The requirement in the Sale of Goods Act 1979, s. 2, that there should be a money consideration also serves to distinguish other types of contract from a contract of sale. For example, it appears that a supply of 'free' goods as part of a sales promotion exercise does not amount to a sale of those goods. Thus in *Esso Petroleum Co. Ltd* v *Commissioners of Customs & Excise* [1976] 1 All ER 117, for the purposes of purchase tax legislation (the predecessor of the modern value added tax) it was considered that Esso had not entered into a contract of sale where they gave away to any customer who purchased four gallons of petrol a free 'World Cup coin'. Although there was a sale of fuel, there was merely a collateral contract to supply the coins, the consideration for which was not the payment of money, but the agreement of the customer to enter into the contract for the sale of the petrol. Unfortunately, this decision may be seen to conflict with the approach adopted in relation to the lottery laws (see chapter 20). Where a consumer is allowed to enter a competition only by virtue of having purchased an article on which the competition entry form is printed, the consumer has paid for the chance of gain as well as the goods on which the form is printed (*Taylor* v *Smetten* (1883) 11 QBD 207).

Since the consideration in a contract for the sale of goods must be in monetary form, it follows that the exchange of material articles under a contract of barter (see *Harrison* v *Luke* (1845) 14 M & W 139) or an exchange of goods for trading stamps will not be classified as contracts for the sale of goods. However, merely because there is an element of exchange of material articles in a particular transaction does not prevent the contract from being one for the sale of goods if some money, no matter how little, is part of the price. Thus in a very common consumer transaction whereby the consumer trades in a used car for a new vehicle, there may be a contract for the sale of goods, provided the difference in value between the two vehicles is paid in monetary form. In *Aldridge* v *Johnson* (1857) 7 El & Bl 885 it was considered that there was a contract of sale where 32 bullocks valued at £192 were exchanged for 100 quarters of barley, valued at £215, on condition that the difference in value was made up by a cash payment.

The facts of such transactions may require close scrutiny, since it is possible to construe this type of arrangement as involving two reciprocal contracts of sale under which there is a set-off of prices, which is what the court in *Aldridge* v *Johnson* appears to have done. On this analysis, both contracts are contracts of sale, each involving a monetary value attributable to the goods sold. But it is equally possible that there may be just one contract for the supply of the principal goods under which the consideration is the list price of those goods, subject to a condition that if the exchanged goods are delivered, an allowance in cash terms will be given (see, e.g., *Dawson (Clapham) Ltd* v *Duttfield* [1936] 2 All ER 232). On this last construction, property in the traded-in goods will not pass until they have been delivered. Moreover, the consideration for that part of the transaction can be viewed as the partial release of a debt, in which case, it should not be properly regarded as a contract for the sale of goods, but rather as one for the supply of goods, now falling within the provisions of the Supply of Goods and Services Act 1982.

6.2.3 Diminishing importance of the distinction between contracts of sale and other contracts

Terms identical to those which apply to sale of goods contracts are implied in contracts of hire purchase by virtue of the provisions of the Supply of Goods (Implied Terms) Act 1973, ss. 8 to 11, and in trading stamp transactions by virtue of the Trading Stamps Act 1964, s. 4. In the case of other contracts involving the transfer of ownership or possession of goods, it was not until the Supply of Goods and Services Act 1982, ss. 2 to 5, that it was made clear in statutory form that similar implied terms also formed part of a contract for work and materials and any other contract involving the transfer of ownership or possession of goods. If the contract is one of hire, different considerations apply since in a contract of hire there is no intention that ownership of the goods should ever be transferred. Accordingly, a modified version of the terms implied in a sale of goods contract apply by virtue of the Supply of Goods and Services Act 1982, ss. 6 to 10.

Although there is little difference in the content of the statutory implied terms applicable to different types of contract for the supply of goods, there are important differences between the contracts in other respects. For example, it has been seen already that so far as the issue of acceptance of the goods is concerned, a more favourable approach can be adopted in determining whether a consumer may still terminate his contractual obligations where he is required to pay instalments under a credit agreement rather than pay the price outright as is normally the case in consumer contracts for the sale of goods (see chapter 4). Moreover, the detailed framework for other aspects of the contract set out in the Sale of Goods Act 1979 applies only to sale of goods contracts. Accordingly, resort will have to be had to common law rules on the issues of transfer of ownership and risk and the matter of remedies if the contract is not classified as one for the sale of goods.

6.3 STATUTORY IMPLIED TERMS ABOUT DESCRIPTION, QUALITY AND FITNESS

In a contract for the supply of goods, there are a number of implied terms which relate directly to the issue of product quality. These include an implied term that the goods supplied will comply with any description which has been given of the goods by the seller, an implied term that the goods will be of satisfactory quality and a term to the effect that the goods supplied will be fit for the particular purpose for which they are intended to be used.

6.3.1 Status of the implied terms

It will be seen that in contracts for the supply of services governed by the Supply of Goods and Services Act 1982 (see chapter 8), the implied terms are not classified as conditions or warranties, with the result that the court should be able to apply the 'innominate terms' doctrine in deciding how serious is a particular breach of a term and what remedial consequences should flow from the breach (see chapter 4). In contrast in contracts of sale, instalment credit contracts and other contracts for the supply of goods the implied terms are referred to as conditions of the contract, with the result that breach will ordinarily allow the consumer to reject the goods and demand return of the price. An exception to this can be found in relation to the implied warranty that the consumer will enjoy quiet possession of the goods after sale and that the goods will be free from encumbrances (see Sale of Goods Act 1979, s. 12(2); Sale of Goods (Implied Terms) Act 1973, s. 8(1)(b); Supply of Goods and Services Act 1982, ss. 2(2) and 7(2)). Breach of this last term will allow nothing more than an action for damages.

6.3.2 Correspondence with a description

The Sale of Goods Act 1979, s. 13(1) (see also Sale of Goods (Implied Terms) Act 1973, s. 9(1); Supply of Goods and Services Act 1982, ss. 3(2) and 8(2)), provides that in a contract for the sale of goods by description, there is an implied condition that the goods will correspond with that description. Unlike the provisions relating to quality and fitness, considered below, s. 13 is not confined to sellers acting in the course of a business, but also covers private sales, which is useful to consumer purchasers in so far as the implied term about description also covers statements relating to the quality of the goods.

The implied term about description covers statements about both quantity and quality. So far as quantitative matters are concerned, if the buyer orders goods of a certain size or gauge or orders a specific quantity of goods and the seller fails to comply with the buyer's requirements, there would appear to be a breach of s. 13, subject to the operation of the principle *de minimis non curat lex*. In the past, the requirement that the seller should deliver the right amount seems to have been construed very strictly in favour of the buyer (see *Arcos Ltd* v *E.A. Ronaasen & Son* [1933] AC 470; *Re Moore & Co. Ltd and Landauer & Co. Ltd* [1921] 2 KB 519 and Sale of Goods Act 1979, s. 30), although for reasons considered below, this may cease to be the case in the future.

6.3.2.1 Meaning of sale by description The phrase 'sale by description' covers a wide range of transactions. It will cover transactions in which the buyer does not see the goods but relies on a written or oral description of the thing ordered, as in the case of mail order transactions. Likewise it will apply where a consumer orders something yet to be made or where the goods are stored in bulk and sold in small quantities, as in the case of draught beer sold in a public house.

It is even possible for a sale to be by description where the consumer has seen the goods before purchase (Sale of Goods Act 1979, s. 13(3)). Thus in a typical supermarket transaction where the consumer selects pre-packed goods from a shelf or freezer cabinet it is unlikely that the precise subject matter of the contract can be examined there and then. The effect of s. 13(3) is that the sale is still one by description even though the buyer has made a personal selection from the goods exposed for sale. Accordingly, if the goods do not correspond with the description on the packaging, there is a potential action under s. 13, provided the goods were sold in accordance with that description.

Even where the goods are specific, in the sense that they are identified at the time of the contract, there are cases which suggest that the sale may be made by description where the goods are sold under a descriptive label. Thus, if a consumer orders 'woollen undergarments' or a 'hot-water bottle', the sale is by description (*Grant* v *Australian Knitting Mills Ltd* [1936] AC 85, 100 per Lord Wright). Even the sale of a second-hand motor car has been held to be a sale by description where the buyer has relied on a document which describes what is purchased (*Beale* v *Taylor* [1967] 1 WLR 1193). If these last two examples are correctly decided, it would seem to follow that there are not many transactions which cannot be regarded as sales by description. It has been suggested that, provided there is some sort of descriptive label on goods supplied in a supermarket, the sale will be by description, but if the consumer buys unlabelled fruit or vegetables, which he selects himself from a retailer's display and no assistance is given by the retailer, the sale will not be by description (Harvey and Parry, *Law of Consumer Protection and Fair Trading*, 4th ed. (1992), p. 83). Likewise, it would appear that there is no sale by description where the goods supplied are unique and are purchased on a 'take it or leave it basis' (see *Smith* v *Lazarus* (1981) (unreported)). Similarly, if it is clear that the buyer places no reliance, at all, on the seller's description, there will be no sale by description (*Harlingdon & Leinster Enterprises Ltd* v *Christopher Hull Fine Art Ltd* [1990] 1 All ER 737).

Cases like *Beale* v *Taylor* and *Grant* v *Australian Knitting Mills Ltd* need to be considered in their historical context, and it may be that the apparent generosity of the courts is simply an accident of history. Initially, the terms implied at common law were confined to cases in which the goods sold were unascertained, generic or future goods, in which case they had to correspond with their description. If the buyer required the goods to reach any particular standard of quality, that was a matter left to the express terms of the contract and if such a term was taken to form part of the contract, it was generally only a warranty, giving rise to an action for damages only. However, the Sale of Goods Act 1893 categorised virtually all the implied terms as conditions of the contract. But at this stage, the implied term about merchantability (replaced in 1994 by the present requirement of satisfactory quality) only applied where the goods were sold by description. The Supply of Goods (Implied Terms) Act 1973 removed the requirement of sale by description in relation to the implied term of merchantability, but by this stage, the courts had already developed a very broad definition of what was a sale by description with a view to protecting the purchaser where goods were defective in quality. In the light of this, some of the pre-1973 decisions affecting s. 13 may need to be treated with some suspicion as they were almost certainly based on a pragmatic judicial approach intended to provide the buyer with a remedy where the implied term of merchantability was inapplicable and where no remedy in damages for misrepresentation was available.

Viewed in this light, the decision in *Grant* v *Australian Knitting Mills Ltd* — an overtly consumer-protectionist decision — might possibly be regarded with some suspicion as an authority on the proper interpretation of s. 13 of the 1979 Act, since it is primarily concerned with the implied terms as to quality and description. Moreover, it was a decision reached at a time when the applicability of the implied term about merchantable quality was dependent upon the goods being sold in accordance with their description. It does not necessarily follow from this that the 'identification test' now applied to s. 13 would be complied with should the same facts be considered in a court today.

The other important accident of history concerns the question of damages for misrepresentation, which only became generally available as of right in the case of a negligent misrepresentation after the enactment of the Misrepresentation Act 1967. In *Beale* v *Taylor* [1967] 1 WLR 1193, the seller sold privately, with the result that there was no available action for breach of s. 14 which applies only where a seller sells in the course of a business. Moreover, at the time the case was decided, damages for misrepresentation would only have been available had the misrepresentation been made fraudulently. As a result, the innocent buyer would have been left without a remedy unless it was possible to invoke s. 13. But to do this involved a certain amount of manipulation of the common law understanding of the difference between terms of the contract and mere representations (see also chapter 4).

6.3.2.2 Should matters of description be the subject of an implied term? By designating s. 13 as an implied term, Parliament has treated as a legally imposed obligation something which may go to the root of the agreement between the parties. As such, matters relating to the description of the thing supplied should be treated as express terms of the contract instead (cf. Uniform Commercial Code art. 2–313(1)(b)).

If a person fails to supply the very thing he has contracted to supply, the breach goes to the root of the contract. Yet if the obligations in s. 13 are contained in implied terms, but for the provisions of the Unfair Contract Terms Act 1977, ss. 6(2) and 7(2), the seller might be able to exclude liability for failing to supply the thing contracted for. At common law, the courts have treated the obligation imposed by s. 13 as fundamental and have refused to allow it to be easily defeated by an exclusion clause (see *Vigers Bros* v *Sanderson Bros* [1901] 1 KB 608).

If the supplier has failed to make his intentions entirely clear, the exclusion clause will be construed *contra proferentem*. In determining the extent to which a supplier can exclude or limit liability for breach of a term describing the thing sold, it is necessary to distinguish between specific and unascertained goods. In the case of specific goods, the consumer is aware of the attributes of the thing he buys, but in the case of unascertained goods, the consumer must rely on the supplier's description, and so a purported exclusion of liability is less likely to be successful as it would render the subject matter of the contract uncertain. It follows from this that where the goods sold are specific and the supplier stipulates that they are purchased as seen, even though there may be a supply by description, the exclusion of liability may still be effective, provided it satisfies the Unfair Contract Terms Act 1977 test of reasonableness (*Cavendish-Woodhouse Ltd* v *Manley* (1984) 82 LGR 376; *Hughes* v *Hall* [1981] RTR 430). Where the goods are unascertained, the supplier cannot exclude liability in respect of a breach which relates to the identity of the thing sold, but he may be able to exclude liability for trivial breaches of contract which are not covered by the *de minimis* principle.

6.3.2.3 Status of descriptive statements Not every descriptive word will take effect as a term of the contract. There are some descriptive words which have no legal effect at all (see *Reardon Smith Line Ltd* v *Hansen-Tangen* [1976] 1 WLR 989) and others which take effect as misrepresentations. In some instances the statement will be a term of the contract, but will not amount to a condition, because the court does not view the consequences of its breach particularly seriously. However, for the purposes of consumer contracts, it is not open to the court to examine the seriousness of breach in relation to the implied terms as to description, quality and fitness. Despite the introduction of a judicial discretion to examine the seriousness of a breach of contract in these respects in the Sale of Goods Act 1979, s. 15A(1), for the purposes of commercial contracts, it is clear that this discretion does not extend to consumer contracts, with the result that a breach of s. 13 will still be regarded as a breach of condition in such cases (see also chapter 4 and *Ashington Piggeries Ltd* v *Christopher Hill Ltd* [1972] AC 441, 503 per Lord Diplock). However, there is no reason why the innominate terms doctrine cannot apply to an express term of a consumer contract.

Where a descriptive statement is made, it is necessary to determine whether it is a term of the contract or a representation. A literal reading of s. 13 would suggest that any descriptive statement may be the subject of the implied term in s. 13, but this is clearly not the case, and some descriptive statements will take effect as representations only (see *Oscar Chess Ltd* v *Williams* [1957] 1 WLR 370 and see also chapter 4). However, there are also cases which appear to have ignored the common law distinction and applied s. 13 where the rule on representations ought to have been applied. In *Beale* v *Taylor* [1967] 1 WLR 1193 the defendant advertised his car for sale as a 'Herald convertible, white, 1961'. The car was in fact an amalgam of parts from two different cars which had been welded together. Part of the car was from a 1961 model but the rest was not. It was held that the words '1961 Herald' formed part of the description of the car. However, the statement could have been treated as an external inducement to enter the contract and not as a term as in *Oscar Chess Ltd* v *Williams* [1957] 1 WLR 370. Perhaps the difference lies in the fact that *Beale* v *Taylor* involved a statement by a seller and the courts tend to construe statements by sellers as terms of the contract, whereas *Oscar Chess Ltd* v *Williams* involved a statement by a consumer to a trade purchaser. It may also have been relevant that *Beale* v *Taylor* was based on the law which applied before the Misrepresentation Act 1967 came into force, and treating a statement as a term of the contract was one way of ensuring that the buyer was compensated for what was essentially a qualitative defect. But the same can also be said of *Oscar Chess Ltd* v *Williams*.

What seems to have persuaded the court in *Beale* v *Taylor* that the statement was a term of the contract was that the buyer had come along to see the car which had been advertised and that it was only on having seen a car which appeared to correspond with the advertisement that the buyer made his offer to purchase ([1967] 1 WLR 1193, 1197 per Sellers LJ).

In order to amount to a contractual description, the words have to identify the goods supplied (*Ashington Piggeries Ltd* v *Christopher Hill Ltd* [1972] AC 441, 503–4 per Lord Diplock). The test to apply is to ask whether the buyer has got what he bargained for according to the standards of the relevant market (ibid. 489 per Lord Wilberforce). The problem this test creates is that it can result in apparently contradictory decisions presumably because the standards of different markets will vary. Thus a mixture of hemp and rape oil did not satisfy the description 'foreign refined rape oil' (*Nicol* v *Godts* (1854) 10 Ex 191), but herring meal contaminated by a toxin generated by an internal chemical reaction can still be described as herring meal (*Ashington Piggeries Ltd* v *Christopher Hill Ltd* [1972] AC 441).

In order for words to identify the goods in question, it is necessary that the words identify an essential part of the description of the goods. Thus words which merely say where goods are to be found are not sufficient to amount to words of description (*Reardon Smith Line Ltd* v *Hansen-Tangen* [1976] 1 WLR 989), but words which identify the very nature of the thing the consumer buys will form part of the description. Thus if the buyer purchases 'a silk scarf', the seller cannot get away with supplying one made of an artificial silk substitute, because the words identify a substantial ingredient in the goods.

6.3.2.4 Importance of reliance

A crucial factor in determining whether a particular statement is a descriptive term or not is whether it is intended by the parties to be an essential term of the contract. In determining whether the parties do intend a particular statement to be an essential term, the identification test in *Ashington Piggeries Ltd* v *Christopher Hill Ltd* [1972] AC 441 shows that the statement must be highly influential on the mind of the buyer. This requirement of a high degree of influence has been interpreted subsequently to mean that the presence or absence of reliance on the statement will be an important factor (*Harlingdon & Leinster Enterprises Ltd* v *Christopher Hull Fine Art Ltd* [1990] 1 All ER 737). However, strictly, this insistence upon an element of reliance is at odds with the general rule that if a statement is a condition of the contract, breach of the condition, no matter how slight, should give rise to a right to reject the goods supplied. However, the requirement of reliance was seen as crucial by a majority of the Court of Appeal in *Harlingdon & Leinster Enterprises Ltd* v *Christopher Hull Fine Art Ltd* in which the buyer was an art dealer who had inspected a painting which was stated by the sellers (also art dealers) in their auction catalogue to be by Gabriele Münter, a German expressionist artist. An important factor was that the sellers, although dealers, had no specific expertise in the field of German expressionist art, but the buyers were known to have such an interest. Some time after purchase, the painting was discovered to be a forgery and the question arose as to whether the descriptive statement disclosed an action for breach of the condition implied by s. 13. In the event, it was held that there was no such breach since it could not be said that the statement in the catalogue had been relied upon by the plaintiffs.

It was considered that in the absence of reliance by the buyer, the descriptive statement would not be incorporated into the contract (ibid. 744 per Nourse LJ). Alternatively, it was also stated that the presence or absence of reliance on the part of the buyer was a powerful indication of the incorporation of the description as a term of the contract (ibid. 752 per Slade LJ). In contrast, Stuart-Smith LJ (dissenting) took the view that a pre-contractual statement would form part of the description of the goods sold unless its effect was expressly negatived prior to the formation of the contract (ibid. 748). The importance of reliance is also underlined by contrasting *Oscar Chess Ltd* v *Williams* [1957] 1 WLR 370 and *Beale* v *Taylor* [1967] 1 WLR 1193. It can be said that it was totally unreasonable for a trader with expert knowledge of motor vehicles to rely on the statement of the consumer wishing to trade in his own vehicle in *Oscar Chess Ltd* v *Williams*. However, it was probably reasonable for the buyer to rely on the seller's statement in *Beale* v *Taylor* as he was not buying just a car, but a car of a particular type identified by the seller's description of it in a newspaper advertisement.

6.3.3 Satisfactory quality

The Sale of Goods Act 1979, s. 14(2) (see also Sale of Goods (Implied Terms) Act 1973, s. 10(2); Supply of Goods and Services Act 1982, ss. 4(2) and (3) and 9(2) and (3)), provides that where the seller sells goods in the course of a business there is an implied condition that the goods supplied will be of satisfactory quality. In historical terms, this is only a very recent introduction in that the requirement of satisfactory quality supplanted the original requirement of merchantable quality which had survived in statutory form since 1893 until its replacement following the enactment of the Sale and Supply of Goods Act 1994, the provisions of which took effect from early 1995. In many respects the new requirement of satisfactory quality differs little from the old requirement of merchantable quality, but the replacement of the old standard does serve to divorce English law from over a hundred years of jurisprudence on the meaning of merchantability.

In one sense, the replacement of the former requirement of merchantability is understandable since the very sound of the word merchantable suggests that its birth lay in the field of commercial transactions. Moreover, the remedies associated with the requirement of merchantability also carried with them a purely commercial flavour in that all a buyer could do was to claim damages or reject the goods outright, claiming back the purchase price paid rather than being able to seek a cure or ask for a replacement at the price paid. However, the twentieth century has seen a substantial increase in the buying power of consumers, which brought with it an increased use of the implied term of merchantability as a tool of consumer protection, to which it was not always adequately suited.

It was not surprising that there was immense pressure from the consumer lobby to move away from the requirement of merchantability towards something more suited to the needs of the modern consumer. Initially, this was done through piecemeal changes to the requirement of merchantability consisting of a statutory definition of merchantable quality (Supply of Goods (Implied Terms) Act 1973, subsequently re-enacted as Sale of Goods Act 1979, s. 14(6)) followed by a consolidating Sale of Goods Act of 1979. But potentially the greatest step forward was a Law Commission Report which recommended the introduction of a new statutory standard of acceptable quality (Law Com No. 160 (Cm 137, 1987)). However, these recommendations did not make their way to the statute book until late 1994 and eventually took effect in early 1995 with the introduction of the phrase 'satisfactory quality' instead of the Law Commission's preferred phrase, 'acceptable quality'.

6.3.3.1 Satisfactory quality and *caveat emptor* One of the basic tenets of nineteenth-century sale of goods law was the maxim *caveat emptor* or 'let the buyer beware'. However, the practical effect of the implied term about merchantability initially, and now the new requirement of satisfactory quality, has been to erode the importance of the principle that the buyer should take care of his own interests, at least in consumer transactions. However, it should not be forgotten that the Sale of Goods Act 1979 is a code intended to deal not just with consumers, but also commercial contracting parties, to whom the *caveat emptor* doctrine has a much greater significance. The opening words of s. 14(1) of the 1979 Act consist of a restatement of the principle that, except as provided for in that Act and any other enactment, there is no other implied term concerning the quality or fitness of goods supplied under a contract of sale. The importance of this is that since the implied term in s. 14 applies only where the seller sells in the course of a business, there is no statutory requirement of quality or fitness where the seller sells privately (see *Beale* v *Taylor* [1967] 1 WLR 1193). However, this will not prevent a commercial agent from being subject to the requirements of quality and fitness where the person he represents is a private seller and the buyer is unaware of this fact. Moreover, the undisclosed seller will also be liable for breach of the implied terms, even if acting in a private capacity (Sale of Goods Act 1979, s. 14(5), and see *Boyter* v *Thomson* [1995] 3 All ER 135). This is particularly important in the growth in the number of second-hand car dealers who regularly advertise in local newspapers suggesting that they can sell a privately owned car more quickly than could the owner himself, since if the dealer fails to make it clear to customers that he is acting on behalf of a private seller, both the seller and the dealer, as agent, will be caught by s. 14(5).

6.3.3.2 The pre-1994 law As has been indicated above, the modern requirement of satisfactory quality replaces the previous requirement of merchantable quality. For the purposes of the old law, the old s. 14(2) of the Sale of Goods Act 1979 provided that there was an implied condition of merchantable quality where the goods supplied under the contract were sold in the course of a business (for the meaning of this phrase, see chapter 1), except that there was no such condition (a) as regards defects specifically drawn to the buyer's attention before the contract was made and (b) where there were patent defects in goods which the buyer had examined before the contract was entered into.

The main problem under the old law was to identify the circumstances in which goods could be said to be unmerchantable, especially in the light of the fact that there was no statutory definition of merchantability until 1973. By virtue of the lack of definition, it is not surprising that there grew up a substantial body of case law on the subject. These judicial definitions fell broadly into two camps. On the one hand goods could be said to be merchantable if they were 'usable', but under another definition, the focus was upon 'acceptability'.

The judicial test of 'usability' which commended itself to a minority of the House of Lords in *Henry Kendall & Sons* v *William Lillico & Sons Ltd* [1969] 2 AC 31 required the court to consider whether the goods could be used for at least one of the purposes for which goods of that kind could commonly be used. The emphasis of this approach was more appropriate for the purposes of commercial transactions since it raised the general question whether the goods as supplied were fit for resale in the condition in which they were delivered to the buyer. For example in *Henry Kendall & Sons* v *William Lillico & Sons Ltd* Lord Reid suggested that unmerchantable meant:

> that the goods in the form in which they were tendered were of no use for any purpose for which goods which complied with the description under which these goods were sold would normally be used, and hence were not saleable under that description.

The problem with a usability test is that consumer purchasers do not purchase goods for the purposes of resale and therefore a different test might be appropriate in such circumstances. In *Henry Kendall & Sons* v *William Lillico & Sons Ltd* an alternative test employed was that of acceptability, which required the court to consider whether the goods were in such a state that a buyer fully acquainted with all relevant facts would buy them without substantial abatement in the price which could be obtained for such goods in reasonable condition. Such a test had been propounded in *Australian Knitting Mills Ltd* v *Grant* (1933) 50 CLR 387, 418 per Dixon J, where it was said that goods:

should be in such an actual state that a buyer fully acquainted with the facts and, therefore, knowing what hidden defects exist and not being limited to their apparent condition would buy them without abatement of the price obtainable for such goods if in reasonably sound order and condition and without special terms.

The later statutory definition of merchantable quality which became consolidated in the Sale of Goods Act 1979 s. 14(6) tended to concentrate more on the question of usability rather than acceptability, describing goods as being of merchantable quality:

if they are as fit for the purpose or purposes for which goods of that kind are commonly bought as it is reasonable to expect having regard to any description applied to them, the price (if relevant) and all the other relevant circumstances.

The major drawback with such a definition is that by concentrating on the functionality of the goods sold, many matters of concern to consumers could be ignored in deciding whether goods were merchantable or not. What must be remembered is that a consumer does not buy goods for the purposes of resale, he buys for use and enjoyment.

Some of the concerns of consumers later came to be recognised by the Court of Appeal in *Rogers* v *Parish (Scarborough) Ltd* [1987] QB 933, in which the buyer had purchased a new Range Rover, which suffered from a number of minor defects which taken together made driving the vehicle a most unenjoyable experience. In this context, Mustill LJ observed that:

. . . the purpose for which 'goods of that kind' are commonly bought . . . would include in respect of any passenger vehicle not merely the buyer's purpose of driving the car from one place to another but of doing so with the appropriate degree of comfort, ease of handling and reliability and, one might add, of pride in the vehicle's outward and interior appearance.

Undoubtedly, this type of approach went some way towards adapting the 1973 definition of merchantable quality as an instrument of consumer protection, but there were always strains as between the rival judicial tests of merchantability which never really went away. The judgments in *Rogers* v *Parish (Scarborough) Ltd* suggested that the statutory definition of merchantability heralded a new era in which the courts could 'wipe the slate clean' and redefine merchantability in the light of the statutory definition, ignoring any previous case law. In contrast, in *Aswan Engineering Establishment Co. Ltd* v *Lupdine Ltd* [1987] 1 WLR 1 it had been suggested (in the context of a purely commercial transaction) that the old case law still remained relevant since the statutory definition did no more than to place in statutory form a succinct distillation of the common law tests of merchantability.

Because of the uncertainties attached to the old definitions, it was eventually decided by the Law Commission (Law Com. No. 160 (Cm 137, 1987)) that it would be appropriate to adopt a test of acceptable quality so as to reflect the concerns of consumer purchasers. In fact Parliament chose not to adopt a test of acceptability, opting instead to set a standard of 'satisfactory quality'. Apparently, the reasoning which underlies the use of this alternative adjective is that many consumers may regard goods as unsatisfactory without wishing to reject them — in other words people are prepared to accept goods with which they are not wholly satisfied. Moreover, if the standard of acceptable quality had been adopted, this might have given rise to confusion since the concept of acceptance is closely related to the separate issue of whether a buyer may terminate his contractual performance obligations and elect to reject the goods delivered by the seller (see further chapter 4).

6.3.3.3 Application of the standard of satisfactory quality The new s. 14 of the Sale of Goods Act 1979 provides:

(2)   Where the seller sells goods in the course of a business, there is an implied term that the goods supplied under the contract are of satisfactory quality.

(2A)   For the purposes of this Act, goods are of satisfactory quality if they meet the standard that a reasonable person would regard as satisfactory, taking account of any description of the goods, the price (if relevant) and all the other relevant circumstances.

(2B)   For the purposes of this Act, the quality of goods includes their state and condition and the following (among others) are in appropriate cases aspects of the quality of goods—

(a)   fitness for all the purposes for which goods of the kind in question are commonly supplied,
(b)   appearance and finish,
(c)   freedom from minor defects,
(d)   safety, and
(e)   durability.

(2C)   The term implied by subsection (2) above does not extend to any matter making the quality of the goods unsatisfactory—

(a)   which is specifically drawn to the buyer's attention before the contract is made,
(b)   where the buyer examines the goods before the contract is made, which that examination ought to reveal, or
(c)   in the case of a contract for sale by sample, which would have been apparent on a reasonable examination of the sample.

It has been noted above that one of the difficulties associated with the 1973 statutory definition of merchantability was that the courts did not always find themselves able to divorce that definition from the earlier judicial definitions of merchantable quality, with the result that some of the problems of the old case law could quite easily permeate more contemporary considerations of the meaning of merchantability. With the introduction of the new standard of satisfactory quality, it is clear that the courts will now be able to approach the issue of product quality afresh and will not be bound by the old case law. However, it should also be observed that in many respects there is very little difference between merchantable quality and satisfactory quality, with the result that in defining satisfactory quality some help may be derived from the old case law. In particular, there are a number of common elements in the present law and that prior to 1994. For example, the implied term about satisfactory quality only applies where the seller sells goods in the course of a business, with the result that judicial interpretations of the meaning of that phrase will continue to have some importance (see chapter 1). Other similarities are considered below.

6.3.3.3.1 *Status of the implied term*   It was clear from the provisions of the old s. 14(2) that the term implied into contracts of sale was a condition. In contrast the new s. 14(2) initially refers to the requirement of satisfactory quality as simply a term of the contract. However, it is later provided in the new s. 14(6) and in the Sale and Supply of Goods Act 1994, sch. 2, para. 5, that in England and Wales this term is to be regarded as a condition. As a result of this, breach of the implied term will continue to allow rejection of the goods on the part of the consumer. Moreover, the introduction of a judicial discretion to consider the seriousness of the breach in determining whether the buyer should be allowed to reject the goods (Sale of Goods Act 1979, s. 15A) applies only to commercial transactions, with the result that in the case of a consumer purchase, the dissatisfied customer may still reject the goods even where the breach of s. 14 is apparently insignificant, but nonetheless sufficient to allow a reasonable person to regard the goods as being of unsatisfactory quality.

6.3.3.3.2 *Goods to which the implied term applies*   The requirement of satisfactory quality applies to 'the goods supplied under the contract'. This wording is identical to that used under the old law, and has been interpreted to mean that the condition applies to anything supplied pursuant to the contract. Thus anything supplied under the contract must satisfy the condition, with the result that 'free' goods supplied by way of a promotional offer will be subject to the requirement of satisfactory quality, although due to the absence of a money consideration, cases of this kind will not fall within the Sale of Goods Act 1979, but will be covered by the provisions of the Supply of Goods and Services Act 1982, s. 4 (see *Esso Petroleum Co. Ltd* v *Commissioners of Customs & Excise* [1976] 1 All ER 117).

It is also clear from the old case law that 'the goods supplied under the contract' will extend to cover the totality of the package supplied. Accordingly, it is not sufficient if the goods required by the consumer are in perfect condition, if the container in which they are supplied is dangerous and capable of causing injury to the consumer. If a consumer is injured by a defective bottle in which a soft drink is supplied, the overall package fails to meet the standard of satisfactory quality (*Geddling* v *Marsh* [1920] 1 KB 668). Similarly, the seller cannot avoid liability by claiming that impurities in goods supplied were not contracted for and therefore are not covered by the implied condition. Thus in *Wilson* v *Rickett Cockrell & Co. Ltd* [1954] 1 QB 598, the seller supplied a quantity of smokeless fuel which contained a detonator. It was not open to the seller to argue that the detonator was not contracted for and that, the detonator apart, the fuel supplied was of merchantable quality. The detonator was supplied pursuant to the contract and was covered by the words 'goods supplied under the contract'. It is also arguable that these words will cover defective instructions for use which render the goods supplied unfit for normal use. If the instructions are such that the goods cannot be used for the buyer's particular intended use there is a possibility that the goods fail to comply with the requirement of fitness for purpose under s. 14(3) (see *Wormell* v *R.H.M. Agriculture (East) Ltd* [1987] 3 All ER 75 and see also MacLeod (1981) 97 LQR 550). If the goods cannot be used for their normal purpose for the same reason, it would seem to follow that the defective instructions can also render the goods unmerchantable.

6.3.3.3.3 Circumstances in which the implied term is inapplicable The Sale of Goods Act 1979, s. 14(2C)(a), provides that the implied condition about satisfactory quality does not apply where the seller has specifically drawn the buyer's attention to defects in the goods prior to the making of the contract. Thus, if a seller points to defects in a second-hand car and the buyer purchases the vehicle knowing of these defects, he cannot later claim that those defects render the car unmerchantable (*Bartlett* v *Sidney Marcus Ltd* [1965] 1 WLR 1013).

Under s. 14(2C)(b) the condition of satisfactory quality is also inapplicable where the buyer has examined the goods and that examination ought to have revealed a patent defect in the goods. It is clear from the present wording of the Act that there must have been an examination, but if there is present an obvious defect, the buyer purchases subject to that defect. However, s. 14(2C)(b) will not affect the buyer in relation to latent defects, which by their nature are not reasonably discoverable on any examination. Accordingly, it has been held under the old law that the presence of arsenic in beer is not a defect of which the purchaser could be aware by means of any sort of reasonable examination (see *Wren* v *Holt* [1903] 1 KB 610).

It has become apparent that the wording of s. 14(2C)(b) is defective in one respect. In *R & B Customs Brokers Co. Ltd* v *United Dominions Trust Ltd* [1988] 1 All ER 847 the plaintiff bought a car on conditional sale, which was delivered immediately. Before the contract was legally concluded the plaintiff discovered a defect which the car dealer agreed to repair. Despite numerous attempts, the defect was not remedied and the plaintiff subsequently purported to reject the car. It was argued by the defendants that because the plaintiff took delivery of the car before the contract was made, he had had a chance to inspect it with the result that the condition of merchantable quality was inapplicable. In the event, the defendants were liable under s. 14(3) because the car was not fit for the particular purpose which the buyer had in mind, and the court did not express an opinion on the wording of what is now s. 14(2C)(b). However, if the defendant's argument is correct, the position of the consumer under a conditional sale agreement is unenviable.

One way in which the problem might be resolved is by resort to the inference of a collateral contract. If the supplier is told of a defect before the contract is made and he undertakes to repair it, he will be liable for a breach of a collateral undertaking if he fails to effect those repairs. In such a case, the finance company may also be liable for the supplier's breach of contract under the provisions of the Consumer Credit Act 1974, s. 56 (see chapters 4 and 11).

6.3.3.3.4 The standard of the reasonable person In defining satisfactory quality, s. 14(2A) of the Sale of Goods Act 1979 indicates that the test to be applied requires the goods to meet the standard which a reasonable person would regard as satisfactory, having regard to matters such as the description of the goods, the price and any other relevant circumstances. It is clear from this that satisfactory quality does not imply perfection, since the description of the goods and the price paid may indicate that the reasonably expected standard of quality may have been lowered. This reflects the variable standards which must, of necessity, be applied to quality standards. It will be seen in chapters 7 and 14 that it is possible to set minimum standards of safety, below which no producer may fall, but the same cannot be said of quality. What is an acceptable standard of quality depends on a number of variables, which is a matter clearly indicated in the old case law on merchantable quality and will continue to affect decisions in the future on the meaning of satisfactory quality. In this respect, it is unfortunate that the new standard of satisfactory quality divorces English law from the 100 years or so of jurisprudence concerning the meaning of merchantable quality and what that phrase means in a particular fact situation.

The definition of satisfactory quality implies that the goods should be reasonably acceptable, since what a reasonable person would regard as satisfactory is that which he would be prepared to accept. Accordingly, the standard that a reasonable person will regard as satisfactory will turn upon all the surrounding circumstances. Thus, merely because the goods delivered suffer from minor or cosmetic defects or are defective in their appearance or finish will not necessarily mean that the goods are unsatisfactory since s. 14(2A) makes it clear that these factors have to be considered alongside the description, price and other relevant circumstances, which taken together may indicate a satisfactory standard of quality. For example, it will be seen below that minced beef could be regarded as perfectly acceptable in qualitative terms despite the presence of a very high fat content if the sample is sold cheaply in comparison with higher-quality minced steak (see *Goldup* v *John Manson Ltd* [1981] 3 All ER 257 and see chapter 15). Similarly, a reasonable person would almost certainly expect a second-hand car to suffer from some minor defects, which is also implied by virtue of the fact that second-hand cars are sold more cheaply than their brand-new counterparts (see *Bartlett* v *Sidney Marcus Ltd* [1965] 1 WLR 1013). But, if the second-hand car is one which falls into the 'luxury' bracket, the higher price paid compared with other second-hand cars may indicate a slightly higher standard of quality (see *Shine* v *General Guarantee Corporation Ltd* [1988] 1 All ER 911).

A further factor to consider is that the standard of quality is based upon the expectations of a reasonable *person* as opposed to a reasonable *buyer*. Accordingly, it is arguable that the test should take on board not just the expectations of purchasers but also the reasonable expectations of retailers as well. From this it should follow that if a consumer unreasonably misuses a product in a manner which could not be expected by a reasonable retailer, the goods should ordinarily satisfy the requirement of quality set out in s. 14. Thus if a consumer buys pre-packed food which contains a clear set of instructions on storage and use, the failure by the consumer to adhere to those instructions ought to mean that the required standard of quality has been reached (see, e.g., *Heil* v *Hedges* [1951] 1 TLR 512 — failure to cook meat properly).

The reference to reasonableness relates to the quality of the goods not their acceptability. It may be the case that defects in goods are not sufficiently serious for a buyer to want to reject. For example, the buyer might choose to keep goods suffering from minor defects and seek to recover damages. The fact that the goods are 'acceptable' does not mean that there is no breach of s. 14(2) if the standard of quality is deemed to be unreasonable. It follows that if the buyer gets exactly what he ordered, there may still be a breach of s. 14(2) if the standard of quality remains unreasonable (see Adams, *Atiyah's Sale of Goods*, 9th ed. (1995), pp. 153–4).

6.3.3.3.5 Description The description applied to goods is a crucial factor, since it may either raise or lower the standard of quality expected of the goods sold. For example, if goods are sold as 'seconds' or under the description, 'one previous owner', there is a clear indication that a reasonable person's expectations of quality will be reduced. It is reasonable to expect second-hand goods to offer a lower standard of quality in most instances, although this does not mean that the standard of quality is reduced to absolute zero. A description can also raise the standard of quality expected. In *Rogers* v *Parish (Scarborough) Ltd* [1987] QB 933, Mustill LJ was of the opinion that the description of the car as a 'Range Rover' was sufficient to conjure up a particular set of expectations, since that type of car could be regarded as falling within the higher end of consumer vehicle purchases. In s. 14(2A), the word 'description' does not carry with it the connotations discussed above in relation to s. 13 of the Act. It is fairly clear from the case law applicable to the old s. 14 that the descriptive statement does not need to satisfy the identification test used in relation to s. 13. It would appear that any statement made by the seller, either orally or in writing, which may be taken as an indication of the expected standard of quality will suffice for these purposes. Thus information contained on food packaging and advertising material generally may suffice to raise the expected standard of quality of goods supplied to a consumer. However, the reasoning of the majority of the Court of Appeal in *Harlingdon & Leinster Enterprises Ltd* v *Christopher Hull Fine Art*

Ltd [1990] 1 All ER 737 was that if the action was not to succeed under s. 13, there was no likelihood of the plaintiff being allowed to circumvent that decision through an action under s. 14. However, the case involved a dispute between two professional art dealers and there may be a willingness to be more lenient in a purely consumer context when it comes to deciding what constitutes a relevant description for the purposes of s. 14.

6.3.3.3.6 State or condition Section 14(2B) of the Sale of Goods Act 1979 indicates that the quality of goods includes their state or condition, which is an indication that not just the functional aspects of goods should be taken into account. Accordingly, although the requirement of satisfactory quality will ordinarily relate to physical characteristics of the goods supplied, this is not exclusively so. For example, goods have been held to be unmerchantable because their legal state is such that they cannot be used as intended (*Niblett Ltd* v *Confectioners' Materials Co. Ltd* [1921] 3 KB 387; cf. *Sumner Permain & Co.* v *Webb & Co.* [1922] 1 KB 55) and there is no reason to suppose that the same approach will not also apply to the requirement of satisfactory quality.

The Court of Appeal was divided on the application of the requirement of merchantable quality to non-physical defects in *Harlingdon & Leinster Enterprises Ltd v Christopher Hull Fine Art Ltd* [1990] 1 All ER 737. Nourse LJ was of the opinion that a mistake as to authorship of a painting rendered it defective, but was not sufficient to make the painting unsaleable (ibid. 745). Accordingly, the painting was of merchantable quality. Slade LJ went even further, expressing the opinion that since the complaint related to the identity of the artist, s. 14 had no application (ibid. 753). However, Stuart-Smith LJ differed in his approach holding that the requirement of merchantable quality extended to factors other than the physical characteristics of the goods supplied. In particular, it was considered necessary to ask what was the description of the goods supplied, and if a painting is said to be by a particular artist, this is a factor relevant to the quality of the work of art (ibid. 750).

The requirement that the court should consider the state or condition of the goods also prevents the seller from arguing that provided certain steps are taken by the buyer, the goods might become perfectly acceptable. For example in *Grant* v *Australian Knitting Mills Ltd* [1936] AC 85, the seller sold woollen undergarments which were contaminated with sulphites used to bleach the cloth. The sulphites in the fabric combined with the perspiration produced by the wearer to create an acidic substance which resulted in the wearer suffering an attack of dermatitis. One of the arguments raised by the seller was that had the consumer washed the garment before wearing it, no harm would have been caused. However, since there was no indication on the packaging that this precaution ought to have been taken, it was held that the goods failed to reach the standard of merchantable quality. It is likely that the same result will obtain under the new law, since a consumer cannot be expected to take substandard goods in the expectation that he should carry out certain precautionary measures before use, unless this has been made abundantly clear in advance. Accordingly, the condition of the undergarments in *Grant* v *Australian Knitting Mills Ltd* was such that under the modern law, the goods would be regarded as being in an unsatisfactory state at the time of sale.

6.3.3.3.7 Price Section 14(2A) of the Sale of Goods Act 1979 expressly stipulates that the price paid for goods may be a relevant factor in determining whether they are of satisfactory quality. This was equally true of the old law regarding merchantable quality under the old s. 14(6). The effect of this is that the buyer is entitled to value for money (*Rogers* v *Parish (Scarborough) Ltd* [1987] QB 933; cf. *Harlingdon & Leinster Enterprises Ltd* v *Christopher Hull Fine Art Ltd* [1990] 1 All ER 737).

The price paid is also a relevant factor in relation to second-hand motor vehicles, since the older the car, the cheaper the buyer expects it to be. At the same time, if the car is second-hand, the buyer can presumably expect a lower standard of quality, although he can reasonably expect it to be roadworthy and perhaps more. If the buyer has paid a substantial price for an 'up-market' second-hand vehicle, he can expect it to do more than move from A to B and can expect it to satisfy his aesthetic requirements (*Shine* v *General Guarantee Corporation Ltd* [1988] 1 All ER 911; cf. *Business Applications Specialists Ltd* v *Nationwide Credit Corporation Ltd* [1988] RTR 332). It is important to emphasise that under s. 14(2A), price is only a determining factor, if relevant. For example, if the seller puts on an 'end of season' sale in which all goods put up for sale are new and not subject to any shop-soiling, it is arguable that the fact that they are sold at a reduced price in order to clear the shop before new lines are brought in should not in any way reflect upon the quality that the consumer can expect of the goods sold.

Conversely, a high price will normally be an objective indication of high quality, signifying to most reasonable people that the product is better than others priced more cheaply or has features which other similar goods do not possess and perhaps even an indication of reliability (see Howells, *Consumer Contract Legislation* (London: Blackstone Press, 1995), p. 14).

6.3.3.3.8 Fitness for all common purposes At common law, before the introduction of any statutory definitions of the required standard of quality, it was sufficient that the goods supplied were fit for *any* of the purposes for which goods of that kind were commonly used (*Henry Kendall & Sons* v *William Lillico & Sons Ltd* [1969] 2 AC 31; *B. S. Brown & Son Ltd* v *Craiks Ltd* [1970] 1 All ER 823). Perhaps more surprisingly, the same view was also taken after the introduction of a statutory definition of merchantable quality in the old s. 14(6) on the spurious grounds that the reference to 'purpose or purposes' in that provision was to allow for the fact that some goods might be of such a quality that they might be expected to reach higher standards than other similar goods sold at a lower price (*Aswan Engineering Co.* v *Lupdine Ltd* [1987] 1 WLR 1). However, under the requirement of satisfactory quality, it is clear that there has been an important change in the law in this respect since s. 14(2B)(a) now normally requires the goods to be fit for *all* of the purposes for which goods of that kind are commonly supplied.

While this appears, at first sight, to represent a substantial change in the law, it should be remembered that the factors listed in s. 14(2B) are, *in appropriate cases,* indicators of the required standard of quality. The mere fact that one of these elements is not complied with does not mean that the goods will be automatically regarded as being of unsatisfactory quality.

If a court holds that the purpose for which the goods are required is uncommon, the implied condition of satisfactory quality will not apply and the buyer will be required to show that he has informed the seller of the purpose to which he intends to put the goods so that s. 14(3) (considered below) may apply. However, where s. 14(3) is invoked, the buyer must show that he has relied on the seller's skill and judgment.

What is a 'common' purpose is difficult to define since the decision will depend on the context of each particular case. What is clear is that the goods supplied do not need to be fit for immediate use if it is clear that something has to be done to them in order to render them fit for use, e.g., food that has to be cooked or furniture sold in kit form which has to be assembled at home (cf. *Grant* v *Australian Knitting Mills Ltd* [1936] AC 85 considered above).

One difficulty which may arise from the requirement that goods should be fit for all common purposes is that if goods of a particular kind can be used for a number of different purposes, the price may differ according to which purpose is intended by the buyer. Suppose food can be used for both human and animal consumption and the buyer expressly purchases it cheaply for the purposes of feeding to his pets. It would be unreasonable to allow the buyer to reject the goods on the ground that they are unfit for human consumption. The price paid for the food would be some indication of the purpose for which the buyer required it, but under the proposed amendment the food might still be regarded as unsatisfactory. In such a case, it would be necessary for the court to treat food for human consumption and food for animal consumption as goods which are not of the same kind. However, one way in which the seller can avoid this particular problem is to inform the buyer that the goods in question are suited only for a limited number of uses, in which case the buyer may be taken to have purchased subject to those express reservations by virtue of s. 14(2C)(a).

6.3.3.3.9 Appearance and finish   Although appearance and finish and free-dom from minor defects (considered below) might appear to be closely related issues, the legislators have properly chosen to separate the two, since minor defects may relate to functional aspects of the goods sold, whereas appearance and finish relate simply to matters of cosmetic defectiveness. Cosmetic defects can be very serious, so as to render the goods sold almost unusable. For example, in a very early decision based on commercial use, the defendants sold a quantity of motor vehicle horns, which, at the time, were displayed prominently on the outside of the motor vehicles to which they were fitted. Because the majority of the consignment was very badly scratched, so that no reasonable car manufacturer would use them, the horns were considered to be unmerchantable (see *Jackson* v *Rotax Motor & Cycle Co. Ltd* [1910] 2 KB 937). In the same vein, some consumer goods may be unsatisfactory due to the presence of some cosmetic defect. Thus a pair of trousers which is badly stained to the extent that the stain cannot be removed, or a dining-room sideboard intended for public display which is so badly scratched as to be unacceptable may be regarded as goods which are not of satisfactory quality, despite the fact that the trousers can be worn and the sideboard will withstand the weight of the purchaser's plates.

6.3.3.3.10 Freedom from minor defects Section 14(2B)(c) of the Sale of Goods Act 1979 states that freedom from minor defects is an aspect of the quality of goods, which would appear to confirm the position in *Rogers* v *Parish (Scarborough) Ltd* [1987] QB 933. However, what is clear is that the presence or absence of minor defects is merely a factor to consider in determining whether goods reach the required standard of satisfactory quality. It would seem to follow that if goods suffer from minor defects, but are still reasonably satisfactory in quality, having regard to other factors, the seller will not be in breach of s. 14(2). Accordingly, it is also relevant to consider the defects in the goods in the light of the price paid and the description applied to the goods, with the result that some minor defects in second-hand or cheap goods may be matters which the consumer must put up with. Conversely, the higher the price paid, the more the consumer can expect from the goods he buys. Thus in *Rogers* v *Parish (Scarborough) Ltd* the buyer could expect a £16,000 Range Rover to offer the appropriate degree of comfort, ease of handling and reliability and to generate pride in the outward and inward appearance of the vehicle, but this was dependent on the market at which the car was aimed (*Rogers* v *Parish (Scarborough) Ltd* [1987] QB 933, 944 per Mustill LJ). Accordingly, defects in the engine, gearbox and body-work were sufficient to render the vehicle unmerchantable and there is no doubt that the car would also be regarded as being of unsatisfactory quality under the present law.

The approach adopted in *Rogers* v *Parish (Scarborough) Ltd* seems to be a departure from past thinking. Mustill LJ dismissed a test based upon whether the car was of a workable character, being able to start and be driven safely from one point to another (ibid.). However, earlier decisions based upon the standard of merchantable quality had taken exactly that stance. Thus it has been held that an incurable oil leak from the power steering mechanism of a new car, which would have cost just £25 to repair in 1973, was not a sufficiently serious defect to allow the court to treat the goods as being unmerchantable (*Millars of Falkirk Ltd* v *Turpie* 1976 SLT (Notes) 66). But in the light of *Rogers* v *Parish (Scarborough) Ltd* it is possible that such defects might now be sufficient to reveal a breach of s. 14(2), especially if the car is placed at the top end of the market and is described as new, in which case consumer expectations might be considerably higher, although it should be observed that in *Millars of Falkirk Ltd* v *Turpie* the defects were far less serious than those in *Rogers* v *Parish (Scarborough) Ltd.*

6.3.3.3.11 Safety Section 14(2B)(d) of the Sale of Goods Act 1979 now makes it clear that the safety of goods is an aspect of their quality. This was not explicit under the old law, but there were decisions which indicated that safety was a relevant consideration. Thus it has been held that a new car which cannot be safely used is not of merchantable quality (*Bernstein* v *Pamson Motors (Golders Green) Ltd* [1987] 2 All ER 220, 226 per Rougier J). Similarly it has been observed of a second-hand car that there are two preconditions to the merchantability of such a vehicle, namely that it can be driven and that it is safe to drive, since a car which will not move is useless and a car which will move but is a death trap is worse than useless (*Bartlett* v *Sidney Marcus Ltd* [1965] 1 WLR 1013)

6.3.3.3.12 Durability A matter which has given rise to controversy is whether the seller impliedly contracts to supply goods which are durable. In *Lambert* v *Lewis* [1982] AC 225 it was held that the implied condition of fitness for purpose in s. 14(3) of the Sale of Goods Act 1979 amounts to a continuing warranty that goods will continue to be fit for a reasonable period after the making of the contract. What is a reasonable time will clearly depend on the circumstances of the case, for example, something bought very cheaply cannot be expected to last for ever. However, in *Crowther* v *Shannon Motors Ltd* [1975] 1 All ER 139 the Court of Appeal took the view that in order to be able to sue under s. 14(3), it had to be shown or presumed that the defect complained of existed at the time the contract was entered into, thereby implying that there was, at that time, no requirement of durability.

Durability is now a matter specifically listed in s. 14(2B)(e) as an aspect of quality. However, this addition may not make a great deal of difference to the consumer who wishes to reject goods on the ground of lack of durability, due to the provisions of ss. 35 and 11(4) (see chapter 4). It is likely that under s. 35(4) the buyer will be deemed to have accepted the goods through lapse of time in which case s. 11(4) will confine him to an action for damages only.

6.3.4 Fitness for purpose

The Sale of Goods Act 1979, s. 14(3) (see also Sale of Goods (Implied Terms) Act 1973, s. 10(3); Supply of Goods and Services Act 1982, ss. 9(4), (5) and 4(4), (6)) provides that where the seller sells goods in the course of a business there is an implied condition that the goods sold are reasonably fit for any purpose expressly or impliedly made known to the seller by the buyer, provided it is reasonable for the buyer to rely on the seller's skill and judgment in selecting goods suited to that purpose. In the case of sales which involve the provision of credit, such as a conditional sale agreement, it is sufficient that the buyer makes known to the dealer the purpose for which the goods are required.

Like the provisions in respect of quality in s. 14(2), s. 14(3) only applies to sales made by the seller in the course of a business and does cover all goods supplied pursuant to the contract of sale.

6.3.4.1 Purpose Section 14(3) of the Sale of Goods Act 1979 requires the goods to be fit for the purpose for which the consumer requires them. If the goods are required for their normal purpose, there will be an overlap between the provisions of the Act in relation to quality and fitness. This overlap is inevitable given that satisfactory quality is defined in s. 14(2A) in terms of fitness for the purpose for which goods of that kind are commonly used. Thus, catapults which break in normal use (*Godley* v *Perry* [1960] 1 WLR 9) and injure the user, and hot-water bottles that burst when used according to the manufacturer's instructions (*Preist* v *Last* [1903] 2 KB 148), are neither of satisfactory quality nor fit for the purpose for which they are required. There are circumstances in which the two provisions do not overlap. For example, a car which suffers from a range of minor defects may be unsatisfactory (*Rogers* v *Parish (Scarborough) Ltd* [1987] QB 933), but if it can be driven, it will probably still be fit for the purpose for which it is intended. Similarly, an animal feed may be fit for feeding to animals generally without being fit for feeding to the particular type of animal which the buyer had in mind (*Ashington Piggeries Ltd* v *Christopher Hill Ltd* [1972] AC 441). In such a case there may be a breach of s. 14(3) without there being a breach of s. 14(2).

If goods can be put to one purpose only, there will be a breach of the requirement of fitness for purpose if they cannot be used for that purpose. In such a case, it is pointless to require the buyer to make that purpose known to the seller expressly and it will be assumed that the seller is aware that the buyer requires the goods for that purpose.

There are circumstances in which goods can be put to a number of purposes. If this is the case, it cannot be assumed that the goods are fit for the particular use to which the buyer wishes to put them. Instead, it is necessary for the buyer to show that he has communicated to the seller the particular purpose for which he requires them (see *Sumner Permain & Co.* v *Webb* [1922] 1 KB 55). In *Griffiths* v *Peter Conway Ltd* [1939] 1 All ER 685 the buyer required a tweed coat, but failed to inform the seller that she had an unusually sensitive skin and was therefore prone to dermatitis. Had the seller been aware of this fact he would have advised the buyer against purchasing a garment made of such a coarse material. It was held that the seller was not in breach of the implied term about fitness for purpose. The buyer's abnormal sensitivity was a matter which should have been communicated to the seller before liability could attach. The coat was required not merely for wearing, but to be worn by someone with an unusually sensitive skin. This approach to idiosyncrasies is confirmed in *Slater* v *Finning Ltd* [1996] 3 All ER 398 where the House of Lords held that if the failure of goods to serve the purpose required by the buyer is due to some abnormality of the buyer or his property which has not been made known to the seller, the buyer cannot rely on s. 14(3). This remaining the case whether or not the buyer is aware of that abnormality. In *Slater* v *Finning Ltd* the buyer's fishing vessel had an unusual engine which meant that three 'off-the-shelf' camshafts fitted by the sellers caused the engine to malfunction. The sellers were held to be entitled to assume that the camshafts fitted by them would be used in a 'normal' engine and that if this was not the case, the onus fell on the buyer to make known to the seller any idiosyncrasy which might affect their property. It was important that the goods were not made to the special order of the buyer for the specific purpose of being fitted to the particular vessel since then the buyer could expect the goods supplied by the seller to be fit for use on the particular vessel nominated (see *Cammell Laird & Co. Ltd* v *Manganese Bronze & Brass Co. Ltd* [1934] AC 402). The seller of a standard part suitable for use on all boat engines of the same type was entitled to assume that the buyer's engine was 'normal' in the same way that the seller in *Griffiths* v *Peter Conway Ltd* could assume that Mrs Griffiths was a normal person.

English law adopts an objective theory of contract law, so what matters is how a reasonable seller in the circumstances under consideration would have understood the buyer's intended purpose (*Slater* v *Finning Ltd* [1996] 3 All ER 398, 409 per Lord Steyn). Accordingly if a consumer buys a new tyre for his car, not being aware that his car suffers from a defect in the steering mechanism with the result that the tyre wears out after only a few hundred miles rather than the expected thousands of miles, it would be wholly unreasonable to hold the seller liable under s. 14(3), since the seller has no knowledge of the specific nature of the buyer's property (ibid. 405–6 per Lord Keith of Kinkel, citing an example given by Lord Griffiths in argument).

6.3.4.2 Reliance on the seller's skill and judgment

Even where the buyer has made known the particular purpose for which he requires goods, it does not automatically follow that the condition of fitness applies to the transaction. It is also a requirement that the buyer has reasonably relied on the seller's skill and judgment in selecting goods suited to that purpose. The burden of proof in this respect lies on the supplier, who must show that the consumer did not rely on his skill and judgment (cf. *Aswan Engineering Establishment Co.* v *Lupdine Ltd* [1987] 1 WLR 1). This burden can be discharged by showing that the buyer has not relied on the seller or that the buyer's reliance is unreasonable.

If the seller knows of the purpose for which the goods are required, as is the case where the goods are purchased for a single, normal purpose, reliance will be readily assumed. In *Grant* v *Australian Knitting Mills Ltd* [1936] AC 85 it was stated that the consumer can assume that the seller has selected his stock with skill and judgment (ibid. 99 per Lord Wright), thereby satisfying the requirement of reliance.

If the buyer has relied solely on his own skill and judgment, he cannot avail himself of the protection afforded by s. 14(3), but there is nothing to prevent the buyer from relying, in part, on the seller's skill and judgment. However, it must be established that the loss suffered by the buyer results from the reliance he has placed on the seller (*Ashington Piggeries Ltd* v *Christopher Hill Ltd* [1972] AC 441). If the buyer has inspected goods prior to purchase, it does not necessarily follow that there is no reliance on the seller's skill and judgment.

Factors which may be relevant in determining whether the consumer does reasonably rely on the seller's skill and judgment include the relative expertise of the parties (cf. *Henry Kendall & Sons* v *William Lillico & Sons Ltd* [1969] 2 AC 31), whether instructions on use have been supplied either before or after the making of the contract (*Wormell* v *RHM Agriculture (East) Ltd* [1987] 3 All ER 75) and whether the supplier is also the manufacturer (*Henry Kendall & Sons* v *William Lillico & Sons Ltd* [1969] 2 AC 31, 84 per Lord Reid).

6.3.4.3 Duration of the duty Strictly, the duties of the seller to supply goods which are of satisfactory quality and fit for the purpose for which they are required apply only at the time of the contract. If a defect manifests itself some time after sale and it is shown that that defect was not present at the time of contracting, the implied conditions would appear not to apply. However, it has been held that the implied condition of fitness for purpose also implies a warranty of durability (*Crowther* v *Shannon Motors Ltd* [1975] 1 All ER 139; *Lambert* v *Lewis* [1982] AC 225).

6.3.4.4 Strictness of the duty The duty imposed by s. 14(3) of the Sale of Goods Act 1979 is strict in the sense that where the goods prove not to be reasonably fit for the purpose for which they are required, the seller is liable, even where no amount of care on his part could have avoided the presence of the defect which rendered them unfit for the buyer's intended use (see *Frost* v *Aylesbury Dairy Co. Ltd* [1905] 1 KB 608).

The fact that s. 14(3) requires the buyer to have reasonably relied on the seller's skill and judgment does not import a requirement of fault into the implied condition of fitness. It follows that s. 14(3) applies to latent defects (*Henry Kendall & Sons* v *William Lillico & Sons Ltd* [1969] 2 AC 31, 84 per Lord Reid).

It is important that s. 14(3) requires the goods to be reasonably fit for the purpose for which the buyer requires them, since this negates the view that the implied condition imposes a form of absolute liability. The standard required of the seller will depend on the preciseness with which the buyer has specified his requirements. In the ordinary consumer supply contract, it is unlikely that the buyer will have spelt out in detail what his requirements are, and so the seller will be required to supply goods which are reasonably fit for the normal purpose for which the goods are used. If the buyer fails to reveal facts which are exclusively within his own knowledge, the seller cannot be expected to anticipate these and s. 14(3) will not come to the buyer's aid (*Griffiths* v *Peter Conway Ltd* [1939] 1 All ER 685, 691 per Lord Greene MR and see also *Slater* v *Finning Ltd* [1996] 3 All ER 398).

6.3.5 The difference between sections 13 and 14(2) and (3)
Where the consumer is faced with qualitatively defective goods, the success of his action against the supplier will depend on whether his case fits s. 13 or s. 14 of the Sale of Goods Act 1979. There are differences between the various provisions which may fashion the consumer's choice.

Prima facie, the difference between the three provisions would appear to be simple to identify — s. 13 applies where the buyer has not received that which he contracted to buy and s. 14 applies where he got what he contracted for but, due to defects in the goods, he cannot put them to their normal use or some special, but identified use. However, the distinction is not that simple. Sometimes, matters of quality will creep into the description of the goods contracted for. For example, a sale of food will also imply that the food is fit for human consumption. While food which cannot be eaten is not of satisfactory quality, it is probably also the case that fitness for consumption would also form part of the description of the goods (see *Christopher Hill Ltd* v *Ashington Piggeries Ltd* [1969] 3 All ER 1496, 1512). In these circumstances, the distinction between s. 13 and s. 14(2) is purely academic, as the consumer would have an action under both provisions.

In other cases, the difference between description, quality and fitness may be more important. For example, goods may be of satisfactory quality in the sense that they are acceptable and can be resold without substantial abatement in price, but at the same time they may not be what the buyer asked for. In such a case, s. 13 must be relied upon. Alternatively, goods may comply generally with their description but, due to some defect, they may not be fit for the particular use to which the buyer wishes to put them. This problem may arise where goods are contaminated by some extraneous matter and it becomes necessary to determine whether the presence of that matter destroys the character of the thing supplied (*Ashington Piggeries Ltd* v *Christopher Hill Ltd* [1972] AC 441, 489 per Lord Wilberforce and see also *Gill & Duffus SA* v *Berger & Co. Inc.* [1981] 2 Lloyd's Rep 233; *Gill & Duffus SA* v *Berger & Co. Inc. (No. 2)* [1983] 1 Lloyd's Rep 622).

6.3.5.1 Sale in the course of a business Perhaps the most important difference between s. 13 and both limbs of s. 14 is that the latter apply only where the supplier acts in the course of a business, whereas s. 13 applies to all sales by description. Thus, if the consumer wishes to proceed against a private seller in respect of a qualitative defect in the goods he has purchased, he must show that there is an express term of the contract which relates to his complaint or that the qualitative defect relates to a matter concerned with the identity of the thing supplied. In *Beale* v *Taylor* [1967] 1 WLR 1193, the plaintiff had to show that the car he purchased had been wrongly described, even though his complaint was one which related to the quality of the thing supplied. An action under s. 14(2) or (3) was denied because the seller did not act in the course of a business.

6.3.5.2 Relevance of reliance The requirement of reliance is a central feature of an action under s. 14(3) in that it must be reasonable for the buyer to rely on the seller's skill and judgment in selecting goods suited for the particular purpose the buyer has in mind.

Reliance also appears to be an important factor in determining the liability of the supplier under s. 13 in the sense that the consumer must rely on the supplier's description of the thing supplied (*Varley* v *Whipp* [1900] 1 QB 513, 516 per Channell J). It is the description that goes to the root of the contract and has such an influence on the buyer that it becomes an essential term of the contract (*Harlingdon & Leinster Enterprises Ltd* v *Christopher Hull Fine Art Ltd* (1990) 1 All ER 737, 744 per Nourse LJ). It is the fact of reliance by the buyer that throws light on the intention of the parties to treat a descriptive statement as an essential term of the contract (ibid. 752 per Slade LJ).

So far as s. 14(2) is concerned, it would appear that reliance is not an essential requirement in that the condition is broken if the goods are not fit for any purpose for which goods of that kind are normally bought. However, on closer examination, reliance may be a factor in determining liability. Because of the provisions of s. 14(2C)(a) and (b), the condition of satisfactory quality does not apply where the buyer has been told of a defect in the goods or where he has examined the goods and that examination ought to have revealed a defect. In both cases, if the buyer purchases the goods, he has no recourse against the seller because he has relied on his own judgment in purchasing the goods despite the presence of the defect in question.

6.4 THE TORT OF NEGLIGENCE AND PRODUCT QUALITY

Because of the apparent defects in the law of contract emanating, in particular, from a strict application of the doctrine of privity of contract, the question has arisen whether the tort of negligence can be used to compensate for those deficiencies (see Markesinis (1987) 103 LQR 354). The principal way in which this can be done is by enlarging the circumstances in which a duty of care is owed by a manufacturer to a consumer of a defective product.

6.4.1 Economic loss and physical harm
The main problem with the issue of product quality is that the consumer's complaint is that the product is not worth as much as he expected when he made his purchase. In some way the product is less valuable due to the presence of qualitative defects and it is that diminution in value which the consumer seeks to recover.

The implications of the House of Lords decision in *Anns* v *Merton London Borough Council* (1978) AC 728 were that in certain circumstances, economic loss such as the damage caused by a defective building to itself was remediable in an action for negligence if the defectiveness of the building was such as to create a present or imminent danger to the occupant of the building. By analogy, if a defective product gave rise to such a danger, damages representing the cost of rectifying the defect could be awarded.

The conceptual difficulty this gave rise to was that the harm complained of in *Anns* v *Merton London Borough Council* was pure economic loss — the plaintiff was given damages to compensate for the diminution in value of the building concerned, and this was not the province of the tort of negligence. Accordingly, the decision was overruled in *Murphy* v *Brentwood District Council* [1991] 1 AC 398 on the ground that it represented an unwarranted extension of the tort of negligence into an area it was never intended to cover.

The effect of overruling *Anns* v *Merton London Borough Council* is that if the only damage suffered is to the defective product itself, the manufacturer of that product will owe the consumer no duty of care. Similarly if the consumer discovers a defect before it becomes dangerous and replaces or repairs the product, the loss he has suffered is purely economic and generally, no duty of care is owed. Apparently, once the defect has been discovered, the product is no longer dangerous and the manufacturer's duty of care ceases to exist when this is the case (*D & F Estates Ltd* v *Church Commissioners for England* [1989] AC 177, 206 per Lord Bridge of Harwich).

In some cases, what appeared to be economic loss was remediable as a variety of physical damage where the 'complex structure' theory applied. This was a theory which had been put forward in the defective building case of *D & F Estates Ltd* v *Church Commissioners for England* and which suggested that damages could be recovered in a negligence action for physical harm to one part of a complex structure which was found to be caused by a defect in another part of same structure. Unfortunately, the theory suffered from inadequate explanation (see Wallace (1989) 105 LQR 46; Cane (1989) 52 MLR 200), but since Lord Bridge in *D & F Estates Ltd* v *Church Commissioners for England* [1989] AC 177, 206; equated defective buildings with other defective products (cf. Lord Oliver of Aylmerton 211), the theory is capable of being applied to products such as defective motor cars and domestic electrical appliances, if these can be described as complex structures.

In *Murphy* v *Brentwood District Council* three members of the House of Lords sought to explain this concept further. It was said that the complex structure theory cannot apply to a product or building which is wholly erected and equipped by the same contractor ([1991] 1 AC 398, 470 per Lord Keith of Kinkel). The whole package is to be regarded as a single unit which is rendered unsound by a defect in part of it. Each part of such a structure is interdependent on the other parts (ibid. 478 per Lord Bridge). The theory is applicable to structures which are erected by more than one contractor and the work of one results in damage to another part of the structure as a whole. Thus, damage to a building owned by A caused by defective electrical wiring installed by B in the same structure might satisfy the requirements of the theory (ibid. at 470 per Lord Keith). Similarly, damage caused to the same building by a defective central heating boiler negligently installed by C or negligently manufactured by D might also be classified as physical harm under the theory (ibid. per Lord Bridge). However, it would appear that an aeroplane which is fitted with a defective engine is not subject to the complex structure theory (*Trans-World Airline Inc.* v *Curtiss-Wright Corporation* (1955) 1 Misc 2d 477).

If a consumer suffers extensive damage to his new car because a tyre bursts when the car is being driven at speed, his likelihood of success will depend on who has manufactured the tyre. If the manufacturer of the car is also the manufacturer of the tyre, the complex structure theory suggests that the consumer will be unable to maintain a negligence action. However, if the manufacturers of the tyre and the car are distinct, the consumer will be able to recover damages in tort from the tyre manufacturer.

For further discussion see Cane, *Tort Law and Economic Interests*, 2nd ed. (Oxford: Clarendon Press, 1996).

6.4.2 Proximity

The House of Lords in *Murphy* v *Brentwood District Council* did admit to the existence of exceptional cases in which economic loss was remediable in a negligence action, namely, where the rule in *Hedley Byrne & Co. Ltd* v *Heller & Partners Ltd* [1964] AC 465 applied and where the relationship of proximity was so great as to fit within the principle laid down in *Junior Books Ltd* v *Veitchi Co. Ltd* [1983] 1 AC 520. Thus if the manufacturer gives information or advice concerning his product which is relied on by the consumer who subsequently suffers economic loss as a result of that reliance, the *Hedley Byrne* principle seems to apply.

It is very unlikely that the very close relationship of proximity required will be found to exist between the manufacturer and consumer of a qualitatively defective product which results in economic loss to the consumer. This much was clear from the decision of the House of Lords in *Junior Books Ltd* v *Veitchi Co. Ltd* (see also *Muirhead* v *Industrial Tank Specialities Ltd* [1985] 3 All ER 705). In *Junior Books Ltd* v *Veitchi Co. Ltd* it was considered that in most cases, the consumer will have relied on the retailer (rather than the manufacturer) to provide goods of the desired quality ([1983] 1 AC 520, 533 per Lord Fraser of Tullybelton and 547 per Lord Roskill). To the contrary, it can be argued that in some instances the primary reliance of the consumer is on the manufacturer rather than the retailer, particularly where the consumer has relied on the general reputation of the manufacturer or where he has been influenced by a national advertising campaign (see Oughton [1987] JBL 370; Palmer and Murdoch (1983) 46 MLR 213). In such a case, the identity of the person from whom the product is purchased would appear to be immaterial, thereby negating the possibility of reliance on the retailer.

The reluctance to allow the tort of negligence to be used in respect of qualitative defects is based on the fact that it is difficult to ascertain the appropriate standard to which the goods supplied should conform. The *Donoghue* v *Stevenson* [1932] AC 562 duty is to take reasonable care to ensure that goods supplied are not dangerous, but to extend that duty to include quality would pose substantial problems since the desired standard of quality in each case will depend on the standard of quality contracted for. It has been seen already that the standard of quality under a contract for the supply of goods will depend on a range of factors, including the price paid for the goods and any description applied to them. Where the defendant is a manufacturer, there is no contractual relationship with the consumer, and the courts, at present, see it as too difficult a task to ascertain the standard of quality required. Accordingly, the buyer is presently required to enter into his contract with the retailer with care and to specify what he requires in the way of quality. While this is a fair argument to employ in relation to business contracts, the same is not necessarily applicable where the buyer is a consumer who does not possess the business expertise to determine in advance what he requires from the supplier.

6.5 MANUFACTURERS' GUARANTEES OF QUALITY

The protection afforded the consumer under the Sale of Goods Act 1979 and related legislation assumes the existence of a contractual relationship between the consumer buyer and the retailer. However, all too often, the ultimate consumer of a product is not the person who has purchased the qualitatively defective product. As an alternative, the consumer might wish to pursue the manufacturer of the defective product, but this can present almost insurmountable hurdles where the complaint is that the product is merely qualitatively defective. It has been seen already that the limitations of the tort of negligence in relation to economic loss are such that the consumer is likely not to make any headway in that area so far as qualitative defects are concerned, but a very common feature of modern-day consumer shopping is the manufacturer's guarantee of the consumer goods he makes. Most typically, a guarantee will operate for a period of 12 months from the date of purchase and will amount to an offer to replace defective parts. Often these guarantees may be extended through the purchase of an insurance policy which offers an 'extended warranty', but often excluding liability in respect of reasonable wear and tear. The attractiveness of some of these guarantees is often undermined by the fact that the consumer must pay for the cost of returning the goods to the manufacturer or an appointed repairer. Moreover, some guarantees also require the consumer to pay for the cost of labour. The difficulties of establishing a contractual relationship between the consumer and the manufacturer of a product are substantial and have been discussed in chapter 4.

As an alternative to the conventional contractual and tortious remedies of the consumer, it is frequently the case that the consumer is given a guarantee of the quality of the product he uses. If fully effective, guarantees are a highly desirable means of consumer protection as they operate as a means of prevention rather than as a cure after things have already gone wrong. The consumer is not left to pursue his remedies through the courts, but has a simple remedy against the person who gives the guarantee. However, the question remains whether these guarantees are worth any more than the paper they are written on.

6.5.1 Features of and purposes served by guarantees

Some manufacturers give guarantees or warranties with their products, which are in addition to the statutory rights of the consumer under the Sale of Goods Act 1979 and related legislation. Most often, these manufacturers' guarantees are to be found in relation to the more expensive consumer purchases such as motor vehicles and domestic kitchen appliances. It is common to find that certain parts of the product are guaranteed for a longer period than others and in some cases, certain parts, particularly of motor vehicles, are excluded from the guarantee altogether. In some instances, the guarantee is subject to a servicing requirement, with the result that a guarantee may be invalidated if the consumer does not have his motor car serviced on a regular basis at an approved garage.

Guarantees are not only a service to the consumer, they also provide the manufacturer with useful product information and act as a promotional device. In particular, it appears to be accepted by manufacturers and retailers that information about complaints is essential to effective quality management (see National Consumer Council, *Competing in Quality* (1989), para. 5.1). Unless a producer knows how well his product is performing in use, it is virtually impossible to gauge consumer satisfaction and improve the product's quality. Guarantees and consumer responses associated with guarantees can help to provide the information required by producers in this respect. Given the various roles served by guarantees, there are a number of competing theories concerning the reasons for giving guarantees with consumer goods and services (see Priest (1981) 90 Yale LJ 1297; Whitford (1982) 91 Yale LJ 1371).

One view is that guarantees are essentially exploitative devices imposed by retailers and manufacturers on consumers because they are aware of the consumer's inequality of bargaining power. This is borne out by those guarantees which seek to exclude or limit the liability of the guarantee giver to a level below that provided by the Sale of Goods Act 1979. The exploitative nature of guarantees has been recognised by Parliament and measures have been taken to deal with guarantees that operate in this fashion (see chapter 12).

An alternative view is that guarantees provide a signal of the reliability of the product. The search costs which face consumers who wish to compare rival products before making a purchase are substantial, but the presence of a wide-ranging guarantee may signal to the consumer that the producer has confidence in his product. In this way the consumer may cut down his search costs by comparing the warranty provisions of competing manufacturers and ignoring other matters. However, with any product, there are likely to be parts which are more prone to suffer from defects and it is likely that the manufacturer will use small print in the guarantee to exclude or limit his liability in these respects. Accordingly, the consumer still has the search costs associated with reading each guarantee to discover how the exclusions of one producer differ from those of another. Given that few consumers ever read the small print in contractual documents, this would seem to destroy the signal theory. Furthermore, in many cases, the guarantee is not discovered until after purchase, because it is contained in the packaging surrounding the goods, in which case, it cannot have figured in the consumer's decision to purchase.

A further theory is the investment theory developed by Priest ((1981) 90 Yale LJ 1297), which seeks to identify which of the consumer or producer is in the best position to insure against a particular risk of loss. In particular, Priest points to the fact that if a particular defect is best avoided by the producer taking precautions at the design stage or by adopting quality control techniques, he is more likely to give a warranty that covers such defects. On the other hand, there may be defects which are best covered by private insurance taken out by the consumer, in which case, such defects are likely to be excluded from the guarantee by the producer. The investment theory is therefore based on the notion of the least-cost avoider namely that if one person is in a better position to accept responsibility for a particular variety of loss, he rather than the other party, should be left to absorb it. On this basis, it is argued that the manufacturer of a motor vehicle ought to be allowed to exclude liability in respect of the failure of his product to satisfy the requirement of satisfactory quality, because the consumer can obtain alternative insurance elsewhere. Furthermore, if the manufacturer is obliged to provide extensive cover beyond that given in his warranty, this will reduce the consumer's incentives to maintain his vehicle or obtain insurance elsewhere, with the result that the number of product defects will increase. Accordingly, less careful consumers will be cross-subsidised by those who are more careful with their purchases. This might seem to suggest that provisions such as the Unfair Contract Terms Act 1977, s. 5, are inefficient in so far as they prevent the use of exclusions of liability in manufacturers' guarantees (see also chapter 12).

6.5.2 Problems of guarantees

Guarantees, if enforceable, provide the consumer with rights of considerable value, but quite often the guarantee is nothing more than a marketing ploy or a means of diverting the consumer's attention from his legal rights.

In some instances in the past, manufacturers' guarantees have even been used to take away rights which the consumer enjoyed under statute or at common law (see *Adams* v *Richardson & Starling Ltd* [1969] 1 WLR 1645, 1648–9 per Lord Denning MR). Arguments of this type are consistent with the exploitation theory considered above, but it also needs to be considered whether countermeasures are efficient in the light of the investment theory.

Exploitation abuses were recognised and the Unfair Contract Terms Act 1977, s. 5, now provides that liability for loss or damage caused by a defective product cannot be excluded by reference to a guarantee if the product is of a type ordinarily supplied for private use or consumption and the damage etc. arises from the product proving to be defective whilst in consumer use and is caused by the negligence of a person concerned with the manufacture or distribution of the product. Accordingly, where a guarantee is now given, it adds to the remedies of the consumer without taking away his existing legal rights. It is a criminal offence for a person acting in the course of a business to make a statement to the effect that the consumer's rights under the Sale of Goods Act 1979, related legislation or the Unfair Contract Terms Act 1977 are in any way restricted or excluded (Consumer Transactions (Restrictions on Statements) Order (SI 1976/1813), art. 3). It is also a criminal offence for a person to publish a statement which relates to consumer rights, for example, a guarantee, without also clearly stating that the statutory rights of the consumer are unaffected (ibid., art. 4).

Whether or not guarantees are used in an exploitative fashion, data collected by the Office of Fair Trading and the National Consumer Council suggest that many consumers are still highly dissatisfied with guarantee provisions. It has been reported that much consumer dissatisfaction emanates from the failure of guarantees to cover labour costs and from the lack of clarity in the language used in guarantee disclaimers of liability (OFT, *Consumer Guarantees* (1986), para. 5.9). The extent of consumer dissatisfaction also appears to be increasing. For example, in 1988 it was estimated that 38 per cent of the adult population was dissatisfied with a purchase made by them (OFT, *Beeline*, issue 88/4, pp. 22–4) whereas in 1986, the relevant figure was 28 per cent (OFT, *Consumer Dissatisfaction* (1986)). Even given trade suggestions that the OFT data were suspect, it has still been conservatively estimated that at least one million people each year fail to resolve complaints concerning faulty new goods (NCC, *The Consumer Guarantee* (1989), para. 3.1.4). It is also uncontroversial that the greatest level of dissatisfaction emanates from the purchase of cars and household appliances (ibid., para. 3.1.5).

6.5.3 Proposals for reform

The level of consumer dissatisfaction indicated above has led the National Consumer Council to propose a regime of consumer product guarantees based on the notions of competition and increased consumer information (NCC, *The Consumer Guarantee* (1989)). The Council's proposals were taken up in the private member's Consumer Guarantees Bill (Session 1989–90, House of Commons Bill 16), which was lost due to absence of Parliamentary time and government opposition in summer 1990. Subsequently, the DTI published a consultation document entitled *Consumer Guarantees* (DTI 1992) at roughly the same time as the European Commission began to show an interest in consumer guarantees (see below).

The DTI paper makes three general proposals:

(a) that a manufacturer should be legally liable under his own guarantee;

(b) that retailers selling goods subject to a manufacturer's guarantee should also be liable on the terms of the guarantee;

(c) that the manufacturer should also be responsible for the quality of goods manufactured by him but sold by someone else under the terms of the Sale of Goods Act 1979.

Clearly, some of these proposals, if implemented, would involve some adjustments being made to the doctrine of privity of contract. There is widespread opposition on the part of the manufacturing industry to the last two of the DTI proposals.

The most recent proposals in respect of consumer guarantees have emanated from the European Commission which has published a *Green Paper on Consumer Guarantees and After-Sales Service* (COM (93) 509) followed by a *Proposal for a Council Directive on the Sale of Consumer Goods and Associated Guarantees* (COM (95) 520 final, 3 September 1996), both of which are premised on the belief that the future will see an increase in cross-border shopping in the single market, particularly in relation to expensive consumer durables such as cars and consumer white goods. This belief is further emphasised by the fact that there are plans to introduce legislation on distance selling (see COM (92) 11, 21 May 1992, OJ C156/14). But whether this belief is well-founded has been the subject of a certain amount of doubt, especially in the light of the fact that most consumers prefer to purchase locally for reasons of convenience, such as being able to return defective goods from whence they came (see Cranston, 'The Green Paper on Guarantees' (1995) Consum LJ 110). Conversely, there probably is good reason for

European intervention on other grounds, namely, in an attempt to achieve the single market, it will be important to create a level playing field Europe-wide in which the rules on consumer guarantees are as similar as possible within all member States, so that there is no disincentive to consumer purchases in one State rather than another due to the disparity in guarantee provisions. This particular ground for intervention seems to underlie the proposals contained in the proposed Council Directive, which is based on the EC Treaty, art. 100a, and is concerned with the establishment of the internal market. But if the proposal is justified on the basis that it will facilitate the completion of the internal market, it seems strange that its provisions concern only transactions made by a natural person who is 'acting for purposes which are not directly related to his trade business or profession' (proposed Council Directive COM (95) 520 final, art. 1). In order to facilitate completion of the internal market, it might have made sense to apply the rule to all purchasers, including those who buy solely for business purposes.

The Green Paper canvasses two possible routes for consumer guarantees. On the one hand it refers to 'legal guarantees', the UK equivalent of which is to be found in the Sale of Goods Act 1979, s. 14. In addition, it also considers the possibility of 'commercial guarantees' which are the equivalent of the familiar high street manufacturers' guarantees, the contractual status of which in English law is the subject of some concern.

The route forward chosen in the proposed Council Directive is based upon the notion of the legal guarantee and consists of three main elements. First, it is proposed to allow consumers to rely upon the producer's advertising in order to found a claim against the retailer where goods are not in conformity with the contract (proposed Directive, art. 2(2)(b)). This differs somewhat from the proposal contained in the Green Paper to the effect that the producer and the retailer should be jointly liable for all goods not in conformity with the contract. If anything, the Green Paper proposal is more in line with current consumer understanding of who should be responsible for defective products, since it would be reasonable to assume that most consumer purchasers of expensive items, such as cars and electrical goods, rely on the brand name of the product purchased rather than upon the skill and expertise of the retailer.

If the proposed Council Directive is adopted in its present form, it will result in important changes in English law on the status of claims made by producers in their advertisements. At present it is very likely that only the most specific of claims by producers will give rise to the inference of a collateral contractual relationship, because it will rarely be the case that there is an intention to enter into contractual relations with those who read advertisements (*Lambert* v *Lewis* [1982] AC 225 and see chapter 4). If this does become law, the problem will still remain that advertisements often contain material on which no reasonable person could expect to rely, namely trade puffs. Accordingly, it will become necessary to identify those parts of an advertisement on which it is reasonable for a consumer to rely.

Given the problems associated with holding the retailer responsible for what the producer might have said about his product, there are a number of escape routes. For example, under the proposed Council Directive, a retailer would not be responsible for statements of which he could have had no knowledge, such as those which are published in another country. Similarly, the retailer will not be responsible for the content of advertising material on which the consumer could not have relied, such as that which is published after a particular transaction is entered into. There is also a provision which will allow the retailer to display a notice which corrects any statement made by the producer. Such corrections, however, will have to be carefully worded so that they do not amount to an attempt to exclude the rights of consumers, contrary to the Unfair Contract Terms Act 1977 and the Unfair Terms in Consumer Contracts Regulations 1994.

Although the Green Paper envisaged a legal guarantee in respect of the quality of goods which should be borne jointly by the retailer and the producer, the compromise position arrived at in the proposed Council Directive is that the seller should be responsible for a failure of goods supplied to conform with the contract within a period of two years from the date of purchase (proposed Council Directive, art. 3(1)). In the light of the remedies for lack of conformity, considered below, the effect of this provision would be to extend the consumer's right of rejection of the goods, given that the present state of English law will take account of whether the buyer has accepted the goods supplied under the contract (see *Bernstein* v *Pamson Motors (Golders Green) Ltd* [1987] 2 All ER 220 and see chapter 4).

Without further definition, a requirement that goods should conform with the contract says little other than that the goods must satisfy the requirements of the express terms of the contract. Accordingly, goods would have to be in accordance with any description applied to them. But in addition to this, the proposed Council Directive adds substance to the meaning of the phrase 'conformity with the contract' by imposing requirements similar to those contained in the Sale of Goods Act 1979 regarding satisfactory quality, fitness for purpose and compliance with a description and with a sample provided. Additionally, it is proposed that the legitimate expectations of the consumer should be taken into account (ibid.). In order to ease the burden of proof which would otherwise rest on the consumer, it is proposed that there should be a presumption that any defect manifesting itself in the goods within six months of the sale existed at the time of sale (ibid., art. 3(3)).

So far as the matter of remedies is concerned, it has been seen that English law offers the alternative remedies of rejection and damages or both, where appropriate, subject to the caveat that where the buyer is taken to have accepted goods supplied under an entire contract, rejection will not be permitted. The proposed Council Directive goes further than this, introducing other remedies, better known in other mainland European States. It is proposed that if a lack of conformity with the contract becomes manifest within one year of the sale, the consumer will be able to reject the goods (misleadingly referred to as rescission of the contract) or demand repair, a partial refund or a replacement (ibid., art. 3(4)). In particular, the right to demand repair of the goods is a remedy which does not exist in English law, although in practice many sellers will offer to have defective goods repaired instead of offering a refund of the price. Moreover, many producers' guarantees (referred to in the Green Paper as 'commercial guarantees') will also make provision for repair of defective goods.

Beyond the one-year period during which the consumer will have the choice of asking for whatever remedy suits him, the consumer will have the alternative remedies of repair or a price reduction which would take into account the use made of the goods by the consumer in the intervening period (ibid., art. 3(4)).

The Commission Green Paper also addressed the problem of 'commercial guarantees'. These are the equivalent of the familiar high street manufacturers' guarantees. There is some concern about their present contractual status in English law due to legal orthodoxy in respect of the requirements of consideration and intention to create contractual relations. The Green Paper takes the view that most commercial guarantees suffer from lack of transparency in that there is no standard-form guarantee. Instead, the remedies available under such guarantees, their duration and their formal preconditions for validity differ from producer to producer. Moreover, commercial guarantees also differ from country to country according to the domestic rules applicable to legal guarantees (Green Paper p. 38). The Paper concludes that the problems associated with commercial guarantees arise from the fact that there is no legal framework within which they can operate so that there is no means of filling gaps in guarantee documents as and when they are seen to arise (ibid., p. 79). The preferred view expressed in the Green Paper is that there should be a Europe-wide commercial guarantee which could be invoked in any member State, regardless of the country in which the guaranteed goods were purchased. However, the point remains that the need for such a guarantee is not clearly established while there is no general consumer trend towards cross-border shopping. What is far more important is that there should be some means by which commercial guarantees should be made enforceable, whatever the nationality of the giver of the guarantee.

Consistent with the line of argument adopted in the Green Paper, the proposed Council Directive provides that commercial guarantees should be legally enforceable (proposed Council Directive, art. 5). The effect of art. 5 would be that if a guarantee is given, it must place the consumer in a more advantageous position than would be the case under other legal provisions affecting the goods subject to the guarantee. The proposed Council Directive would itself provide consumers with a right of rejection within a two-year period, so art. 5 would appear to mean that guarantee periods will have to be longer than two years in order to improve the position of the consumer.

SEVEN

Product safety and the civil law

In addition to product quality, the consumer also has an interest in product safety. Product safety is a matter which goes beyond the quest for compensation when things go wrong: there is a general social interest in ensuring that consumer goods and, to a lesser extent, consumer services reach general standards of safety. For the most part, the criminal law is used to this end and will be considered in chapter 14. Where the consumer suffers physical harm to his person or to his property, that harm may be the subject of a civil action for compensation. The principal means by which this harm is compensated is through the operation of the law of tort in the form of an action for negligence, an action under the Consumer Protection Act 1987, part I, or an action for damages for breach of statutory duty. Where goods supplied to a consumer fail to reach the required standard of satisfactory quality or fitness for purpose and as a consequence cause physical harm, that harm may be taken into account in an award of damages for breach of contract.

7.1 CONTRACTUAL DUTIES AND PRODUCT SAFETY

While the implied terms of satisfactory quality and fitness for purpose considered in chapter 6 are generally concerned with the quality of the goods supplied, it is undoubtedly the case that if goods are unsafe they will fail to reach the required qualitative standard and the retailer will be liable for their lack of safety. Where the consumer suffers harm to his person or damage to property other than the defective product itself, such harm is remediable in an action for consequential loss, provided it satisfies the contractual principles of remoteness of damage (cf. Waddams (1974) 37 MLR 154).

If the consumer purchases food which cannot be eaten safely (*Heil* v *Hedges* [1951] 1 TLR 512) or if he buys clothes which give a 'normal' person a skin complaint (*Grant* v *Australian Knitting Mills Ltd* [1936] AC 85; cf. *Griffiths* v *Peter Conway Ltd* [1939] 1 All ER 685), the goods concerned are neither of satisfactory quality nor fit for the purpose for which they are required. The same applies equally to the packaging in which goods are supplied. Thus if a glass bottle in which a soft drink is supplied causes an injury to the consumer (*Geddling* v *Marsh* [1920] 1 KB 668), it too fails to satisfy the Sale of Goods Act 1979, s. 14. Similarly, solid fuel or other material which causes an unexpected explosion, thereby resulting in property damage (*Wilson* v *Rickett Cockrell & Co. Ltd* [1954] 1 QB 598; *Vacwell Engineering Co. Ltd* v *BDH Chemicals Ltd* [1969] 3 All ER 1681), fails to satisfy the requirements of satisfactory quality and fitness for purpose. Accordingly, consequential loss damages may be awarded to the consumer who suffers personal injury or damage to property other than the defective product itself, provided that loss is not too remote.

7.2 MANUFACTURERS' LIABILITY FOR NEGLIGENCE

The manufacturer of a product is expected to exercise reasonable care in the preparation and putting up of his product so as to ensure the safety of the product he puts into circulation.

According to the 'narrow' rule in *Donoghue* v *Stevenson* [1932] AC 562, 599 per Lord Atkin:

A manufacturer of products, which he sells in such form as to show that he intends them to reach the ultimate consumer in the form in which they left him with no possibility of intermediate examination and with the knowledge that the absence of reasonable care in the preparation or putting up of the products will result in an injury to the consumer's life or property, owes a duty to the consumer to take reasonable care.

The rule is based on the notion of fault which must be proved by the consumer. Accordingly, it is not so favourable to the consumer purchaser as the implied terms in contracts of supply (see chapter 6), which impose strict liability on the supplier. However, the duty of care owed by the manufacturer of a product does extend to anyone whom he can foresee as likely to be affected by his acts or omissions. Accordingly, a wider range of plaintiffs is embraced by the 'narrow' rule.

7.2.1   Parties to the action

7.2.1.1   Manufacturers   The term 'manufacturer' is given a very wide definition with the result that it includes not just the producer of an end product but also the supplier of a service and a retailer. A better way of stating the rule is that it covers any person who fails to take reasonable care when he puts a product into circulation. Thus it has been held that the rule extends to include retailers (*Andrews* v *Hopkinson* [1957] 1 QB 229) and wholesalers (*Watson* v *Buckley, Osborne, Garrett & Co. Ltd* [1940] 1 All ER 174), who have failed to inspect or test goods, repairers (*Haseldine* v *Daw & Son Ltd* [1941] 2 KB 343), assemblers (*Malfroot* v *Noxall Ltd* (1935) 51 TLR 551) and those who hire products to consumers (*White* v *John Warwick & Co. Ltd* [1953] 2 All ER 1021). It is also the case that a donor (*Griffiths* v *Arch*

Engineering Co. Ltd [1968] 3 All ER 217), the builder of a house (*Dutton* v *Bognor Regis Urban District Council* [1972] 1 QB 319; cf. *D & F Estates Ltd* v *Church Commissioners for England* [1989] AC 177) and possibly a local authority building inspector (*Murphy* v *Brentwood District Council* [1991] 1 AC 398) fall within the rule.

7.2.1.2 Consumers Unlike the position of the retailer under the Sale of Goods Act 1979, the manufacturer is liable to any person foreseeably affected by his defective product. There is no requirement that the person affected should have contracted to purchase the product. Accordingly, the rule will extend to cover a purchaser (*Grant* v *Australian Knitting Mills Ltd* [1936] AC 85) or a borrower (*Griffiths* v *Arch Engineering Co. Ltd* [1968] 3 All ER 217), and members of his family and invited guests. Similarly a manufacturer may also owe a duty of care to a donee (*Donoghue* v *Stevenson* [1932] AC 562), an employee of the purchaser (*Davie* v *New Merton Board Mills Ltd* [1959] AC 604) or even a mere bystander (*Stennett* v *Hancock* [1939] 2 All ER 578).

7.2.2 Products
The rule in *Donoghue* v *Stevenson* [1932] AC 562 applied specifically to food and drink, but it was not long before it was extended to cover the full range of manufactured products. Thus it has been held to extend to clothing (*Grant* v *Australian Knitting Mills Ltd* [1936] AC 85), motor cars (*Herschtal* v *Stewart & Arden Ltd* [1940] 1 KB 155), cleaning fluids (*Fisher* v *Harrods Ltd* [1966] 1 Lloyd's Rep 500), hair dyes (*Holmes* v *Ashford* [1950] 2 All ER 76), buildings (*Dutton* v *Bognor Regis Urban District Council* [1972] 1 QB 373; cf. *D & F Estates Ltd* v *Church Commissioners for England* [1989] AC 177) and the packaging in which products are supplied (*Hill* v *James Crowe (Cases) Ltd* [1978] 1 All ER 812).

7.2.3 Failure to take reasonable care
The rule requires the manufacturer to take reasonable care. In general, absence of reasonable care can be established by the consumer of the product if he can point to a breakdown in the production process, a defective design, defective instructions on use or a failure to warn of a known danger.

7.2.3.1 Production process An end product may be defective because of impurities which should have been removed before the product was put into circulation. Since the manufacturer of a soft drink has control over the production process, it will be negligence on his part if some impurity such as a snail manages to get into a bottle of his ginger beer (*Donoghue* v *Stevenson* [1932] AC 562). Similarly, the failure to remove harmful impurities applied to clothing by the manufacturer in the process of bleaching will also constitute a failure to exercise reasonable care (*Grant* v *Australian Knitting Mills Ltd* [1936] AC 85). The impurities may have been naturally present and not removed by the manufacturer. For example, a caterer who leaves a bone in a chicken sandwich may be in breach of his duty of care to the consumer (*Tarling* v *Nobel* [1966] ALR 189).

In other cases, inadequate construction may be the cause of complaint, whether it be the construction of the product itself (*Walton v British Leyland (UK) Ltd* (1978) Product Liability International (August 1980), pp. 156–60) or the packaging in which it is supplied (*Hill v James Crowe (Cases) Ltd* [1978] 1 All ER 812). In *Walton v British Leyland (UK) Ltd* the failure by the manufacturer to take reasonable remedial steps after discovering that a range of its cars suffered from an axle defect which made it possible that a wheel might become detached during use amounted to a failure to take reasonable care. At the very least, a reasonable manufacturer in the same position would take the precaution of warning the public of the danger and making proper arrangements for the repair of any defective component part, rather than leaving the matter to main agent garages to rectify defects as and when vehicles were brought in for service by their owners.

In other cases, the product may be defective if the manufacturer has used inadequate component parts supplied by someone else. In such a case, the manufacturer of the finished product may be liable if there was something he could have done to avoid the presence of the defect in the product, for example, testing it.

7.2.3.2 Design defects A breakdown in the production process tends to produce 'one-off' defective products, whereas defective design produces a whole range of defective products. It may be that a range of products has been designed with the use of insufficiently strong or durable materials or that the whole range creates a health hazard or lacks essential safety features (*Griffiths v Arch Engineering Ltd* [1968] 3 All ER 217).

The difficulty in design cases is that the manufacturer may be at the forefront of technology, with the result that he may not be aware of the potential of a prototype product for causing injury. In such a case, it cannot be said that the manufacturer has failed to comply with the requirement of reasonable care. The reasonable man who sets the standard of reasonable care could not expect a manufacturer to be aware of a potential for harm if the state of scientific and technological development is not sufficient to allow the defect to be discovered.

7.2.3.3 Warnings and instructions for use The presence or absence of a warning or instructions is important in two respects. If the manufacturer gives a warning, this may serve to divert liability elsewhere on the ground of causation. Alternatively, if the manufacturer is aware of a possible defect in his product, or if he is aware that a product may be misused in some way by the consumer, and he fails to give a warning, this may be evidence of negligence on his part (*Andrews v Hopkinson* [1957] 1 QB 229).

Even where a warning is issued, it may be inadequate for what it says or fails to say. Thus, a warning which contains false representations may give rise to liability (*Watson v Buckley, Osborne, Garrett & Co. Ltd* [1940] 1 All ER 174). A warning may be inadequate not for what it says, but for what it omits to say. Thus it has been held to be insufficient to warn that a chemical gives off a harmful vapour when it also has a tendency to react violently in contact with water (*Vacwell Engineering Co. Ltd* v *BDH Chemicals Ltd* [1971] 1 QB 88 and 111). If anything, such a warning tends to lull the user into a false sense of security.

In order to decide whether a failure to give a warning amounts to negligence on the part of a manufacturer, a number of factors will have to be considered. Generally, it can be said that in the case of known latent defects, a warning is a practicable step to take. Thus it is reasonable to expect a warning to be given with products which possess explosive and flammable qualities. The obviousness of the danger should also be considered. Thus, there would be no need to warn of a danger that all consumers would be expected to know of (*Farr* v *Butters Brothers & Co. Ltd* [1932] 2 KB 606). If the product has been put into circulation before its defectiveness can reasonably be discovered, the manufacturer must apply his knowledge of the defect to future supplies (*Wright* v *Dunlop Rubber Co. Ltd* (1972) 13 KIR 255), but it is doubtful whether the negligence principle requires him to recall products already in circulation. However, in *Walton* v *British Leyland (UK) Ltd* (1978) Product Liability International (August 1980), pp. 156–60 Willis J held the defendants liable for a failure to warn of a rear axle defect in Allegro cars which they manufactured. The defendants believed that warning the public might damage the commercial reputation of that range of cars. Willis J concluded that liability was made out, in these particular circumstances, because the defendants had failed to fit a safety device to all Allegro cars in stock and unsold at the time the defect came to their knowledge. However, his lordship also refused to rule out the possibility of liability based on a failure to warn the public of a defect in this range of cars, even after they had been put on to the market. But it was unnecessary to decide the case on this basis.

More recently, the question of what duty rests on a manufacturer after his product has been put into circulation has arisen once more in *Carroll* v *Dunlop Ltd* (1996) Product Liability International (April 1996), pp. 58–9), in which Dunlop disputed liability for tyre defects in a range of their tyres which had been in circulation since 1981 and appeared to be a cause of a motor vehicle accident occurring at a time when the car to which the under-inflated tyres were fitted was being driven at about 85 miles per hour. An important factor in holding Dunlop 80 per cent to blame for the accident was that they, or a company to which they had sold manufacturing rights, had received over 300 complaints from worried motorists about the safety of this brand of tyre, but nothing had been done to alert the public to the danger and no report had been made to the Ministry of Transport. It was concluded that a responsible manufacturer must keep an eye on the number of complaints received and warn users of the product if there is any substantial risk of injury should the product be used normally or in foreseeable conditions which might present a danger.

7.2.4 Proof of negligence

The burden of proof generally lies on the person seeking to establish a particular point. As a result, the consumer of a defective product must prove that the manufacturer is negligent. This requires proof that the product was defective, that the injury was caused by that defect and that the injuries suffered by the consumer were caused by the manufacturer's failure to exercise reasonable care.

This appears to place a heavy burden on the consumer, but there is a rule to the effect that the consumer does not have to identify the exact person responsible for the defect in the product (*Grant* v *Australian Knitting Mills Ltd* [1936] AC 85, 101 per Lord Wright). Negligence can be inferred from the fact that the product leaves the manufacturer in a defective state. The effect of this is that the manufacturer is required to show that he was not negligent in using an improper system and that his employees have not been careless. This would appear to amount to something very close to an application of the doctrine of *res ipsa loquitur*, the application of which to manufacturers' liability cases has been denied elsewhere (see *Donoghue* v *Stevenson* [1932] AC 562, 622 per Lord McMillan). However, the *Grant* v *Australian Knitting Mills Ltd* principle suggests that it is now relatively easy to presume fault in cases of negligent manufacture in the absence of a strong defence called by the producer and has been described by one commentator as making the manufacturer an insurer of his own product (Fleming, *The Law of Torts*, 8th ed, Sydney: Law Book Co, pp. 485–88).

In addition to the doctrine of *res ipsa loquitur*, the Civil Evidence Act 1968, s. 11, provides that the burden of disproving negligence rests on the defendant where he has been convicted of a criminal offence arising out of the facts which also form the basis of the product liability action. This provision could assist the consumer in a civil action against a manufacturer who has committed a criminal offence under the Consumer Protection Act 1987, part II, or the Food Safety Act 1990.

7.2.5 Causation
The manufacturer's negligence must be the cause of the injury suffered by the consumer. It may be that there is some other independent cause of the consumer's injuries or it may be that someone else is expected to examine the product before it reaches the consumer. In either event, the manufacturer may be relieved of responsibility for the defective product.

7.2.5.1 Alternative cause The manufacturer is only responsible for defects caused by his own conduct. Thus if defect results from wear and tear or the consumer has used the product in an unforeseeable way or if another person in the chain of distribution is responsible for the defect, the manufacturer may escape liability. But if the product reaches the consumer subject to the same defect as when it left the manufacturer, this will be evidence that the defendant has caused the harm which flows from the defective product.

It is important that the burden of proof rests on the consumer since it may be the case that there are two plausible explanations of the accident, in which case negligence on the part of the manufacturer is not proved. This can be a particular problem in consumer transactions where there is a lengthy chain of distribution and where the product is assembled using components supplied by a number of different manufacturers so that it is difficult to establish which component was the cause of the accident, particularly if the accident does not occur until some time after the finished product was put into circulation. Thus in *Evans* v *Triplex Safety Glass Co. Ltd* [1936] 1 All ER 283 the plaintiff was injured when a car windscreen manufactured by the defendants, but fitted by the vehicle manufacturer shattered while the car was in normal use. It was held that the onus fell upon the plaintiff to prove negligence by showing that there was no opportunity for examination of the defective product by a third party. The manufacturers had called evidence which showed that the glass had been properly manufactured and would withstand a light blow in the course of the car being driven. Accordingly, there was still a chance that the car manufacturer was responsible, but since no evidence was called in this respect, the plaintiff had failed to prove fault on the part of the defendants.

In other cases, the consumer may be the cause of his own injury. If the consumer is aware of a danger, but continues to use the product, he cannot later complain (*Farr* v *Butters Brothers & Co. Ltd* [1932] 2 KB 606), although simple knowledge of a defect is not sufficient to divert responsibility if there is nothing the consumer can do to avoid the danger (*Denny* v *Supplies & Transport Co. Ltd* [1950] 2 KB 374).

It can be argued that if the manufacturer has created a danger, he should not be excused merely because another person has failed to remove it. However, if the manufacturer has given explicit instructions on the use of his product and if these are ignored, the resultant injury cannot be said to be due to the manufacturer's fault (*Kubach* v *Hollands* [1937] 3 All ER 907).

The problem with a causation argument is that there is no room for apportioning blame. Either the manufacturer is the cause of the consumer's injury or he is not. Since the passing of the Law Reform (Contributory Negligence) Act 1945, the position is different in that the court may now apportion damages by reference to the plaintiff's degree of blameworthiness.

Where the consumer misuses a product in an unforeseeable manner, the manufacturer will not be liable because his responsibility only extends to injury suffered as a result of the contemplated use of his product. In these circumstances, it cannot be said that the product is defective. Had the product been used in the manner intended, no harm would have been suffered (*Aswan Engineering Establishment* v *Lupdine Ltd* [1987] 1 WLR 1, 7 per Lloyd LJ).

7.2.5.2 Intermediate examination

In some instances it may be reasonable to expect someone other than the manufacturer to inspect the product before use. Whether or not there is an opportunity to examine goods before they reach the consumer is essentially a matter of causation, since the person who is required to examine and fails to discover a defect in the product can be regarded as the cause of the harm suffered by the consumer.

The fact that someone other than the manufacturer has had an opportunity to examine the goods is not sufficient to exonerate the manufacturer. It must also be shown that the manufacturer can reasonably expect the other person to take up the opportunity to examine (*Griffiths* v *Arch Engineering Co. Ltd* [1968] 3 All ER 217, 222 per Chapman J). For this reason, the fact that the consumer could have washed clothing before wearing it for the first time will not excuse the manufacturer if that clothing is likely to cause a skin disease unless washed before use (*Grant* v *Australian Knitting Mills Ltd* [1936] AC 85).

An examination by another person can be expected where the manufacturer has issued a warning that tests should be carried out before use (*Kubach* v *Hollands* [1937] 3 All ER 907; *Holmes* v *Ashford* [1950] 2 All ER 76). In these circumstances the failure by the other person to heed the warning may break the chain of causation, thereby relieving the manufacturer of liability. If the failure of the intermediary to inspect is itself negligent, the consumer may be able to sue the intermediary.

7.2.6 Damage

The *Donoghue* v *Stevenson* [1932] AC 562 principle refers to negligence on the part of the manufacturer resulting in an injury to the consumer's life or property. This is consistent with the general rule that tortious rules are concerned with physical damage. Thus the negligence principle protects the consumer against death, personal injury and property damage.

So far as property damage is concerned, it would appear that if the 'complex structure theory' advanced in *D & F Estates Ltd* v *Church Commissioners for England* [1989] AC 177 applies to defective products, one part of a complex product may cause damage to another part of the same product. That damage is regarded as damage to other property. The difficulty in these circumstances is that it may be difficult to say when one part of a product is distinct from the rest of the product. In any case, the usefulness of this theory has been cast into serious doubt in later cases (see chapter 6). If the defective product causes damage to other property belonging to the consumer, that property damage is actionable in a negligence action on ordinary principles. But it may be the case that the property damage also results in additional, consequential losses, which may be financial in nature. It appears that these losses are recoverable in a tort action even if they amount to no more than pure economic loss (*Spartan Steel & Alloys Ltd* v *Martin & Co. (Contractors) Ltd* [1973] QB 27; *Muirhead* v *Industrial Tank Specialities Ltd* [1986] QB 507).

In some instances, a defective product may suffer from qualitative defects as well as those which render it unsafe to use. The question has arisen whether the tort of negligence can be used as a means of recovering these economic losses. This matter is considered in more detail at para 6.4.1 in relation to the qualitative defectiveness of a product, but it would appear that a successful action by a consumer in this respect is now very unlikely.

7.3 CONSUMER PROTECTION ACT 1987, PART I

Part I of the Consumer Protection Act 1987 is intended to supplement common law rules (s. 2(6)) by imposing a strict liability regime (s. 2(1)) on the producer of a defective product. It applies to producers rather than manufacturers and the intention is that a producer should insure his product against its potential for causing harm to consumers.

Section 1(1) of the Act states that it shall have effect so as to make such provision as is necessary in order to comply with the Product Liability Directive (Directive 85/374/EEC (25 July 1985)) and shall be construed accordingly. This wording is important since reference may be made to the Directive as an aid to interpreting the Act, particularly where the wording of the Act differs from the wording of the Directive. Since it is for the European Court to determine the scope of the Directive, principles of interpretation may differ from those employed by English courts in relation to domestic statutory provisions (see Whittaker (1989) 105 LQR 125, 130).

At the time of implementation of the Product Liability Directive, the European Commission came under an obligation to report to the Council of Ministers every five years. The first of those reports in 1990 was considered to be unnecessary, since at that stage the majority of member States were still to transpose the content of the Directive into domestic law. France has only recently adopted a measure intended to give effect to the terms of the Directive, and the Commission has commenced infraction proceedings under the EC treaty, art. 177. There is some sympathy for the French position, since in many respects their existing law is more consumer orientated than will be the new law based on compliance with the Directive. However, the purpose of the Directive is not just to ensure a high level of consumer protection, but also to facilitate the harmonisation of product liability laws so as to encourage the single market under which the laws of member States do not operate as a restriction upon the free movement of goods within the Community.

Despite this objective of achieving the approximation of national laws, the Directive permits a number of optional derogations from its terms. These derogations include the ability not to apply the provisions of the Directive to primary agricultural produce; the ability to adopt a development risks defence and the ability to place a financial ceiling on the overall liability of producers. The application of these derogations by member States means that the Directive has not been implemented uniformly across Europe, creating the possibility of restrictions upon the free movement of goods. For example, Luxembourg, Sweden and France either have included or intend to include primary agricultural produce in their product liability laws whereas all other member States have opted for exclusion in this respect. A development risks defence is permitted by all states except Luxembourg, Finland and Norway; Germany has chosen not to apply the defence to medicinal products, and Spain has chosen to disapply the defence in relation to food products intended for human consumption in Spain. The permitted financial ceiling on liability of not less than 17 million ECU has been taken up only by Germany, Greece, Portugal and Spain.

The Commission was required to deliver a further report on the effects of the Directive in 1995, but because civil proceedings take a long time to filter through, it was considered that there was insufficient experience of the operation of the Directive to warrant any change in the present law or practice (First Report on the Application of Council Directive on Liability for Defective Products 13.12.1995, COM (95) 617 Final). However, the Commission did note that in their opinion, the Directive had been useful in increasing awareness of the importance of product safety and that aspects of the operation of the Directive, particularly its application to unprocessed agricultural produce would continue to be monitored.

7.3.1 Producers

For the purposes of the Consumer Protection Act 1987, primary liability in respect of a defective product rests with the producer rather than the retail supplier. In ideal circumstances there would be only one producer of a product and he would be expected to insure his product against its potential for causing harm to the consumer. This avoids the position which obtains under the 'enterprise liability' system whereby all businesses in the chain of supply are potentially liable for the defectiveness of the product and will take out insurance accordingly.

If the Act succeeds in identifying one producer for each product, this may serve to avoid wasteful multiple insurance (see Merkin, *A Guide to the Consumer Protection Act*, 1987, p. 10). However, it would appear that under the Act there is the possibility that more than one producer will be found to exist and where this is the case, potential defendants are jointly and severally liable (s. 2(5)). In limited circumstances, liability may pass down the chain of supply, in which case a number of partcipants in the supply chain may decide it is in their interests to insure. If this is the case, the effect may be to increase the cost of consumer goods.

Included in the definition of a producer in s. 2(2) and s. 1(2) is the manufacturer of a finished product (s. 1(2)(a)), the manufacturer of a component part (Product Liability Directive, art. 3) the producer of raw materials (Consumer Protection Act 1987, s. 1(2)(b)), a person who has subjected a product to an industrial or other process (s. 2(2)(b)) and a person who imports goods into the EC from elsewhere (s. 2(3)).

7.3.1.1 Supply

In order that a person may be held liable under the Consumer Protection Act 1987, he must have supplied a defective product (s. 4(1)(b)) and that supply must be in the course of a business (s. 46(5) and see chapter 1). It follows that a supply by one member of a family to another will not be covered by the Act. Also, it is a defence for the producer who does act in the course of a business to show that the product was not supplied so as to make a profit (s. 4(1)(b)). Accordingly, produce made for charitable purposes such as bring and buy sales will fall outside the scope of the Act, provided the 'producer' can satisfy the burden of proof.

It is also important to emphasise that the supply does not need to be directly to the ultimate consumer. It is sufficient that the producer has voluntarily put the product into circulation.

For these purposes, supply includes selling, hiring, lending, supply pursuant to a hire purchase agreement and a contract for work and materials, exchange for any consideration, provision pursuant to a statutory function, voluntary transfer by way of gift and the provision of a service by which gas or water is made available (s. 46(1)). For the purposes of credit transactions, the dealer and not the finance company is deemed to be the supplier (s. 46(2)).

In the light of this definition, there is little by way of voluntary transfer which will not amount to a supply. However, the transfer or disposal of an interest in land does not bring the supply of the building within the scope of the product liability provisions of the Act (s. 46(4)).

Difficulties may arise in determining who is liable for the supply of a finished product which is defective because of inadequate component parts supplied by another. In these circumstances, the manufacturer of the finished product has supplied the finished product but the component manufacturer has supplied the component part. Ordinarily, the manufacturer of the finished product will be liable in respect of his supply of that product, provided it is covered by the provisions of the Act, but where the finished product is exempt from the provisions of the Act, the manufacturer of that product is not liable for its defectiveness if this results solely from a defect in a component part (s. 1(3)). An exception to this rule exists in the case of a builder who is not liable in respect of his supply of the building (the finished product) but is deemed to be liable for the defectiveness of components used to construct the building (s. 46(3)).

7.3.1.2 Producers other than manufacturers

Liability under the Act is not confined to those who manufacture a finished product. By virtue of s. 1(2) liability also extends to those who have won or abstracted a raw material and to those who have processed a natural product where the essential characteristics of the product are due to that process. In relation to processing, s. 1(2) is not entirely clear. The Product Liability Directive proposed that a processor should be liable for a defect arising from initial processing (art. 2). The difficulty created by s. 1(2) is that it will be necessary for the courts to determine the essential characteristics of each product so as to determine whether the provisions of the Act apply.

By virtue of s. 2(2)(b) a person who puts his own name on a product, thereby holding himself out as the producer will be treated as a producer. Typically, this will cover the high street supermarket chain that sells its 'own brand' products without revealing the identity of the actual producer. One who, in the course of a business, imports a product into the European Community from outside is also deemed to be a producer under s. 2(2)(c).

Where it is not possible to identify the producer or importer of a product, the Act provides for secondary liability on the part of another supplier of the product (s. 2(3)). This person is not necessarily the retail supplier, although in practice the person who supplies to the consumer is most likely to have to accept responsibility, in addition to his liability under the Sale of Goods Act 1979.

In order that a supplier may be liable for harm suffered by the consumer, four requirements must be satisfied. First, the consumer must have asked the supplier to identify the producer (s. 2(3)(a)). Secondly, the request by the consumer must be made within a reasonable time of the occurrence of damage (s. 2(3)(b)). Thirdly, it must have become impracticable for the consumer to identify the actual producer (s. 2(3)(b)). Fourthly, the supplier must have failed, within a reasonable time of the request, to comply with it or to identify the person who supplied him with the product (s. 2(3)(c)). These provisions make it important for retailers to keep records of purchases for some considerable time after initial supply to the consumer, so that they can identify their own supplier, the producer or importer so as to avoid liability themselves.

If the supplier does identify the producer of the product or the person who supplied him with the product, he has satisfied the requirements of s. 2(3) with the result that he will be no longer liable to the consumer. If it happens to be the case that the person or persons identified are insolvent, the consumer may still be left with no practical remedy under the Act.

A difficulty presented by the provisions of s. 2(3) is to determine what is meant by a reasonable time. If the consumer's request is not made within a reasonable time of the occurrence of the damage, the supplier will not be liable. Likewise, if the supplier fails to comply with the consumer's request within a reasonable time of it having been made, he will face liability under s. 2(3).

The Act does not define a reasonable time, but what is reasonable will depend on the circumstances of each case. For the purposes of the initial request by the consumer, it will be necessary to determine when damage occurs. This is defined for the purposes of property damage, as the earliest date on which a person having an interest in the property had knowledge of the material facts concerning the loss or damage (s. 5(5)). This knowledge test is further qualified in ss. 5(6) and (7) with the result that it amounts to a test of objective discoverability with subjective qualifications. It is necessary to ask, first, whether this particular plaintiff was aware of the damage suffered and secondly, whether he would have been reasonable in reaching the particular conclusion he reached.

There is no parallel provision in respect of personal injury, but it would be reasonable to assume that a discoverability test also applies. Thus a consumer who suffers latent personal injury, for example, through consuming pharmaceutical products, will not be deemed aware of the harm he has suffered until it is reasonably discoverable. This may require the consumer's reasonable suspicions to be confirmed through seeking medical advice. In these circumstances, the request will still be made within a reasonable time even though it may come some years after the initial purchase of the product.

7.3.2 Products

The term 'product' is defined in very wide terms in the Consumer Protection Act 1987, subject to a number of specific exclusions. Generally, a product covers any goods, or electricity, and includes any component part or raw material included in another product (s. 1(2)). Goods are defined as including substances, growing crops, things comprised in land by virtue of being attached to it, ships, aircraft and vehicles (s. 45(1)). These provisions, if unqualified, mean that virtually anything movable or immovable is capable of being a product for the purposes of the Act. However, the Product Liability Directive defines a product as something movable, and so there will be certain 'products' which do not fall within the scope of the Act. Included amongst these are some building work, some forms of agricultural produce and products governed by the provisions of the Nuclear Installations Act 1965 (Consumer Protection Act 1987, s. 6(8)).

7.3.2.1 Buildings and fittings If a building is supplied by way of the creation or disposal of an interest in land, the supply is not subject to the provisions of the Consumer Protection Act 1987 (s. 46(4)). However, this does not prevent the goods incorporated in a building from being treated as goods (s. 46(3)). Thus if a building collapses due to a defect in one of the constituent parts employed in its construction, an action under the 1987 Act may lie in respect of personal injury or damage to property other than the building itself.

7.3.2.2 Agricultural produce Article 2 of the Product Liability Directive allows member States to exclude from their definition of a product any primary agricultural produce and game. Primary agricultural products are defined as products of the soil, stock farming and of fishing (Consumer Protection Act 1987 s. 1(2)), excluding products which have undergone initial processing. The intention to include agricultural produce which has been subject to an initial process is given effect in ss. 1(2) and 2(4), but the wording of the Act differs significantly from that of the main body of the Directive in that it refers to an industrial or other process which changes the essential characteristics of the product, whereas the third recital to the Directive refers to an industrial process rather than the phrase incital process used in article 2.

Arguably, an initial process includes crop-spraying with chemicals or hormone treatment of cattle prior to slaughter, which might serve to bring such agricultural produce within the scope of the Act. Whether these could be described as industrial processes is a different matter. Accordingly, it will remain to be seen whether the wording of the Act achieves what appears to have been intended in the Directive. The terms initial process and industrial process appear to include large-scale processes such as pre-cooking and packaging, canning and possibly freezing. However, the requirement of s. 1(2) that the process should change the essential characteristics of the produce must also be considered. The fact that a chicken has been frozen, does not change the fact that it is still essentially a chicken. This particular requirement appears nowhere in the Directive, so the justification for its inclusion is suspect, to say the least.

Where processed food is subject to the provisions of the Act, the processor appears to be strictly liable for the consequences of his process and for defects introduced at an earlier stage. The wording of s. 1(2) is such that if a person has subjected produce to an industrial process which changes its essential characteristics, he is a producer. Accordingly, he is liable for the defectiveness of the product, even though it may not be attributable to his process. Thus, a commercial food processor will be responsible for defects in meat used to make a pie filling where those defects are caused by a farmer giving his cattle infected animal feed.

Why agricultural produce should be exempt from the provisions of the Act and the Directive is difficult to understand. From the point of view of the consumer, food poisoning is a matter of considerable concern. However, the interests of the farming community appear to have been given priority on the grounds that the imposition of liability might place farmers at a competitive disadvantage.

If it transpires that the consumer has been injured as a result of consuming unprocessed food, whether or not he has any remedy will depend on whether he bought the food himself or whether someone in the chain of supply can be said to be at fault. If there is a contractual relationship, the implied terms in the Sale of Goods Act 1979 will apply, in which case liability may pass up the chain of supply and eventually reach the producer of the agricultural produce, who is protected from the application of the provisions of the 1987 Act.

7.3.2.3 Other products The use of the word 'substance' in the definition of goods in s. 45(1) of the Consumer Protection Act 1987 opens up the possibility of applying the Act to a wide range of products. It can be argued that human blood and organs fall within the definition of a product (see Clark (1987) 50 MLR 614), although it would appear that they are not goods for the purposes of the Sale of Goods Act 1979. Furthermore, it may also be necessary to decide whether 'intellectual' products, such as the ideas that go into a book or computer software can be regarded as products (see Whittaker (1989) 105 LQR 125). So far as computer software is concerned, it would appear that a distinction should be made between software which is commercially produced and sold 'off the shelf' and that which has been tailored to the specific needs of an individual client (Prince (1980) 33 Okla L Rev 848 cited in Whittaker, op. cit.; see also *St Albans City & District Council* v *International Computers Ltd* [1996] 4 All ER 481 where a computer disk containing a program was regarded as goods for the purposes of the Sale of Goods Act 1979). In the former case, the product has been placed in the stream of commerce and the producer is in the best position to control risks. In the latter case, the matter is best equated with the liability of a supplier of professional advisory services, which generally only attracts fault-based liability. So far as books are concerned, it is generally the case that information given by the author will result in economic losses which are excluded from the provisions of the Consumer Protection Act 1987 (s. 5(1) and (2)). However, the author and the publishers of a book of recipes may need to consider if they have published a product where reliance on a defective recipe results in food poisoning (see Whittaker, op. cit., pp. 133–5). Policy arguments based on protecting freedom of speech may justify a decision not to impose liability, but it may be difficult to raise a freedom of expression issue in relation to a mass-produced recipe book.

7.3.3 Defectiveness

The basis of the producer's liability is that his product is defective. For these purposes, s. 3(1) of the Consumer Protection Act 1987 provides that a product is defective if it is not as safe as persons generally are entitled to expect. Accordingly, the Act applies only to unsafe products and not to useless products. A product which is perfectly safe but useless, such as a firework which contains no explosive, is not covered by the provisions of the 1987 Act. Instead, such complaints about quality are dealt with under the provisions of the Sale of Goods Act 1979 and the common law rule on negligence, to the extent that qualitative complaints are covered by the rule in *Donoghue* v *Stevenson* [1932] AC 562.

So far as the incidence of the burden of proof is concerned, the Product Liability Directive is clear. It states in art. 4 that the consumer must prove damage, defectiveness and a causal link between the two. This having been established, it is then for the producer to prove that he is covered by one of the defences to liability. On the issue of the burden of proof, the 1987 Act is silent, but applying the rule that he who affirms must prove, general principles of English law require the consumer to bear the burden of proving defectiveness.

7.3.3.1 Statutory guidelines on defectiveness

Section 3(2) of the Consumer Protection Act 1987 identifies a number of factors which can be considered in order to determine the safety of a product. These include the marketing of the product, its get-up and the provision of instructions or warnings about use, expectations about use of the product and the time of supply.

7.3.3.1.1 Marketing, get-up etc. Due to s. 3(2)(a) the court may consider the reason for manufacture, the way the product has been advertised, the sort of instructions supplied with the product and any warnings about misuse which may have been supplied by the producer. By including this wide range of factors for consideration, the Act is more complex than the simple requirement of the Directive that the presentation of the product should be considered (art. 6(1)(a)).

It will be important to identify the producer's intended market, as safety considerations will be affected by the group of people targeted. For example, it might be reasonable to expect higher standards where a product is intended for use by children rather than adults. Similarly, food products primarily intended for consumption by the infirm or the aged might be expected to reach higher standards of safety than food aimed at the ordinary adult population who might be less prone to illness.

In the context of marketing, s. 3(2)(a) also allows the court to consider the purposes for which a product has been marketed. This would appear to allow the court to engage in a cost-benefit analysis based on the objective of the producer in putting the product into circulation balanced against the risk it creates. Accordingly, the court may be able to treat as sufficiently safe a beneficial pharmaceutical product which contains certain inherent safety defects, provided the risks to the user are not too substantial.

Also relevant in the context of a defective product is whether or not it has been supplied along with adequate instructions on use and appropriate warnings in respect of known dangers (see generally MacLeod (1981) 97 LQR 550; Clark [1983] JBL 130). If the producer provides suitable instructions for use or appropriate warnings, this may prevent the product from being defective. It has been seen already that an appropriate warning can relieve the manufacturer of liability under the rule in *Donoghue* v *Stevenson* [1932] AC 562 and a similar regime applies under the 1987 Act. Accordingly, the fact that a producer supplies an inherently dangerous product does not automatically subject him to the strict liability regime of the Act, since he can negative the danger created by his product if he warns the consumer in a suitable fashion. It may be that considerations similar to those which apply to the liability of an occupier of premises under the Occupiers' Liability Act 1957 may be appropriate to the 1987 Act in relation to the adequacy of warnings about product use. It is clear that a warning will not be of any use unless it enables a visitor to be safe on the occupier's premises (Occupiers' Liability Act 1957, s. 2(4)(a); *White* v *Blackmore* [1972] 3 All ER 158). Furthermore, account is taken of the fact that children are less likely to heed warnings than adults. Thus in the context of the 1987 Act, it will need to be considered whether a product is intended to be used by a supervised or an unsupervised child in determining whether the producer's warning suffices to render the product safe for its expected use.

7.3.3.1.2   Expectations about use   By virtue of s. 3(2)(b) of the Consumer Protection Act 1987 the court may also consider what may reasonably be expected to be done with or in relation to the product in deciding whether it is defective. The Act does not specify whose reasonable expectations should be considered, but since s. 3(1) refers to the expectations about safety of persons generally, it can be assumed that all relevant expectations can be taken into account. These would appear to include the expectations of the producer and the consumer.

It has been seen that in the context of the common law negligence liability of a manufacturer, a product can be defective due to a breakdown in the production process, a design defect and a failure to give adequate warnings about use. In the case of a production process defect which renders a product unsafe, it is likely that the product will be defective under the 1987 Act since it fails to reach the standard expected by the producer himself. Design defects present a different problem, since a whole range of products is produced according to the producer's intentions. Deciding whether the end product satisfies the reasonable expectations of persons generally in such a case may be difficult, since persons generally may not have any expectations at all until they have had a chance to test the product.

It would appear that in relation to design defects, a test similar to the 'expectations' test in s. 3(2)(b) has been abandoned in favour of a cost-benefit test similar to the approach adopted at common law in deciding whether there has been a breach of the duty of care. Factors considered by the courts include the difficulty or otherwise of eliminating the defect, balanced against the benefits to society which would have been lost had introduction of the product been delayed pending further tests etc (see *Barker v Lull Engineering Co* (1978) 573 P 2d 443).

Another relevant factor arising under the heading of expectations about use is that the court may consider whether the consumer has used the product in an unexpected fashion for which the product was not intended. For example, it is unlikely that a producer would be held responsible for the death of a poodle warmed in a microwave oven on a cold day. Similarly the manufacturer of industrial alcohol clearly labelled as a fuel would not be responsible for its use as the base for a party cocktail (*Barnes v Litton Industrial Products* (1976) 409 F Supp 1353). In less extreme cases, the producer would be well advised to issue a warning about the use of his product, if there is a danger that it might be misused. For example, it is common to see warnings concerning inhalation on solvent-based products such as certain types of glue and cigarette lighter fluid. The giving of the warning should serve to exonerate the producer, but it could also be argued that, even in the absence of a warning, the product has not been used in the manner expected by the producer in particular and by persons generally.

7.3.3.1.3 Time of supply   Section 3(2)(c) specifies the time of supply as a relevant factor in determining when a product is defective. It would appear that this provision protects the producer against later developments in terms of product safety. The concluding words of s. 3(2) provide that nothing is to be inferred from the fact that the safety of later products is greater than that of the product supplied by the producer in question.

The time of supply is also relevant in relation to the shelf-life of certain products. It is quite possible that certain products will remain unsold for a considerable period of time. In these circumstances, the producer is judged according to the standards of safety which prevailed at the time he put the product into circulation, not when the product is eventually supplied to the consumer.

7.3.3.2   Defects which do not attract liability under the Act

7.3.3.2.1 Compliance with Community or statutory obligations   Where proceedings are brought against a person under the Consumer Protection Act 1987, he may plead compliance with a mandatory requirement as a defence (s. 4(1)(a)). If the goods supplied comply with the requirements of a Community obligation or a domestic statutory provision, an action against the producer will fail.

7.3.3.2.2 Defects arising after the date of supply   Since the producer is only responsible for the defectiveness of the product at the time he put it into circulation, he will have a defence if the defect in the product only came about after the time of supply (Consumer Protection Act 1987, s. 4(1)(d) and 4(2)(a)). If the defect arises due to wear and tear or misuse by the consumer or some other person, the producer may be able to rely on this defence. A producer who seeks to rely on this defence bears the burden of proving that the product was not defective at the time he put it into circulation. It is important to emphasise that the defence does not apply to defects which existed in the product at the time of supply but which did not come to the attention of the producer until a later date. In these circumstances, the producer might be able to rely on the scientific and technological development defence.

A supplier liable under s. 2(3) will not be responsible for defects which came about after the last date on which the product was supplied by a producer or importer (s. 4(2)(b)).

7.3.3.2.3 Scientific and technological development It is a defence under s. 4(1)(e) for the defendant to show that the state of scientific and technological development at the time the product was put into circulation was not such that a producer of a product of the same description as the product in question might be expected to have discovered the defect if it had existed in his products while they were under his control.

The wording of the defence in s. 4(1)(e) does not exactly follow the wording employed in art. 7(e) of the Directive with the result that it can be argued that the 1987 Act provides for a much wider defence than was envisaged in the Directive (see Merkin, *A Guide to the Consumer Protection Act 1987*, pp. 32–4). If this is the case, the United Kingdom is in breach of its EC Treaty obligations and the Directive, and so the 1987 Act will not state the law on this matter correctly.

The defence is one which member States were permitted to include if they wished, and there is not a consistent practice throughout the Community. One possible consequence of this is that States which have chosen to include the defence may become testing grounds for newly developed products, and supplies to States which have not made the defence available will be delayed until trials have shown that the product is safe for use.

The principal arguments employed to justify the inclusion of the defence were that without it research into the development of new products might be stifled and that the potential liability of producers might be so great as to render their activities uninsurable.

The effect of the defence is that if a product is still on trial and a defect in it is not discoverable at the time of its being put into circulation, the defendant will not be liable. The main problem is to identify what is discoverable, and it is this that lies at the root of the wording of s. 4(1)(e). The argument which convinced the UK government to adopt the more detailed wording of s. 4(1)(e) rather than that of the Directive is that the defect must be reasonably discoverable. It would not be reasonable to make a defendant liable if research which had identified a possible defect was not widely available (see Newdick [1988] Camb LJ 455).

If the approach adopted in s. 4(1)(e) is correct, products developed with the use of new technology are subject to little more than a fault-based regime, since the producer will only be liable if he has failed to take care in keeping abreast of reasonably discoverable relevant research, although the burden of proof will rest on the producer.

Recently, there has been an indication from Germany that the defence is not as broad as might have been previously considered. The German *Produkthaftungsgesetz* (Product Liability Act, introduced in 1990) includes a development risks defence limited to certain types of product. In one of the earliest decisions based upon laws intended to implement the Community Product Liability Directive, the German Supreme Court has held that the defence does not apply to manufacturing defects (see *Product Liability International* (May 1996), p. 73). Accordingly, the defence was considered to have no application to a bottle of mineral water which exploded in the hands of a nine-year-old girl as a result of either a hairline crack in the glass or a hollow in the bottle. The reason why the development risks defence had no application was that it was known that bottles can be subject to hairline cracks and that even if there was no means of detecting these cracks, the presence of such defects cannot be regarded as a development risk. It was said that true development risks must be confined to the risks of design, not the risks of manufacture. Therefore unavoidable manufacturing risks do not fall within the scope of the defence and the manufacturer remains liable.

7.3.3.2.4 Contributory negligence The Law Reform (Contributory Negligence) Act 1945 applies to an action brought under part I of the Consumer Protection Act 1987 (s. 6(4)). Accordingly, it will be open to the court to apportion the plaintiff's damages having regard to his responsibility for the harm he has suffered. If liability under the 1987 Act is viewed as strict, there might be a problem in comparing the blameworthy conduct of the plaintiff against the apparently non-blameworthy conduct of the defendant. However, in some instances under the Act the defendant's liability will be effectively based on fault. Even if the defendant's liability is said to be strict, the courts have faced similar problems in relation to actions for breach of a statutory duty and are likely to treat causes under the 1987 Act in the same way.

7.3.4 Causation
The essential requirements of the Consumer Protection Act 1987 are that the producer has put the product into circulation, that the product is defective and that the defectiveness of the product has caused damage within the meaning of the Act. Although fault on the part of the producer does not have to be proved, the problematic issue of causation still remains and is subject to ordinary principles.

It is clear from the wording of s. 2(1) that the consumer bears the onus of proving that the defect in the product wholly or partly caused the damage he complains of. The wording of s. 2(1) appears to solve one of the problems faced by the consumer in a negligence action, namely, what is the cause of damage resulting partly from a defect in the finished product and partly from a defect in a component used in its manufacture? It is sufficient that a producer is partly responsible for the damage suffered.

While a blameworthy consumer may have his damages reduced by virtue of an application of the contributory negligence 'defence', it is also the case that the 'extremely blameworthy' consumer may be regarded as the cause of the harm he suffers. For example, a person who uses a microwave oven to warm a pet poodle on a cold day can hardly be heard to complain. In these circumstances, the producer may be able to escape liability on the grounds of causation. The issue of causation in this type of case is closely bound up with the meaning of defectiveness considered above. For example, even without an appropriate warning on the microwave oven, it is probably fair to assume that persons generally would not reasonably expect to use the appliance in that way. In these circumstances, the producer can argue either that he is not the cause of the harm suffered or that the appliance is not defective.

7.3.5 Damage

The losses recoverable under the Consumer Protection Act 1987 are fairly clearly defined. By virtue of s. 5(1) damage includes death or personal injury and any loss of or damage to property, including land.

7.3.5.1 Death and personal injury So far as death and personal injury are concerned, the main deficiency of the Act, if it can be considered such, is that it does not specify how damages are to be assessed. It may be assumed that ordinary principles of the law of tort apply, in which case the plaintiff will be able to recover consequential losses such as lost earnings and an award may be made in respect of pain and suffering (see Product Liability Directive, art. 9).

7.3.5.2 Property damage Section 5(3) qualifies the meaning of property damage for the purposes of the Act. It is provided that a producer will only be liable for damage to property which at the time of damage is of a type ordinarily intended for private use, occupation or consumption (s. 5(3)(a)) and was intended by the person suffering the damage to be put mainly to private use, occupation or consumption (s. 5(3)(b)).

The effect of this is that a producer will not be liable for damage to business property. Section 5(3)(b) means that the plaintiff must have intended to put the property mainly to private use, and so property used by a company in the course of business will be excluded. However, it is possible under s. 5(3) for a person to use property for both business and private purposes and so long as it is mainly put to private use, it will be covered by the Act.

In respect of trivial property damage, it is provided that no award of damages shall be made where the claim is for an amount less than £275.

As a result of the definition of damage, economic loss is not recoverable, except in so far as consequential economic losses are recoverable if ordinary tort principles apply. Furthermore, s. 5(2) specifically provides that damage to or loss of the defective product itself (or anything supplied with or comprised in it) is not remediable. This might mean that the damage caused by the explosion of a defective battery fitted to a car manufactured by the defendant is not remediable. However, that conclusion might be questioned on the ground that the battery was not comprised in the car.

7.3.6 Limitation of actions

The limitation period for the purposes of an action under part I of the 1987 Act runs for three years from the date on which damage was caused by the defective product or for three years from the date on which the damage could reasonably have been discovered (Limitation Act 1980, s. 11A(4)). The first of these alternatives will apply to patent damage, but in the case of latent damage it is possible that the normal three year period will have expired before the consumer is aware that he has suffered damage at all. In this case the discoverability test is more likely to be applied.

By virtue of the Limitation Act 1980, s. 11A(3), there is a longstop on the liability of the producer which runs for 10 years from the date on which the product was first put into circulation. Accordingly, if a product first put into circulation in 1985 causes undetectable damage in 1986, which becomes discoverable by the consumer in 1996, the consumer will not be permitted to commence his action because of s. 11A(3).

The court has a discretion under the Limitation Act 1980, s. 33, to extend the time during which an action for personal injuries may be commenced. This discretion is subject to the longstop provision in s. 11A(3) with the result that s. 33 cannot be used to extend the time available to the consumer beyond 10 years from the time the product was put into circulation.

7.4 BREACH OF STATUTORY DUTY

Consumer protection legislation makes wide-ranging use of the strict liability criminal offence in order to regulate trading conduct. Ordinarily, such regulations are regarded as deterrent in effect or at least to encourage businesses to seek to achieve the highest trading standards possible. However, it may be the case that the breach of a statutory duty also gives rise to a civil action for damages in tort, where the consumer can show that he has suffered particular damage as a result of the trader's breach of statutory duty.

7.4.1 The intention of Parliament

In relation to product safety, there are two principal statutes which impose duties on producers and retailers, namely the Food Safety Act 1990 and the Consumer Protection Act 1987, part II. In order to determine whether these statutes allow a civil action for breach of statutory duty, the courts must ascertain the intention of Parliament in this respect. This task is simple where Parliament has expressed its intention, as in the case of the Consumer Protection Act 1987, which provides that an action for breach of statutory duty will lie in the event of the breach of a safety regulation (s. 41(1)). However the matter is more difficult where no such intention has been expressed, as is the case with the Food Safety Act 1990.

Factors which the courts will consider in seeking to identify the intention of Parliament include the size of the class of people protected by the action for breach of statutory duty, the nature of the penalty provided for by the statute and whether there is an adequate alternative available remedy to the consumer.

If the class of people to whom the action for breach of statutory duty might extend is particularly large, it is less likely that the court will find in favour of the plaintiff. Consumers may be regarded as too wide a class of people to be afforded the luxury of a further cause of action in civil law. It is generally thought that if a statutory provision is passed for the protection of the general public and not for the protection of a more closely defined group of people, no action for breach of statutory duty will lie (*Solomons* v *Gertzenstein* [1954] 2 QB 243). However, it has also been argued that it would be strange if an unimportant duty owed to a defined group of people could be enforced by civil action when a comparatively more important duty owed to persons generally could not be so enforced (*Phillips* v *Britannia Laundry Ltd* [1923] 2 KB 832, 841 per Atkin LJ). So far as food legislation is concerned, the courts have generally taken the view that consumers of food constitute such a large group of people that they can be identified with the whole community only (*Buckley* v *La Reserve* [1959] Crim LR 451).

The availability of alternative remedies has also proved to be a stumbling block for the consumer seeking to establish a civil remedy for breach of statutory duties in respect of food. The judicial view appears to be that most breaches of food safety regulations will also give rise to civil action under the Sale of Goods Act 1979, with the result that there is no need to create a further civil action (*Square* v *Model Farm Dairies (Bournemouth) Ltd* [1939] 2 KB 365). However, it should be observed that the existence of common law duties on the part of employers has not prevented the courts from finding new civil actions for breach of statutory duty.

7.4.2 Consumer Protection Act 1987, part II

The Consumer Protection Act 1987 makes it clear that a civil action will lie for breach of a duty imposed by product safety regulations (s. 41(1)). Part II of the Act (see chapter 14) creates a range of obligations which may be based on regulations in respect of the safety of goods generally or particular products (s. 11(1)). The Act also imposes a general safety requirement (s. 10(1)) and allows for the service of prohibition notices and notices to warn (s. 13(1)) and suspension notices (s. 14(1)). Failure to comply with any of these amounts to the commission of a criminal offence, but it is only in respect of the breach of a safety regulation that a civil action for breach of statutory duty will lie (s. 41(1)). No such action will be available in respect of a breach of the general safety requirement, a prohibition notice, a notice to warn or a suspension notice (s. 41(2)).

7.4.3 Incidents of an action for breach of statutory duty

In any action for breach of statutory duty, it must be shown that the duty is owed to the plaintiff. Section 41(1) provides that the duty is owed by the person in breach to any other person who may be affected by a contravention of the safety regulation. The consumer must also be able to show that he has been affected by the failure to comply with the safety regulation and in particular that the injury he has suffered is one which the regulation was intended to guard against. Thus, economic losses suffered by a retailer would not be remediable because the Act is concerned with the safety of goods and because the retailer is not a consumer. However, on the latter point the wording of s. 41(1) may be wide enough to cover a physically injured retailer as he cou d be regarded as a person affected by a contravention of the safety regulation. Other relevant factors in an action for breach of statutory duty are whether there has been a breach of the duty and whether that breach has caused the injury complained of. Important in this last respect might be consumer misuse of a product supplied in breach of safety regulations.

Some actions for breach of statutory duty create torts of strict liability whereas others are construed by the courts as giving rise to fault-based liability on the part of the defendant. The fact that the 1987 Act provides for a due diligence defence (s. 39(1)) might suggest that a breach of safety regulations would be construed as giving rise to fault-based liability only. In these circumstances, it would be for the defendant to discharge the onus of proof on the no-negligence issue.

EIGHT

Defective consumer services

8.1 INTRODUCTION

A frequent cause of consumer complaint is that a service provided by the supplier has not come up to standard. In most instances, the service will have been contracted for, in which case the consumer's remedies will be dependent on the terms of the contract with the supplier. However, in other instances, the service may be provided otherwise than by way of a contract, for example, medical services provided under the National Health Service. In such a case, the consumer's principal remedies will lie in tort. While liability for defective products is symbiotic with the notion of strict liability, (see chapter 6), this is not the case with defective services which continue to be governed by the principle of fault-based liability.

While the civil law obligations of the supplier are important, valuable sources of consumer protection can also be found in the form of criminal law regulation of the supply of services (see chapter 18) and in trade association codes of practice voluntarily submitted to by their members. It has already been seen that in many instances, legal controls may not be the most appropriate means of dealing with consumer problems and that self-regulating codes of practice promulgated by trade associations may be a better response (see chapter 2). The consumer service industry has seen increasing numbers of such codes of practice which are specific to the service to which each code applies. As has been observed, codes of practice can be fashioned to the needs of the particular trade or profession and the needs of the consumers of the service provided. Often, a code of practice will be able to deal with matters which would be extremely difficult to legislate for and because the code is tailor-made for a particular sector of the service market, it will often be more detailed than legislation could be. However, because adherence to a code of practice is a matter of voluntary choice, codes of practice are ineffective in relation to suppliers who choose not to join a trade association. Furthermore, there is also some doubt about the effectiveness of codes of practice where the promoting trade association does not possess sufficient powers of enforcement.

Many codes of practice on services contain similar provisions relating to the speed with which the service is provided and the cost of the service. Sometimes, the provisions about cost require the supplier to give a quotation instead of an estimate of likely cost. It is also common to find a requirement that adequate spare parts should be kept in stock and that guarantees should be given in respect of work done. In respect of disputes, it is common to find provision for a conciliation and arbitration scheme. Many codes also contain provisions in respect of exclusion clauses which provide the consumer with greater protection than that given by the Unfair Contract Terms Act 1977 and perhaps even the Unfair Terms in Consumer Contracts Regulations 1994.

8.2   THE RANGE OF CONSUMER SERVICES AND THE PROBLEMS ENCOUNTERED BY CONSUMERS

Services provided for consumer consumption exist in a variety of forms. Two broad categories can be identified, first, a service related to the transfer of possession or ownership of goods or materials; second, a pure service.

The provision of a pure service requires the expertise or skill of the provider and nothing more. Such services include the professional services of a doctor, a lawyer, a surveyor, a financial adviser or other advice givers. Apart from advice givers, the consumer may also require pure services from the providers of leisure, transport and cleansing services. Services associated with the supply of goods or materials will normally be provided by a skilled tradesman such as a plumber, electrician or double glazing contractor, all of whom will use some material article in addition to the skill they exercise. It is important in this context to identify the source of the consumer's complaint. If the product supplied is defective, an issue of product liability is raised (see chapters 6 and 7) . However, if the manner of installation is the cause of complaint, a defective service has been provided. The other major type of consumer service involves the transfer of possession of goods, without a corresponding transfer of ownership. A typical example of such a service is the contract of hire, for example, the bailment of a rented television for a specified or indeterminate period of time. Important considerations in contracts of this kind are whether the bailor has title to the goods and whether the goods bailed are as described or of the desired quality or fitness. The implied terms relating to description, quality and fitness are almost the same as those implied in a contract for the sale of goods and are considered in chapter 6.

Wherever a service is provided, it must be accepted that the service industry has its fair share of cowboys who may be prepared to engage in unfair practices, detrimental to the consumer. The service provider may be guilty of shoddy or late performance, or of overcharging. All of these issues are intimately concerned with the civil liability of the supplier. However, the criminal law, administrative and business self-control may also alleviate the plight of the consumer. Recourse to law may not always be necessary due to the emergence of numerous trade association codes of practice, which may give greater protection to the consumer than is available through the medium of legal controls. In other instances the consumer may be happy to make a complaint to a consumer protection agency and not pursue an action for damages. For example, a complaint to a trading standards authority may result in the prosecution of the provider of a service, particularly if the provider has given false or misleading information concerning the price, provision or availability of a service (see chapters 18 and 19).

8.3   CIVIL LIABILITY OF THE SUPPLIER

Consumer services may be provided either pursuant to a contract or independently of any such contract. For example, no contract exists between a litigant and a barrister (*Kennedy* v *Broun* (1863) 13 CB NS 677) or between a National Health Service doctor and his or her patient. Similarly, the purchaser of a house who relies on a building society valuation of the property he proposes to purchase may not have dealt directly with the surveyor who provides the valuation (see *Smith* v *Eric S. Bush* [1990] 1 AC 831, below), in which case no contractual relationship exists. However, in all such cases, the provider of the service will still owe a duty to exercise reasonable care in the provision of the service.

Services provided by way of bailment, such as repair, film processing, cleaning and carriage services, will often be subject to the terms of a contract which include an implied term to take reasonable care. In the case of a gratuitous bailment, the provider owes a duty to take reasonable care of the consumer's property. A repairer may also owe a duty of care to a stranger in respect of failure to effect a safe repair. For example, in *Stennett* v *Hancock and Peters* [1939] 2 All ER 578 a garage was liable for negligence where it failed to exercise reasonable care in effecting repairs to the wheel of a vehicle with the result that the wheel flange came loose and struck a pedestrian. Branson J, applying *Donoghue* v *Stevenson* [1932] AC 562, took the view that the requirements laid down by the House of Lords for establishing the liability of a manufacturer of a product to its ultimate consumer, were applicable. Accordingly, the first defendant, the vehicle operator, was not negligent in failing to inspect the wheel to verify that it had been correctly reassembled, because it was reasonable to assume that its assembly had been properly carried out by the garage, the second defendant (see also, *Haseldine* v *Daw & Son Ltd* [1941] 2 KB 343).

8.3.1   Contractual liability
Normal rules of the law of contract apply to consumer contracts, although in some instances the application of such rules can present difficulties (see chapter 4). In particular, the consumer must provide consideration. Unlike contracts for the sale of goods, any consideration will suffice for the purposes of a contract for the supply of services (Supply of Goods and Services Act 1982, s. 12(3)).

8.3.1.1   Terms implied by the Supply of Goods and Services Act 1982
The obligations of the parties are represented by the terms of the contract, which may be express or implied by statute. The Supply of Goods and

Services Act 1982 implies into contracts for the supply of a service, which includes contracts where goods are also supplied, a duty on the part of the business supplier to 'carry out the service with reasonable care and skill' (s. 13) and, in the absence of express contractual provision, a duty to perform the service within a reasonable time (s. 14(1)). Where the contract does not provide otherwise, there is an implied term to the effect that the consumer will pay no more than a reasonable charge for the service, whether or not the supplier acts in the course of a business (s. 15(1)).

Section 13 amounts to a codification of the common law position and imports into the contractual obligation general negligence principles surrounding the ambit of reasonable care and skill (see further, G. Woodroffe, *Goods and Services — The New Law* (London, Sweet & Maxwell, 1982)). It is immediately apparent that liability here is fault-based, so that, for example, a shoe repairer who ruins an expensive pair of boots will avoid liability unless negligence can be proved. It is also evident that the terms implied in a contract for the provision of services are generally less onerous than those implied in a contract for the sale of goods, under which the supplier guarantees the fitness of the goods for the purpose for which the buyer requires them. It has been argued that the standard required of the supplier of consumer services is too low (Stephenson and Clark, National Consumer Council Paper (1985)). By way of riposte, it has been argued that the person who requests a service will frequently specify the nature and extent of the service he requires (see Law Com. No. 156 (Cmnd 9773, 1986), para. 2.24). The response of the Law Commission may, in turn, be criticised on the ground that consumers often fail to specify exactly what they want due to a lack of information on their part. Accordingly, it remains the case that the consumer of services is in a considerably worse position than the consumer of a defective product.

Section 12(1) of the Supply of Goods and Services Act defines a 'contract for the supply of a service' as meaning 'a contract under which a person ("the supplier") agrees to carry out a service'. Some services do not fall within the provisions of the 1982 Act. Consistent with the view that the statute gives effect to the common law, a distinction is drawn between a contract of service and a contract for services. Accordingly, contracts of employment and contracts of apprenticeship are expressly excluded from the scope of the Act (s. 12(2)). Other types of service contract may also be excluded from its provisions by order of the Secretary of State, so as to give effect to the position at common law before 1982. Exemptions have been made in respect of advocates, company and building society directors and arbitrators (see SI 1982/1771; SI 1983/902 and SI 1985/1) with the effect that the implied term relating to the exercise of reasonable care and skill does not apply to the services provided by such persons.

8.3.1.2 Contracts for services and contracts for work and materials

Many contracts for the provision of a service also involve the supply of goods. For example, the consumer may engage the services of a plumber to supply and install a bathroom suite. In such a case, it becomes important to distinguish between the supply of goods element in the contract and the part of the contract that relates to the skill exercised by the plumber. If the reason for the consumer's complaint is that the bath is defective, the consumer will be able to invoke the implied terms which relate to the fitness and quality of the goods supplied and which impose a form of strict liability (see chapter 6). However, if the consumer's complaint is that the bath has been badly fitted, his complaint is in respect of the service provided, and, subject to what has been expressly agreed, the supplier of the service is liable only for failure to exercise reasonable care and skill. In a contract for work and materials, the goods element is governed by Part I of the 1982 Act and the service element by Part II.

Distinguishing between a contract for the supply of a service and one for the supply of goods is sometimes difficult. Some contracts are primarily contracts for the supply of a service which incidentally involve the supply of a material article. For example, in *Perlmutter* v *Beth David Hospital* (1955) 123 NE 2d 792 the plaintiff, a private patient, was given a blood transfusion with contaminated blood. Expert evidence showed that the contamination was undetectable. The plaintiff claimed that the defendants were strictly liable for breach of the implied term relating to product quality. However, the majority of the court held that the contract was one for the provision of a service and that the defendants would only be liable for a failure to exercise reasonable care (see also *Roe* v *Minister of Health* [1954] 2 QB 66). However, in *Dodd* v *Wilson* [1946] 2 All ER 691, where the plaintiff's cattle were harmed as a result of the defendant veterinary surgeon's use of a serum which was not fit for its intended use, the defendant was not negligent but was nonetheless liable for the harm suffered. It is difficult to distinguish these cases and it might be argued that they show scant regard for personal safety compared with the safety of a farmer's cattle. However, a distinction may lie in the fact that a substance such as human blood is not ordinarily regarded as something which is the subject of a commercial transaction (cf. the Consumer Protection Act 1987, s. 45(1) and see chapter 8).

The test employed for distinguishing a supply of goods from a supply of services is to enquire what is the substance of the contract. It is necessary to determine whether the contract is substantially one for the exercise of skill or one which is intended to transfer ownership in goods to the consumer. For example, if a prospective house purchaser engages the services of a surveyor, he will receive a material article in the form of a written report, but the substance of the contract is the skill of the surveyor in surveying the property. Similarly, in *Robinson* v *Graves* [1935] 1 KB 579 a contract for the provision of a service was made where a consumer engaged the services of an artist to paint a portrait, despite the transfer of ownership in the painting. Perhaps surprisingly, it has been held that a contract for the supply of a meal in a restaurant is a contract for the sale of goods (*Lockett* v *A. & M. Charles Ltd* [1938] 4 All ER 170, see also Supply of Goods and Services Act 1982, s. 12(3)(a), which provides that a contract is a contract for the supply of a service whether or not goods are also transferred), despite the undoubted skill which goes into the preparation of the meal. Perhaps a different conclusion might be arrived at if the meal was one prepared by Michel Roux or Anton Mosimann rather than a simple dish of whitebait as in *Lockett* v *A. & M. Charles Ltd*! In *Lee* v *Griffin* (1861) 1 B & S 272, a contract to supply false teeth was held to be a contract of sale. This decision was approved by the Supreme Court of Victoria in *Deta Nominees Pty Ltd* v *Viscount Plastic Products Pty Ltd* [1979] VR 167, which held that a contract to supply plastic moulding dies made to the customer's specification was a sale of goods contract.

8.3.2 Tortious liability

The non-contractual supplier of a service is not immune from liability as he may owe a duty of care to the consumer of the service. Alternatively, the fault of the supplier may consist of giving misinformation which induces the consumer to enter into the supply contract. In such a case, the misleading information may not be regarded as part of the contract, but the supplier of the service may nevertheless be liable for misrepresentation.

8.3.2.1 Negligence In the absence of a contractual nexus between the parties, the supplier of a service may still be liable for a failure to exercise reasonable care. Thus if the service is provided gratuitously, or if the supplier's defective performance foreseeably harms a third party, the supplier may be liable for negligence. Much will depend on the type of harm suffered by the consumer. As a general rule it is much easier for a negligence action to succeed where the consumer has suffered personal injury or property damage than if the harm is of a financial nature.

Even where there is a contractual relationship between the supplier and the consumer, the consumer may choose to sue for breach of a tortious obligation since it is now established that contractual and tortious duties of care may exist concurrently. In *Henderson* v *Merrett Syndicates Ltd* [1995] 2 AC 145 Lord Goff of Chieveley stated that 'unless his contract precludes him from doing so, the plaintiff, who has available to him concurrent remedies in contract and tort, may choose that remedy which appears to him to be the most advantageous' (at p. 194; see also *Midland Bank Trust Co. Ltd* v *Hett, Stubbs & Kemp* [1979] Ch 384; *Forsikringsaktieselskapet Vesta* v *Butcher* [1986] 2 All ER 488 at p. 507; cf. *Groom* v *Crocker* [1939] 1 KB 194; and see also Kaye (1984) 100 LQR 680).

Whether the consumer sues in contract or in tort has practical implications, since different rules on limitation of actions apply to the different causes of action. For contract, the six-year limitation period laid down by the Limitation Act 1980 accrues when the breach occurs. The fact that damage is not suffered by the plaintiff until some later date does not extend the limitation period. However, if the breach gives rise to an action in negligence, the cause of action accrues when damage is in fact sustained. Accordingly, the limitation period starts to run at a later date in tort (see *Henderson* v *Merrett Syndicates Ltd* and *Midland Bank Trust Co. Ltd* v *Hett, Stubbs and Kemp*). Further, there are apparently different rules relating to remoteness of damage and quantification of damages depending on whether the action is framed in contract or in tort.

8.3.2.2 Misrepresentation As with any contract, the supplier of a service may make a number of assertions about his intended performance. Some of these assertions may be treated as express terms of the contract whereas others will amount to representations only. If the representation proves to be false, it may be actionable under the Misrepresentation Act 1967 or under the common law rule concerning negligent misstatements in *Hedley Byrne & Co. Ltd* v *Heller & Partners Ltd* [1964] AC 465. In *Esso Petroleum Co. Ltd* v *Mardon* [1976] QB 801 the Court of Appeal held that in making statements about a petrol station's prospective 'throughput' during pre-contractual negotiations, the plaintiffs owed the defendant a duty of care since they had a financial interest in the advice they were giving and knew that the defendant was relying on their knowledge and expertise. It therefore follows that, provided all the ingredients of a duty of care are present, a duty will arise even in a pre-contractual situation (see Sealy [1976] CLJ 221).

8.4 GENERAL DUTIES OF THE PARTIES TO A CONTRACT FOR THE SUPPLY OF SERVICES

Where a service is provided under a contract, the supplier is subject to a number of implied duties in respect of performance. Some of these duties will apply to the supplier whether or not there is a contractual relationship between the supplier and the consumer. Additionally, the supplier may expressly undertake to do more than is implied by law. As has been noted above, under the Supply of Goods and Services Act 1982 the implied obligations of the supplier include a duty to perform the service with reasonable care and skill, to perform the service within a reasonable time and to charge no more than a reasonable amount. Other factors which may also be relevant are whether personal performance is required and whether the supplier ever guarantees a particular result.

8.4.1 Reasonable care and skill
Whether the action is framed in contract or in tort, the supplier owes a duty to exercise reasonable care in the performance of a service. In a contractual action, the duty is based on the Supply of Goods and Services Act 1982, s. 13, and if the action is one for negligence at common law, the duty is based on ordinary *Donoghue* v *Stevenson* [1932] AC 562 principles, either as a variety of manufacturers' liability or on the basis that the consumer is the supplier's neighbour (see chapter 7).

8.4.1.1 Privity of contract and tortious proximity As a general rule, the duty owed by the supplier will be based on a voluntary assumption of liability, since the relationship between the supplier and the consumer is normally very close, and performance of the service will have been expressly requested. Accordingly, the supplier will be aware of the identity of the person who benefits from the provision of the service. Even if this is not the case, the supplier will usually be aware that someone in the class of persons to which the consumer belongs will rely on the service provided.

In the case of a service provided by way of a contract, a duty of care is implied under the Supply of Goods and Services Act 1982, s. 13. Where a service is provided in a non-contractual setting, the consumer will have to establish that he is sufficiently proximate to the supplier to justify protection in law. Accordingly, where the consumer commissions building services, the builder will be liable under the terms of his contract with the consumer. Whether the builder is also liable for losses suffered by a subsequent purchaser depends on the provisions of the Defective Premises Act 1972 and on the type of loss suffered by the consumer. If a consumer complains of personal injury or damage to property other than the building itself, the loss is prima facie actionable in tort (see *D & F Estates Ltd* v *Church Commissioners for England* [1989] AC 177). For these purposes, property damage appears to include damage by one part of a 'complex structure' to another part of the same complex structure, although what constitutes a complex structure is not entirely clear (see chapter 7).

Establishing the necessary relationship of proximity is difficult in cases where the service has not been requested but the consumer has nonetheless relied on the supplier. This problem may arise where one person gives information to another which is then passed on to a third party who detrimentally relies on it, for example, where a valuation report by a surveyor is given to a building society in the knowledge that it will be passed on to the purchaser of the surveyed house. In such a case, the surveyor does owe the purchaser a duty to exercise reasonable care, provided he is aware that such a person would almost certainly rely on the valuation. In *Smith* v *Eric S. Bush* [1990] 1 AC 831, the plaintiff applied to the Abbey National Building Society for a mortgage to enable her to purchase a house. The Society was under a statutory duty to obtain a written valuation report on the house and instructed the defendant surveyor to inspect the dwelling and provide the necessary report. The plaintiff paid the Society an inspection fee, and signed an application form which stated that she would be provided with a copy of the report. The report also contained a disclaimer to the effect that neither the Society nor the surveyor warranted that the report and the valuation would be accurate and that the report was supplied without any assumption of responsibility. In reliance on the report, and without obtaining an independent survey, the plaintiff purchased the house. The surveyor, who knew that the report would be shown to the purchaser, was found to be negligent in failing to detect a structural defect in one of the chimneys. Although the surveyor had observed that the first-floor chimney breasts had been removed, he failed to ascertain whether or not the chimneys were adequately supported. Eighteen months after the purchase, one of the chimney flues collapsed and crashed through the bedroom ceiling causing considerable damage

With respect to the disclaimer, the House of Lords held that it was governed by the Unfair Contract Terms Act 1977, s. 2(2), and therefore had to satisfy the requirement of reasonableness to be effective. In the circumstances, it was held that it would not be fair or reasonable for mortgagees and valuers to impose on purchasers the risk of loss arising as a result of carelessness on the part of the valuers. Lord Templeman observed:

A valuer who values property as a security for a mortgage is liable either in contract or in tort to the mortgagee for any failure on the part of the valuer to exercise reasonable skill and care in the valuation. The valuer is liable in contract if he receives instructions from and is paid by the mortgagee. The valuer is liable in tort if he receives instructions from and is paid by the mortgagor but knows that the valuation is for the purpose of a mortgage and will be relied upon by the mortgagee.

. . . in my opinion the valuer assumes responsibility to both mortgagee and purchaser by agreeing to carry out a valuation for mortgage purposes knowing that the valuation fee has been paid by the purchaser and knowing that the valuation will probably be relied upon by the purchaser in order to decide whether or not to enter into a contract to purchase the house.

See also, *Yianni* v *Edwin Evans & Sons* [1982] QB 438.

The relationship between the parties in *Smith* v *Eric S. Bush* was 'akin to contract', but if the relationship is less close, it is less likely that a duty of care will be owed. For example, it is clear that the surveyor would have owed no duty of care to a subsequent purchaser of the house who might have been shown a copy of the report and suffered economic loss. So far as economic loss is concerned, the courts have sought to restrict substantially the circumstances in which it is recoverable. The 'two-stage' test of Lord Wilberforce in *Anns* v *Merton London Borough Council* [1978] AC 728, 751–2, has been subject to much criticism on the ground that a general test of that nature cannot take into account the wide range of circumstances relevant to whether or not a duty of care should be imposed in respect of economic losses. Instead the House of Lords in *Caparo Industries plc* v *Dickman* [1990] 2 AC 605 has advocated a more cautious approach Lord Bridge of Harwich stated (at pp. 617–18):

But since the *Anns* case a series of decisions . . . have emphasised the inability of any single general principle to provide a practical test which can be applied to every situation to determine whether a duty of care is owed and, if so, what is its scope. . . . What emerges is that, in addition to the foreseeability of damage, necessary ingredients in any situation giving rise to a duty of care are that there should exist between the party owing the duty and the party to whom it is owed a relationship characterised by the law as one of 'proximity' or 'neighbourhood' and that the situation should be one in which the court considers it fair, just and reasonable that the law should impose a duty of a given scope upon the one party for the benefit of the other. . . . Whilst recognising, of course, the importance of the underlying general principles common to the whole field of negligence, I think the law has now moved in the direction of attaching greater significance to the more traditional categorisation of distinct and recognisable situations as guides to the existence, the scope and the limits of the varied duties of care which the law imposes.

Accordingly, reasonable foresight of harm on its own is not sufficient to give rise to a duty to take care. It is also essential that there is a very close relationship of proximity between the giver and the recipient of the advice, characterised by reasonable reliance (in the sense of its causative effect, see below) on the advice and that the imposition of a duty of care should be fair and just in the circumstances. The requirement of reliance in actions for negligent misstatement is, of course, critical for 'the plaintiff will have no cause of action at all unless he can show damage and he can only have suffered damage if he has relied on the negligent statement' (*White* v *Jones* [1995] 2 AC 207, 272 per Lord Browne-Wilkinson, see also 288 per Lord Mustill).

Regard must be had to the adviser's knowledge of the particular purpose for which the advice is to be used. These elements were explained further in *James McNaughton Paper Group Ltd* v *Hicks Anderson & Co.* [1991] QB 113, where it was said that regard should be had to the purpose for which the statement was made and communicated, the relationship between the adviser, the advisee and any relevant third party, the size of the class to which the advisee belongs, the knowledge of the adviser and the extent of reliance by the advisee. These tests were applied by the Court of Appeal in *Goodwill* v *British Pregnancy Advisory Service* [1996] 2 All ER 161, in which the plaintiff, who became pregnant by a partner who had undergone a vasectomy operation carried out by the defendants, sued in respect of her financial losses resulting from the birth of her daughter. It was held that the defendants were not in a sufficient or any special relationship to the plaintiff such as to give rise to a duty of care. Further, the defendants could not be taken to have voluntarily assumed responsibility to the plaintiff when giving advice to the man, since at that time she was not an existing sexual partner of his. Peter Gibson LJ therefore concluded that she 'was merely, like any other woman in the world, a potential sexual partner of his, that is to say a member of an indeterminately large class of females who might have sexual relations with (him) during his lifetime' (ibid. 169). The conclusion which follows from these cases is that very rarely will an adviser owe a duty of care to a person who relies on his advice, unless the adviser is made fully aware of the nature of the reliance and the transaction the advisee proposes to enter into in reliance on the advice. Thus a company auditor will generally owe no duty of care to a person who relies on audited company accounts to purchase additional shares in the company whose accounts he has audited (*Caparo Industries plc* v *Dickman*). However, a duty of care may be owed by an accountant who negligently prepares accounts to be shown to an identified potential investor (*Morgan Crucible Co. plc* v *Hill Samuel & Co. Ltd* [1991] Ch 295). The basis of liability for economic loss arising from negligent misstatement under the *Hedley Byrne & Co. Ltd* v *Heller & Partners Ltd* [1964] AC 465 principle, has been the subject of extensive review in three recent decisions by an arguably expansive House of Lords. The first of which is *Spring* v *Guardian Assurance plc* [1995] 2 AC 296 in which the plaintiff was unable to take up an offer of a job because the reference provided by his ex-employer wrongfully described him as dishonest. He could not sue for defamation because the reference was covered by the defence of qualified privilege. The plaintiff therefore brought an action in negligence. Lord Goff of Chieveley reviewed the principal speeches in *Hedley Byrne & Co. Ltd* v *Heller & Partners Ltd* and found that:

> . . . although *Hedley Byrne* itself was concerned with the provision of information and advice, it is clear that the principle in the case is not so limited and extends to include the performance of other services, as for example the professional services rendered by a solicitor to his client. . . . Accordingly where the plaintiff entrusts the defendant with the conduct of his affairs, in general or in particular, the defendant may be held to have assumed responsibility to the plaintiff, and the plaintiff to have relied on the defendant to exercise due skill and care, in respect of such conduct. ([1995] 2 AC 296, 318)

In finding for the plaintiff, Lords Goff and Woolf stressed that sufficient proximity exists where the relationship between the parties is 'equivalent to contract'. Lord Goff stressed that: 'It is not to be forgotten that the *Hedley Byrne* duty arises where there is a relationship which is, broadly speaking, either contractual or equivalent to contract' (ibid. 324). *Spring* v *Guardian Assurance plc* is significant because there was no direct reliance by the plaintiff on the defendant, and so it is now doubtful whether reliance, in its strict sense, remains a prerequisite to *Hedley Byrne* liability. But, as noted above, this is not to say that the requirement of reliance has been jettisoned since it will continue to operate under the guise of causation (cf. *Caparo Industries plc* v *Dickman*; see Howarth, *Textbook on Tort* (London: Butterworths, 1995), pp. 286–90 and Murphy, 'Expectation losses and negligent omissions' [1996] CLJ 43).

The second case is *Henderson* v *Merrett Syndicates Ltd* [1995] 2 AC 145, in which the plaintiffs were 'names' (investors) in the Lloyd's insurance market and were members of syndicates managed by the defendant underwriters as agents. The plaintiffs suffered considerable financial losses in respect of a number of policies underwritten by their syndicates. They sued the defendants for the negligent mismanagement of their financial affairs. Although the defendants were in breach of contract in failing to exercise due care as managing agents of the syndicates, the plaintiffs' action was time barred because the limitation period for contract starts to run from the date of the breach not, as in tort, when the damage is suffered.

Lord Goff, delivering the principal opinion of the House of Lords, held that the defendants were liable. He found that *Hedley Byrne* liability arises either where the defendants assume responsibility for the plaintiffs' economic welfare, or where the relationship between the parties is 'equivalent to contract'. The crucial factor for finding liability for negligent misstatement now appears to be the existence of an assumption of responsibility. Having again subjected the speeches in *Hedley Byrne & Co. Ltd* v *Heller & Partners Ltd* to considerable analysis, Lord Goff concluded:

> . . . we can derive some understanding of the breadth of the principle underlying the case. We can see that it rests upon a relationship between

the parties, which may be general or specific to the particular transaction, and which or may not be contractual in nature. All of their lordships spoke in terms of one party having assumed or undertaken a responsibility towards the other. ([1995] 2 AC 145 at p. 180)

Significantly, Lord Goff went on to add that:

It follows that, once the case is identified as falling within the *Hedley Byrne* principle, there should be no need to embark upon any further enquiry whether it is 'fair, just and reasonable' to impose liability for economic loss (p. 181).

Commenting upon Lord Goff's disavowal of the control mechanism afforded by the 'fair, just and reasonable' test, Mr Weir laments that this 'is rather a strong thing to say in an opinion which discounted the importance of reliance, and equated not only speech with action but commission with omission (which in the case of speech means silence)' ((1995) 111 LQR 357, 361).

The final case in the trilogy is *White* v *Jones* [1995] 2 AC 207. The issue before the House was whether two beneficiaries, the daughters of the testator, who lost their intended legacies as a result of the carelessness of their father's solicitor in failing to execute his will when instructed to do so, could sue the solicitor for negligence. The contract was, of course, between the deceased father and his solicitor, and the beneficiaries in question had not relied on the defendant solicitor's skill. Lord Goff acknowledged that there was a lacuna in the law which 'practical justice' required to be filled. He said:

In the forefront stands the extraordinary fact that, if such a duty is not recognised, the only persons who might have a valid claim (i.e., the testator and his estate) have suffered no loss, and the only person who has suffered a loss (i.e., the disappointed beneficiary) has no claim (p. 259).

The loss suffered by the testator's daughters was the value of their expected legacies which would pass to the residuary legatees. Lord Goff therefore held that the assumption of responsibility on the part of the solicitor towards his client should extend to the intended beneficiary.

Lord Browne-Wilkinson, adopting a different route to reach the same conclusion, approached the issue from the stand point of *Hedley Byrne & Co. Ltd* v *Heller & Partners Ltd*. Proximity or, in other words, the existence of a 'special relationship' between the parties, depended upon the solicitor having made 'a conscious assumption of responsibility for the task rather than a conscious assumption of legal liability to the plaintiff for its careful perform-ance' ([1995] 2 AC 207 at p. 274). By way of explanation his lordship said:

The solicitor who accepts instructions to draw a will knows that the future economic welfare of the intended beneficiary is dependent upon his careful execution of the task. It is true that the intended beneficiary (being ignorant

of the instructions) may not rely on the particular solicitor's actions. But
. . . in the case of a duty of care flowing from a fiduciary relationship
liability is not dependent upon actual reliance by the plaintiff on the
defendant's actions but on the fact that, as the fiduciary is well aware, the
plaintiff's economic well-being is dependent upon the proper discharge by
the fiduciary of his duty (p. 275).

Lord Browne-Wilkinson therefore held that the solicitor, by accepting instructions to draw a will, came into a special relationship with the beneficiaries and in consequence owed a duty of care to act with due expedition and
care in relation to the task. The decision in *Smith* v *Eric S. Bush* seems,
therefore, to fit easily within this interpretation of proximity. Similarly, such
a tenuous relationship as existed in *Goodwill* v *British Pregnancy Advisory
Service* between the doctor and the plaintiff clearly fails this test of proximity.

On the face of it, the approach adopted by the majority of the House in
White v *Jones* would seem to offend the notion that the law of negligence
should not countenance liability 'in an indeterminate amount for an indeterminate time to an indeterminate class' (per Lord Bridge in *Caparo Industries
plc* v *Dickman* quoting Cardozo CJ in *Ultramares Corporation* v *Touche* (1931)
174 NE 441 at p. 444). However, Lord Goff stressed that, in his view, the
threat of opening the floodgates was not present since the loss in question was
limited both in amount and in terms of those who were potentially liable.

8.4.1.2   Required standard of care   Whether the consumer's action lies
in contract or in tort, the same basic standard of care applies. The business
supplier of a service has to perform to the standard of the reasonably
competent member of the relevant trade (Supply of Goods and Services Act
1982, s. 13). For the purposes of tort actions, the issue received substantial
consideration by McNair J in *Bolam* v *Friern Hospital Management Committee*
[1957] 2 All ER 118. The plaintiff alleged negligence on the part of a doctor
who had administered electroconvulsive therapy to the plaintiff without first
administering a relaxant drug or applying any restraint to the plaintiff to
prevent convulsive movements. As a result, the plaintiff suffered a fractured
jaw. The learned judge stated (at p. 121):

How do you test whether this act or failure is negligent? In an ordinary case
it is generally said, that you judge that by the action of the man in the
street. He is the ordinary man. . . . But where you get a situation which
involves the use of some special skill or competence, then the test whether
there has been negligence or not is not the test of the man on the top of a
Clapham omnibus, because he has not got this special skill. The test is the
standard of the ordinary skilled man exercising and professing to have that
special skill. A man need not possess the highest expert skill at the risk of
being found negligent. It is well-established law that it is sufficient if he
exercises the ordinary skill of an ordinary competent man exercising that
particular art.

In considering the requisite standard of care to be displayed by members of a profession, the judge went on to say (at p. 122):

A doctor is not guilty of negligence if he has acted in accordance with a practice accepted as proper by a responsible body of medical men skilled in that particular art. . . . Putting it the other way round, a doctor is not negligent, if he is acting in accordance with such a practice, merely because there is a body of opinion that takes a contrary view. At the same time, that does not mean that a medical man can obstinately and pig-headedly carry on with some old technique if it has been proved to be contrary to what is really substantially the whole of informed medical opinion.

A jeweller piercing the ears of a consumer is required to exhibit the standard of care expected of a reasonable jeweller, not the standard expected of a surgical registrar (*Phillips* v *William Whiteley Ltd* [1938] 1 All ER 566). However, a hairdresser who fails to read instructions on how to use a hair dye before applying it to his client's scalp (*Watson* v *Buckley, Osborne, Garrett & Co.* [1940] 1 All ER 174), or a carpet layer who leaves a carpet in a condition whereby the consumer can trip over an exposed edge (*Kimber* v *William Willett Ltd* [1947] 1 All ER 361) both fail to reach the standard of the reasonably competent. Further, it is a requirement of such cases that the service is provided in a workmanlike and safe manner (*Kimber* v *William Willett Ltd* at p. 362 per Tucker LJ).

A relevant factor considered by the court in determining whether the duty of care has been broken is that of general and approved practice. If the supplier of the service has complied with a standard practice, this may be some evidence that he has exercised reasonable care. However, such compliance should not be regarded as conclusive evidence of the exercise of such care. It may be the case that an established practice has become obsolete and that adherence to it is to be regarded as negligence on the part of the service provider (*Brown* v *Rolls Royce Ltd* [1960] 1 WLR 210).

Since the test applied is objective, it is no defence for the supplier to argue that he has done his incompetent best. The supplier is judged by the standards of the reasonably competent supplier of the type he or she claims to be. The law does not countenance varying standards of care. Thus the novice who has just started to supply a service of a particular kind is required to reach the same standard of competence as the supplier with a number of years' experience (*Nettleship* v *Weston* [1971] 2 QB 691). This approach has been applied by the Court of Appeal to the acts of a trainee doctor, even though doctors require clinical training and the health authority in question lacked the financial resources required to staff all of its wards with qualified staff (*Wilsher* v *Essex Area Health Authority* [1987] QB 730; standard of care was not discussed when the case went to the House of Lords, (1988) AC 1074 see further, A. Dugdale and K. Stanton, *Professional Negligence* (London: Butterworths, 1989)).

If the service is not provided in the course of a business, s. 13 of the Supply of Goods and Services Act 1982 does not apply, but the private supplier will still be subject to the tortious duty to take reasonable care. However, since the supplier is not acting in the course of a business, the standard he will be expected to adhere to will be lower than that expected of a professional. Nonetheless, he will be expected to reach the standard of a reasonably competent amateur (*Wells* v *Cooper* [1958] 2 QB 265).

It has been argued that the standard of reasonable care and skill is too low a standard for the purposes of consumer services and that it produces uncertainty about what the consumer can expect from the supplier. However, it would appear that for the time being no changes in the law are likely, since the Law Commission (Law Com. No. 156 (Cmnd. 9773, 1986)) regard the present state of the law as satisfactory. The Law Commission were of the view that the standard of reasonable care is a flexible standard and that decided cases are sufficient guidance on how the test is to be applied in particular instances.

8.4.2 Guaranteeing a result

Since the supplier of a service is ordinarily liable only for a failure to exercise reasonable care, it follows that the supplier will not be deemed to guarantee a particular result. This position holds true even for the contractual supplier of services. But, unlike the contractual supplier of goods, the supplier of a service is not regarded as an insurer in respect of harm suffered by the consumer. It follows that a solicitor does not warrant the success of proposed litigation and a surgeon does not guarantee that an operation will be successful. In *Thake* v *Maurice* [1986] 1 All ER 497 the plaintiffs, a married couple, had five children and wished to prevent further pregnancies. The defendant was a surgeon who contracted to carry out a sterilisation by vasectomy on the husband. The appropriate consents were given, but following the operation, Mrs Thake became pregnant. It was contended by the plaintiffs that the defendant had led a reasonable person in the position of the plaintiffs to believe that he had firmly promised that the operation would lead to sterility. The Court of Appeal found that no such 'guarantee' could be inferred. Nourse LJ, with whom Neill LJ agreed, stated (at p. 511):

The question then is whether the defendant contracted to carry out a vasectomy to render Mr Thake permanently sterile. The latter alternative necessarily involved a guarantee; in other words, a warranty that there was not the remotest chance, not one in ten thousand, that the operation would not succeed. . . . The contract contained an implied warranty that, in carrying out the operation, the defendant would exercise the ordinary skill and care of a competent surgeon. It did not contain an implied warranty that, come what may, the objective would be achieved. . . . The only question is whether it contained an express warranty to that effect. Would the words and visual demonstrations of the defendant have led a reasonable person standing in the position of the plaintiffs to understand that, come what may, Mr Thake would be rendered sterile and incapable of parenthood? . . . In the end the question seems to be reduced to one of determining the extent of the knowledge which is to be attributed to the reasonable person standing in the position of the plaintiffs. . . . I do not suppose that a reasonable person standing in the position of the plaintiffs would have known that a vasectomy is an operation whose success depends on a healing of human tissue which cannot be guaranteed. . . . But it does seem to me to be reasonable to credit him with the more general knowledge that in medical science all things, or nearly all things, are uncertain . . . that knowledge is part of the general experience of mankind.

Interestingly, the position in English law stands in stark contrast to the approach adopted in Australia. Subject to certain limited exceptions s. 74(2) of the Trade Practices Act 1974 (Australia) implies on the part of the supplier of a service, a warranty that the service will be reasonably fit for the purpose made known to him, whether 'expressly or by implication', by the consumer, and that the service is of such quality that it might reasonably be expected to achieve the desired result.

The contractual supplier of a service can guarantee a result, but this will normally arise only where there is an express term of the contract to this effect. Thus in *G K Serigraphics* v *Dispro Ltd* (unreported, CA Transcript 916, 1980) the appellants contracted to stick a laminated surface on printed boards. When the lamination failed to work, the appellants were taken to have agreed expressly to laminate the boards properly. Since they had not performed what they had contracted to do, it was held that their breach went to the root of the contract. The problem with express contractual terms is that the consumer must know exactly what he or she wants and negotiate with the supplier to that end. All too frequently consumers are unsure what they require and their contracts reflect this imprecision. Consumers often find it difficult to articulate requirements with the result that contracts will not always achieve the result anticipated. Accordingly, the contractual expectations of consumers might be better achieved if the law were to imply certain basic standards.

Occasionally, the circumstances of the case may justify the imposition of a standard higher than that of reasonable care, with the result that the supplier of a service may be deemed to have undertaken to produce a particular outcome. Where a stricter duty is held to exist, it is likely to relate to 'design services'. In *Greaves & Co. (Contractors) Ltd* v *Baynham Meikle & Partners* [1975] 3 All ER 99 the designers of a warehouse floor were taken to have impliedly warranted that the floor would be reasonably fit for the use of fork-lift trucks. The circumstances showed that the customer had made it clear that such trucks would be used. Furthermore, there had been a warning by the British Standards Institution that traffic vibration could cause cracks in the type of floor recommended by the defendants. Lord Denning MR reasoned (at pp. 103–4) that:

To resolve this question, it is necessary to distinguish between a term which is implied by law and a term which is implied in fact. A term implied by law is said to rest on the *presumed* intention of both parties; whereas, a term implied in fact rests on their *actual* intention.

It has often been stated that the law will only imply a term when it is reasonable and necessary to do so in order to give business efficacy to the transaction; and, indeed, so obvious that both parties must have intended it. But those statements must be taken with considerable qualification. In the great majority of cases it is no use looking for the intention of both parties. If you asked the parties what they intended, they would say they never gave it a thought; or, if they did, the one would say that he intended something different from the other. So the courts imply — or, as I would say, impose — a term such as is just and reasonable in the circumstances. . . .

Their common intention was that the engineer should design a warehouse which would be fit for the purpose for which it was required. That common intention gives rise to a term implied *in fact*. . . .

In the light of that evidence it seems to me that there was implied in fact a term that, if the work was completed in accordance with the design, it would be reasonably fit for the use of loaded stacker trucks. The engineers failed to make such a design and are, therefore, liable.

While Browne and Geoffrey Lane LJJ concurred, both were at pains to emphasise that the decision laid down no general principle in relation to the obligations and liabilities of professional men. Nevertheless, although the decision concerned a business transaction, it is suggested that the approach adopted by Lord Denning would be of considerable benefit in reinforcing the position of consumers if it were to be applied to consumer services generally.

The decision in *Greaves & Co. (Contractors) Ltd* v *Baynham Meikle & Partners* would seem to suggest that design services fall into a separate category in which the courts are more prepared to imply higher standards. Certainly, it is true that a designer supplies an end product which may be more easily equated with the position of the supplier of goods, thereby justifying a requirement that the design should be reasonably fit for the purpose for which it is intended. In the field of building design services, it is important to relate the designer's obligations to those of the main contractor under his contract with the building owner. In *Independent Broadcasting Authority* v *EMI Electronics Ltd* (1980) 14 BLR 1, the IBA had employed EMI, as main contractors, to design and supply a television mast. BICC were nominated subcontractors responsible for the design. The IBA had raised doubts about the safety of the proposed design, but they had been assured in a letter sent by BICC to EMI that the mast would not oscillate dangerously. Subsequently, the mast did collapse, due to design faults, which failed to take into account the effects of ice accumulating on the structure. In the event, it was held that EMI had warranted the fitness of the mast to the IBA and that BICC had also given the same warranty to EMI. Accordingly, a chain of contractual liability was set up. However, there are also dicta to the effect that where a service only is supplied, a duty to exercise reasonable care alone will arise, but where a chattel is to be delivered there is a strict obligation to ensure that the chattel is fit for its intended purpose, in the absence of an express or implied term negating the liability of the designer. In the circumstances of the IBA case, that warranty would have been given by BICC directly to the IBA (see 14 BLR 1 at pp. 47–8 per Lord Scarman; see also *Samuels* v *Davis* [1943] KB 526).

An important factor in *Greaves & Co. (Contractors) Ltd* v *Baynham Meikle & Partners* was that the supplier knew what the customer required. It would not be reasonable to expect the supplier to comply with the consumer's unstated desires. Thus, it is important for the consumer to voice his requirements as these may increase the cost of the service or require the exercise of new skills (*CRC Flooring* v *Heaton* (8 October 1980 unreported)). At the same time, if the consumer engages the services of an expert, he may expect to pay fees representing the skill of the expert. In such a case, it may be reasonable for him to expect a standard of performance in excess of the reasonably competent (*Duchess of Argyll* v *Beuselinck* [1972] 2 Lloyd's Rep 172 at p. 183 per Megarry J).

8.4.3 Personal performance
The Supply of Goods and Services Act 1982, s. 13, provides, *inter alia,* that the supplier *will* carry out the service, and so it has been argued that the provision implies a requirement of personal performance of the service which the supplier has undertaken to supply (see Palmer (1983) 46 MLR 619). If the 1982 Act does incorporate such a requirement, it would appear to have extended the liability of the supplier as compared with the position at common law, under which delegation is impliedly permitted, where appropriate (see *Davies* v *Collins* (1945) 1 All ER 247; *Stewart* v *Reavell's Garage* [1952] 1 All ER 1191). While this construction would appear to be possible, the Law Commission (Law Com. No. 156 (Cmnd 9773, 1986), para. 2.25) take the view that s. 13 will not be construed by the courts to produce a requirement of personal performance in every case.

8.4.4 Delayed performance
A common consumer complaint is that the work commissioned starts late or takes much longer in performance than was originally anticipated. This is a particular problem in relation to building work including, for example, the installation of double glazing. If the supplier has contracted to supply the service on a specified date, failure to comply with that date is a breach of contract. This, in turn, may give the consumer the right to treat his or her obligation to perform the contract as being at an end. Furthermore, it may be possible to imply an agreed date for performance by reference to a previous course of dealings between the parties. However, in the context of consumer services, particularly those for the supply of expensive building services, it is unlikely that there will be a sufficient degree of regularity to imply the existence of a course of dealing (see also chapter 12). Whether or not the supplier's breach will have this effect will depend on the ratio quantitatively which the breach bears to the contract as a whole. The supplier's breach may be regarded as insufficiently serious to justify repudiation by the consumer, in which case the breach will be treated as a breach of warranty giving rise to an action for damages only.

In deciding whether the consumer can treat his obligation to perform as being terminated, it is necessary to determine whether the provision in the contract relating to the time of performance is of the essence. Generally, time provisions in non-commercial contracts are not treated as being of the essence of the contract, but there are circumstances where this is not so. Thus, time will be of the essence of the contract where the parties have expressly provided for this and where the circumstances of the case suggest that time is of the essence (*United Scientific Holdings Ltd* v *Burnley Borough Council* [1978] AC 904, 958 per Lord Fraser of Tullybelton). If the contract provides for the purchase of shares by a specified date, the time stipulation will be regarded as crucial due to the volatile nature of the subject matter of the contract (*Hare* v *Nicoll* [1966] 2 QB 130). Furthermore, where a consumer who has been the subject of unreasonable delay gives the supplier reasonable notice requiring performance by a specified date, time will be of the essence of the contract. This rule can be a useful device to an aggrieved consumer who believes that there has been unreasonable delay and who, by putting his or her complaint in writing, can demand performance by a specified date. In *Charles Rickards Ltd* v *Oppenheim* [1950] 1 All ER 420, the defendant agreed to buy a modified Rolls-Royce chassis which was to be delivered by 20 March 1948. The chassis was not available by that date, so the defendant pressed for delivery and subsequently, on 29 June, gave notice that if it was not delivered within four more weeks he would not accept it. The chassis was made available in October 1948, but the defendant refused to take delivery. It was held by the Court of Appeal that he was entitled to take this course of action. Denning LJ stated (at pp. 423–4) that:

(Counsel for the plaintiffs) agrees that, if this is a contract for the sale of goods, the defendant could give such a notice. He accepted the statement of McCardie J in *Hartley* v *Hymans* [1920] 3 KB 475 at p. 495, as accurately stating the law in regard to the sale of goods, but he said that that statement did not apply to contracts for work and labour. He said that no notice making time of the essence could be given in regard to contracts for work and labour. . . . in my view, it is unnecessary to determine whether it was a contract for the sale of goods or a contract for work and labour, because, whichever it was, the defendant was entitled to give a notice bringing the matter to a head. . . . Adequate protection to the suppliers is given by the requirement that the notice should be reasonable.

The next question, therefore, is: Was this a reasonable notice? . . .

In this case, not only did the defendant press continually for delivery, not only was he given promises of speedy delivery, but, on the very day before he gave the notice, he was told by the subcontractors' manager, who was in charge of the work, that it would be ready within two weeks. He then gave a four weeks' notice. The judge found that it was a reasonable notice and, in my judgment, there is no ground on which this court could in any way differ from that finding.

The problem posed by this last rule is that it may prove difficult to advise a consumer on what constitutes unreasonable delay given that this is a question of fact in each case. If the consumer has contracted for the supply and installation of a central heating system by a specified date, and the supplier attempts to perform the work after that date, it may be unreasonable for the consumer to refuse to accept the late performance, in which case the consumer will then in breach of contract.

If the contract does not provide for the time of performance, and it is not possible to determine by other means when the service is to be performed, the Supply of Goods and Services Act 1982, s. 14(1), provides that a supplier acting in the course of a business will carry out the service within a reasonable time. What is a reasonable time is a question of fact (s. 14(2)). Therefore, the court will have to consider the nature of the work to be carried out, the availability of the necessary materials for completing the work and the general conditions and customs of the trade under consideration. In deciding whether the supplier is in breach of the implied term, the court will consider what time would have been taken by a reasonably competent tradesman in the particular circumstances of the case in issue. In *Charnock* v *Liverpool Corporation* [1968] 1 WLR 1498 the plaintiff owned a car which was damaged in a collision caused by the negligence of the driver of the other vehicle, an employee of the first defendant. The car was taken to the second defendants for repair. With the agreement of the plaintiff's insurers, it was understood that an estimate of the cost of repair would be submitted to the insurers by the second defendants and that the insurers would pay the full cost of those repairs. The plaintiff overheard that the second defendants had a lot of warranty work to carry out in their capacity as main dealers for a car manufacturer, but no indication was given that the work on his car would be delayed. In the event, the work on the plaintiff's car took eight weeks when a competent repairer would have taken no more than five weeks to complete the work. The plaintiff was awarded £53 damages in respect of the cost of hiring a replacement car for three weeks. Salmon LJ opined (at pp. 1505–6) that:

. . . there was a clear contract to be inferred from the facts between the garage proprietor and the car owner that in consideration of the car owner leaving his car with the garage for repair the garage would carry out the repairs with reasonable expedition and care, and that they would be paid by the insurance company. . . .

The second point is even shorter. The judge found that the garage proprietors broke their contract with the car owner in that they failed to repair the car within a reasonable time. There was ample evidence before him that a reasonable time for carrying out these repairs should not have exceeded five weeks. Since the garage proprietors in fact took eight weeks, they were in breach of their contract. . . . The reason why these garage proprietors were unable to do the work within a reasonable time . . . was that when they took on the work their labour force was very much under strength. Moreover, the holiday period was approaching. Further, and perhaps most importantly, they had an arrangement (which no doubt was commercially of great value to them) with the Rootes group that any warranty work should be given precedence. . . .

It seems to me that, if they had wanted to protect themselves against a claim for damages for unreasonable delay, they could and should have warned the car owner that the repairs could not be carried out in the time which is recognised in the trade as the normal and reasonable time for carrying out such repairs.

The standard required of the supplier is that of the reasonably competent supplier of the service, therefore he will not be liable for delays that are beyond his control. Thus if the delay is due to procrastination or the imposition of unreasonable conditions on the part of the consumer, the supplier will not be in breach of the implied term. Similarly, if the delay is due to external factors beyond the supplier's control, such as a strike by workers, there will be no breach of s. 14(1) (*Hick* v *Raymond & Reid* [1893] AC 22).

8.4.5 Cost
The amount payable by the consumer for a service provided will depend initially on the terms of the contract with the supplier. It has been observed by the National Consumer Council that a consumer who purchases goods will almost always know the price in advance. However, in the case of a supply of services, this will not always be the case (National Consumer Council, *Services and the Law: A Consumer View* (1981), p. 17). Sometimes the supplier will display fixed charges, as do hairdressers, dry cleaners and most entertainment services. However, the supplier of other services may wish to wait to see how much work has to be carried out before valuing the cost of that work. In such a case, the consumer may be surprised at the cost of the service.

If the cost of the service is fixed in advance, generally, the consumer will be bound to pay that amount. Normally, the courts will not reopen a bad bargain. However, consumers may only discover at a later stage that the charge is extortionate. Only in rare cases will it be possible to reopen an agreement. For example, in the case of extortionate credit bargains, ss. 137–40 of the Consumer Credit Act 1974 (see chapter 11) provide for such a power on the part of the court. The Consumer Protection (Cancellation of Contracts Concluded Away from Business Premises) Regulations 1987 (SI 1987/2117) implementing the provisions of the Council Directive on Doorstep Selling (85/5771 EEC, 20.12.1985) are also relevant in this regard. The Regulations require a trader to give the consumer notice of his right to cancel a contract within seven days of making certain types of contract concluded off trade premises (reg. 4(1) and (5)). Further, where the regulations apply, the consumer will be entitled to recover any payments made under the agreement (reg. 5(1)). However, it is clear that the regulations do not apply to all contracts for the supply of services. Specific exemptions are given in relation to contracts for the construction or extension of a building (reg. 3(2)(a)(iv)), although this would appear not to apply to home improvements involving the installation of goods, such as double-glazing units, provided installation has not taken place (reg. 7(2)). Insurance contracts and many contracts for financial services are excluded, since provision is made elsewhere for them. In order for the Regulations to apply, the consumer must have entered into a contract valued at more than £35 (reg. 3(2)(f)) where there has been an unsolicited visit by a trader to a consumer's home or place of work or where the trader has attempted to sell to the consumer goods or services which have not been specifically requested (reg. 3(1))) Despite the provisions of these Regulations, there are still many contracts which will not be provided for in which the consumer may agree to pay an exorbitant amount and not be able to cancel. For example, wherever the consumer has specifically requested the provision of the service and there has been no unsolicited visit by the trader, an agreed charge will be enforceable against him.

At common law, it may also be possible for the court to construe the contract in such a way as to rewrite the terms of payment (see *Staffordshire Area Health Authority* v *South Staffordshire Waterworks Co.* [1978] I WLR 1387) particularly where those terms are onerous. For example, in *Interfoto Picture Library Ltd* v *Stiletto Visual Programmes Ltd* [1988] 1 All ER 348 a contract for the hire of photographic transparencies provided that should the hirer keep photographs for longer than was agreed he should pay £5 per day in respect of each transparency retained. It was considered that the amount charged was excessive and since no steps had been taken to communicate the existence of the onerous provision to the hirer, it would be reasonable to impose a *quantum meruit* payment of £3.50 per transparency per week (see also *J. Spurling Ltd* v *Bradshaw* [1956] 2 All ER 121).

It has been suggested that there should be a discretion on the part of the court to reopen and rewrite consumer contracts in the case of blatant exploitation (Lantin and Woodroffe, *Service Please* (National Consumer Council, 1981), p. 26). However, prospects for reform of the law in this respect appear remote since the Law Commission have concluded that it would not be appropriate to make special provision for consumer services without also making similar provision for supply of goods contracts (Law Com. No. 156 (Cmnd 9773, 1986), para. 4.21).

A difficulty which consumers may encounter is that they have been given an estimate of the cost of work which is subsequently exceeded when the work is completed. An estimate is generally regarded as a prediction which is not binding on the supplier (*Croshaw* v *Pritchard* (1899) 16 TLR 45). One way in which the consumer can protect himself in this respect is to secure a quotation from the supplier. In such a case, the supplier is bound to perform the service for the amount agreed. Thus, even if the work takes longer than was anticipated or if the supplier incurs unexpected costs, the quotation is binding upon him (*Gilbert & Partners* v *Knight* [1968] 2 All ER 248).

If the contract does not provide for the amount payable by the consumer, the Supply of Goods and Services Act 1982, s. 15(1), provides that the consumer will pay a reasonable charge. What is reasonable is a question of fact in each case, but the effect of the section is to order a *quantum meruit* in respect of services rendered (*Way* v *Latilla* [1937] 3 All ER 759). The section will also provide a solution where there is an agreement to pay, but no specific figure has been fixed by the parties. What is a reasonable charge may reflect current market prices. However, this will not always be the case if special considerations apply (see *Acebal* v *Levy* (1834) 10 Bing 376).

8.5 SPECIFIC TYPES OF CONSUMER SERVICE

Clearly, it is not possible to devise a definitive categorisation of the various types of services which are 'consumed'. Such services are as wide ranging as they are varied. In selecting varieties of service for more detailed consideration, the choice is likely to be arbitrary, but since the consumer's two major items of expenditure are his or her house and car, it is proposed to consider home-improvement services, and repair services. The provision of credit is dealt with separately (see chapter 11), as is holiday law (see chapter 9) and consumer insurance (see chapter 10).

8.5.1 Repair services and other bailments
The supply of services to consumers will often involve a bailment relationship. Such a relationship arises wherever the consumer's property is handed over to another for the purposes of safekeeping, repair, processing or carriage on condition that the bailee shall ultimately return the goods to the bailor.
The service supplier is subject to the general duties which apply to bailees. In certain circumstances, the consumer is also subject to the same duties, for example, when taking possession of a television under a consumer hire agreement.

8.5.1.1 The supplier as a bailee   In most cases of bailment there must be a delivery of goods by the bailor to the bailee. The meaning and scope of the term 'delivery' in this context was considered by the Court of Appeal in *Ashby* v *Tolhurst* [1937] 2 KB 242. The plaintiff left his car at a private car park, paid a shilling (5p) and received a ticket from the attendant which stated that the proprietors accepted no responsibility for the safe custody of cars or articles therein and that all cars were left entirely at the owner's risk. When the plaintiff returned to collect his car, he was told by the attendant that he had allowed the plaintiff's 'friend' to take it. In fact the 'friend' did not have the ticket and had gained entry to the car by force. Negligence on the part of the attendant was admitted but liability was denied. In considering whether there had been delivery, Romer LJ said that it must be established that the bailor parted with possession of the chattel in question. He said (at pp. 255–7):

> In the present case there is no evidence whatever of any delivery in fact of the motor car to the attendant on behalf of the defendants. All that the plaintiff did was to leave his car on the car park, paying the sum of 1*s*. for the privilege of doing so. It is true that, if the car had been left there for any particular purpose that required that the defendants should have possession of the car a delivery would rightly be inferred. If, for instance, the car had been left at the car park for the purpose of being sold . . . or

indeed for the purposes of safe custody, delivery of the car, although not actually made, would readily be inferred. But it is perfectly plain in this case that the car was not delivered to the defendants for safe custody. You cannot infer a contract by A to perform a certain act out of circumstances in which A has made it perfectly plain that he declines to be under any contractual liability to perform that act.

In some instances delivery may be effected by an intermediary. For example, it may be that goods entrusted to a repairer are passed to another for the purpose of carrying out specialist work.

Generally a bailment will be contractual in nature, but a bailment relationship can arise independently of a contract, and a bailment relationship can arise despite the absence of consideration. However, this does not mean that the duties of the bailee lie exclusively in the law of tort. It is better to regard bailments as *sui generis* and therefore subject to special rules of their own. In particular, because the bailment relationship is created by the parties themselves, a bailee owes a duty of care to the bailor alone. In contrast, a tortious duty of care is owed to persons generally. The burden of proof in a bailment relationship rests on the bailee. Thus if a garage is entrusted with a consumer's car for repair, and the car is stolen, it is for the garage to prove that reasonable care has been exercised or that the failure to take care did not contribute to the consumer's loss (see *Joseph Travers & Sons Ltd* v *Cooper* [1915] 1 KB 73). On the other hand, if the consumer brought an action in tort, the consumer would have to prove want of reasonable care on the part of the garage. In *Levison* v *Patent Steam Carpet Cleaning Co. Ltd* [1977] 3 All ER 498 the plaintiffs arranged for a £900 carpet to be cleaned by the defendants. When the carpet was collected, Mr Levison signed a form which stated that the maximum value of the carpet was deemed to be £40 and that all merchandise was accepted at the owner's risk. The carpet was never returned, probably because it had been stolen. In the county court, the plaintiffs were awarded £900. The defendants' appeal was dismissed on the basis that the burden of proving what had happened to the carpet was borne by the cleaning company. Since they were not able to explain the loss adequately, negligence was inferred. This case involved the application of the doctrine of fundamental breach to an exclusion clause and is one of a number of cases which must be regarded as wrongly decided, now, in relation to the doctrine of fundamental breach. However, it remains good authority for the points it makes about the onus of proof in bailment cases.

The standard of care required of the supplier is the same whether or not the bailment is for reward, namely, a duty to exercise reasonable care and skill appropriate to the relevant circumstances (*Houghland* v *R.R. Low (Luxury Coaches) Ltd* [1962] 1 QB 694). The fact that the service has been paid for may be relevant in that the parties may be said to have raised the standard required of the supplier.

In some instances the consumer may encounter difficulties related to the tort of conversion. As a general rule, the bailee is obliged to return the bailed chattel to the bailor at the end of the period of bailment. However, where the property is not returned, the bailee may be able to show good cause as, for example, where the consumer has not paid for the work done by the repairer. In such a case, the repairer may wish to sell the consumer's goods in order to cover the cost of the repairs. Generally, it would be wise for the repairer to reserve a contractual right of disposal because without such express permission, the repairer commits the tort of wrongful interference with goods (Torts (Interference with Goods) Act 1977, s. 2(2)). If this is the case, the bailee is liable for the value of the article at the time of being sued, subject to a deduction in respect of the value of any improvement in the chattel effected by the bailee.

Special provision is made for the sale of bailed goods by the bailee in the Torts (Interference with Goods) Act 1977. Section 12 of the Act provides for the bailee's power of sale where the bailor is in breach of an obligation to take delivery of the goods or if the bailee, without success, has taken reasonable steps to trace the bailor in order to impose such an obligation. An obligation to take delivery can be imposed on the bailor by serving a notice specifying that the goods are ready for collection and stating the amount payable in respect of work done. Concurrently with the service of the notice referred to above, the bailee must also notify the bailor that the goods are to be sold on or after a specified date if delivery is not taken by that date. Where a sale is effected, the bailee is liable to the bailor for the proceeds of sale less the costs of sale and any sum payable to the bailee by the bailor in respect of work done.

8.5.1.2 The consumer as a bailee In some instances the consumer will be a bailee and as such will be subject to the normal rules that apply to the bailment relationship. The most notable examples of this arise where the consumer hires goods or takes goods pursuant to a hire purchase agreement. In addition to the ordinary incidents of a bailment relationship, if the bailment is contractual, certain terms relating to the title of the bailor and the description, quality and fitness of the goods bailed are implied into the contract by the Supply of Goods and Services Act 1982, ss. 7 to 10 and the Supply of Goods (Implied Terms) Act 1973, ss. 8 to 11.

8.5.2 Home improvements
A common consumer complaint is that building or other home-improvement work has failed to reach the standard expected by the consumer. The problems encountered by consumers are various, some being extremely serious, others much less important. Sometimes, the basis of the consumer's complaint is a matter of subjective judgment, which may render legal controls inappropriate. For example, the consumer may complain that an extension to a house does not blend with the existing structure (see *Home Improvements — A Discussion Paper* (OFT, 1982), para. 6.1). In the light of this, it may be the case that the use of trade association codes of practice as a means of control is more likely to meet with success, provided some effective means of enforcement of such codes can be found. Other more specific difficulties may arise in determining whether a builder has substantially or only partially fulfilled the obligations under a contract with the consumer. Further grounds

for consumer complaint may also emanate from the fact that some suppliers require advance payment in respect of some or all of the work they do. Additionally, problems may arise in determining whether a tortious duty of care is owed by the builder and in identifying the appropriate standard of performance required.

8.5.2.1 Partial contractual performance As a general rule English law requires complete performance before the obligations of a party to a contract can be regarded as being discharged. Furthermore, if one party's contractual obligations are not performed, it will generally follow that the obligations of the other party to the contract can be treated as being discharged. From this it would seem to follow that a builder will not be able to demand payment for home-improvement work until he has performed in full that which is required of him by the consumer. However, this is not necessarily the case as in English law there is a distinction between entire and severable obligations.

If a contractual obligation is said to be entire, it must be performed completely before the other party is required to pay for that performance. It is said to be a condition precedent to the liability of the recipient of the service that the performance of the other party is complete. Thus in *Sumpter* v *Hedges* [1898] 1 QB 673 the plaintiff agreed to build two houses for the defendant in return for a lump-sum payment of £565. Part of the way towards completion, the plaintiff encountered financial difficulties and informed the defendant that he would not be able to complete the work. In the meantime, the defendant had the houses completed by another contractor. The plaintiff sued to recover the agreed price, but it was held that payment was not due until performance was complete. Furthermore, the plaintiff could not recover on a *quantum meruit* basis in respect of the work he had done as there was no evidence of a voluntary acceptance of any benefit by the defendant. Collins LJ reasoned (at pp. 676–7) that:

> If the plaintiff had merely broken his contract in some way so as not to give the defendant the right to treat him as having abandoned the contract, and the defendant had then proceeded to finish the work himself, the plaintiff might perhaps have been entitled to sue on a *quantum meruit* on the ground that the defendant had taken the benefit of the work done. But that is not the present case. . . . Where, as in the case of work done on land, the circumstances are such as to give the defendant no option whether he will take the benefit of the work or not, then one must look to other facts than the mere taking of the benefit of the work in order to ground the inference of a new contract. . . . The mere fact that a defendant is in possession of what he cannot help keeping, or even has done work upon it, affords no ground for such an inference. He is not bound to keep unfinished a building which in an incomplete state would be a nuisance on his land. I am therefore of opinion that the plaintiff was not entitled to recover for the work which he had done.

The plaintiff had actually been paid £333 in respect of the completed work, although the judgments make it clear that he was not entitled to a penny of it, so that had he been paid nothing, the decision would have been the same. The rule is harsh and can be sidestepped where the court is able to find a contract which imposes severable obligations in relation to the amount of work done.

Where contractual obligations are said to be severable, payment in respect of performance may be due as particular stages of performance are reached. The question which then arises is whether a breach in respect of one stage of performance is sufficiently serious to justify the other party in refusing to make payment in respect of the whole of the defendant's performance. A builder may be able to design a contract which allows for payment as work proceeds subject to the payment of retention moneys on completion of the building work. In such a case there is a series of severable obligations in respect of each stage of the work and an entire obligation to complete the whole of the work in accordance with the terms of the contract.

In *Sumpter* v *Hedges*, the builder's obligation to complete two houses was entire, however, he would not have been disentitled to payment if his breach of contract had been less serious. For example, if the work had been completed a week late (ibid. 676 per Collins LJ), the builder would have been entitled to payment in full subject to a deduction in respect of the late completion. Similarly, qualitative defects in the finished product may not be sufficiently serious to go to the root of the contract which would allow the consumer to refuse payment (cf. *Bolton* v *Mahadeva* [1972] 1 WLR 1009, considered below). In such a case, there may be an entire obligation in relation to the quantity of work performed, but not in relation to the quality of the work performed (see Cheshire Fifoot and Furmston, *Law of Contract*, 12th ed. (London: Butterworths, 1991), p. 533 et seq.) In *Hoenig* v *Isaacs* [1952] 2 All ER 176 the plaintiff had contracted to decorate and furnish the defendant's flat. The work was complete, but the furniture supplied was defective. These defects could be rectified at a cost of £55. The defendant had paid £400 of the £750 due but had refused to pay the balance. The essential issue was whether entire performance was a condition precedent to payment. The Court of Appeal held that on a true construction of the contract it was a lump-sum agreement, so that unless the breach went to the root of the contract the defendant must pay the contract price. The terms of payment were crucial in that they provided, 'net cash, as the work proceeds, and balance on completion'. The court found that the 'balance' was not retention money payable only when the work was entirely finished without defects. Denning LJ found that generally 'retention money' usually accounts for only 10 or 15 per cent of the agreed price (at p. 181). Accordingly, since the contract was substantially performed, it was held that the plaintiff was entitled to payment at the full contract rate of £750 subject to a deduction in respect of the cost of rectifying the defects.

The foregoing does not mean that a consumer who complains of defective quality in the supplier's performance will have no grounds for refusing to pay. It may be the case that defects in quality amount to a sufficiently serious breach of contract to justify rescission by the consumer. The principal consideration is whether the consumer has been substantially deprived of the benefit he contracted for. In deciding whether the consumer is entitled to rescind a number of factors will be considered. First, it is necessary to consider whether an award of damages is adequate recompense. The notion of the 'consumer surplus value' (see also chapter 4 and the discussion of *Ruxley Electronics & Construction Ltd v Forsyth* [1996] AC 344 and see also chapter 9) may be relevant in this context. Sometimes, the consumer contracts for a benefit which is difficult to value in market terms. If this benefit substantially forms the basis of the contract and is not provided, the consumer may be able to decline to pay for the service. Thus it has been held that a funeral director who negligently constructs a coffin so that it cannot be taken into the funeral service is not entitled to payment (*Vigers v Cook* [1919] 2 KB 475). It is possible that a consumer will place such a value on home-improvement work. However, a further factor must also be considered. The work of the builder is likely to have conferred a substantial benefit on the consumer which will have to be taken into account. The courts will be reluctant to allow a person to refuse payment where he has received such a benefit and is not in a position to restore the benefit to the other party. In the case of home-improvements, the consumer is hardly likely to want to restore double-glazing units to the builder and leave a large hole in his living-room wall!

If the consumer is considered to have accepted the benefit conferred on him by the builder, he will have to pay for the benefit received. However, this will not normally involve paying the full contract price. It is relevant that home-improvement work is carried out on the consumer's own property, since taking possession of one's own property is not automatically regarded as acceptance of the benefit (*Sumpter v Hedges* [1898] 1 QB 673). It is not acceptance if the consumer has no real option whether to take the benefit or not (ibid. 676 per Collins LJ). This rule is particularly important where the builder's failure to perform causes the consumer to suffer a loss. However, it may also be the case that the failure to perform does not cause any loss or a loss which is substantially offset by the benefit conferred by the incomplete performance. In such a case, the consumer who is able to take advantage of the builder's non-performance may benefit substantially. For example, in *Bolton v Mahadeva* [1972] 1 WLR 1009 a contractor agreed to install a central heating system for £560. The system was defective in that it circulated fumes inside the consumer's house and, on average, the house was 10 per cent less warm than it should have been. The defects cost the consumer £174 to repair when the installer had refused to attend to his shoddy performance. The Court of Appeal held that the defects were so great as to constitute non-performance of the contract. The end result was that the consumer had acquired an operative central heating system for £174. Cairns LJ said (at pp. 1011–13):

The main question . . . is whether defects in workmanship found . . . to cost £174 to repair — that is, between one third and one quarter of the contract price — were of such a character and amount that the plaintiff could not be said to have substantially performed his contract. . . .

In considering whether there was substantial performance I am of opinion that it is relevant to take into account both the nature of the defects and the proportion between the cost of rectifying them and the contract price.

However, it was observed that had the contractor been prepared to remedy the defects when asked to do so, the position would have been different. The Law Commission (*Pecuniary Restitution for Breach of Contract* (Law Com. No. 121, 1983), para. 2.32) have recommended that a party who in breach of contract fails to complete an entire contract but who has also conferred a benefit on the other party should be entitled to some payment, unless the contract provides otherwise. However, one member of the Law Commission (Brian Davenport QC) dissented strongly on this issue, observing that in most commercial building contracts there will be a provision for payment in stages, in which case, the problem in *Bolton* v *Mahadeva* will not arise.

8.5.2.2 Consumer prepayments

A common feature of the home-improvements sector is that the consumer may be required to make full or partial payment in advance for the work done. The builder can justify such a requirement on the ground that he must purchase materials in advance. However, the building trade is notorious for a high risk of business failure, which may leave the consumer who has made a prepayment in the position of an unsecured creditor and with no discernible benefit on his hands. Furthermore, where the consumer makes an advance payment, he may have placed himself in a very weak bargaining position if the work later proves to be defective.

Whether or not the consumer can recover his prepayment will depend on the terms of the contract. In the case of home improvements, the contract will be one for work and materials and the contractual obligations of the supplier will involve him incurring expenditure before his performance is complete. Because of this, the supplier's right to the payment will be unconditional and the payment will be irrecoverable even though it is not required as security for performance (*Hyundai Heavy Industries Co.* v *Papadopoulos* [1980] 1 WLR 1129). If the supplier has failed to perform at all, the prepayment made by the consumer will be recoverable on the grounds of a total failure of consideration (*Fibrosa SA* v *Fairbairn Lawson Combe Barbour Ltd* [1943] AC 32). If the consideration is regarded as 'whole and indivisible', performance of any part of the thing promised will prevent recovery on the basis of a total failure of consideration. However, the parties may have expressed the intention that the price can be earned incrementally, in which case the consideration may be regarded as divisible, but this will depend on an express term in the contract to this effect.

The fact that the builder has to ask for prepayment may be some indication that he is a credit risk. It has been observed that most builders' merchants will offer one month's credit and that if the consumer is asked for a prepayment, this may indicate that the builder concerned is not considered creditworthy by others in the same sector (*Home Improvements — A Discussion*

Paper (Office of Fair Trading, 1982), para. 3.21). Paragraph 3.22 of the Discussion Paper warns that:

. . . payment in advance for work to be undertaken can be followed by the disappearance of the supplier before the work is started or completed or the trader may become insolvent and go into liquidation before the work is completed. Householders should recognise the possible risks of making payments in advance, before satisfactory completion of the work, which may not be related to any actual costs incurred. They should always approach requests for payment in advance with healthy scepticism and, before agreeing to payment, should satisfy themselves, first that the trader concerned has an established business, secondly, that the advance payment is reasonably related to costs which the trader may be expected to have incurred, and thirdly, that there is every likelihood of the contract being completed.

A major risk faced by consumers is that after having made an advance payment, the contractor may become insolvent or a company cease trading before work is commenced or completed. In such a case, the consumer may be left with little protection and stands a distinct chance of being unable to recover the full amount of his prepayment. Some protection may be found in the form of trade association bonding schemes such as that operated by the Glass and Glazing Federation through their code of ethical practice. Double-glazing contractors who are members of the Federation are required to be covered by a deposit indemnity fund (see the Code of Ethical Practice of the Glass and Glaziers Federation, 1981, para. 5.1). This gives Federation fund managers the option to ensure that the work is completed at a fair market price, less the value of any deposit paid, or to refund the consumer's deposit.

Consumers are not in the same strong market position to be able to protect their deposit as is possible in business transactions. For example, a business-man who wishes to protect his position in a contract for the sale of goods could insist on reserving title in the goods sold until payment is received (*Aluminium Industrie Vaassen BV* v *Romalpa Aluminium Ltd* [1976] 1 WLR 676). However, it is unlikely that the consumer would be in a position to insist upon similar protection unless it were to be provided by law.

Suggestions for reform of the law have included one attempt to legislate for 'customers' prepayment accounts' whereby a contractor would be required to hold prepayments on trust in a separate account. The proposal would have prevented the use of the money for business purposes (Hansard HC, 28 April 1982, coll. 847–9). This might work in relation to some prepayments where the work is likely to take some time to complete, but it would be impractical to apply the same rule to services due to be supplied very soon after the consumer's payment. Compulsion and voluntary choice are different matters. A trader who wishes to do so can create a trust in favour of a customer who has made a prepayment by opening a separate trust account, in which case the payment will be protected should the company later become insolvent. The use of the trust as a device for protecting consumers where a supplier becomes insolvent was recognised by Megarry J in *Re Kayford Ltd* [1975] 1 WLR 279 at p. 282:

> No doubt the general rule is that if you send money to a company for goods which are not delivered, you are merely a creditor of the company unless a trust has been created. The sender may create a trust by using appropriate words when he sends the money . . ., or the company may do it by taking suitable steps on or before receiving the money. If either is done, the obligations in respect of the money are transformed from contract to property, from debt to trust.

See also Richardson [1985] JBL 456.

8.5.2.3 Duty of care and standard of performance

It has been seen that the supplier of a service is ordinarily required to exercise reasonable care and skill. In the case of building work, a higher standard would appear to be appropriate. At common law there is a requirement, based on an implied contractual term, that a builder will carry out work in a good and workmanlike manner with good and proper materials in order to produce a building which is reasonably fit for human habitation (*Perry v Sharon Development Co. Ltd* [1937] 4 All ER 390; see also *Hancock v B.W. Brazier (Anerley) Ltd* [1966] 2 All ER 901, 903 per Lord Denning MR). As this is a contract term it protects only the person who has dealt directly with the builder and will not avail a subsequent purchaser of the property.

The common law rule has been augmented by the provisions of the Defective Premises Act 1972, which applies not only to the erection of buildings but also to conversions and enlargements (s. 1(1)). The non-excludable duty owed under this Act is strict and extends to every person who acquires an interest in the property, but the Act is also subject to a number of important limitations. In particular, the Act does not apply to dwellings protected by an 'approved scheme' (s. 2) and since most new houses are covered by the approved NHBC scheme, the Act is limited to alterations and conversions (see Spencer [1974] CLJ 307, [1975] CLJ 48). The cause of action is deemed to accrue on completion of the building work and runs for six years from that date (s. 1(5)). Unfortunately many building defects take much longer than six years from the date of completion to reveal themselves, in which case the consumer will be time barred before he realises that any damage has been done.

At one stage, the most important extension of a builder's liability was in the tort of negligence, represented by *Dutton v Bognor Regis Urban District Council* [1972] 1 QB 373. Doubts remained about the scope of the duty owed by the builder and the local authority. Subsequent interpretation of the decision in *Anns v Merton London Borough Council* [1978] AC 728 has shown that the builder is liable for foreseeable personal injury and property damage suffered as a result of his negligence but that only limited liability exists in respect of economic loss (*D & F Estates Ltd v Church Commissioners for England* [1989] AC 177). The main difficulty is to determine what is property damage and what is economic loss. In *D & F Estates Ltd* v *Church Commissioners for England* the House of Lords held that the cost of repairing a defective building was pure economic loss and therefore generally irrecoverable in the absence of a contractual relationship between the parties. However, the decision is subject to a number of qualifications. If the building is regarded as a complex structure, one part of that structure can cause damage to another part of the same structure. In such a case there is damage to other property (ibid. 207 per Lord Bridge of Harwich). It would appear to be possible to recover the cost of repair in order to avert a threat of imminent danger to the health or safety of the occupant of the building (ibid. 216 per Lord Oliver of Aylmerton; *Department of the Environment* v *Thomas Bates & Son Ltd* [1991] 1 AC 499, though trying to justify this view by reference to what Lord Bridge said in *D & F Estates Ltd* v *Church Commissioners for England* [1989] AC 177, 207 may be difficult. Nevertheless, in *Department of the Environment* v *Thomas Bates & Son Ltd* Lord Keith of Kinkel expressed the view that 'the builder would be liable under the principle in *Donoghue* v *Stevenson* in the event of the defect, before it had been discovered, causing physical injury to persons'.

NINE

Holiday law

Holiday law is an interesting amalgam of a number of the different techniques of consumer protection outlined in chapter 2 of this book. There are a range of common law rules, which, for reasons considered below, are probably the least effective means of consumer protection. Because of the importance of tourism generally throughout Europe, this is an area which has attracted the concerns of EC institutions with the result that there is important legislative intervention at Community level in the form of the Directive on Package Holidays and Package Tours (90/314/EEC, OJ L158, 23.6.90, p. 59), which has been implemented in English law by the Package Travel, Package Holidays and Package Tours Regulations 1992 (SI 1992/3288). The travel industry has the advantage of a very strong trade association in the form of the Association of British Travel Agents (ABTA), which has promulgated a code of practice, which in many respects is ahead of the law. This code is enforced rigorously against the membership of the association, which, for reasons considered below, covers virtually all travel agents and tour operators who do business in the United Kingdom.

The strength of the position of ABTA in the holiday industry was due largely to a provision in the articles of association of ABTA known as 'stabiliser', which provided that no ABTA tour operator could sell its package holidays through anything other than an ABTA travel agency and that no ABTA travel agency could sell anything other than ABTA tour operators' packages. The practical effect of this patently restrictive trade practice was to ensure virtually 100 per cent membership of the association on the part of tour operators and travel agents. This high level of membership, unrivalled among other trade associations, has meant that the association has been able to exert a strong degree of control, because the threat of expulsion from ABTA would spell the end of any holiday business through inability to trade. Accordingly, the ABTA Codes of Conduct are widely adhered to by members of the association and in many respects those Codes provide consumers with protection greater than that provided by law.

However, since the introduction of the Package Travel, Package Holidays and Package Tours Regulations 1992, all tour organisers are under an obligation to protect the consumer's money by making appropriate insurance or bonding arrangement (regs 16, 17 and 18). The result of this is that previous justifications of 'stabiliser' on the ground of the public good (see *Re ABTA Ltd's Agreement* [1984] ICR 12) no longer hold good with the result that ABTA voluntarily removed 'stabiliser' from its articles of association in 1993. A likely effect of this is that holidays may well be sold through high street shops etc., bypassing the traditional travel agency. Furthermore ABTA agencies will no longer be confined to selling ABTA tour operators' products.

Most of the problems associated with the consumer as a holidaymaker relate to his or her expectations. The main difficulties arise where the consumer has booked a foreign holiday on the strength of statements made by the tour operator in a holiday brochure, only to find that the holiday promised is not what has been delivered. Where a consumer has been misled by false factual statements relating to the holiday, it is possible that a criminal offence has been committed by the tour operator under s. 14 of the Trade Descriptions Act 1968 (see chapter 18). However, it is also possible that the tour operator may have to compensate the consumer in respect of his or her disappointed expectations.

Perhaps as a word of caution, it should be observed that the range of remedies now available to the disappointed holidaymaker may take its toll in the form of substantially increased holiday costs. A recent survey conducted by ABTA shows that the number of complaints about holidays received in 1995 was 17,450 compared with 14,931 in 1994, a rise of nearly 17 per cent. In order to combat this increase in claims being made by consumers, tour operators are having to employ more staff to check all the constituent elements of the holidays they offer. Inevitably, this will lead to more expensive holidays, especially if spurious claims on the part of disappointed holidaymakers have to be met with an offer of compensation (see *The Times*, 11 June 1996, p. 9).

9.1 PACKAGE TRAVEL, PACKAGE HOLIDAYS AND PACKAGE TOURS REGULATIONS 1992

The most important development in relation to holiday law is the introduction of the Package Travel, Package Holidays and Package Tours Regulations 1992 (SI 1992/3288), which implement the EC Package Travel Directive (OJ L158/61, 23.6.1990). While existing common law rules remain effective, these Regulations create additional obligations which impinge on the rights of consumers and add to the duties of tour operators. Some of the provisions create criminal offences, while others allow the consumer to cancel what would otherwise be a valid contract.

The Regulations apply to 'package' travel and holidays, but 'package' is given a broad definition in reg. 2(1), which encompasses a pre-arranged combination of at least two of the following components offered for sale at an inclusive price (covering a period of more than 24 hours or including overnight accommodation), namely transport, accommodation, other tourist services. But the submission of separate accounts for different components does not prevent the arrangement from being a package and the fact that a combination is arranged at the request of the customer in accordance with his instructions does not prevent the package from being pre-arranged.

A difficulty which emerges from the wording of reg. 2(1) is what is meant by pre-arranged. It certainly covers 'off-the-shelf' holidays, such as those advertised in standard brochures. However, pre-arranged could also mean 'arranged before the contract is concluded', in which case customised combinations of travel and accommodation made at the customer's specific request by a travel agent could also be classified as packages within the Regulations. If this is so, the travel agent booking the holiday would be expected to acquire a bond in order to ensure that consumer injuries and holiday failures etc. are adequately covered.

9.2 FORMATION OF THE HOLIDAY CONTRACT

As with any contract, holiday contracts are governed by the rules of offer and acceptance. Normally, the contract will be made between the tour operator and the consumer via the services of a travel agent acting on behalf of the tour operator. However, it appears that a notice displayed in a travel agent's shop which describes the ABTA protection scheme against the financial failure of its members is sufficiently clear in its language to amount to an offer by ABTA to consumers so as to create legal relations in respect of the compensation scheme. See the discussion of *Bowerman* v *ABTA Ltd* (1995) 145 NLJ 1815 in chapter 4.

A tour operator's brochure is much more likely to be construed as an invitation to treat on the reasoning employed in cases like *Grainger* v *Gough* [1896] AC 325 that if an advertisement were to be treated as an offer, there would be a contract with every person who responds to the advertisement. Accordingly, a tour operator with only 500 holidays available for sale at a discount price would be in breach of contract with every customer who responds after the 500th holiday has been sold.

In addition to common law rules on contract formation, the consumer is also provided with important protection in the form of the Package Travel, Package Holidays and Package Tours Regulations 1992. Under reg. 9, there is a requirement that the tour operator will include in the package holiday contract certain information specified in schedule 2 and will set out the terms of the contract in a comprehensible manner. Failure to comply with these requirements is regarded as a breach of condition under reg. 9(3), with the result that the tour operator will be unable to rely on any term which is not sufficiently comprehensible. Moreover, a further effect of non-compliance in this respect is that the consumer may cancel a contract not made in accordance with the communication requirements of reg. 9. Regulation 9(3) provides that the information supply requirement is a condition of the contract so that failure to comply means that the operator will be unable to rely on any term which fails to comply with the communication requirement. Moreover, the consumer may cancel a contract not made in accordance with the communication requirements of reg. 9(3). The requirements of reg. 9 are that the consumer must be supplied with written details of the intended destination or destinations; the intended means of travel including dates and points of departure; the location of any accommodation provided and its tourist category; what meals are included in the package; whether there must be a minimum number of travellers in order to allow the package to take place; any relevant itineraries; any visits or excursions included in the package; the name and address of the organiser, retailer and insurer; the price and whether that price may be revised in accordance with reg. 11; a payment schedule and the methods by which payment may be made; any communicated special requirements, such as special accommodation requested for an invalid or special dietary requirements; and the period during which any complaint is to be made by the consumer in the event of things going wrong during the package holiday.

The wording of reg. 9 makes it clear that the tour operator has two obligations. First all the information required must be provided both before the contract is made (reg 9(1)(b)) and must also be included in the contract (reg. 9(1)(a)). Generally this will not be a problem for conventional package travel arrangements, since the information can be included in the brochure, complying with reg. 9(1)(b), and the brochure information can be incorporated in the contract booking form, thereby complying with reg. 9(1)(a).

The obligations imposed by reg. 9 will not apply where the consumer makes such a late booking that it is not practicable for the information to be given (reg 9(2)). But reg. 9 could cause problems where the consumer books a holiday over the telephone and pays by credit card, in which case the contract is made before the necessary information has been supplied. In this case, arguably, unless the operator refuses to make the contract until the reg. 9 information has been supplied, the consumer will have the right to cancel the contract.

9.3 STATEMENTS MADE IN THE HOLIDAY BROCHURE AND THE BASIS OF THE TOUR OPERATOR'S LIABILITY

A very common source of consumer complaint is that the holiday provided does not live up to the description given of it in the tour operator's brochure. An initial problem is to identify who is responsible for the various statements which have been made. On the face of it, since it is the tour operator who publishes the brochure, it would seem to make sense to hold the operator liable for any misleading information. However, it should not be forgotten that the consumer was probably given the brochure by a holiday retailer, namely, a travel agent. It will be seen below that the effect of the Package Travel, Package Holidays and Package Tours Regulations 1992 is to hold the supplier of the holiday *and* the retailer liable for inaccurate information with the result that a travel agent may have to accept responsibility for a statement which he did not make himself. At common law, the position is somewhat different in that a travel agent who did not originate the statement will not be liable for something said by someone else. The terms of the contract between the travel agent and the tour operator will normally provide for some form of indemnity in favour of the agent.

In analysing statements made in a holiday brochure, it is necessary to distinguish between terms of the contract, misrepresentations and mere puffs. The latter are mere commendatory statements which do not give rise to any liability — generally statements on which no reasonable person could claim to rely, e.g., 'Persil washes Whiter than White'. Although the travel trade has started to clean up its act, there are nonetheless statements in holiday brochures which no reasonable person could regard as anything other than a mere puff. For example in *Hoffmann* v *Intasun* (unreported, 1990) the plaintiff bought a 'Club 18-30' holiday. In the brochure, holiday representatives were described as 'the life and soul of the party, hard working, good timing, trouble shooting, guitar playing, beach partying smooth operators'. Such a general description could not possibly fit all reps who might be employed by Intasun, and there could be no conclusion other than that this statement was a puff. The fact that a particular representative did not play the guitar or did not fall within the description 'smooth operator' could not form the basis of an action for breach of contract or misrepresentation!!

To an extent, the common law distinction between terms and representations (and possibly puffs) becomes irrelevant due to the Package Travel, Package Holidays and Package Tours Regulations 1992, reg. 4, which provides that organisers and retailers incur civil liability if they supply descriptive matter concerning the package, the price of a package and any other conditions applying to the contract which contains any misleading information. It seems reasonable to assume that the word 'matter' only covers written statements, with the result that information contained in a brochure or in press advertisements will incur liability. The important point, however, is that travel agents are just as much liable as tour operators and since a travel agent will supply brochures to customers, the effect of reg. 4 is that the agent can be held responsible for statements made by others which are misleading about the elements listed in reg. 4. A more difficult question is whether a mere puff can be said to relate to 'any other conditions of the contract'. It is possible that most puffs will be treated as so devoid of any meaningful content that they will not be treated as relating to the *conditions* of the contract.

More specific statements may give rise to the possibility of an action for breach of contract. Generally, there will be some specific statement in the brochure which forms part of the contract and is therefore an express term of that contract. However, in some circumstances something may go wrong which has not been specifically dealt with in the holiday literature and the question may arise whether the court can imply a term into the contract.

A term may be implied on the basis of the 'officious bystander' test contained in *Shirlaw* v *Southern Foundries (1926) Ltd* [1939] 2 KB 206. What this entails is a suggestion by the officious bystander that a particular term has been omitted. If the immediate response of both parties as reasonable men would be that the omitted term ought to be part of the contract, then it will be implied. Accordingly, the term suggested will usually be fairly uncontroversial and obvious in most cases falling within the test. If there is any reasonable possibility of one of the parties not agreeing to the presence of a particular term, there will be no room for its implication. The problem in most holiday contracts is that there are two interests involved, namely, the reasonable enjoyment and safety of the holidaymaker and a desire not to saddle a tour operator with responsibility for the deficiencies of, for example, overseas hotel owners over whom the operator may have little or no control. Unfortunately these two interests may conflict with the result that implying a term under the officious bystander test may become impossible.

Two views are possible of the scope of a tour operator's liability on his contract with the consumer. One view is that since the brochure details what the holidaymaker will get and since the contract is with the tour operator, the tour operator is strictly liable for all damage foreseeably suffered by the consumer in a manner similar to the operation of the implied requirements of quality and fitness in a sale of goods contract. However, tour operators would prefer to see the contract as one for services supplied by a number of independent contractors, for whose actions the tour operator is only liable if he has failed to exercise reasonable care in selecting someone competent.

At one stage the latter view appeared to prevail. In *Wall* v *Silver Wing Surface Arrangements* (unreported, 18 November 1981) holidaymakers were injured when they tried to escape from a Tenerife hotel by the fire escape, only to discover that the escape route was padlocked by the hotel management. Instead they tied sheets together to make an escape rope, which unfortunately broke when used by the plaintiffs to escape from a third-floor room. The question arose as to whether a term could be implied into the holiday contract to the effect that travellers would be reasonably safe in using the hotel for the purposes for which they were invited to be there. Evidence showed that a Silver Wing representative had visited the hotel before its details were put in the brochure and that all fire escapes were operational and effective at the time of the visit.

Hodgson J considered it astonishing that anyone could suggest that a tour operator should be accountable for any default on the part of hotel owners, taxi drivers or airlines when they had no control over the way in which such people acted. As was observed by Hodgson J:

> . . . it is perfectly well known that the tour operator neither owns, occupies or controls the hotels which are included in his brochure any more than he has control over the airlines which fly his customers, the airports whence and whither they fly and the land transport which conveys them from airport to hotel. . . . If injury is caused by the default of the hotel owners . . . the customer will have whatever remedy the relevant law allows.

Accordingly, this was not a term which would satisfy the officious bystander test. Moreover, there was no justification for such a term under the *Liverpool City Council* v *Irwin* [1977] AC 239 test of necessity.

Consequences of the *Wall* v *Silver Wing Surface Arrangements* analysis of the tour operator's obligations are that if the consumer suffers harm as a result of some negligent act on the part of a hotel employee or due to the state of the hotel in which he stays, the tour operator will not be liable unless he has failed to exercise reasonable care. Thus if a honeymoon couple arrive a day late at their destination due to industrial action, the tour operator is not liable if the delay is beyond anyone's control (*Usher* v *Intasun* [1987] CLY 418). Similarly, if the consumer complains of a cockroach-infested hotel room, the tour operator is only liable if it can be shown that reasonable care has not been exercised in selecting a suitable hotel (*Kaye* v *Intasun* [1987] CLY 1150).

There is a possible problem with *Wall* v *Silver Wing Surface Arrangements* in that Hodgson J's judgment slavishly applies Lord Wilberforce's judgment in *Liverpool City Council* v *Irwin* when, in fact, other judgments in that case (notably that of Lord Cross of Chelsea) seem to allow a term to be implied on grounds other than necessity, for example, reasonableness. However, the courts have continued to adopt the same general approach to the issue of implying terms into holiday contracts when to do so would saddle the tour operator with responsibility for what someone else has done.

In *Wilson* v *Best Travel Ltd* [1993] 1 All ER 353 it was considered that the tour operator will have complied with his implied obligation to exercise reasonable care if he ensures that the hotel accommodation provided meets the minimum safety requirements imposed by the law of the country in which the hotel is to be found, unless those standards are so low that no reasonable holidaymaker would regard them as acceptable.

It is questionable whether the holidaymaker should be so badly protected. For example, it has been seen already that the buyer of goods is protected under the Sale of Goods Act 1979 by the imposition of strict liability duties on the part of the retailer in so far as the quality and fitness of the goods purchased are concerned. However, the provision of a holiday, being classified as a service is only subject to a fault-based regime under English law (see also chapter 8).

The intolerability of imposing on a tour operator any wider duty than that implied in *Wall* v *Silver Wing Surface Arrangements* has been called into question by the Privy Council in *Wong Mee Wan* v *Kwan Kin Travel Services Ltd* [1996] 1 WLR 38, in which the plaintiff's daughter bought a package tour of part of China, organised by the defendants. When the tour party reached the border of Hong Kong and China, they were joined by a tour guide employed by a travel company acting on behalf of the defendants. The tour party was taken by this employee on a lake crossing in a speedboat owned by the third defendants. This boat was driven at excessive speed, probably in an attempt to overtake another speedboat, with the result that there was a collision with a fishing junk. As a result of this accident, the plaintiff's daughter was drowned. It was accepted that the speedboat had been driven negligently by the driver and the question arose whether the tour operator could be held responsible for the plaintiff's daughter's death. It was held that on a proper construction of the contract, the defendants had undertaken to provide all the services on the tour as opposed to merely arranging those services through others. As such it was an implied term of the contract that any service provided by the defendants would be performed with reasonable care and skill, even if those services were actually performed by others. Since the lake crossing had not been carried out with reasonable care and skill, the defendants could be held liable for the plaintiff's daughter's death. This, however, did not amount to holding that the defendants undertook that the plaintiff's daughter would be reasonably safe and that the defendants had guaranteed the safety of all components of the package tour, it was merely an undertaking that the services provided by the defendants (through others) would be performed with reasonable care and skill. The implied term would not have covered the killing of the plaintiff's daughter by some third party unconnected with the defendants. On the issue of the 'intolerability' of holding the defendants liable for the acts of others over whom they have no control, the point was made that a tour operator can protect himself by negotiating suitable contractual terms with those who provide services for him, or by obtaining suitable insurance cover, or by inserting a suitable exclusion or limitation of liability in his contract with the traveller, so far as permitted by the law. What is important about this decision is that it turns clearly on an interpretation of the contract that it was the defendants who undertook to provide all the services referred to in the contract. The position would have been different if the contract was merely one to *arrange for services to be provided by others*, since in those circumstances there can be no implied term which could render the defendants liable (*Craven* v *Strand Holidays (Canada) Ltd* (1982) 142 DLR (3d) 31).

The cases considered so far all turn on what is meant by the exercise of reasonable care on the part of the tour operator, but there have also been dicta which point to a form of strict liability on the part of the tour operator. For example, it has been said that if a tour operator fails to provide a holiday of the required quality, he is liable in damages (*Jarvis* v *Swans Tours Ltd* [1973] 1 All ER 71, 76 per Edmund Davies LJ). In *Cook* v *Spanish Holiday Tours Ltd* (1960) *The Times* 6 February 1960, the Court of Appeal held that the duty of a tour operator was not merely to book a room, but also to provide the accommodation requested. It appears to follow from this that the tour operator is strictly liable if he fails to provide the full components of the package holiday booked by the customer. However, this may need to be read in the light of the observations in *Wong Mee Wan* v *Kwan Kin Travel Services Ltd* that the extent of the tour operator's liability will turn on a proper construction of the contract and that if the tour operator has undertaken to provide a package, whoever performs elements of that package must do so with reasonable care and skill, and if that required degree of skill is not exercised the tour operator may be held liable.

The liability of tour operators is now clearly affected by the Package Travel, Package Holidays and Package Tours Regulations 1992, reg. 15(1), which holds the tour operator liable for the improper performance of the contract by other service providers. This effectively reverses the basis on which *Wall* v *Silver Wing Surface Arrangements* was decided. The only let-out under reg. 15(2) is where the improper performance is due to neither the fault of the tour operator nor the fault of the service provider because of a specified list of events. This list includes a failure which is attributable to the consumer. For example, in *Hartley* v *Intasun* [1987] CLY 1149 the consumer arrived at the airport a day late. He was flown to his destination, but when he got there the booked accommodation had been let to someone else by the hotel owner.

The consumer had to accept inferior accommodation as a replacement. It is likely that under reg. 15(2) the fault of the consumer would be regarded as the cause of the holiday disappointment.

A second listed reason in reg. 15(2) is that the holiday failure is due to the unforeseeable and unavoidable act of a third party unconnected with the provision of the services contracted for, for example, if damage were to be caused to the hotel swimming pool by vandals. Conversely, if the damage is caused by a third party, but it is foreseeable that this might happen, the tour operator may still be responsible. Thus if the consumer is mugged on the first night of his holiday because he has been booked into a hotel in a notoriously rough area, although the injury is caused by a third party, it might be regarded as foreseeable damage.

The third exception provided for in reg. 15(2) extends to cover *force majeure* events such as war, civil commotion, and extreme weather conditions such as earthquakes and hurricanes, all of which may be regarded as being beyond the control of the tour operator and the service provider. However, it is important to emphasise that the event must be one the consequences of which could not have been avoided even if all due care and attention had been exercised. If a *force majeure* event is established, its effect will be to absolve the tour operator from liability for compensation, but the consumer will still be able to cancel the contract, if, for example, the frustrating event occurs before the departure date under reg. 13 and will be entitled to a full refund. Where the alleged frustrating event occurs after departure, the position is governed by reg. 14, which makes no specific mention of *force majeure* events, but does imply a term into the holiday contract to the effect that if the tour operator is unable to provide a significant proportion of the services contracted for, he will make suitable alternative arrangements and, if necessary, transport the consumer back to the point of departure.

The fourth exception under reg. 15(2) covers any event which the tour operator or service provider could not have foreseen or forestalled even with the exercise of due care. What is likely to fall within this would be events such as a strike by air traffic controllers or by all French seamen.

The way in which reg. 15(2) is set out would seem to suggest that if there is an improper performance due to neither the fault of the tour operator nor the fault of the service provider, but which is not covered by the list of specific events, the tour operator will still remain liable. Under reg. 15 it is likely that there would be no fault on the part of the tour operator or service supplier in such a case.

Quite apart from common law rules and before the provisions of the 1992 Regulations took effect, the provisions of the ABTA Code of Conduct were amended so that in relation to all package tours with a departure date after April 1990 tour operators were required to offer a limited guarantee to holidaymakers before any changes in the law were effected by way of regulations. The reason for this was that ABTA acted swiftly to ensure that their code of conduct fell in line with an earlier proposed EC Directive on package holidays (OJ C96, 12.4.88, p. 5) on this matter. Subsequently, the Code has been re-amended to take account of later developments at European level.

Clause 2.8(i) of the Code provides that it must be a term of all contracts for the sale of foreign inclusive holidays that the tour operator should accept liability for the acts or omissions of their employees, agents, subcontractors and suppliers, resulting in harm other than death, bodily injury or illness. It is clear that this provision also extends to natural events as well as those resulting from the default of the hotelier and that the tour operator will be liable where he has no control over the event giving rise to the complaint. It follows from this that while the law based on the decisions in *Wall* v *Silver Wing Surface Arrangements*, *Usher* v *Intasun* and *Kaye* v *Intasun* remains the same, consumers in a similar position will now be covered by the Code. Clause 2.8(i) also provides that the protection afforded by it will extend to any person whose name appears on the booking form, thus preventing a privity of contract defence on the part of the tour operator (cf. *Jackson* v *Horizon Holidays Ltd* [1975] 1 WLR 1468 considered in 9.4).

Clause 2.8(ii) provides that the tour operator must accept responsibility for death or bodily injury caused by the negligent acts or omissions of employees, agents and subcontractors etc., provided that they act in the course or scope of their employment. Excluded from this is the act of an air or sea carrier which will be covered by specific transport conventions. There is also a requirement that tour operators should be adequately insured against such liability (Code, clause 2.8(iv)). While this does not add anything in relation to agents and employees, clause 2.8(ii) provides protection in excess of the law in relation to the negligent acts or omissions of subcontractors and suppliers. It would appear that the consumer will now have a remedy in a case like *Craven* v *Strand Holidays (Canada) Ltd* (1982) 142 DLR (3d) 31 where a holidaymaker was injured when a bus in which he was travelling overturned due to the negligence of the driver. At the time, the tour operator was held not to be liable because it had no control over the bus company and had exercised reasonable care in selecting the company as a subcontractor.

The Code further provides that tour operators will also contract to provide advice, guidance and financial assistance up to a limit of £5,000 per booking to consumers who, while on holiday, suffer illness, injury or death due to a misadventure not related to the holiday arrangement. The wording of this provision is somewhat ambiguous, and tour operators would be advised to think carefully about the wording of such a contract term so as to avoid construction *contra proferentem* if it were to be tested in legal proceedings. It is intended to mean that tour operators will undertake to provide assistance in the bringing of legal proceedings against the person responsible. However, on its present wording it could be taken to mean that the tour operator will provide up to £5,000 towards the cost of hospital fees incurred by the consumer if he were to fall off a defectively designed motorcycle which has been hired independently of any specific holiday arrangements with the tour operator.

9.4 PRIVITY OF CONTRACT

Privity of contract can cause unfortunate problems in holiday contracts since it is likely that a holiday will have been booked by one person on behalf of other members of his or her family. One way of getting round the problem set up by a strict application of the doctrine of privity is to seek to apply the principle in *Jackson* v *Horizon Holidays Ltd* [1975] 1 WLR 1468 (see also chapter 4) that certain types of contract may be made by one person on behalf of another. A difficulty with this principle is to ascertain precisely what it amounts to. It has been observed already that James LJ appeared to decide the case on the basis that the loss suffered by Mr Jackson's family could be regarded as loss suffered by Mr Jackson himself. However, in a more broad-ranging judgment Lord Denning MR took the view that the contract entered into by Mr Jackson was one made for the benefit of his wife and children with the result that he could recover in damages the amount which his wife and children would have recovered had they been able to sue. The difficulty with this reasoning is that it has been roundly criticised by the House of Lords in *Woodar Investment Development Ltd* v *Wimpey Construction UK Ltd* (1980) 1 WLR 277 on the ground that Lord Denning was wrongly applying a decision which turned on principles of equity applicable only to trusts (see chapter 4).

What is more difficult to understand about the reasoning of the Court of Appeal in *Jackson* v *Horizon Holidays Ltd* was that part of the booking form clearly stated, 'I have read and understood these booking conditions and accept them for and on behalf of myself and all the persons named in the booking form', which had been signed by Mr Jackson. In the light of this, it would seem to follow that the case could have been pleaded and decided on the basis that Mr Jackson contracted as agent for the rest of his family. Even this is an imperfect solution since the Jackson children were so young that they would not have been regarded as contractually capable principals, but at least the problems concerning Mrs Jackson could have been dealt with on the basis of agency.

Many of the problems of privity of contract are circumvented by the Package Travel, Package Holidays and Package Tours Regulations 1992, reg. 2(1) and reg. 10. Under reg. 2(1) the protection afforded to the purchaser of a holiday is also extended to other beneficiaries and transferees. Thus cases like *Jackson* v *Horizon Holidays Ltd* will no longer require the legal gymnastics of Lord Denning MR. Under reg. 10, if the consumer finds that he is prevented from taking up the package holiday, he may transfer his booking to someone else qualified to take it up, on giving the tour operator reasonable notice. In such circumstances, the transferor and the transferee become jointly and severally liable for the amount of price outstanding, but the effect of reg. 10 is to prevent a tour operator from being able to levy a cancellation charge.

One difficulty which may arise in the interpretation of reg. 10 is to determine what is meant by the phrase 'prevented from'. A number of events might suffice, some of which may result from external events and others of which may be related to the consumer's own behaviour or feelings. For example, suppose the would-be holidaymaker is handed down a custodial sentence and becomes unable to take up a holiday booked earlier in the year? If the same approach is taken to reg. 10 as has been applied to the question of frustration of contracts of service, this might be an unacceptable reason for allowing the consumer to cancel a holiday (see, e.g., *Shepherd & Co. Ltd* v *Jerrom* [1987] QB 301). However, simply finding a replacement holidaymaker under reg. 10 is not the same as treating a contract as frustrated, in which case, it ought to follow that the imprisoned consumer has been prevented from taking up the holiday he has booked, provided he can give reasonable notice. Other reasons which are equally likely to allow for the operation of reg. 10 would include illness and redundancy, since neither of these is related to any sort of wrongdoing on the part of the consumer. However, it is doubtful whether reactions such as 'I don't feel like going today' or 'I've changed my mind because I've had a better offer' would necessarily be regarded as sufficient to prevent someone from taking a booked holiday.

There may also be problems under reg. 10 in ascertaining who is a person qualified to take up the package. For example, it seems unlikely that a 65-year-old grandmother should be permitted to take a place on a Club 18–30 Holiday, if only for the protection of the interests of other holidaymakers taking that particular package. Similarly, seeking to send an 18-year-old on a Saga holiday intended for old-age pensioners might attract the same criticism.

9.5 REMEDIES

An award of expectation damages for a breach of contract is ordinarily related to the standard business expectation of making a profit, since the general measure of damages in an action for breach of contract is supposed to put the plaintiff in the position he would have been in had the contract been performed (see *Robinson* v *Harman* (1848) 1 Ex 850, 855). Ordinarily, the appropriate measure might be thought to be the cost of the holiday, but, in the context of disastrous holidays there are other considerations. It may be that what has been provided is worth the money paid for it, in the sense that the value of the flight to the holiday location and the cost of the accommodation provided are equal to the amount paid by the consumer. Even if the court decides that the consumer has only had 'half a holiday', an award of damages based on half the cost of the holiday may not be sufficient compensation for the loss of enjoyment (*Jarvis* v *Swans Tours Ltd* [1973] 1 All ER 71, 74 per Lord Denning MR).

Damages can be awarded under a holiday contract on a number of bases. In the first place, there is the possibility of a difference in value claim. If the consumer only gets half a holiday, he should get back half of what he has paid. Thus in *Jackson* v *Horizon Holidays Ltd* [1975] 1 WLR 1468, £600 damages were awarded against a holiday cost of £1,200. It appears from *Levine* v *Metropolitan Travel* [1980] CLY 638 that if the consumer makes a cheap late booking, his damages should be based not on the price paid, but on the value of the holiday in normal circumstances hence in the case half a holiday was valued at £200 because the holiday, at full cost, was worth £400, though only £323 had been paid for it.

A second basis for awarding damages is to quantify the plaintiff's loss by reference to any out-of-pocket expenses incurred. Thus if the food provided by the hotel is so poor that the consumer feels he must buy meals in a local restaurant, provided receipts are kept, it should be possible to include these incidental expenses in a claim for damages. As an extreme example, the plaintiff in *Davey* v *Cosmos* [1989] CLY 2561 was able to recover the cost of having his clothing cleaned after an attack of dysentery. However, it is not legitimate to claim for lost earnings (*Jarvis* v *Swans Tours Ltd* [1973] 1 All ER 71), since such loss is not caused by the failed holiday, but rather by the consumer's conscious choice to take a holiday.

A third possible head of damage where a holiday fails is that of mental distress or loss of enjoyment. It should be appreciated that a consumer may make a purchase for pleasure or utility conferred which may bear no relation to the price paid (see Harris, Ogus and Phillips, 'Contract remedies and the consumer surplus' (1979) 95 LQR 581). Where the purchase is made for the pleasure or utility conferred, it is quite possible that the consumer places a value on the holiday which is actually in excess of the price paid for the accommodation and travel. This excess over the actual market value is referred to as the 'consumer surplus value' which in the case of a holiday includes the expected relaxation, enjoyment and relief from the tedium of general working life which most people look forward to when they book their annual family holiday. It has been seen already that this consumer surplus value may arise from building services (see *Ruxley Electronics & Construction Ltd* v *Forsyth* [1996] AC 344 discussed in chapter 4) as well as from taking a holiday. Since in most of these cases there is no question of non-performance, specific performance of the contract is not an appropriate remedy. Similarly, it will not be possible to compensate the consumer by giving reinstatement damages so as to allow satisfactory performance by a third party. Much will depend on what the tour operator's brochure has claimed about the holiday in question and how this has been interpreted by the consumer. The origin of recovery of damages for distress and disappointment is to be found in the Court of Appeal decision in *Jarvis* v *Swans Tours Ltd* [1973] 1 All ER 71 where it was observed that a holiday contract is one for enjoyment and if that enjoyment has been compromised, the plaintiff is entitled to a sum of money in respect of his damaged expectations. Mr Jarvis booked a 'house party holiday' in Switzerland on the strength of various statements in the defendant's brochure which described the principal attractions as including a welcome party on arrival; afternoon tea and cake for seven days; Swiss dinner by candlelight; fondue party; yodler evening; Chali farewell party in the 'Alphütte Bar'; service of representative. There were also special claims indicating that suitable skiing equipment was available for hire.

Mr Jarvis booked a 15-day holiday with ski-pack for which the total charge was £63.45. However the holiday proved to be an immense disappointment. The plaintiff expected to be one of a house party of some 30 or so people. Instead, he found that there were only 13 people present in the first week and in the second week there was no house party at all, since everyone else had left! Moreover, no one could speak English and the skiing proved to be a disaster as the nearest slopes were some miles away and there were no ordinary-length skis until the second week, by which time his feet were so rubbed that he could not continue. Lord Denning MR observed (at pp. 74–5):

> It has often been said that on a breach of contract, damages cannot be given for mental distress. . . . The courts in those days only allowed the plaintiff to recover damages if he suffered physical inconvenience. . . . I think those limitations are out of date. In a proper case damages for mental distress can be recovered in contract, just as damages for shock can be recovered in tort. One such case is a contract for a holiday, or any other contract to provide entertainment and enjoyment. If the contracting party breaks his contract, damages can be given for the disappointment, the distress, the upset and frustration caused by the breach. I know that it is difficult to assess in terms of money, but it is no more difficult than the assessment which the courts have to make every day in personal injury cases for loss of amenities.
>
> Take the present case. Mr Jarvis has only a fortnight's holiday in the year. He books it far ahead, and looks forward to it all that time. He ought to be compensated for the loss of it.

Applying these principles in *Jackson* v *Horizon Holidays Ltd* [1975] 1 WLR 1468, in addition to the assessed diminution in value of the holiday of £600, the court awarded a further £500 in respect of the distress suffered by the family (per Lord Denning MR) or by Mr Jackson alone (per James LJ).

The problem remains to consider how far the distress damages factor extends. It is clear from *Hayes* v *Dodd* [1990] 2 All ER 815 that damages will only be awarded under this head in contracts for 'peace of mind' but what does this entail? *Jarvis* v *Swans Tours Ltd* shows that a package holiday is one such contract, but what about 'flight only' holidays or business travel? In the case of flight only holidays, assuming the flight is to a holiday destination and the travel agent or airline is aware of this fact, it should not be too difficult to treat disappointment at not reaching one's holiday destination on time as something which might foreseeably give rise to disappointment. However, in the case of business flights, the justification for disappointment damages seems to be a little less clear.

The basis on which damages were awarded in both *Jarvis* v *Swans Tours Ltd* and *Jackson* v *Horizon Holidays Ltd* was that there had been a breach of contract, but this will not always be the case. For example, it is possible that the misleading statement on which the consumer relies is treated as a mere representation rather than as a term of the contract. In these circumstances, the consumer surplus value may be protected by an award of damages for misrepresentation for loss of enjoyment. In *Chesneau* v *Interhome Ltd* (1983) *The Times*, 9 June 1983 the defendants claimed that a house was in a quiet location near woods with a private swimming pool and was not part of a holiday complex. In fact, the house was part of a complex and had a shared swimming pool. Accordingly, the plaintiff found alternative accommodation at an additional cost of £209. The Court of Appeal held that the plaintiff was entitled to recover the additional expenditure plus damages for distress suffered as a result of the defendant's misrepresentation. It was regarded as a reasonable solution to the problem they faced to pay for additional accommodation which accorded with what had been represented to them, rather than opting to come home and sue for damages for the defendant's misrepresentation.

The extent to which this distinction between terms of the contract and misrepresentations is important is now less than it used to be following the implementation of the Package Travel, Package Holidays and Package Tours Regulations 1992, since if the misleading statement is contained in a tour operator's brochure, reg. 6 now turns those particulars into warranties which will give rise to an action for compensation. Moreover, under reg. 4 there is now a general liability in damages for the provision of any misleading descriptive matter (see above).

A final head under which the consumer may recover damages is that of physical discomfort. If the failed holiday actually causes the consumer to suffer physical pain or suffering this may be included in the statement of claim. In *Cook* v *Spanish Holidays* (1960) *The Times*, 6 February 1960 a couple who had to spend the first night of their honeymoon on a park bench because no accommodation was available could recover a sum of £25 (multiply several times over for the 1990s!!).

As with any action for damages, the plaintiff will only be able to recover loss which can be regarded as a reasonably foreseeable consequence of the defendant's breach of contract. It has been seen above in the discussion of *Jarvis* v *Swans Tours Ltd* that disappointment damages may be regarded as a variety of expectation loss, although many judicial observations liken the process of quantification to that which applies to actions for damages for personal injuries in tort actions. The basic principles of remoteness of loss are set out in *Hadley* v *Baxendale* (1854) 9 Ex 341 and *Koufos* v *C. Czarnikow Ltd* [1969] 1 AC 350 (see further chapter 4), under which losses may be subdivided into those which are the natural consequence of the defendant's breach and, as such, are regarded as foreseeable and those which do not arise naturally from the defendant's breach, but the possibility of which has been made known to the defendant by the plaintiff at the time the contract was entered into. Following the House of Lords decision in *Koufos* v *C. Czarnikow Ltd*, losses which do not arise naturally from the defendant's breach are subject to a stringent test of foresight which requires the defendant to realise that the loss is 'quite likely' or 'a real danger' or 'a serious possibility'. Accordingly, a mere side remark in the course of a casual conversation in a travel agent's shop may not be sufficient to make losses known to the defendant in order to be recoverable.

The tour operator will remain responsible for all normal losses which flow from the breach. However, in relation to unusual potential loss, there is an obligation on the tourist to ensure that the tour operator (through the travel agent) is made aware of any special requirements such as diet, special accommodation requirements or medical provision. (See *Kemp* v *Intasun Holidays Ltd* (1988) 7 TrLR 161 discussed in chapter 4.)

9.6   GETTING THERE AND BACK

When the consumer has booked a holiday, he can reasonably expect to be transported to and from his destination. However, problems can arise where there is a late alteration to the holiday schedule, where a scheduled flight is overbooked or where the tour operator becomes insolvent.

9.6.1   Alterations

Whether or not alterations to the holiday schedule are permitted will depend on the terms of the contract contained in the standard booking conditions. Many such provisions will amount to limitations of the tour operator's liability and will be dealt with in chapter 12. Perhaps the most important type of provision in this respect is one which allows the tour operator to alter itineraries at his discretion. Such a provision must satisfy the Unfair Contract Terms Act 1977 requirement of reasonableness (see *Anglo-Continental Holidays Ltd* v *Typaldos Lines Ltd* [1967] 2 Lloyd's Rep 61 and see chapter 12).

If the alteration is material or amounts to cancellation of the holiday, the tour operator's breach will amount to non-performance of the contract and the consumer will be entitled to recover any pre-payment he has made on the ground of a total failure of consideration. Principles identical to those which apply to pre-payments for home-improvement work are relevant here (see chapter 8).

If the tour operator materially alters holiday arrangements, his conduct may be regarded as a breach of condition and therefore sufficiently serious to allow the consumer to treat his obligation to pay for the holiday as being at an end. In such circumstances, the consumer has two options at common law. He may either accept the breach or waive it and treat the contract as continuing (*Heyman* v *Darwins Ltd* [1942] AC 331; *Johnson* v *Agnew* [1980] AC 367). One difficulty which may face the consumer is whether or not the tour operator's breach is sufficiently serious to allow termination. Some breaches go to the root of the contract, while others may spoil the holiday but only give rise to an action for damages. For example, if the consumer's flight is delayed due to the fault of the tour operator, but an alternative flight is offered four hours later to a destination 100 miles away from the proposed holiday location, it may be that the consumer must accept the alteration and seek to recover damages in respect of any specific expense incurred and for inconvenience and loss of enjoyment. Failure to accept the alternative offered could be construed as unreasonable conduct amounting to a failure to mitigate loss (*Payzu Ltd* v *Saunders* [1919] 2 KB 581). On the other hand, if the alteration consists of sending the consumer to a totally different holiday resort, it would be unreasonable to expect the consumer to stand for this and a decision to return home might be justified in the circumstances.

In relation to alterations and cancellations, the consumer is better protected by the provisions of the ABTA Tour Operators' Code of Conduct (revised April 1993). This deals with the issues of cancellation (clause 2.3) and significant alteration (clause 2.4) separately. In either event the Code requires the tour operator to offer an alternative comparable holiday or a prompt return of all money paid.

The Code provides that the tour operator shall not cancel a holiday after the date on which the balance of the price becomes due for reasons other than the outbreak of hostilities, political unrest or other circumstances amounting to *force majeure*. For these purposes, the Code stipulates that certain events over which the tour operator has no control, such as unilateral action on the part of a hotelier making accommodation unavailable, are not to be regarded as *force majeure* events. A strike by the tour operator's own staff is not regarded as sufficient excuse for cancellation. The ABTA guidelines for booking conditions give a definition of cancellation which goes beyond its dictionary definition. Clause 2.3 of the guidelines provides that changing a holiday in such a way that it amounts to the substitution of an entirely different tour will be regarded as a cancellation. Other examples given in the guidelines include the substitution of a resort unreasonably far from that booked by the client, provision of accommodation of an entirely different type to that booked, changes of flight time by more than 24 hours and changes of itinerary omitting the main advertised event or place.

Clause 2.4 provides that if the tour operator makes a material alteration after a booking, he must give the consumer the choice of an alternative holiday of comparable standard or a full refund of moneys paid. If the alteration is made after the date on which payment of the balance of the price became due, the tour operator is required to pay reasonable compensation. In most cases, the tour operator will itemise, in the brochure, in scale form, the amount of compensation available to the consumer.

The major difficulty is to determine what alterations are to be regarded as material. The code provides little in the way of definition, but the ABTA guidelines for booking conditions, while informal and not binding, provide greater detail in this respect. Alterations caused by departure delays resulting from weather or other technical difficulties including industrial disputes are not to be regarded as material. Changes resulting from overbooking are dealt with separately and must not be regarded as material by the tour operator (clause 2.6). The guidelines for booking conditions provide that any significant change to the tour not amounting to cancellation will be classified as a material alteration. These are stated to include significant changes of resort, flight changes involving substantial inconvenience and inconvenient changes of airport.

9.6.2 Overbooking of flights

While many package deals will involve transport by means of charter flights, tour operators sometimes use scheduled flights. A difficulty which can arise is that a consumer who believes he has a confirmed flight booking finds that he is denied access to that flight. The reason this can happen is that many airlines adopt a deliberate policy of overbooking scheduled flights to allow for 'no-shows', namely businessmen who have booked seats on a number of flights knowing that they will use only one of those flights. With a policy of overbooking, there will be occasions on which more passengers will arrive for a flight than can be legally put on board. Adopting such a policy can result in criminal liability, where the flight operator gives written confirmation of the availability of a seat, but this is no compensation to the disappointed traveller.

An EC Council Regulation (No. 295/91, OJ L36/5, 8.2.91) provides for minimum rules on the provision of compensation in such circumstances. The Regulation requires an air carrier to formulate a set of rules which it will operate in the event of an overbooked flight (art. 3.1), which should include provision for a call on volunteers prepared to take an alternative confirmed reservation (art. 3.3). Special consideration should be given to unaccompanied children and handicapped travellers (art. 3.4).

Where it is necessary to prevent a passenger from boarding a flight on which he is booked, the Regulation gives a passenger the choice of reimbursement of the cost of the ticket, re-routing to his final destination at the earliest possible opportunity or re-routing at a later date at the passenger's convenience (art. 4.1). Irrespective of what choice the passenger makes, he is entitled to compensation of ECU150 for flights of up to 3,500 kilometres and ECU300 for longer flights (art. 4.2). However, where the passenger is re-routed and arrives at his final destination no more than two hours later on flights of less than 3,500 kilometres (four hours in the case of longer flights), the specified compensation may be reduced by 50 per cent (art. 4.3). In any event, the carrier is not required to pay more than the face value of the passenger's ticket (art. 4.4) and the compensation may be paid in cash or travel vouchers or other services, if the passenger agrees (art. 4.5).

In addition to the provisions in respect of compensation, the Regulation requires the flight operator to provide a passenger who is denied boarding free telephone or fax facilities to convey one message, hotel accommodation and refreshments where this proves to be reasonably necessary (art. 6.1).

9.6.3 Tour operator's insolvency

Where a tour operator or a travel agent becomes insolvent, two principal issues arise. First, the consumer will wish to recover advance payments made if the holiday cannot be taken and secondly the consumer will wish to be assured of a safe return home, if the insolvency occurs after the holiday has commenced.

Where a tour operator becomes insolvent prior to the commencement of the holiday, it may be the case that the trustee in bankruptcy will arrange for profitable contracts to be performed by another operator. However, it is more likely that most holiday contracts will be terminated prior to the date of performance. Such termination amounts to an anticipatory breach of contract which, if accepted, will entitle the consumer to a full refund. However, as the holidaymaker will be an unsecured creditor of the tour operator, it is unlikely that he will receive in full the amount he has paid. The Package Travel, Package Holidays and Package Tours Regulations 1992 now apply to all tour operators and make special provision for the solvency of operators. Under reg. 16(1) it is now provided that the tour operator shall at all times be able to provide sufficient evidence of security for the refund of money paid over and for the repatriation of the consumer in the event of insolvency. That security is required to be maintained until the contract has been fully performed.

For the purposes of the security provisions in reg. 16, there are two approved methods of making bonding arrangements under regs 17 and 18 which depend upon whether the bonding arrangement is supported by a reserve fund (reg. 18) or not (reg. 17). If there is no reserve fund or additional insurance provision, the bonding institution must pay such sum as may be reasonably required to cover all moneys paid over by consumers in respect of packages which have not been fully performed by the insolvent tour operator.

One way in which the consumer can protect himself is by paying for the holiday with a credit card. Under the Consumer Credit Act 1974, s. 75, the creditor is jointly liable to the debtor in respect of the supplier's breach of contract (see further chapter 11). The effect of this is that where the consumer has paid the tour operator directly by means of a credit card, the creditor will be bound to satisfy the consumer's claim under s. 75. More difficult, however, is the situation in which the credit card payment has been made to a travel agent. In these circumstances, it is arguable that the collapse of a tour operator does not amount to a breach of contract on the part of the travel agent, in which case the creditor is justified in rejecting the debtor's claim under s. 75.

Where a tour operator ceases trading during the currency of a holiday, it is of prime importance that the consumer is not left stranded. Again, the travel industry bonding arrangements provide the greatest protection. In some instances where the holiday has been paid for in advance by the now collapsed tour operator, the holiday can continue uninterrupted. Even where this is not the case, the bonding arrangement will be such that any balance due to a hotelier etc. will be paid for. However, this does not stop some hoteliers from demanding immediate payment from the stranded consumer. In such a case, the consumer may be forced to return home early and the bonding arrangement will ensure that a flight is provided. This still leaves the consumer uncompensated in respect of the 'lost' portion of his holiday. Suing the tour operator is not an option, but under the bonding arrangements, the consumer can apply for a partial refund of the cost of his holiday. The order of priorities in which bond moneys are applied is first to ensure that stranded holidaymakers enjoy the remainder of their holiday or are repatriated. Any balance can then be used to make refunds. If the consumer booked his holiday through an ABTA travel agent, the agent may have given a money-back guarantee, in which case the consumer will be reimbursed and the agent will seek to recover that amount under the relevant bonding arrangement.

TEN

Consumer insurance

10.1 INTRODUCTION

For the consumer, insurance is assuming an increasing significance. The seller of goods will frequently attempt to convince the purchaser of the importance of entering into a contract with a third-party insurer which extends the manufacturer's guarantee period for the product purchased. This is particularly commonplace in sales of domestic electrical goods, motor vehicles and boats where the purchaser is offered the opportunity, either at the time of the sale or immediately prior to the expiry of a manufacturer's guarantee period, to insure the goods against specified risks, such as repair costs, should the product suffer a mechanical breakdown (see Hellner, 'The scope of insurance regulation: what is insurance for the purposes of regulation?' (1963) 12 Am J Comp L 494). For those who own a motor vehicle, or permit the use of such a vehicle by another on a road, the law has long required some form of compulsory insurance against third-party risks, covering not only personal injuries and death but also property damage (Road Traffic Act 1988, ss. 143 and 145). In this context the importance of insurance as a policy factor underlying many of the decisions on the tort of negligence involving motoring cases should not be underestimated (see, for example, *Nettleship* v *Weston* [1971] 2 QB 691; see also Stapleton, 'Tort, insurance and ideology', (1995) 58 MLR 820).

Modern insurance practice is becoming increasingly complex with much of its focus on the management of investment portfolios on behalf of clients, for example, in the form of personal equity plans and investment bonds, rather than the more traditional underwriting of pure risks. Such contracts, while not contracts of insurance in the strict sense (cf. *Fuji Finance Inc.* v *Aetna Life Insurance Ltd* [1996] 3 WLR 871, discussed in 10.2), are regulated in the same way as life policies by virtue of the provisions of the Financial Services Act 1986 relating to investor protection. Traditionally, insurance is classified into two broad categories: indemnity insurance on the one hand, and contingency insurance on the other. Indemnity insurance will indemnify the

insured against a specified loss, for example, the loss of a car, or of a building due
to fire. The actual amount of loss suffered by the insured will normally
determine the amount of payment, although if the parties have agreed that the
subject matter should bear a specific value for insurance purposes, the insured
will be able to recover an amount based on the agreed value rather than actual
value. Contingency insurance provides a specified payment upon the occurrence
of a contingent event. Thus, in a whole-life policy, the sum of money is payable
on the death of the insured (see Megarry V-C in *Medical Defence Union* v
Department of Trade [1980] Ch 82 at 89). In all cases, there can only be a contract
of insurance if the event insured against is outside the control of the insured.

10.2 DEFINING THE CONTRACT OF INSURANCE

The Insurance Companies Act 1982, having charged the regulation of the
insurance industry to the Department of Trade and Industry, does not go on
to define a contract of insurance. Accordingly, in the event of a regulatory
decision of the DTI being challenged in the courts, it will be for the court to
declare whether or not a particular activity constitutes the carrying on of
insurance business. As insurance contracts are not covered by the Unfair
Contract Terms Act 1977, the necessity for a definition of such a contract can
be crucial. The problem of formulating a comprehensive and precise definition has long been recognised by the courts. For example, in *Medical Defence
Union Ltd* v *Department of Trade* [1980] Ch 82, Megarry V-C opined that a
contract of insurance is a concept which it is better to describe than to
attempt to define (ibid. 95; see also *Department of Trade and Industry* v *St
Christopher Motorists Association* [1974] 1 WLR 99). However, an exhaustive
examination of the elements which go to make up a contract of insurance was
made by Channell J in *Prudential Insurance Co.* v *Commissioners of Inland
Revenue* [1904] 2 KB 658. In consideration of weekly payments of 6d (2.5p)
the appellants agreed to pay a certain sum of money to the insured when he
reached the age of 65. If he died before reaching that age, a smaller sum
would be paid to his executors. It was held that this was a policy of insurance
within the meaning of s. 98 of the Stamp Act 1891. Channell J stated (at
p. 663):

It must be a contract whereby for some consideration, usually but not
necessarily for periodical payments called premiums, you secure to yourself
some benefit, usually but not necessarily the payment of a sum of money,
upon the happening of some event. . . . the event should be one which
involves some amount of uncertainty. There must be either uncertainty
whether the event will ever happen or not, or if the event is one which must
happen at some time there must be uncertainty as to the time at which it
will happen. . . . A contract which would otherwise be a mere wager may
become an insurance by reason of the assured having an interest in the
subject matter — that is to say, the uncertain event which is necessary to
make the contract amount to an insurance must be an event which is prima
facie adverse to the interest of the assured.

The insurer must be under a legal obligation to pay the agreed sum, or money's worth to the insured. If the benefit is payable in the discretion of the insurer, then the contract is not one of insurance. In *Medical Defence Union Ltd* v *Department of Trade* the company had a membership made up of medical practitioners, including dentists, who paid an annual subscription. Its principal object was to conduct legal proceedings on behalf of its members and to indemnify them against claims for damages and costs. However, the company retained its absolute discretion in deciding whether to grant such assistance to its members. It was held that the plaintiff company was not in the business of carrying on insurance and was therefore exempt from the regulatory framework established under the relevant insurance legislation. The member's right was restricted to having his or her request for assistance considered fairly by the union, but this was not of itself a benefit in the nature of money or money's worth. Although the company would only rarely refuse assistance, and then only in extreme circumstances, their element of discretion in determining whether or not a member's claim would be met robbed the contract of its insurance element (see Roberts (1980) 43 MLR 85; Merkin (1979) 1 Liverpool L R 125).

The issue of whether or not investment policies fall within the definition of life assurance contained in s. 1 of the Life Assurance Act 1774 recently came before the Court of Appeal in *Fuji Finance Inc.* v *Aetna Life Insurance Ltd* [1996] 3 WLR 871 on appeal from Nicholls V-C (1994) 4 All ER 1025. The plaintiff policyholder, an investment company, invested a single premium of £50,000 in a capital investment bond. Under the terms of the policy, the policyholder could switch investments by directing at any given time into which funds the allocated units were to be invested. The policy provided for the payment of a sum equal to the bond's value, as determined under the rules of the policy, either upon the death of one Tait, an investor and 'prime mover' behind the plaintiff company, or upon its prior surrender. If the policy was surrendered within five years, a small discontinuation charge would be levied. The policy was taken out in October 1986 and by June 1992 it had appreciated in value to over £1 million, which represented an annual average increase of 90 per cent compounded. This rate of return was due to the acumen of Tait in monitoring the bond's performance and switching its investments under the highly favourable rules of the policy. It was estimated that at this rate of return, the policy, if it continued for the estimated life expectancy of Tait, would be worth £252 thousand trillion! When the defendant tightened the switching procedures, the plaintiff claimed repudiatory breach and surrendered the policy for £1,110,758.

The defendant company claimed that the policy fell within s. 1 of the Life Assurance Act 1774, and was therefore void. Section 1 provides that:

> . . . no insurance shall be made by any person . . . on the life or lives of any person or persons, or on any other event or events whatsoever, wherein the person . . . on whose account such policy . . . shall be made, shall have no interest, . . . and . . . every assurance made contrary to the true intent and meaning hereof shall be null and void.

The preliminary issue before the court was whether the policy was 'insurance . . . on the life . . . of any person' for the purposes of the Act. Nicholls V-C, having reviewed the principal authorities on the meaning of insurance (including *Prudential Insurance Co.* v *Commissioners of Inland Revenue*; *Flood* v *Irish Provident Assurance Co. Ltd* [1912] 2 Ch 597; *Joseph* v *Law Integrity Insurance Co. Ltd* [1912] 2 Ch 581, *Gould* v *Curtis* [1913] 3 KB 84), and the terms of the particular policy in issue, which provided for valuation in the event of death or earlier surrender, found that the policy was not a contract of insurance. The learned judge stated ([1994] 4 All ER 1025 at p. 1032) that:

> . . . it is necessary to identify the uncertain event which triggers a payment by the insurer. I do not see how an event can be regarded as triggering a payment if there is already in existence, irrespective of the happening of that event, an obligation on the insurer to make that very same payment on request. When the event occurs, the insured acquires nothing he did not already have. Nor, I add, does the insured lose anything.

The policy provided for a discontinuation charge, or penalty, to be levied on a descending scale should it be surrendered during the first five years of its term. However, in the event of Tait dying during this period, no such penalty would be deducted so that a larger sum would be paid out. Was this thread of insurance sufficient to render the policy a contract of life insurance on Tait's life? Nicholls V-C took the view that: 'It cannot be that the presence of a minor and insignificant element of insurance suffices to turn a contract otherwise of a different nature into a contract of insurance' (ibid. 1034). In the light of this finding, the defendants went on to argue that the policy was rendered unenforceable by virtue of s. 16(1) of the Insurance Companies Act 1982, which provides :

> An insurance company . . . shall not carry on any activities . . . otherwise than in connection with or for the purposes of its insurance business.

The section does not stipulate what the consequences are for breach of its prohibition, but does state that default is not a criminal offence. The issue then was whether a contract entered into in breach of the section could be considered illegal and unenforceable. The learned judge concluded that s. 16 forms part of the overall regulatory framework of the Act which confers wide powers on the Secretary of State. Breach of the prohibition under the section can 'trigger an exercise of those powers' (ibid. 1037), but Parliament cannot necessarily be taken to have intended that the contract should consequentially be unlawful and unenforceable. Accordingly, it was held that the policy was enforceable.

However, the Court of Appeal, applying recent Commonwealth decisions, allowed the defendants' appeal. It was held that where under a contract of insurance the benefit payable on voluntary surrender is the same as that payable on death, that is sufficient to render the contract a policy of life assurance within the meaning of s. 1 of the Life Assurance Act 1774. Morritt LJ stated that:

> The recent cases [not cited to the Vice-Chancellor] show how the courts of Australia and New Zealand have regarded the newer forms of policy. . . .
>
> (*Marac Life Assurance Ltd* v *Commissioner of Inland Revenue* [1986] 1 NZLR 694) recognised that the investment element of a policy, which has become such a feature of modern insurance, is consistent with its characterisation as a life policy. . . .
>
> In this case . . . the policy came to an end on the death of Mr Tait so that, subject to notification in the prescribed manner, the benefits then crystallised. Thus the right to surrender was related to the continuance of life for it could not be exercised by Fuji after the death of Mr Tait.

If the event on which a benefit was payable was sufficiently life or death related, Morritt LJ could see no reason in principle why it should matter if that benefit was the same as that payable on another life or death-related event. That was a matter for the insurer. In any case, his lordship stressed that, except in the case of unusual stability in the market, it was almost inevitable that the value of the benefits payable on death would be different from the policy's surrender value.

To be considered as carrying on insurance business, the insurer must agree that in return for the payment of a premium, it will assume the risk of some *uncertain future event* occurring in which the *insured has an interest* and over which the insurer has *no control*, and that should that uncertain event occur, the insurer will indemnify the insured either in *money or money's worth*. In *Re NRG Victory Reinsurance Ltd* [1995] 1 All ER 533, Lindsay J, holding that both reinsurance and retrocession (reinsurance of reinsurance) business fall within the ambit of the 1982 Act, adopted the *Oxford English Dictionary* definition of insurance, namely,' . . . a contract by which the one party . . . undertakes, in consideration of a payment (called a *premium*) proportioned to the nature of the risk contemplated, to secure the other against pecuniary loss, by payment of a sum of money in the event of destruction of or damage to property . . . or of the death or disablement of a person'.

10.3 REGULATION OF INSURANCE TRANSACTIONS

The importance of insurance to the consumer is immediately apparent and is likely to continue. For example, during the debate on the 1994 Budget the government announced that the risk of redundancy for mortgage payers is to be shifted away from the social security system to private insurance effected by the borrower at the time of obtaining the mortgage loan (see (1995) 145 NLJ 1418; the changes came into effect on 2 October 1995). Against this background the insurance business has been made subject to increasing State control and regulation, principally aimed at ensuring that companies authorised to conduct insurance business maintain certain solvency margins. This has been achieved largely through the Insurance Companies Act 1982, which contains a complex regulatory structure which implements the three generations of EC Insurance Directives (see MacNeil, 'The legal framework in the United Kingdom for insurance policies sold by EC insurers under freedom of services' (1995) 44 ICLQ 19). By s. 2 of the 1982 Act, a body carrying on insurance business in the United Kingdom must obtain the authorisation of the Secretary of State for Trade and Industry (see *R* v *Wilson* [1997] 1 All ER 119). This requirement is subject to certain exemptions, for example, motoring organisations which provide roadside breakdown assistance are specifically exempted from the scope of the Act (Insurance Companies Regulations 1994 (SI 1994/1516), reg. 2). More significantly, in accordance with the single insurance market established by EC law, an insurer authorised in its home State is able to set up branches in other EC countries, or otherwise sell insurance directly to insureds in other countries, without the authorisation of the host State. An insurer authorised elsewhere in the EC is, therefore, free to insure UK policyholders, subject only to informing them of its home State address. If an insurer is required to be authorised, but has not obtained the necessary authorisation, its policies were regarded as illegal by the common law, but their validity was preserved, with retroactive effect, by the Financial Services Act 1986, s. 132, as construed by the Court of Appeal in *Group Josi Re* v *Walbrook Insurance Co. Ltd* [1995] 1 WLR 1152.

In the event of the insolvency of an insurer, an assured with an outstanding claim against the insurer is entitled to claim 90 per cent of the loss (100 per cent in motor vehicle liability and employers' liability cases) from a fund established under the Policyholders Protection Act 1975. The right extends only to 'private policyholders' (i.e., non-corporate policyholders, or members of partnerships with no corporate members) holding 'United Kingdom policies', a phrase which has been held to mean a policy issued in the course of an insurer's UK business whether or not the policy proceeds are payable in sterling in England (*Scher* v *Policyholders Protection Board (Nos. 1 and 2)* [1993] 3 All ER 384 and [1993] 4 All ER 840. While the conduct of insurance businesses is now extensively controlled through a sophisticated supervisory framework, the relationship between insurers and insureds has been left largely to self-regulation. For instance, there are voluntary Statements of Insurance Practice whereby insurers have undertaken not to exercise some of their strict legal rights against individual policyholders. The first such Statement was adopted in 1977 (revised in 1986), in return for the undertaking that insurance contracts would be excluded from the scope of the Unfair Contract Terms Act 1977. Insurance contracts are, however, within the Unfair Terms in Consumer Contracts Regulations 1994, (SI 1994/3159), although, as will be seen below, the Regulations operate to prevent the courts from considering the validity of policy terms which relate to the scope of cover obtained in return for the premium paid.

10.3.1 Ombudsmen

There are two ombudsman schemes designed to protect the consumer, the first is the Insurance Ombudsman Bureau (IOB) established in 1981, and the second is the Personal Insurances Arbitration Service (PIAS) set up by insurers who feared that the IOB would become too effective as a consumer watchdog. The Bureau has 355 members. In 1993 it received 8,133 applications compared with 5,576 in 1992. Some 6,344 cases were completed as compared with 4,476 the previous year, a 42 per cent increase. Interestingly, in only 33 per cent of cases was the complaint upheld. In 1994 complaints reached their highest level with 8,500 being received, representing an increase of 4.5 per cent on 1993. The Bureau decided 7,182 cases with 60 per cent of decisions going in favour of insurers.

The need for statutory regulation remains given that some insurers, namely, those who are not members of the Association of British Insurers or of Lloyd's, are outside the regulatory framework. The Insurance Ombudsman's terms of reference require the officeholder to reach a decision which is 'fair and reasonable in all the circumstances' and which is in accordance not only with the law but also with 'good insurance practice'. The Ombudsman will hear complaints only when the complainant has exhausted all internal avenues for redress within a member insurance company and is empowered to make a compensation order up to a maximum sum of £100,000, although most complaints are resolved through conciliation. The procedure is informal, issues generally being conducted by 'letters of advice' but, where necessary, informal hearings are held. Paradoxically the Ombudsman has ruled that he can disallow reliance by an insurer on a term which he views as unreasonable despite the fact that contracts of insurance fall outside the ambit of the Unfair Contract Terms Act 1977.

Major inroads into the immunity enjoyed by the insurance industry from the provisions of the Unfair Contract Terms Act 1977 have been made by the Unfair Terms in Consumer Contracts Regulations 1994, which came into effect on 1 July 1995. The Regulations apply to contracts for the supply of goods and services and therefore represent a broad-ranging addition to consumer law generally (see chapter 12). With respect to insurance, although the Department of Trade and Industry originally decided that the Directive should not apply to terms which 'define or circumscribe the insured risk and the insurer's liability', the DTI changed its mind after consultation. The principal aim of the Directive is to prohibit unfair terms which are not individually negotiated, and to address some of the inadequacies of the Unfair Contract Terms Act 1977. Regulation 3(3) provides that 'a term shall always be regarded as not having been individually negotiated where it has been drafted in advance and the consumer has not been able to influence the substance of the term'. As will be seen, an unfair contract term shall not be binding on the consumer (reg. 5(1), see further chapter 12). Given the nature of insurance contracts in this regard, the impact of the provisions contained in the Regulations is of immense significance.

Of particular importance with respect to insurance contracts is reg. 6, which provides that terms in consumer contracts must be 'expressed in plain, intelligible language' and that if the meaning of a particular term is ambiguous, 'the interpretation most favourable to the consumer shall prevail'. The potential effect of this provision may operate as a device for allowing the courts to avoid the inequitable results seen in decisions such as *Dawsons Ltd v Bonnin* [1922] 2 AC 413 and *Thomson v Weems* (1884) 9 App Cas 671, considered below. If the Director General of Fair Trading considers a contract term to be unfair, he may institute proceedings for an injunction, including an interlocutory injunction, 'against any person appearing to him to be using or recommending use of such a term in contracts concluded with consumers' (reg. 8(2)). However, the protection afforded by the regulations may be rendered nugatory by the limiting effect of reg. 3(2) which states that: 'In so far as it is in plain, intelligible language, no assessment shall be made of the fairness of any term which . . . defines the main subject matter of the contract'. Given that generally the terms of an insurance policy relate to the subject-matter of the risk, this provision may well serve to frustrate the objective of including insurance contracts within the ambit of the Regulations.

10.4 CONTRACT FORMATION

Although contracts of insurance are governed by the general law of contract, there are significant points of divergence, not least of which is the fact that an insurance contract is one of *uberrima fides*, whereby the parties are subject to far-reaching duties of disclosure (considered below).

With the exception of marine insurance, there are no strict legal requirements governing the form of a contract of insurance. It can therefore be wholly oral, provided there is agreement on material terms, which includes the amount of the premium, the nature and duration of the risk, and the subject matter of the insurance (*Murfitt v Royal Insurance Co. Ltd* (1922) 38 TLR 334). In practice, however, the parties generally proceed on the basis of a proposal form completed by the insured in which the insured discloses factual information relating to the particular risk and on which the insurer will decide whether or not to accept the risk, and if so, on what terms.

The proposal generally represents an offer on the part of the insured to contract on the insurer's standard terms, or where there have been previous dealings between the parties, on the terms previously agreed between them (*General Accident Insurance Corporation v Cronk* (1901) 17 TLR 233; *Adie & Sons v Insurances Corporation Ltd* (1898) 14 TLR 544). As with any valid contract, an insurance contract will not be concluded until there is unconditional acceptance of the offer. Frequently, the insurer will state that acceptance is conditional upon receipt of the first premium. In this case, there is a counter-offer, which in turn will have to be accepted by payment of the premium by the insured. Such a counter-offer is non-revocable unless there is a change in the risk proposed. In *Canning v Farquhar* (1886) 16 QBD 727, Canning's proposal for life assurance was accepted on 14 December, subject to payment of the first premium. On 5 January he fell over a cliff and seriously injured himself. Four days later his representative visited the insurers to tender the first premium and also told them of Canning's accident. The insurers refused the premium and shortly thereafter, Canning died of his injuries. The Court of Appeal held that the insurance contract had not been concluded and therefore the insurers were not in breach. Lindley LJ found that the insurers' 'acceptance' of Canning's offer was in fact a counter-offer which, but for the change in the risk, would have continued until accepted by payment of the first premium. The tender of the premium was, in the light of the accident, 'a new offer for a new risk which the company were at liberty to decline' (ibid. 733).

While the terms of the insurance contract are generally contained in a policy document, it can be effected through an interim document. For example, in motor insurance the insured will often require immediate cover, in which case a temporary cover note may be issued which, provided there is objective evidence that the insured intends to accept the offer of insurance, will be treated as a valid contractual document (see *Taylor* v *Allon* [1966] 1 QB 304).

10.5   INSURABLE INTEREST

At common law there was no general requirement that the insured should have an insurable interest in the event against which the insurance is effected, nevertheless insurable interest has become a fundamental requirement which governs the validity of an insurance contract. At its root, it is this prerequisite which distinguishes a contract of insurance from a wager. The requirement arises from three sources which, depending upon the type of policy in question, will determine the validity of the contract. For example, in indemnity insurance the very nature of the contract as one of indemnity will require the insured to have an insurable interest at the date of the loss, and the general prohibition of gaming contracts, contained in s. 18 of the Gaming Act 1845, will strike down a policy taken out by an insured who has no interest, and no reasonable expectation of obtaining an interest, in the subject matter of the policy. As is considered below, it is the level of the insured's loss which determines the amount of payment under the policy. There are also non-excludable statutory provisions which require insurable interest. The Life Assurance Act 1774 imposes such a requirement at the date of entering into the contract to prohibit 'a mischievous kind of gaming' (see the preamble to the Life Assurance Act 1774), but not at the date of the loss, thereby facilitating the assignment of life policies (see below). Failure to establish insurable interest at the outset will render the policy illegal. The 1774 Act does not apply to marine policies or to the insurance of goods, which are specifically excluded by s. 4. It is unclear from the wording of the Act whether it applies to other forms of indemnity cover, most importantly property insurance and liability insurance, although the matter has been put beyond doubt by the Court of Appeal in *Mark Rowlands Ltd* v *Berni Inns Ltd* [1985] QB 211 and by the Privy Council in *Siu Yin Kwan* v *Eastern Insurance Co. Ltd* [1994] 2 AC 199, the former relating to buildings insurance and the latter to liability insurance. The Marine Insurance Act 1906, s. 4, requires, as regards marine policies, the insured to possess either actual insurable interest or a reasonable expectation of obtaining an insurable interest, when the policy is taken out, although in contrast to the 1774 Act, an insured's failure to establish an insurable interest does not render the policy illegal, but void (*John Edwards & Co.* v *Motor Union Insurance Co. Ltd* [1922] 2 KB 249). An insurable interest must exist also at the date of the loss, as a marine policy is one of indemnity.

10.5.1 Insurable interest in lives

As has been seen, s. 1 of the Life Assurance Act 1774 provides that a policy of insurance will be void unless the insured has an insurable interest in the life of the assured. Section 2 of the Act requires that the names of those so interested in the insurance to be declared in the policy. In practice this requirement serves little purpose, particularly since often it will be the insured's next of kin who benefit from the insurance and there is no requirement that their names should be specified in the policy: there have been difficulties posed by this section for group policies, e.g., in respect of employees, as it is unclear from the outset exactly who will from time to time, fall within the group, although the problem was averted by s 50 of the Insurance Companies Act 1973, which disapplies s. 2 of the 1774 Act provided that the class of persons covered by the policy is identifiable with reasonable *certainty*.

Moreover, an insured may assign a policy of assurance to another who lacks the requisite insurable interest.

Section 3 of the 1774 Act restricts the amount recovered by the insured to the value of his or her interest. Taking the literal reading of ss. 1 and 3 together, it would appear that the interest of the insured would have to be satisfied both at the time of effecting the policy, and at the time of the loss (this was the decision in *Godsall* v *Boldero* (1807) 9 East 72). However, it was held in *Dalby* v *India and London Life Assurance Co.* (1854) 15 CB 365, that s. 3 merely required the insured to 'value his interest at its true amount when he makes the contract' (ibid. 404). Parke B opined that to hold to the contrary would result in the injustice of the insured paying a fixed premium over the term of the policy, only to find that he could recover some uncertain sum which depended on the value of his interest at the time of the death (ibid. 403).

The nature of the interest required can be deduced from the language of s. 3 itself, which provides that 'no greater sum shall be recovered or received from the insurer or insurers than the amount of value of the interest of the insured in such life'. The inference is that it must be a financial or pecuniary interest. Accordingly, an employer may have an insurable interest in the life of an employee or vice versa, and a secured creditor in the life of a debtor. Spouses are presumed to possess an unlimited insurable interest in each others' lives on the basis that 'a husband is no more likely to indulge in "mischievous gaming" on his wife's life than a wife on her husband's' (*Griffiths* v *Fleming* (1909) 100 LT 765, 769 per Farwell J; see also *Reed* v *Royal Exchange Assurance Co.* (1795) Peake Add Cas 70). Paradoxically, an adult child does not have an insurable interest in the life of a parent. In *Harse* v *Pearl Life Assurance Co.* [1904] 1 KB 558, the plaintiff effected two life policies on the life of his mother who lived with him as his housekeeper and to whom he paid an allowance. The plaintiff's father was alive, but being paralysed he did not work and would therefore be unable to meet the funeral expenses of his wife in the event of her predeceasing him. One of the policies stated that it was to cover funeral expenses. Upon discovering that the policies were void for want of insurable interest, there being no obligation on a child to bury his parent, the plaintiff sued for the recovery of the premiums paid by him which now amounted to more than the original sum assured. It was held by the Court of Appeal that the plaintiff's lack of insurable interest rendered the policy illegal, and on the basis that money paid over under an illegal contract is irrecoverable, the insurers were not bound to return the premiums. Whether or not a minor has an interest in the lives of his or her parents is less clear as there is no common law obligation on a parent to support a child (*Bazeley* v *Forder* (1868) LR 3 QB 559, 565 per Lord Cockburn CJ); *Stopher* v *National Assistance Board* [1955] 1 QB 486, 495 per Lord Goddard CJ). However, such an obligation may arise by virtue of a maintenance order, in which case an insurable interest will exist. The principle that a child has no insurable interest in the life of its parents is generally circumvented by a parent taking insurance on his or her own life and ensuring that it is expressed to be for the benefit of the child (see the Married Women's Property Act 1882, s. 11).

10.5.2 Insurable interest in property
The classic definition of insurable interest in property was formulated by Lord Eldon in *Lucena* v *Craufurd* (1806) 2 Bos & PNR 269 at p. 321, as being 'a right in the property, or a right derivable out of some contract about the property, which in either case may be lost upon some contingency affecting the possession or enjoyment of the party'. Accordingly, the insured must possess some present legally enforceable right, whether legal or equitable, or a contractual right, to the insured property. This will, for example, exclude a beneficiary under a will and also an intestate's next of kin for although 'there is no man who will deny that such an heir at law has a moral certainty of succeeding to the estate; yet the law will not allow that he has any interest, or any thing more than a mere expectation'. Lord Eldon justified a restrictive definition of insurable interest on the basis that it was necessary to ensure certainty and to avoid illusory insurance. This reasoning was emphatically rejected by Wilson J in *Constitution Insurance Co. of Canada* v *Kosmopoulos* (1987) 34 DLR (4th) 208, 217–21), in which the Canadian Supreme Court adopted the more liberal 'factual expectation' test propounded by Lawrence J in *Lucena* v *Craufurd* at p. 302. Put simply, under this test a moral certainty of profit or loss is sufficient to constitute insurable interest. Thus, on very similar facts to *Macaura* v *Northern Assurance Co. Ltd* [1925] AC 619, discussed below, the insured was able to recover under the policies on the basis that as a sole shareholder of the company he 'was so placed with respect to the assets of the business as to have benefit from their existence and prejudice from their destruction. He had a moral certainty of advantage or benefit from those assets but for the fire' (34 DLR (4th) 208, 228 per Wilson J). The factual expectation test has also been adopted by the Australian

legislature, and has been followed in many American states, for example, para. 3401 of the New York Insurance Law, art. 34, defines insurable interest as including 'any lawful or substantial economic interest in the safety or preservation of property from loss, destruction or pecuniary damage' (quoted by Wilson J at p. 228).

Until recently, and in contrast to the position in North Amercan and Commonwealth jurisdictions, English law continued to insist that the insured had a proprietary right in the insured property. This is starkly illustrated in *Macaura v Northern Assurance Co. Ltd* [1925] AC 619, in which the insured, Macaura, was an unsecured creditor and the only shareholder in a limited company which owned a substantial quantity of timber, much of which was stored on his land. Two weeks after effecting insurance policies with several companies in his own name, the timber was destroyed by fire. A claim brought by Macaura on the policies was disallowed on the ground that he lacked insurable interest in the timber. Lord Sumner, proceeding on the basis that neither the company's debt to the insured nor his shares were exposed to fire, observed, at p. 630:

. . . the fact that he was virtually the company's only creditor, while the timber was its only asset, seems to me to make no difference. . . . he was directly prejudiced by the paucity of the company's assets, not by the fire.

His lordship stated, at p. 630, that the insured:

. . . stood in no 'legal or equitable relation to' the timber at all. He had no 'concern in' the subject insured. His relation was to the company, not to its goods.

As a gratuitous bailee he was not liable for the timber and therefore an interest could not be based on bailment. The guiding principle in *Macaura v Northern Assurance Co. Ltd* centres around the separate legal personality accorded to companies, so that a company is, in law, distinct from its members. It was the company which owned the timber and therefore had a proprietary interest in it, not its shareholder. The fact that the timber was in his possession did not give him a proprietary interest. He merely had a factual expectation of loss. On the other hand, if Macaura qua creditor had insured against the company's insolvency, or qua shareholder had insured his shares against depreciation due to the failure of a company venture, then the requirement of insurable interest would have been fulfilled. This decision was distinguished in *Sharp v Sphere Drake Insurance plc* [1992] 2 Lloyd's Rep 501, where the sole shareholder in a company was held to have an insurable interest in a yacht purchased by the company, as the yacht was intended for his use and a power of attorney had been granted to him in respect of it. The English courts have recently adopted a wider approach to insurable interest. In *Petrofina (UK) Ltd v Magnaload Ltd* [1984] QB 127 Lloyd J held that each of the individual subcontractors on a building site had an insurable interest in the entire works despite the fact that they were working only on limited parts of the site, their interest arising not from any ownership or possession but from the fact that, in the event of negligence, they would face liability for any part of the works damaged or destroyed. Accordingly, it was possible for a policy covering the entire works to be taken out on a co-insurance basis by the head contractor and all subcontractors. This decision was followed by Colman J in *National Oilwell Ltd* v *Davy Offshore (UK) Ltd* [1993] 2 Lloyd's Rep 582, although in that case the subcontractor in question was held not to be a party to the policy as he had not authorised the head contractor to insure on his behalf. This expansive approach to insurable interest was approved by the Court of Appeal in *Glengate-KG Properties Ltd* v *Norwich Union Fire Insurance Society Ltd* [1996] 2 All ER 487.

In relation to contracts for the sale of goods, the general rule is that risk follows ownership, *res perit domino*. Thus, a seller who retains title in the subject matter of the contract clearly has insurable interest given that he or she continues to bear the risk of loss. Similarly, an unpaid seller in possession of the goods, or who has parted with possession but has exercised the right of stoppage in transit, will have insurable interest (Sale of Goods Act 1979, ss. 41 and 44–6). Generally, the contract for sale will stipulate which party is under a duty to insure, in which case the issue of insurable interest will be consequential on the contractual obligation. Accordingly, a buyer of goods will have insurable interest if risk has passed, and risk is not necessarily dependent upon ownership. Clearly, the buyer has an economic interest in the goods since if they are lost he will be liable to pay the contract price (Sale of Goods Act 1979, s. 20; see *Stock* v *Inglis* (1885) 10 App Cas 263; *Anderson* v *Morice* (1875) LR 10 CP 609).

Basically, anyone who has a substantial interest in the continued existence of property at the time of its loss will have insurable interest and can validly insure the property for its full value. For example, a bailee who damages goods bailed with him will be liable to the owner and will therefore have insurable interest in the property. Obvious examples arise where a consumer hires goods, for example, where he or she takes possession of DIY equipment from a hire shop, or takes goods, such as a television, pursuant to a hire purchase agreement. The amount recoverable under the policy will be limited to the level of the insured's interest, which is the amount necessary to achieve indemnification. Exceptionally, the contract may expressly or impliedly waive the requirement of insurable interest completely. In *Prudential Staff Union* v *Hall* [1947] KB 685, the insured, an employees' association, effected policies through Lloyd's insuring against loss of premium moneys collected by their members as agents of their employers. It was held that the insured lacked insurable interest but the contractual undertaking given by the insurers to pay the staff association in the event of a claim constituted a waiver of the requirement. One issue which arises from this decision is whether or not a member would have been able to enforce the policy if the union had refused a claim. The doctrine of privity obviously presents a major hurdle here unless the member can show that the union entered into the insurance contract as his or her agent, or held the policy on behalf of the member as trustee (*Trident General Insurance Co. Ltd* v *McNiece Bros. Pty Ltd* (1988) 165 CLR 107). If, in this situation, the insurance was on real property as opposed to money, the requirements of s. 2 of the Life Assurance Act 1774 would have to be satisfied, in which case establishing agency or trusteeship would be fairly straightforward.

10.6   NON-DISCLOSURE AND MISREPRESENTATION

Whereas under the general law of contract there is no positive duty of disclosure, both parties to an insurance contract are bound to disclose every material fact to the other before the contract is concluded (see *Banque Financière de la Cité SA* v *Westgate Insurance Co. Ltd* [1991] 2 AC 249, where it was held that the remedy available to the insured was avoidance of the contract and return of the premiums paid, not damages). The effect of non-disclosure, whether when effecting a new policy or upon its renewal (other than a policy for life insurance which is presumed to be entire), is to render the insurance contract voidable, thereby entitling the insurer to avoid the contract *ab initio*. Accordingly, it 'terminates the contract, puts the parties in *statu quo ante* and restores things, as between them, to the position in which they stood before the contract was entered into' (*Abram* v *Westville* [1923] AC 773, 781, per Lord Atkinson). However, where the insured is in breach of warranty, the insurer is automatically discharged from liability (see below). This can have the effect of ending a policy as soon as it begins, or even before, as where fulfilment of the warranty is a condition precedent to the inception of the insurance contract for 'there is in reality no contract' (*Newcastle Fire Insurance Co.* v *Macmorran & Co.* (1815) 3 Dow 255, 259 per Lord Eldon).

The duty of disclosure has been described as 'an incident of the contract of insurance' (*Bank of Nova Scotia* v *Hellenic Mutual War Risks Association (Bermuda) Ltd* [1988] 1 Lloyd's Rep 514, 546 per Hobhouse J, affirmed [1990] 1 QB 818 (CA), reversed on another ground (1992) 1 AC 233). In *Locker and Woolf Ltd* v *Western Australian Insurance Co. Ltd.* [1936] 1 KB 408, the insured was asked in the proposal form for fire insurance: 'Has this or any other insurance of yours been declined by any other company?' The insured answered 'No'. In fact, two years previously a proposal for motor insurance was refused by another company by reason of non-disclosure. A fire occurred and the insurers repudiated liability for non-disclosure of a material fact. It was held by the Court of Appeal that they were entitled to do so. Slesser LJ stated, at p. 414:

> In the present case it is quite impossible to say that the non-disclosure by those proposing to take out a policy against fire risks that they have had an insurance on motors declined on the grounds of untrue answers in the proposal form is not the non-disclosure of a fact very material for the insurance company to know — a fact which if known to the company might lead them to take the view that the proposers were undesirable persons with whom to have contractual relations.

See also *London Assurance* v *Mansel* (1879) 11 ChD 363.

Where there is a change of circumstance between the submission of the proposal form and its formal acceptance, the insured must disclose the change to the insurer. For example, if a proposer falls ill after submitting a proposal for private medical insurance, but fails to disclose this prior to acceptance, the insurers will be able to avoid the policy since an offer to provide insurance is generally made conditional upon there being no material change in the risk between the time when the offer was made and the time of acceptance (see *Canning* v *Farquhar* (1886) 16 QBD 727). In *Looker* v *Law Union and Rock Insurance Co. Ltd* [1928] 1 KB 554 a policy for life assurance contained a clause which stipulated that: 'The risk of the company will not commence until receipt of the first premium; and the directors meanwhile reserve the power to alter or withdraw the acceptance'. The proposer fell ill after submitting his proposal but before cover had commenced and failed to give notice of his illness to the insurers. He sent a cheque for the first premium which was dishonoured and died from pneumonia four days after the illness began. It was held that the insurers could avoid the policy since the duty of disclosure continued up until payment of the first premium. Acton J stated 'that the acceptance is made in reliance upon the continued truth of the representations', and the proposer 'had failed to disclose the change in his state of health' (ibid. 559).

Unless there is an express term to the contrary, the insured is under no duty to disclose a change of circumstance which occurs during the operation of the insurance contract (*Pim* v *Reid* (1843) 6 Man & G 1; cf. *Kausar* v *Eagle Star Insurance Co. Ltd* (1996) *The Times*, 15 July). During argument in *Baxendale* v *Harvey* (1859) 4 Hurl & N 449, Pollock LJ said, at p. 449: 'If a person who insures his life goes up in a balloon, that does not vitiate his policy'. In his judgment in the case he said: 'A person who insures may light as many candles as he please in his house, though each additional candle increases the danger of setting the house on fire' (ibid. 452).

However, a duty to disclose a change of circumstance can arise by virtue of a so-called 'increase of risk' clause. Generally such clauses, frequently found in fire policies, only operate to require disclosure of changes which are permanent in nature. In *Dobson* v *Sotheby* (1827) Mood & M 90, a barn was insured against fire and the policy stated that no fire or hazardous goods were to be kept on the premises. When the premises required tarring, a fire was lit and a tar barrel was brought into the building. The tar boiled over and the premises were destroyed by the ensuing fire. Lord Tenterden CJ considered that 'the condition must be understood as forbidding only the habitual use of fire, or the ordinary deposit of hazardous goods, not their occasional introduction, as in this case, for a temporary purpose connected with the occupation of the premises. The common repairs of a building necessarily require the introduction of fire upon the premises' (ibid. 92–93). Thus an insured who brings into his or her house some device which by its nature is inherently dangerous, for example, a blow torch for the purpose of redecorating, will not need to notify the insurers unless a clause in the policy expressly imposes such a duty in relation to temporary changes (*Shaw* v *Robberds* (1832) 6 Ad & El 75).

The duty of disclosure arises from the principle that an insurance contract is a contract *uberrimae fidei* (of utmost good faith), the rationale of which was explained by Lord Mansfield in *Carter* v *Boehm* (1766) 3 Burr 1905 at p. 1909:

> Insurance is a contract of speculation. The special facts upon which the contingent chance is to be computed lie most commonly in the knowledge of the assured only; the underwriter trusts to his representation, and proceeds upon confidence that he does not keep back any circumstance in his knowledge to mislead the underwriter into a belief that the circumstance does not exist. . . . Although the suppression should happen through mistake, without any fraudulent intention, yet still the underwriter is deceived and the policy is void; because the *risque* run is really different from the *risque* understood and intended to be run at the time of the agreement.

As with the law of contract, a material misrepresentation of fact which induces the insurer to accept the risk will entitle the insurer to avoid the contract (Marine Insurance Act 1906, s. 20(1)). Where the misrepresentation is negligent or fraudulent, the innocent party will also be entitled to claim damages. With the demise of the so-called 'basis of the contract clause', at least in contracts proposed by individuals, whereby pre-contractual statements of fact contained in the proposal form were converted into fundamental terms, misrepresentation now assumes greater importance for insurance law (see the Statement of General Insurance Practice, para. 1(b), discussed below).

The doctrine of *uberrimae fidei* applies to all classes of insurance whether the contract is for fire, life or marine insurance (*London Assurance* v *Mansel* (1879) 11 ChD 363, 367 per Jessel MR; see also *Joel* v *Law Union and Crown Insurance Co.* [1908] 2 KB 863). With respect to the latter, the duty of disclosure as formulated in *Carter* v *Boehm* has been codified by the Marine Insurance Act 1906 which is, however, of general application (*Lambert* v *Co-operative Insurance Society Ltd* [1975] 2 Lloyd's Rep 485 and *Pan Atlantic Insurance Co. Ltd* v *Pine Top Insurance Co. Ltd* [1995] 1 AC 501 discussed below). Section 17 of the Act restates the applicability of *uberrimae fidei* to insurance contracts. Section 18 provides:

> (1)   Subject to the provisions of this section, the assured must disclose to the insurer, before the contract is concluded, every material circumstance which is known to the assured, and the assured is deemed to know every circumstance which, in the ordinary course of business, ought to be known by him. If the assured fails to make such disclosure, the insurer may avoid the contract.
>
> (2)   Every circumstance is material which would influence the judgment of a prudent insurer in fixing the premium, or determining whether he will take the risk.

The question arises whether such an onerous duty is apposite in an age of instantaneous communications. In this respect, insurers have gone some way towards recognising the harshness which this poses to individuals applying for insurance. Paragraph 2(b) of the Statement of General Insurance Practice, as revised in 1986, now provides that an insurer will not repudiate a contract if the non-disclosed fact is one which 'a policyholder could not reasonably be expected to have disclosed'; or where the misrepresentation is innocent. However, para. 3(a) of the Long-Term Statement states that:

> An insurer will not unreasonably reject a claim. In particular, an insurer will not reject a claim or invalidate a policy on grounds of non-disclosure or misrepresentation of a fact unless:
>
> (i)   it is a material fact; and
> (ii)   it is a fact within the knowledge of the proposer; and
> (iii)   it is a fact which the proposer could reasonably be expected to disclose.
>
> (It should be noted that fraud or deception will, and reckless or negligent non-disclosure or misrepresentation of a material fact may, constitute grounds for rejection of a claim.)

It is therefore only the innocent proposer who has nothing to fear. Negligently failing to disclose a material fact will entitle the insurer to avoid the contract and repudiate any claim. The Insurance Ombudsman has attempted to mitigate the Draconian consequences of non-disclosure by, for example, requiring insurers to pay a proportion of a claim that the premium actually fixed bears to the premium that would have been charged had the fact been disclosed (see the Insurance Ombudsman's Annual Report, 1989, para. 2.17).

10.7   DETERMINING MATERIALITY

The Report of the Law Reform Committee (Cmnd 62, 1957) observed that 'it seems that a fact may be material to insurers . . . which would not necessarily appear to a proposer for insurance, however honest and careful, to be one which he ought to disclose'. While s. 18 of the Marine Insurance Act 1906 attempts to lay down the guiding principle governing materiality of facts, it does not address the critical issue of the meaning of the term 'influence'. Determining whether or not a particular circumstance 'influenced' someone is a nebulous exercise for there is no absolute standard. Degrees of influence are limitless. It is clear that a fact will be regarded as material if it relates either to the physical hazard of the subject matter of the insurance or to its moral hazard. For example, whether or not flammable substances are stored in a building is obviously highly relevant to a proposal for fire insurance. Similarly, in car insurance non-standard modifications carried out to increase the vehicle's performance will be considered pertinent to the assessment of risk. If an enthusiast removes the factory-fitted engine from his small family saloon car, and fits a supercharged model in its place, the premium payable will obviously be much greater to reflect the increased risk of accident.

Moral hazard centres on the circumstances surrounding the particular proposer and will include the proposer's claims history and criminal record (see *Locker and Woolf Ltd* v *Western Australian Insurance Co. Ltd* [1936] 1 KB 408). In *Lambert* v *Co-operative Insurance Society Ltd* [1975] 2 Lloyd's Rep 485, the proposer effected an 'all risks' insurance policy on her own and her husband's jewellery in April 1963. At this time she was not asked about previous criminal convictions and she did not disclose that her husband had been convicted some years earlier of receiving stolen cigarettes. The insurers issued the policy which provided that it would be ipso facto void if there should be an omission to state any fact material for estimating the risk. The policy was renewed every year. In December 1971 the proposer's husband was again convicted of a criminal offence and sentenced to 15 months' imprisonment. This fact was not disclosed when the insured renewed her policy for the year 1972, and in April she claimed £311 for items of jewellery which had been lost. The insurers successfully repudiated the claim on the basis that the insured had failed to disclose a material fact relating to moral hazard at the time of applying for the original policy and at its subsequent renewals. There is no duty to disclose a conviction which is spent under the Rehabilitation of Offenders Act 1974, but a conviction which carries a sentence of two and a half years' imprisonment or more can never become spent. Section 7(3) of the Act confers a discretion on the court to admit evidence about spent convictions if the court is satisfied that 'justice cannot be done in the case except by admitting it'.

The meaning of 'influence' for the purposes of s. 18(2) of the Marine Insurance Act 1906 received extensive consideration in *Container Transport International Inc.* v *Oceanus Mutual Underwriting Association (Bermuda) Ltd* [1984] 1 Lloyd's Rep 476. Shifting the balance firmly in favour of insurers, the Court of Appeal held that an insured is bound to disclose those material facts which *might* influence the judgment of a prudent insurer in deciding whether or not to accept the risk or in setting the premium. This approach was adopted by Steyn J in *Highlands Insurance Co.* v *Continental Insurance Co.* [1987] 1 Lloyd's Rep 109, who applied the Court of Appeal's formulation of the duty to non-marine misrepresentations. Under this test, insurers are placed in a particularly strong position for it is not necessary to prove that the 'influence' was decisive. Nor is it necessary for the actual insurer to prove that the misrepresentation or non-disclosure had induced the contract of insurance (*Zurich General Accident and Liability Insurance Co. Ltd* v *Morrison* [1942] 2 KB 53). The duty of disclosure on a prospective insured is therefore boundless since he or she will have to disclose unlimited information on the basis that the prudent insurer might want to know it even if, ultimately, it does not affect the insurer's decision as to the risk. However, the Court of Appeal's view in *Container Transport International Inc.* v *Oceanus Mutual Underwriting Association (Bermuda) Ltd* that it had correctly interpreted precedent on this issue is open to question. For example, in *Mutual Life Insurance Co. of New York* v *Ontario Metal Products Co. Ltd* [1925] AC 344, Lord Salvesen (at p. 351) accepted the submission of the insurers' counsel that 'the test was whether, if the fact concealed had been disclosed, the insurers would have acted differently, . . . by declining the risk at the proposed premium'. The Court of Appeal distinguished this decision on the basis that the Privy Council was concerned with the interpretation of the phrase 'material misrepresentation' contained in an Ontario statute. However, the particular statute in question was a codification of the English law, and the Privy Council opined that there was no difference between the law in England and Ontario (see Clarke, 'Failure to disclose and failure to legislate: is it material? — II' [1988] JBL 298, who also points out that the Board's definition of materiality was adopted as a statement of the English position by the Law Reform Committee, *Fifth Report: Conditions and Exceptions in Insurance Policies* (Cmnd 62, 1957)).

The opportunity for a complete and authoritative review of the duty of disclosure came before the House of Lords in *Pan Atlantic Insurance Co. Ltd* v *Pine Top Insurance Co. Ltd* [1995] 1 AC 501. The issues were first, should materiality be measured by reference to whether its 'influence' on the prudent insurer's judgment was 'decisive', or should some lesser degree of impact be sufficient? Second, where there has been non-disclosure of a material fact, must it *induce* the actual insurer to enter into the contract?

With respect to the first issue Lord Mustill (with whom Lords Goff and Slynn of Hadley concurred) could see no good reason for departing from the principle formulated by Lord Mansfield in *Carter* v *Boehm* (1766) 3 Burr 1905, which had guided insurance law for more than 200 years. Lord Mustill stated: 'I can see no room within (the principle) . . . for a more lenient test expressed solely by reference to the decisive effect which the circumstance would have on the mind of the prudent underwriter' ([1995] 1 AC 501, 536). On the question of statutory interpretation, the majority view was that since Parliament had left the word 'influence' in s. 18(2) unadorned by phrases such as 'decisively' or 'conclusively', it must bear its ordinary meaning. His lordship stated that:

> . . . this expression clearly denotes an effect on the thought processes of the insurer in weighing up the risk, quite different from words which might have been used but were not, such as 'influencing the insurer *to take* the risk'. (ibid. 531, see also 517 per Lord Goff of Chieveley.)

The majority decision therefore was to reject the 'decisive influence' test, and, in reaffirming *Container Transport International Inc.* v *Oceanus Mutual Underwriting Association (Bermuda) Ltd* the position remains that a circumstance is material and must be disclosed even though the prudent insurer, had he known of the fact, would have insured the risk on the same terms. On this issue, the insured thus remains in a highly vulnerable position. On the other hand, Lord Lloyd of Berwick, in a powerful dissent, agreed with the appellants' submission that there should be a twofold test under which the insurer must show that a prudent insurer, if aware of the undisclosed fact, would either have declined the risk or charged a higher premium and that the actual insurer would have declined the risk or required a higher premium (ibid. 553). The simplicity of the logic here clearly appealed to Lord Lloyd who stated (at p. 557):

> But if the prudent insurer would have accepted the risk at the same premium and on the same terms, it must be because, so far as he is concerned, the risk is the same risk. How, as a matter of ordinary language, can a circumstance be described as material, when it would not have mattered to the prudent insurer whether the circumstance was disclosed or not?

In his lordship's opinion, the appellants' submission 'does full justice to the language of s. 18 of the 1906 Act. It is well defined, and easily applied. It does something to mitigate the harshness of the all-or-nothing approach which disfigures this branch of the law.' (ibid. 560).

In relation to the second issue, the House of Lords unanimously held that non-disclosure, as with misrepresentation, must induce the particular insurer to enter into the contract. In their reasoning, their lordships were clearly influenced by the argument that the 1906 Act codified the common law, and as inducement was a requirement under the general law, the Act must be taken as having the same effect. Lord Mustill stated, at p. 549:

> . . . I conclude that there is to be implied in the 1906 Act a qualification that a material misrepresentation will not entitle the underwriter to avoid the policy unless the misrepresentation induced the making of the contract, using 'induced' in the sense in which it is used in the general law of contract.

Lord Mustill's approach of translating the requirement of inducement into the realms of non-disclosure is curious. Inducement for the purposes of misrepresentation has always taken an active form, in other words, silence cannot, without more, constitute misrepresentation (see *Bell* v *Lever Brothers Ltd* [1932] AC 161, 227 per Lord Atkin). However, Lord Mustill did admit that the proposition that non-disclosure must induce the contract may well involve the House in making new law ((1995) 1 AC 501, 549). Clearly, it did.

Lord Goff, concurring, opined that the need to show inducement on the part of the actual insurer addresses the criticisms directed against the *Container Transport International* decision. He reasoned that it was the absence of this requirement that prompted the call for the test of materiality to 'be hardened into the decisive influence test' ([1995] 1 AC 501, 518). It is suggested that practical considerations render this a hollow victory for the critics, and Lord Lloyd's approach in favouring the 'decisive influence' test is to be preferred since it would provide an objective assessment of materiality. The costs involved in seeking disclosure of documents required for an insured to establish non-inducement are likely to be immense and will therefore stand as an effective deterrent against such claims, and the matter is made more difficult from the assured's point of view by the adoption by Lord Mustill (vigorously opposed by Lord Lloyd) of a 'presumption of inducement', whereby proof of materiality by the insurer casts upon the insured the burden of proving that the insurer was not induced by the breach of duty. That said, whether or not a non-disclosed fact is material is a question of law which will be decided in the light of expert evidence. If materiality is not established in the first place, inducement becomes a non sequitur. While the House recognised the iniquity of the *Container Transport International* test, Lord Mustill considered that the question of reform along the lines argued for by Pan Atlantic must be left to Parliament.

The approach adopted to the issue of inducement in *Pan Atlantic Insurance Co. Ltd* v *Pine Top Insurance Co. Ltd* was endorsed by the Court of Appeal in *St Paul Fire and Marine Insurance Co. (UK) Ltd* v *McConnell Dowell Constructors Ltd* [1995] 2 Lloyd's Rep 116. It is evident that the law is heavily weighted against the insured, and recent judicial pronouncements have perpetuated this inequality. Given the obvious reluctance of the courts to challenge the protected position enjoyed by insurers, it is to be hoped that Parliament will take up Lord Mustill's challenge to intervene and redress the imbalance.

10.8 TERMS OF THE CONTRACT OF INSURANCE

As with contracts generally, the terms of an insurance contract may be incorporated from a number of sources. For insurance contracts, these will include the completed proposal form, the policy document and renewal notices. The terminology adopted in insurance law to categorise terms is curious and often confusing. In contrast to the general law of contract, fundamental terms are classified as warranties, not as conditions. To compound the confusion, in insurance contracts the two terms are sometimes used interchangeably. If the insured is in breach of a warranty the insurer is always entitled to repudiate liability (*Provincial Insurance Co. Ltd* v *Morgan* [1933] AC 240, 253–4 per Lord Wright). However, it does not follow that minor terms are described as 'conditions', for a breach of condition may have the same effect as a breach of warranty unless it is construed as a collateral stipulation. A further category of terms in insurance contracts are so-called clauses 'descriptive of the risk'. The effect of a breach of a particular term is a question of law for the court to decide on the basis of the presumed intention of the parties.

10.8.1 Warranties
A common method of creating warranties is by the inclusion of the so-called 'basis of the contract clause' at the foot of the proposal form whereby the questions and answers contained in the form are stated to be the basis of the contract. As we have seen, if an answer is false, the contract is rendered voidable. Thus, in *Dawsons Ltd* v *Bonnin* [1922] 2 AC 413, the House of Lords held that the insured's inaccurate statement as to where the insured

lorry was garaged entitled the insurer to avoid the contract ab initio even though the statement was immaterial to the risk. The proposal form stated that it was to constitute the basis of the contract. However, the scope for relying on such clauses has been restricted by the Statement of Insurance Practice discussed below.

Where there has been a breach of warranty on the part of the insured, s. 33(3) of the Marine Insurance Act 1906 provides that the insurer 'is discharged from liability as from the date of the breach'. This is so even if the loss claimed for is wholly unconnected with the breach (*De Hahn* v *Hartley* (1786) 1 TR 343; *Dawsons Ltd* v *Bonnin*). Further, a warranty must be strictly complied with and the fact that the insured was blameless is irrelevant, for liability is strict (*Philips* v *Baillie* (1784) 3 Doug KB 374). In the past, the accepted view was that a breach of warranty entitled the insurer to elect whether or not to repudiate the policy. However, in *Bank of Nova Scotia* v *Hellenic Mutual War Risks Association (Bermuda) Ltd* [1992] 1 AC 233 it was held, taking the literal meaning of s. 33(3) of the 1906 Act, that an insured's breach of warranty automatically discharged the insurer from liability. Although strictly speaking this is a marine insurance decision, it has been taken to be of general application. Section 33(3) provides that:

A warranty . . . is a condition which must be exactly complied with, whether it be material to the risk or not. If it be not so complied with, then, subject to any express provision in the policy, the insurer is discharged from liability as from the date of the breach of warranty, but without prejudice to any liability incurred by him before that date.

In considering this provision, Lord Goff stated that the words of the section 'are clear. They show that discharge of the insurer from liability is automatic and is not dependent upon any decision by the insurer to treat the contract of insurance as at an end' ([1992] 1 AC 233, 262). His lordship went on (at p. 262) to observe that there is an:

. . . inveterate practice in marine insurance of using the term 'warranty' as signifying a condition precedent. . . . Once this is appreciated, it becomes readily understandable that, if a promissory warranty is not complied with, the insurer is discharged from liability as from the date of the breach of warranty, for the simple reason that fulfilment of the warranty is a condition precedent to the liability or further liability of the insurer. . . . Here, where we are concerned with a promissory warranty, i.e. a promissory condition precedent, contained in an existing contract of insurance, non-fulfilment of the condition does not prevent the contract from coming into existence. What it does (as s. 33(3) makes plain) is to discharge the insurer from liability as from the date of the breach.

Section 34(3) of the 1906 Act provides that a 'breach of warranty may be waived by the insurer'. Such waiver will occur where the insurer, with knowledge of the breach, renews the policy or continues to accept premiums.

Thus in *Ayrey* v *British Legal and United Provident Assurance Co.* [1918] 1 KB
136, a clause in the proposal form for life insurance provided that if any
information was withheld which should be made known to the insurer, the
policy would be rendered absolutely void. The insured described himself in
the proposal form as a fisherman, his usual occupation. The fact that he was
also a member of the Royal Naval Reserve, which exposed him to additional
risks, was not disclosed. However, his wife did inform the insurer's district
manager of this fact and the manager continued to accept the premiums on
behalf of the insurer. When the insured was killed at sea during a mine-
sweeping operation, the insurer repudiated liability. It was held that the
district manager's knowledge of the true facts could be imputed to his
employers. Lawrence J stated, at p. 140, that:

> . . . the receipt of premiums by the district manager with full knowledge of
> the facts was a waiver by the company of the objection that there had been
> a concealment of a material fact. There was no new contract entered into
> by the district manager, but there was a waiver of the objection to the
> existing contract.

See also *Evans* v *Employers' Mutual Insurance Association Ltd* [1936] 1 KB
505, 515.

Where the insured is in breach of warranty the insurer is not necessarily
bound to terminate the contract but has the option to treat the breach as a
breach of condition, giving rise to a claim for damages only. Although it has
been held in *West* v *National Motor and Accident Insurance Union Ltd* [1955]
1 WLR 343 that the insurer is only entitled to terminate the policy as a whole,
this would appear to be wrong in principle and does not accord with the
general law of contract (See, for example, the Sale of Goods Act 1979,
s. 11(2), which provides that where in a contract for sale the seller is in breach
of a condition, the buyer may elect to treat the seller's breach as a breach of
warranty, and not as a ground for repudiating the contract).

Given the harsh results which flow from the insured's breach of warranty, the
courts have endeavoured to mitigate the effects by adopting the *contra
proferentem* rule of construction towards such terms (considered below; see also,
chapter 12). Under this rule any ambiguity in the wording of such clauses will be
strictly construed against the party, usually the insurer, seeking to rely on them.
In a line of cases it has been stressed that insurers should express themselves in
plain terms so that where the language used is ambiguous, it will be interpreted
in the sense that the insured might reasonably have understood it. Thus in
Kennedy v *Smith* 1976 SLT 110, the Lord President said, at pp. 116–17:

> . . . if insurers seek to limit their liability under a policy by relying upon an
> alleged undertaking as to the future prepared by them and accepted by the
> insured, the language they use must be such that the terms of the alleged
> undertaking and its scope are clearly and unambiguously expressed or
> plainly implied, and . . . any such alleged undertaking will be construed, *in
> dubio, contra proferentem*.

See also *Notman* v *Anchor Assurance Co.* (1858) 4 CB NS 476, 481 per Cockburn CJ; *Fowkes* v *Manchester and London Life Assurance and Loan Association* (1863) 3 B & S 917, 929 per Blackburn J; *Provincial Insurance Co. Ltd* v *Morgan* [1933] AC 240, 250 per Lord Russell of Killowen. Of particular note in this regard is reg. 6 of the Unfair Terms in Consumer Contracts Regulations 1994 (SI 1994/3159), see para 10.3.1 above.

By their very nature, warranties can be classified into three types depending upon whether the insured's promise or undertaking relates to: (a) some past or existing state of affairs; (b) some future state of affairs; or (c) a warranty of opinion by the insured about the truth of a fact.

Generally, a warranty about past or existing facts will arise from the information contained in the proposal form after completion by the insured. It is a question of construction whether it is a warranty about present facts, or whether it also extends to the future, in which case it is termed a 'promissory warranty' or 'continuing warranty'. The distinction is crucial for if a false warranty relates to a state of affairs existing at the time of the proposal, there is an effective breach which will entitle the insurer to terminate the contract from the moment of its conclusion. The appropriate analogy here is rescission for misrepresentation. Conversely, if the insured's statement was true when made, no action will lie for breach if there is a subsequent change in the state of affairs. In practice, however, the insured is often placed under a continuing duty to notify the insurer of any subsequent changes. In determining whether or not a warranty is promissory in nature, the courts have regard not only to the purpose of the warranty, but also the purpose of the policy itself.

In *Hair* v *Prudential Assurance Co. Ltd* [1983] 2 Lloyd's Rep 667, Woolf J held that a warranty in a fire policy that the insured premises were occupied could not be construed as amounting to a continuing obligation but rather as 'an indication of the state of affairs which existed at the time that the answers were given' (ibid. 672). However, where on its construction, a warranty is construed as being promissory in its effect, any breach will operate to terminate the insurer's liability as from the date of the breach only (see *Provincial Insurance Co. Ltd* v *Morgan* [1933] AC 240). In *Beauchamp* v *National Mutual Indemnity Insurance Co. Ltd* [1937] 3 All ER 19, the proposal form asked 'Are any explosives used in your business?' The insured answered that there were none. This was correct at the time it was made but the insured, a builder, did subsequently use explosives when, for the first time in his business, he was contracted to demolish a building. It was held, as a matter of construction, that the question and its answer related to the future. Similarly, in *Hales* v *Reliance Fire and Accident Insurance Corporation* [1960] 2 Lloyd's Rep 391, a question relating to the storage of inflammable oils was construed as a promise about the future, so that there was a breach when the insured shopkeeper took delivery of a quantity of fireworks 17 days prior to 5 November. McNair J accepted that warranties in fire and burglary policies about the condition of the premises and precautions taken to prevent loss will prima facie be construed as continuing. Thus, if in a household contents policy the proposer warrants that the house is fitted with a burglar alarm, this will constitute a promissory warranty so that if the alarm is removed, the liability of the insurers will cease. However, this view is now open to question in the light of Saville LJ's interpretation of *Hales* v *Reliance Fire and Accident Insurance Corporation Ltd* in the recent decision in *Hussain* v *Brown*, [1996] 1 Lloyd's Rep 627. His lordship stressed that there was no principle of insurance law requiring answers on proposal forms to be read as importing promises to the future (see further Hird [1996] JBL 404).

In any case, the futurity of a warranty must be apparent from the words used. In *Kennedy* v *Smith* 1976 SLT 110 the insured warranted in a proposal for motor insurance that: 'I am a total abstainer from alcoholic drinks', which was true at the time it was made. However, after a cricket match the insured drank a small quantity of beer on an empty stomach. He then drove himself and two friends home. His vehicle was involved in an accident and his two passengers were killed. He sought an indemnity from his insurers for the damages he was liable to pay, but the insurers refused the claim on the basis that a continuing warranty had been broken. It was held that the warranty related to the past and was not promissory about the future.

In consumer insurance, i.e., where the insured is an individual as opposed to a business entity, 'warranties of opinion' are now a common species. With this type of term, the insured warrants that the answers given in the proposal form are true to the best of his belief and knowledge. The insured must exercise due care when completing the proposal form (*Huddleston* v *RACV Insurance Pty Ltd* [1975] VR 683; see also Birds, 'Warranties in insurance proposal forms' [1977] JBL 231). As a consequence, such a warranty will only be broken if the insured is dishonest or reckless. In *Confederation Life Assn* v *Miller* (1887) 14 SCR 330 the insured warranted in a life policy that to the best of his knowledge and belief he had suffered no serious injury. Gwynne J held that this would be untrue only if the answer given was wilfully false. Householders who insure possessions against theft or other loss are frequently required to estimate and warrant the value of specific items. Where this is the case, it has been held that the value of a possession, for example, a stamp collection, is a matter of opinion so that, provided the insured gave a bona fide estimate, the warranty would not be broken where a subsequent expert valuation showed the original estimate to be too low (*Timms* v *FAI Insurances Ltd* (1976) 12 ALR 506). Paragraph 1(a) of the Statement of Insurance Practice provides that: 'The declaration at the foot of the proposal form should be restricted to completion according to the proposer's knowledge and belief'. Paragraph 1(b) goes on to provide that: 'Neither the proposal form nor the policy shall contain any provision converting the statements as to past or present fact in the proposal form into warranties'. Taken together these provisions seriously undermine the effect of the 'basis of the contract' clause in consumer policies. As far as individuals are concerned, the harshness exemplified by the decision in *Dawsons Ltd* v *Bonnin* has now, therefore, been largely addressed.

10.8.2 Clauses descriptive of risk
It is important to distinguish promissory warranties from clauses which describe or limit the risk. It is common practice for insurers to reduce the

scope of the risk insured by listing excepted perils. The effect of such clauses is merely to suspend the insurance cover during the period in which the insured engages in an excepted risk. Further, if the insured's loss is not proximately caused by an excepted peril, the insured may still be able to recover under the policy. In *Provincial Insurance Co. Ltd* v *Morgan* [1933] AC 240, the proposer for a motor policy stated in the proposal form that the lorry to be insured was to be used for delivering coal. The insured warranted the truth of his answers and the proposal form was made the basis of the contract. At the time of the accident, the lorry was carrying coal although earlier that day, it had been used to carry timber. The insured's claim was repudiated by the insurers who argued that there had been a breach of warranty. It was held by the House of Lords that the statement in the proposal form did not amount to a warranty but was merely descriptive of the risk insured. Lord Russell of Killowen stated that the insured's statements could not be read as nothing more than mere statements of 'intentions as to the use of the vehicle and the goods to be carried in it' (ibid. 278). Similarly, in *Farr* v *Motor Traders' Mutual Insurance Society* [1920] 3 KB 669, a statement in the proposal form that the insured taxicabs were only to be driven in one shift per 24 hours was held to be descriptive of risk and not a promissory warranty. In *De Maurier (Jewels) Ltd* v *Bastion Insurance Co. Ltd* [1967] 2 Lloyd's Rep 550, the policy contained a 'warranty' that the insured's vehicles would be fitted with approved locks and alarm systems. The insured suffered two losses. When the first loss occurred, the locks were not of the required type, but by the time of the second loss there was compliance with the term. It was held that as a matter of construction of the so-called 'warranty', it was merely a description of risk, with the result that the insurers were not liable for the first loss, the policy being suspended by the breach, but were liable for the second loss (see also *CTN Cash & Carry Ltd* v *General Accident Fire and Life Assurance Corporation plc* [1989] 1 Lloyd's Rep 299). Where a motor insurance policy restricts cover to when the vehicle is being used for 'social, domestic and pleasure' purposes, the insured will not be covered whilst using the vehicle for some other purpose which has a business element (*Wood* v *General Accident Fire and Life Assurance Corporation Ltd* (1948) 82 Ll L Rep 77).

10.8.3 Conditions

Conditions may be classified as either conditions precedent to the validity of the contract, conditions precedent to recovery or merely as collateral stipulations. A condition precedent to validity will often impose a continuing obligation on the insured, for example, in motor insurance the insured will be required to maintain the vehicle in a roadworthy condition and to ensure that the vehicle has a valid MOT test certificate. Breach of this type of condition will entitle the insurer to repudiate the contract as from the date of the breach, although the insurer may elect to affirm it (*Hain Steamship Co. Ltd* v *Tate & Lyle Ltd* (1936) 52 TLR 617; *Jones* v *Provincial Insurance Co. Ltd* (1929) 35 Ll L Rep 135).

An insurer, with full knowledge of a breach, may be estopped from repudiating the contract, as where, for example, the insurer continues to accept premium payments (see *Hemmings* v *Sceptre Life Association Ltd* [1905] 1 Ch 365, *Bentsen* v *Taylor, Sons & Co.* [1893] 2 QB 274 and *Ayrey* v *British Legal and United Provident Assurance Co.* [1918] 1 KB 136). Conditions precedent to recovery generally impose requirements to be complied with by the insured when a loss arises, for example, that a claim is made within a specified time limit and that the insurers receive specified particulars of the loss. Breach of such a condition does not entitle the insurer to repudiate the contract but merely to avoid liability for a particular claim (*Hood's Trustees* v *Southern Union General Insurance Co. of Australasia* [1928] Ch 793). If the insured, in breach of such a condition, fails to notify the insurers of the particulars of a loss, but the insurers are nevertheless in possession of all relevant facts by virtue of being informed by, for example, the police, the court can excuse the insured's breach (*Barrett Brothers (Taxis) Ltd* v *Davies* [1966] 1 WLR 1334). In *Barrett Brothers (Taxis) Ltd* v *Davies* a motorcyclist claimed an indemnity from the insurers in respect of damages he was required to pay to a third party arising from an accident caused by the insured's negligence. The policy contained a condition which provided that 'full particulars' should be communicated to the insurance company 'as soon as possible after the occurrence of any accident . . . and shall forward immediately any . . . notice of intended prosecution'. The accident occurred on 17 May 1964 and the insured received a notice of intended prosecution but did not inform his insurers. In the meantime the insurers received a letter from the police, dated 18 June, notifying them of the proceedings. By letter dated 23 June the insurers wrote to the insured explaining that: 'We understand that proceedings are being taken against you on 2 July. . . . It would be appreciated if you would let us know why you have not notified us of these proceedings since we will wish to arrange your defence.' Subsequently, the insurers denied liability on the basis that the insured was in breach of condition in not notifying them of the intended prosecution. It was held by the Court of Appeal that the letter of 23 June constituted a waiver by the insurers of the insured's breach. Lord Denning MR said at p. 1339:

> The principle of waiver is simply this: If one party by his conduct leads another to believe that the strict rights arising under the contract will not be insisted upon, intending that the other should act on that belief, and he does act on it, then the first party will not afterwards be allowed to insist on the strict rights when it would be inequitable for him so to do. . . .
>
> By not asking for the documents, they as good as said that they did not want them. So he did not send them. I do not think they should be allowed now to complain of not receiving them.

A clause in a policy which, on its construction, does not fall into any of the above categories will be held to be a collateral term not giving the right to avoid or repudiate the contract (*Re Bradley and Essex and Suffolk Accident Indemnity Society* [1912] 1 KB 415), so that at best the insurer will have a right to damages, although there is no reported case in which an insurer has been able to prove loss due to a breach of a collateral term. The courts are most reluctant to construe a clause as a condition precedent to liability, given the severe consequences that may flow from such a finding. Accordingly, unless the wording is absolutely clear — and for this purpose, calling a term a 'condition precedent' will not necessarily suffice — the courts will reject the argument that a condition is a 'condition precedent'. A clear example of this is the Court of Appeal's ruling in *Charter Reinsurance Co. Ltd* v *Fagan* [1996] 2 WLR 726, in respect of a reinsurance policy under which the reinsurer was not to be liable to make payment to the reinsured until the reinsured 'shall actually have paid' its own policyholders, that the wording of the 'to be paid clause' was sufficiently ambiguous not to give rise to a condition precedent, and accordingly the reinsured was entitled to recover from the reinsurer on proof of its liability to make payment rather than on having made payment.

10.9 AGENTS

In common with the conduct of commerce generally, insurance is conducted through intermediaries. Even where the proposer deals 'directly' with the insurance company the issue of agency still arises given that the company, as an artificial person, has to conduct its business through agents (*J. C. Houghton & Co.* v *Nothard, Lowe & Wills Ltd* [1928] AC 1, 18 per Lord Sumner). Consequently, insurance policies are effected either through brokers, or agents and employees of insurance companies. At law, a principal is bound by the acts of an agent with respect to matters which the agent has either actual or ostensible authority to conduct on behalf of the principal. With respect to information made known to an agent by the proposer, but which is not transmitted to the insurer, the insurer may be estopped from asserting breach of warranty. For example, in *Wing* v *Harvey* (1854) 5 De G M & G 265, an agent continued to accept premiums on behalf of the insurers knowing that the assured was in breach of warranty. It was held that the insurers could not repudiate liability. By accepting the premiums through their authorised agent, the insurers affirmed the policy, thereby waiving the assured's breach (see also *Ayrey* v *British Legal and United Provident Assurance Co.* [1918] 1 KB 136).

In determining the legal relationship existing between the parties it can generally be said that brokers are deemed to be the agents of the insured, while canvassing agents (salespersons) and employees, are deemed to be agents of the insurer. It is of particular importance in the insurance law context to determine whether the intermediary's principal is the insured or insurer. This issue assumes crucial significance in pre-contractual situations where it is not uncommon for an insurance agent to complete the proposal form on behalf of the proposer. If a written answer in a proposal form fails to disclose a material fact made known to the agent at the time of its completion because, for example, the agent deliberately concealed the truth, the question arises whether the agent's actual knowledge can be imputed to the insurer. If it cannot, it follows that the insurer will be able repudiate the contract for non-disclosure.

The case law appears to be inconsistent and in a confused state. It is apparent that the guiding principle followed by the judges is that a person is bound by the contents of a document that he or she has signed unless *non est factum* can be pleaded (*L'Estrange* v *F. Graucob Ltd* [1934] 2 KB 394; *Norwich & Peterborough Building Society* v *Steed* [1993] Ch 116. For the plea to succeed the court must be satisfied that the signed proposal form is entirely different from that which the proposer intended to sign, and his or her mistake was not due to carelessness (see Fifoot, *History and Sources of the Common Law, Tort and Contract* (1949)). It is only in exceptional cases that the judges are prepared to deviate from the rule that a signed document is binding. For example, in *Bawden* v *London, Edinburgh and Glasgow Assurance Co.* [1892] 2 QB 534, the insurers' agent completed the proposal form for the proposer who was illiterate and had lost an eye. The form contained a warranty that the applicant was free from any physical infirmity. This was patently untrue, and did not escape the agent's notice. The insured was later involved in an accident in which he lost his other eye. The Court of Appeal held that the agent's knowledge of the insured's condition at the time of the proposal was imputed to the insurer, with the result that the insured could claim under the policy. Lord Esher MR concluded that the agent had authority to complete the proposal form.

On the other hand, in *Newsholme Brothers* v *Road Transport and General Insurance Co. Ltd* [1929] 2 KB 356 a proposer for a motor insurance policy orally gave correct answers to questions relating to previous losses to the insurers' agent. The agent, who was not authorised to complete proposal forms, deliberately recorded untrue answers in the proposal form, which was then signed by the proposer, warranting the truth of the statements contained therein. The proposal form also contained a basis of the contract clause. The Court of Appeal held that the agent's knowledge that the answers were false could not be imputed to the insurers since the agent was the agent of the proposer. Scrutton LJ stated, at pp. 375–6 that:

> If the answers are untrue and (the agent) knows it, he is committing a fraud which prevents his knowledge being the knowledge of the insurance company. If the answers are untrue, but he does not know it, I do not understand how he has any knowledge which can be imputed to the insurance company. In any case, I have great difficulty in understanding how a man who has signed, without reading it, a document which he knows to be a proposal for insurance, and which contains statements in fact untrue, and a promise that they are true and the basis of the contract, can escape from the consequences of his negligence by saying that the person he asked to fill it up for him is the agent of the person to whom the proposal is addressed.

Greer LJ, while noting the agency point in issue (ibid. 381–2), also focused upon the parol evidence rule forbidding the admission of oral evidence of what the agent actually knew in order to vary the terms of the written contract, i.e., the proposal form. The agent's lack of authority to complete proposal forms was, it is suggested, material to the court's reasoning. The decision was distinguished in *Stone* v *Reliance Mutual Insurance Society Ltd* [1972] 1 Lloyd's Rep 469. The insured was visited by an inspector (employed by the insurers) in order to reinstate a lapsed fire policy. The proposal form asked for details of lapsed policies and the insured's claims history. The inspector, who completed the form on the instructions of his employers, did not ask the insured for details but answered incorrectly that there were none. The proposal form was signed by the insured's wife without reading it. The Court of Appeal, approving *Bawden v London, Edinburgh and Glasgow Assurance Co.*, held that the insurers could not avoid the policy. The decision is readily explainable on the basis of the inspector's actual and ostensible authority to complete proposal forms on behalf of prospective applicants. Lord Denning MR, clearly influenced by the fact that the insurers could have discovered the true situation from their records of the insured, stated, at p. 474:

> No doubt it was Mrs Stone's mistake too. She ought to have read through the questions and answers before she signed the form: but she did not do so. Her mistake, however, was excusable, because she was of little education, and assumed that the agent would know all about previous policies and that there had been claims under them.

The duties owed by an agent to the principal arise from the general law of tort, contract and, as a person occupying a fiduciary position, equity. In tort, liability can arise either in deceit or negligence. To support an action in deceit it must be established that the agent made a fraudulent statement which caused loss to the plaintiff. The defendant must either know his statement to be false or else must be reckless, i.e., without knowing whether his statement is true or false he must be consciously indifferent to its truth (*Derry v Peek* (1889) 14 App Cas 337). On the question of damages recoverable in deceit see *Smith Kline and French Laboratories Ltd v Long* [1988] 1 WLR 1. For a claim in negligence, the normal rules apply so that where the loss is purely economic, not arising from a negligent misstatement, no action will lie (note the tripartite test promulgated in *Caparo Industries plc v Dickman* [1990] 2 AC 605; *Murphy v Brentwood District Council* [1991] 1 AC 398; see also *Hedley Byrne & Co. Ltd v Heller & Partners Ltd* [1964] AC 465, 502–3 and 514). Where the intended beneficiary of the insurance suffers loss because the agent failed to properly effect the transaction, the duty of care owed to the proposer may now be extended to the beneficiary (*Ross v Caunters* [1980] Ch 297; *White v Jones* [1995] 2 AC 207). The contractual liability of the agent arises from the express or implied agreement with the principal to fulfil the mandated transaction. The nature and extent of the agent's contractual duties is determined as a question of construction of the agreement between the parties. With respect to the degree of care and skill to be discharged for the purposes of determining liability in both tort and contract, an agent is under a legal duty to exercise reasonable care and skill (*Forsikringstaktieselskapet Vesta v Butcher* [1989] AC 852).

As with agents generally, an insurance agent is subject to the full rigour of fiduciary duties. For present purposes, these can be distilled into two propositions. First, to act bona fide in the interests of the principal. Secondly, to avoid a conflict of interests (*Keech v Sandford* (1726) Sel Cas t King 61; *Boardman v Phipps* [1967] 2 AC 46). The situation becomes complex in insurance because the insured's agent will generally receive commission on the policy from the insurer which can give rise to issues of conflict of interest. As with fiduciaries generally, provided the principal has knowledge that commission is paid to the agent, no breach arises since the principal will be taken to have consented to the payment. Surprisingly, in *Anangel Atlas Compania Naviera SA* v *Ishikawajima-Harima Heavy Industries Co. Ltd* [1990] 1 Lloyd's Rep 167, the court took this to mean that knowledge of the amount was not necessary. This view may be doubted given that fully informed consent must include knowledge of all material facts (*New Zealand Netherlands Society 'Oranje' Inc.* v *Kuys* [1973] 1 WLR 1126; *BLB Corporation of Australia Establishment* v *Jacobsen* (1974) 48 ALJR 372).

The most important form of agent from the insured's point of view is the broker. Brokers are independent, but the law has long been clear that the broker acts as the agent of the insured, so that if the broker is aware of material facts but does not disclose them to the insurer, the insurer has the right to avoid the policy and the insured must turn to the broker for indemnification in a negligence action. In *Dunbar* v *A. & B. Painters Ltd* [1986] 2 Lloyd's Rep 38, the insurers avoided liability for the insured's loss on the basis of non-disclosure. In fact the brokers had answered questions in the proposal form incorrectly and were held liable to the insured in damages to cover the loss. It was material to the court's reasoning that the answers given fell within the broker's knowledge. The scope of the duty of care owed by a broker to an insured was also examined in *McNealy* v *Pennine Insurance Co. Ltd* [1978] 2 Lloyd's Rep 18, in which members of certain designated professions were offered low-premium motor insurance. The broker failed to check that the proposer qualified and was held liable to him. Waller LJ said that it was the duty of the broker 'to make as certain as he reasonably could that the (proposer) came within the categories acceptable to the insurers' (ibid. 21). However, the Court of Appeal stressed that where the broker is not in possession of material facts and there are no special circumstances putting the broker on notice, there is no duty to warn the insured of his or her duty of disclosure.

The role of brokers in placing insurance has been given detailed consideration by the Court of Appeal in two cases decided at the same time but with slightly different facts, *PCW Syndicates* v *PCW Reinsurers* [1996] 1 WLR 1136 and *Group Josi Re* v *Walbrook Insurance Co. Ltd* [1996] 1 WLR 1152. In these cases, an agent acting on behalf of the reinsured was charged with the duty of procuring reinsurance, and a broker was instructed by the agent. The agent had in fact been guilty of serious frauds at the reinsured's expense, and the reinsurer sought to avoid liability on the basis that such fraud was material and ought to have been disclosed. The Court of Appeal held that the reinsured was obliged only to disclose such facts as he knew or ought to have known in the ordinary course of business, and that earlier cases were incorrect in so far as they assumed that the knowledge of an agent could be imputed to his principal. The court further held that the rule, codified in s. 19 of the Marine Insurance Act 1906, that an 'agent to insure' must disclose to the insurer all facts known to the agent, did not defeat the reinsured in the present case, as, first, the agent in question was not an 'agent to insure', as that description applied only to the last agent in the chain, i.e., the broker who places insurance; and secondly, that even if the agent had been a placing broker, the information which has to be disclosed under s. 19 is confined to that which the agent has obtained while acting as the assured's agent and does not extend to information obtained in some other capacity, for example, because the agent was defrauding the insured.

10.9.1 Regulation of insurance intermediaries

The move towards regulating insurance intermediaries began in 1970 following a study carried out by the National Consumer Council, which identified the vulnerability of consumers to those selling insurance in an unregulated market place. This was followed by the British Insurance Brokers' Association Consultative Document (1976), *Insurance Intermediaries* (Cmnd 6715, 1977). The ensuing regulations take two forms: those dealing with intermediaries generally, and those restricted to insurance brokers. With respect to intermediaries, those who are not truly independent but are connected to a particular insurer are required by regs 67–9 of the Insurance Companies Regulations 1981 (SI 1981/1654) to disclose details of the 'connection' in writing (see the Insurance Companies Act 1982, s. 74). Non-compliance with these provisions is rendered a criminal offence. The regulatory framework governing brokers was established by the Insurance Brokers (Registration) Act 1977. The Act established the Insurance Brokers Registration Council which is responsible for registering all those carrying on the business of insurance brokers. To qualify for registration a broker must possess a recognised qualification and have at least three years' experience. The broker must also satisfy the Council of his or her solvency, independence and good character. Those who do not fulfil the educational criteria for registration may apply for registration after five years' full-time experience. By s. 22 of the 1977 Act, carrying on business as a broker without registering with the Council is made a criminal offence, punishable on conviction on indictment by an unlimited fine. Curiously, the Act does not apply to those who choose to carry on the business of brokers under some alternative title, for example, 'financial adviser' or 'insurance consultant', although such persons are regulated by voluntary codes of practice issued by the Association of British Insurers in 1987 and 1989, and they will also be regulated by the stringent requirements of the Financial Services Act 1986 as regards the broking of life policies. The Council established by the 1977 Act oversees a number of Codes of Conduct, has laid down minimum solvency margins to ensure the independence of brokers and stipulates accountancy requirements. In the event of a breach of the Codes, the Council may remove a broker from the register.

10.10 CONSTRUING THE CONTRACT

10.10.1 Scope of cover

In the event of a loss, it is crucial for the insured to demonstrate that the risk is covered by the terms of the contract. This depends on the construction of the policy. The point was compendiously stated in *Cehave NV v Bremer Handelsgesellschaft mbH* [1976] QB 44 by Roskill LJ at p. 71: 'the same legal principles should apply to the law of contract as a whole and . . . different legal principles should not apply to different branches of that law'. Accordingly, the courts follow general contractual principles when construing contracts of insurance, the overriding consideration being to give effect to the intention of the contracting parties (*Want v Blunt* (1810) 12 East 183, 187 per Lord Ellenborough CJ; *Charter Reinsurance Co. Ltd v Fagan* [1995] CLC 1345; *affd* [1996] 2 WLR 726).

In ascertaining the intention of the parties, the underlying presumption which governs the construction of insurance contracts is that words should be given their ordinary meaning. This is sometimes described as being their natural, primary, or popular sense (*Yorke v Yorkshire Insurance Co. Ltd* [1918] 1 KB 662, 666 per McCardie J; *Curtis's & Harvey (Canada) Ltd v North British & Mercantile Insurance Co.* [1921] 1 AC 303, 311 per Lord Dunedin). For example, in *Deutsche Genossenschaftsbank v Burnhope* [1995] 1 WLR 1580, a policy was effected by the bank covering, inter alia, 'theft, larceny or false pretences, committed by persons present on the (bank's) premises'. A customer, the chairman of a company, perpetrated a £9 million securities fraud on the bank by acting through an innocent employee of the company. Consequently, at the material time, the customer (thief) did not enter the bank's premises. The House of Lords, construing the relevant clause, held that the loss was not covered by the policy. Lord Nicholls of Birkenhead stated, at p. 1585, that:

> . . . I find myself constrained to accept that there is here no context enabling the words to be read as covering the case where the securities are removed from the bank and taken to the thief by his innocent agent. . . . 'by' cannot be read as 'through', so as to embrace acts committed by innocent agents personally present. 'Theft . . . committed by persons present on the premises' is naturally to be read as indicative of physical presence of the person committing the theft.

This precept of attributing the ordinary meaning of words to terms in a policy document can also be seen in *Thompson v Equity Fire Insurance Co.* [1910] AC 592, where a shop keeper's premises were destroyed by fire caused by a small quantity of gasoline kept in a cooking stove. The fire policy exempted the insurers from liability for loss if 'gasoline was stored or kept in the building insured'. In holding the insurers liable for the loss, the Privy Council construed the words 'kept or stored' in their ordinary meaning as implying a large quantity. At pp. 596–7 Lord Macnaghten summed up the approach taken thus:

> What is the meaning of the words 'stored or kept' in collocation and in the connection in which they are found? . . . It is difficult, if not impossible, to give an accurate definition of the meaning, but if one takes a concrete case it is not very difficult to say whether a particular thing is 'stored or kept'

within the meaning of the condition. No one probably would say that a person who had a reasonable quantity of tea in his house for domestic use was 'storing or keeping' tea there. . . .

Some meaning must be given to the words 'stored or kept'. Their lordships think those words must have their ordinary meaning.

It follows that the courts will not necessarily adopt a literal approach if this results in an absurdity which does not reflect the intention of the parties (*Smit Tak Offshore Services* v *Youell* [1992] 1 Lloyd's Rep 154, 159 per Mustill LJ). Where there is ambiguity in the policy, the court may invoke the *contra proferentem* rule of construction with the result that the meaning most favourable to the insured will be adopted. The point was clearly expressed by Staughton LJ in *Youell* v *Bland Welch & Co. Ltd* [1992] 2 Lloyd's Rep 127, who said, at p. 134:

> There are two well established rules of construction. . . . The first is that, in case of doubt, wording in a contract is to be construed against a party who seeks to rely on it in order to diminish or exclude his basic obligation, or any common law duty which arises apart from contract. The second is that, again in case of doubt, wording is to be construed against the party who proposed it for inclusion in the contract: it was up to him to make it clear.

In *Houghton* v *Trafalgar Insurance Co. Ltd* [1953] 2 Lloyd's Rep 503, a motor insurance policy contained a clause which excluded liability 'arising whilst the car is conveying any load in excess of that for which it was constructed'. At the time of the accident the insured was carrying five passengers in a car which was designed to carry four. The fifth passenger was sitting on the knees of another. The insurer repudiated liability on the ground that the vehicle was carrying an excess load. The Court of Appeal held that the clause in question was ambiguous and should be construed as referring to weight only. Somervell LJ stated, at p. 504, that:

> If there is any ambiguity, it is the defendants' clause and the ambiguity will be resolved in favour of the assured. In my opinion, the words relied on . . . only cover cases where there is a weight load specified in respect of the motor vehicle, be it lorry or van. . . . We have to construe the words in their ordinary meaning, and I think those words clearly only cover the case which I have put. If that is right, they cannot avail the insurance company in the present case.

The *contra proferentem* rule will only be invoked in cases of real ambiguity and has no place where the ambiguity of a particular term can be resolved by looking at the policy as a whole (*Passmore* v *Vulcan Boiler & General Insurance Co. Ltd* (1936) 154 LT 258). In this regard, where particular words are followed by general words, the latter may be construed *eiusdem generis* thereby limiting their meaning. In *Watchorn* v *Langford* (1813) 3 Camp 422, a coach-plater insured his 'stock in trade, household furniture, linen, wearing apparel and plate' against the risk of fire. A fire occurred at his premises destroying a large stock of linen drapery. He claimed from the insurers arguing that the linen drapery was within the description of 'linen' contained in the policy. His action failed, Lord Ellenborough CJ stated, at p. 423:

> I am clearly of opinion that the word 'linen' in the policy does not include articles of this description. Here we may apply *noscitur a sociis*. The preceding words are 'household furniture', and the succeeding 'wearing apparel'. The 'linen' must be 'household linen or apparel'.

Words which carry a technical meaning, whether legal or scientific in nature, or deriving from a particular trade or industry, will be construed accordingly. For example, 'theft' will be interpreted according to its statutory definition in the Theft Act 1968, even though this may not accord with the insured's understanding (*London and Lancashire Fire Insurance Co. Ltd* v *Bolands Ltd* [1924] AC 836; *Dobson* v *General Accident Fire and Life Assurance Corporation plc* [1990] 1 QB 274; see also *Dino Services Ltd* v *Prudential Assurance Co. Ltd* [1989] 1 All ER 422).

In determining the extent of cover afforded by a policy for 'loss', the insurers are liable only if there has been actual loss or damage to the insured property. In *Eisinger* v *General Accident Fire and Life Assurance Corporation Ltd* [1955] 1 WLR 869 a motor insurance policy stated that: 'The corporation will indemnify the policyholder against loss of or damage (including damage by frost) to any motor car described in the schedule hereto'. The insured sold his car to a rogue in return for a cheque which was dishonoured. The rogue then resold the car and disappeared. The insured claimed under the policy arguing that he had suffered a loss of the vehicle. It was held that there had been no 'loss' of the property within the meaning of that word in the policy, but rather a loss of the proceeds of sale. Lord Goddard CJ stated, at p. 871: 'It is a clear case of obtaining a car by false pretences. But that passed the property in the car. You cannot say that the claimant has lost the car; what he has lost is the proceeds of sale. He has lost the price which the man promised to pay him.' (Cf. *Webster* v *General Accident Fire and Life Assurance Corporation Ltd* [1953] 1 QB 520. The *Eisinger* decision was not cited to the Court of Appeal in *Dobson* v *General Accident Fire and Life Assurance Corporation plc* [1990] 1 QB 274, in which the Court of Appeal held that the insured was entitled to recover for 'loss by theft' in a similar case of theft by trick. It remains uncertain whether the phrase 'loss by theft' has a different meaning to the word 'loss' taken alone, or whether *Eisinger* is no longer good law.

Where a previous decision of the courts has determined the particular meaning of a word, this will be generally followed in subsequent cases on the basis that the parties are presumed to intend such precedents to be respected, the added advantage being that adherence to precedent avoids uncertainty. In *Louden* v *British Merchants' Insurance Co. Ltd* [1961] 1 Lloyd's Rep 155, the court was required to construe the meaning of an exemption clause contained in a motor policy which excluded liability where the insured died from bodily injury 'sustained whilst under the influence of drugs or intoxicating liquor'. Lawton J, at p. 157, adopted the definition attributed to such clauses by Lord Coleridge CJ and Denman J in a decision reported in 1877:

> . . . I adopt the constructions in *Mair* v *Railway Passengers Assurance Co. Ltd* (1877) 37 LT 356, albeit they have been expressed in mid-nineteenth century idiom. I add no gloss, as to do so might add confusion where none may have existed among insurers and policyholders during the past 84 years.

10.10.2 Causation

For the insured to validly claim under a policy of insurance it must be established that the insured risk was the proximate cause of the loss. This has been defined as the 'dominant' or 'effective' cause (*J. J. Lloyd Instruments Ltd* v *Northern Star Insurance Co. Ltd* [1987] 1 Lloyd's Rep 32, 37 per Lawton LJ). In *Leyland Shipping Co. Ltd* v *Norwich Union Fire Insurance Society Ltd* [1918] AC 350 Lord Shaw of Dunfermline analysed the issue in the following terms, at p. 369:

> The true and the overriding principle is to look at a contract as a whole and to ascertain what the parties to it really meant. What was it which brought about the loss, the event, the calamity, the accident? . . .
>
> To treat proximate cause as if it was the cause which is proximate in time is . . . out of the question. The cause which is truly proximate is that which is proximate in efficiency. That efficiency may have been preserved although other causes may meantime have sprung up.

It follows that if the direct cause is within the risks covered, the insurer will be liable. Conversely, if the cause falls within an excepted risk or is outside the scope of the policy as a whole, the insurer will avoid liability. Thus, where property was stolen from a building damaged by a bomb dropped during enemy action, the effective or dominant cause of the loss was the theft, not the air raid which facilitated it (*Winicofsky* v *Army & Navy General Assurance Association Ltd* (1919) 88 LJ KB 1111. In *Coxe* v *Employers' Liability Assurance Corporation Ltd* [1916] 2 KB 629 the insured effected a personal accident policy against death. The policy contained an exception which stated that it did not apply if death was 'directly or indirectly caused by, arising from, or traceable to . . . war'. The insured, an army officer, was killed by a train when he was walking alongside a railway line for the purpose of inspecting sentries who had been posted to guard the track. The spot where the accident occurred would normally be illuminated, but the lights had been dimmed as a result of the prevailing wartime conditions. The insured's personal representatives claimed under the policy, arguing that the accident was not 'directly or indirectly traceable to war'. It was held that the proximate-cause rule was excluded by the terms of the policy. The insured's death was indirectly caused by war because, at the time of the accident, the insured was carrying out his military duties which exposed him to special risks.

Nowadays, personal accident policies are common, and are frequently effected by trade unions and professional bodies for the benefit of their members. The meaning of the term 'accident' in relation to such policies is correlative. In *De Souza* v *Home and Overseas Insurance Co. Ltd* [1995] LRLR 453, the insured, while on holiday in Torremolinos, sustained heatstroke and died. The issue before the Court of Appeal was whether the insured had sustained 'accidental bodily injury' within the terms of his insurance policy. Mustill LJ stressed that 'accident' is synonymous with the notion of something fortuitous and unexpected and 'is to be regarded as the antithesis to bodily infirmity by disease in the ordinary course of events' (ibid. 458). He concluded, at p. 463:

> Did Mr De Souza suffer an 'injury'? I cannot see that he did. To my mind he unfortunately became ill and died. Where was the element of 'accident' in his illness? The plaintiff has never identified what the accident was, or when it happened. So far as we know there was normal sun, normal heat, and normal exposure to them, which for some reason sadly led to Mr De Souza's death.

The scope of the term 'accident' was again considered by the Court of Appeal in *Dhak* v *Insurance Co. of North America (UK) Ltd* [1996] 2 All ER 609. The plaintiff's wife died as a result of acute alcoholism, which caused her to suffocate through the inhalation of her own vomit. She began to drink heavily as a means of alleviating severe back pain caused by lifting a heavy patient at the hospital where she worked. The plaintiff, as executor, claimed under his wife's personal accident, policy which provided £50,000 in respect of 'bodily injury resulting in death . . . caused directly or indirectly by the accident'. 'Bodily injury' was defined in the policy as 'bodily injury caused by accidental means'. The trial judge upheld the insurers' rejection of the plaintiff's claim. The plaintiff appealed to the Court of Appeal. Neill LJ, who delivered the principal judgment, accepted that 'bodily injury' need not necessarily be restricted to circumstances where there was injury to the exterior of the body, but could cover asphyxiation as in the present case. However, he went on to observe (at pp. 621–2) that:

> . . . the terms of this policy require a court . . . to concentrate on the cause of the injury and to inquire whether the injury was caused by accidental means. . . . I have come to the conclusion that the judge was justified in finding that Mrs Dhak must have been aware of the consequences and dangers of drinking alcohol to excess and that she must be taken to have foreseen what might happen in the event of someone drinking to excess. She was a ward sister with many years of experience as a nurse. . . . I am satisfied that there must be a point at which she would have realised that any further drinking would be dangerous and that vital bodily functions might be impaired or interrupted.

Applying the approach of Mustill LJ in *De Souza* v *Home and Overseas Insurance Co. Ltd*, Neill LJ concluded that the insured's death was not the result of some fortuitous cause and was not, therefore, 'accidental' within the terms of the policy.

Generally, the courts construe an exception of negligence restrictively. In *Sofi* v *Prudential Assurance Co. Ltd* [1993] 2 Lloyd's Rep 559, a clause in the all risks section of a 'Private Combined (Hearth and Home) Policy' required the insured to 'take all reasonable steps to safeguard any property insured and to avoid accidents which may lead to damage or injury'. While en route to catch a ferry at Dover, the insured and his family stopped to make a brief visit to Dover Castle. The object of this visit was purely to kill time pending their ferry's departure. In the locked glove compartment of his car, the insured was carrying some valuable jewellery. He had told the insurer's agent that, having experienced a burglary at home, he considered it safer to take the jewellery away on holiday with him. Having parked his car in the unattended car park, the insured and his family decided to take their money and travellers cheques, but left everything else in the car. Upon returning 15 minutes later, they discovered that their vehicle had been broken into and ransacked. The insurers argued that the insured had not taken all reasonable steps to safeguard the jewellery in that he should either have taken the jewellery with him when he went into the castle grounds, or left a member of his family behind in the car. Lloyd LJ, giving judgment for the Court of Appeal, stated (at p. 566) that as a matter of 'common sense, the greater the value of the goods insured, the greater the risk that they be stolen, and the easier it will be for the insurer to establish' recklessness. He went on to agree with the trial judge who, having found that the car was out of sight or sound for only five to seven minutes, and that this was not a case of a car being left unattended for a lengthy period of time in an obviously vulnerable place, concluded that the insured had not been reckless.

In *Sofi* v *Prudential Assurance Co. Ltd* it is apparent that the Court of Appeal drew the distinction between gross negligence or recklessness which is excepted, and mere inadvertence which is not. In *Port-Rose* v *Phoenix Assurance plc* (1986) 136 NLJ 333, the insured's handbag was stolen at Gatwick airport. The insurers repudiated her claim on the basis that she had failed 'to take reasonable steps to prevent loss'. Hodgson J said that the insurers' defence came down 'to a suggestion that, because this lady was inadvertent momentarily, for two or three seconds and took her eye off the handbag during two or three seconds, she was in breach of the condition of the policy. It seems to me inconceivable that such a let-out could be open to an insurance company.' It has been held that if the insured peril is imminent, and reasonable steps are taken to avoid it which in themselves cause the loss, the loss will be treated as having been caused by the peril so that the insured will recover under the policy (*Symington & Co.* v *Union Insurance Society of Canton* (1928) 97 LJ KB 646).

Problems may arise when two or more events operate concurrently to cause the loss and one of them is an excepted risk. In *Wayne Tank & Pump Co. Ltd* v *Employers' Liability Assurance Corporation Ltd* [1974] QB 57, liability for damage caused by the nature and condition of goods installed by the insured was excluded in an accident policy. The insured's premises were destroyed by fire caused by a defect in the insured's equipment coupled with the negligence of an employee, an insured risk, in leaving the equipment switched on overnight. The Court of Appeal held that the defective equipment was the proximate cause of the loss and since this was an excluded risk, the insurers were not liable. The employee's negligence was not a *novus actus interveniens*. Lord Denning MR stressed that ignoring the excepted peril as being the proximate cause would result in rendering the contract ineffective.

10.10.3 Claims
It was seen above that the policy will contain conditions precedent to recovery which must be complied with by the insured when claiming payment to cover an insured loss. In effect then, such terms may be described as conditions precedent to the liability of the insurers. Such conditions may, inter alia, impose requirements as to the requisite notice to be given to the insurers in the event of a loss, the particulars of the loss to be furnished by the insured and, in the event of a dispute arising between the parties, that settlement should be by way of arbitration.

Generally, the insured will be under a duty to notify the insurers of the loss within a specified time limit, or if none is stipulated, within a reasonable time. Oral notice will suffice unless written notice is expressly stipulated. If the condition is clear and unequivocal, the duty is absolute and impossibility is no defence. In *Cassel* v *Lancashire & Yorkshire Insurance Co.* (1885) 1 TLR 495, the insured was involved in a canoeing accident but his injuries were latent for some eight months. IIis claim under an accident policy failed because he had not complied with the 14 days' notice period specified in the policy. While such terms require strict compliance by the insured, they are strictly construed against the insurer. In *Verelst's Administratrix* v *Motor Union Insurance Co. Ltd* [1925] 2 KB 137 a motor policy contained a condition which provided that in the event of a loss 'the insured or the insured's personal representative . . . shall give notice . . . to the . . . company of such loss as soon as possible after it has come to the knowledge of the insured or the insured's personal representative'. While visiting India the insured was killed in a motoring accident. Her administratrix did not know of the insurance company with which the insured had effected cover until nearly a year after the accident had occurred when she came across the policy while sorting out old papers belonging to the insured. The insurers sought to repudiate liability for breach of the notice requirement. It was held that the administratrix could recover. Roche J construed the clause to mean 'as soon as possible in the circumstances which prevail and apply ' (at p. 142).

In addition to notification, the insured will generally be under a duty to submit particulars of the loss to the insurers. The guiding principle seems to be that the insured must provide sufficient detail to enable the insurers 'to form a judgment as to whether or not he has sustained a loss' (*Mason* v *Harvey* (1853) 8 Ex 819, 820–1 per Pollock CB). A condition that 'full particulars' of the loss must be given has been defined as meaning 'the best particulars which the assured can reasonably give' (ibid.). However, it has been held that where the insured failed to give particulars of a loss to the insurers personally, the insurers by their subsequent conduct could be taken to have waived this requirement (*Barrett Brothers (Taxis) Ltd* v *Davies* [1966] 1 WLR 1334).

The insured's duty of utmost good faith continues beyond the time when the policy is initially effected and renewed so that it operates when a claim is made. This is clear from Matthew LJ's observation in *Boulton* v *Houlder Brothers & Co.* [1904] 1 KB 784 at pp. 791–2, that it 'is an essential condition of the policy of insurance that the underwriters shall be treated with good faith, not merely in reference to the inception of the risk, but in the steps taken to carry out the contract'. If the insured makes a fraudulent claim, he will not be able to recover (*Britton* v *Royal Insurance Co.* (1866) 4 F & F 905), and it was stated in the *Britton* case that the insured forfeited his rights under the policy, which has been taken to mean that the policy can be terminated for breach. However, the question whether the policy can be avoided *ab initio* so that the insurer can recover any payments made with respect to an earlier loss, or only from the date of the fraudulent claim, has vexed judges and commentators alike (see *Gore Mutual Insurance Co.* v *Bifford* (1987) 45 DLR (4th) 763; *Black King Shipping Corporation* v *Massie* [1985] 1 Lloyd's Rep 437; *Reid & Co.* v *Employers' Accident & Livestock Insurance Co. Ltd* 1 F 1031; Clarke, *The Law of Insurance Contracts*, 2nd ed. (Lloyd's of London Press, 1994), para. 27–2D). It would seem that the degree of protection required by insurers at the inception of the contract is significantly higher than that at the time of any loss and subsequent claim, so that to allow avoidance *ab initio* would be particularly Draconian in effect. In the most recent decision, *Manifest Shipping & Co. Ltd* v *Uni-Polaris Insurance Co. Ltd* [1995] 1 Lloyd's Rep 651, Tuckey J doubted the independent application of utmost good faith to the claims process, and held that, even if it did operate, there had to be at the very least recklessness by the assured. It was also held that the duty came to an end once legal proceedings had been commenced as after that date false statements were to be dealt with as part of the court's processes rather than as part of the claim.

A material statement in a claim is fraudulent if the insured either knew it to be false or else was reckless as to its truth (*Derry* v *Peek* (1889) 14 App Cas 337, 371 per Lord Herschell). Mere carelessness will not suffice. The onus of proof is on the insurer, and because of the nature of the allegation the burden will be greater than on a mere balance of probabilities (*Hornal* v *Neuberger Products Ltd* [1957] 1 QB 247, 258 per Lord Denning MR). A so-called 'recession-induced claim', where the insured has intentionally destroyed the insured property, is a common example of fraud in this context. While overvaluation is not in itself sufficient, a grossly exaggerated claim of the true value of the loss will raise a presumption of fraud (*Goulstone* v *Royal Insurance Co.* (1858) 1 F & F 276).

It was at one time common for policies of insurance to include a condition providing for the resolution of disputes through arbitration in the first instance. This avoids the expense and delay which are inherent characteristics of civil litigation. Such clauses are enforceable as conditions precedent, with the result that the insured cannot sue on the policy but can bring an action only to enforce an arbitration award in his favour (*Scott* v *Avery* (1856) 5 HL Cas 811). Following the findings by the Law Reform Committee (para 10.7 above) of abuse by insurers in insisting upon arbitration, particularly in the light of the unavailability of legal aid in such proceedings, the Association of British Insurers and Lloyd's announced that their members would not enforce arbitration clauses in cases where the insured indicated a desire to have the issue of liability, as opposed to quantum, determined by a court.

10.11 PRINCIPLE OF INDEMNITY — MEASUREMENT OF LOSS

In indemnity insurance, for example, where the subject matter of the policy is property, whether real or personal, the insured is precluded from recovering more than the value of the actual loss sustained. This is because 'indemnity' means that the insured is to be put back to the position he or she would have been in had the loss not occurred, less any excess which the insured has agreed to bear. The position should be contrasted with contingency insurance, for example, life and accident policies, where the sum recovered is fixed by the terms of the policy. Similarly, if the policy is valued, in that the sum recoverable is fixed by contract (which is the usual position in marine insurance) the sum agreed is not open to challenge at a later date, and the assured is entitled to the full agreed value, or the relevant percentage of it in the case of a partial loss. Leaving aside these special cases, the governing principle was stated by Brett LJ in *Castellain* v *Preston* (1883) 11 QBD 380 at p. 386:

> The very foundation, in my opinion, of every rule which has been applied to insurance law is this, namely, that the contract of insurance contained in a marine or fire policy is a contract of indemnity, and of indemnity only, and that this contract means that the assured, in case of a loss against which the policy has been made, shall be fully indemnified, but shall never be more than fully indemnified. That is the fundamental principle of insurance, and if ever a proposition is brought forward which is at variance with it, that is to say, which either will prevent the assured from obtaining a full indemnity, or which will give to the assured more than a full indemnity, that proposition must certainly be wrong.

The overriding requirement of indemnity can be seen to underlie the rules which operate in the event of an insured loss. We turn now to consider those rules.

10.11.1 Forms and measurement of loss

The 'sum insured' represents the maximum figure which the insured can recover, but it is not necessarily the sum which will be received in the event of a loss. The principle was cogently stated by Cockburn CJ in *Chapman* v *Pole* (1870) 22 LT 306 when summing up for the jury: 'You must not run away with the notion that a policy of insurance entitles a man to recover according to the amount represented as insured . . . he can only recover the real and actual value of the goods' (at p. 307). Accordingly, the sentimental value which an insured places on a lost item is not recoverable even if capable of quantification.

The property which is the subject matter of the policy may be either totally lost or partially lost. There is total loss where the property is damaged beyond economic repair. For example, insurers will sometimes 'write off' a motor vehicle that has suffered extensive damage in a crash where the repair bill would be greater than the value of the insured vehicle. Where goods have been totally lost, indemnity is based on the market value of the item, ascertained as at the time and place of its loss (*Chapman* v *Pole*). Consequently, in 'unvalued policies', where the value of the insured item is not specified, the principle of indemnity will entitle the insured to recover for any appreciation in value that has taken place during the currency of the policy (*Re Wilson and Scottish Insurance Corporation Ltd* [1920] 2 Ch 28). Conversely, in 'valued policies' the agreed value of the item as specified in the policy will be the amount recoverable in the event of total loss. If the value of the property exceeds the sum insured, the insured will bear the excess personally. Where real property is lost, the measure of indemnity is generally determined by reference to the cost of reinstatement, unless the insured has contracted to sell the property, in which case assessment will be based on market value, i.e., the agreed price (*Leppard* v *Excess Insurance Co. Ltd* [1979] 1 WLR 512).

In the event of partial loss, which arises not only where the insured property has been damaged but also where a part of the property has been totally lost, indemnity is usually referable to the cost of reinstatement, subject to any deduction for betterment. The doctrine of betterment operates to take account of depreciation so that a deduction is applied to the amount recoverable where the reinstated property is improved beyond its pre-loss condition (*Dominion Mosaics & Tile Co. Ltd* v *Trafalgar Trucking Co. Ltd* [1990] 2 All ER 246). To avoid this, it is now common to effect insurance on a 'new for old' basis, whereby, in return for a higher premium, insurers will provide replacement cost cover. Where partial loss occurs under a 'valued policy' the insurer is liable to pay a percentage of the stated value. This is calculated by determining the ratio which the actual value of the damaged property bears to the insured sum. In *Elcock* v *Thomson* [1949] 2 All ER 381, a mansion was insured against loss or damage by fire. The agreed value was £106,850. A fire occurred which partially destroyed the property. The value of the property before the fire was £18,000 and after the fire it stood at £12,600, which represented a depreciation of 30 per cent. The property was not reinstated, and the insured claimed under the policy. The issue for the court was how much should the insurers pay. It was held that the agreement about value applied not just in the event of total loss but also to partial loss. The insurers were therefore liable to pay 30 per cent of £106,850, which was £32,055. Morris J, in construing the policy, stated, at p. 387:

> The respective words 'loss' and 'damage', as used in the policy, seem to be synonymous. It would not seem to be the case that the word 'loss' is only referable to complete destruction. . . . The result is that in my judgment,

the percentage of actual depreciation resulting from the fire should be applied to the agreed values as set out in the policy so as to arrive at the amount recoverable.

Where the insured possesses only a limited interest in the insured property, recovery in the event of a loss is limited to the actual value of the interest in question. Examples include creditors who insure the value of their security interests in an asset, and tenants (lessees) who insure the value of their property. Where several creditors have security interests in the same property the total sum recoverable in the event of a loss may exceed the actual value of the property (*Westminster Fire Office* v *Glasgow Provident Investment Society* (1888) 13 App Cas 699). A lessee who has covenanted to repair or insure the property against fire damage will receive the cost of reinstatement. Recovery is not limited to the market value of the lease. The point has also been taken that even in the absence of such a covenant, a tenant will recover more than the value of his interest where the loss results in the tenant losing his home (*Castellain* v *Preston* (1883) 11 QBD 380, 400).

10.11.2 Under-insurance: average
Where the insured undervalues the subject matter of the policy either at the time of its inception or upon renewal, so that the sum insured does not reflect the true value of the property, then strictly speaking the insurer may avoid the policy for non-disclosure or breach of warranty (*Leppard* v *Excess Insurance Co. Ltd* [1979] 1 WLR 512). However, where a partial loss occurs to the insured property and the policy contains an 'average' clause, the insurer's liability will be limited to that part of the loss which the sum insured bears to the actual value of the property. If, for example, property which is actually worth £50,000 is insured for £25,000, and as a result of a partial loss £10,000 is required to repair it, the insured will only recover £5,000.

10.11.3 Double insurance and contribution
There is no prohibition against double insurance, so a person may effect multiple policies on the same property against identical risks. In such a case, the insured is free to claim payment from whichever insurer he or she chooses, but will not be allowed to recover more than is necessary to achieve indemnification against the loss, no matter how many policies are effected. So if the insured claims for the full loss against one particular policy, he or she cannot go on to recover for the same loss against other insurers who have provided the same cover. The position of the co-insurers is governed by the equitable doctrine of contribution. The insurer who has paid the claim can require the other insurers to contribute rateably in proportion to the amount for which the insurer in question is liable, although contribution may be sought only as against an insurer who remains liable at the date of the contribution claim against him: if, therefore, the insured's failure to make a claim under the policy gives the insurer a defence, contribution cannot later be sought from him (*Eagle Star Insurance Co. Ltd* v *Provincial Insurance plc* [1994] 1 AC 130).

Contribution is generally modified by the terms of the insurance contract which commonly include a so-called 'rateable proportion clause'. This has the effect of preventing an insured recovering all of the loss from one insurer only. Instead, the insured is required to claim rateably from each insurer. For example, if property is insured with insurer A for £100 and with insurer B for £200 and the damage is valued at £60, A will be liable for £20 and B for £40. The 'maximum liability' basis of contribution used in this example therefore limits the liability of the respective insurers to the proportion of the risk covered by them and which determined the level of premium charged. Where liability is unlimited, as, for example, in third-party liability motor insurance, the liability of the insurers will be divided equally *inter se* (see Marine Insurance Act 1906, s. 80(1)).

10.11.4 Subrogation

Apparently deriving from Roman law, the restitutionary doctrine of subrogation, as it applies to insurance contracts, serves to reinforce the principle of indemnity in preventing the insured profiting from the loss suffered. The doctrine, as it applies to a policy for fire insurance, was summarised by Cotton LJ in *Castellain* v *Preston* (1883) 11 QBD 380:

> The policy is really a contract to indemnify the person insured for the loss which he has sustained in consequence of the peril insured against which has happened . . . it is only to pay that loss which the assured may have sustained by reason of the fire which has occurred. In order to ascertain what that loss is, everything must be taken into account which is received by and comes to the hand of the assured, and which diminishes that loss.

Subrogation is limited to indemnity insurance and is therefore inapplicable to life or personal accident policies. Further, the right of subrogation triggers only when the insurers have paid the insured under the policy (*Scottish Union and National Insurance Co.* v *Davis* [1970] 1 Lloyd's Rep 1). Where the insured, having been fully indemnified by his or her insurers, goes on to recover damages for the same loss against a third party, the award will be held on constructive trust for the insurers. The correlation between subrogation and the principle of indemnity is clear. If the insured was entitled to retain both the insurance money and the damages awarded, he or she would be doubly compensated. From a restitutionary standpoint, the insured in this situation would be unjustly enriched at the expense of the insurers. However, that said, the insurers cannot reclaim more than the amount paid out by them under the policy, so that if the insured receives damages greater in value, he or she can retain the excess. Whether or not an insured has to account for any payment received in respect of a loss depends upon the intention of the donor. If such a payment was intended to be extra compensation, the insured will be entitled to keep it (*Burnand* v *Rodocanachi, & Sons & Co.* (1882) 7 App Cas 333), whereas if it was intended to diminish the insured's loss it may be claimed by the insurer even though the payment was in the form of a gift (*Colonia Versicherung AG* v *Amoco Oil Co.* [1995] 1 Lloyd's Rep 570).

As we have seen, it is common for an insured to bear an excess in the event of a loss so that, in effect, the insured acts as his or her own insurer for that agreed figure. Is the insured entitled to apply damages recovered from a third party towards defraying any such excess before accounting to the insurers for the balance? This was answered in the negative by the House of Lords in *Lord Napier and Ettrick* v *Hunter* [1993] AC 713, in which it was held that, as a matter of construction, the insurers had agreed only to indemnify in respect of the loss suffered, less any excess figure stipulated in the policy. Accordingly, the insured must bear that element of the loss as contracted for.

Where the insured has received full indemnification under a policy but fails to sue a third party responsible for the loss, the insurer can compel the insured to institute proceedings subject to the costs being borne by the insurers. The position was explained by Brett LJ in *Castellain* v *Preston*:

> In order fully to carry out the fundamental principle (of indemnity) we must carry the doctrine of subrogation so far as to say that, as between the underwriter and the assured, the underwriter is entitled to every right, whether of contract fulfilled or unfulfilled, or in tort, enforced, or to any other right, legal or equitable, which has been diminished. That is the largest form in which I can put the rule. I use the words 'every right' because I think the doctrine requires to be carried to that extent.

This obligation may be modified by the contract itself providing for the insurer to bring a civil claim and requiring the insured to provide all reasonable assistance. Where the policy contains an express assignment of the right to sue, the action will be brought in the name of the insurer, who will be entitled to retain any damages recovered in total. An insured who does commence proceedings against a third party for his loss is under a duty not to prejudice the rights of the insurers in so doing, and if he gives the third party exemption from liability or settles for a wholly inadequate amount, the insurer may be able to bring proceedings against the insured for breach of his duty to safeguard the insurer's interests (*Lord Napier and Ettrick* v *Hunter*).

ELEVEN
Consumer finance

The period immediately following the end of the Second World War saw an increase in the availability of credit. The increase in the amount of credit available caused an increase in the number of problems encountered by consumers in dealing with their creditors. To meet this widespread dissatisfaction, the Crowther Committee on Consumer Credit was set up to examine the existing law and come up with proposals for reform. Their final report (Cmnd 4596, 1971) resulted in the passing of the Consumer Credit Act 1974, which replaced earlier piecemeal legislation in respect of specific types of credit transaction.

The control of credit provision has existed for some time. Examples can be found in the Moneylenders Acts 1900 to 1927 and the Pawnbrokers Acts 1872 and 1960 in relation to the lending of money and in the Hire-Purchase Acts 1938 to 1964 (which were consolidated in the Hire-Purchase Act 1965), in relation to lending connected to the supply of goods. The most comprehensive statutory control of credit provision has come in the form of the Consumer Credit Act 1974. More recently, the European Community has intervened in the form of two Directives on the approximation of the laws of Community States in respect of consumer credit (87/102/EEC, OJ L42/48, 12.2.1987) and the approximation of laws relating to the calculation of the annual percentage rate of charge (the APR Directive, 90/88/EEC, OJ L61/14, 22.2.1990). However, the Directives both appear to be based on the provisions of Consumer Credit Act 1974 and contain little in excess of the provisions of that Act. Accordingly, there has been no additional legislation to implement the requirements of the Directives.

One of the features of the 1974 Act has been a large increase in paperwork. In the White Paper, *Releasing Enterprise* (Cm 512, 1988) there was a recommendation that as many restrictions on business as possible should be removed under what has become known as the 'deregulation initiative'. The problem with deregulation is that although it will facilitate economic recovery by releasing business from some of the legal constraints imposed by regulations under the 1974 Act, it is also potentially dangerous from the point of view of the consumer. Accordingly, care must be taken in selecting the areas of consumer credit law to which the deregulation initiative is applied. As part of this process, the Department of Trade and Industry has issued a consultation document, *Deregulation of UK Consumer Credit Legislation* (1995), in which it proposes a number of changes. In particular, it is suggested that business borrowers do not need the same protection as consumers, so that there should be no need to include within the scheme of the 1974 Act lending and hiring for purely business use, but not mixed business and private use, although there may be dangers in removing the protection of regulation from the likes of sole traders. Also proposed are a number of changes to the monetary limits within which the 1974 Act applies, considered in more detail below, mainly to take into account the effects of inflation. So far as the system of licensing credit businesses and ancillary credit businesses is concerned (see also chapter 2), it is proposed that there should be no need to report certain changes in the licensed business to the Director General of Fair Trading. In particular, the DTI document accepts the view of the Director General that the most important disclosure requirements should relate to matters like criminal convictions for offences of dishonesty and contraventions of anti-discrimination legislation, but that all other requirements of disclosure should be dispensed with. The consultation document also makes proposals to modify the present regulation of rebates on early settlement and proposes the abolition of the Quotations Regulations, both of which are considered in more detail below.

11.1 TYPES OF CREDIT

The 1974 Act does not dispose of the terminology employed prior to its enactment, accordingly the types of credit available remain the same. The three principal types of credit transaction are contracts of hire purchase, conditional sales and credit sales.

11.1.1 Hire purchase, conditional sale and credit sale

A hire purchase agreement is defined as one in which goods are bailed in return for periodic payments by the person to whom they are bailed and passing of ownership is delayed pending compliance with certain conditions, which will normally involve the exercise of an option to purchase the goods (Consumer Credit Act 1974, s. 189). Thus if the bailee is under no obligation to purchase goods hired to him, the contract is likely to be regarded as one of hire purchase rather than one of sale (*Helby* v *Matthews* [1895] AC 471). But if the buyer is obliged to make a specified number of deferred payments after which ownership in the goods will pass to him, the contract is one of conditional sale (*Lee* v *Butler* [1893] 2 QB 318 and see also Consumer Credit Act 1974, s. 189). A conditional sale agreement is governed by the provisions of the Sale of Goods Act 1979, although in so far as it involves the provision of credit, it is also subject to the provisions of the Consumer Credit Act 1974. Where the contract is one of credit sale, ownership in the goods will pass to the buyer at or before the time of delivery, in which case the buyer will have the right to transfer title to another person. Such credit sales are regulated under the provisions of the Consumer Credit Act 1974 despite the fact that very few of the restrictions imposed by the Hire Purchase Acts applied to them.

11.1.2 Terminology of the Consumer Credit Act 1974

The 1974 Act introduces terminology of its own, distinguishing between the debtor, the supplier and the creditor. A consumer credit agreement is defined as a personal credit agreement by which the creditor provides the debtor with credit not exceeding £15,000 (s. 8(2)). For these purposes, the debtor must be an individual, although this includes a partnership, but not a company (s. 189).

The problem with fixed financial limits such as those in s. 8(2) is that in times of inflation, they soon become dated. A DTI consultation document (*Deregulation of UK Consumer Credit Legislation* (1995)) has recommended that the upper limit of application of the 1974 Act to regulated agreements should be raised to £25,000. Moreover, it was also considered whether all the financial limits in the 1974 Act should be index-linked so that they would rise or fall automatically according to changed economic circumstances. However, the DTI document concludes that disadvantages, such as uncertainty about the limits in operation, and the general complication of such a system, militate against index-linking (ibid., para. 3.7).

The types of credit identified by the Act include running-account credit, fixed-sum credit, restricted-use credit and unrestricted-use credit.

11.1.2.1 Running-account and fixed-sum credit Running-account credit is a revolving credit under which the debtor may make withdrawals up to an agreed credit limit, subject to an understanding that the debtor will top up his account with payments to the creditor (s. 10(1)(a)). Examples include the main types of credit card agreement under which the consumer can choose how much of his debt to repay at the end of each month.

For the purposes of such transactions, the credit limit is defined as the maximum debit balance allowed under the agreement (s. 10(2)). So as to allow for the identification of the credit limit in the case of running-account credit, s. 10(3) provides that the overall £15,000 limit is deemed not to be exceeded where the specified credit limit under the agreement is not in excess of £15,000; where the debtor cannot draw more than £15,000 in one transaction; where there is provision for an increase in credit charges should the debt ever exceed an amount specified in the agreement; and where it appears unlikely that the credit limit will ever exceed £15,000 even though it is technically possible under the agreement. The main purpose of s. 10(3) is to prevent evasion of the regulatory regime imposed under the 1974 Act.

A fixed-sum credit agreement is any personal credit agreement which is not a running-account credit agreement (s. 10(1)(b)). This type of credit includes loans made for a specific purpose, such as the acquisition of goods on hire purchase or conditional sale and which are limited to a specified amount.

11.1.2.2 Restricted-use and unrestricted-use credit Section 11(2) provides that any agreement not covered by s. 11(1) is one for unrestricted-use credit. By virtue of s. 11(1) a restricted-use credit agreement is one which performs one of three possible functions.

First, restricted-use credit may finance an agreement between the debtor and the creditor, whether forming part of that agreement or not (s. 11(1)(a)). This will include contracts of hire purchase, credit sale and conditional sale, since in such transactions the creditor is also the legal supplier of the goods, even though they may have been physically supplied by someone else (see s. 56 discussed below).

Secondly, a restricted-use credit agreement includes one which finances a transaction between the debtor and a supplier other than the creditor (s. 11(1)(b)). This will include retail purchases using credit cards and voucher trading agreements where the goods or services are purchased from a person distinct from the creditor.

Thirdly, credit agreements which refinance any existing indebtedness of the debtor (whether to the creditor or some other person) are classified as restricted-use credit agreements (s. 11(1)(c)). This will cover what are called 'consolidation' loans, whereby the consumer's debts to a range of creditors may be settled by taking out a single loan from a further creditor.

In general terms, a restricted-use credit is one in which the debtor can use the credit only in a prescribed manner and an unrestricted-use credit is one in which the debtor is free to use the credit as he chooses (s. 11(3)).

If the supplier is not known at the time the credit agreement is made but the creditor refuses to make the credit available until the supplier is identified, this is still a restricted-use credit (s. 11(4)).

11.1.2.3 Exempt agreements Only regulated agreements are covered by the Act. Certain agreements which would otherwise be regarded as regulated are treated as exempt under the provisions of the Act. These are covered by s. 16 and are mostly loans for the purposes of house purchase given by 'reputable' lenders.

Under the Consumer Credit (Exempt Agreements) Order 1989 (as amended) (SI 1989/869; SI 1989/1841) further exempt agreements have been provided for. These include a debtor-creditor-supplier agreement for fixed-sum credit where payment is not to be made in more than four instalments within a 12-month period, for example, the credit extended to a customer by a newsagent, whereby the customer may pay in arrears. However, this particular exemption does not apply to hire purchase or conditional sale agreements of any kind. Secondly, the 1989 Orders exempt a debtor-creditor-supplier agreement for running account credit under which the whole of the credit extended is to be paid off in a lump sum, provided the agreement is not one for conditional sale or hire purchase. Generally the effect of this is to exempt from the provisions of the Act a large number of high street store budget and option accounts and American Express green card accounts. However, Visa and Access card accounts under which the debtor can choose how much to repay each month would not be covered by this exemption.

Thirdly, the Orders exempt debtor-creditor agreements under which the maximum interest fails to exceed the greater of 13 per cent or 1 per cent above the highest of the London and Scottish clearing bank base rates 28 days before the agreement is entered into. Accordingly, many business loans to employees at low rates of interest are removed from the regime set up under the 1974 Act. Also covered by this exemption would be a credit sale under which the seller allows the customer to pay off the purchase price over a number of months without incurring interest charges, if it is not already exempt under the four-payments-or-less exemption.

Small agreements, namely those where the credit provided does not exceed £50 (s. 17), and non-commercial agreements (s. 189), such as a loan made by one friend to another and not in the course of a business, are also exempt from the provisions of certain parts of the 1974 Act. In particular, the provisions of part V of the Act governing the formalities of entry into credit agreements do not apply to such transactions. So far as small agreements are concerned, there is a proposal that the lower limit on the partial exemption should be raised from £50 to £150 to take account of the effects of inflation and also to ease the burdens of regulation on business generally (DTI, *Deregulation of UK Consumer Credit Legislation* (1995), paras 3.3–3.4).

11.1.2.4 Debtor-creditor-supplier agreements and debtor-creditor agreements

There are generally three ways in which goods can be acquired on credit. First the goods and the credit may be obtained from the creditor himself, in which case, the creditor is also the supplier. Alternatively, the goods may be acquired from a supplier who is connected to the creditor, or in some instances from a supplier who is not connected with the creditor.

Where one person fulfils the roles of supplier and creditor, as is the case where there is a hire purchase or credit sale contract, the credit transaction is a debtor-creditor-supplier (DCS) agreement. Similarly, where there is a link between the creditor and the supplier there is a debtor-creditor-supplier agreement because of the connection between them.

Where there is no link between the creditor and supplier, for example, where the consumer is lent money to spend in whatever way he likes, there is a debtor-creditor (DC) agreement.

The principal difference between the two is that in the case of a DCS agreement, the creditor is responsible for the supplier's misrepresentations and breaches of contract (s. 75). Furthermore, canvassing DC agreements is prohibited off trade premises, whereas canvassing of a DCS agreement is permitted (s. 49).

A connected loan is one made by a person who is also the supplier or by a person who has business connections with the supplier and will normally be for restricted-use credit.

Under the 1974 Act there are three varieties of DCS agreement (s. 12). First, there is a restricted-use credit agreement which falls within s. 11(1)(a) (s. 12(1)(a)). This would include hire purchase, conditional sale and credit sale agreements.

Secondly, a DCS agreement may be a restricted-use credit agreement which falls within s. 11(1)(b) and is made by the creditor under pre-existing arrangements, or in contemplation of future arrangements, between himself and the supplier (s. 12(1)(b)). This will cover a situation in which a supplier refers customers to a specific finance house following arrangements between the creditor and the supplier. Similarly, where a customer uses an Access or Visa card to make a purchase, the credit transaction between the customer and the bank will fall within s. 12(1)(b) because arrangements will have been made between the creditor and the supplier.

A third form of DCS agreement can be found where there is an unrestricted-use credit agreement made by the creditor under pre-existing arrangements between himself and an independent supplier in the knowledge that the credit is to be used to finance an agreement between the debtor and the supplier (s. 12(1)c)). This appears to cover the situation in which a creditor makes a cash advance to a debtor who has been referred to the creditor by an identified supplier with whom the creditor has pre-existing arrangements.

A DC agreement is defined in s. 13 and can take one of three forms. First, it may consist of a restricted-use credit agreement under s. 11(1)(b) which is not made under pre-existing arrangements nor in contemplation of future arrangements (s. 13(a)). This would cover a situation in which the debtor obtains goods or services from a supplier who has no connection with the creditor and the creditor is approached directly by the debtor to provide finance which is tied to the purchase of those goods or services.

Secondly, it may be a restricted-use credit agreement made under s. 11(1)(c) (s. 13(b)), for example where one creditor lends money which is tied to repaying debts owed by the debtor to another creditor.

Thirdly, there is a DC agreement where there is an unrestricted-use credit agreement not made under pre-existing arrangements (s. 13(c)). For the most part, this will cover personal loans made to the debtor, provided he is left free to use the finance facility in whatever way he pleases (see sch. 2, examples 8, 16, 17, 21).

11.1.2.4.1 Pre-existing arrangements It is important to identify what will be regarded as pre-existing arrangements so as to be able to recognise a DCS agreement. By virtue of s. 187(1) and (4) pre-existing arrangements are those previously made between the creditor and the supplier (or their associates). These will include an arrangement between a retailer and banks offering Access or Visa facilities whereby the retailer will accept the use of these credit cards in his shop (see sch. 2, example 21) and an arrangement whereby a supplier is paid a commission for introducing customers to a finance company (see sch. 2, example 8).

Where the creditor is an associate of the supplier, for example, where the creditor and supplier are part of the same group of companies, there is a presumption that there are pre-existing arrangements between the two companies unless the contrary can be proved by the creditor (s. 187(5)).

For the purposes of s. 12, the mere fact that there is or will be an arrangement for the making of payments to suppliers by the creditor is not to be treated as a pre-existing or future arrangement (s. 187(3)). Thus an arrangement entered into by a bank to honour cheque payments supported by a cheque guarantee card will not, of itself, constitute a pre-existing or a future arrangement.

11.1.2.4.2 Future arrangements Future arrangements are those which the creditor expects to make with the supplier (or their associates) (s. 187(2)). For these purposes, it would appear that there need only be an expectation of arrangements. Thus if a creditor issues a credit card to a customer and the supplier only agrees to honour such cards after they have been issued, there is an expectation of future arrangements when the supplier and the creditor reach their agreement.

At first sight, these provisions might lead to the conclusion that an arrangement between a high street supermarket and a bank in respect of electronic transfer of funds from a current account is one made in contemplation of future arrangements. However, it is clear from an amendment to the 1974 Act made by the Banking Act 1986 that this is not the case (s. 187(3A)).

11.1.2.5 Linked transactions It is not just the credit agreement which is affected by the provisions of the 1974 Act: linked or related transactions are also governed (s. 19). Thus a contract of supply associated with the credit agreement or an insurance contract which the lender requires the debtor to enter into so as to protect the goods subject to the credit agreement are subject to some of the provisions of the Act.

11.1.2.5.1 Varieties of linked transaction Contracts for the provision of security are excluded from the definition of a linked transaction (s. 19(1)) and are dealt with under separate provisions of the Act.

A transaction is linked if it is entered into between the debtor (or a relative of his) and another person and the agreement is entered into in compliance with a term of the credit agreement (s. 19(1)(a)). A compulsory requirement in a hire purchase agreement that the debtor should insure the goods bailed would fall within this category. However, the same would not be true of an optional offer of insurance since it is not entered into in compliance with a term of the credit agreement.

If the credit arrangement is a DCS agreement and a further transaction is financed by it, that additional transaction is linked (s. 19(1)(b)). Thus the supply of goods financed by a loan facility made under pre-existing arrangements between the creditor and the supplier will be linked. Similarly, a contract to provide travel facilities where a flight is paid for by Access or Visa would be linked under s. 19(1)(b). However, the same is not true of the supply element in a hire purchase contract since the supply forms part of the regulated agreement and is excluded from the definition of a linked transaction in s. 19(1).

If the agreement has been entered into to induce the creditor to enter into the principal agreement, it is linked (s. 19(1)(c)(i)). Thus if the consumer takes out life assurance in order to persuade the creditor to make a loan facility available, the assurance policy will be a linked transaction. Similar treatment is accorded to an agreement which is entered into for some other purpose relevant to the principal agreement (s. 19(1)(c)(ii)). For example, where credit is provided by a skiing tour operator and, at the operator's suggestion, the debtor takes out accident insurance, the insurance contract is linked. Where the principal agreement is a DCS agreement, and a further contract is made for a purpose related to a transaction financed by that agreement, that additional transaction is linked (s. 19(1)(c)(iii)). This would appear to cover a maintenance contract entered into with the supplier of electrical equipment which has been supplied on credit provided by a creditor who has made pre-existing arrangements with the supplier.

In all of the cases covered by s. 19(1)(c), it is a requirement that a person associated with the creditor or someone who is, at least, aware that the principal agreement may be entered into (s. 19(2)) has suggested entry into the linked transaction.

11.1.2.5.2 Effect of treating a transaction as linked Where a transaction is linked, charges paid under it are treated as part of the total charge for credit (s. 20(2)), a linked transaction has no effect until the principal agreement has been concluded (s. 19(3)) and if the debtor withdraws from or cancels the principal agreement, the linked transaction is also terminated (ss. 57(1) and 69(1)). Any sums paid under a linked transaction will also be taken into account in computing the appropriate rebate to be granted to the debtor on early settlement (s. 95(1)).

11.2 TRUTH IN LENDING

11.2.1 Pre-contract disclosure

One purpose of the Consumer Credit Act 1974 is to ensure that the debtor is given sufficient information regarding the proposed transaction, before it becomes binding. A creditor is required to give adequate information to the debtor in advertisements (s. 44) and quotations (s. 52) to allow him to be aware of the commitment he might be taking on. Adverse consequences for the contract follow if the creditor fails to provide the necessary information.

Regulations (SI 1983/1553) pursuant to s. 55(1) require the document containing the terms of the agreement to be signed, legible and to provide financial information, including the annual percentage rate of charge (APR), the required deposit, the amount of credit provided, a comparison of the cash price and the credit price, the total charge for credit and the total amount payable.

Failure to comply with these requirements renders the agreement improperly executed (s. 55(2)) with the result that the agreement is unenforceable against the debtor in the absence of a court order (s. 65). The Act gives no definition of the word 'unenforceable', but for the purposes of the legislation on hire purchase it has been held that it means that the debtor may enjoy possession of the property without having to pay for it (*Eastern Distributors Ltd* v *Goldring* [1957] 2 QB 600).

Under s. 60(1) regulations may be made regarding the form and content of agreements (see SI 1983/1553). The Act also requires the debtor to be supplied with copies of the unexecuted and the executed agreement and with notice of cancellation rights (ss. 62 and 64). Failure to comply with these requirements in respect of copies and cancellation notices renders the agreement improperly executed (ss. 62(3) and 64(5)) with the result that it can only be enforced by the creditor if he obtains a court order.

If the relevant document is posted to the debtor, a copy of the agreement must be sent at the same time along with any other document referred to in it, for example, an insurance contract or a legal charge.

If the unexecuted agreement is presented to the debtor personally for his signature and at that stage, the agreement becomes executed, he must be given a copy of the executed agreement immediately (s. 63(1)). This will probably be an unlikely occurrence as the agreement will normally be sent to the creditor for signature, in which case the agreement remains unexecuted until signature on behalf of the creditor. In normal cases, s. 63(2) provides that a copy of the executed agreement must be sent to the debtor within seven days of the making of the agreement. If the agreement is subject to the cancellation provisions of the Act, s. 63(3) provides that a copy of the executed agreement must be sent by post. Since the sending of the copy constitutes acceptance, the postal acceptance is subject to contractual rules on this method of acceptance.

Before the agreement can be said to be properly executed, it must be contained in a document which embodies the terms of the contract in legible form and is signed by both the debtor, in person, and the creditor, or someone acting on his behalf (s. 61(1)). It is also essential that all blank spaces on the standard form are filled in. It is not sufficient that the debtor signs the contract, leaving the details to be filled in by the dealer at a later stage. If the debtor does sign a blank form, which is filled in by the supplier at a later stage, and no copy is given to the debtor at the time of signature, there is a failure to comply with s. 61(1), with the result that the court may use its discretion to decline to enforce the agreement against the debtor in the event of an attempt to cancel (see *PB Leasing Ltd* v *Patel & Patel* [1995] CCLR 82). Moreover, in such a case, there is no agreement as to the essential terms of the contract such as the price of the goods supplied (*Campbell Discount Co. Ltd* v *Gall* [1961] 1 QB 431).

The court has a discretion whether or not to enforce an improperly executed agreement against a debtor by virtue of s. 65. If there is likely to be extreme prejudice to the debtor if the agreement is enforced in the face of a serious breach of the supply of information requirements of the 1974 Act, it is highly likely that the court will decline to grant an enforcement order. Thus if the debtor is not told that the agreement he has entered into will require substantial accelerated payments in the event of default, it is possible that the court may substantially reduce the amount the creditor is entitled to recover under the agreement because of the lack of disclosure (see *Rank Xerox* v *Hepple* [1994] CCLR 1). However, if there is no evidence that the debtor's position would have changed had there been full disclosure, an enforcement order is likely to be made (*Nissan Finance UK* v *Lockhart* [1993] CCLR 39).

11.2.2 Disclosure of information during the currency of the agreement

A key feature of the 1974 Act is that the debtor is entitled to be kept aware of the state of his indebtedness. If the debtor under a fixed-sum credit agreement makes a request in writing concerning the amount he owes, the creditor must respond within 12 days of the request by providing the debtor with a statement of the total amount he has paid under the agreement and the amount which remains to be paid or will become due (s. 77(1)). It is in the interests of the creditor to ensure that the information he gives is correct, since the statement is binding on him (s. 172(1)).

In the case of a running-account credit agreement, there is a similar provision, except that the type of information which the creditor must supply differs. Section 78(1) provides that the debtor must be informed, within 12 days of his written request of the state of the account, of the amount presently payable and amounts which will become payable and the dates on which they are to be paid. In addition to the required response to a written request from the debtor, the creditor is also required to provide periodic statements of account under a running-account credit agreement whether these have been requested or not (s. 78(4)). These statements should be sent out at least once every 12 months.

11.3 WITHDRAWAL AND CANCELLATION

11.3.1 Withdrawal

Under the Consumer Credit Act 1974 the debtor is permitted to withdraw from a prospective agreement. The provisions of s. 57 are in addition to the common law rule which allows a person to revoke an offer before acceptance.

Section 57 operates only in favour of the debtor and allows notice of withdrawal to be given to persons other than the offeree. The notice of withdrawal extends to linked transactions. In the event of withdrawal, the parties should be returned to their prior position.

11.3.2 Cancellation

In addition to the right of withdrawal from a prospective agreement, and the limited power to cancel contracts concluded away from business premises under the Consumer Protection (Cancellation of Contracts Concluded away from Business Premises) Regulations 1987 (SI 1987/2117), the debtor may also cancel certain concluded credit agreements under the provisions of s. 67 of the Consumer Credit Act 1974. The right under the 1974 Act will depend on where the contract is made. There is a degree of overlap between the provisions of the Act and the 1987 Regulations, since the latter do not exclude the possibility that both rights may arise simultaneously. However, as a matter of practice, if the rights conferred by the 1974 Act operate, there will be no need to apply the 1987 Regulations.

11.3.2.1 Cancellable agreements
A cancellable agreement is one made off trade premises (s. 67(b)) as a result of oral representations made to the

debtor (or a relative) in the course of antecedent negotiations. The representations may be made by the creditor, any party to a linked transaction or the
negotiator in the antecedent negotiations. The general effect of this provision
is to strike at unsolicited 'door-to-door' selling, which may involve remarks
made to a consumer in his or her own home.

The withdrawal and cancellation provisions of the Act and the requirements in respect of copies of the agreement do not apply to non-commercial
agreements, small agreements, most agreements for the provision of a current
account and agreements providing for payments to be made on death (s. 74).

It is important for the purposes of the cancellation provisions that there
have been antecedent negotiations which include oral representations. These
representations must have been made in the presence of the debtor or a
relative of his, although not necessarily to him. For example, antecedent
negotiations could consist of passing remarks made by a salesman to someone
other than the debtor which the debtor overhears. However, because of the
requirement that the representations should be made in the presence of the
debtor, mailshot and telephone representations will not fall within the
cancellation provisions of the Act.

The definition of the phrase 'oral representations' in s. 189 is very wide and
on a literal interpretation of that definition it might be possible to regard as
oral representations, any statement made in the course of the antecedent
negotiations leading up to the making of the contract. However, in *Moorgate
Services Ltd* v *Kabir* (1995) *The Times*, 25 April 1995, Staughton LJ held that
it is necessary for the statement to be material in the sense that it should relate
to a matter of fact or opinion or an undertaking about the future, which is
capable of inducing the borrower to enter into the agreement. However, there
is no need for it to be shown that the statement did, in fact, induce the debtor
to make the contract, nor need the maker of the statement intend it to operate
as an inducement. Statements which might satisfy this test were thought to
include an indication of the suitability of goods for their intended use or a
statement concerning the amount of credit proposed, but a simple statement
to the effect that the negotiator would have to contact the creditor to obtain
further financial details could not be regarded as material.

Antecedent negotiations are defined in s. 56, but it is possible for these
negotiations to commence before the creditor is aware of the debtor's
identity, since s. 56(4) provides that negotiations can include communication
by means of an advertisement, although there must also be an oral representation.

The debtor may give notice of cancellation to the creditor or his agent or
any person specified in the notice of cancellation rights (s. 69(1) and (6)).

Cancellation is permitted during the cooling-off period specified in s. 68.
The debtor has five days in which to exercise his right and the relevant period
runs from the day after the second copy of the agreement or notice of
cancellation has been received (s. 68(a)).

Alternatively, if the creditor is exempt from delivering a separate cancellation notice under s. 64(4), the debtor has a cooling-off period of 14 days from
the date of signing the agreement (s. 68(b)).

11.3.2.2 Effects of cancellation If an agreement is cancelled, it, and any linked transaction (s. 69(1)), is treated as if it had never been entered into (s. 69(4)). It has been held that the effect of s. 69(4) is to render the contract void *ab initio* rather than voidable until the date of cancellation (*Colesworthy* v *Collman Services Ltd* [1993] CCLR 4). Thus payments made by the debtor can be recovered and goods delivered to the debtor must be redelivered. The debtor's right of cancellation is only lost if he fails to deliver the required cancellation notice within the period specified in s. 68.

Since the effect of cancellation is that not just the principal agreement is void, but also any linked transaction, any additional contract which falls within the latter category is also terminated. Thus in *Global Marketing Europe* v *Berkshire County Council* (1994) *Consumer Law Today*, December 1994 a credit agreement was entered into in order to finance a timeshare agreement. Because the credit agreement fell within the cancellation provisions of the 1974 Act, it was held that the timeshare agreement was also cancellable, as a linked transaction, whether or not the provisions of the Timeshare Act 1992 also applied to the transactions.

11.3.2.2.1 Money paid by the debtor Any money paid by the debtor as part of the total charge for credit can be recovered (Consumer Credit Act 1974, s. 70(1)(a)). Thus deposits and interest payments made to the creditor are recoverable. Furthermore, the debtor also ceases to be responsible for sums of money due after cancellation (s. 70(1)(b)). The dealer is also required to pay back to the creditor any sum he has received where there is a DCS agreement under s. 12(b).

As a general rule, the debtor's claim for repayment will be made to the person to whom the payment was made (s. 70(3)). Thus if money has been paid to an agent of the creditor, the debtor will be able to recover what has been paid from the agent and leave him to sort out matters with the debtor (see *Colesworthy* v *Collman Services Ltd* [1993] CCLR 4). However, where there is a DCS agreement under s. 12(b), the dealer and the creditor are jointly and severally liable for the amount due (s. 70(3)). Thus the creditor may hold the debtor liable under a purchase-loan agreement arranged by the dealer and where payment has been made to the dealer alone. However, in such cases, the creditor may be entitled to an indemnity against the dealer (s. 70(4)).

11.3.2.2.2 Continuation of unrestricted-use loan agreements After cancellation, an unrestricted-use credit agreement remains in force so far as it relates to the repayment of credit and and the payment of interest (s. 71(1)).

The motive behind this is to prevent a creditor from advancing a cash loan in anticipation of an executed agreement, since by s. 71(2), if the debtor repays the credit, or any part of it, within one month of service of the notice of cancellation, or before the first repayment is due, no interest is payable on the loan. However, if the credit is not repaid in time, the terms of the agreement remain in force and by virtue of s. 71(3) the interest then payable is calculated by reference to the terms of the cancelled agreement.

11.3.2.2.3 Return of goods by the debtor The general effect of the cancellation provisions of the 1974 Act is that the parties should be returned to their position before entering the contract. Thus, goods in the possession of the debtor are returnable (s. 72).

Under s. 72(3) the debtor is under a duty to retain possession of the goods during the cancellation period and to take reasonable care of them during that period. The duty only applies to a restricted-use DCS agreement and to a transaction linked to such an agreement (s. 72(1)). Thus the duty to return does not apply to an unrestricted-use credit agreement, or to a debtor-creditor agreement since the supply of goods in such cases is independent of the credit agreement.

While the duty to return the goods implies that they should be returned to the creditor, in fact it is sufficient that the debtor makes the goods available for recollection at his own premises (s. 72(5)). Furthermore, the notice of cancellation can be sent to anyone specified in the cancellation notice, with the result that return to the supplier will suffice (s. 72(6)).

When return is effected, the debtor's duty to take care of the goods comes to an end (s. 72(7)). However, if the debtor refuses to surrender the goods after receipt of a reasonable request, he exposes himself to an action for damages for breach of statutory duty (s. 72(11)). If the debtor receives a notice requiring him to redeliver the goods within 21 days of cancellation, and he refuses to comply, the duty of care which rests on him continues until actual redelivery (s. 72(8)). Conversely, if no such notice is received, the debtor's duty to take care of the goods in his possession terminates 21 days after the notice of cancellation was received by an authorised person.

Certain types of agreement are exempt from the provisions of s. 72, namely those which relate to perishable goods, goods which are consumed by use and have been consumed before cancellation, goods supplied to meet an emergency and goods which have been incorporated in land (s. 72(9)).

11.3.2.2.4 Return of goods given in part exchange Goods given in part exchange by the debtor are returnable (s. 73). Under s. 73(2), unless part-exchange goods are returned to the debtor within 10 days of cancellation, the debtor is entitled to a cash equivalent of the cost of those goods.

11.4 CONTINUANCE OF THE AGREEMENT

11.4.1 Terms of the contract
During the currency of the agreement, the debtor may have cause to complain that the goods supplied are defective. In this event, the debtor's remedies will be based on the express terms of the contract or the implied terms arising out of the provisions of the Sale of Goods Act 1979, the Supply of Goods (Implied Terms) Act 1973 or the Supply of Goods and Services Act 1982 (see chapter 6).

11.4.2 Creditor's liability for the acts of the supplier

11.4.2.1 Effect of the form of credit provision The person against whom the debtor should proceed when he has a complaint concerning the

goods supplied will depend on the type of credit made available to him. In some instances, the supplier will have provided the credit himself ('vendor credit') in the form of a conditional or credit sale agreement, or there might be separate contracts of sale and loan. In these circumstances, the lender and the supplier are the same person and the consumer will be able to proceed against him as a seller in respect of the quality of the thing supplied.

In other instances the credit will be provided by a person other than the physical supplier of the goods. One way in which this can be done is through the medium of 'lender credit' or 'sales financing', under which the supplier enters into a contract of sale with the consumer and the creditor lends the consumer the money to make that purchase. In these circumstances, the consumer would have his normal sale of goods remedies against the supplier, and the loan agreement would be subject to the requirements of the 1974 Act. In the past, such arrangements were unpopular since they fell within the restrictive provisions of the Moneylenders Acts 1900 to 1927, but these Acts have now been repealed and it may be that the number of lender credit arrangements will increase.

Because of the difficulties encountered under the Moneylenders Acts, the more familiar type of credit arrangement has involved a system of 'direct financing'. In the typical hire purchase contract, the dealer sells the goods to the creditor for their cash price, less the amount of any deposit paid to the dealer. The creditor then enters into an instalment contract with the consumer debtor. In these circumstances the creditor is not engaged in a business which has as its primary object the lending of money (Moneylenders Act 1900, s. 6) and thereby avoided the provisions of the Moneylenders Acts. The effect of such an arrangement is that the creditor also becomes the legal supplier of the goods subject to the instalment contract and is primarily responsible for the quality of the goods supplied. It is also the case that no contract exists between the dealer and the consumer. However, it is possible that a collateral contract may be found to exist (*Brown* v *Sheen & Richmond Car Sales* [1950] 1 All ER 1102; *Andrews* v *Hopkinson* [1957] 1 QB 229).

A number of problems arose due to the fact that there was no contract between the dealer and the consumer. In particular, the deposit was paid to the dealer, but the contract was made with the creditor and it became necessary to decide if the dealer was an agent for one or other of the parties to the instalment contract.

11.4.2.2 The dealer as an agent

11.4.2.2.1 Position at common law The normal common law rule is that a person is only liable for his own breaches of contract. Thus it follows that the creditor should not be made responsible for the acts or omissions of the dealer who supplies the goods subject to the credit agreement, unless the dealer is the creditor's agent.

At common law, there was a divergence of opinion on this issue. On one view, the dealer is not an agent for the finance company where he receives a deposit paid by the consumer. In such a case, he is a party in his own right,

acting primarily on his own behalf (*Mercantile Credit Ltd* v *Hamblin* [1965] 2 QB
242, 388 per Pearson LJ, adopted by the House of Lords in *Branwhite* v
Worcester Works Finance Ltd [1969] 1 AC 552). In *Branwhite* v *Worcester Works
Finance Ltd* the appellant arranged to purchase a car under a hire purchase
contract with the respondents. A dealer took the plaintiff's car (valued at £130)
in part exchange. Subsequently, the respondents refused to proceed with the
contract on the ground that there were irregularities in the way in which the
forms had been completed. The appellant argued that the dealer was an agent
for the respondents and held the £130 deposit on their behalf, thereby
rendering the contract complete. However, the House of Lords held that while a
dealer may be an agent for the creditor if he has been held out as such, the dealer
is normally a contracting party in his own right who is acting in his own interests
when he sells goods to the creditor (ibid. 573 per Lord Morris of Borth-y-Gest).

It would appear that the mere fact that a dealer holds stocks of a finance
company's standard forms will not be sufficient to give rise to an agency
relationship (see *J. D. Williams & Co.* v *McCauley, Parsons & Jones* [1994]
CCLR 78). The finance company can put the matter beyond doubt by
stipulating in the hire purchase contract that the dealer has no authority to
commit the finance company in any respect. If the finance company expressly
takes steps to notify the consumer of this, there is unlikely to be any apparent
or ostensible authority to bind the creditor on the part of the dealer
(*Overbrooke Estates Ltd* v *Glencombe Properties Ltd* [1974] 3 All ER 511).

There may be circumstances in which the dealer is authorised to deal as an
intermediary. For example, in the absence of any indication to the contrary,
the dealer may have an ostensible authority to receive communication of the
revocation of an offer on behalf of the finance company (*Financings Ltd* v
Stimson [1962] 3 All ER 386).

11.4.2.2.2 Agency under the Consumer Credit Act 1974 Where the credit
agreement is regulated under the provisions of the 1974 Act the position is
different. The Act refers to the dealer as a negotiator in antecedent negotiations and further provides that an agreement is void if it purports to treat a
negotiator as an agent for the debtor (s. 56(3)(a)). This avoids the problem
which surfaced under the Hire Purchase Act 1965 whereby a clause in the
hire purchase contract deemed the dealer to be the debtor's agent rather than
that of the creditor.

Under the Consumer Credit Act 1974, s. 56(2), a person other than the
creditor who conducts 'antecedent negotiations' leading to the making of a
regulated agreement is deemed to be the agent of the creditor.

According to s. 56(1)(a), antecedent negotiations include any negotiations
with the debtor conducted by the creditor in relation to the making of a
regulated agreement (see sch. 2, examples 1 and 4). This will cover the case
where the negotiations are led by a dealer who finances the transaction
himself under a conditional sale agreement or where an employee of a
moneylender leads the negotiations.

By virtue of s. 56(1)(b) antecedent negotiations also include those conducted by a credit broker in respect of goods sold or proposed to be sold by the

credit broker to the creditor before the goods become the subject of a DCS agreement under s. 12(a) (see sch. 2, examples 2 and 4). Thus if a hire purchase contract is entered into after the consumer debtor has read a poster describing the goods in question and displayed on the dealer's premises, there have been antecedent negotiations, provided there is a business relationship between the dealer and the creditor.

Negotiations conducted by the supplier in relation to a transaction financed or proposed to be financed by a DCS agreement within s. 12(b) or (c) are antecedent negotiations for the purposes of s. 56(1)(c) (see sch. 2, example 3). This would cover a conversation between a shop assistant and the customer concerning the merits and demerits of goods the customer proposes to purchase using an Access or Visa card.

The effect of s. 56 is to treat the negotiator as the creditor's agent, but it is important that statements made in the course of negotiations are related to the credit transaction. In *United Dominions Trust* v *Whitfield* [1986] CLY 375 the defendant traded in a car which was still subject to a hire purchase contract with UDT and wished to acquire a further vehicle on credit. The dealer had promised the defendant that he would pay off UDT using credit provided by a second finance company (FNS). The dealer failed to pay UDT and the defendant elected to pay FNS. Accordingly, he was sued by UDT, who brought in FNS as third parties, claiming that the dealer's promise to pay UDT bound FNS. It was held that the promise was sufficiently related to the purchase of the car to form part of antecedent negotiations. It followed that FNS were required to pay UDT as they were bound by their agent's promise.

The particular purpose of s. 56 is to prevent the debtor from being persuaded by the dealer or other negotiator to enter into a transaction which is not to his benefit. This is particularly so where the antecedent negotiations contain statements which amount to persuasion to enter into an uneconomic deal. For example, in *Woodchester Leasing Equipment* v *Clayton & Clayton* [1994] CLY 500, the defendants were persuaded to enter into a consumer hire agreement relating to a fax machine rather than an outright purchase, which they had originally preferred. The persuasion was done by the supplier of the equipment, who had existing arrangements with the plaintiffs (the finance company). Under that arrangement, the greater the monthly rental negotiated by the supplier with the defendants, the greater was the price paid for the machine by the plaintiffs to the supplier. In the event the price paid to the supplier was in fact £1,751 (plus VAT), whereas the advertised price of the machine at which the defendants would have purchased was as little as £995 (plus VAT). Since the whole tenor of the supplier's persuasion was geared towards the benefits of leasing, he was considered to be the agent of the finance company under the principle in *Branwhite* v *Worcester Works Finance Ltd* [1969] 1 AC 552.

It is interesting that in *Woodchester Leasing Equipment* v *Clayton & Clayton* s. 56 was raised in argument, but not used to justify the decision, since before the statutory agency provisions operate, there must have been representations in respect of the provision of *credit* or other financial accommodation. Since a consumer hire agreement does not involve the provision of credit, it would appear that s. 56 will not allow the consumer to hold the hirer responsible where a dealer makes representations about goods which are the subject of a lease-back arrangement (*Moorgate Mercantile* v *Isobel Gell & Ugolini* [1986] CLY 371).

11.4.2.3   Vicarious liability of the creditor   Under s. 75 the debtor has a remedy against the creditor in respect of the supplier's breaches of contract or misrepresentations, subject to an upper limit of £30,000 and a lower limit of £100, both being based on the value of the transaction (s. 75(3) and SI 1983/1878). It has been recommended that the former of these two figures be reduced to £25,000, provided it is related to the amount of credit advanced rather than the value of the transaction (DTI, *Deregulation of UK Consumer Credit Legislation* (1995), para. 3.6; see also OFT, *Connected Lender Liability* (1995)).

Section 75 overlaps with the statutory agency provisions of s. 56 in so far as both sections cover DCS agreements falling within s. 12(b) and (c). The effect of this is that all consumer hire contracts, debtor-creditor loans are not covered by s. 75. Furthermore, if the agreement falls within s. 12(a), as does a hire purchase contract, s. 56 is the appropriate provision to apply (cf. *Porter* v *General Guarantee Corporation* [1982] RTR 384 — incorrectly decided?). For the relationship between ss. 75 and 56 see Fairest and Rudkin (1978) 128 NLJ 243; Lowe (1981) 97 LQR 532; Dobson [1983] JBL 312; Hill-Smith (1983) 133 NLJ 1012, 1063. For other problems of s. 75 see Dobson [1981] JBL 179; Lowe (1981) 97 LQR 533.

An important effect of s. 75 and s. 56(1)(c) is that they cover the typical three-party credit card agreement, whereby goods are paid for with the use of an Access or Visa card, provided it was entered into after 1 April 1977 (SI 1977/802). However, it appears that the major credit card companies have been resisting liability as far as possible, especially as a lot of consumers pay for their holidays with their credit cards. Their view is that the consumer should first pursue the supplier if he is solvent, then any special fund which might have been set up by, for example, ABTA or some other bonding institution (see chapter 9). In *Connected Lender Liability* (OFT, 1994), the OFT expressed the view that it is highly undesirable that this stance is being taken and hoped that litigation would produce a definitive decision on the position of the major credit card companies. The view expressed in the OFT paper is that s. 75 does apply where, for example, payment is made directly to a travel agent if acting as agent for the tour operator, but consumers booking holidays are probably better advised to make payment directly to the tour operator to remove any doubt that s. 75 operates in their favour so as to render the credit card company liable for any breach of contract or misrepresentation on the part of the supplier (i.e., the tour operator).

A more difficult problem arises where a credit card is used to pay for services or property under a contract which is governed by the law of a foreign country. For example, in *Jarrett* v *Barclays Bank plc* (1996) *The Times*, 18 November 1996 a Barclaycard had been used to pay for a timeshare in a

Portuguese property, but the bank sought to rely on the argument that s. 75 had no application to contracts not subject to English law, on the basis that English courts had no jurisdiction over claims in respect of a tenancy over property situated in a foreign State, by virtue of the Brussels Convention, art. 16 (Civil Jurisdiction and Judgments Act 1992, sch. 1). Although the bank's argument was accepted by the county court, the Court of Appeal reversed that decision, holding that the object of the proceedings in the present case was not the tenancy, but the DCS agreement which financed the arrangement. Accordingly, the consumer's action was allowed to proceed.

The effect of s. 75 is to give the debtor a 'like claim' against the creditor. Thus any action he would have had against the supplier for damages for breach of contract or misrepresentation may be asserted against the creditor.

A broad interpretation of s. 75 would extend this right to rescission of the contract, and such an interpretation was given to s. 75 in *United Dominions Trust Ltd* v *Taylor* 1980 SLT 28 (cf. Davidson (1980) 96 LQR 343). Conversely, it can be argued that the word 'claim' suggests a claim for money.

Section 75 also refers to 'a like claim in relation to' the supply agreement, thus the claim must refer to the supply agreement and not to the credit agreement.

Where the creditor is liable to the debtor under s. 75(1), he has a right of recourse against the supplier in respect of his breach, with the result that the creditor can claim an indemnity against the supplier (s. 75(2)). In this respect, the creditor can make the supplier a party to any proceedings which may be brought against him by the debtor. However, there always remains the danger that the supplier is insolvent, in which case, the creditor will have to accept full responsibility for the supplier's misrepresentation or breach of contract.

11.4.3 Variation of the agreement

The ability to vary the terms of an agreement may be conferred in one of two ways. There may be an express term of the contract which permits this, most commonly found in long-term arangements such as running-account credit agreements, under which the creditor will wish to alter the rate of interest applied to the debtor's account in the light of changes in the prevailing base rate of interest. In such a case, the variation will not take effect until a notice in the prescribed form has been delivered to the debtor (s. 82(1) and SI 1977/328 (as amended by SI 1979/661 and 667)). Alternatively, the right to vary may arise from a subsequent agreement between the parties, for example, where the debtor has experienced difficulty in keeping up repayments and asks for his debt to be rescheduled over a longer period.

In some instances, the original agreement will leave the matter of variation to the absolute discretion of the creditor. In such a case, the creditor can unilaterally modify the rate of interest under the agreement, although he should not use this power in a capricious manner so as to treat old customers less favourably than potential customers (*Lombard Tricity Finance Ltd* v *Paton* [1989] 1 All ER 918).

11.5 TERMINATION OF THE CONTRACT BY THE DEBTOR

11.5.1 Early settlement of the debt

The debtor is not obliged to wait for the agreement to run its course. He has an inalienable right to demand early settlement under the Consumer Credit Act 1974, s. 94, at any time. Any attempt to exclude this right is void under s. 173(1). Where there is an early settlement, the principal agreement and linked transactions are discharged (s. 96(1)), except where the linked transaction itself provides credit (s. 96(2)).

To facilitate early settlement, the debtor is entitled to be provided with settlement information, including a statement of the total amount repayable and any rebate due on early settlement. The amount of the rebate is calculated according to the provisions of the Consumer Credit (Rebate on Early Settlement) Regulations (SI 1983/1562). Should the creditor give an incorrect indication of the amount payable on early settlement, which is in the consumer's favour, the creditor will be subsequently estopped from claiming the correct amount, provided there is evidence to show that the debtor has altered his position in reliance on the incorrect forecast (*Lombard North Central* v *Stobart* [1990] CCLR 53).

The mathematical formula used to calculate the rebate on early settlement is a matter which has given rise to substantial consumer complaint, since it is possible under the present formula for the cost of settling early to be higher than the cost of leaving the agreement to run its course. To meet this criticism, it has been suggested that a more equitable formula should be used, based on what is known as 'actual reducing balance' together with a fixed fee to cover administrative costs, so as to make the whole process more transparent and so that consumers may be made aware from the outset, what costs will be involved if they decide on early settlement (see DTI, *Deregulation of UK Consumer Credit Legislation* (1995), chapter 5).

Problems may arise where the creditor brings proceedings for default and ordering payment of the full amount might give the creditor an advantage because the rebate on early settlement would have been ignored. But if the full rebate at the date of judgment is given, the creditor might lose out if payment of the judgment debt is deferred. One view is that judgment for the full debt should be given, subject to a deduction in respect of the applicable rebate at the time of judgment (*Forward Trust* v *Robinson* [1987] BTLC 12, county court). However, a different view has been taken in *Forward Trust Ltd* v *Whymark* [1990] 2 QB 670, in which it was held that judgment should be made for the full amount without deduction if the case is heard in the county court, since the rebate represents future interest on the loan. However, if the case is heard in the High Court, judgments in that court bear interest and the early settlement rebate can be deducted.

A further complication is that the date for assessing the rebate under the Regulations is the date of payment by the debtor. If, at the date of judgment, the full amount was still outstanding, judgment would be entered for the full amount. However, when the debtor does pay, he may pay the amount ordered, less any rebate due to him at the time payment is tendered.

In principle a judgment debt of £100 can only be satisfied by the payment of £100 (*Foakes* v *Beer* (1884) 9 App Cas 605; *Re Selectmove Ltd* [1995] 2 All ER 531), but it appears that the rebate regulations are an exception to this rule following the decision in *Forward Trust Ltd* v *Whymark*.

11.5.2 Termination of hire purchase agreements

Special provision is made for voluntary termination of the hire purchase agreements. Under s. 99(1), the debtor may give written notice terminating the contract at any time before full performance. Notice may be given to anyone entitled to receive payments under the agreement (effectively the creditor or the dealer). For the reasons considered below, termination of the contract is not in the debtor's interest, as he will be subject to liabilities and will lose possession of the goods subject to the agreement.

11.5.2.1 Events constituting termination

11.5.2.1.1 Mutual agreement A contract can be terminated by mutual agreement between the parties. Ordinarily, this agreement will be followed by the substitution of a new agreement, for example, one which allows the debtor to spread payments over a longer period than that allowed by the earlier agreement. Where a later agreement modifies or varies an earlier arrangement between the parties, the 1974 Act provides that the earlier agreement is to be treated as revoked and the new agreement is deemed to contain provisions reproducing the combined effect of both agreements (s. 82(2)).

11.5.2.1.2 Exercise of a power to terminate An agreement will often provide for voluntary termination of the contract on the part of the debtor. However, the contract may also stipulate that the debtor is required to make some payment in addition to outstanding instalments. Such a stipulation is known as a minimum payment clause and may give rise to problems concerning the doctrine of penalties where it operates in the event of the debtor's breach of contract (see below).

If the contract allows the debtor to terminate, his exercise of that right is not a breach of contract, but the minimum payment clause may require him to make what appears be an excessive payment. The justification for such provisions is that they protect the creditor's investment by ensuring that he gets a minimum return from the contract. If the agreement is not regulated under the 1974 Act, common law rules will apply and the minimum payment clause will be treated as an agreement to pay the amount stipulated in return for the right to terminate at an early date (*Associated Distributors Ltd* v *Hall* [1938] 2 KB 83). This may not always be a satisfactory solution, since the amount required of the debtor may be excessive, in which case the court may be inclined to place a strained construction on the conduct of the debtor by regarding it as a breach of contract, thereby bringing the common law doctrine of penalties into play (*Bridge* v *Campbell Discount Ltd* [1962] AC 600). In particular, the court is not likely to hold that the debtor has voluntarily terminated the contract unless he is fully aware of the consequences of his actions (*United Dominions Trust Ltd* v *Ennis* [1968] 1 QB 54).

Where the agreement is regulated under the 1974 Act, the provisions of ss. 99 and 100, considered below, apply with the result that a term of the contract will only be enforceable if it provides for a payment of less than that stipulated under the Act or for no payment at all (ss. 100(1) and 173).

11.5.2.1.3 Debtor's breach of contract A particularly serious breach of contract on the part of the debtor may give rise to a right on the part of the creditor to terminate the contract. This matter is considered in more detail below.

11.5.2.2 Effects of termination In the event of the termination of a hire purchase contract, title to the goods remains vested in the creditor. Furthermore, the debtor must discharge all outstanding liabilities (s. 99(2)). Any sums already due under the agreement will remain payable and the creditor will be able to sue for damages in respect of breaches of contract on the part of the debtor prior to termination.

The rights of termination and cancellation coexist for a brief period at the commencement of a hire purchase agreement. Because of s. 99(2), it is better for the debtor to cancel rather than terminate, if he has the option, since s. 69(4) provides that the agreement is treated as if it had never been entered into and the debtor will be able to recover all payments made by him.

Where the debtor terminates the agreement, the goods must be returned to the creditor. He may also be liable to pay sums of money in accordance with the provisions of s. 100 (see below).

11.5.3 Termination of credit sale and conditional sale agreements
In the case of a credit sale agreement, ownership of the goods passes to the debtor when the contract is made, but liability to pay for the goods is staggered. Thus, the buyer will be the owner of the goods before he has fully paid for them. If the debtor defaults, the creditor or seller, where the agreement is regulated, will be able to sue for the amount still outstanding, subject to the requirements of the 1974 Act in relation to default.

Since the debtor under a credit sale agreement is the owner of the goods from the outset, there is no right on the part of the creditor to recover possession of the goods subject to the agreement. Furthermore, the matter of 'protected goods' considered below is irrelevant for the purposes of credit sale agreements for the same reason. Where there is a conditional sale agreement the date on which property passes to the debtor may be deferred until payment of the price, but the contract is still one of sale in that the debtor has committed himself to purchase the goods subject to the agreement. In these circumstances, a disposition to a third party will pass a good title, which will ordinarily prevent the creditor from recovering the goods. Where the debtor is in breach of contract, becomes bankrupt or dies, the contract may provide for recovery of the goods by the creditor. In such a case, the term of the contract will be enforceable subject to the operation of the common law rules on damages and penalties.

At common law there is no general right to terminate a conditional sale agreement, but s. 99(1) gives a statutory right of termination to the debtor under a regulated conditional sale agreement. The consequences of termination are generally the same as those which apply to hire purchase contracts considered above, but special provisions apply so as to prevent the debtor from terminating a conditional sale agreement where there has been a valid disposition of the goods to a third party (s. 99(4)).

Under s. 99(5), goods revest in the 'previous owner' (or his successor in title or trustee in bankruptcy) where the debtor terminates a regulated conditional sale agreement and property in the goods has already passed to him. Thus the creditor will become, once more, the owner of the goods.

11.6   ENFORCEMENT OF THE CONTRACT BY THE CREDITOR

There is always the danger that for a number of reasons, a consumer debtor cannot keep up payments under an instalment credit agreement, and the creditor may have provided for such an event in the contract. Some of these provisions may be designed to protect the creditor's investment by ensuring that he receives a specified amount or is paid in full at an earlier date than originally agreed. For example, it is common to find minimum payment clauses in hire purchase contracts under which the creditor claims to be entitled to a minimum amount in the event of the debtor's breach of contract. In conditional sale and credit sale agreements, a commonly found term is an accelerated payment clause under which the debtor may be required to pay the balance of any remaining indebtedness in the event of default or some other specified occurrence.

The use of such provisions in instalment credit contracts is understandable since creditors view the goods subject to the contract as security for the credit which has been made available. Where minimum payment clauses are concerned, the sort of goods normally subject to credit arrangements are of a type that rapidly depreciate in value. The creditor will want to pass on the cost of this depreciation to the consumer, since he has had the benefit of the use of the goods. Furthermore, where the debtor's default results in repossession of the goods supplied, the creditor is left with a second-hand article on his hands which he will find more difficult to dispose of than an article which is brand new.

Where the creditor relies on a minimum payment clause or an accelerated payment clause, it is important that its effect is not to entitle the creditor to more than he would have received had the agreement gone its full course. In particular, accelerated payment clauses should provide for a rebate to the consumer since the debt is being paid off at an earlier date than would otherwise have been the case. Similarly, a minimum payment clause must not amount to a penalty, intended to punish the consumer for his breach of contract — to be valid, it must be a genuine estimate of the loss likely to flow from the debtor's breach of contract.

11.6.1   Procedure on default where the agreement is regulated
Where the debtor is in breach of a regulated agreement, the creditor may wish to pursue one of a number of avenues. He may wish to sue for debt in respect

of instalments due but not paid; he may wish to recover damages in respect of specific losses suffered as a result of the debtor's breach; he may wish to treat his own obligations of performance as terminated where there is a serious breach of contract; he may wish to repossess goods in the debtor's possession, or he may wish to demand early payment of a sum of money, for example, under the provisions of an accelerated payment clause.

Where, in the event of the debtor's default, the creditor seeks to take a course of action which would involve the debtor in doing more than just honour the agreement, the debtor must be served with a default notice (s. 87(1)). Thus, such a notice must be served where the creditor wishes to terminate the agreement, demand early payment, recover possession of goods, terminate or restrict a right of the debtor or enforce any security, since all of these courses of action can be viewed as a kind of threat designed to induce the debtor to honour the agreement.

Where the debtor's breach of contract consists of overdrawing on credit facilities made available to him, the creditor may immediately restrict the availability of further credit facilities. Such action is not subject to the requirement of service of a default notice (s. 87(2)). Thus, if the consumer exceeds the credit limit stipulated under his agreement with Access or Visa, steps may be taken by the creditor to prevent any further overrun on the credit facility.

The Act stipulates in s. 88(1) the required form of a default notice. It must identify the nature of the debtor's breach, state what action is necessary to remedy the breach and the time by which this must be done. Thus if the debtor has failed to pay a number of instalments or has broken a covenant to keep the goods maintained in a satisfactory state of repair, the default notice should specify what should be done to remedy the breach.

If the breach is not capable of remedy, the default notice must specify the sum of money required to be paid by the debtor and the date by which it should be paid. For example, if the debtor has sold goods subject to a credit sale or conditional sale agreement and has thereby conferred a good title on the third party, the default notice will have to specify the amount required from the debtor to pay for the goods in question.

There must also be a statement of the consequences for the debtor if he fails to comply with the default notice (s. 88(4)). For example, the creditor must state that he proposes to repossess the goods and terminate the agreement in the event of the default not being remedied by the debtor.

If the debtor complies with the requirements of the default notice by remedying the breach or by paying the amount specified in the default notice, the breach is to be treated as if it had never occurred (s. 89).

Special provision is made for the situation in which breach of one term of the contract brings into force another term. An example of this arises in the case of an accelerated payment clause, which requires the debtor to pay the full outstanding debt due under the agreement if he has failed to pay one or more instalments due to the creditor. The Act provides that failure to comply with the second term is not to be treated automatically as a breach of contract for the purposes of the default notice (s. 88(3)). Instead, if the first breach (non-payment of the instalment) is not remedied within seven days of service of the default notice, only then can the failure to comply with the second term (non-payment of the outstanding balance) be treated as a breach of contract. If this stage is reached, the creditor must serve a second default notice and start the default procedure once more.

11.6.2   Enforcement of regulated agreements in the absence of default

11.6.2.1   Enforcement of the agreement on death   Where the debtor dies, his rights and liabilities will pass to his personal representatives, with the result that the creditor could serve a default notice in the event of non-payment. However, it is normal practice for the credit agreement to contain a term to the effect that the death of the debtor will terminate the agreement or that on death any outstanding balance shall become due.

Where the agreement is regulated, the 1974 Act provides that the creditor cannot claim to be entitled to do any of the acts which trigger the default procedure in the event of the debtor's death if the agreement is fully secured (s. 86(1)). In the case of an unsecured or partially secured agreement, which is for a period specified in the contract, which has not yet expired (s. 86(3)), the creditor may do one of the acts listed in s. 87(1) if he seeks a court order (s. 86(2)). It follows that the requirement of seeking a court order does not extend to an agreement of unlimited duration, with the result that such credit agreements can be enforced at any time after the death of the debtor.

11.6.2.2   Non-default enforcement   In certain circumstances, the creditor may wish to enforce a term of the contract at a time when the debtor is not in breach of contract. For example, the contract may provide that the creditor is entitled to immediate payment of any outstanding balance or that he may repossess the goods subject to the agreement in the event of the debtor's bankruptcy. Similar provisions may also apply where the debtor changes his address, becomes unemployed or is convicted of an offence of dishonesty. In these circumstances, there may be a risk to the creditor, but there is no default on the part of the debtor.

To deal with enforcement in the absence of default, ss. 76 and 98 of the 1974 Act provide for a procedure similar to that which applies to enforcement in the event of default (see ss. 87 and 88), although these provisions only apply to agreements of specific duration (ss. 76(2) and 98(2)). It follows that if a bank overdraft agreement allows the bank to demand immediate payment, s. 76 will have no application. Section 76(1) requires the creditor to serve notice on the debtor if he proposes to demand early payment of any sum, recover possession of the goods or treat any right of the debtor's as restricted. If the creditor proposes to terminate the agreement, he must give the debtor at least seven days' notice of his intention (s. 98(1)).

11.6.3   Judicial powers in enforcement proceedings

11.6.3.1   Enforcement orders   Where the creditor applies for an enforcement order, the court must determine whether there has been a fatal or a non-fatal irregularity. A fatal irregularity is one which leaves the court with no option but to refuse the application for an enforcement order (see s. 127(3) and (4)). Examples of such irregularities include failure to secure the signature of the debtor (s. 61(1)(a)); failure to specify the prescribed terms of the agreement (s. 60(1)) and failure to supply notice of cancellation rights (s. 64(1)).

Non-fatal irregularities do not render the agreement unenforceable, but a discretion rests in the court to determine whether or not enforcement is appropriate. There is a non-fatal infringement where the contractual document is not legible (s. 61(1)) or where not all the terms of the contract are expressed in writing (s. 61(1)). Similarly, the court has such a discretion where the agreement is not in the form set out in the Agreements Regulations (SI 1983/1553) or where there is a failure to supply copies of the agreement (ss. 62(3) and 63(5)).

For the purposes of these 'non-fatal' infringements, the court has a discretion under s. 127(2) whether to order enforcement and if so, whether to reduce or discharge any sum payable by the debtor, as compensation to the debtor for prejudice suffered as a result of the creditor's infringement. Since the intention is to compensate the debtor for prejudice suffered, it is essential that there has been some prejudice, thus if the debtor's position would have remained the same whether the creditor was in breach of his regulatory obligations or not, the debtor should receive nothing (*Nissan Finance UK* v *Lockhart* [1993] CCLR 39). But if a debtor might have obtained a much lower rate of interest elsewhere had he been provided with the required information, there is clear evidence of prejudice which will justify a substantial reduction in the interest rate applicable to the transaction (*National Guardian Mortgage Corporation* v *Wilkes* [1993] CCLR 1).

Under s. 135(1) the court has a general power to make any term of the contract subject to the doing of a specified act by any party to the proceedings and under s. 136, the court may alter the terms of the agreement as a consequence of any enforcement order which might be made. Thus it has been held possible for the court to order a reduction in the interest rate applied, where appropriate (*Southern & District Finance plc* v *Barnes* (1995) *The Times*, 19 April 1995).

The county court has jurisdiction over enforcement orders and may exercise one of three options in the event of an application for one. It may enforce the agreement according to its terms or subject to modifications or decline to make any order at all.

11.6.3.2 Time orders If it appears just to do so, the court may make a time order in favour of the debtor (s. 129). The effect of such an order is to allow the debtor more time to comply with his obligations under his contract with the creditor.

The debtor has a limited right to apply for a time order after a default notice under s. 87 or a non-default notice under s.s 76 or 98 has been served upon him. There is also a wider right where the creditor has applied to the court for enforcement of the agreement.

The court's powers consist of giving time to pay sums due, giving time to rectify a breach and conferring the right to continued possession after making a time order.

11.6.3.3 Other orders So as to protect the creditor's position pending a claim for repossession, the court may issue a protection order under s. 131, so that the goods are preserved until trial. Other orders which may be made include return orders (s. 133) and transfer orders (s. 133) in the case of proceedings in relation to hire purchase and conditional sale agreements.

11.6.3.4 Power to reopen extortionate credit bargains One of the most important court powers relates to extortionate credit bargains. If a contract (regardless of value) requires the payment of grossly exorbitant sums or otherwise grossly contravenes ordinary principles of fair dealing (s. 138(1)), the bargain may be reopened (s. 137(1)). The creditor bears the onus of proving that the bargain is not extortionate (*Bank of Baroda* v *Shah* [1988] 3 All ER 24) once the debtor or a surety has first raised the issue (s. 139(1)).

Where a credit bargain is considered to be extortionate, the debtor may be relieved of his obligations under the contract, and the creditor may be ordered to repay sums paid under the agreement. The power relates not only to the credit agreement but also to any related agreement and to both the primary and secondary obligations of the debtor. Thus, these provisions will apply to terms of the contract which operate on default and linked transactions (s. 138(5)).

A number of factors are specified in s. 138 as being relevant to the question whether a credit bargain is extortionate or not. In particular s. 138(2) provides that regard should be had to matters such as interest rates at the time of making the agreement (see *A. Ketley Ltd* v *Scott* [1981] ICR 241; *Davies* v *Direct Loans Ltd* [1986] 2 All ER 783); personal factors such as the age, experience, business capacity and health of the debtor; the degree of risk undertaken by the creditor; the relationship of creditor and debtor and whether an inflated cash price has been quoted to the debtor.

The meaning of 'extortionate' is not fettered by percentage limits as used to be the case under the Moneylenders Acts 1900 and 1927, with the result that seemingly high rates of interest can be justified where the circumstances permit.

Other factors may also be taken into account in determining whether a credit bargain is extortionate or not. For example, in *Castle Phillips & Co.* v *Wilkinson* [1992] CCLR 83 it was considered relevant to take account of the facts that the interest rate charged was almost four times that charged by a building society, and that the security for the loan exceeded the amount advanced together with the inexperience of the applicants for the loan.

11.7 CREDITOR'S REMEDIES ON DEFAULT BY THE DEBTOR

Where the debtor is in default, certain remedies are conferred on the creditor by law. He is entitled to sue for each instalment payable under the agreement as it falls due. He may be able to sue for damages in respect of losses suffered as a result of the debtor's breach. If the debtor's breach is so serious as to amount to repudiation at common law, the creditor may be able to treat the contract as being at an end and recover damages in respect of the breach.

The agreement itself may also confer remedies on the creditor, such as a power to demand immediate payment of the outstanding balance or a power to terminate the agreement in specified circumstances. Likewise, the agreement may allow the creditor to take possession of the goods subject to the agreement or may empower him to remedy a breach and charge the cost to the debtor. Sometimes the contract contains a liquidated damages clause which specifies a fixed sum to be paid in the event of certain breaches of contract on the part of the debtor.

11.7.1 Actions for sums due under the agreement

Where the debtor has failed to make payments required by the agreement he has entered into, the creditor can recover each payment as it becomes due. In *Yeoman Credit Ltd* v *Apps* [1962] 2 QB 508 a car subject to a hire purchase agreement proved to be unfit for use on the roads. The debtor had chosen not to reject the vehicle until after he had made payments under the agreement. It was held that as they had become due prior to the date of rejection they were sums due under the agreement and were therefore deductible from any award of damages made to the debtor in respect of the unfitness of the vehicle.

It is important to distinguish this action from one for damages for breach of contract, as they are quite different in nature (*Overstone Ltd* v *Shipway* [1962] 1 WLR 117). The action for instalments due is one for debt in respect of the hire-rent due as a result of the hirer's use of the goods subject to the agreement. In contrast, the action for damages is based on some specific breach on the part of the debtor which has caused additional loss to the creditor over and above any debt due under the agreement. Since the action for debt is based on hire-rent becoming due under the agreement, it is essential that the hiring period has commenced. If the debtor has refused to take delivery, hiring has not commenced, in which case, there will be no action for debts due, although an action for damages for failure to take delivery may be available (*National Cash Register Co.* v *Stanley* [1921] 3 KB 292). Similarly, if no agreement is reached, hire-rent is not due and no action will lie for debt (*Campbell Discount Ltd* v *Gall* [1961] 1 QB 431 (overruled on other grounds)).

Once the hiring period has commenced, the debtor is liable to make payments according to the terms of the agreement, while he remains in possession of the goods. However, if the debtor gives up possession of the goods, the hire-rent ceases to be payable by him (*Belsize Motor Co.* v *Cox* [1914] 1 KB 244).

If the contract contains an accelerated payment clause, its effect may be to convert into debts sums which would otherwise be due in the future. Whether the acceleration clause is valid or not depends on a number of factors. If the agreement is regulated, the creditor has to give the debtor at least seven days' notice of an intention to invoke the clause and demand full payment earlier than was originally agreed (s. 76(1) (non-default) and s. 87(1) (default)). If the notice is served on the debtor following his default and the debtor subsequently complies with the requirements of the default notice (for example, by paying an outstanding instalment) the breach is treated as if it had never occurred (s. 89).

If the acceleration clause merely requires payment of the cash price of the goods, there can be no question of its validity since all it serves to do is to bring forward the date on which the debtor must pay for the subject matter of the contract. But in most cases, the creditor will want to recover the interest due in respect of the period of credit. In these circumstances, it is important that the contract provides the debtor with a rebate for early settlement, otherwise it could be struck down on the ground that it is penal (see *Wadham Stringer Finance Ltd* v *Meaney* [1980] 3 All ER 789).

If the agreement is regulated, the creditor cannot rely on a term which subjects the debtor to a rise in interest rate following his default under the agreement (s. 93).

11.7.2 Termination and repossession by the creditor

In the event of the debtor's repudiation or a breach of condition, the creditor may wish to terminate the contract and in a case where ownership in the goods has not passed to the debtor, the creditor may wish to retake possession. It is important to distinguish between termination after the debtor's repudiation and termination under a term of the contract. In some instances, a term of the contract allows the creditor to bring the contract to an end in the event of the debtor's breach of contract or upon some other specified occurrence. Where this is the case and the breach does not amount to a repudiation, the creditor is treated as the cause of the termination of the contract. Where there is a repudiation, the debtor is regarded as the cause of termination, which could have adverse consequences for him if the creditor also sues for damages.

11.7.2.1 Repudiation The debtor will be treated as having repudiated the contract where he does some act which is totally repugnant to the agreement. Thus if the debtor sells goods which are subject to a hire purchase contract (*Bowmakers Ltd* v *Barnet Instruments Ltd* [1945] KB 65) or indicates that he has no intention of proceeding with the hiring (*Overstone Ltd* v *Shipway* [1962] 1 WLR 117), he may be treated as having repudiated the agreement. While it is possible for the court to infer repudiation from a person's conduct, it is clear that such an inference will not be lightly made. For example, repeated failure to pay instalments punctually, as required by the agreement, does not necessarily amount to repudiation (*Lombard North Central plc* v *Butterworth* [1987] QB 527). However, failure to pay any instalments at all is likely to be construed as repudiatory conduct (*Yeoman Credit Ltd* v *Waragowski* [1961] 1 WLR 1124).

11.7.2.2 Non-repudiatory breaches of contract Some breaches of contract may not be sufficiently serious to amount to repudiation, but may give the creditor a contractual right to terminate the contract. This may be the case where the debtor fails to pay instalments on time or fails to take reasonable care of the goods which are the subject of the agreement. Where the agreement is regulated, the 1974 Act provides that the debtor must be given the chance to remedy his default (see s. 87(1)) and that if he does so, the default is treated as if it had never occurred (s. 89).

11.7.2.3 Recovery of the goods on termination Where an agreement has been terminated, the common law rule is that the debtor no longer has a right to possession of the goods. Accordingly, the creditor is entitled to retake possession whether the contract specifically allows this or not (*Bowmakers Ltd v Barnet Instruments Ltd* [1945] KB 65). The creditor can either commence proceedings for damages for conversion or physically take possession of the goods. The difficulty with the latter option is that if the goods are on the debtor's premises, the creditor will be guilty of trespass if he enters those premises without the debtor's permission. This problem could be avoided where the contract contains a term which authorises the creditor to enter the debtor's premises for the purpose of retaking possession.

11.7.2.3.1 Restrictions on repossession In the case of regulated agreements, the Consumer Credit Act 1974 limits the last option by providing that the creditor cannot enter premises to take possession of goods or land without leave of the court (s. 92). A creditor who fails to comply with s. 92 is guilty of a breach of statutory duty and may be liable in damages (s. 92(3)).

11.7.2.3.2 Protected goods status Where the goods are classified as 'protected' under s. 90 the creditor in a regulated hire purchase or conditional sale agreement may not recover them without a court order. Goods are protected if the debtor is in breach of the agreement (s. 90(1)(a)), has paid more than one third of the total price of the goods (s. 90(1)(b)) and property in the goods remains with the creditor (s. 90(1)(c)).

It follows from this that goods are not protected where the debtor exercises his right of voluntary termination. Accordingly, it is important to determine whether a debtor's communication constitutes breach or voluntary termination, since in the case of voluntary termination by the debtor, the creditor will be able to take possession of the goods, provided the necessary notice has been given to the debtor. In these circumstances, the court will order the debtor to deliver the goods to the creditor and will not give the debtor the option of paying for them except where it would not be just to make such an order (s. 100(5)). For this reason, the debtor who finds himself in financial difficulties is advised not to be precipitate in returning the goods to the creditor. Instead, he is in a better position if he defaults and waits for the creditor to act against him. The courts are mindful of the debtor's position in the event of a voluntary termination and may be reluctant to regard his conduct as amounting to such a termination, particularly if its consequences have not been fully explained (*United Dominions Trust Ltd* v *Ennis* [1968] 1 QB 54).

The effect of s. 90(1)(c) is that goods subject to a conditional sale agreement under which the debtor is obliged to purchase will not be protected since property in the goods must remain with the creditor.

The definition of protected goods requires the debtor to have paid one third or more of the total price of the goods. It will be necessary to total the amounts paid by the debtor, including any deposit, instalments paid prior to default and the option fee. If this comes to more than one third of the total price for the goods, they are protected. However, s. 90(2) provides that any amount paid by the debtor by way of an installation charge is to be deducted from the amount paid by the debtor and is not to be regarded as part of the total price of the goods. If the debtor has paid £200 of the total price of a £600 gas cooker, but that £600 includes a £60 installation charge, it is necessary that he should have paid the whole of the installation charge and one third of the remainder. In this example the cooker is not protected because in order to achieve protected goods status the debtor must have paid the installation charge of £60 plus one third of the price of the cooker ignoring the installation charge, i.e., £60 plus one third of £600 − £60, or £60 plus one third of £540, which is £60 + £180 = £240.

11.7.2.3.3 Effect of ignoring protected goods status Where a creditor wrongly takes possession of protected goods, he commits no crime, but the agreement is automatically terminated and no further liabilities on the part of the debtor arise under it (s. 90(3)). Furthermore, the debtor can recover all sums paid to the creditor in an action for moneys had and received (s. 91(b)). In *Capital Finance Co. Ltd* v *Bray* [1964] 1 All ER 603, the creditor wrongly took possession of a car subject to a hire purchase agreement. The debtor asked for return of all sums paid by him so the creditor returned the car to the debtor. The debtor used the car on a number of occasions but paid no further instalments. In a subsequent action by the creditor it was held that the initial repossession without a court order meant that the creditor had no defence to a counterclaim by the debtor for the return of all sums paid by him under the agreement.

11.7.2.3.4 Loss of protected goods status If the debtor or his agent has consented to repossession, s. 91 will not apply (s. 173(3)). Thus if the debtor has failed to read his copy of the agreement, does not realise that the goods are protected and agrees to repossession, he cannot later claim repayment of sums paid under the agreement because of his consent (*Mercantile Credit Ltd* v *Cross* [1965] 2 QB 605). It is essential, in this respect, that the debtor's consent is fully informed (*Chartered Trust plc* v *Pitcher* [1988] RTR 72). Consent given by a third party will not suffice (*Peacock* v *Anglo Auto Finance Ltd* (1968) 112 SJ 746).

Similarly, if the debtor has abandoned the goods or if he has sold the goods to a third party, s. 91 will not apply because s. 90(1) refers to recovering possession from the debtor. In the case of a disposition to a third party, the rights of the third party will have to be considered, but the right to seize the goods would appear to be available (see *Bentinck* v *Cromwell Engineering Ltd* [1971] 1 QB 324).

11.7.3 Damages for breach of contract

A breach of contract by the debtor may have caused loss to the creditor which is remediable in the form of an award of damages. Ordinarily, the principal cause of loss to the creditor will be the fact that the debtor has fallen into arrears, in which case it will be necessary to decide whether the default amounts to a repudiation of the contract or not.

The creditor may also have a legitimate claim where the debtor has wrongly failed to take delivery of the goods subject to the agreement or where the debtor has failed to take care of goods in his possession. Furthermore, if the debtor wrongly refuses to give up possession of the goods when properly asked to do so, he may be liable in damages for conversion.

11.7.3.1 Failure to take delivery Provided the goods delivered are in accordance with the contract, the debtor is under an obligation to accept them. If the debtor fails to take delivery, the creditor's action is not one for instalments due, because hire-rent does not become due until the hiring has commenced (*National Cash Registers Co.* v *Stanley* [1921] 3 KB 292). Instead, the appropriate action is one for damages for non-acceptance. Ordinary principles of contract damages will apply in these circumstances. Thus the creditor will be able to recover any loss arising naturally from the breach of contract. This will include the difference between the price paid for the goods by the creditor and the market value of the goods on resale and the creditor's lost finance charges. However, in quantifying the award, the court will have to take into account the fact that the creditor is being paid back earlier than would have been the case had the agreement run its course.

11.7.3.2 Failure to take care of the goods Where the debtor is not the owner of the goods, he owes a duty to the creditor to take reasonable care of the goods in his possession. Ordinarily, the creditor will take no chances and there will be express terms of the contract defining the nature of the debtor's responsibility. But even in the absence of such terms, the debtor is a bailee and is therefore responsible for harm caused to the goods by his negligence (see *Brady* v *St Margaret's Trust Ltd* [1963] 2 QB 494).

11.7.3.3 Refusal to give up possession If the hiring terminates for some reason, the creditor may be entitled to retake possession of the goods, subject to certain restrictions. If the debtor wrongly refuses to give up possession, he may be liable in the tort of conversion. The measure of damages will normally be the value of the converted goods at the date of conversion, with the result that an award of damages in such a case will amount to a compulsory sale of the goods concerned. Account will be taken of any instalments already paid under the agreement, but the debtor will be required to pay the amount which would have become payable under the agreement had it not been terminated (*Wickham Holdings Ltd* v *Brooke House Motors Ltd* [1967] 1 WLR 295). This does not mean that account will not also be taken of the fact that the creditor may receive accelerated payment, in which case a reduction in the award will be made.

11.7.3.4 Damages for breach of instalment payment obligations
Where the debtor fails to pay instalments due under a conditional sale or credit sale agreement, the creditor will be able to sue for the price or for damages for loss of profit, but not for both. In the case of a hire purchase, the creditor will be able to recover the goods subject to the agreement and hire-rent due in respect of the period of hire. This double recovery on the part of the creditor may be added to where the contract contains a minimum payment clause which requires a payment by the debtor in respect of future instalments due under the agreement.

In seeking to find a solution to the problem created by minimum payment clauses in conjunction with apparent default on the part of the debtor, it is necessary to determine whether the debtor's default amounts to a voluntary termination of the contract, a repudiation of the contract or a breach not amounting to repudiation.

11.7.3.4.1 Voluntary termination If the debtor's conduct is construed as a voluntary termination of the contract, no question of damages for breach of contract will arise, assuming the agreement or statute confers such a right (see s. 99). However, a minimum payment clause may still provide for payment of future hire-rent in such a case. At common law the position appears to be that the minimum payment clause is to be construed as an agreement to pay the amount stipulated as compensation for loss of future interest. Since there is no breach of contract, the doctrine of penalties, considered below, has no application (see *Associated Distributors Ltd* v *Hall* [1938] 2 KB 83).

If the agreement is regulated by the Consumer Credit Act 1974 the debtor is given some protection against what might otherwise be a requirement to pay an exorbitant amount. In particular, the debtor will be required to pay no more than half of the total price (s. 100(1)). Thus if the debtor's payments including the deposit and sums due but not yet paid come to that amount, the creditor can expect to be paid nothing more. If the debtor's payments have not reached the 50 per cent threshold, the court can require him to pay up to that amount, subject to a discretion to reduce the sum payable in accordance with the actual loss suffered by the creditor (s. 100(3)).

In addition to any payment made under s. 100(1), the debtor will also be liable to the creditor for his failure to take care of the goods in his possession (s. 100(5)). This liability is superimposed on any payment made under s. 100(1).

The provisions of s. 100(1) apply only where the terms of the contract concerning payment are less favourable than those stipulated in the Act. Thus, if the contract provides for no payment, or payment of a sum less than half of the total price, the relevant term will be applied (s. 100(1)).

11.7.3.4.2 Default amounting to repudiation Where the debtor's default amounts to a repudiation, that default is regarded as the cause of the termination of the contract and the amount the creditor receives by way of damages may exceed the amount payable under a minimum payment clause. The repudiation may come in the form of an express statement (*Overstone Ltd*

v *Shipway* [1962] 1 WLR 117), or it may be inferred from a substantial failure
to perform (*Yeoman Credit Ltd* v *Waragowski* [1961] 1 WLR 1124). In *Yeoman
Credit Ltd* v *Waragowski* the creditor could have relied on a minimum
payment clause which would have allowed him a 50 per cent payment, but
sought damages for repudiation instead. He recovered damages which put
him in the position he would have been in had the agreement run its course
even though the agreement was terminated after six months of the envisaged
three-year period. This element of overcompensation has since been recognised and the court is likely to reduce damages so as to take into account the
earlier settlement date (*Overstone Ltd* v *Shipway*).

11.7.3.4.3   Non-repudiatory default   If the debtor's default does not go to the
root of the contract, the decision of the creditor to terminate the contract
cannot be attributed to the breach. Termination in such a case is caused by
the creditor rather than the debtor and the latter is treated more favourably.
The creditor cannot claim damages for loss of future payments and is limited
to the arrears outstanding at the time of termination (*Financings Ltd* v *Baldock*
[1963] 2 QB 104).

In the light of the decision of the Court of Appeal in *Financings Ltd* v
Baldock, there has been a judicial tendency to regard the debtor's conduct as
not amounting to repudiation, given the adverse consequences that follow
from the decision in *Yeoman Credit Ltd* v *Waragowski*. Thus a creditor cannot
write to the debtor saying that unless payment is received within a specified
period, it is to be assumed that the debtor no longer wishes to continue with
the agreement (*Eshun* v *Moorgate Mercantile Co. Ltd* [1971] 1 WLR 722).
Generally, it cannot be assumed from the failure to pay two instalments that
a person has repudiated the contract. Thus in *Kelly* v *Sovereign Leasing* [1995]
CLY 720 the debtor failed to make two payments under an unregulated hire
purchase agreement with the result that the creditor repossessed the vehicle
and sold it against the debtor's wishes. In an action by the debtor for damages
for conversion, it was held that, since the agreement did not indicate when
payments had to be made, the time of payment could not be regarded as
being of the essence of the contract. Accordingly, the breach of contract could
not be regarded as repudiatory conduct, with the result that the debtor's
action for conversion was bound to succeed.

While the courts may be reluctant to hold that a debtor has repudiated the
contract, the creditor may be able to get round the decision in *Financings Ltd*
v *Baldock* by making prompt payment of the essence of the contract (*Lombard
North Central plc* v *Butterworth* [1987] QB 527). Where this is the case, default
in the form of persistent late payment may go to the root of the contract, with
the result that the creditor can rely on a minimum payment clause in the
contract. Where there is no time of the essence clause and no repudiation,
any purported termination of the contract cannot be blamed on the debtor
with the result that the creditor will be confined to recovery of outstanding
instalments.

11.7.4 Application of the doctrine of penalties to minimum payment clauses

It is clear from the decision in *Financings Ltd* v *Baldock* [1963] 2 QB 104 that a minimum payment clause may be struck down on the ground that it is penal, in the sense that the clause operates *in terrorem* over the head of the debtor (see *Dunlop Pneumatic Tyre Co. Ltd* v *New Garage and Motor Co. Ltd* [1915] AC 79; *Landom Trust Ltd* v *Hurrell* [1955] 1 WLR 391). In particular, a minimum payment clause will be penal if it requires the payment of an extravagant or unconscionable amount which is out of proportion to the greatest possible loss that the creditor could suffer. In particular, if a minimum payment clause requires the debtor to pay more than the amount he would have paid had the contract run its full course, it will be struck down as penal (*Lombank Ltd* v *Excell* [1964] 1 QB 415).

In considering the application of the penalty doctrine, it is necessary to distinguish between the operation of a minimum payment clause in the event of breach of contract by the debtor, voluntary termination by the debtor and the death or bankruptcy of the debtor. As the law stands at present, the doctrine only applies where there has been a breach of contract on the part of the debtor and not where the contract comes to an end by virtue of a voluntary termination or by virtue of the death or bankruptcy of the debtor (cf. Law Commission, *Penalty Clauses and Forfeiture of Monies Paid* (WP 61), 1975, para. 26).

Where there is a default in the form of a late payment the contract may provide that it shall terminate automatically thereby immediately triggering the minimum payment clause. In such a case, the clause is penal and will be struck down (*Cooden Engineering Ltd* v *Stanford* [1953] 1 QB 86). The problem with most minimum payment clauses is that they cannot be regarded as a genuine estimate of the loss likely to be suffered by the creditor in the event of the debtor's breach of contract.

If the clause requires payment of the same amount regardless of the number of payments made by the debtor before breach, it will be struck down as penal, since it operates in relation to one of a number of different events which may be of differing importance (*Landom Trust Ltd* v *Hurrell* [1955] 1 WLR 391).

Finance companies have sought to get round the problem of the doctrine of penalties by drawing up a scale of compensation, providing for payment of a variable percentage of the total price at each stage of the repayment period. Such minimum payment clauses have been held to be genuine liquidated damages clauses (*Phonographic Equipment Ltd* v *Muslu* [1961] 1 WLR 1379), but it now appears that following the decision of the House of Lords in *Bridge* v *Campbell Discount Co. Ltd* [1962] AC 600, these too can be regarded as penal.

The typical minimum payment clause is claimed to operate as a means of securing compensation for depreciation, but depreciation in the value of a motor vehicle increases as time passes by, whereas the amount required under a variable-percentage minimum payment clause gets smaller as time passes. Accordingly, the majority of minimum payment clauses do work on a sliding scale, but one which operates in the wrong direction.

In order to comply with the requirements of *Bridge* v *Campbell Discount Co. Ltd* a minimum payment clause will have to give the debtor due allowance for the value of repossessed goods, make allowance for early payment, produce a scale of compensation sliding in an upward direction and take account of the condition of the goods at the time of breach, thereby compensating the creditor for his true loss. In *Anglo Auto Finance Co. Ltd* v *James* [1963] 1 WLR 1042 these requirements were satisfied except that no allowance was made for early payment. Accordingly, the clause was regarded as penal. Where a minimum payment clause is held to be a penalty, it will not be enforceable against the debtor. Instead, the creditor will be confined to an action for unliquidated damages in respect of the debtor's breach.

TWELVE

Exemption clauses and other unfair terms in consumer contracts

12.1 REASONS FOR THE CONTROL OF EXEMPTION CLAUSES

The principle of freedom of contract suggests that it should be open to the parties to a contract to agree to whatever terms they see fit. However, where one of the parties is a consumer, the courts and Parliament have taken a stand against the indiscriminate use of exclusion and limitation clauses, particularly where they are contained in standard-form documents.

12.1.1 Inequality of bargaining power and paternalism

One view of these standard-form contracts containing exemption clauses is that they have developed out of the concentration of business in a relatively small number of hands (*A. Schroeder Music Publishing Co. Ltd* v *Macaulay* [1974] 3 All ER 616, 624 per Lord Diplock). It may also be objected that such contracts are not the subject of negotiation between the parties and that they may be described as weapons of consumer oppression (Yates, *Exclusion Clauses*, 2nd ed., p. 2). These arguments are consistent with the 'exploitation theory' of exemption clauses in consumer contracts (see Kessler (1943) 43 Colum LRev 629; Slawson (1971) 84 Harv LRev 529).

The exploitation theory may not fully explain the Unfair Contract Terms Act 1977, which seeks to prevent or limit to a reasonable extent the use of exemption clauses in consumer contracts. The use of exemption clauses in relation to certain types of contract term, such as the implied terms about quality in contracts for the supply of goods, is prohibited altogether. It is doubtful whether the use of exemption clauses in this context is any more exploitative than in the context of the supply of services. But in the latter case, an exemption of liability in a consumer contract is permitted where reasonable. In these circumstances, it may be that Parliament has acted out of paternalist motives to protect what may be perceived as inalienable rights which should never be subject to an exemption of liability.

12.1.2 Transaction costs

Arguments based on the notion of inequality of bargaining power assume a monopoly or near-monopoly situation in which the consumer is faced with little or no choice but to take the terms offered to him if he wishes to make use of the goods or services on offer. Sometimes it may be argued that the standard-form contract is not the instrument of consumer oppression outlined above, but a means of reducing transaction costs with the result that goods and services may be made available to consumers at lower cost than would otherwise be the case. For example, in relation to the sale of insurance, there is a wide choice of policies available, if the consumer cares to look, but there appears to be little or no negotiation over the terms of those policies. It has been argued that the fact that there is no negotiation over terms is not that insurance companies wish to browbeat consumers but because it is not cost-effective to negotiate individual contracts with each consumer (Posner, *Economic Analysis of Law*, 2nd ed., p. 84; see also Trebilcock in Reiter and Swan (eds), *Studies in Contract Law* (1981), p. 381). If the consumer compares competing policies, he will find what he wants and the insurer with the least attractive terms will be compelled by market forces to produce something more attractive.

12.1.3 Information

While it may be true that the consumer can shop around in the market place, it would appear that this is not always done. There are rules at common law which require a business seeking to rely on an exemption clause to communicate its existence to the consumer. However, the consumer may not read the terms of the standard-form contract thrust at him by the other party. Accordingly, it may be that the objection to the use of exemption clauses in standard-form consumer contracts is to be based on the notion of information asymmetry. The consumer can only make an effective choice if he has the necessary information at his finger tips. In this respect, it may sometimes be necessary for Parliament to legislate for the form and content of certain contract terms.

12.2 COMMUNICATION TO THE CONSUMER

Since an exemption clause is a contract term, it is subject to ordinary principles of contract law. In particular, before a consumer can be said to have contracted on terms which are unfair to him, it must be shown that the other party, or *proferens*, has adequately communicated the effect of the exemption to the consumer. In most consumer contracts, the *proferens* will make use of a standard-form document containing the terms on which he wishes to contract. In some instances the consumer will not sign the document and may not even read it. In the latter event, it is for the *proferens* to show that he has done sufficient to convey his intention to rely on the term as part of his contract with the consumer.

12.2.1 Reasonable notice

The *proferens* must show that he has taken steps to give reasonably sufficient notice of the existence of an exemption clause to the other party to the contract (*Parker* v *South Eastern Railway* (1877) 2 CPD 416). This may be a lot easier in some contracts than in others, especially where the particular standard form under consideration is one which people generally realise will contain contractual terms. Thus in *Parker* v *South Eastern Railway* the view was expressed that consumers generally are aware that railway tickets refer to the terms on which the railway company offer their services. But the same cannot be said of all documents. For example, it is common practice for computer software manufacturers to shrink-wrap their products, so that the buyer does not have access to all the terms of the software licence until he has opened the packaging. In these circumstances, where what is sold is an 'off-the-shelf' package not specifically produced for the special purposes of the buyer, it was held in *Beta Computers (Europe) Ltd* v *Adobe Systems (Europe) Ltd* [1996] CLC 821 that there was no concluded contract despite the warning printed on the outside of the packaging that 'Opening the . . . software package indicates your acceptance of these terms and conditions'. What was important was that by shrink-wrapping the product, the sellers had prevented the buyer from intimating his acceptance until after the package had been opened.

A further consideration is whether the document which contains the exempting term, on which the *proferens* later seeks to rely, is normally regarded as a contractual document. A time sheet presented to the customer by an employee of the *proferens* is not normally regarded as a contractual document, since it amounts to no more than a record of performance of an existing contractual obligation and is usually presented some time after the contract has been concluded (*Grogan* v *Meredith Plant Hire Ltd* (1996) 15 TrLR 371). Thus if an old-age pensioner in failing health were to engage the services of an itinerant nurse through a nursing agency, terms referred to on the back of the time sheet which is normally presented to the patient at the end of each week's work would have no effect on the contractual relationship between the parties, unless signing the time sheet could be regarded as a variation of the existing contractual relationship (cf. *Thompson* v *T. Lohan (Plant Hire) Ltd* [1987] 2 All ER 631). In a consumer contract of this kind an inference of agreement to a variation is unlikely, especially in a case where no terms have been specifically alluded to at the time the contract was made. Where the other party is a consumer, it would appear that the *proferens* may need to take special steps to ensure that the consumer not only knows that there are purported exemptions of liability but also how far they go (*Thornton* v *Shoe Lane Parking Ltd* [1971] 2 QB 163). The difficulty this creates is that if the requirement is applied to all terms in consumer contracts, contract documents may become excessively bulky. In some instances, communication of all of the terms on which the consumer is expected to contract is feasible, as where the consumer books a holiday and is supplied with a brochure containing the terms of contracting of the tour operator (*Hollingworth* v *Southern Ferries Ltd* [1977] 2 Lloyd's Rep 70). However, in other cases this is not so. For example, it would not be possible to print on a standard railway ticket all the terms on which railway travel is sold. Accordingly, reference on the ticket to the document in which those terms can be found is permitted, provided the reference is clear (*Sugar* v *London, Midland & Scottish Railway Co* [1941] 1 All ER 172).

What constitutes reasonable communication will depend on the circumstances of each case. If the consumer possesses peculiar characteristics, it may be that additional steps must be taken to communicate the intention to rely on the exclusion or limitation of liability. Where the *proferens* frequently deals with consumers who do not speak English, it may be necessary to provide a translation of the terms in question (*Geier* v *Kujawa* [1970] 1 Lloyd's Rep 364; cf. *Saphir* v *Zissimos* [1960] 1 Lloyd's Rep 490).

The nature of the purported exemption is also important. It would appear that in addition to the reasonable notice rule there is a 'red hand' rule (see Macdonald [1988] JBL 375) which applies to individual terms as opposed to all of the proposed terms of the contract. Some terms are so onerous in effect that before notice could be said to be sufficient, they would need to be printed in red ink with a red hand pointing towards them (*J. Spurling Ltd* v *Bradshaw* [1956] 1 WLR 461, 466 per Denning LJ). It can follow from this that the majority of the terms proposed by the *proferens* satisfy the reasonable notice test, but one or two may be subject to the more onerous 'red hand' test because of what they purport to do. Thus it has been said that some exemptions may be so unreasonably wide and destructive of rights that only the most explicit reference to them will suffice (*Thornton* v *Shoe Lane Parking Ltd* [1971] 1 QB 163, 170 per Lord Denning MR). How far the rule extends is not entirely clear. Alternative formulations apply it to unreasonable contract terms (ibid.), to terms which are unusual in the class of contract under consideration (ibid., 172 per Megaw LJ), or to terms which are onerous or unusual (*Interfoto Picture Library Ltd* v *Stiletto Visual Programmes Ltd* [1988] 1 All ER 348, 350 per Dillon LJ and see also *AEG (UK) Ltd* v *Logic Resource Ltd* [1996] CLC 265).

12.2.2 Signed contractual documents

A consumer who signs a document which contains contractual terms is bound by those terms even where the contractual document has not been read (*L'Estrange* v *F. Graucob Ltd* [1934] 2 KB 394). The signature of the consumer is regarded, in law, as the clearest objective evidence of acceptance of the terms proposed in the document. Exceptionally, a signed document is not binding, for example, where the signature has been obtained by fraud or misrepresentation (*Curtis* v *Chemical Cleaning & Dyeing Co. Ltd* [1951] 1 KB 805) or where an express oral statement overrides the terms of the written agreement (*J. Evans & Sons (Portsmouth) Ltd* v *Andrea Merzario Ltd* [1976] 1 WLR 1098).

12.2.3 Implied communication

In some instances it will not be possible for the *proferens* to show that the consumer has actual knowledge of an exemption clause. For example, a notice which refers to a purported exemption of liability may have fallen down, or the notice may be displayed where it can be read only after the contract has been entered into (*Olley* v *Marlborough Court Hotel Ltd* [1949] 1

KB 532). Where this is the case, the court may be prepared to infer awareness of the relevant term by reference to a previous course of dealing between the parties.

Normally, this inference of awareness is made in the case of business transactions where the parties have consistently dealt with each other over a long period of time. The nature of many consumer transactions is such that a consistent course of dealing will rarely be encountered except in the case of the frequent use of travel services and possibly consistent use of the same garage for the purposes of maintaining the family car (see also *Mendelssohn* v *Normand Ltd* [1970] 1 QB 177, 182 per Lord Denning MR). Where knowledge of a contract term is implied, two conditions must be satisfied. First, the *proferens* must show that there is a consistent course of dealing between the parties. If there are inconsistencies in business practice, it is unlikely that a course of dealing will be established. Thus in *McCutcheon* v *David MacBrayne Ltd* [1964] 1 WLR 125 the defendants sought to rely on exempting conditions in a ferry travel contract on an occasion on which the plaintiff had not been asked to sign the customary 'release note'. Although the plaintiff had used the defendant's ferries in the past, what proved fatal for the defendants was that they had failed to adopt any consistent business practice in relation to the 'release note'. On some occasions they would ask for one to be signed and on other occasions this was not done.

Secondly, if the course of dealing is sporadic, the element of consistency is not satisfied and knowledge of the exemption will not be inferred. In *Hollier* v *Rambler Motors (AMC) Ltd* [1972] 2 QB 71 the consumer had his car serviced at the defendant's garage on three or four occasions in a five-year period, but because of the infrequency of dealing between the parties, it could not be said that a consistent course of dealing had come into existence. Where the plaintiff is a consumer, there may be the problem of inequality of bargaining power, which may justify a restrictive approach to the inference of knowledge of contract terms (*British Crane Hire Ltd* v *Ipswich Plant Hire Ltd* [1975] QB 303, 310 per Lord Denning MR).

12.2.4 Exemption clauses and third parties

Sometimes it is necesssary to decide if an exemption clause can affect the liability of a person who is not a party to the contract with the consumer. Problems of this kind have been encountered more frequently in business transactions where the question has arisen whether C can claim the protection of an exemption clause contained in a contract between A and B, where A, B and C are all parties to a chain of related contracts. In these cases, whether or not the exemption can be relied on by C has depended on how clearly it has been stated by A that the term of the contract protects C and whether A contracts as agent for C (*New Zealand Shipping Co. Ltd* v *A M Satterthwaite & Co. Ltd* [1975] AC 154).

Ordinarily, where consumer contracts are concerned, the courts are likely to apply the doctrine of privity of contract strictly so as to prevent the *proferens* from broadening the scope of the exemption of liability to include employees, agents and subcontractors. Thus a passenger on board a ferry may proceed against members of the crew whose alleged negligence has caused harm to the passenger's property, even though the ferry operator has excluded his own liability and purported to extend that exemption to include employees (*Adler* v *Dickson* [1955] 1 QB 158).

12.2.5 Non-contractual exemptions

An exemption of liability that does not form part of a contract between the consumer and the person seeking to rely on it will not affect the contractual liability of the parties, but it could serve as a disclaimer in respect of tortious liability. Thus if a purported exemption of liability is contained in a document regarded as a receipt rather than a contractual document (*Chapelton* v *Barry Urban District Council* [1940] 1 KB 532) or the manufacturer of a product purports to exclude his liability in respect of certain losses by means of a statement on the packaging of his product, there may not be a contractual relationship, but it must be considered whether the disclaimer affects the defendant's liability.

For the purposes of disclaiming tortious liability, the reasonable notice rule still applies in that the disclaimer must be sufficiently clearly worded and displayed in a prominent position so that the plaintiff can take precautions for his own safety (*Ashdown* v *Samuel Williams and Sons Ltd* [1957] 1 QB 409). Any ambiguity in the disclaimer will be construed *contra proferentem* in the same way as a contractual exemption clause (*Vacwell Engineering Co. Ltd* v *BDH Chemicals Ltd* [1971] 1 QB 88). Where the disclaimer relates to negligently caused death or bodily injury, it will have no effect (Unfair Contract Terms Act 1977, s. 2(1)), but if it relates to negligently inflicted economic loss or property damage, it will be permitted, but only in so far as it complies with the reasonableness test laid down by the Unfair Contract Terms Act 1977, s. 11, which may be particularly difficult to satisfy where the other party is a consumer (see *Smith* v *Eric S. Bush* [1990] 1 AC 831).

12.3 JUDICIAL CONSTRUCTION OF EXEMPTION CLAUSES

Before the advent of statutory controls on exemption clauses, where a term was said to have been adequately communicated to the other party, the greatest excesses of the business community were controlled through a process of judicial construction of the terms of the contract.

12.3.1 The *contra proferentem* rule

If a term of the contract is intended to benefit one party to the contract, it will be construed against the person seeking to rely on it in the case of any ambiguity. This process of construction would seek to identify whether the exemption clause was sufficiently clearly worded so as to cover the breach of contract under consideration. Thus if the supplier of goods purported to exclude liability for breach of an implied term, this would not cover the breach of an express term of the contract (*Andrews Brothers Ltd* v *Singer & Co. Ltd* [1934] 1 KB 17) and the purported exclusion of liability for a breach of warranty would be ineffective in relation to a breach of condition (*Wallis, Son & Wells* v *Pratt & Haynes* [1911] AC 394).

The courts came to look very closely at the wording of the contract and very often engaged in a hostile approach to the construction of contract terms perceived to be unreasonable. Generally, terms which purported to exclude liability altogether were treated more harshly than those which sought to limit liability to a reasonable level. This led to the view that limitation clauses would normally be construed literally whereas it might be appropriate to construe an exclusion clause in a hostile manner (*Ailsa Craig Fishing Co. Ltd* v *Malvern Fishing Co. Ltd* [1983] 1 All ER 101, 124 per Lord Wilberforce). Thus in *George Mitchell (Chesterhall) Ltd* v *Finney Lock Seeds Ltd* [1983] 2 AC 803 the House of Lords held that cabbage seed which produced cabbages with no heart had to be regarded as qualitatively defective cabbage seed and could not be treated as being something other than cabbage seed. This literal interpretation of the wording of a limitation of liability was more appropriate than the strained construction adopted by the majority of the Court of Appeal.

It would appear that whether the term is a limitation clause or an exclusion clause, it will continue to be construed against the person seeking to rely upon it where it derogates from common law rights ([1983] 1 All ER 101, 105 per Lord Fraser of Tullybelton). The approach adopted by the Court of Appeal was criticised heavily on the ground that it amounted to a back-door reintroduction of the doctrine of fundamental breach, which is considered below. A further aspect of the *contra proferentem* rule is the extent to which a term can be used to restrict liability for negligence. The courts have taken the view that if the *proferens* would have been liable for his negligence but for the provision in the contract, he will still be so liable unless the clause is very clearly worded (*Alderslade* v *Hendon Laundry Ltd* [1945] 1 All ER 244). Thus generally worded provisions such as 'no liability accepted for damage howsoever caused' could be struck out on the ground that they did not cover liability for negligence.

12.3.2 The doctrine of fundamental breach of contract
A particular aspect of the *contra proferentem* rule which developed in the 1950s and 1960s was that the *proferens* could not rely on an exclusion or limitation clause where it sought to restrict liability in respect of the breach of terms which were fundamental to the contract. Thus if a person delivered a thing which was different in kind from the thing ordered, the *proferens* would not be able to rely on a term of the contract which purported to restrict the supplier's liability in that respect (*Karsales (Harrow) Ltd* v *Wallis* [1956] 2 All ER 866; see also the 'peas and beans' cases, e.g., *Chanter* v *Hopkins* (1838) 4 M & W 399).

The development of this doctrine involved a process of identifying breaches which were fundamental to the contract. In particular, it was said that there would be such a breach if the party not in default is deprived of substantially the whole benefit it was intended that he should obtain from the contract.

With a view to consumer protection the doctrine of fundamental breach came to be regarded as a rule of law, with the result that every time there was such a breach of contract, an exclusion clause in the contract would automatically fail (*Karsales (Harrow) Ltd* v *Wallis*). Whilst this provided a useful tool in respect of consumer protection, the general principle also applied to commercial contracts with the result that sensible business allocations of risk might be upset on the ground that there had been a serious breach of contract.

Ultimately, the rule of law approach was abandoned (*Photo Production Ltd* v *Securicor Transport Ltd* [1980] AC 827). Instead, the doctrine of fundamental breach was regarded as laying down nothing more than a rule of construction which required the court to consider whether the exclusion clause as worded was sufficiently clear to cover the particular breach under consideration. As such it is merely an aspect of the *contra proferentem* rule.

12.4 CONTROL OF EXEMPTION CLAUSES UNDER THE UNFAIR CONTRACT TERMS ACT 1977

12.4.1 Background
While common law rules on the communication and construction of exemption clauses in contracts served to curb some of the excesses of business, it became apparent that those rules alone were not wholly capable of protecting the consumer interest. A widespread practice had evolved of excluding liability for breach of the implied terms in the Sale of Goods Act 1893. Exemption clauses were also prevalent in other consumer contracts, such as contracts with railway operators and other providers of consumer services.

The issue was passed to the Law Commission for consideration and in two reports (Law Com. No. 24 (1969); Law Com. No. 69 (1975)), legislation was recommended first in relation to the exclusion of liability for breach of the implied terms in supply of goods contracts and later in respect of the use of exemption clauses in standard-form contracts generally. In particular, the Law Commission believed that in many instances the consumer was unaware of how he was being treated, but even where he was, he was often powerless to do anything but accept the terms offered, because alternative, more favourable terms were not available (Law Com. No. 24 (1969), para 68). Furthermore, the effect of some exclusions of liability was to deprive the consumer of rights which social policy required that he should have (Law Com. No. 69 (1975), para. 146).

One of the underlying assumptions of the Law Commission appears to be that consumers are not in a position of equal bargaining strength in comparison with the business with which they deal. However, it has been seen that the reasons for this inequality have to be closely examined and that there are cost reasons for the use of standard-form contracts which contain exclusions and limitations of the supplier's liability to the consumer.

Since the passing of the Unfair Contract Terms Act 1977, the European Community has also taken an interest in unfair terms in consumer contracts, publishing the Unfair Terms in Consumer Contracts Directive (93/13/EEC), which has since been implemented as part of English law in the Unfair Terms in Consumer Contracts Regulations 1994 (SI 1994/3159), many of the provisions of which are similar to those contained in the Unfair Contract

Terms Act 1977 but which also go further than the 1977 Act in other respects (see below).

12.4.2 Scope of the Unfair Contract Terms Act 1977
The 1977 Act applies to purported exclusions of both contractual liability and liability under the tort of negligence. It covers unlilateral exclusions of liability such as notices displayed by the occupier of premises which do not necessarily form part of a contractual relationship. The regime created by the 1977 Act includes two principal means of controlling exemption clauses. In some instances an exemption clause is rendered statutorily invalid on the ground that it impinges on some inalienable right on the part of the consumer. In other cases, an exemption clause may be treated as valid only if it satisfies a test of reasonableness.

12.4.2.1 Business liability Subject to exceptions in respect of supply of goods contracts and misrepresentations (see ss. 6(4) and 8), exemptions of liability in private transactions are not covered by the provisions of the Act. This follows from the assertion that the Act applies only to the purported exclusion of business liability (s. 1(3)). The Act defines a business as including a profession and the activities of government departments or local or public authorities (s. 14), but a person who grants access to premises for recreational or educational purposes does not fall within the regime created by the Act unless this is done as part of the business activities of the occupier (s. 1(3)(b)). Apart from this brief definition of the word 'business', there is no other reference in the Act to the concept of business liability, which might appear strange, given the importance of this phrase to the application of the Act. Accordingly, there are doubts about whether a purported exclusion or limitation of liability by a charity shop, a student union or a private club would fall within the provisions of the Act.

12.4.2.2 Primary and secondary obligations The Act is concerned with contract terms or notices which exclude or limit liability. On a literal interpretation this might suggest that the Act only applies to the secondary obligations of the parties which follow from the breach of a primary obligation. On this basis, the Act is concerned mainly with provisions which exclude or limit the liability of the *proferens* where he has admitted a breach of duty. However, the drafters of the legislation were aware of the possibility that someone might try to draft an exemption clause in such a way as to seek to minimise the effect of the legislation, for example, by dressing up an exemption clause in language which relates to the primary obligations of the parties, thereby becoming a definition of their contractual obligations. For the most part, the Act will not apply to terms of the contract which operate in this way since this would involve an interference with the root of the contract. Thus if the consumer buys a car and the seller expressly states that the vehicle is guaranteed fit for all use other than for competitive racing, the seller is not excluding his liability should the car be raced, he is stating that he is selling a car suitable for purposes other than racing.

To this general rule there are two exceptions. First, the ability of a person to exclude the duty of care giving rise to liability in negligence is substantially limited (ss. 2, 5 and 13(1)). Secondly, the supplier of goods is not allowed to exclude his duties to a consumer which arise out of the terms implied by the Sale of Goods Act 1979 and related legislation (ss. 6 and 7). In particular, the Unfair Contract Terms Act 1977, s. 13(1), provides:

To the extent that this part of this Act prevents the exclusion or restriction of any liability it also prevents—
 (a) making the liability or its enforcement subject to restrictive or onerous conditions;
 (b) excluding or restricting any right or remedy in respect of the liability, or subjecting a person to any prejudice in consequence of his pursuing any such right or remedy;
 (c) excluding or restricting rules of evidence or procedure;
and (to that extent) ss. 2 and 5 to 7 also prevent excluding or restricting liability by reference to terms and notices which exclude or restrict the relevant obligation or duty.

The practical effect of this provision is that the courts will now look very closely at the intended effect of the particular term of the contract to determine whether it is in essence a term which excludes or restricts liability rather than look simply at its form (*Phillips Products Ltd* v *Hyland* [1987] 1 WLR 659). Accordingly it was observed by Lord Griffiths in *Smith* v *Eric S. Bush* [1990] 1 AC 831 that the provisions of s. 13(1) introduce:

. . . a 'but for' test in relation to the notice excluding liability. They indicate that the existence of the common law duty to take reasonable care . . . is to be judged by considering whether it would exist 'but for' the notice excluding liability. The result of taking the notice into account when assessing the duty of care would result in removing all liability for negligent misstatements from the protection of the Act.

12.4.2.3 Application to liability for negligence The Act clearly applies to an attempt by the *proferens* to exclude or restrict his liability for negligently caused harm. For the purposes of the Act negligence is defined in s. 1(1) as including the breach of a contract term requiring the exercise of reasonable care and skill, the breach of a common law duty of care and a breach of the common duty of care owed under the provisions of the Occupiers' Liability Act 1957.

For the purposes of the Act it does not matter whether the breach of duty was inadvertent or intentional (s. 1(4)), which would seem to include the commission of any tort which requires the exercise of reasonable care. This would appear to include torts such as trespass to the person (see *Fowler* v *Lanning* [1959] 1 QB 426) and nuisance (see *Bolton* v *Stone* [1951] AC 850; *Goldman* v *Hargrave* [1967] 1 AC 645) in so far as they require the exercise of reasonable care.

So far as the provisions on negligence liability are concerned, it will not be open to the *proferens* to argue that an exemption clause prevents a duty of care from coming into existence where but for the exclusion, he would have been guilty of a failure to exercise reasonable care (s. 13(1)). Thus a building surveyor cannot provide a valuation report on a domestic dwelling which is qualified by a statement to the effect that the surveyor accepts no responsibility for the contents of the report (*Smith* v *Eric S. Bush* [1990] 1 AC 831). In this respect, it is important to distinguish between the compilation of the report itself and the work which leads up to its compilation.

12.4.3 Statutory invalidity

12.4.3.1 Death and bodily injury caused by negligence Any attempt to exclude or restrict liability for death or bodily injury resulting from negligence is void (s. 2(1)). Thus it is not open to a carrier of passengers to display a notice on a bus to the effect that passengers travel at their own risk (see also Public Passenger Vehicles Act 1981, s. 29). Where the defendant is in breach of a strict duty with the result that the consumer suffers bodily injury, s. 2(1) of the 1977 Act will not apply. However, other statutory provisions may serve to restrict the *proferens*'s ability to exclude his liability (see Defective Premises Act 1972, s. 1(1); Consumer Protection Act 1987, s. 7).

12.4.3.2 Implied terms in consumer contracts for the supply of goods Where the recipient of goods deals as a consumer and the supplier seeks to exclude or restrict his liability in respect of a breach of the implied terms in the Sale of Goods Act 1979 or related legislation, the exclusion will be regarded as void (Unfair Contract Terms Act 1977, s. 6(1) and (2); s. 7(2) and (3A)). If the recipient of the goods deals otherwise than as a consumer, liability for breach of the implied terms about title (Sale of Goods Act 1979, s. 12; Supply of Goods (Implied Terms) Act 1973, s. 8; Supply of Goods and Services Act 1982, s. 2) cannot be excluded (s. 6(1) and (2)). In relation to the remaining implied terms about description, quality and fitness, liability for breach may be excluded in non-consumer transactions, provided the exclusion clause satisfies the statutory test of reasonableness.

As a general rule, the 1977 Act applies only to business liability, but in relation to contracts of hire purchase and those for the sale of goods, the provisions of s. 6 apply to any such contract (s. 6(4)). Since the total invalidity provisions of s. 6 apply only where the buyer or hirer deals as a consumer and since a requirement of dealing as a consumer is that the supplier should act in the course of a business, it follows that the invalidity provisions will not apply to private supplies. However, where the goods are sold privately, a purported exclusion of the supplier's liability will be subject to the reasonableness test. This extension will only be relevant for the purposes of the implied terms about description (Sale of Goods Act 1979, s. 13), since the implied terms about quality and fitness only apply where the seller sells in the course of a business (Sale of Goods Act 1979, s. 14(2) and (3)).

12.4.3.3 Guarantees of consumer goods A particular form of abuse which once adversely affected the consumer arose out of the use of exemptions of liability in guarantees provided by the manufacturer of consumer goods. The unfortunate effect of such guarantees was that on closer examination they gave the consumer fewer rights than he already possessed at law. If appropriately worded, the guarantee could negative the consumer's rights against both the retailer and the manufacturer himself, by confining the consumer's 'rights' to those provided by the guarantee itself.

Guarantees are now regulated by the Unfair Contract Terms Act 1977, which provides that where goods of a type ordinarily put to private use or consumption cause loss or damage, either as a result of the defectiveness of the goods themselves or as a result of negligent manufacture or distribution, liability for such loss or damage cannot be excluded or restricted by reference to a guarantee (s. 5). For these purposes, a guarantee is anything in writing which purports to contain some promise or assurance that defects in the goods will be made good in some way (s. 5(2)(b)).

Section 5 does not affect the relationship between the consumer and the retailer (s. 5(3)), it merely applies to the relationship between the consumer and the producer. Since the 1977 Act applies to notices as well as to contract terms, it does not matter that there is no contractual relationship between the manufacturer and the consumer.

12.4.4 Exemption clauses subject to the requirement of reasonableness
While some exemption clauses are rendered totally invalid by the 1977 Act, a variety of others are permitted provided they are regarded as reasonable. The onus of proving reasonableness rests on the *proferens* rather than the consumer being required to establish its unreasonableness (s. 11(5)).

12.4.4.1 Damage other than death or bodily injury caused by negligence If the *proferens* seeks to exclude or restrict liability for negligently inflicted harm other than death or personal injury, the relevant term or notice must satisfy the test of reasonableness (s. 2(2)). Thus a purported exclusion of liability in respect of property damage or economic loss resulting from the failure of a supplier of services to exercise reasonable care may be struck down on the ground that it is unreasonable for the *proferens* to rely upon it. Section 2(2) is not confined to contract terms as it also applies to notices which purport to exclude or restrict liability. Thus a notice displayed in a multi-storey car park to the effect that the owner accepts no responsibility for damage to property, howsoever caused, will be ineffective unless regarded as reasonable.

It might be argued that it is undesirable to allow a person to restrict his liability for any form of negligently caused damage, since this might encourage people to behave carelessly. However, in relation to property damage and economic losses, the insurance position must be considered. The consumer is sometimes in the best position to insure his property against the risk of loss, in which case it may be reasonable to allow the defendant to restrict his liability in some way (see Law Com. No. 69 (1975), para. 56). Conversely, where personal injury and death are concerned, it would be unacceptable to regard the consumer as the best insurer or least cost avoider and place the risk of loss on the consumer.

12.4.4.2 Residual consumer contracts While exemption clauses in respect of the implied terms in consumer contracts for the supply of goods are widely catered for by the invalidity provisions of the 1977 Act, there still remains a residual category of consumer contracts. Exemption clauses in such contracts are subject to a requirement of reasonableness (s. 3(1)). It follows that in consumer contracts for the supply of services and other consumer contracts not otherwise provided for by the 1977 Act, a purported exclusion or limitation of the liability of the *proferens* must be reasonable.

For the purposes of s. 3(1), the Act further provides that the *proferens* cannot exclude or restrict liability in respect of his own breach of contract (s. 3(2)(a)) or claim to be entitled to give a contractual performance substantially different to that which could be reasonably expected of him (s. 3(2)(b)(i)) or claim to be able to offer no performance at all in respect of any part of his contractual obligations (s. 3(2)(b)(ii)), unless to do so satisfies the test of reasonableness.

Where the *proferens* is in breach of contract, s. 3(2)(a) provides that he cannot exclude or restrict liability in respect of his own breach unless the exclusion or restriction is reasonable. Thus, a provision in a consumer contract which attempts to limit the liability of the *proferens* to a particular amount or one which requires notification of damage within a specified period in the event of a breach of contract will have to satisfy the test of reasonableness.

Section 3(2)(a) refers specifically to liability, therefore there must be a breach of contract on the part of the *proferens*. Accordingly, if the term of the contract is worded in such a way as to define the primary obligations of the parties, s. 3(2)(a) will have no application since there will be no breach of contract if the *proferens* has clearly defined what he is prepared to provide under the terms of the contract.

Under s. 3(2)(b)(i) the *proferens* cannot claim to be entitled to render a performance substantially different from that which was reasonably expected of him, unless the relevant contract term satisfies the requirement of reasonableness. This provision would appear to take on board the majority of cases which were previously dealt with by means of the doctrine of fundamental breach of contract, since the failure to do what can reasonably be expected will ordinarily go to the root of the contract. If this is to add anything to s. 3(2)(a), it must cover something other than a breach of contract. Thus it would appear to cover a contract term which specifies that a particular method of performance is not to be regarded as a breach of contract. In the context of travel services, if a tour operator states that he is free to change itineraries, the advertised route or the nature of the accommodation initially advertised, it would appear that such provisions would have to satisfy the test of reasonableness (see *Anglo-Continental Holidays Ltd* v *Typaldos Lines Ltd* [1967] 2 Lloyd's Rep 61; Law Com. No. 69 (1975), paras 143–6). Certain expectations of performance arise independently of the contract itself, in which case those expectations may be defeated by a contract term which seeks to define the obligations of the tour operator. Accordingly, it may be reasonable to expect a performance on the part of the tour operator in excess of that which he purports to provide.

Section 3(2)(b)(i) assumes that it is possible to identify a reasonably expected performance. However, the 1977 Act does not specify whose view of the matter should be taken into account. One possible approach is to consider the expectations of the unreasonably suspicious person who reads all small print in every document before committing himself to anything (see Beale, Bishop and Furmston, *Contract Cases and Materials*, 2nd ed. (1990), p. 717). However, if this were to be the case, s. 3(2)(b)(i) would be totally ineffective. Instead, it would be preferable if courts were to consider the matter from the position of the person who is aware of what the contract provides, but expects the exemption clause to be applied fairly. This would amount to something similar to the 'main purpose of the contract' rule applied at common law under the doctrine of fundamental breach of contract. On this basis, if a carrier agrees to transport the consumer from A to B, but reserves the right to depart from the agreed route, any deviation must be in accordance with the main purpose of the contract, namely to transport the consumer from A to B. Thus if the deviation takes the consumer wildly off course, the deviation clause would probably be struck down as unreasonable (*Glynn* v *Margetson & Co* [1893] AC 351). Similarly, a provision in a holiday contract which allows the tour operator to change destinations and itineraries must be fairly applied so as not to place the holidaymaker in accommodation which could not have been reasonably expected at the time the contract was entered into.

By virtue of s. 3(2)(b)(ii) the *proferens* cannot claim to be entitled to render no performance at all in respect of any part of his contractual obligations. This would appear to cover partial or total cancellation of the contract and would therefore include a provision in a holiday contract to the effect that the tour operator may refuse to comply with his contractual obligations on economic grounds. Similarly, it would also seem to cover the cancellation at short notice, of a dramatic production at a theatre. So far as total non-performance is concerned, it can be argued that s. 3(2)(b)(ii) adds nothing to the position at common law, since if a person renders no performance at all there would appear to be a total failure of consideration. Furthermore, if the *proferens* claims to be entitled to offer a partial non-performance, there is a danger that what is offered may be substantially different from that which could reasonably be expected, in which case s. 3(2)(b)(i) might apply.

12.4.4.3   Indemnity clauses in consumer contracts   A consumer cannot be made to indemnify another in respect of liability arising due to negligence or breach of contract, except where it is reasonable for that other to rely on the indemnity clause (s. 4). Indemnity clauses may be of two kinds, namely reflexive indemnities and insurance indemnities (see Adams and Brownsword [1982] JBL 200). A reflexive indemnity is one whereby a contracting consumer is required to indemnify another party to the contract in respect of that other's liability to the consumer. Thus if a consumer engages a removal firm to transport his personal property to a new house, the contract may provide that the consumer shall indemnify the contractor against all claims and demands in excess of £500 in the event of damage to the consumer's effects resulting from negligence or other breach of contract on the part of the removal firm (see *Gillespie Brothers & Co. Ltd v Roy Bowles Transport Ltd* [1973] QB 400). Such indemnity clauses can be described as being the obverse of an exemption clause (*Smith v South Wales Switchgear Co. Ltd* [1978] 1 All ER 18, 22 per Viscount Dilhorne).

An insurance indemnity requires the consumer to indemnify the other party to the contract in respect of his liability to a third party for negligence or breach of contract. This would appear to cover a provision in a contract with a removal firm whereby the consumer agrees to indemnify the contractor in respect of liability he might incur to a third party in the course of unloading the consumer's personal effects. For example, it would apply where the consumer's dining-room table is dropped on the foot of his next-door neighbour or where one of the contractor's employees stands on the neighbour's prize rose bush. That both types of indemnity clause (see s. 4(2)(b)) and that the vicarious liability of the contractor (see s. 4(2)(a)) are covered is clear from the provisions of s. 4.

12.4.4.4 Exemption of liability for misrepresentation Section 8 of the 1977 Act amends the Misrepresentation Act 1967, s. 3, which also requires a purported exemption of liability for misrepresentation to satisfy a test of reasonableness.

A number of difficulties surround the interpretation of the Misrepresentation Act 1967, s. 3. In particular it refers to liability by reason of any misrepresentation made by a party before the contract was made. If the misrepresentation is incorporated as an express term of the contract, it would appear not to be subject to the provisions in respect of excluding liability for misrepresentation and since express terms not contained in standard-form documents, for the most part, fall outside the provisions of the Unfair Contract Terms Act 1977, the innocent party might be prejudiced.

Furthermore s. 3 of the Misrepresentation Act 1967 is intended to cover terms which exclude liability and restrict remedies. However, if the term can be drafted in such a way that it does neither of these things, it would appear to escape statutory control (*Overbrooke Estates Ltd v Glencombe Properties Ltd* [1974] 1 WLR 1335). Thus if a term provides that the representee does not rely on the statement of the representor, there would appear to be no actionable misrepresentation due to the absence of reliance or inducement, unless the reference to the absence of reliance is a pure sham (*Cremdean Properties Ltd v Nash* (1977) 244 EG 547, 551 per Bridge LJ).

12.4.5 The tests of reasonableness

12.4.5.1 The general test The Unfair Contract Terms Act 1977, s. 11(1), provides that the appropriate test to apply is to ask whether an exclusion or limitation clause is fair and reasonable having regard to the circumstances which were or ought reasonably to have been known to the parties at the time the contract was entered into. The onus of proving reasonableness lies on the *proferens* who seeks to rely upon the exclusion clause (s. 11(5)).

Because the test is applied at the time of contracting, subsequent events which might influence the court's decision are not to be taken into account in deciding whether the relevant term is reasonable or not. Accordingly, the nature of the breach of contract and its seriousness in relation to the contract as a whole should not be taken into account, unless such matters were within the contemplation of the parties at the time of contracting.

What is reasonable is not defined in the Act since this is bound to be a factual issue, thereby giving the courts considerable scope for the exercise of discretion (see Adams and Brownsword (1988) 104 LQR 94). The factors relevant to the question of reasonableness will change from case to case, but some guidelines have been judicially indicated. Generally, since the issue of reasonableness is a question of fact, appellate courts are unlikely to interfere with the trial judge's ruling on the matter unless it is clear that a perverse decision has been arrived at (see *George Mitchell (Chesterhall) Ltd* v *Finney Lock Seeds Ltd* (1983) 2 AC 803, 816 per Lord Bridge and see also *St Albans City & District Council* v *International Computers Ltd* [1996] 4 All ER 481 per Sir Iain Glidewell).

In a number of cases, the courts have openly considered which of the parties could have best insured against the risk of loss under consideration (*Photo Production Ltd* v *Securicor Transport Ltd* [1980] AC 827, 843 per Lord Wilberforce; *Smith* v *Eric S. Bush* [1990] 1 AC 831, 858–9 per Lord Griffiths). This may be a relevant factor in consumer transactions, particularly where property damage is concerned. The consumer may be in the best position to insure against the risk of loss at minimal cost, in which case the use of an exclusion or limitation clause on the part of the *proferens* could be justified.

In some instances, the court may be forced to consider the complexity and comprehensibility of the purported exclusion of liability in order to determine whether it is reasonable (*Stag Line Ltd* v *Tyne Shiprepair Group Ltd* [1984] 2 Lloyds Rep 211, 222 per Staughton J). This matter would be particularly relevant to consumer transactions in which the consumer rarely has access to independent legal advice and may not be in a position to understand a particularly complex exclusion or limitation of liability (see also *Levison* v *Patent Steam Carpet Cleaning Co. Ltd* [1978] QB 69).

There has been a growing tendency to resort to the list of guidelines contained in sch. 2 to the 1977 Act, even though these are specifically relevant only to supply of goods transactions between business contracting parties. Clearly, some of the factors listed in those guidelines will be relevant in other contexts (see *Phillips Products Ltd* v *Hyland* [1987] 2 All ER 620). Accordingly, it will be relevant to consider the relative bargaining strengths of the parties and whether the goods or services contracted for could have been acquired elsewhere and at what cost (*Smith* v *Eric S. Bush* [1990] 1 831, 858; see also *Woodman* v *Photo Trade Processing Ltd* (7 May 1981) Exeter County Court, unreported, see *Which?* July 1981). In particular, it will be necessary to consider whether the consumer has received any sort of representation. Sometimes, the content of a standard-form contract will have been negotiated in consultation with a trade association (see *R. W. Green Ltd* v *Cade Brothers Farms* [1978] 1 Lloyd's Rep 602; cf. *George Mitchell (Chesterhall) Ltd* v *Finney Lock Seeds Ltd* [1983] 2 AC 803). In some instances, it may be the case that the consumer interest is considered through consultation with consumer bodies. The difficulty this may present is that contract terms may represent the wish of the majority with the result that some individual preferences may not be catered for (cf. *Woodman* v *Photo Trade Processing Ltd*).

Other factors which may be taken into account include an assessment of the difficulty of the task undertaken by the *proferens* and a consideration of the practical consequences of the court's decision on the reasonableness issue. Thus if the supplier of a service has undertaken to perform a particularly simple task, it is unlikely that an exclusion of liability would be appropriate. The court would also need to consider the sum of money at stake, including the possibility of the consumer being faced with a financial catastrophe or a loss of an emotional kind (see *Woodman* v *Photo Trade Processing Ltd*).

12.4.5.2 Limitation clauses Where the contract term purports to limit the liability of the *proferens* to a specified sum of money, the 1977 Act gives specific guidance. It is provided that the court should have particular regard to the insurance position by considering whether insurance was available to the *proferens* and whether he had sufficient resources to meet liability should it arise (s. 11(4)).

12.4.5.3 Statutory reasonableness guidelines A list of guidelines relevant to the issue of the reasonableness of exemption clauses in non-consumer contracts for the supply of goods is contained in sch. 2 to the Act. While not specifically applicable to consumer transactions, no doubt these factors will be taken into account where appropriate. The relevant factors include the relative bargaining strength of the parties; whether there was any inducement to agree to the exemption clause; whether any condition as to the enforcement of liability could practicably be complied with; whether the buyer could have bought elsewhere without being subject to the exclusion or limitation of liability and whether the goods were made to the special order of the buyer.

The list of guidelines is not exclusive, and other factors may be considered according to the factual circumstances of the case. Because of this, it is probably unlikely that an appellate court will readily interfere with the decision reached at first instance since there is considerable scope for the exercise of discretion on the part of the courts and there may be room for differences of judicial opinion (*George Mitchell (Chesterhall) Ltd* v *Finney Lock Seeds Ltd* [1983] 2 AC 803, 815–16 per Lord Bridge).

12.4.6 Secondary evasion of liability
In order to prevent secondary evasion of the provisions of the 1977 Act, s. 10 provides that a person is not bound by the terms of a contract which seeks to

prejudice or take away rights which arise under or in connection with the performance of another contract. Thus if a consumer contracts to purchase a television and at the same time enters a separate service agreement in respect of the television, the terms of the service agreement will be ineffective if they purport to limit the supplier's liability in respect of the quality or fitness of the television.

12.5   THE UNFAIR TERMS IN CONSUMER CONTRACTS REGULATIONS 1994 (SI 1994/3159)

These Regulations, albeit six months late (thereby exposing the UK government to *Francovich* damages, see chapter 2) implement the EC Directive on Unfair Terms in Consumer Contracts (93/13/EEC, OJ L95/29, 21.4.1993) and stand alongside the provisions of the Unfair Contract Terms Act 1977. Accordingly, English traders, consumers and their advisers have two overlapping sets of rules to contend with when considering the effectiveness of exclusion clauses, limitation clauses and other unfair terms in consumer contracts as well as existing common law rules on incorporation of terms and judicial construction of contractual documents. As will be seen there are areas of overlap between the two sets of provisions, but there are also areas in which the 1977 Act applies when the 1994 Regulations do not and vice versa.

12.5.1   Application of the 1994 Regulations

In two particular respects, the 1994 Regulations have a very narrow focus: they apply only to consumer contracts with a seller or supplier which have not been individually negotiated (reg. 3(1)). Because of these limitations, the Regulations will not apply to a contract entered into between a small business and another business, as does the 1977 Act. Moreover, the Regulations will have no application to contracts which are tailor-made for an individual consumer as opposed to being based on a standard-form set of contract terms.

For the purposes of the Regulations, a consumer is defined as a natural person who in making a contract acts for non-business purposes (reg. 2(1)). Accordingly, the buyer in *R & B Customs Brokers Co. Ltd* v *United Dominions Trust Ltd* [1988] 1 All ER 847 (see chapter 1) would not be treated as a consumer for the purposes of the Regulations, although the 1977 Act did operate in its favour, despite the fact that the buyer was a company. Since a natural person may include a sole trader or a member of a partnership, such people may be protected by the Regulations, but it is clear that they must contract for purposes which are not related to their business. For these purposes, it is likely that a similar test to that applied under the 1977 Act will be used, with the result that the purchase of a car by a doctor which he intends to use partly privately and partly for the purposes of his medical practice will still be regarded as a non-business-related purchase since a doctor does not buy cars as an integral part of his business (see chapter 1).

For the purposes of the 1994 Regulations, the seller or supplier must also act 'for purposes relating to his business' (reg. 2(1)). The wording of this differs somewhat from that familiar in domestic consumer protection legislation which has been interpreted to require the supplier to supply goods as an integral part of his business (see chapter 1). It is quite possible that under the 1994 Regulations the phrase 'relating to his business' may be construed more widely so that, for example, the sale by a doctor of his car or his computer is regarded as a business sale, since both of these articles will have been used for business purposes.

Consistent with the approach adopted under domestic legislation, there is a minimalist definition of what constitutes a business activity, with the result that there is the usual uncertainty about whether a sale of goods by a student union, a charity shop or a church bazaar is to be regarded as a sale relating to a business.

In addition to the uncertainties over what is to be regarded as a business transaction, it is also essential, if a term is to be regulated under the Regulations, that it has not been individually negotiated. For these purposes, the burden of proving that a term has been individually negotiated lies on the supplier (reg. 3(5)) and a term will always be regarded as falling within the scope of the Regulations if it has been drafted in advance and the consumer has not had the chance to influence the substance of the term (reg. 3(3)).

Clearly this will cover standard-form contracts, but the wording of reg. 3(3) is such that other terms may also fall within the regulatory regime. For example, a set of terms may have been prepared with a specific consumer in mind, but if the consumer has not been consulted so that he or she can have some influence over what is agreed, reg. 3(3) would appear not to have been complied with.

In addition, the 1994 Regulations introduce the concept of severance in that they provide that nothwithstanding the fact that a particular term has been individually negotiated, this will not prevent the court from regarding the rest of the contract as being a pre-formulated standard-form contract on the basis of an overall assessment (reg. 3(4)). The difficulty this provision creates is that by introducing the notion of the standard-form contract, the wider protection suggested under reg. 3(3) could be watered down so that only standard-form contracts fall within the scope of the regulations. Clearly this would be an undesirable development from a consumer perspective. However, this fear may be misfounded, since the Directive upon which the 1994 Regulations are based makes it clear that implementing legislation should apply not just to written contracts, but also those which are made orally (Directive 93/13/EEC, recital 11).

In the process of assessing whether the terms of the contract are unfair, the regulations state that no assessment will be made of its 'core' terms (reg. 3(2)), which for present purposes cover terms which define the main subject matter of the contract or relate to the adequacy of the cost of the goods or services supplied under the contract.

Accordingly, terms of the contract which are susceptible to market forces are matters to be left to agreement between the parties and will not be the subject of legislative interference. However, there are difficulties in determining what constitutes the main subject matter of the contract, although the experience of the Unfair Contract Terms Act 1977, s. 13, shows that the courts are prepared to adopt a purposive approach to exemption clauses by looking at the effect of a particular clause rather than at its specific form (see above para 12.4.2.2). If any term in a consumer contract is to be regarded as fair, it must be drafted in plain and intelligible language. This requirement applies to all terms including those which are regarded as 'core' terms under reg. 3(2), with the result that a failure to state in clear terms what price or charge is payable for goods or services may still result in the application of the 1994 Regulations. Thus suppose in a case like *Woodman* v *Photo Trade Processing Ltd* (considered in 12.4.5.1) there is an exemption clause which operates in relation to all levels of service both at high prices and at simple holiday photograph level, even the core terms of the contract may come under scrutiny, if necessary.

12.5.2 Meaning of unfairness

The 1994 Regulations are concerned with unfairness in terms contained in consumer contracts. As such they are much broader in their application than the Unfair Contract Terms Act 1977, which, despite its misleading title, is concerned only with exclusion and limitation clauses. The key requirement for the purposes of the Regulations is that terms in consumer contracts should not be unfair. The concept of unfairness is defined in the following way in reg. 4(1):

> . . . any term which contrary to the requirement of good faith causes a significant imbalance in the parties' rights and obligations under the contract to the detriment of the consumer.

12.5.2.1 Detriment to the consumer An essential feature of this definition is that the term, if it is to be challenged under the Regulations, must be to the detriment of the consumer. However, what the Regulations do not say is at what stage the question of detriment has to be assessed, other than a provision to be found in reg. 4(2), which directs a court to consider the circumstances relating to the terms of the contract at the time of the conclusion of the contract.

What might be regarded as detrimental at the time the contract was entered into may not be regarded as so detrimental in the light of the events which unfold after there has been a breach of contract. Conversely, a term might appear to be perfectly fair at the time the contract is made, but may subsequently appear to operate unfairly in the light of post-breach events. For example, insurance contracts commonly include a provision to the effect that if an insured risk occurs, it should be reported to an appropriate authority, such as the police, within a specified period of time. But suppose the consumer's house is broken into while he is on holiday and the first opportunity on which a report can be made is some days after the cut-off date for reporting losses to the insurer. It is clear that the term may appear to be unfair in the light of the particular events which surround the failure to report.

12.5.2.2 Good faith The Regulations also introduce into English law what has hitherto been regarded as the completely alien notion of good faith, apart from the requirement which relates to insurance contract proposals (see chapter 10). Because the notion of good faith is not generally an aspect of English law, it is likely that should the European Court of Justice be asked to adjudicate on the meaning of the phrase, regard will be had to other mainland European jurisdictions where the notion of good faith is more securely planted within the legal system, such as in France or Germany.

For the purposes of the 1994 Regulations, sch. 2 provides that the following matters should be considered:

(a)   the strength of the bargaining positions of the parties;
(b)   whether the consumer has been induced to agree to the presence of the term;
(c)   whether the goods or services had been supplied to the special order of the consumer; and
(d)   the extent to which the supplier has dealt fairly and equitably with the consumer.

Generally, the first three of these matters should not cause an English court any difficulty since they are all matters which English courts take into account in determining whether an exemption clause is reasonable for the purposes of the Unfair Contract Terms Act 1977. But the last of the criteria may be more problematic, not least because it poses once more the question which sch. 2 seeks to answer, namely what is an unfair term, since an unfair term is one which does not comply with the requirement of good faith and a term which fails to comply with the requirement of good faith is one under which the supplier has failed to deal fairly and equitably with the consumer. However, an important aspect of the failure to comply with the requirement of good faith is that that failure should result in a significant imbalance in parties' rights and obligations under the contract.

For the purposes of the good faith test, the Regulations include, in sch. 3, an indicative, but non-exhaustive (reg. 4(4)) list of terms which may be regarded as unfair. This list has been taken more or less directly from the Unfair Terms Directive. Since the list is non-exhaustive, terms other than those to be found in the list may also be regarded as unfair if they fail to satisfy the requirement of good faith. But on the other hand, since the list is merely indicative, there may be circumstances in which a term listed in sch. 3 is not necessarily unfair, when other circumstances are taken into account. It is perhaps unfortunate that the Regulations do not specify that the onus of proving fairness should lie on the trader who seeks to rely upon the term under consideration.

Broadly, the listed terms which may be regarded as unfair fall into four groups (see Howells, *Consumer Contract Legislation* (London: Blackstone Press, 1995), pp. 46–8 and Brownsword, Howells and Wilhelmsson, *Welfarism in Contract Law* (Dartmouth, 1994)), which may be described as (a) terms which give one party control over the contract terms or the method of performing the contract; (b) terms which govern the duration of the contract; (c) terms which prevent the parties from having equal rights and (d) terms which exclude or limit liability under the contract.

The first of these groups, namely, terms which give one party control over the contract or its performance, seems to cover any term which seeks to bind a consumer to a set of terms before he has had a chance to become acquainted with their content.

Accordingly, rules on sufficient notice of contractual terms discussed above in relation to exemption clauses will remain relevant for the purposes of the 1994 Regulations. Also included within this category would be terms which enable the supplier to alter the terms of the contract without a valid reason for doing so and terms which allow the supplier unilaterally to vary the characteristics of the goods or services contracted for. Similarly, a term which allows the supplier to alter the price charged at the time of delivery without also giving the consumer the right to cancel the contract might be regarded as giving the supplier excessive control over the manner in which the contract is to be performed, as would a term which allows the supplier to transfer his obligations under the contract if this would be detrimental to consumer rights under a guarantee.

The second group of terms encompasses those which relate to the duration of the contract. This would include a term which enables a supplier to terminate a contract, the duration of which is not specified, unless there are reasonable grounds for that termination. Likewise, a term which allows the extension of a contract agreed to last for a fixed period beyond the date agreed would fall within this category.

The third group, consisting of terms which prevent the parties from acquiring equal rights appears to cover terms such as those which render an agreement binding on a consumer while also allowing the supplier to escape from the contract for reasons known only to himself. Also this group would encompass terms which permit the supplier to retain moneys paid by the consumer where the consumer fails to conclude a contract, if the contract does not also provide for the consumer to be compensated if the supplier fails to perform his obligations under the contract. Likewise, should the contract provide that the supplier can require the consumer to fulfil all his obligations under the contract even in the face of a failure by the supplier to do the same, the term is potentially unfair.

The final group of terms consists of those most familiar to English lawyers, namely exemption clauses and the list in sch. 3 seems to include all of the terms dealt with under the Unfair Contract Terms Act 1977. The list includes terms which exclude or limit the legal liability of the supplier in the event of death or bodily injury suffered by the consumer in the event of the supplier's negligence; terms which inappropriately exclude or limit the legal rights of consumers in relation to the supplier or another person in the event of a total or partial non-performance or an inadequate performance of any contractual obligation. Also falling within this group of terms is one which requires a defaulting consumer to pay a disproportionately high sum in compensation and one which limits the supplier's obligations to fulfil commitments undertaken by his agents. Finally, falling within this last group are terms which exclude or hinder the consumer's ability to pursue a legal remedy, such as an arbitration clause, or those which prevent the consumer from collecting evidence sufficient to allow him to proceed with an action against the supplier or impose on the consumer a burden of proof which ought to lie on the other party to the contract according to law. In particular, where the term is one which amounts to a consumer arbitration agreement, it is clear that the Unfair Terms in Consumer Contracts Regulations 1994 now apply (Arbitration Act 1996, s. 89(1)). For these purposes, a term which constitutes an arbitration agreement may be regarded as unfair if it relates to a claim for a pecuniary remedy which does not exceed any amount which may be specified by any order made under the Arbitration Act 1996 (ibid., s. 91(1)).

For the purposes of assessing what is meant by good faith, reg. 4(2) stipulates a number of guidelines which include consideration of the nature of the goods or services provided; the circumstances attending the conclusion of the contract and the remaining terms of the contract or any other related contract.

The responsibility for investigating unfair terms in consumer contracts rests with the Office of Fair Trading, although individual consumers also have the right to challenge a term if they see fit. In this regard, the Office of Fair Trading has issued guidance on terms which they regard as unfair (*Unfair Contract Terms*, OFT Bulletin, Issue 1, May 1996). It was observed by the Office of Fair Trading that traders who use plain and intelligible language and adhere to industry benchmarks in codes of practice should have little to fear. However, it is also observed that a number of terms commonly found in consumer contracts could be regarded as unfair. The most common unfair terms were considered to be entire agreement clauses, hidden clauses, penalty clauses, exclusion clauses and variation clauses (ibid.).

Entire agreement clauses are those which seek to exclude from the contract anything said or implied by a representative or agent of the *proferens*, effectively insisting that the entire contract is encapsulated in the written document presented at the time of contracting. The Office of Fair Trading concluded that since most consumers do not understand complicated legal language, an entire agreement clause would have to be drafted in very blunt terms in order to be regarded as fair. For example, it would need to say that even if a salesman happens to make an untrue or misleading statement, the *proferens* will not be bound by it and the *proferens* should also adopt procedures which ensure that the clause is specifically drawn to the consumer's attention and give the consumer the opportunity either to accept or reject any disadvantage or burden imposed by the clause.

THIRTEEN

The criminal law as a means of consumer protection

While civil law remedies serve to provide a means of compensation for harm suffered by consumers as a result of a breach of contract or as a result of the breach of a tortious obligation on the part of a trader, the criminal law is also widely used as a means of deterring traders and producers from engaging in certain types of trading abuse which operates to the detriment of consumers. The principal means of control, in this regard, is the strict-liability criminal offence which is employed as a means of encouraging the business community to achieve high standards of trading conduct. Examples of the use of the criminal law as a means of consumer protection include primary legislation such as the Trade Descriptions Act 1968, the Consumer Credit Act 1974, the Consumer Protection Act 1987, parts II and III, the Food Safety Act 1990 and the Property Misdescriptions Act 1991, which between them seek to lay down broad statutory standards designed to safeguard the consumer's interests in economic well-being and safety. Moreover there are numerous statutory instruments concerned with specific types of trading abuse which make it a criminal offence to engage in the proscribed conduct. Examples of these include the Consumer Transactions (Restrictions on Statements) Order 1976, the Package Travel, Package Holidays and Package Tours Regulations 1992 and the General Product Safety Regulations 1994.

The statutory offences created by primary and secondary legislation are enforced by public bodies at public expense and thus avoid one of the failings of the civil law which, for the most part, can only be enforced by the private initiative of the individual, aggrieved consumer.

13.1 THE USE OF THE STRICT-LIABILITY CRIMINAL OFFENCE AS A MEANS OF CONSUMER PROTECTION

If a criminal offence is said to be one of strict liability, this means that the prosecution are relieved of the responsibility of proving that the alleged offender has the necessary *mens rea* as to one or some of the elements of the *actus reus* of the crime. Sometimes the phrase 'absolute liability' is used to describe this phenomenon, but this is a misleading description as the defendant must be aware that the activity he carries on (or his omissions in relation to that activity) are capable of leading to the commission of offence. Virtually all offences in consumer protection legislation are subject to a due diligence defence which operates in favour of traders who have taken all reasonable precautions to avoid the commission of an offence by themselves or persons under their control. If such a defence is established, a contravention of a statutory provision may be excused, in which case liability cannot be said to be absolute.

The practical effect of the availability of these due diligence defences is that where an offence is made out by the prosecution, the trader will have been guilty of negligence. However, in the context of consumer protection legislation, very often it is necessary to consider the nature of the wrong committed by the trader. What should be appreciated is that consumer protection legislation is concerned with two quite separate consumer interests, namely, economic interests and safety interests, the latter of which appears to be held by the courts in higher regard than the former. Very high standards are required of businesses which prepare and supply food for human consumption or produce goods which pose a safety threat to particular types of consumer. There have been occasions in the past when a food producer has been convicted of supplying food not of the nature, substance or quality demanded by the consumer despite the fact that evidence suggested that there was nothing more the producer could do to comply with the legislation then in force (see *Parker* v *Alder* [1899] 1 QB 20; *Smedleys Ltd* v *Breed* [1974] AC 839). However, both of these cases should be considered in the light of the fact that at the relevant time, there was no statutory due diligence defence available to food producers. Under the Food Safety Act 1990, s. 21, such a defence is now provided for, but, as will be seen below, what constitutes due diligence in the context of consumer safety cases may demand very high standards compared with what is regarded as due diligence where economic interests are concerned.

What is important is that where the criminal law is used as a means of protecting consumer interests, liability should not be imposed merely for the sake of securing a prosecution. Since the purpose of using the criminal law in a regulatory context is to encourage traders to improve their business practices in the interests of consumers, setting impossibly high standards can serve no useful purpose if there is nothing more the trader can do to achieve the objective set by the legislation. Thus it has been said in the context of legislation designed to reduce the risk of environmental pollution that a person should not be convicted of a strict-liability criminal offence if its commission was due to the act of a stranger or an act of nature and where no reasonable precautions could have been taken to prevent the occurrence of the event which precipitated the commission of the offence (*Alphacell Ltd* v *Woodward* [1972] AC 824). If this approach had been adopted in relation to the defendants in *Parker* v *Alder*, in which the commission of the offence resulted from the act of a third party not under the defendant's control, and *Smedleys Ltd* v *Breed*, where food contamination resulted from a natural occurrence which was undetectable even with the use of the most up-to-date equipment, it is likely that neither would have been convicted of the offence charged.

13.2 WHEN IS STRICT LIABILITY IMPOSED BY CONSUMER PROTECTION LEGISLATION?

Ordinarily there is a presumption in favour of *mens rea* with the result that the prosecution must prove that the defendant intended to commit the crime charged. However, this presumption may be displaced by the wording of the statute creating the offence or by the subject matter with which the statute deals (*Sherras* v *De Rutzen* [1895] 1 QB 918, 921 per Wright J). It may be necessary to go outside the words of the statute and examine the context in which the statutory words are used and the mischief aimed at by the provision (*Sweet* v *Parsley* [1970] AC 132).

13.2.1 Reading the words of the statute
Some statutory provisions contain clear words to the effect that proof of *mens rea* is a requirement. For example, if the statute provides that an offence is committed where a person knowingly or recklessly makes a false statement of a prohibited nature, it would seem to follow that the offence is not one of strict liability. The Trade Descriptions Act 1968, s. 14(1), contains these words, yet the placement of the word 'knowingly' in the relevant section has been construed by the House of Lords in *Wings Ltd* v *Ellis* [1985] AC 272 to create an offence of 'semi-strict' liability. In *Wings Ltd* v *Ellis* it was held that a person can make a false statement innocently, but if he later discovers the falsity of that statement and takes insufficient precautions to correct the false impression created by it, he commits an offence. The offence created by s. 14 is one of making a statement knowing it to be false, rather than knowingly making a statement which is false. It follows that a person can make a statement without knowledge of its falsity, but become aware of the incorrectness of what has been said at a later stage, and if no precautions are taken to guard against the misleading nature of the statement made, an offence is committed.

If the statute contains provisions which require an offence to be committed knowingly and other provisions which make no reference to the word, it can normally be assumed that the provisions which do not require knowledge on the part of the offender create offences of strict liability. In *Pharmaceutical Society of Great Britain* v *Storkwain Ltd* [1986] 1 WLR 903, the question arose whether the Medicines Act 1968, s. 58(2)(a), created an offence of strict liability or not. The relevant provision prohibits the sale by retail of specified substances except in accordance with a medical practitioner's prescription. Other provisions of the same Act required the offences they created to be committed knowingly, but s. 58(2)(a) was silent on the matter. It was held that the offence created was one of strict liability. Since Parliament had gone to the trouble of identifying the offences which required proof of *mens rea* it could be assumed that where the statute remained silent, there was an intention on the part of Parliament to create an offence of strict liability.

A further aid to the interpretation of consumer protection legislation lies in the presence or absence of 'no-negligence' defences such as those which can be found in the Trade Descriptions Act 1968, s. 24, the Fair Trading Act 1973, s. 23, the Consumer Protection Act 1987, s. 39 and the Food Safety Act 1990, s. 21. It may be assumed that if Parliament has gone to the trouble of providing an escape route for a person who has offended without negligence, there is an intention to punish the negligent offender (*Clode* v *Barnes* [1974] 1 WLR 544).

Consumer protection legislation often makes use of certain words which have been interpreted to imply that proof of *mens rea* is a requirement. For example, it would be unusual for an offence of 'permitting' something to happen to be treated as one of strict liability, since a person cannot permit a state of affairs to come about without being aware of what has happened (see *Grade* v *Director of Public Prosecutions* [1942] 2 All ER 118; *Sweet* v *Parsley* [1970] AC 132). However, a person can unwittingly 'cause' an event with the result that the offence of causing the sale of a short measure of whisky is a crime of strict liability (*Sopp* v *Long* [1970] 1 QB 518). Similarly, since the acts of sale and supply can be performed by a person other than the contractual seller, the presence of the words 'selling' or 'supplying' imply the existence of a strict-liability offence. It appears to be the case that if the words of the statute define the offence in terms of 'using' a particular substance, this creates an offence of strict liability (*Green* v *Burnett* [1955] 1 QB 78).

When reading the words of a statute, the courts will also have regard to other provisions within the enactment, since these may cast light on whether there is a *mens rea* requirement. For example, if there are two similar statutory provisions, both of which create criminal offences and there is a specific requirement of *mens rea* in one case, but the other provision is silent on the matter, this may be some indication that Parliament intended the latter to be a crime of strict liability (*Pharmaceutical Society of Great Britain* v *Storkwain Ltd* [1986] 1 WLR 903).

13.2.2 Context and subject matter of the statutory provision
If the mischief aimed at by the statute is one which public policy demands should be kept under control, the imposition of strict liability may be justified.

The social purposes served by consumer protection legislation appear to fall into two broad categories. On the one hand, a number of statutory provisions are designed to protect the health and safety of consumers (for example, the Food Safety Act 1990 and the Consumer Protection Act 1987, part II), whereas other enactments are more concerned with the economic interests of the consumer (examples include the Trade Descriptions Act 1968, the Consumer Protection Act 1987, part III, the Fair Trading Act 1973, the Consumer Credit Act 1974 and the Property Misdescriptions Act 1991). The social purpose of a statute is not the only relevant factor. It may also be relevant to consider the nature of the crime, the prescribed punishment, the absence of social obloquy, the particular mischief aimed at and the field of activity in which it occurs (*Sweet v Parsley* [1970] AC 132, 156 per Lord Pearce).

Consideration of these matters in the context of consumer protection legislation has led the courts to the view that if there is something a business can do to improve its operations, this justifies the imposition of strict liability. Accordingly it was observed in *Tesco Supermarkets Ltd v Nattrass* [1972] AC 153 at p. 194 by Lord Diplock that:

> Consumer protection . . . is achieved only if the occurrence of the prohibited acts or omissions is prevented. It is the deterrent effect of penal provisions which protects the consumer from the loss he would sustain if the offence were committed. . . .
>
> The loss to the consumer is the same whether the acts or omissions which result in his being given inaccurate or inadequate information are intended to mislead him, or are due to carelessness or inadvertence. So is the corresponding gain to the other party to the business transaction with the consumer. . . . Where, in the way that business is now conducted, they are likely to be acts or omissions of employees of that party and subject to his orders, the most effective method of deterrence is to place upon the employer the responsibility of doing everything which lies within his power to prevent his employees from doing anything which will result in the commission of an offence.
>
> This I apprehend is the rational and moral justification for creating in the field of consumer protection . . . offences of 'strict liability'.

It does not follow that liability should be imposed in every case, because a conviction might not serve any useful purpose. It is considered to be important that convicting an offender should assist in the overall enforcement of the statutory provision by promoting greater vigilance on the part of the trading community or those who are subject to the operation of the statute (*Gammon (Hong Kong) Ltd v Attorney-General of Hong Kong* [1984] 2 All ER 503, 508 per Lord Scarman). Accordingly, if the impression is given that the law has searched for a luckless victim, it can be said that the imposition of strict criminal liability has served no useful purpose. It could be said that this principle went astray in *Smedleys Ltd v Breed* [1974] AC 839 in which the defendants were convicted of the offence of supplying food not of the substance demanded by the purchaser, contrary to what is now the Food Safety Act 1990, s. 14, when a tin of their processed peas was found to contain a well-sterilised caterpillar. The conviction stood despite the fact that Smedleys had made use of the most modern equipment available to them, since, at the time, the relevant legislation (Food and Drugs Act 1955) contained no due diligence defence, but rather a defence which required the accused to establish that the occurrence which led to the prohibited act was an 'unavoidable consequence' of the defendant's process of preparation. Unfortunately, the view taken of this defence in the House of Lords was that

an event is only 'unavoidable' if it occurs every time, and for a food
manufacturer to plead such a defence would be tantamount to commercial
suicide since it would constitute an admission that every tin of peas produced
would be subject to the same deficiency as the tin which led to the
prosecution! The fact that the prosecution was brought at all was regarded as
a matter of concern by Viscount Dilhorne, who expressed the view that
enforcement authorities ought to consider whether bringing a prosecution
was in the interests of consumers generally (ibid. 856). He also pointed out
that there was no obligation on the part of the enforcement authority to bring
a prosecution in every case and he could see no justification for commencing
the proceedings against Smedleys when they had done everything in their
power to prevent the contamination of their processed foods. Also of some
significance in cases of this kind was the cost in terms of court time and the
legal costs incurred by the prosecution and the defence in preparing for an
appeal to the House of Lords (ibid.).

The result in *Smedley's Ltd* v *Breed* might not be the same today, as the
Food Safety Act 1990, s. 21, now gives food producers and retailers a defence
in the event that they have exercised due diligence and taken all reasonable
precautions in order to ensure compliance with the requirements of the Act.
This, of course, is no compensation for the likes of Smedleys Ltd, and the
fact that it took until 1990 to provide such a defence in favour of the food
industry may be taken as an indication that the protection of consumers from
unsafe and unsatisfactory food products was a high priority at the time. To
the contrary, however, it might also be questioned whether the setting of such
impossibly high standards by Parliament served any useful social purpose, if
the end result was the successful prosecution of a reputable company which
had done everything it could to comply with the law.

13.3 CRITIQUE OF STRICT LIABILITY

It has been argued by some that the imposition of strict criminal liability
involves the punishment of the morally blameless and is therefore at variance
with the basic purpose of the criminal law. In some instances, this criticism
may appear to have been borne out, especially in cases where there is little
the defendant can do to avoid liability. In cases of this kind, the exercise of
prosecutorial discretion can avoid any unnecessary public expense, and on
occasions, enforcement authorities have been urged by the courts to be more
discriminatory in selecting targets for prosecution, if the only value in
bringing a particular case before the courts is to seek an exposition of the law
(see *Smedleys Ltd* v *Breed* [1974] AC 839, 856 per Viscount Dilhorne; *Wings
Ltd* v *Ellis* [1985] AC 272, 290 per Lord Hailsham of St Marylebone LC). It
should always be appreciated that the criminal law should not be used to
bring upon respectable traders who have acted honestly, the unjustified
reputation of having acted fraudulently (ibid., loc. cit.).

In contrast, if a statute is passed in order to protect the public, that
protection should not be undermined in any way (ibid. 293 per Lord
Scarman), particularly if the enactment is concerned with maintaining trading

standards. This view may be defended on the ground that the role of the law in the field of trading standards is largely preventative rather than punitive and the deterrent effect of the statutory provision lies in the stigma of criminal liability.

It may be argued that these statutes are regulatory and do not create 'real' crimes, with the result that there is no need to talk of the 'innocent' defendant as Lord Hailsham did in *Wings Ltd* v *Ellis*. However, there are dangers in downgrading these offences, since a conviction can still be quite damaging to the person convicted. While the type of criminal offences with which we are concerned are generally regarded as 'regulatory' in nature without the stigma of criminality attached to them, the public may not always take the same view. For example, in a very different context, in *Sweet* v *Parsley* [1970] AC 132, the defendant had been convicted, at first instance, of the offence of 'managing premises used for the purposes of smoking cannabis'. It is true that the *actus reus* was made out in the sense that Ms Sweet did own the premises concerned, but she had no idea what her tenants were up to. Although the conviction was overturned on appeal to the House of Lords, this did not prevent Ms Sweet from losing her job and having her name appear in local newspapers, branded as a criminal. Perhaps, at the time, drugs-related offences were regarded as more serious than regulatory trading offences, but the practical effect of the conviction was quite devastating as far as Ms Sweet was concerned.

A further objection to the use of criminal sanctions in the field of trading law is that its continued use may create a disrespect for the law (see Tench, *Towards a Middle System of Law* (Consumers' Association, 1981)). This argument is based on the premise that since the crimes created by consumer protection legislation are not morally reprehensible, it becomes easy to ignore them, treating a conviction as an inevitable consequence of the business in which the trader deals. Thus it has been observed that the ordinary man considers 'crime' to be conduct that is disgraceful or morally wrong, but he cannot be expected to do so for ever if the law jumbles morals and sanitary regulations together and teaches him to have no more respect for the Ten Commandments than for the Woodworking Regulations (Devlin, *Enforcement of Morals* (1965), p. 31). It may also be argued that the types of criminal offence under consideration are 'man-made evils' which may be bitterly resented if they are regarded as unjust by the trading community (Williams, *Textbook of Criminal Law*, 2nd ed., (1983), p. 931).

Certainly, there is some evidence that even the judiciary do not regard regulatory crimes in the same way as morally reprehensible crimes such as murder or robbery. For example, infringements of the licensing laws have been described as 'acts which are not criminal in the real sense' (*Sherras* v *De Rutzen* [1895] 1 QB 918, 922 per Wright J) and a failure to comply with certain provisions of the Misuse of Drugs Act 1971 as 'quasi-criminal' not involving the disgrace of criminality (*Sweet* v *Parsley* [1970] AC 132). If this is the attitude of the judiciary, it is not surprising that traders may regard some of these regulatory provisions as 'tiresome pinpricks' which are an inevitable part of business life (Borrie (1980) JBL 315, 320). For example, before their repeal, the Sunday trading laws based on the Shops Act 1950 were routinely ignored by some of the larger do-it-yourself hypermarkets on the basis that it was more profitable to flout the law and risk conviction than to abide by the law and remain closed on Sundays.

This last example also raises a further defect in the present criminal law system, namely the matter of penalties for infringement. Under the present state of the law, the fines imposed for the commission of a regulatory crime tend to be nominal, possibly because the courts are aware that by imposing a fine, they are nonetheless stigmatising the offender as a criminal (see Tench, *Towards a Middle System of Law*, (Consumers' Association, 1981), p. 21).

It has been suggested that crimes which are not criminal in the real sense should not be regarded as crimes at all and that civil penalties should be introduced to cover inadvertent transgressions (ibid. 20–1; Justice, *Breaking the Rules — The Problem of Crimes and Contraventions* (1980)). In this way, large parts of the criminal law might be decriminalised and replaced by a middle system between the criminal and the civil law. It is argued that if the stigma of criminality is removed there would be a greater respect for the law in that a business paying a civil penalty to the victim of the transgression would see this as serving a purpose by compensating someone rather than paying a pointless fine which gets lost in the State machinery. The adoption of such a middle system of law might encourage a greater willingness on the part of enforcement authorities to press for a civil penalty in marginal cases, instead of deciding not to prosecute for reasons which may never be publicly disclosed (Tench, *Towards a Middle System of Law*, p. 20).

The proposal to decriminalise aspects of consumer protection law would not, and should not, cover all of the present range of criminal offences. There is a strong case for retaining the criminal conviction for the purposes of cases in which the offender has acted fraudulently or intentionally with a view to deceiving consumers, or the offender who, with wilful disregard for the safety of the public, puts on to the market goods which he knows are unsafe. Thus, a car dealer who deliberately turns back the odometer reading on a second-hand car in order to enhance its retail value at the expense of consumers should still be guilty of a criminal offence under the Trade Descriptions Act 1968, s. 1(1)(a), and the supplier of services who knowingly or recklessly misdescribes his product should remain subject to the criminal penalties imposed under the Trade Descriptions Act 1968, s. 14.

While the use of the criminal law as a means of consumer protection has its critics, it does serve a useful enforcement role. Enforcement authorities argue that it would be too difficult and time-consuming to prove fault in every case. Where it is clear that there is little the offender could have done to avoid the commission of the offence in question, enforcement authorities will exercise their discretion by deciding not to prosecute. It has been demonstrated that a non-prosecution policy may be adopted where there is insufficient evidence to proceed and where there is evidence of an absence of fault on the part of the offender (Smith and Pearson [1969] Crim LR 5). Recent experience of the Food Safety Act 1990 shows that the use of this discretion not to prosecute, for example, in the case of first offenders, places the local authority enforcement agency in the position of educator and adviser rather than just being the instigator of penal proceedings.

However, a persistent problem over this exercise of discretion is that, in the past, there has been more than a strong suspicion of inconsistency of approach as between one local authority and another, with the result that traders in one area may feel that they are being treated more harshly than traders who operate in another local authority area. One way in which this problem can be counteracted is for a consistent policy to be adopted on a countrywide basis, which is a role taken on by LACOTS, the local authorities' coordinating body for trading standards matters.

13.4 STATUTORY DEFENCES

While many consumer protection measures impose strict criminal liability, the truly innocent offender will often be able to escape liability where he can show that one of the statutory defences provided for in most consumer protection legislation applies in his case. By far the most important of these is the defence that the person charged has taken all reasonable precautions and has acted with due diligence in order to avoid the commission of the offence charged (Trade Descriptions Act 1968, s. 24(1)(b); Fair Trading Act 1973, s. 25(1)(b); Consumer Credit Act 1974, s. 168(1)(b); Weights and Measures Act 1985, s. 34(1); Consumer Protection Act 1987, s. 39(1); Food Safety Act 1990, s. 21(1); Property Misdescriptions Act 1991, s. 2(1)). Some variants of this defence are coupled with other requirements to the effect that the defendant must show that the commission of the offence was due to a mistake, reliance on information supplied by another, the act or default of another, an accident or some other event beyond the defendant's control (Trade Descriptions Act 1968, s. 24(1)(a)), but generally the modern tendency is to place the emphasis upon the exercise of due diligence and the taking of reasonable precautions.

Where the person charged raises a defence, the effect of doing so is to accept that an offence has been committed, but to aver that there is some excuse which exonerates the defendant. For this reason, the defences considered below do not operate in the same way as the disclaimer doctrine considered in relation to the offences under s. 1 of the Trade Descriptions Act 1968 (see chapter 17). Under that doctrine, the effect of a valid disclaimer of responsibility is to nullify the effect of any description applied to goods so that it has no effect on the mind of the consumer and therefore does not exert any influence (see *R* v *Hammertons Cars Ltd* [1976] 1 WLR 1243). In contrast, by raising one of the statutory defences, there is an admission that an offence has been committed, but the defence itself operates as a form of confession and avoidance.

Because the effect of raising one of the statutory defences is that the accused admits that an offence has been committed, occasionally, there may be a reluctance to use the defence provisions in consumer protection statutes. This appears to be especially the case where the offences under the Trade

Descriptions Act 1968, s. 14, are concerned, since this section contains language which suggests the existence of *mens rea* offences (see chapter 18). Section 14 creates two offences of recklessly making a statement as to services which is false or making a statement about services provided which the maker knows to be false. If these are properly understood to be *mens rea* offences, which is doubtful after the House of Lords decision in *Wings Ltd* v *Ellis* [1985] AC 272, so far as the second offence is concerned, the effect of raising the due diligence defence would be to admit that there has been an element of excusable dishonesty on the part of the defendant. This appears to have been a consideration in the tactics adopted by the defendants in *Wings Ltd* v *Ellis*. They were charged with making a statement about the holiday services they provided, knowing it to be false, contrary to s. 14(1)(a) of the 1968 Act. They appeared to have taken a range of reasonable precautions to ensure that potential clients did not receive incorrect information regarding the misdescribed holiday, yet oddly the defendants did not seek to plead the due diligence defence. It may be argued that the reason for this failure was that, at the time, most people regarded s. 14(1)(a) as creating a genuine *mens rea* offence with the result that if the due diligence defence were to be pleaded, the defendants would have been taken to have admitted that they had committed an offence of dishonesty, which would have been highly damaging to their trading reputation.

However, the interpretation placed upon s. 14(1)(a) by the House of Lords was that it created an offence of 'quasi-strict' liability. It follows from this that it will be possible for a person charged with the commission of that offence to plead the due diligence defence, if he can show that he has put in place a system which is designed to prevent the communication of inaccurate information to service customers. This would not have been possible if the section had been construed as creating a true *mens rea* offence, since it is inherently unlikely that a person who has acted recklessly or knowingly could be said to have taken reasonable precautions to avoid the commission of the offence. It follows from this that the due diligence defence will definitely have no application to the offence of recklessly making a statement which is false under s. 14(1)(b), since the *mens rea* requirement is inconsistent with the nature of the due diligence defence (see *Coupe* v *Guyett* [1973] 2 All ER 1058). Consistent with the approach taken in *Coupe* v *Guyett* to the availability of the statutory defence where an offence of dishonesty has been committed under the Trade Descriptions Act 1968, s. 14(1)(b), it also appears that the due diligence defence will have no application where the defendant has committed the offence of applying a false trade description to goods contrary to s. 1(1)(a) of the 1968 Act (*R* v *Southwood* [1987] 1 WLR 1361). It would be difficult to argue that a person who has himself applied a false description to goods, such as by deliberately turning back the odometer reading on a second-hand car, should be allowed to turn round and say that he has acted diligently to avoid the commission of an offence. As was observed in *R* v *Southwood* by Lord Lane CJ, 'by his initial actions in falsifying the instrument, he has not taken any precautions, let alone reasonable precautions'.

13.4.1 Reasonable precautions and due diligence

It is necessary for the person charged with the commission of an offence to prove that he has both taken reasonable precautions *and* exercised due diligence to avoid the commission of an offence by himself or any person under his control. The defence contains two distinct elements. It is first necessary to show that the initial precautions taken by the defendant are sufficient, and he must also show that he has continued to act diligently thereafter in order to secure compliance with the regulatory scheme.

13.4.1.1 Reasonable precautions

What is reasonable is a question of fact, which will vary according to the circumstances of each case. Factors which may be relevant include the nature of the establishment operated by the alleged offender, the sort of goods sold and the extent to which a reasonable person would think it right to take the precautions which are being canvassed (*Ashurst* v *Hayes & Benross Trading Co.* (1974 unreported) per Lord Widgery CJ). The test applied is an objective one which will take account of what could reasonably have been expected in the circumstances, with the result that the resources available to a particular defendant may be a relevant consideration as will be the nature of the risk posed to consumers. For example, as will be seen below, there is a greater likelihood that the precautions taken by a defendant will be regarded as insufficient where his operation poses a threat to health or safety as opposed to cases in which the offence merely causes economic harm to consumers.

13.4.1.1.1 The source of supply In particular cases it may be relevant for the person charged to show that he has obtained supplies from a reputable source (*Sherratt* v *Gerald's the American Jewellers Ltd* (1970) 68 LGR 256) or that where there is doubt about the truth of a particular description, a retailer has taken steps to verify it (*Sutton London Borough Council* v *Sanger* (1971) 135 JP 239).

13.4.1.1.2 Second-hand cars In relation to the supply of a second-hand car, the odometer of which has been turned back, a number of reasonable precautions may be taken. For example, the car can be checked over by a garage mechanic to ensure that its condition roughly corresponds with the mileage reading on the odometer (*Lewis* v *Maloney* [1977] Crim LR 436). Alternatively, a previous owner can be consulted in order to discover the mileage reading on the car at the time he disposed of it (*Wandsworth London Borough Council* v *Bentley* [1980] RTR 429; cf. *Crook* v *Howells Garages (Newport) Ltd* [1980] RTR 434). Where it is not possible to discover the truth, a suggested precaution is that the supplier should seek to disclaim responsibility for the accuracy of the mileage reading (*Zawadski* v *Sleigh* [1975] RTR 113) but the extent to which a disclaimer is effective is subject to fairly stringent requirements which are not easy to satisfy (see chapter 17). However, it does not follow from these cases that a second-hand car dealer must, in every case, issue a disclaimer or check with the previous owner (*Ealing London Borough Council* v *Taylor* (1995) 159 JP 460). It is important to emphasise that what the law requires is that the defendant should exercise all reasonable precautions rather than every possible precaution to avoid the commission of an offence. For example, in *Ealing London Borough Council* v *Taylor* it was considered pointless to consult the previous registered owner, a car hire company, since the car in question had been sold on within the trade several times before it reached the defendant.

13.4.1.1.3 Sampling If a retailer supplies goods which are capable of posing a threat to consumer safety, it is a reasonable precaution to make random safety checks (*Garrett* v *Boots the Chemist* (1980) 88 ITSA Monthly Rev 238; *Rotherham Metropolitan Borough Council* v *Raysun (UK) Ltd* (1988) 8 TrLR 6). It is quite likely that more in the way of sampling will be expected of a large-scale operation than would be expected of a smaller enterprise with fewer resources to devote to a sampling procedure (*Garrett* v *Boots the Chemist*; *Riley* v *Webb* (1987) 151 JP 372). If the defendant relies upon an overseas agent to ensure compliance with domestic legislative requirements in relation to product safety for the purposes of the Consumer Protection Act 1987, part II, it is more than likely that such precautions will not be regarded as reasonable. Thus in *Rotherham Metropolitan Borough Council* v *Raysun (UK) Ltd* taking just one sample out of 10,000 packets of crayons which were found to contain toxic lead by an overseas agent was considered to be insufficient to satisfy the requirements of the 1987 Act.

What is a sufficient sample may depend upon the size of the defendant's operation. An indication of what is to be expected can be derived from the case law. For example, a sample of a mere 0.49 per cent of almost 77,000 soft toys was considered to be inadequate where the eyes of some of the toys could be easily removed by a child (see *P & M Supplies (Essex) Ltd* v *Devon County Council* [1991] Crim LR 832). What lay behind the decision was that the defendant had failed to produce any statistical evidence of what reasonable traders would do in the circumstances. Accordingly, since the onus of proving the reasonableness of the precautions taken lay on the defendant, that onus had not been discharged by the failure to call any evidence at all on the issue. Similarly in *Sutton London Borough Council* v *Halsall* (1995) 159 JP 431, taking only five samples out of a total import consignment of 4,600 flammable Hallowe'en capes was considered insufficient, even though the sampling procedure complied with BSI requirements. Presumably, an important factor in this case was that the whole of the consignment was likely to be directed towards child consumers, in which case, more rigorous precautions could be justified.

13.4.1.1.4 Warnings Where a producer or an importer becomes aware of a defect in goods for which he is responsible, a simple precaution which can be taken is to warn any person to whom those goods have been supplied in the course of a business. For these purposes, any warning given must make it clear that in order for the goods to be safely used the warning must be complied with. Accordingly, a mere indication that it is desirable that a warning be passed on to consumers will not suffice, since in such a case *all* reasonable precautions have not been taken (*Coventry City Council* v *Ackerman Group plc* [1995] Crim LR 140).

13.4.1.1.5 Corporate precautions Where, as is commonly the case, the alleged offender is a body corporate which employs a large number of people, it must be shown that an adequate training programme has been put into place (*Tesco Supermarkets Ltd* v *Nattrass* [1972] AC 153). In these circumstances, it would be unreasonable to expect the 'directing mind and will' of the company to exercise personal control over all employees within the organisation, but it is necessary for the company to show that it has set up a tiered structure to ensure that employees at all levels of the company do what is necessary to comply with the legal requirements imposed by consumer protection legislation. In particular, it is important to ensure that junior, subordinate employees to whom an important task has been delegated are adequately supervised in carrying out the delegated task (*Amos* v *Melcon (Frozen Foods) Ltd* (1985) 149 JP 712).

13.4.1.1.6 Food production Perhaps the fastest developing area of consumer protection law so far as the reasonable precautions or due diligence defence is concerned is that of food law, where the defence has only been in operation since the enactment of the Food Safety Act 1990. Food producers and retailers must show that they have taken specific steps to avoid the presence of, for example, some undesired substance in food. One way in which this can be done is to adopt an HACCP (hazard analysis critical control point) system, which in the majority of cases should eliminate the possibility of unwanted foreign objects in processed food. However, for such a system to be effective it must be capable of identifying the critical control points at which errors may be made; establish appropriate means of monitoring those points and provide for adequate remedial action if the safe limits of a critical control point are exceeded. On a much simpler level, if any defect detection system is used, it must be strategically placed otherwise it will be of little use at all. In *R* v *F. & M. Dobson Ltd* (1995) 14 TrLR 467, a Stanley knife blade was found in a chocolate nut crunch (initially marketed under the curiously apt name of 'Cock-ups') produced by the defendants. In the Crown Court, the defendants were convicted of selling food which did not comply with food safety requirements and were fined £25,000, despite the fact that they did have a metal detection system. The problem was that the metal detector was not positioned at the end of the production line, but had done its job at a much earlier stage of production. From this, it is clear that the knife blade penetrated the confectionery at a late stage of production and remained undetected before the offending 'Cock-up' reached the public. The defendants sought to argue that they had taken reasonable precautions for the purposes of the Food Safety Act 1990, s. 21. After the incident, the company spent some £280,000 in upgrading their detection system, but this could have no bearing on the question whether reasonable precautions were taken at the time of the commission of the alleged offence.

In upholding the conviction (but reducing the fine to £7,000) the Court of Appeal considered that reasonable precautions had not been taken. To install a metal detector is one thing, but to position it where it will work to best effect is a precaution which any food manufacturer would take.

13.4.1.1.7 Reasonable precautions and matters relevant in mitigation of penalty In determining whether reasonable precautions have been taken by the defendant, the only matters which will be considered will be precautions taken before the commission of an offence. If the defendant takes remedial action after the events which constitute the commission of the offence, this will be relevant only in mitigation of any penalty which might be imposed (*Haringey London Borough Council* v *Piro Shoes Ltd* [1976] Crim LR 462). If a person is charged with selling food which does not comply with food safety requirements contrary to the Food Safety Act 1990, s. 8, it will be no defence to show that several thousands of pounds have been spent in improving safety procedures (see *R* v *F. & M. Dobson Ltd* (1995) 14 TrLR 467). Similarly, explanations of the reason for committing an offence should not be confused with the taking of reasonable precautions. If a retailer commits an offence due to staff shortages, for example, he is still guilty of an offence, but the explanation may be pleaded in mitigation of penalty (*Marshall* v *Herbert* [1963] Crim LR 506).

13.4.1.2 Due diligence The second limb of the statutory defence requires the defendant not just to acquire equipment or take other precautions which are capable of detecting defects or otherwise preventing the commission of an offence, but also to exercise diligence in taking those precautionary measures. Thus it will be insufficient to have a 'paper system' for avoiding the commission of an offence if that system has not been put into operation in a diligent manner. For example in *Tesco Supermarkets Ltd* v *Nattrass* [1972] AC 153 a branch manager employed by the defendants had allowed a misleading indication of the sale price of packets of soap powder to be displayed in the store he managed. The defendants were charged with the commission of an offence under the (now repealed) Trade Descriptions Act 1968, s. 11(2), but claimed that they had set up a proper system of education and training with the result that they had taken reasonable precautions and acted with due diligence to avoid the commission of an offence. It was held by the House of Lords that it was not sufficient for the defendants to show that they had a system of training on paper; they also had to show that they had diligently put that system into operation. In the event, the defendants were held to have complied with the second element of the defence since the 'brains' or the 'directing mind and will' of the company had devised a system to ensure compliance with the law and had taken all proper steps to put that system into operation. It could not be said to be the fault of the company that a 'cog in the machine' had failed to do as he had been directed by his superiors. All that could be said was that the branch manager had certain duties which were the result of the company having taken reasonable precautions and having exercised due diligence, and his breach of those duties could not be said to be the responsibility of the company. Stating that the reasonable precautions taken by the defendant must be diligently put into operation is very easy to state, but in practice it is very difficult to apply. For example, when there has been a major aircraft or passenger ship disaster, a public inquiry into the corporate precautions for avoiding accidents can take months or even years, possibly involving many visits to the company head office and local offices to inspect and sample procedures. In contrast, in a case like *Tesco Supermarkets Ltd* v *Nattrass* the same feat has to be achieved, often by lay magistrates, in a very much shorter period.

Perhaps the most important lesson to come out of the decision in *Tesco Supermarkets Ltd* v *Nattrass* is that proper regard must be had to the way in which a protective system operates in practice. The system adopted by Tesco was considered to be sufficient to ensure compliance with the then requirements of the Trade Descriptions Act 1968, s. 11, but special care may need to be taken with staff training so that all employees are aware of the reasons for certain forms of action. In *Turtington* v *United Co-operative Ltd* [1993] Crim LR 376 employees were given instructions which allowed them to identify goods which failed to comply with relevant safety regulations, but they had not been given any instructions on why those goods should be rejected. In the circumstances, it was held that the employer had failed to act diligently by reason of this failure.

A recently considered problem is whether a person can rely upon the due diligence defence where he has assumed that goods are in compliance with statutory standards because they have been so certified by a third party. In *Balding* v *Lew-Ways Ltd* (1995) 159 JP 541 (see also *Whirlpool UK Ltd* v *Gloucestershire County Council* (1995) 159 JP 123) the Divisional Court has held that *blind* reliance on a certificate of compliance with British Standards Institution standards is not sufficient to establish that due diligence has been exercised. In that case, the defendants supplied a 'Tipper Trike' which was unsafe by virtue of a dangerous and accessible protrusion. This contravened provisions of the Toys (Safety) Regulations 1989 and therefore amounted to the commission of an offence under the Consumer Protection Act 1987, s. 12(1). In allowing the prosecution's appeal, it was considered that there were material differences between BSI standards and the standards required by the Regulations made under the 1987 Act. Moreover, where BSI certification was given, the producer was warned that this did not confer immunity from legal obligations. What the defendants should have done in order to satisfy the defence was to ask the tester they had employed to say whether the 'Tipper Trikes' complied with the law of the land. Reliance on a safety certificate issued by a third party is particularly hazardous where it is clear from the certificate itself that it is out of date. In such a case, the defendant would be well advised to make alternative safety tests (see *Suffolk County Council* v *Rexmore Wholesale Services Ltd* (1995) 159 JP 390). Similarly, it is unreasonable to expect to rely on a canine pedigree certificate where it is obvious that the certificate has not been signed by the breeder (*Sutton London Borough Council* v *Perry Sanger Ltd* (1971) 135 JPN 235).

The decision in *Balding* v *Lew-Ways Ltd* should not be taken to mean that, in all circumstances, there will be a conviction where the defendant has relied upon third party certification. For example, in *Carrick District Council* v

Taunton Vale Meat Traders Ltd (1994) 92 LGR 335, the defendants had consigned meat which was unfit for sale, but had done so because the meat had been certified as fit by a local authority inspector. In the circumstances it was considered that there was no reason for doubting the reliability of the certificate. This might be regarded as an unusual decision, given that there are now a number of decisions which suggest that reliance on third-party certification is not usually sufficient evidence of the exercise of due diligence, but it may be viewed from a public policy angle. Surely it is not in the public interest for a public body charged with the enforcement of the Food Safety Act 1990 to certify food as fit for sale and then proceed to bring a prosecution based upon the incorrect advice given by their own inspector. The decision also emphasises that it is important to consider how reliable is the person who advises that the law has been complied with. Presumably, a person representing a body charged with the responsibility of enforcing the law ought to be taken to be a reliable indicator of whether the law has been complied with.

An interesting development so far as the due diligence defence is concerned is the apparent difference in approach taken to the issue of consumer safety as compared with the matter of consumer economic interests (see Parry, 'Judicial approaches to due diligence' [1995] Crim LR 695). The Food Safety Act 1990 and the Consumer Protection Act 1987, part II, are concerned with safety interests, but the Trade Descriptions Act 1968, the Consumer Protection Act 1987, part III, and the Property Misdescriptions Act 1991 are concerned with purely economic harm to consumers in the form of false or misleading descriptions regarding goods, services, property and price indications. The way in which recent case law has developed suggests that it is far easier for a defendant charged with the commission of an offence which affects consumer economic interests to satisfy the due diligence defence than it is for a defendant charged with the commission of an offence which relates to the issue of consumer health or safety. This apparent distinction between safety and economic interests is of comparatively recent origin, since a fairly strict approach to the applicability of the due diligence defence had been maintained under the Trade Descriptions Act 1968, which is concerned with economic interests only. For example in *Sherratt* v *Gerald's the American Jewellers Ltd* (1970) 68 LGR 256 a retail jeweller charged with the commission of an offence under the Trade Descriptions Act 1968, s. 1(1)(b), had displayed a watch described by its manufacturer as waterproof. The jeweller was held not to have taken reasonable precautions or to have acted diligently to avoid the commission of an offence because he had failed to immerse his stock of timepieces in a bucket of water, as did the customer to whom a waterproof watch had been sold. If nothing more, this serves to illustrate the principle that no one in business can rely upon a description applied to goods by someone else, if there are other measures which could be taken to ensure compliance with the law.

While some of the case law on the Trade Descriptions Act 1968 indicates a somewhat hardline approach to what constitutes due diligence, more recent case law might be taken to indicate a softening of the stance taken by the courts. For example, the cases on 'clocked' odometer readings might have suggested, at one stage, that a wise move would be to check the mileage on a second-hand car with its previous owner or to issue a disclaimer in any case in which there was doubt over the accuracy of the reading. However, more recent cases indicate that these precautions need not be taken in every case (see *Ealing London Borough Council* v *Taylor* (1996) 159 JP 460).

Centre stage for the purposes of the distinction between safety cases and economic interest cases must be the Consumer Protection Act 1987, s. 39, which applies to both types of case, being equally applicable to the pricing offences created by part III of the Act and to the consumer safety offences created by part II. What the case law is beginning to reveal is that it is increasingly difficult to establish that all reasonable precautions have been taken to guard against an offence which prejudices consumer safety, if there is something else the defendant could have done, whereas in economic loss cases, there appears to have developed a much more relaxed approach which may result in an acquittal even where further precautions might have been taken. For example in *Berkshire County Council* v *Olympic Holidays Ltd* (1993) 13 TrLR 251 a customer booked a holiday based upon a misleading price display on a computer screen which showed the price of the holiday to be £182 less than the price actually charged by the tour operator. The defendant travel agents, who were charged with the commission of an offence under the Consumer Protection Act 1987, s. 20(1), had issued no disclaimer of responsibility for the accuracy of the price display, but were nonetheless acquitted. The court accepted that the cause of the error was an inexplicable 'blip' in the computer software for which the defendants could not be held responsible. It was also considered that the risk of a misleading statement being made had to be balanced against the difficulty of taking steps to guard against the provision of misleading information. Given these difficulties, it was considered that, in the circumstances, the defendants had taken reasonable precautions despite the fact that they had not done everything to guard against the consumer being misled. Consistent with other cases in which misleading information has been given which adversely affects the consumer's economic well-being, Roch LJ emphasised that what the Consumer Protection Act 1987, s. 39, requires is that the defendant should take all *reasonable* precautions, not *every practical step* to avoid the commission of an offence (ibid. 256).

13.4.2   Other aspects of the statutory defences

It has been observed above that older variants of the statutory defences, such as that found in the Trade Descriptions Act 1968 and the Fair Trading Act 1973, require the defendant to prove not just that he has acted diligently and has taken all reasonable precautions, but also that the commission of the alleged offence was due to some trigger event recognised by the relevant legislation. More recent legislation, such as the Food Safety Act 1990, generally omits reference to most of these events on the basis that it can be assumed that the reasonable precautions and due diligence defence takes account of the specific trigger events.

The relevant events for the purposes of these earlier statutory measures include those of mistake, reliance upon information supplied by another person, act or default of another person, accident and some other cause beyond the defendant's control.

13.4.2.1 Mistake (Trade Descriptions Act 1968, s. 24(1)(a); Fair Trading Act 1973, s. 25(1)(a); Consumer Credit Act 1974, s. 168(1)(a)). In order for a mistake to operate as a defence, it must be a factual mistake on the part of the person charged. It has been held that a mistake on the part of an employee will not suffice for these purposes (*Birkenhead Co-operative Society* v *Roberts* [1970] 1 WLR 1497; *Hall* v *Farmer* [1970] 1 All ER 729). In the case of employee mistakes, the proper aspect of the defence to plead is that of act or default of another person, considered below, although this is subject to certain procedural requirements.

If the mistake is to be operative, it must be a mistake of fact, thus it will not be open to the person charged to plead that acting in a particular way constitutes the commission of an offence as this will amount to a plea of mistake of law. This supposes the defendant in *Stone* v *Burn* [1911] 1 KB 927 had claimed that he did not realise it was an offence to put his beer in bottles marked with the names 'Bass' or 'Guinness'. The defence of mistake would not be available.

There appears to be little authority on what type of mistake will suffice for the purposes of this aspect of the defence, but it would appear reasonable to assume that an inadvertent misdescription might suffice or a mistake in reading a price list (*Butler* v *Keenway Supermarkets Ltd* [1974] Crim LR 560). Possibly a person could mistakenly believe a description to be correct, although authority under the Merchandise Marks Act 1887, s. 2, suggests that this would not be a defence, amounting in effect to a plea of mistake of law (*Kat* v *Diment* [1951] 1 KB 34).

The reason why more recent legislation has not included a specific reference to mistake as an aspect of the general defences is that it is difficult to imagine circumstances in which a genuine mistake has been made if reasonable precautions have been taken by the defendant.

13.4.2.2 Reliance on information supplied by another (Trade Descriptions Act 1968, s. 24(1)(a); Fair Trading Act 1973, s. 25(1)(a); Consumer Credit Act 1974, s. 168(1)(a); Food Safety Act 1990, s. 21(3)(a); Property Misdescriptions Act 1991, s. 2(3)(b)). This is generally regarded as a defence for the likes of advertising agencies and publishers who may rely upon information supplied to them by their clients. However, the defence can also apply to retailers who rely on product information supplied to them by a producer. Accordingly, this was an appropriate defence in *Sherratt* v *Gerald's the American Jewellers Ltd* (1970) 68 LGR 256, where a retailer relied on the description 'waterproof' applied to watches supplied by a manufacturer. However, as has been seen already, this reliance will not suffice to exonerate the defendant if he has failed to take reasonable precautions to avoid the commission of the offence or has not acted diligently in putting those precautions into effect. Thus blind acceptance of information supplied by another will not be a defence if it is unreasonable to rely on the information supplied. In *Rotherham Metropolitan Borough Council* v *Raysun (UK) Ltd* (1989) 8 TrLR 6 the defendants had imported a consignment of crayons which contained more than the amount of lead permitted under the consumer safety legislation then in force. The defendants were also charged with the commission of an offence under the Trade Descriptions Act 1968, s. 1(1)(b), in that they had supplied the crayons subject to the description 'poisonless' when in fact the crayons did not comply with that description. As part of their defence under s. 24, the defendants argued that they had expected their Hong Kong agents to have inspected the crayons and to have submitted samples for analysis and that since no defects had been reported they were entitled to rely on that silence as an indication that the crayons were in compliance with legal requirements. When the crayons arrived in this country, all the defendants did was to arrange for a single sample test to be carried out. The Divisional Court was prepared to accept that some pre-cautions had been taken, but they were insufficient to satisfy the requirements of s. 24. Blind reliance on what someone else might have said or not said cannot satisfy the requirements of the Trade Descriptions Act 1968. In contrast in *Hurley* v *Martinez & Co. Ltd* (1990) 9 TrLR 189 the defendants sold bottles of German wine which were inaccurately labelled as being of 8 per cent alcohol strength, when the accurate figure was 7.2 per cent. Evidence showed that incorrect information had been supplied by the German bottlers. Despite the fact that the English importers and retailers had made no sample checks or obtained certification of alcoholic strength, it was held that they had reasonably relied upon the information supplied to them due to the exercise of what could be assumed to be 'Teutonic thoroughness' on the part of the West German laboratory analyses of alcohol strength. In the event, the Divisional Court was not prepared to disagree with the magistrates' conclusion that the s. 24 defence had been satisfied, but this does seem to fly in the face of a substantial number of cases which suggest that blind reliance on information supplied by another does not constitute the exercise of due diligence. What seemed to make the difference between *Martinez* and *Raysun* was that the overseas agents in the latter were not subject to any statutory control in their activities, and as such could not be regarded as reliable, whereas the German testers were a State laboratory who could be implicitly relied upon as having given accurate information since the activities of the testers were subject to European Community law. What this serves to emphasise is that reliance upon certification by a third party may be regarded as reasonable if the third party can be regarded as sufficiently reliable not to warrant any further action on the part of the defendant (see also *Carrick District Council* v *Taunton Vale Meat Traders Ltd* (1994) 92 LGR 335, considered in 13.4.1.2). For example, it would not be reasonable to rely upon a MOT certificate as evidence of the roadworthiness of a car, since the certificate specifically states that it should not be relied upon in that respect (see *Barker* v *Hargreaves* (1981) RTR 197).

It would appear that the odometer reading on a car and information printed on the packaging of goods by the manufacturer can be regarded as information on which a person may rely, although it has been argued that the information referred to in s. 24(1)(a) should be confined to information supplied exclusively to the defendant rather than to information which is generally available to the public (see Mickleburgh, *Consumer Protection* (1979), p. 306).

Where the defence is relied upon, it is necessary for the person charged to give seven days' notice to the prosecution. All available information relating to the identity of the supplier of the information must be disclosed in order to assist the prosecution should they decide to pursue the supplier instead (Trade Descriptions Act 1968, s. 24(2); Fair Trading Act 1973, s. 25(2); Consumer Credit Act 1974, s. 168(2); Consumer Protection Act 1987, s. 39(2); Food Safety Act 1990, s. 21(5); Property Misdescriptions Act 1991, s. 2(3)(b)).

13.4.2.3 Act or default of another person (Trade Descriptions Act 1968, s. 24(2); Fair Trading Act 1973, s. 25(2); Consumer Credit Act 1974, s. 168(2); Consumer Protection Act 1987, s. 39(2); Food Safety Act 1990, s. 21(3); Property Misdescriptions Act 1991, s. 2(3)(a)). If the person charged gives seven days' notice of an intention to rely upon this defence in order to allow for the identification of the person concerned (Trade Descriptions Act 1968, s. 24(1)(a); Fair Trading Act 1973, s. 25(1)(a); Consumer Credit Act 1974, s. 168(1)(a); Consumer Protection Act 1987, s. 39(1); Food Safety Act 1990, s. 21(5); Property Misdescriptions Act 1991, s. 2(3)(a)), the person identified in the notice may be proceeded against directly under what is known as the 'bypass' procedure (Trade Descriptions Act 1968, s. 23; Fair Trading Act 1973, s. 24; Consumer Protection Act 1987, s. 40(1); Food Safety Act 1990, s. 20), considered below.

13.4.2.3.1 The bypass procedure The effect of the 'act or default' defence is that a retailer who technically offends against the Trade Descriptions Act 1968, for example, may be able to set up the defence that the commission of the offence was due to the actions or inactions of another person, and it may be determined by the enforcement authority that the policy of the Act is best served by prosecuting that other person, although who may be proceeded against will depend on the wording of the parent legislation.

The defence is most widely used where a retailer seeks to rely on the act or default of a corporate supplier or manufacturer, but there is nothing in the wording of the Trade Descriptions Act 1968, s. 23, to prevent the procedure from being used against an individual. Accordingly, an employer has been able to name an employee within his organisation as a person due to whose act or default an offence came to be committed, with the result that that employee was also proceeded against (see *Whitehead* v *Collett* [1975] Crim LR 53). Similarly, in *Olgiersson* v *Kitching* [1986] 1 All ER 746 the private owner of a car the odometer reading of which had been turned back before the vehicle was traded in part exchange to a car dealer was successfully prosecuted under s. 23, despite the fact that had the original owner been prosecuted under the Trade Descriptions Act 1968, s. 1(1)(a), the prosecution would have failed on the ground that the defendant had not acted in the course of a trade or business. This result, although clearly correct on the wording of s. 23 must be regarded as questionable. It surely serves little useful purpose in terms of implementation of the general scheme of a consumer protection measure to use it against private individuals. While the defendant in *Olgiersson* v *Kitching* was clearly seeking to gain an advantage for himself by enhancing the trade-in value of his car, the general purpose which underlies the Trade Descriptions Act 1968 must be that of improving trading standards. It is suggested that the proper vehicle for a prosecution in a case like *Olgiersson* v *Kitching* would be the Theft Act 1968, on condition that the prosecution could prove the necessary *mens rea* on the part of the private individual. It must be questioned how far prosecutions of employees under s. 23 bring about an overall improvement in trading standards.

There is a noticeable difference in the wording of the Trade Descriptions Act 1968, s. 23, and its counterpart in the Consumer Protection Act 1987, s. 40(1), which requires the person charged under the bypass procedure to have acted in the course of a business of his. Even the branch manager of a retail outlet cannot be proceeded against under this provision, since the business he runs is that of the company which employs him rather than being his own business (*Warwickshire County Council* v *Johnson* [1993] 1 All ER 299).

While there is authority under both the Trade Descriptions Act 1968 and the Consumer Protection Act 1987 which indicates how the bypass procedure may be used in relation to private individuals, the same is not true of the Food Safety Act 1990. Oddly, although this Act is of more recent origin than the Consumer Protection Act 1987, the wording of the Food Safety Act 1990, s. 20, is such that it will be possible to adopt exactly the same approach as that adopted for the purposes of the Trade Descriptions Act 1968.

In order for the bypass procedure to operate effectively, there must be a causal connection between the offence committed by the first defendant who pleads the act or default defence and the second defendant's act or default. Accordingly if the act or default of D2 does not result in D1 committing the crime charged, procedings under s. 23 of the Trade Descriptions Act will fail (see *Tarleton Engineering Co. Ltd* v *Nattrass* [1973] 1 WLR 1261). In order to bring the bypass procedure into operation, D2's act or default must be wrongful. For example, if a supply of goods by D2 is lawful at the time of his supply, the fact that the law later changes with the result that a supply by D1 becomes unlawful means that D2 will be immune from prosecution since there was no initial wrongful act or default and the law should not be allowed to operate retrospectively to hold someone responsible for an action which was not illegal at the time it was performed (see *Noss Farm Products Ltd* v *Lilico* [1945] 2 All ER 609). Similarly, if the initial supplier of a second-hand motor vehicle the odometer of which has been turned back has successfully disclaimed responsibility for the accuracy of the mileage reading, he has done no wrong, with the result that the initial supplier will not be responsible, after the event, by virtue of the bypass procedure (see *K. Lill Holdings Ltd* v *White* [1979] RTR 120).

The counter-argument to these two cases is that if Parliament had intended the act or default to be wrongful, it would have said so in the wording of the

Trade Descriptions Act, s. 23. Moreover, both *K. Lill Holdings Ltd* v *White* and *Noss Farm Products Ltd* v *Lilico* can also be explained on the ground that in neither case was D2 a cause of the commission of an offence by D1.

13.4.2.3.2 Ingredients of the act or default defence Before a person charged with the commission of an offence will be allowed to raise the act or default defence, it is necessary that he should be able to give sufficient information to allow the other person to be identified. It is not sufficient for the person setting up the defence to argue that some unidentified person, in general terms, is to blame for the commission of the offence. Thus a corporate defendant cannot avoid liability by saying that one of a number of employees must have been to blame. Instead, a particular employee has to be identified, whose actions caused D1 to commit the crime charged (see *McGuire* v *Sittingbourne Co-operative Society Ltd* [1976] Crim LR 268).

Once it has been decided that there has been an act or default, it must then be determined whether it is that of another person. In the case of individual offenders this will be a simple process, but problems may arise where a corporate offender wishes to set up the act or default of an employee as the basis for the defence. In *Tesco Supermarkets Ltd* v *Nattrass* [1972] AC 153, it was held that it is necessary to distinguish between the corporate identity of a company and mere employees. An officer who forms part of the directing mind and will of a company is identified with the company itself, and an act or default on the part of such a person will be treated as the act or default of the company. In such a case, the officer, such as a director, senior manager or company secretary may be liable along with the company he represents (Trade Descriptions Act 1968, s. 20; Fair Trading Act 1973, s. 132; Consumer Credit Act 1974, s. 169; Consumer Protection Act 1987, s. 40(2); Food Safety Act 1990, s. 36). A wrong committed by a junior employee or even a branch manager is regarded as an act or default of another person (see *Beckett* v *Kingston Brothers (Butchers) Ltd* [1970] 1 QB 606) with the result that a corporate offender may set up this act or default as a defence, provided it can also be shown that reasonable precautions have been taken and that those precautions have been diligently put into operation in order to avoid the commission of an offence by the person charged or any person under his control. The effects of this identification test may be criticised on the ground that a person such as a branch manager of a supermarket is surely acting on behalf of the company in supervising the workforce in his branch, thereby carrying out the wishes of the directors and area managers. If this is the case, it surely makes sense to hold the company responsible for the acts of such persons rather than going completely in the opposite direction, allowing the company to set up the actions of such individuals in order to avoid a conviction.

13.4.2.4 Accident or some other cause beyond the defendant's control (Trade Descriptions Act 1968, s. 24(1)(a); Fair Trading Act 1973, s. 25(1)(a); Consumer Credit Act 1974, s. 168(1)(a)). The word 'accident' must be read in the light of the words 'beyond the defendant's control'. This means that where an employee accidentally causes the commission of an offence, the appropriate defence is that of act or default of another, considered above, since the employer will be taken to have the ability to control his employees (see *Hall* v *Farmer* [1970] 1 All ER 729).

What constitutes an accident within these provisions is not entirely clear, but it would appear that an unforeseen production breakdown might be covered (*Bibby-Cheshire* v *Golden Wonder Ltd* [1972] 1 WLR 1487). However, it remains essential to show that reasonable precautions have been taken to avoid the commission of an offence and that those precautions have been diligently put into practice.

FOURTEEN

Product quality and safety under the criminal law

14.1 PRODUCT QUALITY AND SAFETY GENERALLY

Civil law rules in respect of product safety form an important part of consumer protection law, but they cannot satisfy all the requirements of a modern consumer society. In particular, while rules of the law of contract and the law of tort can provide consumers with valuable individual rights in respect of harm caused by one-off defects, the criminal law performs an important preventative role. On the basis that prevention is better than cure, a range of statutes have attempted to introduce broad standards of safety in respect of consumer goods generally and specific items such as food, medicines and poisons.

These broad statutory standards apply mainly to the matter of safety. The enforcement of the law in respect of qualitative defects in consumer products is left to the individual consumer. However, where food and medicines are concerned, Parliament has chosen to legislate with the result that it is a criminal offence for a person to sell food or medicinal products which are not of the nature or quality demanded by the consumer (Medicines Act 1968, s. 64; Food Safety Act 1990, s. 14). Sections 16 to 19 of the Food Safety Act 1990 permit regulations to be made in respect of the quality and composition of specified food items.

14.1.1 Rationales for consumer safety legislation
No one would dispute the need for a regime which seeks to promote the safety of consumer goods, but it is necessary to consider how far such a regime should go and what it should seek to achieve. It might be possible to aim for absolute safety, but some would argue that the cost of doing so would be prohibitive. As an alternative, Parliament could seek an acceptable standard of safety, whereby the benefits of regulation do not exceed the costs imposed by it (see *Safety of Goods*, Cmnd 9302, 1984), para. 10; *Building*

Businesses . . . not Barriers (Cmnd 9794, 1986)). For example, excessive safety measures could easily make some consumer goods so expensive that they fall out of the reach of poorer consumers. Enforcement costs also have to be considered. A regime enforced by means of the criminal law or through some administrative agency has to be paid for and the more elaborate the scheme, the greater those enforcement costs are likely to be.

Some risks of harm may be viewed more seriously than others. In balancing the benefits created by a particular activity against the costs it creates, it is necessary to place a value on those social costs. Some risks, such as death and serious bodily injury may be regarded as so great that a substantial level of intervention is justified, even where the cost of compliance is also great.

As in other areas of consumer law, the issue of consumer information is a primary consideration in regard to product safety. In some instances, the consumer will be unaware of any risk at all and in others he may not be able to appreciate the risks created by purchasing goods of a particular type because the scientific information available is too complex for the ordinary consumer to understand. Accordingly, one of the rationales for a consumer safety regime is that the consumer should be provided with sufficient information to allow him to assess those risks. For example, regulations may require the producer of processed foods to give comprehensible information about the composition of the food he produces.

Consumer safety legislation may also be justified on the ground that persons other than the immediate purchaser may be affected by unsafe goods. While the immediate purchaser will be able to pursue a civil action for breach of contract against his immediate supplier this does not provide a full response to the problem. First, prevention is surely better than cure and a consumer safety regime involving the use of penalties for contravention will go some way towards cutting out the problem of unsafe consumer goods, rather than simply providing for the payment of damages for breach after the event. Secondly, persons other than the immediate purchaser have no contractual action in their favour, but an injury to such a person will impose considerable social costs. Avoidance or reduction of these costs can be achieved by means of a safety regime directed at those consumer goods presenting the greatest risk.

Consumer safety regulation may also be justified on paternalist grounds where there is a social distrust of the ability of the consumer to protect himself against risks created by unsafe products.

14.1.2   Legislative background

The need to regulate the safety and quality of food in the interests of both consumer protection and public health has been recognised for some time. The modern legislative framework in the form of the Food Safety Act 1990 contains a number of provisions of considerable antiquity. In particular, the offence of selling food not of the nature, quality or substance demanded by the purchaser dates back to the Sale of Food and Drugs Act 1875. There is also a range of controls in respect of injurious food, food hygiene, food labelling and food composition (see chapter 15).

Public regulation of the safety of products other than food has progressed slowly since the early 1960s. The most important legislation in this field is now the Consumer Protection Act 1987, part II, which replaces the provisions of the Consumer Protection Acts 1961 and 1971 and the Consumer Safety Acts 1978 and 1986. Tracing the history of the earlier legislation shows a gradual awareness of the problems surrounding the issue of general product safety and reveals a range of different techniques designed to meet those problems.

14.1.2.1 Consumer Protection Acts 1961 and 1971 The principal contribution of the Consumer Protection Act 1961 was to confer on the Secretary of State the power to make regulations in respect of any class of goods so as to prevent or reduce the risk of death or personal injury created by that class of goods (s. 1(1)). Regulations under s. 1(1) could cover matters such as composition, design, contents and packaging. It was also possible to make regulations requiring a warning or special instructions to accompany any goods. Under the regime imposed by the 1961 Act, it was an offence for a person to sell or have in his possession for the purposes of sale any goods which failed to comply with safety regulations (ss. 2(1) and 2(2)).

14.1.2.1.1 Regulations under the 1961 Act A number of regulations were made under the 1961 Act, although most did not appear for some time. Indeed in the first 10 years, only three sets of regulations were developed, although regulatory activity increased in the period between 1971 and 1978.

The range of regulations made under the 1961 Act included specific safety requirements in respect of goods likely to be used by children and infants such as carrycot stands (SI 1966/1610), prams and pushchairs (SI 1978/1372 replaced by SI 1985/2047), babies' dummies (SI 1978/836) and hood cords on children's clothing (SI 1976/2).

A number of regulations were made in respect of the safety of electrical appliances. In particular about colour codes used on electrical wiring (SI 1969/310; SI 1970/811; SI 1977/931), the use and safety of electric blankets (SI 1971/1961) and insulation of certain types of lighting equipment (SI 1975/1366; SI 1976/1208; SI 1987/603).

There were also attempts to regulate the content of paints used on consumer products, particularly those used by children and as coatings on cooking utensils (SI 1972/1957; SI 1976/454). For example, there were particular controls on the lead and cadmium release capability of vitreous enamel glazes (SI 1976/454) and ceramic coatings (SI 1975/1241). Similarly, in relation to children's toys the Toy Safety Regulations (SI 1974/1367) placed controls on the use of poisonous materials in paint used on toys in addition to a number of other requirements in respect of the protection of protruding metal edges, electrical safety and the securing of facial features on dolls. In the interests of the health of consumers there was also a detailed list of substances which could not be used in cosmetic products on the ground that they might cause an allergic reaction (SI 1978/1354; SI 1978/1477; SI 1984/1260; SI 1985/1279).

A number of regulations were made in respect of the safety of domestic heating appliances. In particular, about carbon monoxide emissions, flame control and draught emission in oil heaters (SI 1977/167), the adequacy of fireguards on heaters (SI 1973/2106) and the safety of paraffin-burning oil lamps (SI 1979/1372).

14.1.2.1.2 Criticisms of the 1961 Act The principal drawback of the regime imposed under the 1961 Act was that it operated very slowly. It has already been observed that in the first 10 years, only three sets of regulations were introduced. The main reasons for this were that regulations were based on standards of safety agreed between the government and manufacturers. If no standard existed in relation to a particular type of product, it remained unregulated and the process of drafting new standards proved to be very cumbersome.

Even where regulations had been implemented, enforcement authorities were merely empowered to enforce them, there was no statutory compulsion in this respect. As a result, there was a marked difference in enforcement patterns in different parts of the country.

Perhaps most seriously, the offences created under s. 2 of the Act were confined to retailers who sold goods not in compliance with established safety regulations. Accordingly, it was possible for a supplier to continue to sell a product which was known to be unsafe, because there was no regulation in force which related to it. Moreover, there was no power to intercept unsafe goods imported from abroad, since the enforcement powers of local authorities only allowed them to act when the goods had reached the point of sale to consumers.

Under s. 2 of the 1961 Act, a retailer committed an offence if he sold or had in his possession for the purposes of sale any goods which failed to comply with safety regulations. By virtue of s. 2(6) letting goods by way of hire purchase also fell within the statutory regime, but other forms of supply fell outside the 1961 Act. Thus, a person who gave goods away as part of a promotional exercise or a person who supplied goods in return for trading stamps was not subject to the statutory regime.

14.1.2.2 Consumer Safety Acts 1978 and 1986 In an attempt to remedy some of the shortcomings of the earlier legislation, the Consumer Safety Act 1978 implemented a number of proposals for change contained in a consultative document on consumer safety (Cmnd 6398, 1976).

14.1.2.2.1 Supply In order to meet the criticisms of the 1961 Act based on its application to the sale of unsafe goods, the 1978 Act gave a comprehensive definition of supply in the course of a business, which included, subject to a number of exceptions (s. 9(2)), selling, lending, hiring, entering into a hire purchase agreement or a contract for work and materials, exchanging goods for any consideration and giving goods away as a prize (s. 9(1)). In order to widen the scope of the Act, it also became an offence for a person to supply, offer to supply, agree to supply, expose for supply or have in one's possession for the purposes of supply any goods which did not comply with safety regulations.

14.1.2.2.2 Safety regulations The 1978 Act, like its predecessor was an enabling provision which allowed the Secretary of State to make such regulations as he considered appropriate in order to ensure that goods were safe, that appropriate information about goods was made available and that inappropriate information was not given (s. 1(1)). Also like its predecessor, the 1978 Act contained an extensive list of matters in respect of which the Secretary of State could issue regulations (s. 1(2)). These included, for the most part, the matters now covered by the Consumer Protection Act 1987, s. 11, and are considered in more detail below.

A wide range of regulations were brought in under the 1978 Act, including a prohibition on the use of flammable materials in children's night attire (SI 1985/127; SI 1985/2043; SI 1987/286) and in upholstered furniture (SI 1983/519). Other regulations were introduced to restrict the supply of potentially dangerous children's toys, particularly toys which look like or smell like food, such as strawberry-scented erasers (SI 1985/99; SI 1985/1191), and novelties which contain injurious or obnoxious chemicals such as stink bombs and tear-gas capsules (SI 1980/958; SI 1985/128). In the light of increasing instances of firework-related injuries, a ban on the sale of fireworks to a person who appears to be younger than 16 years of age was introduced (SI 1986/1323).

Regulations were also made in respect of the safety of a diverse range of products including pushchairs (SI 1985/2047), bicycles (SI 1984/145), cosmetic products (SI 1984/1260), child-proof packaging (SI 1986/758), motor vehicle tyres (SI 1984/1233) and products containing blue and brown asbestos (SI 1985/2042).

14.1.2.2.3 Enforcement powers Perhaps the most important effect of the 1978 Act was to introduce a number of enforcement powers which sought to address the criticism of the 1961 Act that it permitted the supply of patently unsafe goods in the absence of a safety regulation. The 1978 Act allowed the Secretary of State to issue 'prohibition notices' which prohibited a named person from dealing in unsafe goods specified in the notice (s. 3(1)(b)). It also provided for the issue of 'prohibition orders' which prohibited the supply of goods considered to be unsafe by any trader (s. 3(1)(a)). The power to issue such orders has since been removed from the provisions of the Consumer Protection Act 1987, since it is no longer necessary following the introduction of a general safety requirement.

The important effect of the enforcement powers conferred by the 1978 Act was that speedy action could be taken against the threatened supply of unsafe goods which were not at the time covered by safety regulations. In general, orders and notices would expire after one year, but could be renewed. However, in practice, many of these temporary prohibitions became permanent in the form of new safety regulations.

In addition to prohibition notices and orders, the Secretary of State also had the power to issue a 'notice to warn' which could require a supplier,

at his own expense, to warn consumers that particular goods were unsafe
(s. 3(1)(c)).

Despite the important steps forward taken in the 1978 Act, a number of
weaknesses still remained:

(a)   The Act was still over-concerned with the retail supplier and did not
pay sufficient attention to the problem of unsafe goods imported into the
country. As a result, even where enforcement authorities were aware of the
impending arrival of a consignment of unsafe foreign goods, nothing could be
done until they had been dispersed throughout the country to retail suppliers.

(b)   The enforcement powers contained in the 1978 Act only applied to
regulations made under that Act. Because of this, the substantial number of
regulations eventually made under the 1961 Act were still governed by the
inadequate procedures provided for by the earlier legislation, until those
regulations were re-introduced under the 1978 Act.

(c)   The law was still based on the power of the Secretary of State to make
regulations in respect of specific goods. For the most part, the regulation-
making process required close cooperation between the government and
industry, with the result that there were still delays in formulating safety
standards.

The problem of imported goods was eventually addressed in the Consumer
Safety (Amendment) Act 1986 following yet another report on the state of
consumer safety law (Cmnd 9302, 1984). Section 2 of this Act conferred on
the Commissioners of Customs and Excise the power to seize and detain
imported goods for a period of 48 hours, thereby enabling trading standards
officers to inspect the goods before deciding whether to act. In addition, new
enforcement procedures were introduced, allowing enforcement authorities
to serve a suspension order on a named person (s. 3). The effect of such an
order was to prohibit the supply of identified goods for a period of up to six
months. Where appropriate, the enforcement authority could also apply for
the forfeiture of goods which failed to comply with safety provisions (s. 6). A
court, if satisfied that a contravention of safety requirements had been
established, could order the destruction of the goods concerned.

14.2   SAFETY OF GOODS UNDER THE CONSUMER
PROTECTION ACT 1987, PART II

The law in respect of consumer safety is now contained in the Consumer
Protection Act 1987, part II, which comprises most of the features of the
earlier law, but adds a general safety requirement, breach of which will
amount to the commission of a criminal offence. Some of the matters dealt
with by the 1987 Act will, in time, become otiose in the light of the General
Product Safety Regulations 1994 (SI 1994/2328), which implement the EC
Directive on General Product Safety (92/59/EEC of 29 June 1992).
In particular, the general product safety requirement in the 1987 Act
will, in most circumstances, become unnecessary in the light of the 1994

Regulations, which take precedence over domestic measures concerning product safety.

Generally, for the purposes of the 1987 Act, a person is only caught by the provisions of part II of the Act if he has supplied goods in the course of carrying on a business (whether or not a business of dealing in the goods in question) and either as principal or agent (s. 46(1) and (5)). The importance of the words in parentheses should not be underestimated since their effect would appear to be to cover the facts of *Southwark London Borough Council* v *Charlesworth* [1980] CLY 3311 where a shoe repairer sold an unsafe electric fire. The reference to someone acting in the capacity of principal or agent would seem to include the sale by a car dealer of a car owned by a private individual, where the supplier would be acting in a business capacity as agent of the owner.

14.2.1 Safety regulations

14.2.1.1 Powers of the Secretary of State The 1987 Act allows the Secretary of State to make safety regulations so as to ensure that goods are safe (s. 11(1)(a)) and that where goods are unsafe, whether generally or to a specific group of people, they are not made available to the consumer market (s. 11(1)(b)). Regulations may also be made so as to ensure that appropriate information about goods is made available to consumers or that inappropriate information is withheld (s. 11(1)(c)).

For the purposes of s. 11, safety would appear to be subject to the same definition as applies to the general safety requirement considered below. While the Secretary of State may make regulations in respect of consumer goods, he can only do so in respect of products which fall within the scope of the Act. Some products are already subject to a separate regime and are therefore excluded from the provisions of the 1987 Act.

Like its predecessors, the 1987 Act contains a list of the matters in respect of which the Secretary of State may make regulations. The list is similar in content to that contained in the Consumer Safety Act 1978 and includes composition, contents, design and construction, approval, testing and inspection, warnings or instructions given with goods, prohibitions on supply and information (s. 11(2) and (3)).

Before making safety regulations, the Secretary of State is under a duty to consult any person or organisation he considers appropriate (s. 11(5)). It is likely that relevant trade associations and consumer organisations will be involved in the regulation-making process, but it appears from the wording of s. 11(5) that it is a matter for the Secretary of State to determine which bodies or persons are appropriate to consult.

If a particular body or organisation feels that it ought to have been consulted, the remedy lies in an action for judicial review of the decision taken by the Secretary of State. This matter was considered in *R* v *Secretary of State for Health, ex parte United States Tobacco International Inc.* [1992] QB 353. The Secretary of State had introduced the Oral Snuff (Safety) Regulations 1989 without consulting the applicants who were the sole manufacturers and packagers of snuff in the UK and had been encouraged by the government to set up business in Scotland. The effect of the regulations was to introduce very strict controls on the supply and manufacture of snuff and, given the applicants' unique position, they were considered to be a body which ought to have been given the chance to know of the government's intentions and to be given an opportunity to respond. Since this opportunity had not been given, the procedure adopted was regarded as unfair, with the result that the Regulations were quashed. Effectively the decision of the Divisional Court was that if Draconian measures are introduced, the principle of proportionality requires that there is procedural propriety and fair treatment for all concerned parties.

In addition to the power to make regulations under the 1987 Act, the Secretary of State also has the important power, under s. 50(5) of the Act, to order that regulations made under the Consumer Protection Act 1961 shall take effect as if made under s. 11 of the 1987 Act. The defects inherent in the enforcement procedure applicable to the 1961 Act are avoided once the provisions of the 1987 Act apply to such regulations.

14.2.1.2 Consequences of a breach of safety regulations Where a safety regulation has been made, it does not of itself create a new criminal offence (s. 11(4)), but an offence is committed where the provisions of s. 12 apply. This states that if a safety regulation prohibits a person from supplying goods, offering to supply goods, agreeing to supply goods or exposing goods for supply, a person commits an offence if he contravenes the regulation (s. 12(1)). An offence is also committed by a person who, having been required by regulations to test goods, fails to comply with the testing requirement (s. 12(2)(a)) or fails to deal properly with goods that fail to satisfy the test (s. 12(2)(b)). Where a regulation requires a person to mark goods in a particular way or to give specified information, failure to comply with that requirement will amount to the commission of an offence (s. 12(3)). In order to assist in the enforcement of the safety provisions of the Act, it is an offence for a person to fail to provide information required to be supplied by a safety regulation or knowingly or recklessly to give false information so required (s. 12(4)).

Where the breach of a safety regulation causes death or personal injury, it will give rise to an action in tort for breach of statutory duty (s. 41(1)). Since the purpose of part II of the 1987 Act is to guard against death and bodily injury only, it follows that no civil action for breach of statutory duty will lie in respect of property damage or economic loss. To recover such losses, the consumer will have to pursue his alternative remedies under the Sale of Goods Act 1979 or under part I of the Act. Moreover, since the 1987 Act is geared towards *consumer* safety, it is arguable that injury suffered by a retailer on his own retail premises may not be covered by an action in tort for breach of statutory duty.

14.2.2 The general safety requirement
One of the major problems of consumer safety law prior to 1987 was that it was tied to limited categories of goods covered by existing regulations. The

only way of dealing with new hazards was by means of the prohibition notices and orders provided for by the Consumer Safety Act 1978. In order to meet this problem, s. 10 of the 1987 Act makes it an offence for a person to supply, offer to supply, agree to supply, expose for supply or possess for the purposes of supply any consumer goods which are not reasonably safe.

The duty to trade safely, as the general safety requirement may be described, is couched in negative terms. In this respect, the duty differs from that contained in the General Product Safety Regulations 1994 (SI 1994/2328), reg. 7, which is couched in positive terms, requiring suppliers to place only safe products on the market. Whether this makes any substantial difference is considered in more detail below.

14.2.2.1 Safety Goods must be reasonably safe (Consumer Protection Act 1987, s. 10(2)) which means that there must be no risk, or a risk reduced to a minimum, of death or personal injury (s. 19(1)). Thus, unlike the product liability provisions of the 1987 Act (see chapter 7), goods which only pose a danger to other property or which are merely defective in the sense that they are not fit for use do not fall within the regime provided for by part II of the Act.

It is clear from the definition of safety that regard must be had not only to the intended use of the goods, but also to the condition in which they are kept and the way they are assembled or supplied (s. 19(1)). The key concern of part II of the Act is safety as opposed to quality. The word 'safe' is defined in s. 19(1) as meaning that:

. . . there is no risk, or no risk apart from one reduced to a minimum, that any of the following will (whether immediately or after a definite or indefinite period) cause the death of, or any personal injury to, any person whatsoever, that is to say —
    (a)   the goods;
    (b)   the keeping, use or consumption of the goods;
    (c)   the assembly of any of the goods which are, or are to be, supplied unassembled;
    (d)   any emission or leakage from the goods or, as a result of the keeping, use or consumption of the goods, from anything else; or
    (e)   reliance on the accuracy of any measurement, calculation or other reading made by or by means of the goods,
and 'safe' and 'unsafe' shall be construed accordingly.

It is not just the goods per se which have to be safe in order to comply with the Act, since their keeping, use and consumption have to be considered (see s. 19(1)(b)). It follows from this that an article may be unharmful in itself, but if it proves to be useless at preventing harm it was designed to prevent when put into use, it may be regarded as unsafe. Thus a parachute which is incapable of opening, or a fire extinguisher which does not extinguish fires, may be regarded as unsafe under the s. 19 definition.

Factors in the s. 19 list also seem to include flat-pack furniture which when assembled causes an injury (s. 19(1)(c)); household cleaning fluids which emit noxious fumes or hot-water bottles which deposit their contents on an unwitting user (s. 19(1)(d)); tyre pressure gauges which tell you your tyres are inflated to 1.9 bar when in fact they are inflated only to 1.5 bar or speedometers which indicate that you are travelling at 70 m.p.h. when in fact the speed is 95 m.p.h. (s. 19(1)(e)).

Since goods must be reasonably safe, regard must be had to all the circumstances in which the goods are made available. Whilst this does not preclude the consideration of any relevant factor, the Act does specify three matters which should be taken into account (s. 10(2)). These are the way in which the goods are marketed (s. 10(2)(a)), published safety standards (s. 10(2)(b)) and means of making the goods safe (s. 10(2)(c)).

14.2.2.1.1 Marketing etc. The reference to the way in which the goods have been marketed is based on wording identical to that used in s. 3(2)(a) in defining defectiveness for the purposes of the product liability provisions of the Act (see chapter 7) and therefore raises the same considerations. This approach may be criticised on the ground that it is not necessarily appropriate to apply an identical test of safety to both civil compensation and criminal prosecution in the interests of consumer health and safety. The latter is surely a matter of great concern, in respect of which very high standards can be expected.

14.2.2.1.2 Safety standards Regard is also to be had to published safety standards. However, these are not the only factors which may be taken into account, especially where the enforcement authority serves a suspension notice under s. 14 of the Act. It has been observed that the paramount concern of the 1987 Act is the safety of the consumer and even if there is no proof that goods contravene an existing safety provision, a suspension notice may still be served, provided the enforcement authority has reasonable grounds for believing that there has been a contravention of a safety provision (*R v Birmingham City Council, ex parte Ferrero Ltd* [1993] 1 All ER 530, 537 per Taylor LJ). Even if the enforcement authority takes account of regulations which have been prepared but are not yet in force this will not be a ground for interfering with the service of a suspension notice if it transpires that the goods in question are unsafe (ibid. per Taylor LJ). Conversely, the failure by the enforcement authority to have regard to the fact that goods do comply with the requirements of existing safety provisions will be fatal should the authority attempt to prosecute the producer under other provisions of the 1987 Act.

On the wording of s. 10(2)(b) the standards which may be considered can be published by anyone with the result that there is always the possibility of what has been described as 'window dressing' (*Rotherham Metropolitan Borough Council* v *Raysun (UK) Ltd* (1989) 8 TrLR 6, 12 per Woolf LJ), namely, the preparation of bogus standards by some private body and an appearance of reliance upon such standards. However, it seems that the courts are unwilling to allow a trader to rely on standards which carry no weight and which have not been prepared with care and precision (ibid.).

14.2.2.1.3 Means by which goods could be made safer The third relevant criterion is the existence of means by which the goods could have been made safer. Since the standard is one of reasonable safety, we are not concerned with methods of making goods totally safe. Factors such as cost and the likelihood and extent of improvement have to be considered. For example, motor cars could be made much safer by fitting a control device which prevents the vehicle from travelling faster than 10 m.p.h., but the social cost would be too great to bear. Similarly, if the proposed safety measure would push the purchase price of certain domestic appliances out of the reach of most consumers, it could hardly be regarded as reasonable, unless there was some unacceptable danger to consumers. The express reference to cost might lead consumers to believe that cheap goods need not be safe. If this is the case, the 1987 Act is defective in that there must be certain minimum expectations of safety for all goods.

14.2.2.1.4 Compliance with safety requirements In determining whether goods are safe, regard must be had to safety requirements laid down by any enactment or European Community obligation, since compliance with such requirements will mean that the goods cannot be found to be unsafe (s. 10(3)). The effect of this is to place a very heavy burden on legislators to ensure that no lacunae are to be found in safety legislation (National Consumer Council, *Response to the Proposed EC Product Safety Directive* (PD31/89, 1989), para. 3.2).

14.2.2.1.5 Liability of retail suppliers The main thrust of the 1987 Act is against the producer of goods, but this should not detract from the important role which may be played by a retail supplier in ensuring product safety. In particular, the general safety requirement applies to possession of goods for the purposes of supply (s. 10(1)(c)) and to the keeping of goods (s. 19(1)). The role of the supplier is important, since the way in which he deals with goods can render them unsafe. For example, he may store food at the wrong temperature or supply a number of apparently safe products which when used together are unsafe. Similarly, a retailer may supply a product such as a solvent-based glue or butane gas which when improperly used by a youthful purchaser can present a grave danger of death or physical injury. If the retailer is aware of the likelihood of solvent abuse, it is arguable that he breaches the general safety requirement.

The 1987 Act provides the retail supplier with a defence where he is unaware that goods do not comply with the general safety requirement or where he does not have reasonable grounds for believing that the safety requirement has been broken (s. 10(4)(b)). Moreover, the general defence of taking reasonable precautions and acting with due diligence (s. 39) will exonerate the truly innocent retailer. The 1987 Act does not give any guidance on what is a reasonable precaution or what constitutes due diligence, although the courts have developed guidelines on this matter (see chapter 13) and it would appear that making random safety checks on goods intended for retail supply is some evidence of taking reasonable precautions (*Garrett* v *Boots the Chemist* (1980) 88 ITSA Monthly Rev 238; *Rotherham*

Metropolitan Borough Council v *Raysun (UK) Ltd* (1989) 8 TrLR 6), although expectations of what should be done may differ according to the size of the retail organisation concerned.

14.2.2.2 Consumer goods It is clear from the wording of the 1987 Act that the general safety requirement and the power of the Secretary of State to make safety regulations do not apply to all goods. Safety regulations cannot be made in respect of growing crops and things comprised in land, food, water, feeding stuffs and fertilisers, gas, and controlled drugs and medicinal products (s. 11(7)). The general safety requirement applies only to consumer goods, which are defined as those intended for private use or consumption (see chapter 1), but not including the products referred to in s. 11(7) and also not including aircraft, motor vehicles and tobacco (s. 10(7)). In contrast, the General Product Safety Regulations 1994, considered below, do not exclude food products from their provisions and also include any other manufactured or processed product.

The fact that different products are subject to different regimes is a matter which may be criticised, since fundamentally different rules may apply according to the type of product under consideration (National Consumer Council, *Response to the Proposed EC Product Safety Directive* (PD31/89, 1989, para. 2.6). For example, different rules apply to injuries caused by defective transport equipment or by the consumption of food and drugs and medicines. Instead, it is preferable that there should be a general safety net which applies to all products used by consumers.

Further omissions from the 1987 Act relate to goods which are not new (s. 10(4)(c)) and goods intended for export (s. 10(4)(a)). The policy of the 1987 Act in relation to goods intended for export was that domestic criminal law should not be used to protect the world in general and that other countries should develop their own laws in this regard. Moreover, if United Kingdom exporters were to be required to comply with the provisions of the 1987 Act, they would be placed at a competitve disadvantage if they exported to a country which did not have equivalent laws in respect of the safety of consumer goods.

So far as goods which are not new are concerned the reasons for the inapplicability of the 1987 Act are less clear. The danger to the consumer from a second-hand car is just as great, if not greater than, that presented by a new car. There may be some difficulty in determining when goods are new, since it is always possible that goods may have been manufactured some time before they are first supplied to a consumer or may have been repaired following factory damage (see *R* v *Ford Motor Co. Ltd* [1974] 1 WLR 1220). For the purposes of the 1987 Act, it would appear that the principal issue for the purposes of s. 10(4)(c) is whether the goods have previously been sold to a business or private user (Merkin, *A Guide to the Consumer Protection Act 1987* (London: Financial Training, 1987), p. 63).

14.2.3 Follow-up powers of enforcement
The 1987 Act re-enacts a number of provisions found in earlier legislation concerning powers of enforcement. These powers include the issue of

prohibition notices, notices to warn, suspension notices and forfeiture orders. Failure to comply with a prohibition notice, a notice to warn or a suspension notice constitutes the commission of a criminal offence (s. 13(4); s. 14(6)).

Unlike the 1978 Act, the 1987 Act does not allow for the service of a prohibition order by which the Secretary of State could prevent all traders from dealing in a particular type of goods considered to be unsafe. These orders have been rendered unnecessary following the introduction of the general safety requirement in s. 10, since if a range of goods is considered to be unsafe, a criminal offence is committed by a supplier even where no specific regulations exist.

Under the Consumer Safety Act 1978, a breach of one of these follow-up powers gave rise to an action for damages for breach of statutory duty. The same position no longer prevails under the 1987 Act, since only a breach of safety regulations made under s. 11 will give rise to an action for breach of statutory duty (s. 41(2)).

14.2.3.1 Prohibition notices
A prohibition notice may be served on a specific trader, requiring him not to supply, offer or agree to supply, expose for supply or possess for the purposes of supply any goods specified in the notice as being dangerous (s. 13(1)(a)).

Where such a notice is served, it may be subject to such conditions as are considered appropriate by the Secretary of State (s. 13(3)). Thus, a prohibition notice may direct the trader not to supply the goods referred to in the notice to a specific group of consumers such as children or pensioners while leaving him free to supply to others not specified in the notice.

Goods subject to such a notice are restricted to those in respect of which safety regulations may be made (s. 13(6)(a)). It follows that a prohibition notice cannot be served in respect of goods such as food, water, gas, medicines and things attached to or forming part of land.

Where a prohibition notice is served on a named trader, it is incumbent on the Secretary of State to give his reasons for imposing the restriction on the goods concerned. In doing so, he must state why he considers the goods to be unsafe. He must also state the date on which the prohibition is to take effect and he must inform the trader that he may make written representations seeking to establish that the goods covered by the notice are safe (sch. 2, para. 1). Where representations are made, the Secretary of State must either revoke the notice or appoint an expert to consider the representations and report on the matter within 21 days, after having considered the evidence. After the consultation process, the Secretary of State may revoke, confirm or vary the notice, but in the case of a variation, the notice cannot be strengthened (sch. 2, paras. 2, 3, 4 and 5).

14.2.3.2 Notices to warn
A notice to warn may be served on a trader requiring him, at his own expense, to publish a warning about goods considered by the Secretary of State to be unsafe (s. 13(1)(b)). In circumstances such as those which arose in *Walton* v *British Leyland (UK) Ltd* (1978) Product Liability International (August 1980) 156 (and see chapter 7), where

a serious defect was discovered in a range of the defendant's cars after they had been put into circulation, it would now be possible to require the manufacturer to warn consumers of the danger.

The range of goods to which a notice to warn may apply is wider than that which can be the subject of prohibition notices. While the latter may be made only in respect of goods for which safety regulations may be made under s. 11, notices to warn may be served in respect of all goods, including growing crops and things comprised in land by virtue of being attached to it (s. 13(6)(b)).

As in the case of prohibition notices, the service of a notice to warn is subject to certain procedural requirements. These require the service of a draft notice specifying the Secretary of State's reasons for regarding the goods as unsafe and allowing for written representations (sch. 2, para. 6). The Act also provides for a 28-day consultation period, during which time evidence in respect of the proposed notice may be considered and at the end of which the Secretary of State must decide whether to withdraw the notice or issue it in its final form (sch. 2, paras 8 and 9).

14.2.3.3 Suspension notices   The power to issue a suspension notice was first created by the Consumer Safety (Amendment) Act 1986 and is re-enacted in the Consumer Protection Act 1987. Where an enforcement authority has reasonable grounds for suspecting that there has been a breach of the general safety requirement, a safety regulation, a prohibition notice or another suspension notice, it may serve a suspension notice on the person considered to be in breach, requiring him to retain possession of the goods and not to supply them without the consent of the enforcement authority (s. 14(1)). If such consent is given, it may be conditional (s. 14(5)). A suspension notice may not continue in force for longer than six months, but after service, it may prevent the trader from supplying, offering or agreeing to supply or exposing for supply any goods referred to in the notice (s. 14(1)).

The importance of such a power is that during the currency of the notice, tests may be carried out on goods and additional time is made available to allow a prosecution to be brought. At the same time the public is protected from potentially dangerous goods as a result of the suspension.

The policy underlying s. 14 was explained in *R v Birmingham City Council, ex parte Ferrero Ltd* (1993) 1 All ER 530 in which a child had swallowed a 'Pink Panther' toy supplied by the defendants in their 'Kinder Surprise' chocolate eggs. As a result of this the child died and the enforcement authority immediately issued a suspension notice despite the fact that the producers had offered to give an assurance in terms identical to those set out in the notice. Instead of pursuing the appeal procedure set out in s. 15 (considered below), the producers sought judicial review of the decision to issue a suspension notice. In overturning the decision of the Divisional Court that judicial review should be granted, Taylor LJ observed at p. 537:

As one would expect, . . . the statutory emphasis is on the safety of the consumer. The provisions aim at withholding goods from the public if there is reasonable suspicion that they are unsafe. Unless they are then cleared of the danger, it is right that the suspension should remain, even if the process by which the enforcement authority reached its decision was flawed. It cannot be right that dangerous goods should continue to be marketed simply because of some procedural impropriety by the enforcement authority in the process of deciding to issue a suspension notice. Common sense dictates that protection of the public must take precedence over fairness to the trader. So, if goods are in fact dangerous, it would be nothing to the point to show that, in deciding to issue a suspension notice, the local authority took into account an irrelevant matter or failed to take account of one which was relevant.

Generally, a suspension notice cannot be renewed after the expiry of the initial six-month period unless proceedings have been instituted against the trader for forfeiture of the goods or in respect of a breach of a safety provision other than a contravention of a suspension notice (s. 14(4)).

Since the service of a suspension notice is based on suspicion that there has been a breach of a safety requirement, it is always possible that it may later be revealed that there has been no such breach. In these circumstances, the enforcement authority is liable to pay compensation in respect of loss or damage caused by virtue of service of the notice and regardless of the reasonableness of their belief that there has been a breach of a safety provision (s. 14(7)). Since the most likely loss to be suffered by the trader is loss of profit which would otherwise have been made, it may be argued that the basis of assessment should be similar to that adopted in relation to the award of contractual damages (Cardwell and Kay (1990) 7 TrL 212, 215–16). It is also possible that in the course of testing, goods may have suffered damage in which case the diminution in value of the goods ought to be recoverable.

The Act also provides for an appeals procedure in s. 15 under which the trader can apply for an order setting aside a suspension notice. The magistrates' court may set aside the order only if it is satisfied that there has been no contravention of a safety provision (s. 15(3)).

It seems that until the s. 15 appeal procedure has been exhausted, it will only be in very rare circumstances that any other remedy, such as judicial review will become operative. Generally, it is regarded as a cardinal principle of English law that, save in the most exceptional circumstances, judicial review does not become available while other remedies are available and have not been used (*R* v *Epping & Harlow General Commissioners, ex parte Goldstraw* [1983] 3 All ER 257, 262 per Donaldson MR applied in *R* v *Birmingham City Council, ex parte Ferrero Ltd* [1993] 1 All ER 530).

14.2.3.4 Forfeiture orders Where there has been a contravention of a safety provision, an enforcement authority can apply to a magistrates' court for a forfeiture order (s. 16(1)). For these purposes, it is not necessary that the trader should have been convicted of an offence, since no offence is committed where a suspension notice has been issued and complied with, yet a suspension notice is a safety provision for the purposes of the 1987 Act (Cardwell (1987) 50 MLR 622, 632).

It is not necessary for all goods in a consignment to be inspected and tested before an order for forfeiture is made since all goods in a given batch can be assumed not to comply with safety requirements where it is shown that a representative sample is dangerous (s. 16(4)).

Where a forfeiture order is made, goods are to be destroyed in accordance with the instructions of the court (s. 16(6)), although, if it is appropriate to do so, the goods may be released to a person specified by the court, provided the goods are not supplied to another other than as scrap or to a person who carries on a business of repair or reconditioning (s. 16(7)(a) and s. 46(7)) and the costs of the enforcement authority in bringing the procedings are paid by that person (s. 16(7)(b)).

14.2.3.5 Other possible powers   One power which exists elsewhere but has not been provided for in the 1987 Act is the ability to serve a 'recall' notice. While the Act does enable the Secretary of State to issue a notice to warn, the only obligation of the person served with such a notice is to warn of a specified danger. In certain circumstances it might be appropriate to order a producer to recall consumer goods which are known to be dangerous.

In relation to motor vehicles, members of the Society of Motor Manufacturers and Traders are subject to the provisions of the SMMT Code of Practice, which operates a recall procedure in association with the Department of Transport. However, experience of this has shown that a surprisingly low percentage of consumers actually return their vehicle for repair.

It appears that the Government's view at the time the 1987 Act was passed was that manufacturers could be relied on to recall dangerous goods voluntarily and that, in practice, the service of a notice to warn would achieve the same purpose (Merkin, *A Guide to the Consumer Protection Act 1987*, p. 69).

14.2.4 Defences
Where a person is charged with the commission of an offence under ss. 10, 12, 13 or 14 it is a defence for him to show that he took all reasonable precautions and exercised all due diligence to avoid the commission of an offence (s. 39(1) and see chapter 13).

Where, in addition to raising the s. 39(1) defence, it is alleged that the commission of the offence is due to the act or default of another person or due to reliance on information supplied by another, the person first charged must give seven days' notice to the prosecution, which should provide the information which the defendant has identifying or assisting in the identification of the other person (s. 39(2) and (3)).

If an offence is shown to have been committed as a result of the act or default of another person, that person is taken to be guilty of the offence and may be proceeded against and punished accordingly (s. 40(1)). Thus it may be possible for an individual employee to be prosecuted where his act or default has caused the commission of an offence by his employer.

14.3 SAFETY OF GOODS UNDER THE GENERAL PRODUCT SAFETY REGULATIONS 1994

One of the problems associated with UK domestic product safety legislation is that it operates on a vertical basis, that is, specific regulations are introduced on a piecemeal basis to deal with particular problem goods as and when dangers are identified. The nearest UK domestic law has come to horizontal legislation is the general safety requirement in the Consumer Protection Act 1987, s. 10. However, despite its title, it merely imposes on suppliers a duty not to supply unsafe goods. In 1989 the EC Commission first started work on its Directive on General Product Safety (92/59/EEC, OJ L228, 11.8.1992), since there was a perceived imbalance between the approach to consumer safety adopted in different member States. Some States, for example, the United Kingdom, Germany and France, had horizontal legislation of sorts on the matter of safety, but others had only specific vertical legislation. One of the problems associated with the introduction of a Community-wide horizontal safety requirement was how to dovetail existing domestic laws with the laws introduced to comply with the Directive. In the event, it was decided that any attempt at seeking to identify areas of overlap would be too difficult with the result that the General Product Safety Regulations 1994 and the Consumer Protection Act 1987 are quite separate provisions, not in any way related to each other. However, as will be seen, there are definite areas of overlap between the two, with the result that a person could contravene both sets of rules. In other respects the two sets of rules differ with the result that a trader might comply with one set of rules but offend against another set.

In other areas, the 1994 Regulations effectively mean that the provisions of the Consumer Protection Act 1987 are no longer of any use. In particular, the general safety requirement in s. 10 is now redundant in all cases where the Regulations apply (reg. 5). Section 10 remains in force for the time being, thus it may continue to apply to any case which is discovered to fall outside the scope of the 1994 Regulations. For example, if Community rules are put into effect in relation to a particular type of product, the Regulations will be disapplied since reg. 3(c) provides that they will have no effect if there are specific provisions in Community law governing all aspects of the safety of the relevant product. If these Regulations apply only to manufacturers, s. 10 could be applied in relation to distributors or retailers where appropriate, provided, of course, that other aspects of Community law are not infringed such as general Community policies on the freedom of movement of goods and services. However, distributors are covered by the Regulations to a certain extent, since reg. 9 provides that they must act with due care in order to ensure compliance with the safety requirement in reg. 7. Regulation 9 has two general effects in that a distributor must not supply products which he knows or should have presumed to be dangerous and secondly, within the limits of his activities, a distributor must monitor the safety of products placed on the market, in particular by passing on information regarding product risks and cooperating in action taken to avoid such risks.

The contrast between reg. 7 and reg. 9 is clear. Regulation 7 creates an offence of strict liability, whereas reg. 9 is essentially fault-based, since it applies a subjective test based on knowledge in the distributor's possession. Moreover, the second of the duties imposed on distributors by reg. 9 is confined to the limits of their own activities.

The primary concern of the 1994 Regulations is that producers should produce safe products. For the purposes of the regulations, a producer includes not just a manufacturer, but also those who present themselves as manufacturers by affixing their name, trade mark or other distinguishing feature to goods (reg. 2(1)). Thus 'own-branders' such as high-street supermarket chains may be regarded as producers for the purposes of the 1994 Regulations. Regulation 2(1) also includes in the definition of a producer persons who recondition products.

Since the Regulations are a Community-wide measure, they are concerned only with manufacturers who are based in a Community State. Accordingly, if unsafe goods are brought in from outside the Community, the manufacturer's representative or the importer of the goods is to be regarded as the manufacturer for the purposes of the Regulations.

14.3.1   The general safety requirement

The key element of the 1994 Regulations is the general safety requirement stated in reg. 7, which provides that 'No producer shall place a product on the market unless the product is a safe product'. For these purposes, reg. 2(1) defines a safe product as one which:

> . . . under normal or reasonably foreseeable conditions of use, including duration, does not present any risk or only the minimum risks compatible with the product's use, considered as acceptable and consistent with a high level of protection for the safety and health of persons.

In order to ascertain whether this standard is reached, reg. 2(1) further provides that regard must be had to:

> (a)   the characteristics of the product, including its composition, packaging, instructions for assembly and maintenance;
> (b)   the effect on other products, where it is reasonably foreseeable that it will be used with other products;
> (c)   the presentation of the product, the labelling, any instructions for its use and disposal and any other indication or information provided by the producer; and
> (d)   the categories of consumers at serious risk when using the product, in particular children,
> and the fact that higher levels of safety may be obtained or other products presenting a lesser degree of safety may be available shall not of itself cause the product to be considered other than a safe product.

On the face of it there is a difference between supplying 'only a safe product', as required by reg. 7, and not supplying an unsafe product, which is the gist of the Consumer Protection Act 1987, s. 10. However, the list of factors relevant to the issue of safety in the 1994 Regulations is very similar to the matters relevant under part II of the 1987 Act, for example, both include the target market, composition, packaging and labelling. Moreover, the reference to that fact that higher levels of safety may be obtained should not prevent a product from being regarded as safe imports the same cost-benefit test applicable under the 1987 Act. The Regulations do not seek to set a standard of absolute safety, since this would be economically inefficient. As with the 1987 Act, the aim is to reduce risks to an acceptable level compatible with the intended use of the product.

What is clear from the 1994 Regulations is that safety has to be assessed by looking at all aspects of the goods concerned. Accordingly, even if the contents of a phial of analgesic tablets are safe for consumption by adults, the fact that the container is not childproof may be sufficient to render the product unsafe under the Regulations. Similarly, as is clear from the guidelines in reg. 2(1), instructions for use must be taken into account, with the result that misleading instructions which render electrical goods unsafe to use will fail to comply with the general product safety requirement.

The definition of safety in the 1994 Regulations may be wider than that employed in the 1987 Act in one important respect. It has been seen already that for the purposes of the 1987 Act, safety is defined in terms of what consumers generally are entitled to expect, whereas the 1994 Regulations require goods to contain no risks or only those compatible with use. It follows that a lawnmower will be excused for having a sharp blade, but if it has a wholly inadequate shield to protect the user from cutting himself, it could be regarded as an unsafe product. Moreover, the test applied by the 1994 Regulations prevents producers from narrowing the range of uses to which a product can be put by insisting that goods must be safe under both normal and reasonably foreseeable conditions of use. This contrasts sharply with the 1987 Act, s. 10, which is confined to safety in respect of the purposes for which the goods were marketed.

14.3.2 Products covered by the Regulations
Regulation 2(1) defines a product as:

> . . . any product intended for consumers or likely to be used by consumers, supplied whether for consideration or not in the course of a commercial activity and whether new, used or reconditioned; provided, however, a product which is used exclusively in the context of a commercial activity even if it is used for or by a consumer shall not be regarded as a product for the purposes of these Regulations provided always and for the avoidance of doubt this exception shall not extend to the supply of such a product to a consumer.

Since the supply must be in the course of a commercial activity, it is clear that private sales are not intended to be covered. Moreover, only consumer goods are included in the definition. Thus if an individual were to hire an earth-removing tractor intended for use only by building contractors it is possible that the transaction would fall outside the Regulations. But if a person hires such equipment for use in his extensive back garden, it is arguable that the piece of machinery might become a product which is 'likely to be used by a consumer' for the purposes of reg. 2. Similarly large vans normally used by business contractors could be regarded as consumer goods if they are hired out for a day at a time to effect a private removal of house furniture.

The proviso contained in the words commencing 'provided, however' after the semicolon are not contained in the EC Directive, but seem to have been inserted to prevent the regulations from applying to a purely commercial use of goods which are ordinarily regarded as consumer goods. This would cover, for example, use of shampoo by a commercial hairdresser.

The definition clearly includes second-hand goods, which are not covered by the 1987 Act. However, some second-hand goods are excluded by reg. 3, which states that the Regulations do not apply to antiques and products supplied for repair or reconditioning before use.

It is also important to note that the 1987 Act excluded a number of consumer goods because there was more detailed regulation elsewhere, for example, food, medicines, tobacco products, water, gas, motor vehicles and aircraft. These products are not excluded from the scope of the 1994 Regulations, with the result that food will fall within this set of safety requirements. This is particularly important, since there is no provision in the Food Safety Act 1990 equivalent to the general product safety requirement to be found in both the 1994 Regulations and the Consumer Protection Act 1987. For the purposes of food, perhaps the greatest importance of its inclusion within the scope of the 1994 Regulations will be in relation to novel foods, namely, substances used as a food not previously so used. For example, on 23 January 1996 certain varieties of lupin seeds were declared to be a novel food. If it transpires that these seeds are harmful in some respect the Regulations would be applicable and it could be an offence to put such substances on the market.

14.3.3 Defences
Consistent with other consumer protection legislation, the 1994 Regulations provide for a due dilgence defence (reg. 14). Details of this defence are considered in chapter 13, but the tenor of it is that a person who has set up a safety system which is designed to prevent unsafe goods from being placed on the market and has acted diligently in putting that system into operation will not be guilty of an offence under the Regulations. Also consistent with other consumer protection legislation, should the person charged seek to allege that his commission of an offence was due to the act or default of another person or to reliance upon information supplied by another, it is incumbent on the person charged to serve a notice giving sufficient information to allow that other person to be identified (reg. 14(3)).

14.3.4 Information and monitoring
In addition to the general obligation to produce safe products imposed on producers and the lesser duty imposed on distributors to do their best to

prevent unsafe goods from reaching consumers, a monitoring role is imposed on producers by reg. 8. This specifies that a producer shall, within the limits of his activity, provide consumers with the relevant information to enable them to assess the risks inherent in a product throughout the normal and foreseeable period of its use in cases where those risks are not immediately obvious without an adequate warning. Appropriate precautions should be taken to guard against those risks (reg. 8(1)(a)).

A producer must adopt measures commensurate with the characteristics of his product to enable him to be informed of the risks it presents so as to allow him to take appropriate action, including, where necessary, withdrawing it from the market (reg. 8(1)(b)). Included in the range of suggested monitoring measures are the marking of products in such a way as to allow them to be identified; sample testing of marketed products; complaints investigation procedures and keeping distributors informed of such monitoring (reg. 8(2)).

14.4 EC TREATY, ARTICLE 30 AND DOMESTIC CONSUMER LAW

Domestic consumer protection laws are potentially capable of destroying the notion of an internal market within the European Community (see chapter 2). Such provisions may be distinctly or indistinctly discriminatory and, according to which description applies, the relevant provision will be subject to different rules.

14.4.1 Distinctly applicable provisions
A distinctly applicable provision amounts to a formal restriction on imports and therefore discriminates between goods coming from other parts of the Community and those which have been produced in the domestic market.

The power of customs and excise officers to detain imported goods for a period of up to two working days so as to allow an enforcement authority to take action (Consumer Protection Act 1987, s. 31(1)) would appear to infringe art. 30 of the EC Treaty on the ground that it is discriminatory. However, such directly applicable measures may be justified under art. 36 on the ground that they are necessary for the protection of the health and safety of humans (see chapter 2). In this respect, it is essential that the restriction is proportionate to the purpose it is intended to serve and must not be excessively restrictive of inter-community trade (see *Commission* v *United Kingdom* (case 261/85) [1988] 2 CMLR 11). Thus, a ban on imports may not be justified if a system of checking imported goods can achieve the desired effect.

14.4.2 Indistinctly applicable provisions
An indistinctly applicable provision does not formally restrict imports, but may have an equivalent effect in the sense that it may have a potentially restrictive effect on trade (see chapter 2). It has been seen already that such measures may be justified under the 'rule of reason' in the *Cassis de Dijon* case (*Rewe Zentrale AG* v *Bundesmonopolverwaltung für Branntwein* (case 120/78)

[1979] ECR 649 and see chapter 2) on the ground that they are necessary to satisfy mandatory requirements relating to consumer protection.

In relation to product safety, regulations will usually require consumer goods to comply with certain standards and it is quite possible that these standards may differ from requirements imposed by other member States. The second principle in *Cassis de Dijon* (see chapter 2) stipulates that if goods can be lawfully supplied in one part of the Community, an additional restriction imposed by another member State will be presumed invalid, in the absence of a very strong justification. It is clear that one way in which regulations can comply with the requirements of *Cassis de Dijon* is to recognise the principle of equivalence. For example, the Child Resistant Packaging (Safety) Regulations (SI 1986/758) provide that if goods fail to comply with British Standards requirements, but satisfy requirements laid down in the exporting member State, they must be admitted. However, there are also some safety regulations which do not contain similar provisions and will therefore potentially contravene art. 30 if they do not recognise the possibility of compliance with requirements applicable to exporters in other member States.

Where regulations appear to infringe art. 30, they may be challenged in the European Court or in national courts and if the challenge is successful, the relevant provision may be declared contrary to the requirements of art. 30. This process of 'negative harmonisation' is destructive (Weatherill (1988) 13 EL Rev 87, 99) since it is piecemeal and dependent on the willingness of individuals to litigate. Instead, it would be preferable to see a detailed programme of positive harmonisation, particularly since this would tend to produce a greater degree of certainty in trading and safety standards. Instead, the position which prevails under the *Cassis de Dijon* principle is that standards of safety are dependent on the plethora of different systems which operate throughout the European Community and no one can be entirely sure whether the goods he proposes to export to the United Kingdom will satisfy safety standards or not.

FIFTEEN

Food law

Regulation of the safety, composition and quality of food has existed for many years and while the consumer interest in the safety and quality of food is apparent, there is also a public interest justification for such regulation on the grounds of maintaining standards of public health. Generally, the role of enforcing food law falls to local authority trading standards or consumer protection departments and environmental health departments.

The basis of modern food law is now the Food Safety Act 1990, which, despite its misleading title, covers a range of matters relevant to food, including food safety, consumer protection and food quality, the composition of food, food labelling and the advertising of food. Comprehensive coverage of all these matters is not possible in a book of this nature and the interested reader is directed to titles such as Painter and Harvey (eds), *Butterworths, Law of Food and Drugs*; Howells, Bradgate and Griffiths, *The Food Safety Act 1990* (Blackstone Press), Thompson, *The Law of Food and Drink* (Shaw & Sons, 1996).

This chapter will consider the major criminal offences in respect of food safety and quality created by the 1990 Act, local authority follow-up powers of inspection and seizure, food regulations and defences available to a person charged with the commission of an offence.

15.1 PRELIMINARY CONSIDERATIONS

15.1.1 Food

The Food Safety Act 1990, amongst other things, governs the safety of food. It is therefore important to identify the scope of the Act by defining the term 'food'. The provisions of s. 1(1) make it clear that food includes drink (which includes bottled water, but not that governed by the Water Act 1989), substances of no nutritional value used for human consumption (e.g., food colourings), chewing gum and ingredients used in the preparation of the foregoing. Anything supplied to a consumer which purports to be food will be treated as such (*Meah* v *Roberts* [1978] 1 All ER 97). Thus, a supply of caustic soda in response to a request for lemonade, cannot be defended on the ground that caustic soda is not food since what has been supplied purported to be lemonade.

The definition of food excludes live animals, birds and fish which are not used for human consumption when they are alive. The Act does apply to animals which are ordinarily consumed by humans in their live state, so a fishmonger will fall within the scope of the Act where he supplies live oysters. A more difficult problem might arise in relation to other types of fish normally supplied in their live state to establishments which prepare food for human consumption, but where the fish concerned is killed in the process of preparation, as may be the case with certain types of crustacean such as lobsters. Strictly, on the definition of food in s. 1(1), these are not ordinarily consumed by humans in their live state, in which case they will not be classified as food. What would be the position if an enforcement officer were to discover a diseased lobster in a restaurant presentation tank from which diners could select a lobster for consumption? Other substances excluded from the definition of food include feeding stuffs for animals, controlled drugs and medicines (s. 1(2)). This should not be taken to mean that these substances relevant to consumer safety are unregulated, since in each case there is an alternative regulatory regime under either the Medicines Act 1968 or the Agriculture Act 1978.

So far as water is concerned, although the principal regulatory regime is to be found in the Water Act 1989, the definition of food in the Food Safety Act 1990, s. 1(1), does extend to cover water by virtue of the fact that food is defined as including drink. At face value, this would suggest that there are two competing regimes, both of which apply to water. For the present purposes, once water has passed beyond the controls imposed by the Water Act 1989 and Regulations made thereunder, it will become regarded as food and therefore regulated by the 1990 Act. In contrast, the Food Safety Act 1990 has no application to mains supplies of water (see Food Safety Act 1990, ss. 55, 56), since these are clearly regulated under the Water Industry Act 1991, which requires a water undertaker supplying water for domestic or food preparation purposes to supply only water which is wholesome at the time of supply and if water supplies prove to be unfit for human consumption, the undertaker commits an offence (Water Industry Act 1991, s. 70). Moreover, a statutory duty rests on water undertakers to ensure, so far as is practicable, that there is no deterioration in the water which is supplied up to the time when the water leaves the undertaker's pipes.

These regulatory provisions create general public law standards, some of which may result in criminal proceedings. Whether or not there would be an available civil law action for breach of statutory duty is a matter considered in chapter 5. However, in general terms, since the protected class of persons, namely, water consumers, can be equated with the whole of society, it is highly unlikely that the common law would impose liability in damages for breach of such a duty on pure policy grounds (see especially *Atkinson* v *Newcastle & Gateshead Waterworks Co.* (1877) 2 ExD 441).

15.1.2 Food businesses and food premises

Since many of the provisions of the Food Safety Act 1990 only apply where a person carries on a food business, or where food is stored on premises described as 'food premises', the meaning of these phrases takes on an increased importance. For the purposes of the 1990 Act, s. 1(3), a business 'includes the undertaking of a canteen, club, school, hospital or institution, whether carried on for profit or not, and any undertaking or activity carried on by a public or local authority'.

On the assumption that the definition of business in s. 1(3) is broad enough to catch the majority of activities carried on in relation to food, it is important to emphasise that even if an organisation is classed as a business, it will only fall within the scope of the 1990 Act if it has carried on 'commercial operations' with respect to food, food contact materials or food sources. For the purposes of s. 1(3) a 'commercial operation' includes the acts of (a) selling, possessing for sale and offering, exposing or advertising any food; (b) consigning, delivering or serving food by way of sale; (c) preparing for sale or presenting, labelling or wrapping food for the purposes of sale; (d) storing or transporting food for the purposes of sale and (e) importing and exporting food. For these purposes, however, the word 'preparing' should be taken to refer to the process whereby food changes its physical state. Accordingly, it is not 'preparation' if a butcher uses a slicing machine to cut cooked meats since this form of secondary activity has nothing to do with changing the primary state of the food concerned (see *Leeds City Council v J. W. Dewhurst Ltd* (1991) 10 TrLR 146).

The definition of a commercial operation is most obviously concerned with the later stages of food processing, distribution and sale, but the 1990 Act also applies to food sources and there is a specific reference to what constitutes a commercial operation in this context. There will be such an operation where a person derives food from a particular source for the purposes of sale or for purposes connected with sale. Food sources include growing crops or live animals, birds or fish from which food is intended to be derived, whether by harvesting, slaughtering, milking, collecting eggs or otherwise. A farmer who owns and breeds dairy cattle which are infected with BSE does not deal in food per se, since the cattle, while alive, are not in a form in which they would be consumed by humans, but the cattle will be food sources. The BSE infection would be regarded as an unacceptable potential danger to human health if milk from an infected animal were to be introduced into the food chain. A similarly infected animal in a beef herd, in contrast, would not fall within the scope of the 1990 Act, if the farmer handled only food sources as opposed to food. The dairy farmer, by milking his cows, derives food from the food source, namely his cattle, and if he proposes to sell that milk, he operates a food business for the purposes of s. 1(3). However, the livestock farmer who sells his cattle to an intermediary in the food supply chain would not have derived food from the food source at that stage.

A number of the provisions of the Food Safety Act 1990 relate to what are described as 'food premises'. For example, there is a requirement that food premises be registered (Food Safety Act 1990, s. 19) with a view to providing enforcement authorities with information about the number and type of food premises operating within their area of administration, so as to allow the authority to plan inspections etc. Food premises are defined as those used for the purposes of a food business and are stated to include any vehicle, stall or movable structure and for such purposes as may be specified by ministerial order, any ship or aircraft (Food Safety Act 1990, s. 1(3)). The definition of food premises appears to be very wide, and at first sight might suggest that virtually all permanent and temporary structures from which food is sold become subject to the requirement of registration introduced by order under the powers created by the Food Safety Act 1990, s. 19. However, the Food Premises (Registration) Regulations 1991 (SI 1991/2825 as amended) make it clear that in certain circumstances, premises from which food is sold or supplied may be exempt from registration. For example, although the phrase 'permanent premises' is defined as 'any land or building', places where grouse shooting and fishing by way of sport take place are exempt from registration. Similarly, an owner of premises from which food such as beverages, biscuits, crisps, confectionery or other similar products are sold in a manner ancillary to a principal activity which does not involve the sale of food are also freed from the obligation to register. Thus a petrol filling station which also sells snacks would not need to register. However, a motorway service area at which there is a restaurant or transport cafeteria would be registrable food premises. Other exemptions granted by the regulations include premises operated by charitable organisations or used irregularly (which includes premises used regularly once per week), such as a village hall, and premises which are required to be registered under other regulations, such as slaughterhouses and dairies.

The registration procedures established by the Food Safety Act 1990 do not amount to a system of licensing, such as operates in relation to estate agents under the Estate Agents Act 1979 or the consumer credit industry under the Consumer Credit Act 1974. Perhaps the problem with licensing systems generally is that government may be operating under the maxim, 'once bitten, twice shy', especially on the experience of the Consumer Credit Act 1974. It has been seen that the licensing system under the 1974 Act has proved to be very expensive and time-consuming to bring into operation and that a more flexible system of negative, as opposed to positive licensing has been preferred in relation to estate agents (see chapters 2 and 11). However, in relation to food businesses, there was widespread support amongst opposition parties and consumer groups, at the time the Food Safety Bill was passing through Parliament, for a system of licensing in the interests of consumer safety. The only provision which allows for the setting up of a licensing system is s. 19, which gives a Ministerial power to order the licensing of premises for the purposes of running a food business, and to prohibit the use of unlicensed premises. However, this power has not been made use of to any great extent, except in relation to premises used for the purposes of food irradiation. Moreover, it is clear from s. 19(2) of the 1990 Act that these powers are limited to securing compliance with food safety requirements, ensuring public safety or promoting the interests of consumers.

The fact that there has been no attempt to introduce a licensing system is regrettable, especially when the social, economic and public health considerations attendant on the issue of food poisoning are taken into account.

15.2 INJURIOUS FOOD

Under the Food Safety Act 1990, s. 7(1), it is an offence for a person to render food injurious to health by adulterating it, or removing a constituent or subjecting it to any other process or treatment, with the intent that it shall be sold for human consumption. The concluding words of s. 7(1) indicate that this is not a strict liability offence, since intent to supply for human consumption is a requirement. However, the legislation apparently does not require proof of *mens rea* in connection with the actual process of rendering food injurious to health.

The extent to which s. 7 will form the basis of prosecutions must be questioned given that in the late 20th century, it seems unlikely that there will be many instances of deliberate adulteration of food on the part of the food industry. However, on a closer examination of the wording of s. 7 (1)(a) it is clear that the provision applies to any person who adds an article or substance to food, whether he is responsible for the preparation of the food or not. The importance of this provision is that it is sufficiently broadly worded to be used in cases of food terrorism, such as recently highlighted cases of putting ground glass in baby foods displayed for sale to the public (see also Public Orders Act 1986, s. 38).

15.2.1 Injurious to health
A central feature of food safety law is the notion of injury to health. Food that is injurious to health fails to satisfy the general safety requirement in the Food Safety Act 1990, s. 8, and the enforcement powers of the Act may be invoked (Food Safety Act 1990, ss. 9–13).

An injury to health is defined as an impairment, whether permanent or temporary (s. 7(3)). In deciding whether food is injurious to health, regard should be had to the probable effect of the food on the health of a person consuming it (s. 7(2)(a)) and the probable cumulative effect of similarly constituted food on the health of a person consuming it in ordinary quantities (s. 7(2)(b)). In other words, it is necessary to consider both the immediate and long-term effects on a hypothetical consumer of consuming food of the kind under consideration.

The wording of s. 7(2) is important, since it does not refer to the consumer who has registered the complaint. Instead, the court must consider the matter from the position of the 'consumer in the Clapham High Street'. Thus, if the complaint is that food has brought on an allergic reaction, it will be necessary for the court to consider whether only a small percentage of consumers would be likely to be affected. Conversely, in *Cullen* v *McNair* (1908) 6 LGR 753 it was considered that if an ingredient in cream is harmless to adults, but potentially harmful to invalids and young children, it will be injurious to health, since children and invalids are likely to form a substantial proportion of the consumers of cream.

The reference to 'ordinary quantities' in s. 7(2)(b) means that food will not be regarded as injurious to health merely because the consumer has over-indulged himself. Section 7(2)(b) also requires the court to consider the likely effects of the food for the future. For example, some foods may not have an immediate effect but when consumed over a period of time may result in an increased likelihood of heart disease or some other condition based on continued consumption. On this basis, it is arguable that food businesses such as fish and chip shops or breweries may be regarded as having prepared potentially injurious food (see Howells, Bradgate and Griffiths, *The Food Safety Act 1990* (London: Blackstone Press, 1990), pp. 15–16).

15.2.2 Rendering

The central feature of s. 7 is that something must have been done to food to render it injurious to health. Accordingly, most of s. 7 is aimed at preparers rather than retailers of food, although it has been observed above that s. 7(1)(a) may also be used in cases of alleged food terrorism.

In order to be guilty of an offence, the person charged must have done some positive act which has resulted in the food becoming injurious to health. Such acts include adding an article to food (e.g., colourants; food sabotage), using an article as an ingredient in the preparation of food, abstracting a const'tuent from food (e.g., removal by evaporation) and subjecting food to any process or treatment (s. 7(1)(a)–(d)).

The way in which some of these words have been defined means that s. 7 has a very broad scope. In particular, the word 'preparation' is defined as including any form of processing and treatment. 'Treatment' includes subjecting food to heat or cold (s. 53(1)). The reference to processing and treatment would seem to cover not just the final stages of preparing food for human consumption, but also much earlier stages, such as crop spraying and other forms of treatment in the course of growth.

Generally, s. 7 requires a positive act on the part of the food processor, with the result that defects in food resulting from inaction will not fall within its remit. Thus, the natural growth of mould would appear not to amount to rendering food injurious to health, although this will be covered by other provisions of the Act. Similarly, not removing a natural feature of food does not infringe s. 7. Thus the failure to remove natural toxins present in red kidney beans does not amount to rendering food injurious to health.

15.3 FOOD SAFETY REQUIREMENTS

Under s. 8 of the 1990 Act it is an offence for a person to sell, offer for sale, expose or advertise for sale, possess for the purposes of sale or preparation for sale any food intended for human consumption which fails to comply with food safety requirements (s. 8(1)(a)). It is also an offence to deposit with or consign to another any food intended for human consumption which fails to comply with food safety requirements (s. 8(1)(b)). For the purposes of s. 8 where any food which fails to comply with food safety requirements forms part of a batch or consignment, it is presumed (in the absence of evidence to the contrary) that the whole consignment also fails to satisfy the food safety requirement. Section 8 has the effect of broadening the range of possible offences capable of being committed in relation to food, but it does not go as far as some would like. In particular, there is no general safety requirement such as that which applies to other consumer goods by virtue of the Consumer Protection Act 1987, s. 10(1) (see further chapter 14). However, it has been noted already that the 'shelf-life' of the general product safety requirement of the 1987 Act is strictly limited since it will have no application where the General Product Safety Regulations 1994 (SI 1994/2328) also apply. These Regulations require that no producer should place a product on the market unless it is safe (reg. 7). They apply to food as well as other consumer goods (regs 2 and 3). The important effect of the Regulations is that they impose a positive duty to supply safe goods (reg. 7) as opposed to the negative duty in the 1987 Act to supply goods which are not unsafe. Accordingly, if loopholes are found to exist in the regime created by the 1990 Act, they will be filled by the general safety requirement. For example, if the 1990 Act does not apply to a failure to remove harmful toxins naturally present in food, it is possible that such food might be covered by the general safety requirement. Similarly, until progress is made on how to deal with novel foods, it is arguable that the general safety requirement may provide, at least, a fall-back position.

15.3.1 Sale etc.
The extended definition of sale for the purposes of the Food Safety Act 1990, s. 8(1)(a), appears to cover almost any sort of supply in the course of a business. Clearly, the wording of the Act does not confine offences to sales within the narrow meaning of the Sale of Goods Act 1979, s. 2. It is also possible for the s. 8 offence to be committed by a person who merely exposes food for sale or stores food items in an area from which they may later be moved for the purposes of sale. The phrase 'offer for sale' would not apply to a retailer, who generally does not offer to sell anything, but merely invites customers to make offers to him (see *Fisher* v *Bell* [1961] 1 QB 394 and chapter 4). However, other provisions of s. 8(1)(a) mean that the mere exposure or advertising of goods for sale may equally constitute the commission of an offence.

For the purposes of the whole of the 1990 Act, s. 2(1) extends the meaning of the word 'sale' to include (a) the supply of food otherwise than on sale, in the course of a business and (b) any other thing done with respect to food as is specified in a Ministerial order, and s. 2(2)(a) specifies that the Act will apply to food given away as a prize (including promotional 'give-aways': s. 2(2)(b)) or food which is given away in connection with any entertainment to which the public are admitted, whether for payment or not. The importance of s. 2 is that the broadened definition of a sale has the effect of including within the scope of the 1990 Act a number of supplies which would not ordinarily be described as sales. For example, the supply of free school meals by a local education authority or the supply of food to a patient in a National Health Service trust hospital would probably be regarded as a supply of food in the course of a business within s. 2(1)(a). A person can also supply food without being aware that this is the case. For example, food may be supplied by an agent or employee of the owner of the premises from which the food is sold (see *Gardner* v *Akeroyd* [1952] 2 QB 743). In such a case the owner is the supplier of the food, but he may be able to raise the due diligence defence in s. 21 of the Act (see chapter 13). The person responsible for the commission of the offence may also be proceeded against under the bypass provisions of s. 20 (see further chapter 13).

15.3.2 Depositing and consigning

Under the Food Safety Act 1990, s. 8(1)(b), a person commits an offence if he deposits food with or consigns food to another for the purposes of sale or preparation for sale, if that food fails to satisfy the food safety requirement. This would appear to be aimed at manufacturers and producers who supply others in the food chain. Under previous legislation, the word 'deposit' was given a very broad meaning. For example, meat carried in a cart on its way to premises used for the preparation of food was held to be deposited 'in a place' (*Williams* v *Allen* [1916] 1 KB 425).

15.3.3 Human consumption

For the purposes of s. 8, no offence is committed unless the food is intended for human consumption. In this respect, there are two important presumptions. First, it is presumed that food commonly used for human consumption is intended for human consumption where it is sold, offered for sale, exposed or kept for sale, unless the person charged with the commission of an offence proves the contrary (s. 3(2)). Where food is found on premises used for the preparation, storage or sale of food, it is presumed, unless the contrary is proved, that it is intended for human consumption (s. 3(3)).

It follows from these provisions that where unsafe food is found on food premises, it is not open to the person charged to argue that the food was not intended for human consumption unless he can prove otherwise. For example, evidence might be called to the effect that the food was to be supplied to a pig farmer for use as animal feed. Similarly, if the person charged has prevented a local authority official from gaining access to food stored on his premises, the prosecution will not fail for want of proof that the food was intended for human consumption (see *Hooper* v *Petrou* [1973] Crim LR 198), since this is presumed in the absence of evidence to the contrary.

15.3.4 Food safety

The basis of the s. 8 offence is that food has failed to comply with the minimum food safety requirement laid down by the 1990 Act. Unsafe food is defined as that which is injurious to health under s. 7 (see 15.2.1 above); that which is unfit for human consumption and that which is contaminated within the meaning of the Act (s. 8(2)).

15.3.4.1 Unfit for human consumption

The requirement in the Food Safety Act 1990, s. 8(2)(b), that food should not be unfit for human consumption represents no change in the existing law, with the result that case law relevant to earlier controls on unfit food will be applicable (see generally Stephenson (1982) 131 NLJ 871).

Whether or not food is unfit for human consumption is a question of fact in each case. In *David Greig Ltd* v *Goldfinch* (1961) 105 SJ 367 pastry contaminated with penicillin mould, which is not harmful to human beings, was still held to be unfit for human consumption. Lord Parker CJ drew a distinction between food which is merely unsuitable for human consumption, such as a stale loaf of bread, and that which is unfit for human consumption such as the mouldy pastry. Similarly, it has been observed that game which contains lead shot is not to be regarded as unfit for human consumption merely because it contains extraneous matter, especially since those who eat game realise that the presence of lead shot is quite likely (*J. Miller Ltd* v *Battersea Borough Council* [1956] 1 QB 43, 46–7 per Lord Goddard CJ); likewise, a loaf of bread which contains a piece of string (*Turner and Son Ltd* v *Owen* [1956] 1 QB 48) or a cream bun which contains a piece of metal (*J. Miller Ltd* v *Battersea Borough Council*). What seemed to persuade the court that these last two cases did not invlove the supply of unfit food was that the loaf of bread and the bun, in each case, were perfectly good in themselves (*Turner and Son Ltd* v *Owen* [1956] 1 QB 48, 51 per Lord Goddard CJ).

What seems to be required for the purposes of s. 8(2)(b) is that the food should be 'putrid, diseased or unwholesome' (*J. Miller Ltd* v *Battersea Borough Council* [1956] 1 QB 43, 47 per Lord Goddard CJ). Thus if a person prepares bread which contains a toxic, dirty, used bandage (*Chibnall's Bakeries* v *Cope-Brown* [1956] Crim LR 263), or where caustic soda is supplied as lemonade (*Meah* v *Roberts* [1978] 1 All ER 97), the food will not be fit for human consumption. Although there is no requirement in s. 8 that the food should be harmful to the consumer, if it appears that what has been supplied is positively dangerous, an offence is committed. Thus in *R* v *F. & M. Dobson Ltd* (1995) 14 TrLR 467 the defendants were held to have sold food which did not comply with food safety requirements when they manufactured and supplied a chocolate nut crunch which contained a Stanley knife blade which had cut the mouth of a consumer. The distinction between unfit and unsuitable food is now less important than used to be the case, since food which is unsuitable for human consumption due to the presence of some unwanted extraneous matter may be regarded as contaminated for the purposes of s. 8(2)(c). In any case, the presence of unwanted extraneous material will also fall within the provisions of s. 14, which prohibits the sale of food not of the substance demanded by the consumer (see 15.7.2.2 below).

15.3.4.2 Contaminated food The Food Safety Act 1990, s. 8(2)(c), introduces the entirely new concept of contaminated food. Under the previous legislation there was a loophole where food proved to be merely unsuitable rather than unfit for human consumption. For the purposes of s. 8, food may be contaminated either by extraneous material or by something internal to the food supplied, provided that it is not reasonable to expect the food to be used for human consumption in that state. Thus if food is mouldy, rancid, stale or suffers from minor infestation it would be reasonable to infer that it is contaminated. Likewise, if the food is contaminated with extraneous material such as pesticides or internal ingredients such as unauthorised additives, it is arguable that s. 8(2)(c) is not complied with.

The use of the words 'in that state' in s. 8(2)(c) implies that something may be done to food in order to render it capable of consumption. Accordingly, it would not be appropriate to write food off as contaminated where some later process might have the effect of removing the contamination, thereby rendering the food reasonably fit for human consumption. For example, in *R v Archer, ex parte Barrow Lane & Ballard Ltd* (1983) 82 LGR 361 (decided under the Imported Food Regulations 1968, now replaced by the Imported Food Regulations 1984, SI 1984/1918) it was held that dates infested with insect excrement and fragments could be rendered wholesome (and therefore fit for human consumption) if they were subsequently subjected to a process, the end product of which was brown sauce. It was observed by Lord Donaldson MR (at 365) that food may be unwholesome in the context of an untreated use, but wholesome provided it is subject to some later treatment. For example, fermenting apples would not be regarded as wholesome as eating apples, but they are perfectly acceptable when it is known that they are to be used to manufacture cider (ibid. 366).

From an enforcement officer's perspective, this decision might create problems. For example, in order to be sure whether a prosecution is justified, environmental health officers will now have to examine in some detail the shipping documents before they intercept what is believed to be an unwholesome cargo. There may also be instances in which an importer states one intended use, but in fact has a rather different use in mind.

15.4 ENFORCEMENT POWERS

In order to ensure proper enforcement of the provisions of the Food Safety Act 1990, enforcement authorities are given a number of important powers. In particular, there are powers of inspection and seizure and powers to apply to the court for an improvement notice, prohibition order or an emergency order so as to deal with suspected offenders.

15.4.1 Inspection, seizure and destruction

Under the Food Safety Act 1990, s. 9(1), an enforcement officer has, at all reasonable times, the power to inspect food intended for human consumption which has been sold or is in the hands of a person for the purposes of supply or preparation for supply. After such an inspection has taken place, an enforcement officer may serve a notice preventing the sale of the food (s. 9(3)(a)(i)) or ordering that the food be removed to a specified place (s. 9(3)(a)(ii)) or requiring the food to be taken immediately before a magistrate so as to secure an order for its destruction (s. 9(3)(b)).

These powers of inspection etc are exercisable only at reasonable times. At one stage this was taken to mean that a proposed inspection on a Sunday afternoon when the shop in question was normally closed could be regarded as unreasonable (see *Small* v *Bickley* (1875) 40 JP 119). However, now that Sunday trading is commonplace, Sunday inspections might not be considered unreasonable. Where food is seized under s. 9(3), the enforcement authority has a maximum of 21 days in which to decide whether the food complies with the food safety requirement (s. 9(4)). If the authority is of the opinion that the food safety requirement has not been satisfied, the food is to be seized and dealt with by the magistrates' court (s. 9(4)(b)). Where the court is of the opinion that the food fails to comply with the food safety requirement, it may order the destruction of the food and require the owner to meet any expenditure incurred in disposing of it (s. 9(6)).

Where an enforcement authority decides to withdraw a notice issued under s. 9(3) or where the magistrates' court decides that the food does not infringe the food safety requirement, the enforcement authority is liable to pay compensation in respect of the depreciation in value of the food resulting from action having been taken (s. 9(7)). This is particularly important where the enforcement authority takes speculative action. However, what s. 9(7) does not allow is a claim for compensation in respect of matters such as general loss of business profit or loss of goodwill.

While s. 9(1) envisages a prior inspection of food before any further action is taken, it is possible for an enforcement authority to issue a notice under s. 9(3) without a prior inspection, if it appears likely that food may cause food poisoning or any disease communicable to human beings (s. 9(2)). If an enforcement authority acts under s. 9(2), there is the danger that a mistake might be made, in which case the compensation provisions will come into play.

Where an enforcement officer is not satisfied that food complies with food safety requirements, he must seize the food and apply to a magistrate for further orders. In this event, the enforcement officer will issue a food condemnation warning notice, which must state the reasons for issuing the notice and must give the person on whom the notice is served the right to give reasons why the food should not be condemned (Detention of Food (Prescribed Forms) Regulations 1990, SI 1990/2614).

If the court concludes that the food does fail to comply with food safety requirements, it must be condemned and an order for its destruction or disposal will be made. In reaching a decision to order condemnation, it is important that the court takes account of all the available evidence, including any evidence presented by the owner of the food under consideration and not just evidence presented by the Public Health Laboratory Service (PHLS). Unfortunately, there is no provision for an appeal against a decision to order condemnation made under s. 9. All that is left for the owner of such food is to challenge the decision, after the event, by way of judicial review. For example, in *Errington* v *Clydesdale District Council* (1995, sheriff court, unreported), known as the Lanark Blue Cheese case the owner successfully challenged what some regarded as an overzealous decision on the part of the local authority to apply for a condemnation order in respect of a consignment of Lanark blue cheese which was shown by PHLS tests to contain more than the suggested safe level of *Listeria monocytogenes* (Lm). The local authority application was made despite the fact that tests conducted on behalf of the owner showed that the cheese consistently recorded either zero or minuscule Lm levels. In the event, the sheriff court accepted that the PHLS tests were biologically implausible and that an order for condemnation was inappropriate.

15.4.2 Improvement notices

While the powers of inspection and seizure etc. apply only in relation to unsafe food, there are other enforcement powers which allow other courses of action. An improvement notice may be issued which requires the owner of a food business to comply with regulations made in respect of the processing or treatment of food or for the purposes of securing that food premises are in a hygienic condition (Food Safety Act 1990, s. 10(1) and (3): the required format of the notice is set out in the Food Safety (Improvement and Prohibition — Prescribed Forms) Regulations 1991, SI 1991/100). Given the breadth of the definition of a food business in s. 1(3), an improvement notice could be served on a substantial number of businesses, including those concerned with the sale, advertising, serving, preparation, delivery, wrapping, labelling, storage or transport of food. Businesses associated with food sources are also covered, with the result that an improvement notice could be served on an agricultural business if necessary. So the power to serve an improvement notice encompasses the whole of the food chain, without exception.

Where an improvement notice is served, the enforcement officer is required to state the grounds on which he believes the food business is failing and what steps are necessary in order to secure compliance with the matters set out in the notice and must specify the period within which the necessary steps should be taken (s. 10(1)). Unlike some of the other enforcement powers created by the 1990 Act, there appears to be no provision for the payment of compensation by the enforcement authority where an improvement notice is either wrongly or unreasonably served upon a food business. If a person fails to comply with an improvement notice, he commits an offence (s. 10(2)).

In making use of the power to issue an improvement notice, the enforcement authority is encouraged to comply with the contents of one of a number of codes of practice issued under the Food Safety Act 1990. *Code of Practice No. 5: The Use of Improvement Notices* (revised 1994) sets out informal guidance on what is good practice. An improvement notice should not normally be the first option taken where defects have been discovered following an inspection of a food business. However, there may be exceptions to this rule of guidance where there is a serious danger to public health. Where a particular business has a record of non-compliance with food hygiene or food processing regulations, the service of an improvement notice is considered to be the appropriate course of action to take.

An improvement notice must state as precisely as possible what is required from the person upon whom it is served. For example, in *Bexley London Borough Council* v *Gardiner Merchant plc* [1993] COD 383 an improvement notice merely specified that there had been a breach of the Food Hygiene

(General) Regulations 1970, which themselves specified five requirements, all of which had to be complied with. In the High Court it was considered that the improvement notice was not sufficiently precise, having regard to the guidance set out in Code of Practice No. 5, since the enforcement authority had failed to specify the particular failure to comply with the Regulations on which they sought to rely.

15.4.3 Prohibition orders

If a person has been convicted of an offence under the food processing and hygiene regulations to which the improvement notice regime applies, an enforcement authority is also empowered to apply to the court for the issue of a prohibition order (Food Safety Act 1990, s. 11(1)(a)). Before a prohibition order is issued, the court must be satisfied that the food business presents a health risk (s. 11(1)(b)). For these purposes, a business presents a health risk if there is a risk of injury to health resulting from the use of any process or treatment, the construction of premises, the use of any equipment or the state or condition of any premises or equipment (s. 11(2)). Where a health risk is established, a prohibition order must be issued, but the nature of the order will differ according to the nature of the health risk concerned. For example, the prohibition may relate to specified premises, a particular process or method of treatment or the use of certain types of equipment (s. 11(3)), and the order must clearly specify what is prohibited.

Where the enforcement authority is satisfied that a health risk no longer exists, they must issue a certificate, within three days, lifting the order (ss. 11(6) and (7)). The person upon whom the order was served may apply for a certificate, in which case the enforcement authority must decide whether there is still a health risk within a period of 14 days (s. 11(7)).

As with improvement notices, there is guidance on the use of prohibition orders in the statutory codes of practice made under the 1990 Act. *Code of Practice No. 6: Prohibition Procedures* applies to both s. 11 and the special provisions in s. 12 concerning emergency orders (see below). The code gives examples of circumstances in which it might be appropriate to invoke the prohibition procedures under the 1990 Act. These include, in relation to premises, serious vermin infestation, serious contraventions of food hygiene regulations and cases of serious food poisoning. In relation to equipment, examples of instances in which prohibition procedures would be appropriate include cases of gross contamination of equipment which can no longer be properly cleaned and milk pasteurisation equipment which cannot be kept at the right temperature.

15.4.4 Emergency orders and food scares

Where there is an imminent health risk, the Food Safety Act 1990 confers special emergency powers on enforcement authorities (s. 12(1), (2) and (4)). The procedure consists of the immediate issue of an emergency prohibition notice in terms identical to those which apply to prohibition notices (see s. 11(2) and (3) considered in 15.4.3). Alternatively, the enforcement authority can apply to a magistrates' court for an emergency prohibition order

(s. 12(2)), but such an order will not be granted unless one day's notice has been given to the proprietor of the food business (s. 12(3)):

Where a prohibition notice has been issued, it will lapse after three days unless an application has been made to the magistrates' court under s. 12(2) for a court order to the same effect (s. 12(7)). Compensation is payable to the proprietor of the business where the court refuses to grant a prohibition order or where the enforcement authority decides not to apply to the court (s. 12(10)).

In addition to the powers of local authority enforcement officers, the 1990 Act also confers a power of emergency control on the Minister of Agriculture, Fisheries and Food (s. 13(1)). In the light of recent food scares, such a power is an important element in the control of food presenting a substantial health risk. The Act provides that an emergency control order may be made by the Minister in respect of commercial operations relating to food, food sources or contact materials and may be subject to such conditions as the Minister considers appropriate (ss. 13(1) and (3)).

The emergency procedure established under the Food Safety Act 1990 is particularly useful in relation to food scares under which a harmful hazard may come to public attention, resulting in widespread confusion over what is safe to eat. In recent years there have been scares in relation to salmonella in eggs and BSE in British beef. While the emergency procedure outlined above is effective in certain respects, it has also become necessary to set up a mechanism whereby local enforcement authorities are alerted to pertinent dangers at as early a stage as possible. The system in operation in the United Kingdom has three main aims, namely, to detect food hazards, to evaluate them and to control the hazard. If a decision is taken to withdraw food which has been identified as contaminated, immediate communication of this decision will be sent to 60 local authorities and in turn each of those authorities has a responsibility to pass on the communication to other authorities within their general area. At the same time the European Commission will also be kept informed of the position, so that appropriate action may also be taken at a European level, if necessary.

The necessary action to avert a food hazard is now set out in *Code of Practice No. 16: Enforcement of the Food Safety Act 1990 in relation to the Food Hazard Warning System*, which requires local enforcement authorities to determine the probable scale of the problem, the possibility that the problem was caused by malicious action and the extent of the risk to health. In order to make these determinations, the authority is expected to communicate with experts such as the Public or National Health Laboratory Service, the public analyst or a consultant microbiologist.

15.5 FOOD REGULATIONS

One of the powers conferred on the Ministry of Agriculture Fisheries and Food (MAFF) is that of making food regulations, so as to facilitate the development of food policy. Prior to exercising this power, MAFF is obliged to consult interested bodies (Food Safety Act 1990, s. 48(3)). These include the National Consumer Council, major food producers and representatives of enforcement agencies. Also consulted are advisory bodies consisting of experts in a given field such as the Food Advisory Committee, the Advisory Committee on Pesticides, the Veterinary Products Committee, the Committee on the Microbiological Safety of Food, the Steering Group on Food Surveillance and the Advisory Committee on Novel Foods.

Under the Food Safety Act 1990, ss. 16 to 19, there are wide-ranging powers to create regulations in relation to food. The broad areas set out in the 1990 Act in respect of which this power exists include food safety and consumer protection (s. 16), compliance with European Community requirements (s. 17), special provision for particular types of food (s. 18) and the registration and licensing of food premises (s. 19).

Under s. 59(3) and sch. 4, the numerous regulations which were made in respect of food under the predecessors of the 1990 Act, namely, the Food and Drugs Act 1955 and the Food Act 1984, remain in force and shall take effect as if they had been made under the present enabling legislation.

15.5.1 Food safety and consumer protection

The Food Safety Act 1990, s. 16(1) (see also sch. 1), gives the Minister the power to make regulations in respect of a wide range of matters related to the safety and quality of food. In particular, regulations may be made in respect of the composition of food (s. 16(1)(a)), the means of securing that food is fit for human consumption (s. 16(1)(b)), processes or treatments used in the preparation of food (s. 16(1)(c)), hygiene (s. 16(1)(d)), labelling, marking, presenting or advertising food and descriptions which may be applied to food (s. 16(1)(e)) and any other matter which ensures that food complies with the food safety requirement and that the best interests of consumers are protected and promoted (s. 16(1)(f)).

These powers to make regulations are particularly important in the light of developing practices in the food industry. For example, it would be possible to introduce regulations in respect of novel practices such as food irradiation under s. 16(1)(c), on the basis that food irradiation is a form of food treatment or, failing that, as a process. Where necessary, such matters can be brought to the attention of consumers by means of regulations made under s. 16(1)(e). It is also important that the power to make regulations is not confined to the food itself, but also covers food sources and contact materials. Regulations in respect of food sources could relate to matters such as how animals or crops which are a source of food are dealt with. It was easy to make the wide range of regulations needed to meet the BSE crisis in the beef industry under the enabling provisions of the Food Safety Act 1990.

The reference to contact materials is intended to take in matters such as containers and other materials in which food is wrapped. It is possible to make regulations under s. 16(2) which lay down requirements in respect of materials such as cling film which might be harmful if they come into contact with food in some circumstances, such as during the process of microwave cooking.

The 1990 Act also recognises the capacity of the food industry for innovation by conferring on the Minister a power to make regulations in respect of novel foods. These foods include both foods which have not been previously used for human consumption in Great Britain and foods which have been used for human consumption to only a limited extent. This appears to cover both innovatory foods, for example, new slimming products, and those which have existed for years, in another part of the world, but have not been widely consumed in this country, for example, some exotic fruits (see Howells, Bradgate and Griffiths, *Blackstone's Guide to the Food Safety Act 1990*, para. 5.5).

15.6 FOOD LABELLING AND ADVERTISING

15.6.1 False and misleading descriptions
In addition to the labelling requirements considered below, the Food Safety Act 1990, s. 15(1), creates a general offence of falsely describing, advertising or presenting food. It is an offence for a person to sell, offer, expose or possess for the purposes of sale any food which is labelled in such a way that the label either falsely describes the food (s. 15(1)(a)) or is likely to mislead as to the nature, substance or quality of that food (s. 15(1)(b)). For the meaning of nature, substance or quality, see the discussion of s. 14, below (para 15.7 *et seq*).

For the purposes of the offence in s. 15(1)(a) what is required is an explicit false description on the food label in question. Since the offence is confined to labelling, unlike the Trade Descriptions Act 1968 (see chapter 17), an oral misdescription will not suffice. However, there appears to be no reason why the requirement in the Trade Descriptions Act 1968, s. 3, that a statement should be false to a material degree should not also apply to s. 15 of the 1990 Act (see chapter 17 on the issue of falsity to a material degree).

Although the term 'false description' might be taken to mean that there has to be an actively false statement, it is clear that for the purposes of English law, a statement may be false not only by virtue of what it contains, but also by virtue of what it omits. Accordingly, a statement which is literally true, but which is false by reason of a material omission, may also be regarded as a false statement (*R v Kylsant* [1932] 1 KB 442). For example in *Van den Berghs & Jurgens v Burleigh* (1987, Lewes Crown Court, unreported) the defendants produced cream substitutes under the descriptions 'Elmlea Single' and 'Elmlea Whipping', which, it was alleged, when taken together with depictions of a rural scene, might mislead a consumer into thinking he was buying real cream. It was held that despite the presence of the words, 'the real alternative to cream' on the packaging, the overall effect of the method of presentation was such that an average consumer who was not a food technologist might be misled. Accordingly, an offence under the predecessor of s. 15 was committed.

Since the offence under s. 15 is one of strict liability, it will make no difference if the maker has no knowledge of the falsity of his statement (*R v Cummerson* [1968] 2 QB 534). Nor will it be a defence to demonstrate an honest belief in the truth of the statement. In *Holmes v Pipers Ltd* [1914] 1 KB 57, the defendant described as 'British Tarragona wine' a concoction, of which 85 per cent was wine made from dried English raisins and 15 per cent was a heavy form of Tarragona wine, which was unsuitable for consumption. Overall, the description was considered to be false, so that an offence was held to have been committed. Similarly, the defendant in *Kat* v *Diment* [1951] 1 KB 34 committed an offence when he described as 'non-brewed vinegar' something which consisted of pure acetic acid.

In determining whether a particular statement is false, the test applied is one of fact, based upon what an ordinary man would understand by the description given by the defendant. In *Wolkind* v *Pura Foods Ltd* (1989) 85 LGR 782, the defendants described a cooking fat made of 100 per cent vegetable oils as 'Vegetable lard'. Without qualification, the word 'lard' would be construed by an ordinary man as containing pig fat, but due to the qualification 'vegetable' lard, and the wording on the packaging, 'Made with 100 per cent vegetable oils', no reasonable person could be in any doubt about what was being sold, and no offence was committed. Similarly, in *Amos* v *Britvic Ltd* (1984) 149 JP 13 there was no offence where twice-pasteurised orange juice exported in concentrated form was described as 'natural', despite the fact that, before it was marketed, the concentrate would be diluted with water. Applying the reasonable man test, what was conclusive was that the packaging made it clear that the contents consisted of 'a blend made with concentrated orange juice and orange juice'. Under s. 15(1)(b) of the Food Safety Act 1990 it is an offence to label food in a manner 'likely to mislead as to the nature or substance or quality of the food'. This is a change of wording from previous legislation which placed upon the prosecution the extremely difficult burden of establishing that the defendant's statement was 'calculated to mislead'. The new wording also assists the prosecution in another respect, in that a statement may be likely to mislead a person without actually misleading the particular complainant. Thus an enforcement officer may not be misled by a particular label, but if, in the opinion of the court, the statement might be misleading to ordinary consumers, an offence is still committed under s. 15. Whether a particular label is likely to mislead is a question of fact to be determined by reference to the understanding of an ordinary person. Thus it has been held that even if an expert might not have been misled, an offence is nonetheless committed if an ordinary person would misunderstand the label (*Concentrated Foods Ltd* v *Champ* [1944] 2 KB 342). Moreover, since the emphasis in s. 15 is upon the misleading nature of the statement made, there is no equivalent to the requirement of prejudice to the consumer to be found in s. 14 (*R* v *Mayling* [1963] 2 QB 717).

15.6.2 Food Labelling Regulations 1996 and the Food (Lot Marking) Regulations 1996

In recent years the food industry has made a much greater use of packaging, which can be used to provide consumers with greater quantities of information. For example, some consumers may react adversely to certain ingredients in food, which would not have the same effect on others. If the packaging in which food is supplied gives adequate information, such consumers will be able to discover whether or not a particular item is safe to use. A warning may be printed on packaging which advises consumers on how best to cook a particular item so as to avert any safety risk which might arise if different cooking methods were to be employed.

Most consumers now shop for food at supermarket outlets which purchase food from primary suppliers in large batches. The particular problem associated with large batch purchases is of identification should there be a subsequent consumer complaint. In order to deal with this matter and to give effect to the Council Directive on Lot Marking (89/396/EEC) the Food (Lot Marking) Regulations 1996 (SI 1996/1502) now set up a flexible framework for batch identification, which will facilitate the tracing and identification of a product along the relevant section of the food chain. Some food products are not subject to these regulations. The principal exemptions include primary agricultural produce which has not undergone initial processing and is delivered to temporary storage stations or collection units. The assumption in these circumstances is that someone lower down the food chain will be responsible for lot marking after some subsequent process such as packaging has been applied to the food in question. Other exemptions also apply to foods which are not pre-packed when sold to the ultimate consumer; foods pre-packed at the request of the consumer; foods pre-packed in containers with minimal surface area; small individual portions of substances such as ice cream, salt, sauce or sugar, provided that any larger packaging in which larger quantities of these individual portions might be supplied is appropriately lot marked and foods marked with a 'best before' or 'use by' date.

The law on information labelling is now contained in the Food Labelling Regulations 1996 (SI 1996/1499), which consolidate and replace the Food Labelling Regulations 1984 as from 1 July 1996. The 1984 Regulations (SI 1984/1305) had implemented the requirements set out in the EC Directive on Food Labelling (79/112/EEC) and covered only foods which were not governed by their own specific labelling requirements. The 1996 Regulations, in addition to being a consolidating measure, also implement a number of European Community measures relating to nutrition (Council Directives 89/398/EEC and 90/496/EEC), alcoholic strength (Council Directive 87/250/EEC) and the labelling, advertising and presentation of foodstuffs (Council Directives 79/112/EEC and 94/54/EEC), except in relation to the matter of net quantity, which is covered by the Weights and Measures Act 1985.

Certain types of food are specifically excluded from the remit of the 1996 Regulations under reg. 4 because they are covered by other specific legislation. They include sugar products, cocoa and chocolate, honey, condensed or dried milk, coffee, eggs, spreadable fats, wines, spirit drinks, fresh fruit and vegetables and tuna fish. There is also a general exemption in respect of any food brought into Great Britain from a member State of the European Union or the European Economic Area in which that food was lawfully produced and sold (reg. 3).

The general tenor of the Regulations is towards accurate information supply in respect of pre-packed foods. By virtue of reg. 27 there are certain instances of food supply and preparation to which the application of the Regulations is somewhat limited. These include food prepared on business premises for the benefit of the person preparing it, food which is ready for delivery to the consumer and food supplied by catering establishments such as restaurants, canteens and roadside food dispensing vehicles from which the food is dispensed directly to the consumer for immediate consumption.

15.6.2.1 General labelling requirements One of the general requirements of the 1984 Regulations was that food was not to be presented in a manner likely to mislead the consumer, to a material degree, about its nature, substance or quality (Food Labelling Regulations 1984, reg. 4). This requirement is not repeated in the 1996 Regulations, so as to avoid duplication of the requirement in the Food Safety Act 1990, s. 15(3), that it is an offence to sell, offer or expose for sale or to have in one's possession for the purposes of sale, any food, the presentation of which is likely to mislead as to the nature or substance or quality of the food. For the purposes of s. 15(3) misleading presentation includes the shape, appearance or packing of the food and its manner of display.

The general labelling requirement in reg. 5 of the 1996 Regulations specifies that food to which the Regulations applies must be marked with a label which sets out the name of the food, its ingredients, minimum durability, storage requirements, instructions as to use, the identity of the manufacturer and, in some cases, the origin or provenance of the food. The word 'provenance' is an addition to the original wording of the 1984 Regulations, but is undefined in the 1996 Regulations. What it adds to the word 'origin' is difficult to ascertain, since the two words seem to refer to the same thing, namely the source from which the food is derived or the place in which it originated. Moreover, the guidance notes issued with the 1996 Regulations also state explicitly that the words 'origin' and 'provenance' should be taken as having the same meaning.

The requirement that the origin of certain foods be stated appears to arise from the belief that food of a certain variety which comes from a stated origin may be better than similar produce from other areas. For example, in *Re Labelling of Dutch Poultry* (case 6 U 173/87) [1990] 2 CMLR 104 the Cologne Oberlandesgericht required a Dutch exporter of poultry to state the origin of his exports, since, without such a statement, the manner of packaging was such that the poultry could be taken for German products. The basis for the decision was that a statement of origin serves to individualise a product, thereby establishing a relationship between the product and the customer's expectations of quality.

So far as naming food is concerned, the 1996 Regulations state that certain names are obligatory for certain types of food (reg. 6). For example, certain types of fish must be named in accordance with specific requirements laid out in sch. 1, and spreadable fats require names such as 'butter' or 'margarine', according to their composition. Where there is no obligatory name, the producer may use a name which is customary for that type of food (reg. 7). The term 'customary' has no established definition, but it is clear from the guidance notes issued with the regulations that customary is to be equated with long-term user. Examples include names imported from other countries such as 'lasagne' and 'pizza'. Similarly, if a particular type of food has come to be described in a particular way over a period of time, that name may be used without further elaboration. Examples given in the guidance notes issued with the Regulations include 'fish fingers' and 'Bakewell tart'.

Even if there is a customary name for a particular variety of food, it may be a name which has only localised significance. For example, the terms 'stotty cake' and 'blind scouse' might have significance for those who originate, respectively, from the North-East of England or Merseyside, but it is not certain that others would be aware of the ingredients used in these delicacies. In these circumstances, it would be wise for a producer to provide an indication of the true nature of the food in question despite the fact that the customary names might have been used for generations in certain parts of the country. Moreover, even if there is a customary name for a particular type of food, there is no obligation upon the producer to use it, provided that a descriptive name is used instead.

Where there is no customary name for a type of food, the producer may call his product what he likes, provided the name adequately describes the true nature of the food in question and is not a name which might allow the product to be confused with a different type of food (reg. 8). The effect of the requirement that the 'true nature' of the food should be described is to introduce an element of specificity. Thus if fish fingers contain cod, it would not be sufficient to describe the contents as merely including fish. Similarly, in the case of multi-ingredient foods, such as 'apple and blackberry pie' the requirement that the true nature of the food be described will impose on the producer a duty to state the predominant ingredient first.

Regulation 8 also makes it clear that any name applied to food should be such that the food is not capable of being confused with another product. For example, in *Bird's Eye Wall's Ltd v Shropshire County Council* (1994) 158 JP 961, decided under the 1984 Regulations, the appellants had marketed certain of their products under the names 'Chilli Beef Quarter Pounders' 'Chicken Quarter Pounders' and 'Prize Burgers', all of which contained less than 15 per cent textured vegetable protein (TVP), a soya derivative. TVP was listed as an ingredient, but it was alleged by the prosecution that the names applied to these products failed to reveal their true nature, since TVP did not appear in the name applied to the burgers. The Crown Court had convicted the appellants in relation to the 'Prize Burgers' but allowed appeals against conviction in relation to the 'Chilli Beef Quarter Pounders' and the 'Chicken Quarter Pounders'. In the Divisional Court, appeals by both parties against the Crown Court decision were dismissed. In relation to the two acquittals, it was considered that the public would not expect the quarter pounders to contain 100 per cent pure meat and that it was not misleading to describe the products in this way, especially since it was the general view in the meat industry that meat products could contain up to 30 per cent of rehydrated TVP without any overall detriment to the product concerned. Moreover, in determining whether the name of a product contravenes the Food Labelling Regulations, it is irrelevant to consider the purpose for which TVP is used, namely, to extend the protein content of the burgers containing it. In contrast, the purpose for which TVP is used is directly relevant on the issue of confusion. This is apparent because the conviction in respect of the 'Prize Burger' was upheld mainly because a further type of burger marketed by the appellants contained 100 per cent meat and sold at exactly the same price as the 'Prize Burgers'. Accordingly, the failure to indicate in the product description that it consisted of almost 15 per cent TVP might cause confusion on the part of consumers.

By virtue of reg. 11, a producer must not mislead the purchaser through the omission of an indication that the food is in a particular physical condition (for example, powdered) or has been freeze-dried, frozen, concentrated or smoked. If the possibility of confusion on this issue might arise, the producer is obliged to label the food so as to avoid misleading the purchaser. Particular care must be taken when using the words 'roasted', 'smoked' or 'filleted' since some of the practices adopted by the food industry may not necessarily accord with the ordinary consumer's understanding of these words. For example, it is common for chicken and vegetables to be either steam cooked or parboiled before being subject to a short period of 'flash roasting' prior to the application of food colourants. A producer preparing food in this way might need to be more specific in describing the cooking process used.

In relation to certain products specified in sch. 2 to the Regulations, there are obligatory labelling requirements. For example, meat which has been treated with proteolytic enzymes must be described as 'tenderised' and any food which has been subject to a process of irradiation must be labelled as such.

15.6.2.2 Ingredient labelling The 1996 Regulations make certain specific requirements in relation to the ingredients used in food products. Any list of ingredients should be preceded by an appropriate heading which includes the word 'ingredients' (reg. 12). That list of ingredients must also be set out in descending order of weight, at the time the food was prepared (reg. 13(1)). If an ingredient comes in dehydrated or concentrated form, the relevant weight is that recorded before dehydration or concentration (reg. 13(3)).

15.6.2.3 Prohibited claims Certain claims may not be made on food packaging. In particular, the Regulations provide that there may be no claim, whether express or implied that food has tonic or medicinal properties (regs. 40 and 41 and sch. 6), subject to an exception in the case of 'Indian tonic water'). Schedule 6 also lists as prohibited any unjustified claim to the effect that food is suited to any particular nutritional purpose or any claim to the effect that food has a reduced or low energy value. The extent to which claims may be made about the cholesterol levels in food is severely restricted. Moreover, if medicinal claims are made in respect of a particular product, it is essential that the product is licensed for the purposes of the Medicines Act 1968. Failure to comply with this requirement will constitute the commission of an offence. The difficulty is to determine what constitutes a medicinal claim. This matter received consideration in *Cheshire County Council* v *Mornflake Oats Ltd* (1993) 157 JP 1011, decided under the 1984 Regulations, in which the respondents had claimed that their product helped to 'reduce excess cholesterol levels . . . thereby cutting down the risk of heart disease'. In the Divisional Court, it was considered that if the advertisement containing this claim was read as a whole, the phrase 'cutting down the risk of heart disease' would be construed by some ordinary people to mean that heart disease will be prevented by the use of the product in question. So interpreted, the claim could be regarded as a medicinal claim, with the result that if the product was not licensed under the Medicines Act 1968, an offence was committed. Schedule 6 to the 1996 Regulations also makes it clear now that included in the list of prohibited claims is any suggestion to the effect that food is beneficial to human health by virtue of its level of cholesterol.

15.7 FOOD QUALITY

While the principal concern of the Food Safety Act 1990 is that of public health and safety, there are also provisions of the Act which seek to prevent the consumer from being misled over the nature, substance or quality of the food he or she purchases.

Section 14(1) makes it an offence for a person to sell to the purchaser's prejudice any food which is not of the nature or substance or quality demanded by the purchaser. In order for this offence to be committed, the food must be intended for human consumption (s. 14(2)), with the result that the sale of a cream which is consumed internally, but which is in fact intended for external application would not fall within s. 14.

15.7.1 Sale

If the person charged is to be convicted of an offence under s. 14, there must have been a sale of food which contravenes the requirements of that provision. Without further explanation, the offence would be confined to the circumstances in which the Sale of Goods Act 1979, s. 2(1), applies. However, for the purposes of the 1990 Act, 'sale' is given an extended meaning discussed at 15.3.1 above.

Unlike s. 8, considered in 15.3.4, s. 14 has no application to the mere exposure of food for sale, since s. 14 is concerned with the demand for food made by the customer coupled with a judgment about the quality of the food compared with that demand. It follows from this that it is open to the supplier to refuse to sell to a person he believes may be an enforcement officer. However, due to the extent of the overlap between s. 8 and s. 14, food which is not of the nature or substance or quality demanded will often fail to satisfy the food safety requirement under s. 8 as well, especially in the light of the offence of selling contaminated food.

15.7.2 Nature or substance or quality

The way in which s. 14 of the 1990 Act is worded creates three separate offences, with the result that enforcement authorities must select between the three elements when framing a prosecution. It is no longer sufficient, as was once the case, for all three elements of s. 14 to be cited without any attempt to distinguish between them. While it is often the case that food may fall within more than one of the three elements of s. 14, it is essential for the enforcement authority to make it clear which element or elements of s. 14 form the basis of the prosecution, otherwise the prosecution could fail on the grounds of uncertainty (*Bastin* v *Davies* [1950] 1 All ER 1095; see also Magistrates' Court Rules 1981, r. 12).

15.7.2.1 Nature The distinct offences of selling food which is not of the nature or substance or quality demanded may overlap, so that the selection of one element of s. 14 by the enforcement authority does not mean the prosecution is destined to fail merely because the facts forming the basis of the complaint fall into more than one of the s. 14 categories.

Generally, if food is not of the nature demanded by the purchaser, it will not be of the variety ordered. As a result, it is quite likely that if there is an offence as to the nature of the food demanded, there will also be a breach of the Sale of Goods Act 1979, s. 13, allowing an action for damages for breach of the implied term that the goods sold will correspond with their contract description.

In *Meah* v *Roberts* [1978] 1 All ER 97 it was held that if the buyer asks for lemonade and is supplied with caustic soda, an offence is committed under the Food Safety Act 1990, s. 14, since the food supplied is not of the nature demanded. Wien J said, at p. 105:

. . . Meah sold food on the basis that (the purchaser) asked for lemonade for his children. It was lemonade that was agreed to be supplied and the waiter genuinely thought he was supplying lemonade. There was an agreement for the sale . . . of lemonade. . . . The fact that in pursuance of the sale something different was provided does not alter the fact that, through the waiter, Meah . . . sold lemonade.

A further consideration in this case was that caustic soda is not ordinarily supplied as a food, but the answer to this problem is that although caustic soda was, in fact, supplied, it purported to be a sale of lemonade. Accordingly, the important question to ask is: What was it that the defendant purported to supply?

Section 14 is not confined to food which is harmful to health. What matters is whether the purchaser received food of the variety demanded. Thus if the seller supplies margarine when butter has been asked for or monkfish when the customer has ordered scampi, there is an offence under this limb of s. 14 (see *Preston* v *Greenclose Ltd* (1975) 139 JPN 245). Similarly, in *Shearer* v *Rowe* (1986) 84 LGR 296 it was considered that where the retailer contracted to supply 'minced beef' and what was in fact supplied contained 10 per cent lamb and 10 per cent pork, it was not of the nature demanded by the purchaser.

In order to decide whether food is of the nature demanded, it is necessary to consider the way in which it has been described and ask what the ordinary purchaser would expect to receive. Thus the description 'butter toffee' implies that the confectionery contains no fat other than butter, with the result that if it contains coconut oil, an offence under s. 14 is committed (see *Riley Brothers (Halifax) Ltd* v *Hallimond* (1927) 44 TLR 238).

15.7.2.2 Substance In the past, food which contained unwanted additives or foreign bodies has been held not to be of the substance demanded by the purchaser. The presence of the unwanted article gives the food a substance to which the customer may reasonably object. It may be asked whether food is of the substance demanded where traces of pesticide or fertiliser are present, not having been washed off prior to sale.

This limb of s. 14 was found not to have been complied with in *Smedleys Ltd* v *Breed* [1974] AC 839 where a caterpillar was found in a tin of peas. Similarly, the presence of a beetle in a can of strawberries (*Greater Manchester Council* v *Lockwood Foods Ltd* [1979] Crim LR 593) and the presence of penicillin mould on a fruit pie (*Watford Corporation* v *Maypole Ltd* [1970] 1 QB 573) have been considered to render food not of the substance demanded. In cases of this kind, there may also be an overlap with s. 8 if the food is regarded as contaminated.

All of the cases so far considered have involved the presence of some foreign object which may be regarded as distasteful and perhaps harmful, but it is clear that if a reasonable person might object to the presence of some unwanted extraneous material an offence is still committed even where that material is completely harmless. For example in *Barber* v *Co-operative Wholesale Society Ltd* (1983) 81 LGR 762 a sterile drinking straw was found in a carton of milk supplied by the defendants. Despite the fact that the straw posed no danger, it was held that the milk was neither of the substance nor of the quality demanded by the customer. The relevant test was to ask if the purchaser could reasonably object to the presence of the straw in the carton of milk (at p. 768 per Robert Goff LJ). In the event, this extraneous material was considered to be sufficiently objectionable to justify a conviction. On the basis of this test, if the food supplied by the defendant contains something in respect of which no reasonable person would make a complaint, no offence is committed. Accordingly, it has been held that a bottle of milk is still of the substance demanded where it contains an extra sterile foil cap (*Edwards* v *Llaethdy Meirion Ltd* (1957) 107 LJ 138). However, with respect, it is arguable that the extra foil cap might be harmful if the milk got into the hands of a young child who might choke on the cap, not realising that there was more than one such article in the milk purchased by his parents. Certainly where food is supplied along with extraneous material which is capable of and does, in fact, cause injury, the courts have had no hesitation in regarding the food as something which is not of the substance demanded (see *Southworth* v *Whitewell Dairies Ltd* (1958) 122 JP 322 — sliver of glass in bottle of milk).

Whether or not food is of the substance demanded may also be affected by the existence of statutory or other accepted trade standards, since if food does not comply with such a standard it can be said to lack the substance expected of it by a reasonable consumer. In *Tonkin* v *Victor Value Ltd* [1962] 1 All ER 821 the defendants supplied a 'mock salmon cutlette' which contained only

33 per cent salmon. Although there was no statutory standard for mock salmon cutlettes, there was a standard for salmon fishcakes which demanded at least a 35 per cent salmon content. On the basis that a reasonable person would expect a mock salmon cutlette to be superior to a fishcake, a fish content which was inferior to that expected of the comparator inevitably rendered the cutlettes supplied by the defendants not of the substance demanded.

In addition to statutory standards, it is also clear from the views expressed in *Tonkin* v *Victor Value Ltd* that other benchmarks may be applied in determining whether food is of the substance demanded. For example, in *Tonkin* v *Victor Value Ltd*, the justices were considered to have acted properly in listening to the evidence of the public analyst in determining what fish content could be expected. It would also be appropriate to consider whether there is any general trade practice which establishes a minimum acceptable content for a particular ingredient and whether the particular item has been on the market for many years and it has become accepted that certain ingredients should be combined in particular proportions (at p. 823 per Lord Parker CJ).

It is implicit in the reasoning in *Tonkin* v *Victor Value Ltd* that if there is a statutory standard against which food can be judged, failure to meet that standard will render that food not of the substance demanded. However, some early cases seemed to regard the predecessor of s. 14 as being confined to cases of adulteration of food. Accordingly, it has been held that milk is of the substance demanded provided it comes from a cow, even though its fat content infringed requirements laid down by statutory regulations (*Few* v *Robinson* [1921] 3 KB 504). However, it is clear that s. 14 is not to be confined solely to cases of adulteration, although matters such as fat content may be better dealt with under the issue of quality considered below (see *Goldup* v *John Manson Ltd* [1981] 3 All ER 257).

15.7.2.3 Quality Whether food is of the quality demanded is a question of fact which may depend upon a number of variables. For example, it has been seen in relation to the implied terms in sale of goods contracts that relevant considerations may include the price paid, any description applied to the goods and any other relevant circumstance (see chapter 6). However, it is important to emphasise that quality is not the same as description, so that if the customer gets the type of food he asks for he may still complain that it is substandard in quality (see *Anness* v *Grivell* [1915] 3 KB 685).

In determining whether food reaches a satisfactory standard of quality, the test applied is one of fact with the result that what may appear to be conflicting decisions may be reached simply because of slight, but nonetheless important, factual variations. For example in *Goldup* v *John Manson Ltd* [1981] 3 All ER 257 minced beef containing 33 per cent fat, which was sold cheaply in comparison with better quality minced beef, was held not to be defective in terms of quality, given the price at which it was sold. This remained the case despite the fact that the public analyst had testified that minced beef should not contain more than 25 per cent fat and that most samples of minced beef sold commercially tended to comply with that standard. Since the issue is one of quality, the court needs to know whether the particular consignment of mince is being sold as first or second quality (ibid. 264 per Ormrod LJ). However, in *T. W. Lawrence & Sons Ltd* v *Burleigh* (1981) 80 LGR 631 a butcher who sold minced beef which contained 30.8 per cent fat was held to be guilty of an offence under s. 14 on the ground that the nature of the order placed by the customer had raised the standard of quality required. The order was placed over the telephone, so the customer had no chance to look at what she was purchasing. All she could be taken to have demanded was mince of a reasonable quality, which, as the public analyst's evidence in *Goldup* v *John Manson Ltd* indicated, required a maximum fat content of around 25 per cent.

A description applied to food may determine whether it is of the desired quality, although this may also be relevant to the question whether the food is of the nature demanded. Thus in *McDonald's Hamburgers Ltd* v *Windle* (1986) 6 TrLR 81 the defendant displayed a notice explaining the nutritional attributes and energy content of their cola and diet cola. A customer asked for diet cola and was supplied with ordinary cola. In the circumstances, it was held that the justices were entitled to conclude that the drink was not of the quality demanded. However, an alternative view of this case is that the cola was not of the nature demanded by the consumer, since what he asked for and what he was supplied with were different entities. Since there was nothing wrong with the ordinary cola other than that it was not what the customer asked for, it seems strange that it was regarded as qualitatively defective.

It will be apparent that there is a considerable degree of overlap between the three elements of s. 14 in that food may fail to be of the substance demanded as well as not being of the quality demanded. For example, it has been seen above that in some cases where food contains extraneous material, the court may treat this as a matter relating to the substance of the food (see *Edwards* v *Llaethdy Meirion Ltd* (1957) 107 LJ 138). But in other cases, the presence of a fly in a bottle of milk (*Newton* v *West Vale Creamery Co. Ltd* (1956) 120 JP 318), the presence of a nail in a packet of sweets (*Lindley* v *George W. Horner & Co. Ltd* [1950] 1 All ER 234) and the presence of a sterile, harmless straw in a carton of milk (*Barber* v *Co-operative Wholesale Society Ltd* (1983) 81 LGR 762) have all been treated by the court as involving an issue of quality. Whether the difference is important or not does not appear from the case law, and it would appear that the courts are prepared to use the two elements of s. 14 interchangeably and will not strike out a prosecution on the ground that the charge relates to substance when it should have related to quality. Indeed, it would appear that the test applied in determining whether s. 14 has been infringed is very similar in relation to both the issues of substance and quality. It has been seen already that in deciding whether food is of the substance demanded, the relevant test is to ask: What does the customer expect? and if the customer gets what he expects plus something else which may be reasonably objected to, the food is not of the substance demanded (see *Edwards* v *Llaethdy Meirion Ltd* (1957) 107 LJ 138 per Lord Goddard CJ). Similarly, in relation to the offence of supplying food not of the quality demanded, Robert Goff LJ said, in *Barber* v *Co-operative Wholesale Society Ltd* (1983) 81 LGR 762 at p. 768 that:

> It is sufficient for the prosecution to prove that the presence of . . . extraneous matter will give rise to the consequence that a purchaser could, in the context of the particular transaction, reasonably object to the presence of that matter in the article of food supplied.

Food may fail to satisfy s. 14 on the basis that both its nature and its substance or quality are not that which was demanded. For example, there appears to be little doubt that the caustic soda supplied in place of the lemonade ordered in *Meah* v *Roberts* [1978] 1 All ER 97 could also have been regarded as qualitatively defective, although the matter was not pursued in that case. It has also been accepted judicially that there is an area of overlap between nature, substance and quality with the result that even though one particular offence may be the most immediately relevant, the prosecution will not fail, if the facts of the case are capable of falling within another limb of s. 14. In *Preston* v *Greenclose Ltd* (1975) 139 JPN 245, the supply of monkfish instead of the scampi ordered by the customer would normally be regarded as raising the issue of the nature of the food, but the prosecution did not fail where it had been alleged that the food was not of the substance demanded. This view is defensible on the basis that monkfish does not have the same substance as scampi.

15.7.3 Sale to the purchaser's prejudice
It is essential that the food supplied should prejudice rather than benefit the purchaser. Without these words, an offence under s. 14 would be committed every time the retailer supplied the consumer with more than was asked for or supplied something of better quality. Accordingly the food needs to be inferior in some way to that which could reasonably be expected by the purchaser (*Hoyle* v *Hitchman* (1879) 4 QBD 233, 240 per Lush J).

For the purposes of s. 14, the word 'prejudice' is not confined to cases in which actual damage or pecuniary loss is suffered by the purchaser. As s. 14 is concerned with nature, quality and substance, there is no need for the food to be unwholesome or deleterious, since this would impose an unnecessary restriction on liability. Instead, the view expressed by Mellor J in *Hoyle* v *Hitchman* (1879) 4 QBD 233 at p. 240 was that:

> The prejudice is that which the ordinary customer suffers, viz. that which is suffered by any one who pays for one thing and gets another of inferior quality. . . . It appears to me that the prejudice the Act intends is the general prejudice done to customers.

An enforcement officer making a test purchase could be said to have suffered no prejudice as a consumer. This problem was avoided under earlier legislation by deeming the enforcement officer to be an ordinary purchaser, so that he could be said to have suffered prejudice as a consumer. This might be thought to be a somewhat artificial approach, which is now avoided under the 1990 Act, which simply states that it is not a defence to argue that the food was bought for testing or analysis (s. 14(2)).

Whether or not the purchaser has suffered prejudice can only be judged by reference to the demand made by that person, since before it can be determined whether prejudice has been suffered, it is necessary to know what has been asked for. In *McDonald's Hamburgers Ltd* v *Windle* (1986) 6 TrLR 81 an offence was committed where the customer had asked for diet cola but had been supplied with ordinary cola, containing sugar, in perfect condition, since what was supplied was not what had been asked for and an ordinary customer making such a demand would expect to receive a low-calorie drink. The test applied is effectively a consumer expectation test: if the consumer gets what would be expected by an ordinary purchaser in the light of the demand, even evidence from the public analyst to the effect that what has been supplied is substandard may be disregarded. Thus in *Goldup* v *John Manson Ltd* [1981] 3 All ER 257 the fact that the consumer chose a cheaper variety of mince on display in a butcher's shop indicated that he was prepared to accept meat of a lower standard than usual. No offence was committed under s. 14 when the mince was found to contain 33 per cent fat, despite the fact that the public analyst testified that mince should normally contain no more than 25 per cent fat.

Under the Food Act 1984, s. 3(1), it used to be a defence for the person charged to show that he had clearly notified the purchaser of defects in the food he bought. This provision has not been re-enacted in the 1990 Act, but it would be reasonable to regard the supplier as having a defence where a clear notice has been displayed, since the sale of the food cannot be to the purchaser's prejudice if he has gone into the transaction with his eyes open. Accordingly, a clearly worded notice which contains no ambiguities and brings it home to the consumer what he is being served with ought to mean that there is no prejudice to the consumer. Moreover, in the light of the comments above on the importance of the damand, it can be said that the consumer has demanded that which is identified by the clearly worded notice.

Under the previous law it was necessary to show that adequate notice had been given to an average purchaser (see *Rodbourn* v *Hudson* [1925] 1 KB 225). For the purposes of the present legislation, there appears to be no reason to depart from this approach, so that any sort of ambiguity will be construed against the retailer seeking to argue that the customer knew what he was getting.

15.7.4 The food demanded

Closely associated with the issue of prejudice is the requirement that the customer must have demanded food of a particular nature, substance or quality. It is because he does not get what he demands that there is prejudice (*Collins Arden Products Ltd* v *Barking Corporation* [1943] 1 KB 419).

The problem with many consumer purchases is that a detailed demand may not have been made. However, the courts have developed a number of tests which assist in determining when a relevant demand has been made. For example, the expectations of an ordinary consumer may be ascertained by reference to relevant statutory standards, since it can be assumed that the ordinary consumer expects those standards to be met (*Tonkin* v *Victor Value Ltd* [1962] 1 All ER 821). It will also be possible to hear the evidence of the public analyst on what is a normally acceptable standard (*T. W. Lawrence & Sons Ltd* v *Burleigh* (1981) 80 LGR 631), although such evidence is not always conclusive as is demonstrated in *Goldup* v *Manson Ltd* [1981] 3 All ER 257.

In the majority of cases, a demand will have to be assumed since it is often difficult to identify any sort of overt demand where a customer selects food from a supermarket freezer cabinet without passing any sort of comment. In cases of this kind, the general view is that the customer demands goods which correspond with the description represented by the supplier (*Smedleys Ltd* v *Breed* [1974] AC 839).

15.8 DEFENCES

15.8.1 Abandoned defences

Two defences to what is now liability under s. 14 used to exist under the Food Act 1984 but have not been re-enacted. One such defence was that the defect complained of was an unavoidable consequence of the defendant's manufacturing process. However, the word 'unavoidable' was interpreted to mean that the defect would occur every time the process was put into effect. This made the defence completely unworkable as no food producer would seek to argue that every time he produced a tin of peas, there would be a caterpillar in each tin (see *Smedleys Ltd* v *Breed* [1974] AC 839). In place of this unworkable defence, the Food Safety Act 1990 has introduced the due diligence defence, which is considered in more detail in chapter 13 and would almost certainly have come to the aid of the appellants in *Smedleys Ltd* v *Breed* since they had taken every precaution possible in the circumstances to avoid the presence of caterpillars and the like in their processed produce.

The second abandoned defence was that the person charged had been given a written warranty by his immediate supplier that the food complied with legal requirements. The fact that this defence has disappeared has been compensated for by the presence of a number of presumptions in the Food Safety Act 1990, ss. 21(3) and (4) which also affect the operation of the due diligence defence.

For the purposes of the due diligence defence, it is presumed that a person selling food under his own name or mark has taken reasonable precautions if he has relied on information supplied to him by another person and he or some other person has carried out reasonable checks on the food and the person charged has no reason to suspect that an offence has been committed (s. 21(3)). Where a person does not sell under his own name or mark, for example, where branded goods are sold, reasonable precautions are presumed to have been taken where the person charged has relied on information supplied to him by another person and he has no reason to suspect that an offence has been committed (s. 21(4)). The effect of this last presumption is

to put the retailer into the same position he would have been in had the
written warranty defence been re-enacted.

15.8.2 Reasonable precautions and due diligence

The main defence now contained in the Food Safety Act 1990, s. 21(1), is
that the person charged has taken all reasonable precautions and exercised
due diligence to avoid the commission of an offence by himself or a person
under his control. The elements of this defence are considered in more detail
in chapter 13.

SIXTEEN

Regulation of marketing, advertising and sales promotion practices

16.1 INTRODUCTION

While much of what can be described as consumer protection law is concerned with the quality and safety of goods and services provided for consumption, an equally important aspect of the subject is the control of marketing, advertising and sales promotion practices, which, if taken too far, can prove to be highly misleading and therefore detrimental to the consumer's economic interests. It has been seen already that common law rules may provide some protection, albeit only limited, if it can be shown that a statement in an advertisement amounts to a misrepresentation or a contractual term (see chapter 4) or if it can be construed to amount to an actionable negligent misstatement (see chapter 5). However, since the remedy for breach of these common law rules is generally damages, or possibly rescission of the contract made with the advertiser, such rules are hardly likely to serve a preventative role. The policing role so far as advertisers and marketers are concerned is played by the criminal law in conjunction with important voluntary controls in the form of the British Codes of Advertising and Sales Promotion (BCASP) (Committee of Advertising Practice, 1995), which apply to all advertisements in newspapers, magazines, brochures, circulars, mailings, catalogues and posters, cinema and video commercials, electronic media, mailing lists, sales promotions, advertisement promotions (BCASP, para. 1.1). Certain forms of advertising and sales promotion are not covered by these codes, such as commercials which are the responsibility of the Independent Television Commission or the Radio Authority, and the contents of premium-rate telephone calls, which are regulated by the Independent Committee for the Supervision of Standards of Telephone Information Services. Also excluded from the scope of the Codes are classified private advertisements, works of art, official notices, private correspondence, regular competitions such as newspaper crosswords and flyposting (BCASP, para 1.2).

Advertising may be defined as a passive form of promotion via printed or audio-visual media. The description of advertising as a passive form of promotion indicates that it merely appeals to the consumer's senses and as a consequence develops product awareness. Sales promotion, in contrast to advertising, is an active product purchase incentive such as on-pack or point-of-sale inducements. Since these are displayed in the arena in which purchases are made by consumers they amount to an incentive to purchase and as such can be described as an active form of promotion.

Advertising can relate to a number of different aspects of a particular business — not just the product advertised. For example, it may be used to promote a corporate identity as well as the specific products which may be referred to at the same time.

16.2 CRITIQUE OF THE ROLE OF ADVERTISING

It has been said that 'Advertising is the central symbol of the consumer society, so that it is hardly surprising that regulation of advertising raises fundamental questions concerning the objectives and techniques of consumer protection' (Ramsay, *Consumer Protection: Text and Materials*, p. 369).

It may be said that in a modern consumer society, advertising plays a central role in making available to consumers information which the producer of the advertised product wishes the consumer to have. But advertising can also be said to promote consumption by playing on emotions, while at the same time providing little useful, objective information for the consumer to use effectively in evaluating the competing claims of rival products. Accordingly, there is the possibility that advertising is capable of inducing an imprudent shopping decision if it encourages a person to buy something he does not want. It may also be argued that producers can use advertising in order to create wants on the part of consumers which the producer can subsequently satisfy with his product (Galbraith, *The Affluent Society*, 4th ed. (1984) p. 129). The counter-argument to this is that advertising can encourage production, which is important in maintaining a high standard of living and promoting a buoyant economy.

Differences of ideology are at the root of differing approaches to advertising in the consumer society. On the one hand, it is arguable that, from an economic point of view, advertising is useful in a market economy because it gives information and allows consumers to make choices. But a legal and a sociological perspective might suggest different considerations, such as the ability of the advertiser to manipulate consumers by playing on their emotions. Coase, 'Advertising and free speech' in Hyman and Johnson (eds), *Advertising and Free Speech* (1977), pp. 8–10 argues that advertising may provide information for consumers, but at the same time it can also change people's tastes. He observes that because advertising is selective, in that it only emphasises those aspects of a business which the advertiser wishes to advertise, the information provided is necessarily limited. He also takes the view, contrary to that of many economists, that changing consumer tastes is not necessarily a bad thing, since it can make the economy more competitive.

Assuming it is desirable to regulate advertising, there still remains the problem of identifying the best method of achieving effective regulation. Some would argue that regulation is only necessary where misleading and deceptive advertising has the effect of producing market failures, in which case regulation is necessary to correct those failures. A wider argument is that some forms of advertising not only mislead consumers but also strike at social values by offending taste and decency, in which case regulation is justified on this much wider plane.

There is also the important question whether legislative control is the best solution, especially where there is a desire to strike at advertisements which offend social standards of taste and decency, since the law is often a singularly poor means of dealing with such values, in which case self-regulation seems to be the more appropriate tool, provided there are effective sanctions against offending advertisements.

An important effect of misleading advertising is that consumers receive imperfect information or are unable properly to process complex information about a product or service. Since accurate information on matters such as price, quality and the terms of contracting is essential in the promotion of effective competition, regulation of advertising practices is justified.

Whether or not these criticisms are justified, it is undoubtedly the case that advertising is a very powerful tool, which, if misused, can result in the consumer receiving misleading information. Where this is the case, regulation of misleading advertising practices is justified on the ground that it can correct any market failures resulting from the inaccurate information which might otherwise be given to consumers.

16.3 BRITISH CODES OF ADVERTISING AND SALES PROMOTION

While there are a variety of statutory provisions which concern themselves with the more deceptive trading practices and misleading statements which may be found in advertisements and sales promotion literature, perhaps the most important controls on advertising and sales promotion can be found in the system of self-regulation based on the British Codes of Advertising and Sales Promotion, which set out a number of broad principles designed to ensure that both forms of promotional activity are kept within reasonable bounds.

The codes of practice which apply to advertisements and sales promotion practices do not carry with them much in the way of a sanction, apart from the important market deterrent of withdrawal of advertising space and adverse publicity (Advertising Code, para. 68.35). As is stated above, there are a number of statutory provisions specifically concerned with particular types of advertising. For example, there are controls on misleading statements in respect of goods, property and services in the Trade Descriptions Act 1968 and the Property Misdescriptions Act 1991 (see chapters 17 and 18), restrictions upon price comparisons and other misleading price statements in the Consumer Protection Act, part III (see chapter 19), and restrictions on misleading advertising in relation to credit facilities in the Consumer Credit Act 1974 (see chapter 11). There are also important administrative functions conferred on the Director General of Fair Trading under the Control of Misleading Advertisements Regulations 1988 (SI 1988/915 and see chapter 2), under which injunctive relief may be sought in respect of a misleading advertisement.

16.3.1 Advertising Code

It has been observed already that voluntary codes of practice may be perceived as having advantages over laws in the sense that they tend to be more flexible and can promote principles which cannot be effectively dealt with by laws, which by their nature need to be much more precise (see chapter 2). Because of this flexibility and because codes of this kind operate outside any form of statutory framework, it is possible for the Advertising Code to make requirements of advertisers which would be difficult to enforce by legal means. For example, para. 2 of the Code sets out a number of broad principles which, if contained in a statutory framework which created strict-liability criminal offences, would not be tolerated by the business community. For example, there are general principles to the effect that all advertisements will be legal, decent, honest and truthful; that advertisements should be prepared with a sense of responsibility to consumers and society; that advertisements should respect the principles of fair competition and that the Code will be applied in the spirit as well as in the letter.

Generally, the Code works on the basis that it is for the advertiser to substantiate any claim he makes about his product, with the result that there is a requirement that before an advertisement is submitted for publication, the advertiser, with the exception of political parties (Advertising Code, para 12.1) must hold documentary evidence to prove all claims, whether express or implied (ibid, para. 3.1).

The catchphrase most commonly associated with the Advertising Code is that all advertisements must be legal, decent, honest and truthful. In this regard, understandably, the Code stipulates that it is the primary responsibility of advertisers to ensure that their advertisements comply with legal requirements and include all information required by the law (ibid, para. 4.1). On the issue of decency, the Code urges advertisers not to publish material which is likely to cause serious or widespread concern. In particular, advertisements should not cause offence on the grounds of race, religion, sex, sexual orientation or disability (ibid. para. 5.1), notwithstanding the general provisions on decency, the Code makes it clear that an advertisement may be regarded as distasteful even if it complies with the decency provision (ibid, para. 5.2). Closely associated with the matter of decency are the Code provisions concerning fear, distress and antisocial behaviour. Generally, advertisers are required not to cause fear or distress without good reason, especially if this is merely to attract attention (ibid, para. 9.1). Nor should an advertisement contain any material which condones or promotes violence or antisocial behaviour (ibid, para. 11.1).

The Code urges advertisers not to exploit the credulity, lack of knowledge or inexperience of consumers (ibid, para. 6.1), although an exemption from this requirement is given to advertisements for political parties (ibid, para 12.1) other than those concerning government policy. The Code also requires that advertisements should not mislead by inaccuracy, ambiguity, exaggeration or omission (ibid, para. 7.1).

In relation to promotional advertising through the use of endorsements etc., the advertiser must have dated proof in writing that the person giving the endorsement consents to its use (ibid, para. 14.1). The Code also specifies that testimonials etc. cannot be used to satisfy the substantiation requirements of the Code considered above (ibid, para. 14.3).

Other matters identified in the Code as practices which advertisers should avoid include making unfair comparisons with the product of a competitor. The Code recognises that comparisons can form the basis for vigorous competition (ibid, para. 19.1), but what will not be permitted is 'knocking copy' or unfair denigration of a competing product (ibid, para. 20.1). Also in the interests of other traders, there is a requirement that advertisements should not make unfair use of the goodwill attached to a trademark, name, brand or advertising campaign of another business (ibid, para. 21.1), nor should there be any advertising campaign which can be confused with that of another trader (ibid, para. 22.1).

16.3.2 Sales Promotion Code

The Sales Promotion Code (1995) is now consolidated alongside the Advertising Code and is also supervised by the Code of Advertising Practice Committee. The Sales Promotion Code lays down a number of basic principles for the guidance of the advertising and sales promotion industry. It is the responsibility of the promoter of a particular campaign to ensure that the requirements of the code are complied with and if the promotion is considered to contravene the Code, the promoter will be required to make such changes as are considered appropriate and to pay compensation to consumers who have been adversely affected, where it appears suitable to do so. Furthermore, if the promoter fails to take action when requested to do so, he will be the subject of adverse publicity (Advertising Code para. 68.35).

The primary general principle stipulated by the Code is that all sales promotions should be legal, decent, honest and truthful (Sales Promotion Code, para. 27.1). In particular, this means that a sales promotion campaign should deal fairly and honourably with consumers and should be prepared with a sense of responsibility to society and should not cause unnecessary disappointment (ibid, para. 27.2). Promotions should respect the principles of fair competition and the provisions of the Code should be applied in the spirit as well as the letter (ibid, paras 27.3 and 27.8). Like the Advertising Code, there is a requirement that sales promotions should not operate against the public interest by encouraging antisocial or violent behaviour (Sales Promotion Code, para. 28.1).

The requirements of legality, honesty and truthfulness are defined in similar terms to the same requirements in the Advertising Code, so that the promoter should not seek to abuse the trust of consumers or take advantage of their lack of experience or knowledge (ibid, para. 31.1) and should not mislead by inaccuracy, ambiguity, exaggeration or omission (ibid, para. 32.1).

A particular problem with sales promotions is that of likely demand. What is important is that consumers should not be left disappointed by discovering that the promoted goods have been sold out. Accordingly, the Code urges promoters to ensure that they have made a reasonable estimate of the likely consumer response to the promotion (ibid, para. 35.1). Should promoted goods become unavailable, normally the promoter should supply as a replacement goods of a similar or better quality (ibid, para. 35.3). The only case in which adequate provision does not have to be made is in the case of prize competitions where the number of prizes may be limited, but the public must have been informed of the limited number of prizes (ibid, para 35.1).

On the running of a promotional campaign, the Code sets out in detail that the promoter should specify how to participate; any applicable closing date or a date for final purchases; any proof of purchase requirements; if there is likely to be a limitation on the availability of promotional packs and if there are any age or geographical restrictions on participation (ibid, para 37.1).

Special provision has also been made for promotions with prizes. In this respect, the Code appears to have been made considerably more detailed, probably in the light of the high-profile Hoover promotion, which a number of consumers discovered was subject to a number of qualifications which often made it difficult for participants to select the prize (overseas air trips and holidays) they really wanted. The Code now provides that all prizes, conditions of entry and restrictions on those able to participate must be made known to participants (ibid, para. 40.2) and that any restrictions on the number of prizes, whether there is a cash alternative to those prizes, how participants will be notified of the results of the competition and the criteria for judging entries must all be made known to consumers (ibid, para. 40.3). If there is a poor response or if the quality of entries proves to be poor, neither matter should justify the extension of a promotion beyond its stated date of conclusion unless that option has been clearly stated as a possibility by the promoter (ibid, para. 40.6). Also to be avoided are unnecessarily complex rules of participation and, unless absolutely necessary, additional rules should not be applied to a promotion once it has started (ibid, para. 40.4).

SEVENTEEN

Trade descriptions in relation to goods

Given the ineffectiveness of the civil law as a means of controlling misleading claims made in advertising material (see chapters 4 and 5) and given that prevention is normally regarded as better than cure, statutory intervention in the form of regulatory criminal offences has become necessary. This is particularly the case since many misleading practices are capable of producing information deficiencies on the part of consumers. Accordingly, legislation might tend to encourage high standards of truthfulness on the part of traders, thereby helping consumers to make better-informed choices when they make a purchase. The best known incursion into this area can be found in the Trade Descriptions Act 1968, which is concerned not simply with advertising per se but also with unfair trading practices generally.

17.1 MISDESCRIPTIONS OF GOODS

For some time, Parliament has recognised the need to protect consumers and honest traders alike against the misleading practice of misdescribing goods supplied in the course of trade. The earliest legislation of this type was to be found in the Merchandise Marks Acts 1887 to 1953, but the present controls are now to be found in the Trade Descriptions Act 1968, a more overtly consumer protectionist statute than its predecessors.

The 1968 Act creates two major criminal offences of strict liability, namely, applying a false trade description to goods in the course of a trade or business (s. 1(1)(a)) and supplying or offering to supply in the course of a trade or business any goods to which a false trade description is applied (s. 1(1)(b)).

17.2 CONDITIONS OF APPLICATION OF THE TRADE DESCRIPTIONS ACT 1968, SECTION 1

For the purposes of both parts of s. 1, there must be a trade description which is false to a material degree and which relates to goods. Goods include ships, aircraft, things attached to land and growing crops (s. 39(1)).

The s. 1 offences can be committed only by a person who acts in the course of a business, which means dealing in goods of the kind under consideration with some degree of regularity (see *Davies* v *Sumner* [1984] 3 All ER 831 and see chapter 1). The 1968 Act is not intended to apply to private suppliers, particularly where they do not deal with a view to profit (but cf. *Blakemore* v *Bellamy* (1982) 147 JP 89). However, where the act or default of an individual employee results in the commission of an offence by his employer, the employer may plead that act or default as a defence (s. 24(1)(a) and see chapter 13) and the individual employee may be prosecuted instead (s. 23 and see chapter 13).

After a period of uncertainty, it has been decided that the 1968 Act does cover the activities of professional persons. Most of the case law in this area has tended to concentrate on s. 14 of the Act, which relates to the provision of services and is discussed in chapter 18. However, some professionals also deal in goods. In *Roberts* v *Leonard* (1995) 94 LGR 284 the defendants were veterinary surgeons who had been appointed as veterinary inspectors of calves being exported to mainland Europe. Under a contractual arrangement with a company which exported calves aged between seven and 14 days, the defendants certified that a total of 557 calves were fit for export when the evidence showed that they had examined only 207 of the animals. The defendants were charged with applying a false trade description to the calves which had not been examined, and despite arguments to the effect that professionals such as veterinary surgeons did not act in the course of a business, it was held that the provision of export certificates by the defendants was an integral part of the business of live cattle exporting, with the result that the defendants could be taken to have acted in the course of a business.

While the person charged, in most cases, is likely to be a retail or other business supplier, the wording of s. 1 does not specifically require this. Clearly s. 1(1)(b) is exclusively concerned with supplies or purported supplies in the course of a business, but s. 1(1)(a) is concerned with applying a false trade description to goods. Nothing in s. 1(1)(a) specifies that the person applying the description must supply the goods to a consumer: the offence can be committed by 'any person'. Thus an offence under s. 1(1)(a) may be committed by a person who buys in the course of a business, such as an antique dealer, a second-hand car dealer (*Fletcher* v *Budgen* [1974] 1 WLR 1056) or by a third party who has an interest in the disposition of the goods in the course of trade, with the result that the defendant does not necessaily have to be a party to the contract of supply (*Fletcher* v *Sledmore* [1973] RTR 371). Presumably, a commission agent who makes false representations about the goods he has authority to sell would also have a sufficient interest to commit an offence under s. 1(1)(a).

In contrast, it would appear that a person with no interest in the subsequent transaction does not commit an offence where he makes a misleading statement about goods which the consumer subsequently purchases, since the statement is not associated with a supply of goods. Thus if a garage mechanic refuses to give a MOT certificate because he wrongly believes the car tested is not roadworthy, no offence is committed because the statement does not relate to a supply of goods (*Wycombe Marsh Garages Ltd v Fowler* [1972] 1 WLR 1156). However, this does not mean that a statement made by an MOT tester is immune from prosecution, since there may be circumstances in which the tester is also a supplier. For example, in *R v Coventry City Justices ex parte Farrand* [1988] RTR 273 a garage agreed to sell a car subject to the completion of certain repairs and the issue of an MOT certificate. The garage claimed to have carried out those repairs and issued its own MOT certificate, which contained inaccuracies. Because the MOT tester was considered to have an interest in the transaction, it was considered that a trade description had been applied to the vehicle. For the purposes of the offence under s. 1(1)(a) it also appears to be the case that the act constituting application of a false description must be done at a time when the defendant is acting in the course of a business. In *R v Shrewsbury Crown Court, ex parte Venables* (1994) Crim LR 61 the defendant was a car dealer who used a car for his own business purposes. The car had been fitted with a replacement odometer, because the original instrument had malfunctioned. Subsequently, the car was sold to another car dealer in what can be described as a chance transaction. When charged with the commission of an offence under s. 1(1)(a) it was concluded that at the time the trade description was applied, the defendant was not acting in the course of a business, because the car was being used solely within the defendant's business as a car dealer. Accordingly, there was no offence of applying a false trade description to the car.

Offences under the Act can be committed by a company. The actions of a senior company officer such as the managing director or company secretary will be treated as the actions of the company itself, but there is nothing to prevent the individual officer forming part of the directing mind and will of the company from being prosecuted as well (s. 20(1)).

The two offences created by s. 1 are both regarded as offences of strict liability. The offence of applying a false trade description contrary to s. 1(1)(a) may be regarded as the more serious of the two, since in the majority of cases, a person who applies a false trade description to goods will have acted dishonestly. For example in *R v Southwood* [1987] 3 All ER 556 the defendant had sold on to members of the public cars, the odometers of which he had personally turned back with a view to enhancing their resale value. The sales invoices handed to each purchaser stated that the defendant could not guarantee the accuracy of the recorded mileage. The Court of Appeal upheld the defendant's conviction and in so doing held that he could not rely on the purported disclaimer of liability, since the defendant had disqualified himself from claiming that he had taken reasonable precautions to avoid the commission of an offence. On the distinction between s. 1(1)(a) and s. 1(1)(b) Lord Lane CJ considered the view expressed in *R v Hammertons Cars Ltd* [1976] 1 WLR 1243, 1250 per Lawton LJ that:

> The Trade Descriptions Act 1968 was intended by Parliament to provide protection for the public against unscrupulous and irresponsible traders. Section 1(1)(a) deals with those who are proved to have been actively unscrupulous, as for example, by turning back mileometers; and s. 1(1)(b)

with those who do not take the trouble to check as best they can that mileometer readings are genuine.

Although, in the event, the defendant in *R* v *Southwood* was considered to have been unscrupulous, the Court of Appeal was not prepared to accept that a rigid distinction between dishonesty and carelessness could be maintained in separating out the respective roles of the two parts of s. 1 ([1987] 3 All ER 556, 561 per Lord Lane CJ).

That s. 1(1)(a) can apply to persons other than the unscrupulous and the dishonest has been confirmed in *R* v *Bull* (1996) 160 JP 240 in which the defendant sold a car with an inaccurate mileage recording, for which the defendant was not personally responsible. Although normally this would constitute the commission of an offence under s. 1(1)(b), the defendant had recorded the mileage reading on a sales invoice with the result that he was charged with the offence of applying a false trade description contrary to s. 1(1)(a). The Court of Appeal accepted that the s. 1(1)(a) offence would have been made out but for the fact that, from the outset, there had been a prominently displayed disclaimer notice which had nullified the effect of the inaccurate mileage reading from the time the vehicle came into the defendant's hands and which had been operative well before the time at which any false trade description was applied by the defendant.

17.2.1 Applying a false trade description

Under s. 1(1)(a) it is an offence for a person to apply a false trade description to goods. The meaning of the word 'applies' is also relevant to s. 1(1)(b) since a supplier of goods will only be guilty of an offence under that provision if a trade description has been applied to the goods which are the subject matter of the prosecution.

On a literal interpretation, any application of a trade description to goods would appear to be sufficient for the purposes of the 1968 Act. However, the judicial approach to the interpretation of this word has involved an examination of the mischief which the 1968 Act and its predecessors, the Merchandise Marks Acts 1887 to 1953 were designed to prevent, and so it has been held that the application of the trade description must be associated with a supply of goods. Thus a false statement made after a sale of goods has been effected does not amount to the commission of an offence since it is incapable of inducing a purchase (*Hall* v *Wickens Motors Ltd* [1972] 1 WLR 1418; see also *Wycombe Marsh Garages Ltd* v *Fowler* [1972] 1 WLR 1156). Conversely, a statement which relates to the future is capable of inducing a purchase, and if it can be construed as containing a statement describing a state of facts which existed at the time the statement was made, it may be regarded as having been applied to goods. In *Cavendish Woodhouse Ltd* v *Wright* (1985) 149 JP 497, the defendants displayed items of furniture, representing that what would be delivered would be the same as the showroom display goods. The Divisional Court concluded that this could be regarded as applying a trade description to the goods sold despite the fact that this could be said to be an application by implication only.

The word 'applies' is given a statutory definition in the Trade Descriptions Act 1968, s. 4, which covers a comprehensive list of methods of application. By virtue of s. 4(2) the statement does not have to be in permanent form, since an oral statement will suffice, although the time limit for bringing a prosecution in respect of an oral description is shorter than in the case of a permanent description (s. 19(4), cf. Magistrates' Courts Act 1980, s. 127).

17.2.1.1 Affixing and annexing, marking and incorporating a description (s. 4(1)(a))

A person applies a description to goods if, in any manner, he marks them with it or affixes or attaches it to the goods, their packaging or anything supplied with the goods (s. 4(1)(a)). This would clearly cover descriptive labels attached to goods such as a description of shoes manufactured from man-made materials as being made of leather (*Haringey London Borough Council* v *Piro Shoes Ltd* [1976] Crim LR 462). Since the definition also covers things supplied with goods, a description contained in an invoice, an order form (*R* v *Ford Motor Co. Ltd* [1974] 1 WLR 1220) or an instruction leaflet, provided it is read before purchase, will also amount to the application of a trade description. The reference to applying a description 'in any manner' would cover a description other than by way of a written or oral statement. Thus a misleading pictorial illustration or an active attempt to disguise a defect (see *Cottee* v *Douglas Seaton (Used Cars) Ltd* [1972] 1 WLR 1408, 1417 per Milmo J) would suffice for this purpose.

17.2.1.2 Placing the goods in anything to which a description has been affixed etc. (s. 4(1)(b))

A person also applies a description to goods if he places them in, on or with anything to which a description has been applied (s. 4(1)(b)). Thus a dairy supplier who puts his milk in bottles embossed with the name of another dairy applies a description to the milk (*Donnelly* v *Rowlands* [1970] 1 WLR 1600; see also *Stone* v *Burn* [1911] 1 KB 927).

Section 4(1)(b) also covers the act of placing a marked object with the goods. Thus a trade description has been applied where a petrol filling station is prominently marked with signs indicating that a particular brand of petrol is sold there, but the garage in fact sells another brand (*Roberts* v *Severn Petroleum and Trading Co. Ltd* [1981] RTR 312).

17.2.1.3 Using a description in relation to goods (s. 4(1)(c))

A trade description is also applied when it is used in any manner likely to be taken to refer to the goods (s. 4(1)(c)). For the purposes of s. 4(1)(c) a person must be aware of the description applied in order to have used it in relation to the goods (*Newham London Borough Council* v *Singh* [1988] RTR 359).

Section 4(1)(c) would appear to cover general statements displayed in a shop window, which on a reasonable interpretation may be taken to refer to goods on display inside the shop (Lawson, *Advertising Law* (1978) p. 206). It may also apply to cases in which a description is contained in a document such as a trade journal (*Rees* v *Munday* [1974] 1 WLR 1284) or an order form or invoice which is not physically supplied with the goods purchased (see *R* v *Ford Motor Co. Ltd* [1974] 1 WLR 1220; *Routledge* v *Ansa Motors (Chester-le-Street) Ltd* [1980] RTR 1). Moreover, a trade description can also be applied by implication, for example where goods other than those subsequently supplied are displayed for public view together with an indication that what will be delivered will resemble the displayed goods (see *Cavendish Woodhouse Ltd* v *Wright* (1985) 149 JP 497).

17.2.1.4 The position of advertisers A person who publishes an advertisement which contains a false trade description may also be said to use the description in relation to the goods. This conclusion is confirmed by the provisions of s. 5. This states that if an advertisement is used in relation to a class of goods, it shall be taken to refer to all goods in that class, whether or not they are in existence at the time of publication, for the purpose of deciding whether an offence has been committed under s. 1(1)(a) (s. 5(2)(a)) and where a person both supplies goods and publishes the advertisement, whether an offence is committed under s. 1(1)(b) (s. 5(2)(b)).

The provisions of s. 5 apply to advertisements, catalogues and price lists (s. 39(1)) which may have been in circulation for some time and may become out of date, with the result that the advertisement may be accurate in respect of some goods, but not others. In order to counteract this possibility, s. 5(3) provides that the court should have regard to matters such as the form and content of the advertisement, the time, place, manner and frequency of the advertisement and matters which make it unlikely that the person receiving the goods would think of them as forming part of the class referred to. Thus the fact that a customer has relied on an out-of-date advertisement and that the advertisement has been recently published but the goods purchased are old stock may be considered in deciding if an offence is committed by the advertiser.

A further consideration in relation to advertisements is that the advertiser may publish material supplied to him by another. In these circumstances, provided the advertiser has taken reasonable precautions and has acted with due diligence, a defence of reliance on information supplied by another will be available to him (s. 24(1) and see chapter 13). An innocent advertiser also has a defence of innocent publication under s. 25.

17.2.1.5 Compliance with the customer's order A trade description may be applied where a consumer orders goods using a trade description and goods are supplied which fail to comply with that description (s. 4(3)). Thus if the consumer orders a pair of 'all-leather shoes' and is supplied with shoes with a man-made sole, a trade description has been applied. Similarly, if a customer orders a 1975 model but is supplied with a car in fact manufactured in 1972, a trade description is applied (*Routledge* v *Ansa Motors (Chester-le-Street) Ltd* [1980] RTR 1). It has been observed that there may be occasions when a supplier or manufacturer cannot guarantee that goods will comply with the requirements of the customer and that an offence may be committed due to s. 4(3) (*Review of the Trade Descriptions Act* (Cmnd 6628, 1976), para. 170). However, this problem will be averted where the discrepancy is insignificant since in order to attract liability, the trade description must be false to a material degree (ibid, para. 172 and see also Trade Descriptions Act 1968, s. 3), furthermore, if there is any doubt, the trader could dissociate himself from the description with a suitable statement to that effect (Cmnd 6628, para. 173 and see also *Newham London Borough Council* v *Singh* [1988] RTR 359).

17.2.2 Supplying or offering to supply goods to which a false trade description is applied

Section 1(1)(b) of the Trade Descriptions Act 1968 makes it an offence for a person acting in the course of a business to supply or offer to supply goods to which a false trade description has been applied.

The offence created by s. 1(1)(b) is committed passively by a retailer who supplies goods which have been misdescribed by another, and the offender may be described as merely irresponsible as opposed to offenders under s. 1(1)(a) who may be described as unscrupulous in the majority of cases (*Newman* v *Hackney London Borough Council* [1982] RTR 296; cf. *R* v *Bull* (1996) 160 JP 240). Although s. 1(1)(b) refers to the act of 'supplying goods to which a trade description is applied', it does not follow from this wording that a defendant must both apply the description and supply the offending goods. The words 'is applied' have been taken to indicate merely a state of affairs. In *Swithland Motors Ltd* v *Peck* [1991] Crim LR 386 it was accepted that the defendants were not aware that the odometer reading on a car sold by them was false at the time the sale was concluded. However, it was regarded as irrelevant that the defendants had not applied the description themselves. It was regarded as sufficient that, at some stage, a false description had been applied by any person. Accordingly, the offence was made out.

17.2.2.1 Supply The word 'supply' is not defined in the Act, but it is clear that the defendant must have provided the consumer with something whether by way of sale or part exchange (*Davies* v *Sumner* [1984] 3 All ER 831), pursuant to a hire purchase contract or by way of gift in a promotional exercise. It has been held that a supply involves any form of distribution (*Cahalne* v *Croydon London Borough Council* (1985) 149 JP 561, 565 per Stephen Brown LJ). Thus a contract of hire is a form of supply, even if property in the goods does not pass to the consumer. Whether the person charged acts as agent or principal makes no difference, especially where the customer has little or no means of ascertaining whether the person who actually supplies the goods is the owner or his agent. Provided the disposition of an asset is part of the normal trading activities of the 'agent' there will be a supply for the purposes of the 1968 Act even if it is a supply from which the accused does not derive a profit (*Kirwin* v *Anderson* (1991) 11 TrLR 33).

The supply must be of a commercial nature, so a supply of goods by a private club to one of its members will not ordinarily fall within the scope of s. 1(1)(b) (*John* v *Matthews* [1970] 2 QB 443).

17.2.2.2 Offering to supply Without further qualification, the words 'offers to supply' would be insufficient to allow the conviction of a retailer, because the position at common law is that a retailer does not, generally, offer to sell goods displayed for sale on his premises (see *Fisher* v *Bell* [1961] 1 QB 394), nor does an advertisement stating that goods are available for supply ordinarily amount to an offer to supply (see *Partridge* v *Crittenden* [1968] 1 WLR 1204), since, in both cases, the supplier merely makes an invitation to treat. The 1968 Act avoids this conclusion by providing that a person who exposes goods for supply or has goods in his possession for the purposes of supply is deemed to offer to supply them (s. 6). It follows from this that there does not need to be a purchase in order that a prosecution may be mounted under s. 1(1)(b). For example, an enforcement officer will be able to bring procedings if goods to which a false trade description has been applied are displayed for sale on retail premises (*Stainthorpe* v *Bailey* [1980] RTR 7).

17.2.2.3 Awareness of the falsity of the description Since the offence created by s. 1(1)(b) usually consists of a supply of goods which have been misdescribed by someone else, there is always the danger that a retailer may be convicted of an offence when he is unaware of the falsity of the description. If the supplier has taken reasonable precautions and has acted with due diligence, he may be able to rely on the general defences provided for in s. 24(1) (see chapter 13). In addition to these defences, where the defendant is charged with the commission of an offence under s. 1(1)(b) only, he may also plead that he did not know, and could not with reasonable diligence have ascertained that, the goods did not conform to the description applied to them or that the description had been applied to goods (s. 24(3)).

The defence in s. 24(3) is essentially one of excusable ignorance and does not raise the same issues as the general defences in s. 24(1). One view of s. 24(3) is that it ought to be confined to latent defects in goods (*Naish* v *Gore* [1971] 3 All ER 737) and that it should have no application to representations about goods, since the truth or falsity of these can be discovered. Generally, if the representation takes the form of a false odometer reading, the defence is unlikely to succeed since it is almost certainly possible to discover the falsity of such a representation with the exercise of due diligence (*Lewis* v *Maloney* [1977] Crim LR 436).

It would appear that, for the purposes of s. 24(3), it is necessary for the defendant to show that he did not know of the facts constituting the offence charged and that he could not with reasonable diligence have ascertained that the goods did not conform to their description (*Barker* v *Hargreaves* [1981] RTR 197, 202 per Donaldson LJ). Proof that reasonable precautions have been taken is entirely irrelevant (ibid.). Thus if a car suffers from a latent corrosion defect, which is not immediately discoverable, the defence may be available (ibid.).

17.3 TRADE DESCRIPTIONS

It is central to the regime created by the Trade Descriptions Act 1968 that goods should have been subject to a false trade description.

The essence of a trade description is that it is factual in nature, thereby allowing the court to determine whether it is true or false. It follows that if it is not possible to ascertain the truth of a statement, it will not be regarded as a trade description. Thus, a promise to the effect that a central heating system will operate silently is not a trade description because it is not a factual statement (*R* v *Lloyd* (13 February 1976), Deputy Circuit Judge Whittey, unreported). It has also been stated, in another context, that the Act was never intended to make a criminal offence out of what is really a breach of warranty (*Beckett* v *Cohen* [1972] 1 WLR 1593, 1596–97 per Lord Widgery CJ).

A consequence of this is that what amounts to a misrepresentation at common law will probably also amount to a trade description for the purposes of the 1968 Act, but statements of opinion and intention and mere puffs generally will not fall within the ambit of s. 2, although there appears to be an exception applicable to second-hand car dealers, considered below.

Section 2 seeks to provide a comprehensive list of what is capable of amounting to a trade description. It has been observed already that one of the drawbacks of this approach is that traders may develop claims in respect of goods which do not fall within the list of prohibited statements and that it might be better to introduce a general duty to trade fairly, an aspect of which would be a prohibition on the use of any misleading statement (see chapter 2). Section 2 does not adequately deal with a number of potentially misleading statements in respect of goods which have come to light since the draftsman's attempt to define a trade description (see 17.3.11 below).

Section 2 defines a trade description as an indication direct or indirect of any of the following matters:

(a) quantity, size or gauge;
(b) method of manufacture, production, processing or reconditioning;
(c) composition;
(d) fitness for purpose, strength, performance, behaviour or accuracy;
(e) any physical characteristics not included in the preceding paragraphs;
(f) testing by any person and results thereof;
(g) approval by any person and results thereof;
(h) place or date of manufacture, production, processing or reconditioning;
(i) person by whom manufactured, produced, processed or reconditioned;
(j) other history, including previous ownership or use.

17.3.1 Quantity, size or gauge (s. 2(1)(a))

For the purposes of the Act, quantity includes matters such as height, length, width, capacity, weight, volume and number (s. 2(3)). It is important to emphasise that for the purposes of s. 2, a trade description may be either a direct or an indirect indication of the quantity or amount the consumer is likely to receive. Accordingly, it is not necessary for there to be a written statement as such. For example, in *R* v *A. & F. Pears Ltd* (1982) 90 ITSA Monthly Review 142, the defendants were convicted of applying a false trade description to a jar of moisturising cream when they marketed their product in a jar with a very thick glass false bottom. The overall impression of the size of the jar was taken to be an indication that it contained more than was in fact the case. Today, the same result might not obtain, since packers of goods are now obliged to mark containers with a statement of quantity in prescribed units of weight or volume (Weights and Measures Act 1985, s. 48(1)) and if there is compliance with this requirement there is deemed to be no offence under the Trade Descriptions Act 1968.

17.3.2　Method of manufacture, production, processing or reconditioning (s. 2(1)(b))

This covers statements to the effect that consumer goods have been made or processed in a particular manner, such as 'home-grown' or 'handmade'. It appears that s. 2(1)(b) is broad enough to apply to a claim that eggs are 'free-range' since free-range poultry farming can be regarded as a method of production (*Shropshire County Council* v *Peake* (1982) 2 TrLR 13). Even if s. 2(1)(b) does not apply, either para. (e) or para. (nj) of s. 2(1) might also be applicable.

17.3.3　Composition (s. 2(1)(c))

This would certainly cover statements concerning the materials from which an article is made, for example, a statement to the effect that stockings are made of silk (*Allard* v *Selfridge & Co. Ltd* [1925] 1 KB 129), that bread is made with wholemeal grain, that a knife is made of Sheffield steel or that the contents of a specified package include sardines (*Lemy* v *Watson* [1915] 3 KB 731) would all fall within s. 2(1)(c). A manufacturer who claims to produce 'vegetable lard' also represents the composition of his product since the word 'lard', without further qualification, denotes the use of pig fat (*Wolkind* v *Pura Foods Ltd* (1987) 85 LGR 782). A retail butcher is taken to indicate the composition of what he sells when he claims to supply a particular cut of meat. To describe beef as 'rump' when it is in fact silverside is to make a statement about the composition of that which is sold to the customer (*Amos* v *Melcon (Frozen Foods) Ltd* (1985) 149 JP 712).

Section 2(1)(c) also appears to go further than the ingredients from which a thing is made and may also include parts missing from goods intended to be supplied as a package. For example, if goods are described in an advertisement and the customer is wrongly told that he will receive something identical to the description (*Cavendish Woodhouse Ltd* v *Wright* (1985) 149 JP 497; *Denard* v *Smith* (1990) 155 JP 253), a factual statement relating to composition may have been made. If a statement indicates the manner in which component parts are arranged, this may be regarded as a matter falling within s. 2(1)(c). Thus a newspaper advertisement which suggests that furniture will be supplied in an assembled state when it is in fact supplied as a flat-pack may be taken to be an indication of the composition of the goods advertised (*Queensway Discount Warehouses Ltd* v *Burke* (1985) 150 JP 17). Similarly, if a customer is told that he will receive a free gift when he purchases a particular item, this too may relate to the composition of the package (*British Gas Corporation* v *Lubbock* [1974] 1 WLR 37). However, it might be better to regard these cases as falling within the residual category covered by s. 2(1)(e) if s. 2(1)(c) is properly confined to materials from which a product is made (*British Gas Corporation* v *Lubbock* [1974] 1 WLR 37, 43 per May J).

17.3.4 Fitness for purpose, strength, performance, behaviour or accuracy (s. 2(1)(d))

The matters listed here are all of a qualitative nature, which is inevitably likely to produce problems, since the required quality of goods will depend on a range of factors including the price paid for the goods. Where a car dealer makes an extravagant statement about the physical performance of a second-hand car s. 2(1)(d) may apply. Thus to describe an unroadworthy vehicle as beautiful, as a good little runner or as having a good engine would appear to amount to the application of a trade description relating to the quality of its performance (see *Robertson* v *Dicicco* [1972] RTR 431; *Furniss* v *Scholes* [1974] Crim LR 199). The question to consider is what interpretation would the ordinary man place on the words used in the description (*Kensington and Chelsea London Borough Council* v *Riley* [1973] RTR 122).

These statements appear to be remarkably similar to trade puffs which do not attract liability for misrepresentation in the civil law and which did not attract criminal liability in *Cadbury Ltd* v *Halliday* [1975] 1 WLR 649. Perhaps they illustrate a deep-seated public distrust of the ability of the motor vehicle trade to control their less scrupulous members.

Less difficulty has been encountered in respect of objectively quantifiable statements about performance. Thus to describe a watch as waterproof when it leaks (*Sherratt* v *Gerald's the American Jewellers Ltd* (1970) 68 LGR 256) or to state that a microscope is capable of magnifying up to 455 times when its maximum useful magnification is only 120 times (*Dixons Ltd* v *Barnett* (1989) 8 TrLR 37) is to misrepresent the performance capabilities of the article to which the description is applied.

Apparently also falling within s. 2(1)(d) is an indication that goods are new, although, for reasons considered below, it might be better to regard such cases as involving an indication of the past history of the goods described so that they fall within s. 2(1)(j). While the description 'new' is an indication of lack of previous use, it may also be taken to be an indicator of the likely performance of the article in question. In *R* v *Anderson* (1987) 152 JP 373, in order to prevent Nissan from having its import quota reduced, UK representatives of the Japanese manufacturer, which included the defendants, were asked to register Nissan cars in their own name so that it appeared that more Nissan cars had been sold than was in fact the case. The defendants sold one of these cars under the description 'new'. Despite the fact that the car was in mint condition, it was held that the word 'new' would normally be taken to mean that the vehicle had no registered previous owners, with the result that the defendants were considered to have committed an offence. While the word 'new' indicates no previous owners, it should not be taken as an indication that a car has not suffered any damage at all. Generally, where the word 'new' is used to describe a vehicle this should mean that it has not previously been sold by retail and that it has not been subject to extensive use (*R* v *Ford Motor Co. Ltd* [1974] 1 WLR 1220).

The factors listed in s. 2(1)(d) all relate to physical characteristics of the goods sold, but the reference to strength should not be taken to refer only to the strength of physical performance. It may also cover the alcoholic strength of a drink (*Hurley* v *Martinez & Co. Ltd* (1990) 9 TrLR 189).

Although the cases considered above all involved express statements which could be taken to indicate the fitness of the goods sold for a particular purpose, the way in which the 1968 Act has been interpreted is such that even implied indications of performance or fitness for purpose are capable of falling within the scope of its provisions. If instructions for use provided with goods supplied by the defendant are defective, so that the goods cannot be used as intended, an offence is committed even if the goods can be put to their intended use employing a different method of fitting which has not been described in the instructions supplied (*Janbo Trading Ltd* v *Dudley Metropolitan Borough Council* (1993) 12 TrLR 190).

17.3.5   Other physical characteristics (s. 2(1)(e))

In case anything has been omitted from the list of physical characteristics in s. 2(1)(a) to (d), s. 2(1)(e) provides a general safety net. It would appear that statements relating to component parts supplied with goods sold, such as free gifts (*British Gas Corporation* v *Lubbock* [1974] 1 WLR 37) or additional accessories such as a tool kit or a sunroof fitted to a car are best explained as relating to physical characteristics not covered by the earlier paragraphs of s. 2(1).

17.3.6   Testing by any person and the results thereof (s. 2(1)(f))

The wording of this paragraph seems to require a statement to the effect that goods have been tested and that they have passed the test. Thus a bare statement that a car has been 'AA tested' without a further indication that the test has been passed would probably not be a trade description. This is considered to be a defect in the Act and it has been proposed that where there is a reference to testing, it should be presumed, in the absence of a statement to the contrary that there is an indication that the test has been passed (*Review of the Trade Descriptions Act 1968* (Cmnd 6628, 1976), para. 129). A statement to the effect that a car has an MOT certificate would fall within this subsection since the granting of the certificate is conditional on the goods having satisfied the test requirements. The seller of a car who claimed it had a certificate when it had not passed the test would be guilty of an offence, but the content of the certificate is not to be taken as a trade description applied by the garage providing the certificate since it clearly states that it is not to be relied on (*Corfield* v *Sevenways Garage Ltd* [1985] RTR 109) and in any event the statement is not associated with a supply of goods.

17.3.7   Approval by any person or conformity to a type approved by any person (s. 2(1)(g))

A statement to the effect that goods conform to British Standards requirements (*Downland Bedding* v *Retail Trading Standards Association* (1959) *The*

Times, 17 January 1959), or merely displaying the 'Kitemark' would fall within this provision (see also *Texas Homecare Ltd* v *Stockport Metropolitan Borough Council* (1987) 152 JP 83). Similarly, a claim to the effect that goods are approved by a particular body such as the AA or a trade union would also suffice. It may also be the case that the use of the trademark of a manufacturer with a national reputation can be said to imply conformity with a type approved by another person (*Durham Trading Standards* v *Kingsley Clothing Ltd* (1990) 9 TrLR 50), although this does appear to stretch the wording of s. 2(1)(g) somewhat and it would be better to treat such cases as falling within s. 2(1)(i).

False representations of royal approval (s. 12) and claims that goods have been supplied to another person (s. 13) constitute the commission of offences in their own right.

17.3.8 Place or date of manufacture, production, processing or reconditioning (s. 2(1)(h))

A description of a commodity as a 'Norfolk King Turkey' (*Beckett* v *Kingston Brothers (Butchers) Ltd* [1970] 1 QB 606) or 'Havana cigars' (*R* v *Butcher* (1908) 99 LT 622) would appear to fall within s. 2(1)(h). But conventional descriptions arising out of trade usage probably do not. Thus frozen Yorkshire puddings or Cheddar cheese are not required to be produced only in the area their name suggests.

The paragraph also covers false statements about the date of manufacture. Thus a car registered in 1975 but manufactured in 1972 cannot be sold as a new 1975 model (*Routledge* v *Ansa Motors (Chester-le-Street) Ltd* [1980] RTR 1). Even a qualified statement of the age of a vehicle may not be sufficient to escape liability. Thus it would be unwise for a car dealer to state that the approximate year of manufacture of a vehicle is 1971 when he is not entirely sure how old the car is (*R* v *Coventry City Justices, ex parte Farrand* [1988] RTR 273).

17.3.9 Person by whom manufactured, produced or reconditioned (s. 2(1)(i))

Brand names very often make it easier to sell goods to a particular market, since it may be important to the consumer that he purchases a product made by a nationally recognised producer. This is especially so in the teenage segment of the mass-market fashion industry. Many self-respecting 14 and 15-year-olds would not be seen dead in certain types of T-shirt and only certain recognised brands of training shoe will gain the respect of their peers. Accordingly brand name copying can prove to be lucrative, but whether such practices offend against the Trade Descriptions Act 1968 by virtue of s. 2(1)(i) or possibly s. 2(1)(g) is a moot point. It has been held that a trade description is applied where a petrol filling station advertises its product as Esso petrol when another brand is in fact supplied (*Roberts* v *Severn Petroleum and Trading Co. Ltd* [1981] RTR 312). Similarly, the supply of sweatshirts bearing a famous brand name which is a registered trade mark has been held to fall within the scope of s. 2(1)(i) (*Durham Trading Standards* v *Kingsley*

Clothing Ltd (1990) 9 TrLR 50). In these cases, the inference is that the advertised brand is being supplied, but if it follows from this that where a name is printed on goods it indicates that they have been manufactured by the person named, many suppliers of 'own-brand' products would be in serious difficulties.

While the supply of counterfeit goods is capable of amounting to the application of a false trade description, it does not always follow that an offence has been committed, since there are other factors to consider. For example, in order to fall within s. 2(1)(i) there must have been an indication that goods have been produced by a particular person or body when that is not the case. Merely displaying a logo normally associated with a particular manufacturer may have that effect, but not always. In *Durham Trading Standards* v *Kingsley Clothing Ltd* it was accepted that since the importers, wholesalers and distributors of 'Marc O Polo' shirts dealt only in clothing, the use of their brand name could be taken to be an indication that the shirts had been produced by them but the same result will not always follow from the fact that the defendant has sold what appear to be counterfeit goods. For example, in *R* v *Veys* (1992) 157 JP 567 the defendant sold T-shirts which carried an emblem similar to the 'Manchester United' badge, but had given no indication that he was authorised by the football club to produce and sell the articles. Accordingly, it could not be said that he implied that the shirts were the official produce of Manchester United or that the shirts were approved by the club, thereby bringing the description within s. 2(1)(g).

Since the decision in *R* v *Veys* makes it clear that misuse of a trade mark will not necessarily amount to applying a trade description, it is even less likely that copying the get-up associated with a famous product, in the absence of any confusion about the identity of the product, will suffice for the purposes of the 1968 Act. Thus in *Surrey County Council* v *Clark* (1992) 156 JP 798, no trade description was considered to have been applied to a cube which was similar in size, colour, construction and design to the more famous 'Rubik's cube' manufactured by Matchbox Ltd. What was important was that the word 'Rubik' did not appear anywhere on the packaging and that the defendant's toy had been given a completely different name, namely the 'IQ Wonderful Puzzle'. Since there was no indication that Matchbox Ltd was the manufacturer of the puzzle, the mere similarity could not be said to fall within s. 2(1)(i). However, the Divisional Court was prepared to conclude that the misuse of the get-up was a trade description which, though not false, was misleading within the meaning of s. 3(2), because the 'Rubik's cube' was a relatively recent phenomenon which most people at the time the offending product was put on the market would still remember (ibid. 803 per Taylor LJ).

Even if the defendant's statement about goods can be taken to fall within s. 2(1)(i) there is no offence unless the statement is false to a material degree (see below). Accordingly, if the misuse of a trade mark is nullified before any sale is concluded, no offence is committed if it cannot be said that the statements made to the public were false. In *Kent County Council* v *Price* (1993) 157 JP 1161 the defendant was a market trader who openly sold 'brand copies' of famous-name T-shirts. He did not deny that they were copies, but advertised them as such and informed customers that a genuine branded T-shirt would cost £12 instead of the £1.99 charged by him. The Divisional Court held that the description as a whole had to be considered to ascertain whether it was false to a material degree and that the defendant's oral statements were sufficient to bring it home to customers that they were not purchasing genuine branded articles, so that no offence was committed under the Trade Descriptions Act 1968, although this would not prevent an action by the brand-name owner under the Trade Marks Act 1994 or the Copyright Designs and Patents Act 1988, where appropriate.

17.3.10 Other history including previous ownership or use (s. 2(1)(j))

The majority of cases which have fallen within this paragraph have involved inaccurate odometer readings on motor vehicles (*Tarleton Engineering Co. Ltd v Nattrass* [1973] 1 WLR 1261; *R v Hammertons Cars Ltd* [1976] 1 WLR 1243), but other matters relating to the past history of goods made available for supply will also be relevant. For example, statements to the effect that goods are 'shop-soiled', 'salvaged' or 'fire-damaged' stock would appear to relate to their past history. False statements about the number of previous owners of a car fall within s. 2(1)(j) (*R v Inner London Justices, ex parte Wandsworth London Borough Council* [1983] RTR 425).

Since s. 2(1)(j) is a safety-net provision, it may apply to marginal cases which just fail to be covered by other more specific provisions relating to the past life of the goods described. For example, it has been seen above that there has been some difficulty in fitting some descriptions which indicate implied approval into s. 2(1)(g), but it seems that an indication by a non-approved egg-packing station that its eggs are 'EEC approved' may fall within s. 2(1)(j) despite the fact that the EEC is probably too large an organisation to be described as a 'person' under s. 2(1)(g) (*Benfell Farm Produce Ltd v Surrey County Council* [1983] 1 WLR 1213).

17.3.11 Matters not covered by s. 2(1)

One of the major drawbacks of a closed list of prohibited statements is that there will be circumstances in which a statement is apt to mislead but does not fall within any of the listed categories of trade description. For example, it has been held that an assertion that goods are worth a particular amount or represent extra value cannot amount to trade descriptions as the assertion is not factual and is therefore incapable of precise ascertainment (*Cadbury Ltd v Halliday* (1975) 1 WLR 649). The matter of value is one on which people will express different opinions. However, it is at least arguable that a reasonable person might regard a statement such as 'extra value' as implying 'extra chocolate for the same price' and might therefore fall within s. 2(1)(a). The matter is now largely academic since value and worth claims are covered by the misleading pricing provisions in the Consumer Protection Act 1987 ss. 20 and 21 (see chapter 19).

Other matters which may not be covered by s. 2(1) and which may give a misleading impression include indications of the identity of the supplier or distributor of goods (see *Review of the Trade Descriptions Act 1968* (Cmnd

6628, 1976), para. 126); statements concerning the commercial standing of the manufacturer, supplier or distributor of goods, such as the ability to provide an after-sales service (ibid. para. 125) and false statements of the content of printed and recorded materials (ibid. para. 128).

17.4 IMPLIED TRADE DESCRIPTIONS

Section 2(1) of the Trade Descriptions Act 1968 provides that a statement in respect of one of the listed matters may be made directly or indirectly, but this still requires an express written or oral statement to have been made about the goods to which the description applies. It would appear that in addition to express statements, a trade description may be implied from the conduct of the defendant. Support for this view can be gleaned from s. 3(3) of the Act, which extends the definition of a trade description to include anything likely to be taken as an indication of a matter listed in s. 2(1). Thus a set of instructions for use may be regarded as an implied trade description by virtue of what it omits rather than by virtue of what it says (*Janbo Trading Ltd v Dudley Metropolitan Council* (1993) 12 TrLR 190).

The fact that there may be liability for an implied trade description is borne out by the large number of falsified odometer reading cases. In each of these, there is strictly no express statement, but the courts have had no difficulty in applying the provisions of the 1968 Act to them. Cars may be repaired in such a way that they tell a lie about themselves (*Cottee v Douglas Seaton (Used Cars) Ltd* [1972] 1 WLR 1408, 1416 per Lord Widgery CJ). However, taking this principle too far might be dangerous, since it would also apply to restorers of antiques and artistic works, whose job it is to ensure that their work is not easily detectable (ibid. 1415 per Lord Widgery CJ). There must be a positive statement on the part of the defendant in order to give rise to liability (ibid.), so that no offence is committed where the defendant remains silent on a particular matter relating to the goods in question. However, a person can give an indirect indication of a matter listed in s. 2(1) by way of an opinion offered to a private individual. In *Holloway v Cross* [1981] 1 All ER 1012 a car dealer had purchased, through the trade, a car with an odometer reading of just 716 miles. In fact the true mileage was closer to 70,000 miles. When interest was shown in the car by a customer, the defendant said he would make inquiries about the true mileage figure, but could not ascertain the truth. At first he attempted to persuade the customer to estimate the likely mileage reading, but later he expressed an opinion that an accurate estimate would be about 45,000 miles. While members of the court doubted whether an opinion could be regarded as an indication under s. 2(1), they were content to regard this as a matter caught by s. 3(3), namely something likely to be taken for an indication of the past history of the car.

It is important to note that in *Holloway v Cross* the opinion was expressed to an ordinary member of the public. Had the communication been to another trader it is possible that no offence would have been committed (*Norman v Bennett* [1974] 1 WLR 1229, 1233 per Lord Widgery CJ and see also *R v Shrewsbury Crown Court, ex parte Venables* [1994] Crim LR 61).

17.5 FALSITY

17.5.1 False to a material degree

By virtue of s. 3(1) a false trade description is one which is false to a material degree. This definition is based on the requirement that the description must be of such substance that it is capable of inducing a purchase (*Final Report of the Committee on Consumer Protection* (Cmnd 1781, 1962), para. 634). Thus a statement which amounts to nothing more than a trade puff will not be treated as a false trade description on the basis that such statements are not capable of inducing a purchase (see *Cadbury Ltd v Halliday* [1975] 1 WLR 649; cf. *Robertson v Dicicco* [1972] RTR 431). Similarly, it has been seen already that even where the defendant does something which is clearly wrong, such as selling counterfeit clothing bearing the name of a famous manufacturer, no wrong is done under the Trade Descriptions Act 1968 if he is open about what he is selling and makes the customer aware that it is a cheap copy which is for sale, since it cannot be said that the description is false to a material degree (see *Kent County Council v Price* (1993) 157 JP 1161 discussed in 17.3.9).

Where a statement is capable of verification, it will attract liability only if it is false to a material degree. This suggests that a statement can be technically false, but if it is not likely to mislead anyone, no offence is committed. In *Donnelly v Rowlands* [1970] 1 WLR 1600, a dairyman supplied milk in bottles which were embossed with the name of another dairy, but which were also sealed by means of a silver foil cap, embossed with the dairyman's own name. It was held that, although there was a trade description, it was not false to any degree because no one was likely to be misled by it and the words on the foil cap could be regarded as an accurate description of the milk. The description in its entirety must be considered, which required consideration of both the bottles and the foil cap.

The language used by the court in *Donnelly v Rowlands* suggests that the effect of the foil cap was to correct any misleading impression created by the bottles, in which case the correction seems to have operated as if it were a disclaimer of liability, which if correct gives rise to its own difficulties, since it would appear that a disclaimer can rarely be used to negative the effect of a self-applied description (see 17.6 below).

The test applied in *Donnelly v Rowlands* appears to be objective, in that it is necessary to consider whether a reasonable consumer would have been misled, accordingly, if the statement is objectively misleading, it does not matter that the actual consumer has not been misled (*Chidwick v Beer* [1974] Crim LR 267; *Dixons Ltd v Barnett* (1989) 8 TrLR 37, 41 per Bingham LJ).

A statement may also be false to a material degree not by virtue of what it says, but by virtue of what it leaves out. It has been said that the appropriate test to apply in this context is to ask 'What impression is given by the words used to the reasonable man, the purchaser in a given case?' (*Routledge v Ansa Motors (Chester-le-Street) Ltd* [1980] RTR 1, 5 per Kilner Brown J).

In *Routledge v Ansa Motors (Chester-le-Street) Ltd* the defendant told only half the truth, when he described as a 1975 model, a motor vehicle which had been manufactured in 1972 but registered in 1975 as a new. The statement was held to be materially false since an average person would take it to mean that the vehicle was manufactured in 1975 (ibid. 5 per Kilner Brown J). However, to call a car new when it has suffered superficial damage which has been repaired using new parts does not amount to the commission of an offence (*R* v *Ford Motor Co. Ltd* [1974] 1 WLR 1220). In such a case, the description falls within the principle *de minimis non curat lex*, but if the damage to the car had been more serious, it is possible that repairs would have been so extensive that to call the vehicle new would have been misleading. It is clear from the cases so far considered that whether or not a description will be held to be false to a material degree will depend on the context in which the words are used (*R* v *Anderson* [1988] RTR 260, 266 per Waterhouse J). For example, if what has been done to a 'new' car is likely to diminish its value (such as registering it in the name of the dealer), the description 'new' may be regarded as false (ibid.). The language used by the defendant will also matter. For example, one word taken on its own may be materially false, but if it is qualified by other words it may become accurate. For example, the word 'lard' implies the presence of pig fat, but the words 'vegetable lard' imply a completely different commodity, particularly when statements on the packaging make a virtue of the fact that 100 per cent vegetable oils are used (*Wolkind* v *Pura Foods Ltd* (1987) 85 LGR 782).

17.5.2 Literally true statements
In addition to the basic rule on the materiality of the statement, s. 3(2) the 1968 Act provides that a literally true but misleading statement, namely, one which is likely to be taken by the average man (*Southwark London Borough Council* v *Elderson* (1981 unreported)) for an indication of a matter listed in s. 2(1), is deemed to be false. Thus if a car is described as beautiful when it is in poor mechanical condition, an offence is committed since there is a statement which is misleading about a matter listed in s. 2(1)(d) (*Robertson* v *Dicicco* [1972] RTR 431). Similarly, if a car dealer advertises a vehicle as having had one owner, but does not state that the one owner was a leasing company which had leased the car to a number of different users, s. 3(2) renders this a false indication of a matter covered by s. 2(1)(j) (*R* v *Inner London Justices, ex parte Wandsworth London Borough Council* [1983] RTR 425).

17.5.3 Misleading statements not amounting to a trade description
By virtue of s. 3(3), a statement which is not a trade description within s. 2(1) can still attract liability if it is false to a material degree and is likely to be taken as an indication of one of the matters listed in s. 2(1). For example, s. 2(1) seems to require a statement of fact with the result that s. 3(3) is the more appropriate provision to apply to misleading estimates of the mileage accumulated by a motor vehicle (*Holloway* v *Cross* [1981] 1 All ER 1012).

17.6 DISCLAIMERS OF LIABILITY

Although not mentioned in the Trade Descriptions Act 1968, a practice has developed, with judicial approval, of disclaiming liability in respect of the falsity of trade descriptions (*Waltham Forest London Borough Council* v *T. G. Wheatley (Central Garage) Ltd* [1978] RTR 157, 162 per Lord Widgery CJ). The practice has been most prevalent in the second-hand car trade in relation to inaccurate odometer readings, although examples of their use can also be found in other areas of trade.

17.6.1 Legal status of disclaimers

The use of disclaimers is relevant to, although not directly analogous with, the general defences contained in s. 24(1) (see chapter 13). In particular, it has been held that the use of a disclaimer by a car dealer who is not sure that an odometer reading is accurate is an example of taking reasonable precautions (*Zawadski* v *Sleigh* [1975] RTR 113). But this view must not be taken to mean that an effective disclaimer must be issued in every case, since there may be exceptional circumstances in which other reasonable precautions have been taken in order to make out the s. 24(1) defence (*Ealing London Borough Council* v *Taylor* (1995) 159 JP 460). To insist that a disclaimer is issued in every case in which a car is sold subject to its mileage recording might not be desirable, since a rule to this effect might encourage the use of blanket disclaimers as an alternative to taking time to check the accuracy of descriptions applied to goods before the time of sale (Borrie [1975] Crim LR 662, 667–9).

A disclaimer is not a defence to liability in the sense that it is not a form of confession and avoidance. Instead, it has been held that it is better to regard an effective disclaimer as displacing any inference which arises from the initial trade description (*R* v *Hammertons Cars Ltd* [1976] 1 WLR 1243, 1248 per Lawton LJ) and that it amounts to saying, 'I am not making any representations at all' (*Wandsworth London Borough Council* v *Bentley* [1980] RTR 429).

Because of the judicial emphasis placed on displacing the inference arising from the initial trade description, a practice grew up, again with judicial approval, of 'zeroing' odometer readings so that the customer could not possibly regard the reading as accurate. However, what this judicial acceptance failed to appreciate was that by returning the reading to zero, the car dealer was in fact applying a description himself, with the result that he might be charged with the commission of an offence under s. 1(1)(a) (*R* v *Southwood* [1987] 3 All ER 556).

One consequence of the decision in *R* v *Southwood* is that, as a general rule, a disclaimer cannot be used where the defendant is charged with the commission of an offence under s. 1(1)(a), since it would be illogical to allow a person to assert that a statement is false and then claim that because the customer knows the statement is false, no description has been applied (ibid. 1370 per Lord Lane CJ). Thus it will not be open to an auctioneer who has falsely described a painting as one by J. M. W. Turner RA to cover himself with a blanket disclaimer in the auction catalogue (*May* v *Vincent* (1990) 154 JP 997). However, the offence under s. 1(1)(a) is one of strict liability and there may be circumstances in which a person who is charged with the commission of the offence of applying a false trade description has acted diligently and honestly, in which case he ought to be able to disclaim responsibility for the accuracy of a car odometer reading. For example, in *R v Bull* (1996) 160 JP 241, the defendant was a car dealer who displayed for sale a car which had passed through the hands of a number of owners and car dealers. It had a recorded mileage reading of more than 47,000 miles, which the defendant was unable to confirm and which was later discovered to be false. Before displaying the car for sale, the defendant took the precaution of placing a sticker on the odometer which indicated that the mileage reading could not be regarded as accurate. However, subsequently, that inaccurate reading was copied on to a sales invoice. That last act was considered to constitute an application of a false trade description, on which basis the prosecution was brought. In his defence, the defendant argued that there was no trade description on the basis that his disclaimer meant that any reasonable purchaser would realise that the mileage recording could not be regarded as accurate. However, in the light of statements made in *R v Southwood* and *Newman v Hackney London Borough Council* [1982] RTR 296, there was a sustainable argument that a defendant charged under s. 1(1)(a) could not be allowed to disclaim responsibility at all, but this is clearly not the case in the light of the Court of Appeal decision in *R v Bull*, since a properly worded disclaimer used in the context of a prosecution brought under s. 1(1)(a) can have the effect of preventing the trade description from being false at the time of application by the defendant (*R v Bull* (1996) 160 JP 240, 247 per Waterhouse J). This conclusion, however, will not assist the car dealer who deliberately turns back an odometer and then attempts to disclaim responsibility for his own deliberate wrongdoing, since in that case, the false trade description has been applied, and an offence committed before any attempt to issue the disclaimer (*Newman v Hackney London Borough Council* [1982] RTR 296, 302 per Ormrod LJ).

The outstanding difficulty with the decisions in *R v Southwood* and *R v Bull* is that they were both reached at Court of Appeal level but *R v Southwood* appears not to have been cited in *R v Bull*, rendering the latter a decision reached *per incuriam*. While it may be argued that the *ratio* in *R v Bull* is that there was no false trade description, this decision was reached on the basis that the disclaimer prevented the description from being false. In contrast, the *ratio* in *R v Southwood* may be said to be that 'it is not open to a person charged under s. 1(1)(a) to rely on any disclaimer' ([1987] 3 All ER 556, 564 per Lord Lane CJ). Moreover, in *R v Southwood* the preferred solution in cases in which there is an 'innocent' offender under s. 1(1)(a) was that the defence in s. 24 would come to his aid if he could show that he took all reasonable precautions to avoid or to attempt to avoid the commission of an offence. Thus if there have been inquiries by the defendant which reveal the falsity of a mileage recording, he can avoid liability by frankly disclosing the results of his inquiry so as to put the customer in the same state of knowledge as himself (ibid.).

Fewer difficulties arise in relation to the offence contained in s. 1(1)(b), under which it is it is well established that a disclaimer may be used by the person charged. Since under s. 1(1)(b) the defendant is not the person who has applied the description to the goods, he may not have any means of discovering its inaccuracy.

17.6.2 Form and content of disclaimers

Since the most frequent use of disclaimers has been in relation to car odometer readings, the commonest form of disclaimer is a notice displayed on or near the car to which it applies. There is also something akin to a disclaimer where a trader qualifies what amounts to a false description with words which correct what would otherwise create a false impression. For example, the word 'lard' might ordinarily imply a product made of pig fat, but if the finished product is described as vegetable lard, with a clear statement to the effect that it is made of 100 per cent vegetable oils, there is no false trade description (*Wolkind* v *Pura Foods Ltd* (1987) 85 LGR 782). It is suggested that this type of case is better dealt with on the basis that the description is not false to a material degree rather than by reference to rules on disclaimers, although there have been judicial pronouncements to the effect that it is not wise to separate out into pigeon-holes the aspects of the evidence which establish whether a trade description has been applied and those relating to whether there has been an effective disclaimer of the description (see *R* v *Hammertons Cars Ltd* [1976] 1 WLR 1243, 1247 per Lawton LJ; *R* v *Bull* (1996) 160 JP 240, 246 per Waterhouse J).

The problem with applying the disclaimer doctrine to cases in which the defendant actively makes a statement about the goods available for supply is that the person who seeks to rely on the disclaimer is also the person who has applied the description to the goods and on the basis of *R* v *Southwood* [1987] 3 All ER 556, the defendant should not be allowed to disclaim liability in respect of a self-applied description. However, the two issues do overlap, since there may be circumstances in which the reason why a trade description does not create a false impression is that the defendant has made it clear to his customers that he believes a mileage reading on a car's odometer to be inaccurate, that he accepts no responsibility for the accuracy of the reading and that he has not been responsible for turning back the mileage recording, as in *R* v *Bull* (1996) 160 JP 240. Clearly this is not the same as giving a correct statement of the contents of a packet of vegetable lard, and may be a suitable case in which to invoke the disclaimer doctrine.

17.6.2.1 Tests for an effective disclaimer

If a disclaimer is to be effective, it has been held that it must be 'as bold, precise and compelling as the trade description itself' and must be communicated at or before the time of committing the offence (*Norman* v *Bennett* [1974] 1 WLR 1229, 1232 per Lord Widgery CJ), so as to nullify the effect of the false trade description. An alternative formulation of this test is that the disclaimer must 'equal the trade description to the extent to which it is likely to get home to anyone interested in receiving the goods' (ibid.).

Very clear words are required, so that the misleading effect of the trade description is displaced. In *R* v *Hammertons Cars Ltd* [1976] 1 WLR 1243, Lawton LJ said that the defendant must take positive steps to ensure that the customer understands that the milometer reading is meaningless (ibid. 1248). Alternatively, it has been said that the disclaimer must sit beside the trade description and cancel it out as soon as its first impression can be made on the purchaser (*Waltham Forest London Borough Council* v *T. G. Wheatley (Central Garage) Ltd (No. 2)* [1978] RTR 333, 339 per Lord Widgery CJ). It will be insufficient if a written disclaimer notice appears anywhere in a car other than immediately next to the odometer reading (*Ealing London Borough Council* v *Taylor* (1995) 159 JP 460). A small written notice in an inconspicuous position in a salesman's office is hardly likely to be sufficient (*Waltham Forest London Borough Council* v *T. G. Wheatley (Central Garage) Ltd* [1978] RTR 157). It has also been held to be insufficient for a trader to use words such as 'may be incorrect' (*R* v *King* [1979] Crim LR 122). Disclaimers in small print or made by way of a casual remark during a conversation will not suffice (*R* v *Hammertons Cars Ltd* [1976] 1 WLR 1243). However, this should not be taken to mean that an oral disclaimer will be ineffective in all cases. For example in *Lewin* v *Fuell* (1991) 10 TrLR 126 the defendant had sold counterfeit 'Cartier' and 'Rolex' watches, subject to an oral disclaimer. Although the prosecution appeal against the defendant's acquittal was allowed on the ground that the oral disclaimer came after the offence was committed, there is no suggestion that oral disclaimers, per se, are unacceptable. See also *Kent County Council* v *Price* (1993) 157 JP 1161, discussed in 17.3.9, in which Stuart-Smith LJ said, at p. 1168, that it is a question of fact in each case whether the cumulative effect of the description itself and any disclaimer, whether written or oral, made before any offence is committed is such that the description could be regarded as false to a material degree.

17.6.2.2 Timing of the disclaimer Where the use of a disclaimer is permitted, it must operate so as to nullify any effect the trade description might have had on the mind of the consumer. It follows from this that the disclaimer must be in the public domain before any offence is committed, and this, in turn, means that the time at which the disclaimer must be made may differ according to the offence charged. Understandably, most of the case law on the subject is concerned with the offence created by s. 1(1)(b), since this is the provision most likely to be used against 'innocent' car dealers selling on a car with an odometer which has been tampered with by someone else. For the purposes of s. 1(1)(b), it is clear that the disclaimer must be effective before there is a supply. Accordingly, the defendant will have had to have taken steps to communicate his disclaimer of liability adequately to the customer before the time at which any supply of goods is effected. This might suggest that the applicable test is the same as that used by civil courts when determining whether a contracting party has given adequate notice of an exemption clause (see chapter 12). The Trade Descriptions Act 1968 imposes criminal liability and a test relevant to contractual liability may not always be appropriate. Nevertheless, there are similarities in the two tests. For example, a disclaimer which comes after the consumer has taken delivery cannot be effective in relation to the offence charged under s. 1(1)(b), since the offence is committed at the time of supply and if the trade description is still effective at that stage, whatever happens thereafter can only be relevant to sentence. More difficult is whether a disclaimer made at the time of supply will suffice. What is clear from the tests considered above is that unless the disclaimer is in very strong language, it may not suffice to displace the trade description which has been applied to the goods.

Until the decision in *R* v *Bull* (1996) 160 JP 240, the general view was that the disclaimer doctrine had no application to the s. 1(1)(a) offence. However, it is now clear that in very limited circumstances a person might wish to disclaim responsibility for a description he has applied himself. In the majority of cases this option will be regarded as inappropriate, particularly where the defendant has acted unscrupulously, for example, where he knowingly turns back an odometer reading and then claims not to have knowledge of the accuracy of the mileage reading. The only motive in such cases is dishonest enhancement of the car's market value and clearly it would be inappropriate to allow the fraudulent defendant to dislaim responsibility. But there are other cases such as *R* v *Bull* (considered in 17.6.1) in which the defendant has acted honestly and wishes to inform a customer of what would be a misleading description unless corrected. For example, in *Southend Borough Council* v *White* (1991) 156 JP 463 the defendant had fitted a set of dashboard instruments to a damaged second-hand car with the result that the mileage reading on the odometer did not accurately reflect the mileage travelled by that vehicle. The defendant had to rectify damage to the vehicle in order to be able to sell it, but the repairs involved fitting new dashboard instruments which would not tell the truth about the car. Despite the fact that the defendant had no option but to sell the car subject to the inaccurate odometer reading, it was held that it was not open to him to display a disclaimer which indicated that the odometer had been replaced and the reading was therefore inaccurate. Nolan J said that even a reasonable explanation of the inaccuracy did not prevent the description from being false in a material respect. The route which should have been adopted by the defendant was to have pleaded the s. 24 defence of due diligence, but it is implicit in Nolan J's judgment that this would not have been satisfied as there was no attempt to display the actual mileage of the car at the closest possible point to the inaccurate odometer reading.

In cases such as *R* v *Bull* and *Southend Borough Council* v *White* if a disclaimer is to be effective, it must operate before any offence is committed, which for the purposes of s. 1(1)(a) means that the disclaimer must have been communicated to the customer before any description is applied. On the strange facts of *R* v *Bull,* that requirement was satisfied since the act constituting an application of a false trade description did not come until the very late stage of copying the mileage reading on to a sales invoice, by which time the customer was aware of the disclaimer. But this will not normally be the case as *Southend Borough Council* v *White* illustrates, since in most cases the application of the false trade description, such as by turning back the mileage recording on an odometer, compiling an auction catalogue which falsely describes a painting or fitting a new odometer, all occur before the disclaimer is communicated to the consumer. As suggested in *R* v *Southwood*

[1987] 3 All ER 556, the more appropriate way of dealing with the 'innocent' s. 1(1)(a) offender is by using the s. 24 due diligence defence under which it will be necessary for the defendant to show that he has taken all reasonable precautions to avoid misleading the consumer.

EIGHTEEN

Misdescriptions of services and property

18.1 SERVICES, ACCOMMODATION AND FACILITIES

The modern consumer is just as much concerned with the quality and safety of the services she or he consumes as with the goods she or he buys. Indeed, the purchase of many consumer goods will also involve making arrangements for services in the form of a maintenance agreement. The civil law obligations of the supplier of services have already been considered in chapter 10, but it is also important to ensure that the consumer is not misled by inaccurate statements made about the services she or he contracts for.

The Trade Descriptions Act 1968, s. 14, went beyond the recommendations of the *Final Report of the Committee on Consumer Protection* (Cmnd 1781, 1962, para. 5, in providing for misdescriptions of services, accommodation and facilities. In recognition of the fact that s. 14 broke new ground, the liability imposed on suppliers was less stringent than that which applied to the supplier of goods in that Parliament included a limited requirement of *mens rea*. This requirement may not have been based solely on sympathy for the service industry, since it has been admitted subsequently that any assessment of the quality of services involves a very subjective element (*Review of the Trade Descriptions Act 1968* (Cmnd 6628, 1976), paras 43–9).

18.1.1 Conditions of application of the Trade Descriptions Act 1968, s. 14

The Trade Descriptions Act 1968, s. 14(1), provides that it shall be an offence for any person in the course of any trade or business:

(a) to make a statement which he knows to be false; or
(b) recklessly to make a statement which is false;

as to a number of matters concerning the provision, nature and other aspects of services, accommodation and facilities. Not all misdescriptions of services etc. are covered by s. 14, but only those in the detailed list of the matters in respect of which an offence may be committed (s. 14(1)(i)–(v)).

Since s. 14(1)(a) and s. 14(1)(b) create two distinct offences, it is important that when framing an indictment it is made clear by the prosecution which element is being relied upon. The prosecution will have to identify the statement on which they intend to rely and also call evidence to show why it should be considered to be false, which means that there must be some identification of the element or elements of s. 14(1)(i) to (v) which it is alleged has been infringed (*R* v *Piper* (1996) 160 JP 116, 122 per Roch LJ).

18.1.1.1 Acting in the course of a trade or business Section 14(1) provides that it is an offence for any person acting in the course of a trade or business to make a prohibited statement. It follows that, as in the case of s. 1, an offence may be committed by any person, whether he be the supplier of the service or not, provided he acts in the course of a trade or business (see chapter 1). Thus an offence may be committed by someone who is not the supplier, but has an interest in the outcome of the transaction entered into by the consumer. For example, if a garage proprietor states that the cars he sells are covered by a guarantee provided by an insurance company, there is an infringement of s. 14 if the guarantee is not in fact provided, since the guarantee may be regarded as a facility made available with the goods supplied (*Bambury* v *Hounslow London Borough Council* [1971] RTR 1). The 1968 Act does not specifically state that a business includes the activities of a profession (cf. Unfair Contract Terms Act 1977, s. 14; Sale of Goods Act 1979, s. 61(1)). For the purposes of s. 14, this is likely to be important as many services are provided in a professional capacity and should, it is submitted, fall within the scope of the section. It has been held that s. 14 is capable of applying to false statements concerning professional qualifications since such an indication is likely to be taken to refer to the quality of the service provided. Thus if a person claims to be an architect or conducts himself in a manner which leads the consumer to believe he is an architect when he is not, in fact, qualified as such, he commits an offence under s. 14 (*R* v *Breeze* [1973] 1 WLR 994). This would seem to suggest that s. 14 ought to apply to the provision of professional services. Moreover, it has been seen already that for the purposes of s. 1 of the Act, the activities of a professional veterinary surgeon in certifying animals as fit for export may be regarded as business activities (*Roberts* v *Leonard* (1995) 94 LGR 284). This being the case, there now seems little doubt that the same reasoning should also apply to s. 14. In contrast, it seems that an organisation such as the Law Society, as opposed to individual solicitors who are members of that organisation, does not carry on a trade or business (*R* v *Bow Street Magistrates' Court, ex parte Joseph* (1986) 150 JP 650).

18.1.1.2 When is a statement made? For the purposes of both parts of s. 14, a statement must have been made. One obvious example of making a statement arises when it is communicated to another person (*R* v *Thomson Holidays Ltd* [1974] QB 592), but it does not follow that an offence is only committed when the statement is read by another person (*Wings Ltd* v *Ellis* [1985] AC 272, 296 per Lord Scarman). It is possible for a statement to be made without it being communicated to another. For example, a statement is made when it is published, when brochures are posted in bulk to travel agents, when a message is passed on by telephone, when information is posted to clients and when the information is read by the person to whom it is communicated (ibid., 285 per Lord Hailsham of St Marylebone LC).

It has been seen that for the purposes of s. 1 of the 1968 Act, an offending statement must be connected with a supply of goods (see *Hall* v *Wickens Motors (Gloucester) Ltd* [1972] 1 WLR 1418). However, s. 14 is not so confined, principally because a supply of services involves continuing obligations which the service provider may be called upon to fulfil in the future. As a result, it has been held that s. 14 is not concerned with statements that induce a contract and it does not matter that the offending statement is made after the conclusion of the relevant contract. Thus, a mechanic who makes a false statement about the work he has carried out on his client's car may still be guilty of an offence under s. 14 even where he has already been paid for the work he has done. In *Breed* v *Cluett* [1970] 2 QB 459 the respondent, a builder, had contracted to sell a bungalow. After the contract had been concluded but before completion of the work, he made a number of assertions to the effect that the bungalow was covered by a 10-year guarantee. Despite the fact that the contract was already concluded at the time of making the false statement, it was held that an offence under s. 14 had been committed, since there was no requirement in s. 14 that the false statement had to induce the customer to enter into the contract.

What seems to matter is that the statement must be related to a supply of services, but does not have to precede that supply. Thus it is possible for an offence to be committed where it relates to past services such as where the defendant implies that he has carried out an inspection of goods before recommending that certain repair work be carried out. In *R* v *Bevelectric Ltd* (1992) 157 JP 323 a company engaged in the business of repairing washing machines had adopted a policy of always advising customers who had complained that their washing machine motor did not work that a new motor would be required. Customers were informed that the price of the new unit was £47, which included a £20 credit in respect of the old motor. This remained the case regardless of the actual cost of repairing a defective motor. On two particular occasions, customers were advised of the need for a replacement motor when the cost of repair would have been negligible. In the Court of Appeal a conviction under s. 14(1)(b) was held to be justified as the defendants used language likely to be taken for a statement that a genuine assessment had been made of the extent of any necessary repair. Of necessity, this entailed an argument that s. 14 applies not only to services which are to be provided but also those which have already been provided. This proved not to be controversial since there is good authority to show that, unlike other provisions of the Trade Descriptions Act 1968, s. 14 can apply to a service which has already been provided. For example, the section applied where the nature of building services was misdescribed in a receipt (*Parsons* v *Barnes* [1973] Crim LR 537).

Where a person is charged with the commission of an offence under s. 14, the general defences in s. 24 may be pleaded. However, because of the *mens rea* requirement, considered below, it seems unlikely that these defences will be of much use in all events. If a defendant is shown to have recklessly made a statement contrary to s. 14(1)(b) or if he knows that a statement made by himself is false, thus committing an offence under s. 14(1)(a), it is likely to be difficult to establish that reasonable precautions have been taken and that due diligence has been exercised (cf. *Sunair Holidays Ltd* v *Dodd* [1970] 1 WLR 1037; *Wings Ltd* v *Ellis* [1985] AC 272).

18.1.2 The *mens rea* requirement

It is clear from the wording of s. 14(1) that knowledge of the falsity of the offending statement or recklessness in the making of the offending statement are alternative requirements. However, it will be seen below that the requirement of knowledge in s. 14(1)(a) is not related to the making of the statement and so this element of s. 14 does not imply that a convicted defendant is guilty of fraudulently misleading a consumer.

18.1.2.1 Knowledge of the falsity of a statement

At first sight, the wording used in s. 14(1)(a) would appear to suggest a *mens rea* offence, however, the House of Lords in *Wings Ltd* v *Ellis* [1985] AC 272 has held that the offence created is, in fact, one of 'semi-strict' liability. The important issue is that while the defendant must have knowledge of the falsity of the statement he makes, that knowledge may exist at any time and does not have to exist at the time the statement is first published.

Section 14(1)(a) does not make it an offence knowingly to make a false statement, it merely requires that the defendant should have made a statement and that, at some time subsequently, the defendant knew the statement was false. In *Wings Ltd* v *Ellis* tour operators published and distributed to travel agents a 1981/82 winter brochure which incorrectly indicated that a hotel in Sri Lanka was air-conditioned. The mistake was discovered in May 1981 and all Wings' staff and associated agents were notified. Furthermore, all clients who had already booked that holiday were informed of the position. However, no erratum slip was produced and the complaint which gave rise to the prosecution came from someone who booked the advertised holiday in January 1982. At that stage Wings were aware of the error, although they had not been aware of the falsity of the statement at the time the brochure was published. Since the appellants had made a statement in their brochure and since they knew it was false when they were notified of the absence of air-conditioning facilities in the hotel, an offence was committed. Further offences were committed every time the brochure was read and relied upon by a person who wished to do business with Wings.

Since the offence can be committed without knowledge of the act of statement, it is one of strict liability but as Lord Scarman pointed out at p. 295, this advances the legislative purpose embodied in the 1968 Act by striking against false statements irrespective of the reason for or explanation of their falsity.

It follows from the reasoning employed in *Wings Ltd* v *Ellis* that if the person charged is unaware of the falsity of his statement at the time it is relied on by a customer, no offence is committed under s. 14(1)(a). Thus a sleeping partner who has not been kept informed of events by an active partner may not be convicted under s. 14(1)(a) (*Coupe* v *Guyett* [1973] 1 WLR 669).

18.1.2.2 Recklessness The offence created by s. 14(1)(b) is that of recklessly making a statement which is false. At one stage, it was thought that recklessness under s. 14 imported no more than the common law understanding of that word and did not extend so far as to include simple negligence (see *Sunair Holidays Ltd* v *Dodd* [1970] 1 WLR 1037). However, the statutory definition of recklessness in s. 14(2)(b) provides that a statement is made recklessly if it is made regardless of whether it be true or false and regardless of whether the maker had reasons for believing it might be false. This definition clearly encompasses within the meaning of *Derry* v *Peek* (1889) 14 App Cas 337 in the sense of a fraudulent misstatement, but it also goes beyond this in that dishonesty need not be proved. For example, it has been held that the prosecution need only show that the person charged did not have regard to the truth or falsity of his statement. It is not necessary to establish that the defendant deliberately closed his eyes to the truth. In *MFI Warehouses Ltd* v *Nattrass* [1973] 1 WLR 307, a mail order company advertised goods for sale on 14 days' free approval, indicating in the advertisement that no charge would be made for carriage. A customer placed an order for goods referred to in the advertisement and complained when he was charged a fee for carriage. The problem lay in the fact that the advertisement was ambiguous and could reasonably be interpreted as applying the offer of free carriage to all goods detailed in the advertisement, when it was the defendants' intention that the special offer should apply only to some articles. Through an oversight on the part of the chairman of the company, the advertisement had not been read properly before it was sent for publication. Accordingly, the defendants were convicted under s. 14(1)(b) of recklessly making a false statement. On the meaning of recklessness, it was observed by Lord Widgery CJ, at p. 313:

> I am inclined to think that it was the fact that the word 'reckless' has more than one meaning which prompted the draftsman to give a special definition. . . . this Act is designed for the protection of customers and it does not seem to me to be unreasonable to suppose that in creating such additional protection for customers Parliament was minded to place upon the advertiser a positive obligation to have regard to whether his advertisement was true or false.
>
> I have accordingly come to the conclusion that 'recklessly' . . . does not involve dishonesty. . . . I think it suffices for present purposes if the prosecution can show that the advertiser did not have regard to the truth or falsity of his advertisement even though it cannot be shown that he was deliberately closing his eyes to the truth, or that he had any kind of dishonest mind.

It is necessary that the defendant is reckless at the time of the commission of the offence, which is the time the statement is made. Thus, if the defendant's statement is true at the time of making, no offence is committed if later events cause a change of circumstance (*Sunair Holidays Ltd* v *Dodd* [1970] 1 WLR 1037). However, this view must be considered in the light of the House of Lords interpretation of when a statement is 'made' in *Wings Ltd* v *Ellis* [1985] AC 272. The state of mind required by s. 14(1)(b) is generally to be inferred. If it is shown that a statement is known to be false at the time of making and no steps are taken to correct it, recklessness can be inferred (*Yugotours Ltd* v *Wadsley* (1989) 8 TrLR 74).

Generally, what happens after the defendant has recklessly made a statement will be irrelevant to the question of liability. Thus if the defendant apologises for his mistake and tries to make up for the falsity of his statement this will not affect his liability for the commission of an offence, but it may be a relevant consideration in mitigation of sentence (*Cowburn* v *Focus Television Rentals Ltd* [1983] Crim LR 563).

18.1.3 The meaning of services, accommodation and facilities

18.1.3.1 Services The Trade Descriptions Act 1968 at various points makes a clear distinction between goods and services. One result of this is that the term 'service' when given its natural meaning does not, except in very rare cases, embrace the supply of goods (*Newell* v *Hicks* [1984] RTR 135). Generally, a service involves doing something for somebody (ibid. 148 per Robert Goff LJ). However, in an unfortunate decision of the Divisional Court in *Ashley* v *Sutton London Borough Council* (1994) 159 JP 631 the distinction between a supply of goods and a supply of services has been blurred. The defendant marketed a book which contained a betting strategy for fixed-odds pools gambling. The mailshot which advertised the book also offered a 90-day money-back guarantee should customers not find the system satisfactory, but a number of people who sought return of the money they had paid were refused a refund. It was held that the defendant had recklessly made a statement as to the nature of a service contrary to s. 14(1)(b) on the basis that, although a book is a product rather than a service, what was purchased in this case was, in reality, the information contained in the book rather than a collection of pages bound together. However, it is suggested that what the customers were complaining about was not the book, but the fact that the money-back guarantee had not been honoured.

In reaching its decision it was emphasised that what matters is to consider the essential nature of the transaction and see what in reality is being provided to the customer (ibid. 634 per Scott Baker J). What served to support the court's decision was that an inflated price had been paid for the book which was taken as an indication that it was the information which customers were interested in.

It is suggested that to regard this as a supply of services is probably incorrect on more than one count, despite the undoubted desire to provide redress in respect of an unfulfilled money-back guarantee, which is all too common a problem encountered by consumers. In particular, while it is attractive to think that what students want from a book on consumer law is the information contained on its pages, it is unlikely that the sale of a copy of this book would be regarded as anything other than a sale of goods. Only very rarely will a supply of goods be so closely related to the provision of a service that the two may be regarded as part of the contract for the provision of a service. For example, when a car is repaired at a garage, oil may be supplied as part of the service provision.

The mistake made by the Divisional Court was to concentrate on the book rather than the guarantee. Since a service involves doing something for somebody, it would be difficult to maintain that a book is a service without also accepting that cars allow the purchaser to drive from A to B or that washing machines provide the consumer with the ability to keep the clothes of the family clean. If anything, these articles do not 'do something for somebody' but rather they allow someone to do something for himself, in which case it would be better to regard them as providing a facility rather than a service (see 18.1.3.3 below).

Even if the court in *Ashley* v *Sutton London Borough Council* had concentrated on the issue of the guarantee, matters would not have been any more easy since it has been held that the provision of a promised refund on the price of goods found to be cheaper elsewhere does not fall within the scope of s. 14 (*Dixons Ltd* v *Roberts* (1984) 82 LGR 689). If a promise to refund to a customer part of the price he has paid is not to be regarded as the provision of a service or a facility, then presumably the same reasoning must apply to a promise to refund the whole price (see Cartwright, 'A service fault in the Divisional Court' [1996] JBL 58). However, there are instances in which statements about a guarantee have been treated as falling within s. 14. For example, to promise that a house was covered by a 10-year NHBRC guarantee was considered to form part of the overall service of building the house and as such fell within s. 14. (*Breed* v *Cluett* [1970] 2 QB 459).

18.1.3.2 Accommodation It is clear from the number of cases involving inaccurate statements in tour operators' brochures that s. 14 embraces statements about short-term holiday accommodation. But it does not follow from this that any statement about longer-term property lettings and dispositions will fall within the provisions of the 1968 Act. In particular, inaccurate statements related to the disposition of land or an interest in land fall outside the scope of the 1968 Act, but are now covered by the Property Misdescriptions Act 1991, considered below.

18.1.3.3 Facilities It would appear that the word 'facility' should be construed *eiusdem generis* with the words 'service' and 'accommodation' with the result that a representation that a retailer is willing to supply goods should not be treated as a facility (*Westminster City Council* v *Ray Alan (Manshops) Ltd* [1982] 1 WLR 383). Accordingly a closing-down sale held at a shop which does not close down cannot be described as a facility. Generally, if there is an indication that a third party will provide some facility, this will fall within the scope of the section, with the result that if a motor-vehicle dealer indicates the availability of insurance cover when supplying a motorcycle, there is a statement which relates to a facility provided by a third party (*Kinchin* v *Ashton Park Scooters Ltd* (1984) 148 JP 540). Similarly, a tour operator's brochure which states that shopping facilities are available at a hotel complex probably does give an indication as to the availablity of a facility, but the same reasoning does not apply to cases like *Westminster City Council* v *Ray Alan (Manshops) Ltd* since the availability of shopping facilities in that case is not linked to the provision of any accommodation as is the case with statements contained in holiday brochures.

A facility may be described as something which is made available to customers to use if they are so minded (*Westminster City Council* v *Ray Alan (Manshops) Ltd* [1982] 1 WLR 383, 386 per Ormrod LJ). It has also been held that while the word 'facility' is capable of a very broad interpretation, for the purposes of penal statutes, it should be construed narrowly to mean that the trader is prepared to provide his customers with the wherewithal to do something for themselves (*Newell* v *Hicks* [1984] RTR 135, 148 per Robert Goff LJ). The provision of a car park or a swimming pool constitutes the provision of a facility. It appears that where a retailer displays a credit card logo on his premises he indicates that he is prepared to provide a service. Where a trader offers a refund if goods can be purchased more cheaply elsewhere, it appears that he does not offer a facility (*Dixons Ltd* v *Roberts* (1984) 82 LGR 689; cf. Consumer Protection Act 1987, ss. 20 and 21 and see chapter 19). However this must now be considered in the light of the decision in *Ashley* v *Sutton London Borough Council* (1994) 159 JP 631 considered in 18.1.3.1.

The difficulty which the refund and guarantee cases throw up is that where a retailer offers his customers an inducement of this kind the 'service' or 'facility' he provides is very closely related to a supply of goods. Rather than regard these cases as falling within s. 14, perhaps a better approach would be to treat the statements made by the retailer as an indication of the overall composition of the package of goods which is supplied, thereby bringing the matter within s. 1 and s. 2(1)(c) or (e) (see also *British Gas Corporation* v *Lubbock* [1974] 1 WLR 37).

18.1.4   Statements to which s. 14 applies

In order to secure a conviction, the prosecution must establish that the *actus reus* of the offence has been committed. This means that it must be established that a false statement has been made in respect of one of the matters listed in s. 14. For these purposes a statement is false if it is false to a material degree (s. 14(4)). It follows from this that, as in the case of prosecutions under s. 1, the courts will apply the *de minimis* principle and ignore trifling departures from the truth.

In order to broaden the scope of the prohibition in s. 14, it is further provided that anything likely to be taken for a statement in respect of services etc., if false, shall be treated as such (s. 14(2)(a)). For example, in *R* v *Clarksons Holidays Ltd* (1972) 57 Cr App R 38, the offending 'statement' was an artist's impression. Strictly a picture is not a statement, but it can be taken to refer to the accommodation provided.

It has been seen that if the defendant's statement relates to what has been done already or what he is doing at present, it is a statement of fact and is covered by s. 14 (*Breed* v *Cluett* [1970] 2 QB 459). Under s. 14, considerable difficulties have been experienced in relation to tour operators' claims in brochures about holiday accommodation. Such statements may amount to nothing more than a warranty which may give rise to an action for breach of contract, but do not give rise to criminal liability under the 1968 Act. The mischief aimed at by s. 14 is the factually false or misleading statement. In this regard it has been observed by Lord Widgery CJ in *Beckett* v *Cohen* [1972] 1 WLR 1593 at pp. 1596–7 that:

> . . . if before the contract has been worked out the person who provides the service makes a promise as to what he will do, and that promise does not relate to an existing fact, nobody can say at the date when that statement is made that it is either true or false. . . . Parliament never intended or contemplated for a moment that the Act of 1968 should be used in this way, to make a criminal offence out of what is really a breach of warranty.

It follows from this that if a tour operator predicts what will be available at a foreign holiday resort because the accommodation is undergoing improvements at the time he prepares his brochure, no offence is committed by the tour operator if the statements prove to be inaccurate because of the failure of the hotel owner to provide what has been predicted (*R* v *Sunair Holidays Ltd* [1973] 1 WLR 1105). In such cases, the statement relates to the future and cannot be said to be true or false at the time of making (ibid. 1109 per McKenna J).

In some instances, a promise may imply a factual statement, in which case it may result in a successful conviction. For example, it may be possible to imply that the person making the forecast believes his prediction will come true (ibid. and see also *British Airways Board* v *Taylor* [1976] 1 WLR 13, 17 per Lord Wilberforce). Similarly, if the circumstances of the case are such that the defendant knows that it is possible that his 'promise' cannot be fulfilled, the statement may be treated as one of fact. For example, in *British Airways Board* v *Taylor* an airline confirmed the availability of a seat on a specified flight at a time when the airline policy was to overbook scheduled flights. It was inevitable that a passenger holding a confirmed booking might be denied the right to board. Had the offending statement been made by the defendants rather than another company which they had taken over, an offence under s. 14(1)(a) would have been committed.

What matters in this respect is the understanding of the ordinary person rather than the interpretation which would be placed upon particular words by a trained legal mind (ibid. 18 per Lord Wilberforce; see also *Smallshaw* v *PKC Associates Ltd* (1994) 159 JP 730). If a passenger receives a confirmation slip which informs him of the departure time of a flight on which he has been booked, he can reasonably assume that there is a place available for him on that flight. An ordinary person receiving a confirmation slip of this kind would assume that a certain place had been booked for him and if that proved not to be the case then there was every reason for regarding the statement made by the defendants as one which was covered by s. 14.

A similar result will also be obtained where a traveller books a return ticket which specifies the flight time and the name of the flight operator, with the result that if either is changed an offence is committed. Although the statement appears to relate to the future, it may be regarded as a statement of the facts existing at the time the ticket was issued. Moreover, it makes no difference to the outcome that the contract with the customer contains a term which allows the flight operator to cancel or vary the flight booked (*R* v *Avro Ltd* (1993) 12 TrLR 83).

Just as statements of intention may give rise to problems, the same is equally true of statements of opinion, since an opinion may not be regarded as a statement of fact. However, it has been seen already that at common law, there may be circumstances in which the evidence shows that the defendant could not possibly have held the opinion he expresses or that the apparent opinion amounts to an expression of the *present* state of mind of the person making the statement (see chapter 4). A similar approach also seems to be applicable to s. 14. In *R* v *Bevelectric Ltd* (1992) 157 JP 323 the defendants advised any customer who complained that a washing-machine motors was not working that the motor would require replacement, even if the defect was capable of repair. One issue was whether the defendants' statements were mere expressions of opinion. It was concluded that the statements that motors required replacement were statements of the fact that the motor were so badly damaged that they had to be replaced. But even if this was not the case, it was held that a misleading expression of opinion to the effect that a motor requires replacement is likely to be taken for an indication that a genuine assessment of the need for repair had been made (applying *Holloway* v *Cross* [1981] 1 All ER 1012, on which see chapter 17).

The list of matters in respect of which a false statement may be made, either recklessly or with knowledge of its falsity, include the following:

(a)   the provision in the course of any trade or business of any services, accommodation or facilities (s. 14(1)(i));

(b)   the nature of any services, accommodation or facilities provided in the course of any trade or business (s. 14(1)(ii));

(c)   the time at which, the manner in which or persons by whom any services, accommodation or facilities are so provided (s. 14(1)(iii));

(d)   the examination, approval or evaluation by any person of any services, accommodation or facilities so provided (s. 14(1)(iv));

(e)   the location or amenities of any accommodation so provided (s. 14(1)(v)).

It is considered important that Parliament has gone to the trouble of setting out in detail the various elements contained in these five paragraphs. It follows that when framing the indictment, the prosecution must identify which of these elements applies so as to render the defendant's statement false. It will not suffice for the prosecution to allege simply that the statement was false in relation to the provision of services since there may be some statements about services which do not fall within paras (i)–(v) (*R v Piper* (1996) 160 JP 116, 122 per Roch LJ).

18.1.4.1 The provision in the course of any trade or business of any services, accommodation or facilities (s. 14(1)(i))
It would appear that the word 'provision' cannot be taken to refer to anything other than the fact of providing services etc. Thus s. 14(1)(i) will not extend to cover statements relating to the terms on which services are provided, such as their price (*Newell v Hicks* [1984] RTR 135, 149 per Robert Goff LJ). If a different interpretation were to be placed on s. 14(1)(i), this would render redundant the remaining matters referred to in s. 14, since all matters relating to services would be covered by the one paragraph.

Generally, statements which relate to the provision of a service will inform the customer what is provided. For example, s. 14(1)(i) will apply to statements which describe the features of hotel accommodation, such as whether it has a swimming pool and bedrooms with terraces (*R v Clarksons Holidays Ltd* (1972) 57 Cr App R 38). Similarly, if a builder gives an indication of how the finished product will look (*Beckett v Cohen* [1972] 1 WLR 1593) or if an airline reserves a seat for a passenger (*British Airways Board v Taylor* [1976] 1 WLR 13), a statement is made as to the provision of a service.

18.1.4.2 The nature of any services, accommodation or facilities provided in the course of any trade or business (s. 14(1)(ii))
This appears to cover statements in respect of the quality of the service provided. Thus statements to the effect that a hotel provides a 'good, efficient service' will relate to the nature of a service (*R v Clarksons Holidays Ltd* (1972) 57 Cr App R 38).

More controversially, in *Ashley v Sutton London Borough Council* (1994) 159 JP 631 the provision of a money-back guarantee on the supply of a booklet providing information on how to succeed at fixed-odds pools betting was considered to relate to the nature of the service provided. However, it has been noted already that the court probably wrongly concentrated upon the question whether the booklet was a service rather than upon the more important question whether the provision of the guarantee itself was capable of falling within the scope of the 1968 Act. If anything, what the statement did was to indicate what was available, which, if anything, is a matter concerned with the provision of a service. However, it has been observed above that the word 'provision' should not be taken to refer to the terms on which goods or services are provided, which is effectively what was done in *Ashley v Sutton London Borough Council* (see *Newell v Hicks* [1984] RTR 135).

18.1.4.3 The time at which, manner in which or persons by whom any services, accommodation or facilities are so provided (s. 14(1)(iii))
This would appear to cover an airline reservation which stipulates the time of

the flight and a claim that a dry-cleaner offers a 24-hour service. Also apparently falling within s. 14(1)(iii) is an inaccurate indication that the service provider is a member of a known trade association (*R* v *Piper* (1996) 160 JP 116). However, the elements set out in s. 14(1)(i) to (v) inevitably overlap and there are cases in which a particular indication will fall into more than one of the specified types of statement.

18.1.4.4 The examination, approval or evaluation by any person of any services, accommodation or facilities so provided (s. 14(1)(iv))
Statements to the effect that a hotel or restaurant is 'AA and RAC Approved' or is listed in the Egon Ronay Guide fall within this provision.

18.1.4.5 The location or amenities of any accommodation so provided (s. 14(1)(v))
It may be that this provision is redundant in that it may well overlap completely with s. 14(1)(i) (*Sunair Holidays Ltd* v *Dodd* [1970] 1 WLR 1037). Statements to the effect that holiday accommodation has a balcony with a sea view and a swimming pool relate to the amenities of the accommodation (see *Airtours plc* v *Shipley* (1994) 158 JP 835) but these are matters which also relate to the provision of the accommodation. However, the fact that there is overlap between different elements is not to be objected to if it ensures that as broad a range of statements as possible is covered by the provisions of s. 14 (see *R* v *Piper* (1996) 160 JP 116). Perhaps, s. 14(1)(v) goes further in that the reference to location and amenities may include statements about the locality in which a hotel is to be found, which may not necessarily be covered by s. 14(1)(i).

18.1.5 Disclaimers of liability and s. 14
It has been seen already that in relation to the offence of supplying goods to which a false trade description is applied, the courts have sanctioned the use of disclaimers on the part of a defendant who has no alternative means of avoiding the effects of the strict-liability provisions of s. 1(1)(b) of the 1968 Act.

Whether the disclaimer doctrine applies to s. 14 or not is a matter shrouded in uncertainty. In the first place, it is arguable that the use of disclaimers in relation to the offences set out in s. 14 is not in line with the view expressed by Lord Scarman in *Wings Ltd* v *Ellis* [1985] AC 272 that the Trade Descriptions Act 1968 is concerned with improving trading standards. Moreover, it is also clear from the case law on disclaimers and s. 1 of the Act that the disclaimer must be effective before any offence is committed. Since the offences under s. 14 are committed when a statement is made and since it is clear that a statement may be 'made' several times over, it is possible that a disclaimer might be in the public domain before an offence is committed, in which case it would then become necessary to consider whether the disclaimer did serve to nullify the effect of the false statement. However, an alternative view of s. 14 is that it creates a continuing offence, which is repeated each time the defendant does business on the strength of the inaccuracy. In this case it might be necessary for the disclaimer to be operative before the first occasion on which the offending statement was made.

It has been seen that in order for a disclaimer to be effective under s. 1, it must be 'as bold, precise and compelling as the trade description itself' (*Norman* v *Bennett* [1974] 1 WLR 1229, 1232 per Lord Widgery CJ). Thus far cases which have raised the issue of disclaimers and s. 14 all appear to have stumbled at this hurdle. For example, if the disclaimer does not appear on the page of a holiday brochure on which the false statement appears, it will not suffice (*R* v *Clarksons Holidays Ltd* (1972) 57 Cr App R 38). Likewise, if the attempt at disclaiming liability comes in small print, consistent with cases under s. 1, the *Norman* v *Bennett* formula will not be satisfied (*Savory & Assoc Ltd* v *Dawson* (1976) 84 ITSA Monthly Review 128). Also if the consumer is supplied with more than one document, it is unlikely that a disclaimer in one of them will negative the effect of a false statement contained in another (*Smallshaw* v *PKC Associates Ltd* (1994) 159 JP 730).

18.1.6   Reform of s. 14

It has been observed that s. 14 was enacted without the benefit of proposals from the Molony Committee on Consumer Protection. Since its enactment, s. 14 has revealed a number of deficiencies which were outlined in the *Review of the Trade Descriptions Act 1968* (Cmnd 6628, 1976). As has been noted, one of the most serious criticisms of s. 14 is that the reference to 'accommodation' appears not to include false statements related to residential property sales (see now the effect of the Property Misdescriptions Act 1991 considered in 18.2).

Section 14 does not cover all descriptions of services to be provided, since some statements of this kind relate to the future. It is possible for a statement about the future to be misleading (see *Beckett* v *Cohen* [1972] 1 WLR 1593) and to persuade the consumer to contract with one person rather than another. The Review document concluded that there should be a new offence of supplying services which do not comply with a description given of them (Cmnd 6628, paras 96–8). It was also suggested in relation to future statements that if the truth or falsity of the statement can be tested, it should be an offence to make a false statement about the future supply of services and that it should be an offence to make statements about services which the maker of the statement has no intention of supplying (Cmnd 6628, para. 104).

Because the use of the criminal law in relation to the misdescription of services was novel in 1968, it was considered more appropriate to introduce a *mens rea* requirement. However, in the interests of consistency with other provisions in the Trade Descriptions Act 1968, it was proposed that s. 14 offences should impose strict liability, subject to the operation of the general defences in s. 24.

18.2   PROPERTY MISDESCRIPTIONS

It has been observed above that one of the failings of the Trade Descriptions Act 1968 was that it failed to deal with false and misleading statements regarding residential property sales and lettings, usually by members of the estate agency profession. Although the 1968 Act created criminal offences in relation to a wide range of misdescriptions of goods by reference to their physical attributes and past history and also introduced novel provisions in relation to the misdescription of services, accommodation and facilities, it became clear that the word 'accommodation' was not likely to be construed as including anything other than short-term holiday lettings and that transactions involving land or interests in land fell outside the scope of the 1968 legislation (*Review of the Trade Descriptions Act 1968* (Cmnd 6628, 1976), para. 70). There was some coverage of the estate agency profession in the Estate Agents Act 1979, but this is largely an administrative measure allowing the Director General of Fair Trading to prohibit unfit persons from engaging in estate agency work (Estate Agents Act 1979, s. 3) and set minimum standards of competence (s. 22) and does not impose criminal penalties in respect of property misdescriptions.

The Property Misdescriptions Act 1991 seeks to fill these gaps by creating a strict-liability criminal offence of making, in the course of an estate agency or property development business, a false or misleading statement about a prescribed matter (s. 1(1)) to be specified in an order made by the Secretary of State (s. 1(5)(d)). A link between the 1979 and the 1991 Acts may also prove useful in the long run since it is clear that the licensing system under the Estate Agents Act 1979 will be able to make use of convictions under the Property Misdescriptions Act 1991 in determining whether a particular applicant should be refused a licence on the grounds of unfitness.

18.2.1 Property subject to the provisions of the 1991 Act

The Act applies to statements in respect of both domestic and commercial property. It appears that commercial property was not exempted from the provisions of the Act because other legislation, such as the Trade Descriptions Act 1968, does not distinguish between the use to which goods subject to its provisions are put, particularly where the legislation aims to protect consumers and reputable traders. Also many small concerns starting a new business might be weakly resourced and might not be able to afford professional advice. Thirdly, to distinguish between the uses to which different types of property are put could create enormous problems. For example, it would result in estate agents having to consider the nature of all the property on their books, which would be difficult where there is a gradual change of use. In some instances, property in a residential area might gradually become used for business purposes and vice versa. Considerable difficulties would be encountered in deciding how to market a single building with multiple uses, such as a shop with private living accommodation above it. Finally, if anything, accuracy in relation to descriptions of commercial property is more important than in relation to domestic property since rental and rateable values may be based on estate agents' measurements. A matter which is not clear from the provisions of the 1991 Act is whether the property which has been misdescribed must be located in the United Kingdom. Section 1(6) of the Act defines an interest in land in terms which seem to confine the scope of the Act to properties located in England, Wales, Northern Ireland and Scotland. If this is correct the consequence is that misdescriptions concerning property located in southern Spain, even if made by a UK estate agent to a domestic consumer, remain outside the scope of the Act.

18.2.2 Persons subject to the provisions of the 1991 Act

The Property Misdescriptions Act 1991 strikes at false and misleading statements made by a person carrying on an estate agency business or a property development business. An estate agency business is said to be operated by a person who, in the course of a business, pursuant to instructions given by a person who wishes to dispose of or acquire an interest in land, introduces potential purchasers and seeks to secure the disposal or acquisition of that interest (Estate Agency Act 1979, s. 1(1)). To this there are a number of exceptions, with the result that solicitors, credit brokers, insurance brokers and persons providing surveying services are not regarded as engaging in estate agency work (Estate Agents Act 1979, s. 1(2)) provided they act in that particular professional capacity. This does not mean that a solicitor, for example, cannot engage in estate agency work, since when a solicitor sells houses he does not act in his professional capacity as a solicitor. However, where a solicitor makes a statement in the course of providing conveyancing services, that statement is specifically excluded from the provisions of the 1991 Act (Property Misdescriptions Act 1991, s. 1(1) and (5)(g)). Certain other organisations such as banks and building societies are not subject to the provisions of the Act, apparently on the basis that of 900 complaints per annum received by the Consumers' Association concerning property misdescriptions, none had related to either of these varieties of institution. Builders who market newly built properties are also included within the regime created by the 1991 Act, principally because not all newly built houses are covered by the National House Builders' Council insurance scheme and that builders are more likely to be aware of the past history of the land on which their houses are built and other matters such as site conditions and relevant land charges. While new house provision is a concern of the Act, it is not confined solely to that type of property and extends to builders who renovate older properties and subsequently seek to sell on the market (s. 1(5)(f)). This would cover dispositions by housing associations and other commercial developers of existing property.

Consistent with other legislation which makes it an offence to perform a prohibited act in the course of a trade or business, it is clear from the wording of the 1991 Act that if the person making the statement is not wholly or substantially concerned with property development, the Act will not apply. Thus a newsagent who privately sells his shop will not be guilty of an offence if he makes misleading statements concerning the property he sells, since the business of newsagency does not wholly or substantially involve property development (see also chapter 1).

Both the definition of estate agency work in the Estate Agents Act 1979, s. 1(1), and the definition of a property development business in the Property Misdescriptions Act 1991, s. 1(5)(f), make it clear that an offence may be committed by a person who is employed in the business concerned. Thus offences may be committed by individual receptionists, salesmen and other employees of the business concerned, provided they act in the course of their employment. Moreover, where the misleading statement is made by a senior corporate officer, such as a company director, manager or other person representing the directing mind and will of the company, both the officer and the company are guilty of an offence and may be proceeded against accordingly (Property Misdescriptions Act 1991, s. 4(1)).

18.2.3   False or misleading statements about prescribed matters
The offence created by the Property Misdescriptions Act 1991 is that of making a false or misleading statement about a matter prescribed by the Secretary of State. The Property Misdescriptions (Specified Matters) Order 1992 (SI 1992/2834) sets out a number of matters to which the 1991 Act applies, including location, address, aspect, environment, outlook, the availability and nature of any services, amenities and facilities, the nature of the accommodation, measurements and sizes, fixtures and fittings.

18.2.3.1   Prescribed matters   The matters set out in the Property Misdescriptions (Specified Matters) Order 1992 are fairly predictable, being based upon an Office of Fair Trading guidance document (Office of Fair Trading, *Estate Agency* (1990), paras 4.1 to 4.4). The Schedule to the Order indicates that statements relating to a range of matters relevant to physical characteristics, past history and future use should be included in the prescribed list. These include statements about the location or address of the property, its aspect and proximity to amenities and services and any facilities available. Thus marketing material which describes a house situated in Battersea as one to be found in 'South Chelsea' or a statement that a house has a rural aspect when planning permission for a 2,000-house estate has been granted might fail to satisfy these requirements. Similarly, to claim that a flat is situated two minutes from Tower Bridge without also specifying that this is two minutes by train might also be regarded as misleading. Likewise, to claim that a property is conveniently close to the station would be a misstatement about amenities if the nearest station is in the next village and a good 30 minutes' walk away. Other matters dealt with in the Order include false statements which relate to tenure, the nature and characteristics of title, the time remaining on a lease, the amount of any ground rent and the amount payable by way of community charge or council tax and any other service charge. Accordingly, a false statement to the effect that a property is freehold rather than leasehold would constitute the commission of an offence, as would a misleading statement about the council tax band of a property. In this last instance, estate agents would need to exercise caution before relying on information supplied by contacts in a local authority finance department, since, subject to available defences, liability under the 1991 Act is strict.

The Order also makes subject to the provisions of the 1991 Act, any false or misleading statement which relates to structural characteristics, conformity or compliance with any standard, regulations, guarantee or scheme, the fact of a survey or inspection and the results thereof, the person by whom any part of the building was manufactured or designed and repairs or improvements carried out on the property and the results thereof. Thus false statements to the effect that a house is built of sandstone or is covered by an architect's guarantee or that a house has recently been the subject of a successful treatment by a nationally known contractor for dry rot or common furniture beetle (woodworm) and has a 30-year guarantee in that respect ought to be regarded as offending statements.

Misleading statements concerning the accommodation provided, measurements and sizes, physical characteristics, fitness for purpose, strength or condition, fixtures included in or excluded from sale also appear within any list of prescribed matters. Thus a statement to the effect that a house consists of two reception rooms, a conservatory and three bedrooms would be misleading where the conservatory is a back passage, there are, in fact, only two bedrooms and the two reception rooms consist of a single L-shaped room, the measurements for which have been taken from wall to wall without revealing that one part of the 'L' has been measured twice. Statements to the effect that a house is suited for business use would also offend if there is some legal impediment to its use for business purposes. Finally, the Order also applies to false statements about previous history, restrictive covenants, easements, the existence or nature of planning permission and the existence or extent of any listed building status should be included in any list of prescribed matters. The importance of the past history of the property is a matter of particular relevance to property developers, since there may be facts of which only the developer is fully aware which might affect the purchaser's decision to buy. For example, a developer would not be wise to make positive claims to the effect that a house is built in an area noted for its healthy environment when the house is built on land formerly used as a tip for hazardous chemical waste products.

18.2.3.2 Statements The offence contained in s. 1(1) of the Property Misdescriptions Act 1991 refers to making a statement about a prescribed matter. Ordinarily this will be a statement in writing, as in the case of statements contained in property particulars prepared by estate agents, but it is also clear from the provisions of the Act that an offending statement may be made orally, by pictures or by any other method of signifying meaning (s. 1(5)(c)). Thus statements made in the course of a conversation between an estate agent and a potential purchaser may give rise to liability, provided there is evidence of the making of a false statement.

The inclusion of a reference to statements made by way of a picture is also important where a misleading impression is created by a photograph taken from an unusual angle or where a property developer misleads a potential purchaser by means of an artist's impression of the intended appearance of a particular building. This is consistent with the approach taken under the Trade Descriptions Act 1968 in relation to misleading statements about services, although the wording of the 1991 Act is more explicit. The Trade Descriptions Act 1968 refers to anything, whether or not a statement, 'likely to be taken for' a statement as to a prohibited matter, and this has been taken to cover a misleading artist's impression of the appearance of holiday accommodation (see *R v Clarksons Holidays Ltd* (1972) 57 Cr App R 38 and see also chapter 17 regarding the issue of falsity).

For the purposes of the 1991 Act, an offending statement may also be made by any method of signifying meaning. It is generally thought that this provision is intended to cover 'off-plan' sales of new houses by property developers. Thus if property details are prepared by a builder which give a false indication of the nature of the houses to be built as part of a particular development, this may constitute the commission of an offence. A difficulty which may arise in this context is whether non-factual statements, such as a future warranty, may give rise to liability. It has been seen already that such statements may not give rise to liability under the Trade Descriptions Act 1968, s. 14, if they amount to no more than an aspiration regarding the nature of the service to be provided. However, in the case of property particulars prepared by a builder, it is likely that detailed advance planning by the builder will normally make it possible to ascertain whether an indication given in the particulars is believed in by the builder. If this is the case, it is more likely that indications given in those particulars will be treated as containing implied statements of fact. What matters in this context is what a reasonable person may be expected to infer from the statement made by the developer (Property Misdescriptions Act 1991, s. 1(5)(b)).

A further consideration is whether an offending statement must be made for any particular purpose in order to attract liability. It has been held that some provisions of the Trade Descriptions Act 1968 require an offending statement to be capable of inducing a purchase (see chapter 17), but it would appear that the Property Misdescriptions Act 1991 is not so confined. The 1991 Act appears to be concerned with the mischief of misleading a possible house purchaser into incurring unnecessary expense in viewing property which is unsuited to his needs. If this is the case, it would seem to follow that the 1991 Act is concerned with misleading statements made before the stage of exchange of contracts (Office of Fair Trading, *Estate Agency* (1990) para. 4(1)(c)), but there is no requirement in the Act that the statement must be capable of inducing a purchase. Provided the offending statement is made in the course of an estate agency or property development business and it is capable of causing unnecessary expenditure to be incurred, an offence would appear to be committed. Thus, a misleading statement made in the course of a business by estate agent X, which is relayed by estate agent Y to a potential purchaser might result in the successful prosecution of X if Y is able to show that he has taken reasonable steps and exercised due diligence to avoid committing an offence.

Since the 1991 Act appears to be concerned with factual statements which are capable of misleading a potential purchaser, it is necessary to consider whether mere trade puffs fall within the provisions of the Act. It has been seen already that trade puffs normally do not generate civil liability for misrepresentation (see chapter 4) and that apart from certain trade puffs uttered by car dealers which reflect upon the roadworthiness of the vehicles they sell, a trade puff will not amount to an actionable trade description (see chapter 17). Some statements to be found in estate agents' promotional material may fall within this category. For example, purchasers have been told, uninformatively, that a property has a unique location with panoramic views or is magnificently decorated. The general rule applied in misrepresentation cases would seem to suggest that no offence is committed in such circumstances, but it should also be appreciated that apparent puffs may contain an implied factual element capable of misleading a purchaser. The important question to ask is what interpretation would an ordinary person give to the words used by the defendant. In the same way, apparent puffs relating to property should be regarded as falling within the prohibition created by the 1991 Act if an ordinary person could attribute some factual meaning to the statement in question. Thus if property has been described, in general terms, as being in immaculate condition when it has an untidy garden or has defective guttering or foundations, it might be possible to regard the word 'immaculate' as misleading because of what it fails to disclose.

A further consideration is whether references in the 1991 Act to statements can include an omission to mention relevant facts. In this regard, the 1991 Act provides that a statement is misleading (though not false) if what a reasonable person may be expected to infer from it, or from any omission from it, is false (Property Misdescriptions Act 1991, s. 1(5)(b)). What this would appear to cover is a failure to qualify a positive statement capable of misleading a purchaser rather than a simple omission of information which some purchasers might regard as relevant to their potential purchase. Thus if a house is described as having a 'fine slate roof', the statement would be misleading if half the slates on the roof are missing, since the word 'fine' disguises the fact that the roof is not in good order. The guiding principle in these circumstances is that if the estate agent has any doubts about the accuracy of his lyrical prose, he should leave it out altogether.

Pure omissions appear not to give rise to liability on the ground that the 1991 Act does not impose a duty of positive disclosure of relevant facts. However, it is a well-established principle of the law of misrepresentation that a statement can be misleading by virtue of what it does not say. Being economical with the truth can be as misleading as deliberately telling a lie. Thus it might be open to a court to regard as misleading a literally true statement to the effect that a house has panoramic cliff views when the house is about to fall into the sea or when a house built on a dirty canal bank is described as having a pleasant waterfront aspect. It is important to appreciate that this does not amount to a general duty of positive disclosure, but merely requires the maker of the statement to give facts which are relevant to the statement he has made, particularly where that statement is capable of acting as an inducement to a prospective purchaser.

18.2.3.3 False to a material degree The 1991 Act provides that a person will only be guilty of an offence if his statement is false to a material degree (s. 1(5)(a)). This appears to use wording identical to that found in the Trade Descriptions Act 1968 (see chapter 17). Accordingly, statements which are literally inaccurate, but would not mislead a potential purchaser should not attract liability under the 1991 Act. For example, suppose houses on a new development were described as having 'Georgian' windows. On a literal interpretation, 'Georgian' windows could be said to be those installed during the reign of George III, but it would be patently obvious to a purchaser that a house on a recent development would not have windows of such antiquity. Strictly, it would be more accurate to describe the windows as being of 'Georgian style', but it is unlikely that the description 'Georgian' would be regarded as false to a material degree.

Whether or not a description is false to a material degree is likely to be judged objectively, with the result that if a reasonable person would be misled, an offence is committed under the 1991 Act whether or not potential purchasers have shown any interest in the house concerned.

18.2.3.4 Statutory defences Consistent with other consumer protection legislation which creates criminal offences of strict liability, the truly innocent offender is provided with a range of defences. It is provided that it is a defence for a person charged with an offence to show that he took all reasonable steps and exercised all due diligence to avoid the commission of an offence (Property Misdescriptions Act 1991, s. 2(1) and see also chapter 13). If this defence is raised in conjunction with an allegation that the offence was committed due to reliance on information supplied by another, the person charged must prove that reliance on that source of information was reasonable in all the circumstances of the case (s. 2(2)(a)). The reasonableness of this reliance is to be judged by reference to those steps which were taken or might reasonably have been taken in order to verify the truth of the information given (ibid.) and whether the person charged had any reasonable ground for disbelieving the information supplied (s. 2(2)(b)).

It follows from these provisions that an estate agent may commit an offence if he publishes inaccurate information based on what he has been told by the prospective vendor of the property or by another estate agent. Under s. 2(2), the onus rests on the estate agent charged with the commission of an offence to establish the reasonableness of his reliance on the information supplied. There is nothing in the 1991 Act which allows the prosecution of the vendor, even where he has deliberately fed the estate agent with false information. It is for the estate agent to ensure that the information given to him by the vendor is accurate which might serve to destroy the client–agent relationship, since in order to be safe, estate agents might feel inclined to disbelieve virtually all information supplied by the client. For example, estate agents might consider it necessary to check whether property is protected by a valid woodworm and dry rot guarantee, whether local authority permission has been granted to lower the kerb outside a house so as to allow vehicular access and whether the slates on the roof of a 100-year-old cottage are really 'Welsh slate'. The time taken to glean this information might be such that the estate agent is forced to delay putting the house on the market with the result that a potential sale could be lost. It seems, however, that the courts may not insist upon every possible precaution being taken. For example in *Enfield London*

Borough Council v *Castle Estate Agents* (1996) 160 JP 618 the defendants were
instructed to sell a four-bedroom semi-detached house with an annexe which
had been fitted out as a one-bedroom bungalow. The defendant's surveyor
asked if planning permission had been granted for the annexe and was told,
falsely, that it had. Despite the fact that the defendants failed to check the
accuracy of the owner's assertion with the local authority register, it was held
that reasonable precautions had been taken.

The Act provides that where the person charged seeks to allege that the
offence is committed due to reliance on information supplied by another or due
to the act or default of another, the defence will not be available unless seven
clear days' notice has been served on the prosecution (s. 2(3)). This notice must
specify such information identifying or assisting in the identification of the
person guilty of the act or default or of supplying the inaccurate information as is
in the possession of the person charged at the time of serving the notice (s. 2(4)).

18.2.3.5 Disclaimers of liability A further issue is whether an estate
agent or property developer may escape liability under the 1991 Act by means
of a disclaimer notice, a practice first developed under the Trade Descriptions
Act 1968 (see chapter 17).

It has been seen that for the purposes of the Trade Descriptions Act 1968,
the greatest use of disclaimers has been in relation to the passive offence of
supplying goods to which a trade description is applied and that generally a
disclaimer will be of no use in relation to the active offence of applying a false
trade description. It has been held that in order to be effective the disclaimer
must be communicated to the purchaser at or before the time the offence is
committed and must be as bold, precise and compelling as the trade
description itself, so that the effect of the description on the mind of the
purchaser is nullified. Understood in this sense, the disclaimer prevents the
consumer from being misled at all by wiping out the effect of the erstwhile
misleading statement before any offence is committed.

The offence under the Property Misdescriptions Act 1991, s. 1(1), is
committed when a false or misleading statement about a prescribed matter is
made in the course of a business. Accordingly, the disclaimer would have to
be communicated to the purchaser at or before the time at which a false
statement is made by or on behalf of the estate agent.

For the purposes of the offence of making a statement which is known to
be false in the Trade Descriptions Act 1968, s. 14(1), it has been held that a
statement can be made in a number of different ways, for example, by
communication of information to others and by doing business on the
strength of uncorrected and misleading material (see 18.1.1.2 above). On this
basis, a statement is made by an estate agent when property particulars are
published and on each occasion a prospective purchaser reads a misleading
statement and is induced to view the property therein described. In the light
of this interpretation, a disclaimer would have to be issued at or before the
time the misleading information was first published because, from that time
onwards, an offence is committed if the property particulars contain false or
misleading information.

NINETEEN

Misleading price indications

All manufacturers and suppliers will want to promote their products in a way that will increase sales. A common promotion practice is the publication of claims about the price at which goods or services are supplied, since consumers will often make a purchase if they think they are getting good value for money. If such price campaigns are to be considered acceptable by the law and by relevant codes of practice, it is essential that they do not mislead the consumer.

19.1 BACKGROUND TO THE PRESENT LEGISLATION

The history of the regulation of price claims dates back to the Trade Descriptions Act 1968, s. 11, the provisions of which were subsequently augmented by the Price Marking (Bargain Offers) Orders (SI 1979/364, 633 and 1124). It has been seen already that the provisions of s. 1 of the Trade Descriptions Act 1968 were seen as augmenting and improving existing legislation (i.e., the Merchandise Marks Acts 1887 to 1953) but that the other provisions of the Act, s. 11 included, were novel provisions. Because of the novelty of the provisions in s. 14 of the 1968 Act it was considered appropriate to expect the prosecution to satisfy a limited *mens rea* requirement, but the same was not considered appropriate under s. 11 in respect of price indications.

In the relatively short period between 1968 and 1987 it was considered necessary to replace the provisions of s. 11 with what proved to be the almost unenforceable provisions of the Price Marking (Bargain Offers) Orders 1979, which, in turn, were replaced by the provisions of the Consumer Protection Act 1987, part III. Little thought appeared to have been given to the most effective means of controlling price comparisons, which probably explains why so many amendments to the relevant legislation became necessary. Certainly, unlike the provisions of s. 1 and s. 14, which were based upon a detailed consideration by the Molony Committee on Consumer Protection

(Cmnd 1781, 1962), what became s. 11 was not based upon any law reform body proposals. Legislation in this area seems to have been a late after-thought.

The Trade Descriptions Act 1968, s. 11, was too limited in its scope, and there were numerous misleading statements about price were not covered by its provisions. It prohibited three types of price indication in relation to the supply of goods only, namely, false comparisons with a recommended price (Trade Descriptions Act 1968, s. 11(1)(a)), false comparisons with the retailer's own previous price (s. 11(1)(b)), and false or misleading indications that the price of goods was equal to or less than the actual selling price (s. 11(2)).

The provisions on recommended prices, if anything, may have contributed to an increased use of this type of comparison by highlighting the fact that such price indications could be used legitimately within the framework created by the 1968 Act. A particular problem in this regard was that manufacturers of certain goods adopted the practice of recommending unrealistically high retail selling prices so as to allow retailers to advertise their products at apparently amazingly reduced prices. However, in fact, few retailers ever sold goods at the price recommended by the manufacturer.

The offence of falsely comparing a selling price for goods with a price previously charged by the retailer making the comparison also attracted criticism. In particular, for reasons considered below, it was possible to use s. 11(1)(b) as a means of legitimately disguising a price rise in such a way as to put it across as a price reduction! Nothing in the 1968 Act had any effect on comparisons with the price charged by other traders, 'value' and 'worth' claims and, perhaps more seriously, misleading price information in relation to the supply of services, accommodation or facilities.

Perhaps the most successful provision to be found in the old s. 11, reflected in the fact that it was the provision that generated the most case law, was s. 11(2), which created the offence of giving a false or misleading indication that the price of goods was equal to or less than the actual selling price. Much of what was contained in s. 11(2) has been retained and reappears as part of the Consumer Protection Act 1987 with some additions to take account of new practices developed to try to get round the 1968 legislation.

The Price Marking (Bargain Offers) Orders 1979 were very badly drafted with the result that enforcement authorities were never too sure whether to mount a prosecution or not and the business community could not be sure that what appeared to them to be perfectly legitimate advertising practices would not infringe their provisions. A number of apparently misleading practices remained lawful because of the poor drafting of the Orders and, perhaps most seriously, the Orders allowed businesses to devise new price comparisons, some of which were uninformative at best and downright misleading at worst.

To meet these criticisms, ss. 20 to 26 of the Consumer Protection Act 1987 introduce an entirely new regime based on a general offence of misleading pricing (s. 20(1)) supplemented by the Code of Practice for Traders on Price Indications (Department of Trade, 1988) indicating what statements are to be regarded as misleading and what is acceptable (Consumer Protection Act 1987, s. 25) and a rule-making power which will allow the Secretary of State to regulate the circumstances in which and the manner in which specified price indications may be made and to identify indications which may be regarded as misleading (s. 26). Regulations can be made in response to any new practices developed by retailers.

Section 20 provides:

(1)   Subject to the following provisions of this part, a person shall be guilty of an offence if, in the course of any business of his, he gives (by any means whatever) to any consumers an indication which is misleading as to the price at which any goods, services, accommodation or facilities are available (whether generally or from particular persons).

(2)   Subject as aforesaid, a person shall be guilty of an offence if—

(a)   in the course of any business of his, he has given an indication to any consumers which, after it was given, has become misleading as mentioned in subs. (1) above; and

(b)   some or all of those consumers might reasonably be expected to rely on the indication at a time after it has become misleading; and

(c)   he fails to take all such steps as are reasonable to prevent those consumers from relying on the indication.

(3)   For the purposes of this section, it shall be immaterial—

(a)   whether the person who gives or gave the indication is or was acting on his own behalf or on behalf of another;

(b)   whether or not that person is the person, or included among the persons, from whom the goods, services, accommodation or facilities are available; and

(c)   whether the indication is or has become misleading in relation to all the consumers to whom it is or was given or only in relation to some of them. . . .

(6)   In this part—

'consumer'—

(a)   in relation to any goods, means any person who might wish to be supplied with the goods for his own private use or consumption;

(b)   in relation to any services or facilities, means any person who might wish to be provided with the services or facilities otherwise than for the purposes of any business of his; and

(c)   in relation to any accommodation, means any person who might wish to occupy the accommodation otherwise than for the purposes of any business of his;

'price', in relation to any goods, services, accommodation or facilities, means—

(a)   the aggregate of the sums required to be paid by a consumer for or otherwise in respect of the supply of the goods, or the provision of the services, accommodation or facilities; or

(b)   except in s. 21 below, any method which will be or has been applied for the purpose of determining that aggregate.

The principal offence created by s. 20(1) consists of giving an indication which is misleading, which includes an indication that the price payable for goods, services, accommodation or facilities is lower than the amount actually charged by the supplier. The Act also applies to indications which although initially true, later become misleading (s. 20(2)), thereby creating an alternative offence to that in s. 20(1), which is a general umbrella offence in relation to price indications which are misleading from the outset.

The difference between the two offences was a matter considered in *Toys 'R' Us* v *Gloucestershire County Council* (1994) 158 JP 338, in which the appellants had sold certain toys at the price displayed on the check-out visual display, which was a higher price than that shown on a ticket attached to the goods. The appellants were charged with the commission of an offence under s. 20(1), in that they had given a misleading indication as to the price at which goods were available. The appellants argued that it was their intention to sell at the ticket price rather than the visual display price, since counter assistants had instructions always to alter the selling price in the customer's favour should there be a discrepancy. It was therefore their contention that the commission of the offence was due to a failure by a member of staff to follow procedures. Because of this it was argued that the visual display could not be regarded as an indication of the price at which the goods *were available* since that price was always intended by the appellants to be the ticket price. It was therefore suggested that if any offence had been committed, it was under s. 20(2) which was not referred to in the indictment.

It was observed that the wording of s. 20(1) does not require the court to ascertain whether the goods were sold at the correct price, merely to ascertain whether any price indication relating to the price at which goods are available is misleading or not (ibid. 342 per Kennedy LJ). For these purposes, the relevant time to consider is the time when the price indication was given, which in this case was when the goods were displayed on the shelf. Accordingly, no offence under s. 20(1) was committed. Conversely, if there was evidence that check-out assistants consistently charged the higher price on the visual display rather than the ticket price, s. 20(1) would apply (ibid. 343 per Kennedy LJ), but in the present case, there was sufficient evidence that the appellants intended to charge the ticket price.

The appellants' concession that there might have been an offence under s. 20(2) was also considered inappropriate since it could not be said that the ticket price became misleading when a different price was shown on the visual display. What s. 20(2) was intended to cover was the correct price indication which is subsequently overtaken by later events, for example, where X compares his price with that of Y and Y subsequently changes his prices, but X fails to alter his price indication.

19.2 CODE OF PRACTICE AND REGULATIONS

Some difficulties have arisen over the status of the Code of Practice and proposed Regulations. The Consumer Protection Act 1987, s. 25(2)(a), provides that a contravention of the Code may be relied upon as evidence of the commission of an offence under s. 20 and for the purposes of negativing a defence. Section 25(2)(b) provides that compliance with the requirements of the Code may be taken as evidence that no offence has been committed or that the person charged has a defence. The final wording of s. 25(2) represents a victory for the consumer protection lobby, since the original intention of the government was to make compliance with the Code an absolute defence. The effect of the present provisions, however, is to create an element of uncertainty in relation to the question of criminal liability.

The Code of Practice lists a number of practices which have been recognised as misleading for some time. Consumer groups, representatives of enforcement authorities and the Retail Consortium have argued, with some justification, that such recognised practices should be governed directly by regulations which render them unlawful. However, it would appear that the government is resisting such a move (see Bragg (1988) 51 MLR 210, 211). If such practices are not declared illegal, it follows from the provisions of s. 25(2) that contravention of the Code of Practice is merely evidence of the commission of an offence.

19.3 LIABILITY FOR THE COMMISSION OF AN OFFENCE UNDER SECTION 20

The offences created by s. 20 possess some common elements. In particular, the offender must act 'in the course of a business of his' and there must be an indication of price given to a consumer within the definition of those words given in the 1987 Act.

19.3.1 Business activities
The general rules on what constitutes a business activity will apply (see chapter 1), but, because of the words 'business of his', the only person who may be guilty of an offence is the person who runs the business. This was decided by the House of Lords in *Warwickshire County Council* v *Johnson* [1993] 1 All ER 299, in which it was held that a branch manager of a national retail store committed no offence under s. 20 where he had displayed a notice to the effect that Dixons would beat any price for televisions, hi-fi and video recorders by £20 'on the spot' but failed to honour the pledge. It was accepted that the employers were able to rely on the statutory due diligence defence under s. 39 of the 1987 Act (see chapter 13), but the enforcement authority decided to prosecute the defendant under the bypass procedure (as to which see chapter 13). In reaching the conclusion that the prosecution should fail, the House of Lords held that the intention of Parliament was clearly that individuals should not be prosecuted since the view had been expressed in Parliamentary debate that the inclusion of the words 'in the course of any business of his' should be taken to mean 'any business of which the defendant is either the owner, or in which he has a controlling interest' ([1993] 1 All ER 299, 304 per Lord Roskill; cf. *Whitehead* v *Collett* [1975] Crim LR 53 under the Trade Descriptions Act 1968, s. 11). Immunity from prosecution does not extend to more senior officers of a company, such as

members of the board of directors or the company secretary, and perhaps even area managers if they are classified as part of the directing mind and will of the company (see chapter 13). Senior officers are treated as being part of the company, and they too may be proceeded against personally if the offence was committed with their consent or connivance or where the offence is attributable to the neglect of the senior officer concerned (Consumer Protection Act 1987, s. 40(2)).

If a person does act in the course of a business of his, it does not matter that he acts in a secondary capacity, since s. 20(3)(a) applies the provisions of s. 20(1) and (2) to price indications made by an agent. Thus, commission agents selling goods on behalf of the owner may be guilty of an offence under the Act where they give a misleading indication of the price at which the goods are sold. But it is the agent acting in the course of his business who is liable rather than the principal he represents.

19.3.2 Consumer

An offence under s. 20 is committed only where a misleading indication is given to any consumer. Thus a misleading price indication given in the course of negotiations between two business contracting parties will give rise to no liability under the 1987 Act. It has been observed that the reason for the wording of s. 20(1) in this respect is to exclude liability in cases where a retailer buys from a wholesaler (*Toys 'R' Us* v *Gloucestershire County Council* (1994) 158 JP 338, 344 per Kennedy LJ). Similarly, the supply of goods which by their nature cannot have been intended for private use or consumption, such as the supply of dental equipment which would be used only by a dentist in the course of a business would not fall within the scope of s. 20 (*MFI Furniture Centre Ltd* v *Hibbert* (1996) 160 JP 178, 181 per Balcombe LJ). Conversely, the language used does not prevent a successful prosecution where a misleading price indication is noticed by a trading standards officer on duty. While the officer might not want to be supplied with the goods or services for personal use, he does still act on behalf of members of the public who might wish to be supplied with the goods or services concerned (ibid.).

A consumer is defined as a person who might wish to be *supplied* with goods for his own private use or consumption (s. 20(6)(a); see further chapter 1) with the result that a car dealer who falsely understates the trade-in value of a second-hand car with a view to buying it cheaply from a consumer commits no offence, since the misleading indication is not related to a supply to a consumer. If the same statement is linked to a part-exchange deal, it is arguable that it would fall within the provisions of s. 20, since it would then be partly related to the supply of the new car (see Bragg (1988) 51 MLR 210, 214).

The fact that s. 20(1) makes it an offence to give a misleading indication to any consumers, might be taken to indicate that a specimen consumer must be produced to give evidence about the misleading nature of the price indication under consideration. However, it is clear now that this is not the case (*MFI Furniture Centre Ltd* v *Hibbert* (1996) 160 JP 178) since to hold otherwise would deprive s. 20 of much of its effect (ibid. 181–2 per Balcombe LJ).

The provisions of the 1987 Act in relation to services, facilities and accommodation and those relating to the supply of goods have slightly different wording, and it is possible that they provide different protection. For the purposes of services, facilities and accommodation, the definition of 'consumer' covers only persons who might wish to be supplied with the service etc. otherwise than for the purposes of a business (s. 20(6)(b) and (c)). The emphasis in relation to goods is whether the consumer might wish to be supplied with goods for his own private use (s. 20(6)(a)) whereas the emphasis in relation to services etc. is whether the consumer does not wish to be supplied with a service for business purposes.

19.3.3 Price
In order for giving a misleading indication to be an offence under the Consumer Protection Act 1987, s. 20, the misleading indication must relate to a price, which is defined as meaning the aggregate (or the method of calculating the aggregate) of the sums required to be paid by the consumer (s. 20(6)). Accordingly, if a mandatory payment requirement, such as the VAT element, is omitted from the price quoted, an offence is committed (s. 21(1)(c) and see also *Richards* v *Westminster Motors Ltd* [1976] RTR 88 decided under the 1968 Act, s. 11(2)).

A matter which raises some difficulty is whether an estimate or a quotation for the purposes of s. 20. Since a quotation is an unconditional offer to supply at the price quoted (*Gilbert & Partners* v *Knight* [1968] 2 All ER 248) it will relate to a price, and an offence will be committed if the quotation is not adhered to. However, an estimate is not a fixed price, and is not capable of acceptance as an offer to supply at the price stated (*Croshaw* v *Pritchard* (1899) 16 TLR 45) with the result that the supplier could make a reasonable charge which may not be the same as the amount estimated (Supply of Goods and Services Act 1982, s. 14, and see also chapter 8). On this basis, it is difficult to see how an inaccurate estimate can be regarded as an indication of price (cf. Merkin, *A Guide to the Consumer Protection Act 1987*, p. 95), unless estimates can be taken to fall within the meaning of the phrase 'a method which will be applied' in s. 20(6)(b). However, it seems more likely that estimates will not be covered by the 1987 Act since the definition of a 'price' in s. 20(6) refers to a sum which the consumer will be required to pay. Since the supplier is not bound to charge the amount specified in his estimate, the amount specified can hardly be regarded as something which is required to be paid.

19.3.4 Misleading indications as to the price at which goods, services, accommodation or facilities are available
Section 20(1) applies to misleading indications as to the price at which goods or services etc. are available. While this will apply to a very wide range of misleading statements, it would appear that if the indication relates to something which is not available, no offence is committed. Thus, the indication 'Special Offer Widgets only 50p' would not amount to the commission of an offence if Widgets are not stocked on the premises

concerned. However, if the promotional offer relates to 'free' goods supplied with a specified purchase, the Trade Descriptions Act 1968, s. 1, may apply (*Denard* v *Smith* (1990) 155 JP 253 and see chapter 17). If the price indication is given in a post-contractual invoice it cannot relate to the availability of the goods, particularly if a different price indication was given at the time of contracting (*Miller* v *F.A. Sadd & Son Ltd* [1981] 3 All ER 265). Accordingly, if such an indication does not relate to the price at which the goods are available, it would appear that s. 20 also fails to apply in such circumstances (see Merkin, *A Guide to the Consumer Protection Act 1987*, p. 93).

Since the offence is giving a misleading indication of the price at which goods are available, it is necessary to consider when the relevant indication is given (see *Toys 'R' Us* v *Gloucestershire County Council* (1994) 158 JP 338 considered in 19.1, above).

Section 20(1) specifies that the indication may relate to availability generally or from particular persons. So a misleading indication in respect of the price charged by the advertiser himself or that charged by another trader or traders generally will fall within the prohibition. Thus inaccurate indications such as 'Was £50, now £40' or 'Smith's price £30' or 'West End price £60' will offend against s. 20(1). Section 20 is concerned with indications rather than comparisons, so that the reference to 'Smith's price' does not have to involve a comparison between the advertiser's price and that charged by Smith.

19.3.5 Indications which become misleading
By virtue of s. 20(2) an indication which is initially true but which later becomes misleading may result in the commission of an offence if it is reasonable to expect some consumers to rely on it subsequently and the person giving the indication has not taken all reasonable steps to prevent consumers from relying on it. For example, if a tour operator stipulates in its summer holiday brochure that a price for a self-catering holiday is inclusive of additional charges, but subsequently discovers that the owner of the accommodation proposes to make additional charges on site, the tour operator would need to take reasonable action (as to which see Code of Practice, paras 3.4.2. and 3.4.3) to inform clients who had read the brochure before the operator was informed of the change. Newspaper and magazine advertisements which refer to the price of goods or services are liable to become out of date, and so are capable of falling within s. 20(2). The supplier of the advertised goods should specify for how long the advertised price will last and if he fails to do so, it is assumed that the price advertised remains in force for seven days or until the publication in which the advertisement appeared is next published (Code of Practice, para. 3.2; see also para 3.3 regarding mail order advertisements).

Where a person has already entered into a contract in reliance on a statement which later becomes inaccurate, but the consumer is not due to make payment until a later stage, the trader is advised to cancel any such transaction (Code of Practice, para. 3.1.1).

19.3.6 Misleading indications

The cornerstone of the pricing regime created by the 1987 Act is the definition of 'misleading'. Earlier attempts at the control of misleading price indications were tied to a supply or an offer to supply goods, but s. 20(1) refers simply to 'an indication which is misleading'.

19.3.6.1 Indication It will be sufficient that a misleading statement about a price is displayed or published. Thus a price display in a supermarket window which does not accord with the price printed on the goods or on the shelves may result in an offence being committed and there will be no need to consider whether the offer price or the shelf price is the price to be charged (cf. *J. Sainsbury Ltd* v *West Midlands County Council* (1982) 90 ITSA Monthly Review 58).

How the indication is given does not matter due to the inclusion of the words 'by any means whatever' in s. 20(1). Standard methods of communicating price indications will fall within these words, but so also will an oral communication by an employee of the seller or a display read from a bar code at the checkout. Thus if there is a difference between the display and a price marked on the goods or the shelf, an offence is committed, subject to whether or not there has been an earlier, accurate, indication of the price at which the goods are available (see *Toys 'R' Us* v *Gloucestershire County Council* (1994) 158 JP 338 considered in 19.1).

The use of the word 'indication' in s. 20 is deliberate and is apt to cover a much wider range of statements than would be covered by the word 'representation'. Speaking of the Trade Descriptions Act 1968, s. 11(2), which also successfully used the word 'indication' in the definition of the offence it created, Melford Stevenson J said in *Doble* v *David Greig Ltd* [1972] 1 WLR 703, at p. 710, that:

> The use of the word 'indication' as distinct from some such word as 'representation' plainly shows . . . that the section . . . is intended to extend over conduct or signs of many different kinds, and its width and significance cannot be too widely and clearly recognised.

19.3.6.2 Misleading The definition of the word 'misleading' is to be found in s. 21, which has to be read in conjunction with the Code of Practice for Traders on Price Indications which, without specifically identifying which parts of s. 21 apply, does give guidance on what type of price indication should not be used. Section 21(1) states:

> For the purposes of s. 20 above an indication given to any consumers is misleading as to a price if what is conveyed by the indication, or what those consumers might reasonably be expected to infer from the indication or any omission from it, includes any of the following, that is to say—
> (a)   that the price is less than in fact it is;
> (b)   that the applicability of the price does not depend on facts or circumstances on which its applicability does in fact depend;
> (c)   that the price covers matters in respect of which an additional charge is in fact made;

(d)   that a person who in fact has no such expectation—
    (i)   expects the price to be increased or reduced (whether or not at a particular time or by a particular amount); or
    (ii)   expects the price, or the price as increased or reduced, to be maintained (whether or not for a particular period); or
(e)   that the facts or circumstances by reference to which consumers might reasonably be expected to judge the validity of any relevant comparison made or implied by the indication are not what in fact they are.

Section 21 provides that in order to determine whether an indication is misleading, it is necessary to consider what is conveyed by the indication and what those consumers to whom it is addressed might reasonably infer from it or any omission from it.

The fact that an omission may give rise to liability is important, since this places the onus on the promoter to ensure that his price indications are as explicit as possible. Thus if the price indication does not reveal that it is only available to old age pensioners or is limited to the first 100 purchases made in the shop, or that a promotional offer on a three-piece suite applies only to suites of a particular colour (*Sweeting* v *Northern Upholstery Ltd* (1982) 2 TrLR 5), it is misleading by virtue of what it omits.

The opening words of s. 21(1) import both objective and subjective elements. What is conveyed by the indication is presumably to be judged objectively. It is also necessary to consider what might reasonably be inferred from the indication by those consumers to whom it is addressed, thereby importing a subjective element to the test. If a consumer places an unusual interpretation on a particular indication, it may be regarded as misleading, provided it is not an unreasonable interpretation. This would appear to be roughly consistent with the approach adopted under the Trade Descriptions Act 1968, s. 11(2), in *Doble* v *David Greig Ltd* [1972] 1 WLR 703 where it was emphasised that what matters is the effect of the misleading indication upon the mind of the consumer. It follows that the provision was intended to apply to ambiguities. Thus in *Doble* v *David Greig Ltd* a label on a bottle of fruit cordial was interpreted by the consumer to mean that the price would be 5s 5d (5s 9d − 4d. deposit) whereas the retailer understood the label to mean that the price was 5s 9d after the 4d deposit had been deducted. Since either was considered to be a possible interpretation of the language used, it was considered that there was a misleading indication since the consumer interpretation was a reasonable one to apply.

Similarly, if a price is stated exclusive of VAT and the purchaser reasonably believes that the price stated is that which he will have to pay, an offence is committed, because what is important is not the amount which the seller seeks to obtain, but the effect of the price indication on the mind of the person to whom goods or services are being offered (*Richards* v *Westminster Motors Ltd* [1976] RTR 88, 93 per Waller J).

19.3.6.3 Indications that the price is less than in fact it is (s. 21(1)(a))   This amounts to a re-enactment of the offence created by the Trade Descriptions Act 1968, s. 11(2), except that it is not confined to a supply or an offer to supply, but covers any indication and, unlike the 1968 Act, the new provision covers more than just goods. An offence is committed where a consumer is misled as to the amount he will have to pay for goods, services, accommodation or facilities. It appears that a *de minimis* approach will be adopted to the question whether an isolated occurrence of the giving of a misleading price indication amounts to the commission of an offence. For example, in *Berkshire County Council* v *Olympic Holidays Ltd* (1993) 13 TrLR 251 the defendants technically offended against s. 20(1) when there was a difference of some £182 between the price of a holiday advertised in a tour operator's brochure and the price displayed on a computer screen in a travel agent's shop, caused by a computer error. Even though the higher price was charged, it was considered that no offence was committed, principally on the ground that the due diligence defence had been made out (see also 13.4.1.2). A further matter accepted on appeal was that this was a unique case and since the computer had not previously malfunctioned, the risk of a consumer being misled was so small that it would be wrong to convict.

Since s. 21(1)(a) includes the offence created by s. 11(2) of the 1968 Act, the case law under that provision remains relevant. Established contraventions of s. 11(2) included overcharging where a price list has been displayed (*Whitehead* v *Collett* [1975] Crim LR 53); quoting a price applicable only to cash sales (*Read Brothers Cycles (Leyton) Ltd* v *Waltham Forest London Borough Council* [1978] RTR 397); indicating a reduced price which applies only to a limited range of goods (*North Western Gas Board* v *Aspden* [1975] Crim LR 301; Code para. 2.2.2) and quoting a VAT-exclusive price (*Richards* v *Westminster Motors Ltd* [1976] RTR 88).

In respect of VAT-exclusive prices, the Code of Practice gives useful guidance to traders, stipulating that where they deal with private consumers, prices should always include VAT (para. 2.2.6.). Prices may be indicated exclusive of VAT where the preponderance of business is with trade customers, but if consumer customers also frequent a trader's premises, there should be a clear indication that prices exclude VAT (para. 2.2.7.). Special provision is made for suppliers of professional services and for building work where the final charge may be uncertain. For example, an estate agent is advised either to quote a fee which includes VAT or to state 'fee 1.5 per cent of purchase price plus 17.5 per cent VAT' (para. 2.2.8).

Since VAT rates can change, there is the possibility that a trader may commit an offence where his statement of charges later becomes misleading. In these circumstances, the trader is advised to make the change clear to the consumer before he is committed to buying goods affected by the change (Code, para. 3.5.1).

If the trader displays goods in a particular form, but supplies them in a different state, any price indication must state that the price indicated does not apply to the goods in the state they are displayed. Thus, a supplier of flat-pack furniture should make it clear that the price advertised does not apply to ready-assembled furniture (Code, para. 2.2.3).

There is also special advice for suppliers who make an additional charge for postage and packaging or for delivery. Such traders are advised to make a consumer aware of any such additional charges before he is committed to buy (Code, paras 2.2.4 and 2.2.5). If there is any doubt about what the charge might be, it will be sufficient to state that, for example, current Royal Mail rates apply.

Retailers may also be faced with problems emanating from promotional material printed on goods supplied by the manufacturer. These 'flash offers', which may either offer a reduction in price or offer additional goods free of charge or at a reduced rate should be complied with by the retailer in order to avoid the commission of an offence (Code, para. 1.7.1). Since the test of what is misleading is based on the reasonable interpretation of the particular consumer reading the price indication, any ambiguity in the flash offer will be construed against the retailer (*Doble* v *David Greig Ltd* [1972] 1 WLR 703).

The provisions of the Trade Descriptions Act 1968 applied only to price indications in respect of goods, but the Consumer Protection Act 1987 applies also to indications in respect of services, facilities and accommodation. It has been seen in chapter 18 that the Trade Descriptions Act 1968, s. 14, did not give any definition of what constitutes a service, a facility or any accommodation and that the matter was left for judicial definition. In contrast, for the purposes of its provisions on price indications, the Consumer Protection Act 1987, s. 21(1), provides a non-exhaustive list of what may be regarded as services or facilities, which includes credit, banking and insurance services; the purchase of foreign currency; the supply of electricity; the provision of off-street car parks and arragements for keeping caravans on land where the caravan is not used as a permanent residence.

Restaurants and hotels may require customers to pay a mandatory service charge. Such a charge must be clearly displayed where it can be seen by customers before they place their orders (Code, para. 2.2.10). Charges for holidays may differ according to the time of year when they are taken, but it is common practice for travel agents to display a range of different holidays and their respective costs. In these circumstances, it is important that the consumer understands what he will get for the price paid. Travel agents are advised that consumers should be made fully aware of the basic price for a holiday and what is included in the price. Details of optional extras and their cost should also be provided (Code, para. 2.2.12).

Some tradesmen, such as plumbers and electricians may impose a call-out charge. If this is the case, the supplier is advised to ensure that the consumer is made aware of such charges prior to the supply of the service (Code, para. 2.2.17).

19.3.6.4 Prices dependent on facts which have not been made clear (s. 21(1)(b)) Arguably such an indication may also amount to an indication that the price of goods is less than in fact it is. For example, advertising a promotional offer on a three-piece suite which is only available in respect of goods of a particular colour (*Sweeting* v *Northern Upholstery Ltd* (1983) 2 TrLR 5) might come within either provision. Other price indications which would appear to fall within this provision include promotional offers which require a purchase by a specified date or in conjunction with another purchase. Thus an indication that consumers will be supplied with a free garden hose with every lawnmower purchased will fall within this provision if there is an unstated condition that the offer is only available on purchases above a specified amount.

19.3.6.5 Indications that the price includes matters in respect of which an additional charge is made (s. 21(1)(c)) Again there would appear to be a certain element of overlap with s. 21(1)(a), in that a failure to include a mandatory additional charge, such as VAT in the price stated may fall within both provisions. Section 21(1)(c) also appears to cover offers of free goods, where there is a charge for postage (Code, para 1.10.4 and see Bragg (1988) 51 MLR 210, 217; Howells (1990) 7 TrL 194).

19.3.6.6 Indications that the price is to be increased, reduced or maintained at its present level (s. 21(1)(d)) A price indication is misleading if it suggests that a price is to be increased, when the person giving the indication has no such expectation. An indication will still come within s. 21(1)(d) whether or not the amount of the price rise is specified and whether or not the date of the intended rise is stated. It would appear that the seasonal bout of predictions of the content of the Chancellor of the Exchequer's Budget speech, heralded by notices to the effect that customers should 'Buy now to beat the Budget' could well fall within this provision, if the person giving the notice does not in fact expect that prices will rise. Section 21(1)(d) will also cover the 'everlasting sale', namely the situation in which a retailer displays a sale notice, in the knowledge that prices will not change for some considerable time (see *Westminster City Council* v *Ray Alan (Manshops) Ltd* [1982] 1 WLR 383 decided under the 1968 Act).

Under the Price Marking (Bargain Offers) Order 1979 (SI 1979/364 (as amended)) price comparisons were permitted if the price used as the basis for comparison was one which had been charged in specified different circumstances. The problem this threw up was that some retailers managed to devise bogus prices for the purposes of the Order, so as to be able to suggest that consumers were getting a good deal. One of the more dubious examples of this, which escaped a successful prosecution because the enforcement authority was not satisfied that it would succeed, was the NYPM (next year's price maybe), but misleading indications of this kind would now fall within s. 21(1)(d), on the assumption that the trader has no expectation that a different price will be charged.

These provisions have particular importance in relation to introductory offers and after-sale or after-promotion prices. The guidance given to traders in the Code of Practice is that a promotion should not be called an introductory offer unless the trader intends to continue to offer to sell the product at a higher price after the expiry of the offer period (Code, para. 1.3.1). Where a comparison is made with a future price, the exact nature of the price used as the basis for comparison should be explained. Misleading abbreviations such as ASP (After Sale Price) or APP (After Promotion Price) should be avoided (Code, para. 1.2.4).

The reference in s. 21(1)(d) to intended price reductions is presumably to cover the situation in which a retailer uses a price indication which encourages customers to buy immediately when the retailer expects prices to fall in the future. The paragraph also applies to indications which suggest that a price is to be maintained at a particular level, whether or not for any particular period, when the retailer has no such expectation. This appears to cover statements to the effect that prices will remain at a particular level for a limited period only, when the retailer has not prepared any plans for a change in price.

The effect of s. 21(1)(d) is to render a person criminally liable for a false statement about his intention. The main difficulty which is likely to be encountered in this respect is that it will be necessary to prove, some time after the event, that a person did or did not have a particular intention. This is likely to be no mean feat!

19.3.6.7 Comparisons with another price or value where the facts on which the comparison is based are not stated (s. 21(1)(e))

For the purposes of s. 21(1)(e) and (2)(e), a comparison is defined as a comparison of the price or a method of determining that price with another price or value or any method of calculating such a price or value (whether express or implied and whether past, present or future) (s. 21(3)). This definition is very wide, and it is difficult to imagine any price comparison which escapes the net it creates.

The Code of Practice gives general guidance on the use of comparisons. In particular, it advises traders not to leave the customer guessing and to avoid the use of language which suggests that a comparison is being made (Code, para. 1.1.1). One feature of the previous law was the widespread use of seemingly meaningless abbreviations for prices used as the basis for comparison, some of which were bogus. Examples included the RRP (recommended retail price), the MRP (manufacturer's recommended price), the RAP (ready assembled price), the SOP (special order price), the ASP (after sale price) and the NYPM (next year's price maybe). One feature of the Code of Practice is that abbreviations of this kind should be avoided on the ground that they cause confusion. The Code of Practice is not concerned solely with comparisons with other prices, it also advises traders not to make comparisons with a claimed value of a product or that goods or services are worth a particular amount (Code, para. 1.8). Such claims were prevalent under previous legislation, but the difficulty with the word 'value' is that it has a different meaning to different people. A prohibition of this kind may, however, infringe EC law concerned with free movement of goods (see 19.5, below).

19.3.6.8 Previous selling prices

A common basis for price comparison is the previous price charged by the person giving the price indication for the same or similar goods. Provided the comparison is not misleading, there is no objection to its use, but the unfortunate wording of previous legislation resulted in the development of a number of abuses.

Generally, the trader is advised to state both his present selling price and the higher previous price used as the basis for comparison (Code, para. 1.2.1). Without further qualification, this requirement would still allow the use of 'stale' prices charged many years ago and those charged by chain-stores in another retail outlet (see *Westminster City Council* v *Ray Alan (Manshops) Ltd* [1982] 1 WLR 383) from being used as the basis for comparison.

In order to defeat such misleading practices, the Code of Practice states that the previous price referred to in the indication should be the last price charged and that the goods, service, accommodation or facility should have been available in the outlet at which the indication is given for at least 28 consecutive days in the six months preceding the publication of the indication unless otherwise stated in the indication (Code, para. 1.2.2). A similar provision was to be found in the Trade Descriptions Act 1968, s. 11(3), except that its effect was to operate as part of the definition of the offence, which meant that the onus of proving that the higher price had not been charged in the relevant 28-day period fell upon the prosecution. This meant that the offence under the 1968 Act was virtually unenforceable. In contrast, the operation of the 28 days in six months rule in the Code of Practice operates by way of a defence, which should mean that the onus of proof will be on the trader charged with the commission of an offence.

A further complication with the 28 days in six months rule under the 1968 Act was that there was no requirement that the 28-day period had to immediately precede the publication of the price indication and there was no requirement that the price used as the basis for comparison should have been the last higher price in time to have been charged. The overall effect of the provisions of s. 11(3) of the 1968 Act was that it could be used to disguise a rise in price rather than a price reduction (*House of Holland Ltd* v *Brent London Borough Council* [1971] 2 QB 304).

Many of the difficulties associated with the rule would appear to have been disposed of by the guidance in the Code of Practice that the higher price referred to in the price indication should be the last higher and different price in time to have been charged (Code, para. 1.2.2). Although not a legal requirement, it is clear that failure to comply with this Code provision will be prima facie evidence that a misleading price indication has been given by the person charged. In *A. G. Stanley Ltd* v *Surrey County Council* (1995) 159 JP 691 the defendants sold an occasional table on 2 April 1992 for £7.99. On 14 October of the same year the same tables, were advertised for sale at a reduced price, the offer being stated to be open until March 1993. In November 1992 the tables in question were offered for sale in a 13-day event under the slogan 'Was £7.99 — Now £4.99'. Some time after the 13-day event had supposedly ended, the same tables were still being offered for sale at £4.99, compared with a previous selling price of £7.99. The defendants were charged with and convicted of an offence under s. 20(1) on the basis that the circumstances by reference to which consumers might reasonably be expected to judge the validity of the price comparison were not what in fact they were. In the Divisional Court, it was considered that if an earlier price is to be used for the basis of comparison, it must be a higher price and it must be the last such higher price in time. Otherwise, the comparison will be misleading. The defendants changed the wording of the point-of-sale material on each occasion a new 'promotion' was started, but the price of £4.99 remained constant. The price of £7.99 should have been charged immediately before the most recent offer for sale at £4.99 in order to avoid the commission of an offence. As a result, the price of £4.99 charged after the conclusion of the so-called '13 day event' was misleading since it is suggested that the immediately higher price charged was £7.99.

An exception to the 28 days in six months rule is provided for in the case of food and other short shelf-life goods, for which the Code requires the previous price used as the basis for comparison to be the last price charged for products of that kind (Code, para. 1.2.4).

In some cases, it may not be possible to comply fully with the requirements of para. 1.2.4 of the Code of Practice. If this is the case, the Code provides that goods can be sold in contravention of its provisions if the advertiser gives a full and unambiguous explanation. It is possible for a trader to state that a product has only been available at the higher price for a period of 10 days or that the higher price was charged in a specified number of retail outlets owned by the group giving the price indication. Where such a comparison is made, it must be fair and meaningful (Code, para. 1.2.3). It would appear that outrageous departures from the basic requirements of the Code of Practice will be deterred by market forces — if the trader has to give explicit details of what he is doing consumers will realise that they are being misled. However, it is suggested that past practice indicates that notices of this kind are probably not read by the majority of consumers and even if they are, they may not be fully understood.

If a trader wishes to make a series of reductions on a product line that is not selling well, the 28-day rule does not apply to intermediate price reductions and unless a full explanation of the nature of the series of reductions is given, the highest price in the series must comply with the 28-day rule and all other prices, including the current selling price, must be stated (Code, para. 1.2.6).

19.3.6.9 Recommended prices

A further practice widely used in the past has been to compare a current selling price with one recommended by a manufacturer. However, there have been difficulties resulting from the use of bogus recommendations or genuine manufacturers' recommendations that have been set at an unreasonably high level for the benefit of preferred trade customers. To clarify matters, the Code of Practice provides that the price must be one recommended by the manufacturer as the sale price to consumers; the trader must deal with the manufacturer on commercial terms and the price should not be significantly higher than the price at which the product is sold generally (Code, para. 1.6.3).

Generally, abbreviations should not be used, but the Code is prepared to countenance the use of the initials RRP as an indication of a recommended retail price. Terms such as 'list' price should not be used unless there is a clear indication of whose list price is used as the basis for comparison.

19.3.6.10 Other traders' prices   At one stage, comparisons with another trader's product might have been regarded as 'knocking copy' and discouraged as an advertising practice, however, in a more competitive environment, such comparisons have become more prevalent.

In order to avoid misleading comparisons with a price charged by someone else, the Code provides that the person giving the indication should only engage in such a practice if he knows that the price quoted is accurate and up-to-date; that the name of the other trader and the premises at which the price is charged is clearly identified and that the price relates to products which are substantially similar to those offered by the person giving the price indication (Code, para. 1.5.1). If there are any differences between the products compared, these should be identified in the price indication.

A practice frequently used in the past has been the claim that if a product can be purchased elsewhere at a lower price than that charged by the person giving the price indication, the difference will be refunded. Attempts were made to fit these into the regime created by the Trade Descriptions Act 1968, s. 14, in relation to services, but the courts found difficulty in treating an indication of a charge made as a facility or a service (*Dixons Ltd* v *Roberts* (1984) 82 LGR 689). However, following the controversial and possibly suspect reasoning of the Divisional Court in *Ashley* v *Sutton London Borough Council* (1994) 159 JP 631 the sale of a book subject to a 90-day money back guarantee may fall within the provisions of s. 14 (see chapter 18).

Under the Consumer Protection Act 1987, claims to the effect that a refund will be given are permitted, but not in relation to 'own-brand' products which cannot be purchased elsewhere, unless the offer extends to equivalent products stocked by others (Code, para. 1.5.2). If there are conditions attached to the offer to the effect that the product must be purchased in a particular area, these must be made clear to the consumer.

19.3.6.11 Comparisons with prices charged in different circumstances
The Code of Practice lists the most familiar comparisons with a price charged in different circumstances. These include the price charged for a different quantity of the goods subject to the price indication (10p each — 30p for four); the price charged for goods in a different condition (shop-soiled £5 — when new £20); the price charged for different availability, for example, special order prices; the price charged for goods in a totally different state (ready assembled price £75 — self-assembly kit price £45) and the price charged for special groups of people (pensioners £5 — others £10).

The main problem encountered under the Trade Descriptions Act 1968 and the Price Marking (Bargain Offers) Orders 1979 was that there was no requirement that the trader should have been prepared to do business at the price used as the basis for comparison. Thus in the case of special order prices, it was perfectly lawful to use as the basis for comparison the price that would have been charged for the dress in the violent shade of puce and lime green that few people would ever consider buying and which had never been stocked in any case. To avoid this problem the code requires the trader to have the product available in the different quantity, condition etc. at the price stated (Code, para. 1.4.2).

Where the price for goods in perfect condition is used as the basis for comparison, the Code recognises that the goods may not be available in their perfect form, but goes on to require the trader to identify the nature of the price of those goods. In other words, the trader is required to say whether the price of the goods in perfect condition is the previous selling price of the person giving the indication, that of another trader or a recommended retail price (Code, para. 1.4.3). In each case, the price indication has to comply with the guidelines applicable to such comparisons.

If a trader wishes to compare a selling price with the price for those goods when in a different state, he is required to have a reasonable proportion (stated to be about one third) of the goods in that different state available for supply at the price quoted (Code, para. 1.4.4). Thus it will not be possible to stock a single item at a ludicrously high price so as to give a basis for price comparisons.

19.4 DEFENCES

19.4.1 Defences specific to s. 20
In addition to the general defence of taking reasonable precautions and acting with due diligence in s. 39, the provisions of which are dealt with in more detail in chapter 13, the Consumer Protection Act 1987 provides for a number of other defences specific to the offences created by s. 20.

It is a defence to show that a price indication complies with Regulations made by the Secretary of State (s. 24(1)). If a misleading indication of price is given in editorial material, it is a defence for the publisher to show that the indication was not contained in an advertisement (s. 24(2)). So a magazine article comparing prices charged by retailers for particular commodities would not constitute the commission of an offence under s. 20 if it cited inaccurate information on presently charged prices.

A person who, in the course of business, publishes advertising material supplied to him by others is also able to raise the defence that, at the time of publication, he did not know and had no reasonable grounds for suspecting that the publication would involve the commission of an offence (s. 24(3)). If there are facts which the publisher could not reasonably be expected to know, such as the price previously charged by the person giving the indication or the price charged by another retailer, the defence will protect the publisher of the advertising material. However, the publisher can reasonably be expected to be aware of the provisions of the Code of Practice, with the result that the s. 24(3) defence would not be available where he publishes an advertisement which compares a selling price with an amount the product is worth.

Where a person has indicated a recommended price for goods, services, accommodation or facilities and a third party supplies the advertised materials at a higher price than that recommended, the person making the recommendation is able to raise a defence if he did not indicate the availability of the product from himself and it was reasonable for him to assume that the product would be mainly sold at the recommended price

(s. 24(4)). Thus if a car manufacturer advertises nationally, indicating a recommended price for a particular type of vehicle, no offence is committed by the manufacturer where a dealer sells at a higher price than that stated in the advertisement, if the price is one recommended to all franchised dealers. One difficulty which has arisen in the past is the practice of recommending a bogus retail price to a small number of preferred retailers. In such a case, the s. 24(4) defence would not be available since it is not a price recommended to all retailers. One of the more serious implications of this defence is that while the manufacturer has a defence in the circumstances outlined, the retailer charging the higher price commits no offence because he has given no indication. Accordingly, there may be scope for avoiding liability altogether under s. 20 through collusion between manufacturers and retailers.

19.4.2 Disclaimers

While a disclaimer does not provide a defence, it does have the effect of negativing the liability of a person giving a misleading indication. The principal use of the disclaimer doctrine has been in relation to offences under the Trade Descriptions Act 1968, s. 1, and is considered in more detail elsewhere in chapter 17.

For the purposes of the Trade Descriptions Act 1968, s. 1, a disclaimer of liability, generally, will not be available in respect of a self-applied description (*R* v *Southwood* [1987] 1 WLR 1361). Since all price indications are descriptions of the price charged by the person giving the indication, it should follow that a disclaimer in general terms ought to be ruled out by the courts. It is difficult to imagine circumstances in which a person may legitimately use a price comparison based on currently available information and subsequently claim that any false impression which might be created should be ignored. Even if disclaimers of liability are to be permitted, they will have to comply with the requirement that they should be as bold, precise and compelling as the initial price indication (*Norman* v *Bennett* [1974] 1 WLR 1229). Given the likely effect of most price indications on consumers, the disclaimer would have to be so powerful in effect that any benefit derived from the price indication might be negated.

19.5 PRICE INDICATIONS AND EUROPEAN COMMUNITY REQUIREMENTS

It has been observed already that much of our domestic law in favour of consumers must be considered in the light of European Community policies, particularly those which relate to free trade in the single market (see EC Treaty, art. 30, and chapter 2).

So far as domestic rules on price indications are concerned, the domestic legislature has to be careful to ensure that regulations on the use of price indications do not forbid practices which are regarded as acceptable in other member States of the European Community, since the ECJ has tended to adopt a policy of equalisation which has regard to the fact that if a certain practice is permitted in one part of the EC then it should also be permitted

Misleading price indications

elsewhere. If domestic legislation is capable of limiting the extent to which goods can be freely sold across the EC then the restriction may be regarded as unlawful. In *Schutzverband gegen Unwesen in der Wirtschaft eV* v *Yves Rocher GmbH* (case C-126/91) [1993] ECR I-2361 domestic regulations on price comparisons in Germany provided that the use of such sales promotion devices were lawful provided they were not unfair or likely to mislead consumers, which included a provision to the effect that 'eye-catching' price comparisons using individual prices were unlawful (Gesetz gegen den un-lauteren Wettbewerb (UWG) of 3 June 1909, art. 6(c)). The French defend-ants sold cosmetic products by mail order using, as a sales promotion device, a brochure which was prepared individually for each country in which their products were marketed. The brochure prepared for the purposes of sales in Germany showed former prices which had been crossed out to be replaced by lower prices in bold red characters. At first instance it was held that the method of sales promotion was unlawful on the ground that it was excessively 'eye-catching' contrary to UWG, art. 6(e). On appeal to the ECJ it was accepted that trading rules applied by member States could constitute a measure amounting to a quantitative restriction on imports since they are capable of limiting the volume of imports between member States. In this case, the domestic regulations went too far. The German law prohibited not just 'eye-catching' material, but also price comparisons which were genuinely applied and which could be helpful to consumers. It was decided that art. 30 prevented the use of the German law.

A similar approach also seems to apply to claims printed on goods by their manufacturer to the effect that they represent 'extra value'. It has been seen already that such claims are discouraged by the Code of Practice for Traders on Price Indications and that implicit in that discouragement is that such claims could be regarded as misleading under the Consumer Protection Act 1987, s. 20. However, domestic legislation forbidding such claims may infringe art. 30 of the EC Treaty. In *Verein gegen Unwesen in Handel und Gewerbe Köln eV* v *Mars GmbH* (case C-470/93) [1995] ECR I-1923 Mars ice creams were supplied in wrappers marked '+10 per cent' which were marketed across Europe. Proceedings were brought in a German court to prevent the use of this form of promotion on the ground that 'extra value' claims were anti-competitive and contrary to German law. However, such practices were perfectly acceptable according to the laws of other member States with the result that these ice creams could be lawfully marketed in those States. Because such claims were acceptable elsewhere, the adoption of a prohibition such as that in the relevant German law was bound to hinder intra-Community trade by forcing producers to package their products differently in order to comply with the law in Germany. It followed that unless Germany could justify its prohibition, the relevant law had to be taken to infringe article 30. Attempts at justification on the ground that consumers might be misled into the belief that they would be required to pay no more than they previously paid for the lesser weight goods and that consumers might think they were getting considerably more for their money both failed. There was no evidence that Mars had taken advantage of the promotion to increase their prices nor was there evidence that retailers had increased prices either. Moreover, there was no likelihood that reasonably circumspect consumers would be misled by the size of the lettering used into believing they were getting more for their money than was in fact the case.

TWENTY
Sales promotion

In a market economy it is important for retailers and manufacturers to publicise the products they sell or produce in order to ensure that they sell at a sufficiently high level to warrant continued sales or production. Towards this end a number of sales promotion techniques may be employed, which may attract legal consequences. It has been seen already in chapter 19 that one method of sales promotion is the use of price reductions, comparisons and other forms of price indication, some of which may be acceptable, but others not. Sales promotion exercises considered in this chapter include offers of free gifts, loss-leading, under which goods may be put up for sale at a price which will generate a loss in the hope that consumers will purchase other goods at full price at the same time, and the use of lotteries and competitions. All of these practices are governed, to some extent, by domestic law, but domestic regulation of sales promotion practices may be regarded as a barrier to free trade, in which case, it becomes necessary to consider whether this form of regulation offends against general principles of European Community law (see also chapter 2).

Other remedial possibilities, where a sales promotion scheme fails thus causing upset to consumers who might have expected more from the promotion concerned, may arise in the law of contract, provided it is possible to establish a contractual relationship between the promoter and the consumer. It has already been observed in chapter 4 that the doctrine of privity of contract may create problems in this regard if the consumer complaint is directed towards the manufacturer rather than the retailer, unless a collateral contractual relationship can be established. However, should such a relationship be established, the question will then arise whether the failure to fulfil promotional scheme promises can be regarded as a sufficiently serious breach of contract to give rise to an appropriate remedy, in the form of a full refund of the cost of any promotional gift offered by the promoter, so as to allow the consumer to purchase an alternative replacement elsewhere (or use the money to buy something else). These problems were thrown into sharp perspective in one case based on the notorious Hoover promotion, in which

Hoover offered free airline flights to consumers who purchased its products. In *Jack* v *Hoover (UK) Ltd* (6 August 1993, Kirkcaldy Sheriff Court, unreported) the pursuer sued for damages of £300 representing the value of the flight he had ordered under the Hoover promotion which had not been delivered to him at the time of issue of the writ. Hoover did not contend that there was no breach of contract, but did argue that it was not sufficiently serious to allow repudiation and recovery of the amount promised, since they were still prepared to honour the offer to provide tickets. However, if the pursuer was able to show that the defenders' failure to honour their promise sufficiently swiftly could amount to a fundamental breach of contract then the breach of condition would allow the consumer to refuse to fulfil his side of the contract and recover from the defendant the value of that which was promised. The key issue was therefore whether there was a fundamental breach of contract. In the event, it was decided that there was insufficient evidence that the defenders' tardiness could be regarded as a fundamental breach, especially in the light of the conduct of the pursuer, who had continued to press for alternative flights to those which he had initially asked for or the distibution of free air miles instead.

20.1 FREE GIFTS AND LOSS-LEADERS

A technique frequently used by traders to attract customers is the so-called 'free gift' or loss-leader promotion. However, as has been observed in another context, there is no such thing as a free lunch. At some stage, the customer will pay for the free gift, if he makes other purchases in the same retail outlet. Even if legal controls do not prevent recouping the cost of the promotion by other means, the British Code of Advertising and Sales Promotion (BCASP, 1995; see also chapter 16) provides that it is not legitimate for promoters to recoup such costs by making charges which would not normally be made or by altering the quality of products which must be bought in order to qualify for the offer (BCASP para. 39.3; see also chapter 16).

It has been observed in chapter 19 that free gifts must be what they say they are and that if any sort of direct payment is required, for example, postage charges, it is not a free offer and an offence under the Consumer Protection Act 1987, s. 20, may have been committed.

The thing given away must also comply with civil law requirements about quality and fitness for purpose and the criminal law requirements about product safety, since there is a supply of goods within the meaning of the Supply of Goods and Services Act 1982 (see chapter 8) and the Consumer Protection Act 1987 (see chapter 7). If the gift comes in the form of a free sample of food, the provisions of the Food Safety Act 1990 in relation to the food safety requirement and food quality apply (see chapter 15).

Loss-leading occurs when a retailer purchases from the manufacturer a substantial quantity of a particular product and sells it at a substantially discounted price, sometimes even less than the wholesale price. This may involve making a trading loss, but may be to the advantage of the retailer by attracting customers to his outlet. When this occurs, the manufacturer of the product may be tempted to refuse to supply the retailer concerned. Whether such action is permissible is governed by the Resale Prices Act 1976 concerning anti-competitive practices.

The main provisions of the Resale Prices Act 1976 concerned with the practice of loss-leading are to be found in ss. 11, 12 and 13.

Section 11(1) provides that it is unlawful for a supplier to withhold supplies of goods from a dealer seeking to obtain them for resale in the UK on the ground that the dealer:

(a)   has sold in the UK at a price below the resale price for goods obtained, either directly or indirectly, from that supplier, or has supplied such goods, either directly or indirectly, to a third party who has done so; or
(b)   is likely, if the goods are supplied to him, to sell them in the UK at a price below that price, or supply them, either directly or indirectly, to a third party who would be likely to do so.

Section 12(1) clarifies the meaning of 'withholding supplies', treating the following actions of a supplier as falling within the provisions of s. 11, namely:

(a)   refusing or failing to supply goods to the order of the dealer;
(b)   refusing to supply to a dealer except at prices, or on terms or conditions as to credit, discount or other matters, which are significantly less favourable than those at which or on which he normally supplies those goods to other dealers carrying on business in similar circumstances; or
(c)   treating the dealer in a manner significantly less favourable than that in which he normally treats other such dealers in respect of the times or methods of delivery or other matters arising in the execution of the contract.

By virtue of s. 12(3), if it is shown that a supplier has withheld supplies and that supplier was previously doing business with the dealer from whom supplies are withheld up to the time of withholding and the supplier was aware of loss-leading practices on the part of the dealer in the previous six months, it is presumed that the reason for withholding supplies is a matter which falls within s. 11.

Section 12(2) provides that a supplier is not to be treated as withholding supplies if he has grounds other than those specified in s. 12(1) which, standing alone, would justify a refusal to supply. Section 12(2) would apply where, for example, the dealer is in breach of an earlier contract which would justify refusal to deal with him.

Section 13(1) provides that it is not unlawful to withhold supplies if there is reasonable cause to believe that within the previous 12 months the dealer (or any person to whom he supplies) has used the same or similar goods for loss-leading purposes. That is, loss-leading is permitted, but the dealer must not use the same or similar goods for a promotional exercise more than once in a 12-month period.

Under s. 13(2), loss-leading is defined as the resale of goods, not for the purpose of making a profit, but for the purpose of attracting to a retail establishment customers likely to purchase other goods or otherwise for the purpose of advertising the business of the dealer.

It is questionable whether giving goods away free of charge is the same as loss-leading in the light of the wording of s. 13(2) which requires a 'resale'. If resale requires compliance with the definition of a sale of goods contract in the Sale of Goods Act 1979, s. 2(1), giving something away free of charge may not involve the element of consideration required for the purposes of the 1979 Act (see *Esso Petroleum Co. Ltd* v *Commissioners of Customs & Excise* [1976] 1 WLR 1 and chapter 4 and chapter 6). Despite the legal position, there are undoubted benefits to the retailer in engaging in the practice of loss-leading, but these also have to be balanced against the disadvantages which may be suffered by the producer of the product subject to such a promotional exercise. On the one hand the retailer who runs the loss-leader promotion may benefit from increased turnover because consumers attracted by the loss-leader will buy regularly priced goods as well. Conversely, the producer of the loss-led product may be less happy with the prospect of such promotions since he will still sell at the regular wholesale price and make his profit, but it is possible that there will be damage to the reputation of the loss-led product in that it may be viewed as overpriced. Also there may be damage to the trading relationship betwen the supplier and other dealers in the area who may think that discounts are being offered to the loss-leading dealer. Furthermore, consumers might think that the manufacturer has sacrificed his product to allow a bargain offer to be made and they may be persuaded that there is something wrong with the product because it is being offered so cheaply.

The main remedies against loss-leading tend to be of the self-help variety, namely, the producer of the product subject to the promotion may refuse to supply any products of his to the retailer who engages in the practice of loss-leading. Alternatively, the producer could threaten to withdraw a trade discount normally offered to that supplier or he could ration supplies of products normally made available to that retail outlet.

The producer has to be careful to ensure that the exercise of any such remedy is permitted under the Resale Prices Act 1976, ss. 11, 12 and 13. A common move is to withhold supplies until the dealer gives a written assurance that he will not persist in loss-leading, however, the language of the written assurance must be such as not to amount to price-fixing since this is forbidden by the 1976 Act. If the retailer sells at a profit of just 1 per cent, he does still make a profit, in which case, he does not engage in the practice of loss-leading within the definition in s. 13(2).

20.2 UNSOLICITED GOODS AND SERVICES

Where goods are given away free of charge, ownership passes to the consumer immediately. However, in the case of what is known as 'inertia selling', something may be sent to the consumer with the expectation that he should pay for it in order for ownership to pass. This practice is now controlled by the provisions of the Unsolicited Goods and Services Acts 1971 and 1975.

The Unsolicited Goods and Services Act 1971 provides that a recipient of unsolicited goods may treat them as an unconditional gift if they have not been reclaimed by the sender within six months of their arrival and the recipient has not prevented the sender from recovering them (s. 1(1) and (2)(a)). The six-month period may be shortened to 30 days where the recipient serves written notice on the sender to collect the goods within the 30-day period, provided the recipient does not prevent the goods from being recovered (s. 1(2)(b)).

In order for the provisions of s. 1 to apply, the recipient of the goods must have no reasonable cause to believe that the goods were sent with a view to their purchase for business or trade purposes (s. 1(2)): the Act only protects consumers. A recipient of goods who has agreed to acquire them has no right to treat them as unsolicited (s. 1(2)). Accordingly, a consumer who has signed a form agreeing to buy a book club's 'book of the month' or, more seriously, has failed to insert a cross in the box on his monthly order form, indicating that he does not wish to receive the book of the month is deemed to have agreed to acquire the goods. Similarly, a consumer who has filled in a coupon in a newspaper or a magazine requesting the delivery of certain items cannot treat the goods as unsolicited when they are delivered.

Where a person, acting in the course of a business, demands payment or asserts a present or prospective right to payment for goods which he knows are unsolicited, he commits an offence (s. 2(1)). It is also an offence to make threats regarding payment, amounting to a threat to bring legal proceedings or to place the name of any person on a list of defaulters or debtors or to invoke any other collection procedure (s. 2(2)).

Particular problems can arise where a supplier has received a request for goods from someone other than the person to whom they are sent. Ordinarily, if the name of the person making the request and the person to whom they are sent happen to be substantially different, the goods may properly be regarded as unsolicited, in which case an offence is committed under s. 2. However, it may also be the case that a bogus request is sent in in a name substantially the same as that of the recipient. In such a case it is possible that no offence is committed under s. 2 where a collection procedure is invoked, because the goods may not be unsolicited if the court concludes that the recipient and the person submitting the request are the same person. Alternatively, if the two people are regarded as distinct, the threat to invoke the collection procedure may be regarded as being directed at the person making the request rather than at the person who received the goods (*Corfield v World Records Ltd* (1979, DC unreported) see also Lawson (1975) 125 NLJ 568). An offence under s. 2 is not committed by a person unless the person does not have any reasonable cause to believe that there is a right to payment. There may be a reasonable belief where an honest mistake has been made. Thus if a junior employee of the defendant mistakenly fails to re-program a computer after a consumer has cancelled his subscription to a book club with the result that the computer continues to send out demands for payment, there may be a reasonable cause to believe in a right to payment on the part of the defendant (*Readers Digest Association Ltd v Pirie* 1973 SLT 170).

20.3   LOTTERIES AND PRIZE COMPETITIONS

Games and competitions have been used for many years as a means of sales promotion. The number of such competitions is considerable, including those which require substantial thought and skill down to those dependent on pure chance, such as newspaper bingo. While such games are useful as a means of sales promotion, they may be regarded as illegal, either because they amount to an illegal lottery (Lotteries and Amusements Act 1976, s. 1) or because they constitute an unlawful prize competition (Lotteries and Amusements Act 1976, s. 14).

Apart from the legal controls on lotteries and prize competitions, considered below, there is also business self-control in the form of the British Code of Advertising and Sales Promotion (BCASP), which requires that sales promotion exercises should be prepared with a sense of responsibility, should be conducted equitably and should be seen to deal fairly and honourably with consumers (BCASP, para. 27.2). The Code makes special provision for the availability of results (BCASP, para. 40.3). The duration of a prize competition should be clearly stated (BCASP, para. 40.3).

20.3.1   Lotteries

One of the main reasons for exercising controls over lotteries as a means of sales promotion was that their promotion tended to offend Victorian morality on the ground that they amounted to a form of gambling. In particular, it was seen to be immoral that a person should be able to get something for nothing and, since there was no other means of control, the lottery laws were drafted into use (*R* v *Crawshaw* (1860) Bell CC 303).

The law governing lotteries is now contained in the Lotteries and Amusements Act 1976, which lays down a general rule to the effect that all lotteries not permitted by the Act are unlawful (s. 1). Permitted lotteries include small lotteries (s. 3), private lotteries (s. 4) and societies' lotteries (s. 5). Small lotteries include those organised at school fêtes where participation is confined to those who attend the fête and in which no money prizes are given. Private lotteries consist of those organised by a society for the benefit of its members. Societies' lotteries cover registered promotions on behalf of an organisation set up for charitable, sporting or other purposes and not for private gain. Since lotteries designed to increase sales do not fall within any of these categories, they are potentially unlawful.

It now remains to consider the definition of a lottery, which is to be derived from common law rules, in the absence of a statutory definition. A lottery appears to have three essential elements: it must amount to a distribution of prizes dependent on chance under which the customer has given some payment for the chance of winning a prize (*Imperial Tobacco Ltd* v *Attorney-General* [1981] AC 718, 736 per Viscount Dilhorne).

Other matters such as fraud on the part of the promoter and profit made by the promoter have also been considered to be relevant in the past, but can probably be disregarded. Accordingly, the three main elements in the definition of a lottery are distribution, payment and chance. Of these, distribution has not given rise to any difficulty of definition, provided something of value, whether it be money, some material article or anything else to which a value can be ascribed, is given as a prize (*Director of Public Prosecutions* v *Bradfute & Associates Ltd* [1967] 2 QB 291, 296 per Lord Parker CJ). However, some difficulties have arisen in relation to the meaning of payment and chance, resulting from a battle between the courts and competition promoters seeking to find ways of defeating the lottery laws. If promoters could find a way of devising a completely free competition or one which was not dependent solely on chance but which nonetheless promoted sales, the battle was won.

More recently, the advent of the telephone competition using premium-rate 0898 numbers has also attracted the attention of the lottery laws. Since the basis on which such competitions are operated is that the cost of the phone calls is somewhat inflated so as to allow for a profit on the part of the competition promoter, it is evident that participants actually pay, at least in part, for the prizes they receive. In what is known as the *Telemillion case* (see Lawson, 'Sales promotion after the *Telemillion case*' (1996) 15 TrL 209) the promoters of the game 'Telemillion' invited television viewers to dial a telephone number, whereupon they were asked a number of questions. The names of those who answered correctly were then placed in a draw which determined who was to win a prize. The organisers were convicted of running both an unlawful lottery contrary to the Lotteries and Amusements Act 1976, s. 1, and of operating an illegal prize competition contrary to s. 14 of the 1976 Act, despite the fact that there was a 'free entry route' for participants who wished to post their answers to the questions which had been set by the promoters.

For more on lotteries see Merkin [1981] LMCLQ 66.

20.3.1.1 Payment

If competitors are required to make some sort of a payment for the prize they receive, the promotion will amount to a lottery. This remains the case even if the promoter does not actually make any direct profit from the promotion, since it will be assumed that a profit is made through an increase in custom. Thus in *Taylor* v *Smetten* (1883) 11 QBD 207 there was considered to be a lottery where a retailer sold packets of tea which contained coupons entitling the purchaser to a prize. Since the coupons and the packets of tea were indivisible, it was considered that customers had paid for the chance of winning the prizes offered in the promotion, since it was 'impossible to suppose that the aggregate prices charged and obtained for the packages did not include the aggregate prices of the tea and the prizes' (ibid. 211 per Hawkins J).

If the customer is required to pay an entry fee, the promotion is clearly a lottery, but the same is true where the customer has to make a purchase in order to become a participant as in *Taylor* v *Smetten*. Likewise, if a newspaper runs a competition of chance, making proof of purchase of the newspaper a condition of entry, the promotion is a lottery (*Stoddart* v *Sagar* [1895] 2 QB 474).

To get round the payment rule, promoters devised competitions which did not impose a mandatory requirement of purchase, but nonetheless hoped that extra custom would follow. Even this did not escape the attention of the courts, since in *Willis* v *Young* [1907] 1 KB 448 it was held that even though there was no requirement of payment, in practice the promotion resulted in a 20 per cent increase in sales of a newspaper. The essential nature of the promotion was to increase sales with the result that the lottery laws extended to cover both gambling and genuine cases of offering free gifts (cf. *contra Express Newspapers plc* v *Liverpool Daily Post and Echo plc* [1985] 1 WLR 1089).

The rule in *Willis* v *Young* was subsequently undermined in a series of cases in the 1960s and 1970s which did not overrule the earlier decision, but left the position very unclear. For example, it was found that a free bingo game in a public house which undoubtedly increased sales was not financed by the drinks purchased by customers (*McCollom* v *Wrightson* [1968] AC 522). Similarly, a competition, organised by a national brewery in their chain of public houses which involved giving an envelope containing the competition to anyone who requested one, involved no payment, even though most of those who took part would be customers of the promoter (*Whitbread & Co. Ltd* v *Bell* [1970] 2 QB 547). The conflict between *Willis* v *Young* and *Whitbread & Co. Ltd* v *Bell* was considered by the House of Lords in *Imperial Tobacco Ltd* v *Attorney-General* [1981] AC 718, in which the respondents had run a 'spot-cash' promotion, printing 265 million cards which entitled winning participants to a prize ranging from a packet of cigarettes to £100,000. 262.25 million of these cards were inserted in packets of cigarettes manufactured by the respondents and the remaining 2.25 million cards were available to the public either from Imperial Tobacco or over the counter in some shops. It was held that the scheme was a lottery since those customers who entered the competition using the cards inserted in packets of the cigarettes had paid for both entry to the competition and the cigarettes, but this decision ignored the 2.25 million cards available to anyone. If the proportion of free cards had been much greater, the House of Lords might have been forced to consider the true position of these 'mixed' competitions (see Lawson, *Sales Promotion Law* (1987), p. 11), instead of just sweeping the matter under the carpet. Indeed, it is implicit in the reasoning employed in *Reader's Digest Association Ltd* v *Williams* [1976] 1 WLR 1109 that because entry forms to a lucky draw sent to 5 million households could be returned to by those who wished to buy a book offered for sale by the defendants and by those who did not wish to purchase the book, there was no lottery. What seems to underlie the decision is that there were substantial numbers of participants who could (and did) take part free of charge. In contrast, in *Imperial Tobacco Ltd* v *Attorney-General* and the recent *Telemillion case* (see (1996) 15 TrL 209) the number of free entries was strictly limited. In the *Telemillion case* participants could request a free postal entry form, although the expectation was that the majority of participants would use the premium telephone call route instead. Moreover, the organisers of the competition only employed between one and four people to deal with postal enquiries, with the result that intending participants might be disappointed. The limited number of free entries, amounting to no more than 0.184 per cent of the overall number of entries, could be ignored and the scheme remained a lottery. However, there is a difference between *Telemillion* and *Imperial Tobacco* since in the latter there was a definite limit to the number of free entries whereas in *Telemillion*, no limit had been set, although the reality was that the number of free entrants was very small. The reasoning implicit in *Reader's Digest Association Ltd* v *Williams* will require a court to consider the actual number of free entrants compared with the number of paying entrants and if the gulf between the two figures is 'substantial' the promotion may be regarded as a lottery, despite the fact that the *potential* number of free entries is quite large.

20.3.1.2 Chance If a competition does involve a payment, it can still avoid the lottery laws if its outcome is not dependent on pure chance. If customers have no idea how or when a prize will be awarded, the promotion must be dependent on pure chance and will be regarded as a lottery. In *Howgate* v *Ralph* (1929) 141 LT 512 the defendant employed canvassers to give out leaflets which offered cash gifts to customers who bought tea regularly at the defendant's shop. Qualification for a gift was dependent on the customer's name being entered on a register and reaching the top of the list, subject to that person still being a regular customer at the shop. Since customers had no idea when their name would reach the top of the list and no means of ascertaining when a prize might be won, the whole arrangement was considered to depend purely on chance, with the result that the scheme was held to be an illegal lottery.

The essence of a game of skill is that there is something a competitor can do to influence the result, and it seems that only minor merit or skill will be sufficient for these purposes. Thus forecasting the result of a horse race involves skill since those with better knowledge of horse racing are considered more likely to win (*Stoddart* v *Sagar* [1895] 2 QB 474). Similarly, if the competition can be won by detailed research it will not be a lottery. In *Hall* v *Cox* [1899] 1 QB 198 a £1,000 prize was available to any customer who could correctly predict the number of births and deaths in London during a named week. It was considered that the person most likely to win would be someone skilled in drawing conclusions from available reference books. Accordingly, there was sufficient skill involved to prevent the scheme from being treated as a lottery. However, it has also been held that a requirement of observation alone is probably not enough to escape the application of the lottery laws. Thus the ability to count the number of spots in a diagram does not involve the exercise of skill (*Hall* v *McWilliam* (1901) 85 LT 239). It might be asked how counting spots differs from identifying the number of triangles in a diagram, which was considered to involve the exercise of skill in *Director of Public Prosecutions* v *Bradfute & Associates Ltd* [1967] 2 QB 291 considered below.

Even if skill is involved, the lottery laws may still apply if the exercise of that skill does not determine the outcome of the competition. The promoter must judge the competitors on the skill they have used and not simply on the basis of a pre-set result picked at random. In *Coles* v *Odhams Press Ltd* [1936] 1 KB 416 the competition involved skill in filling in a crossword grille, but

there were many different ways of completing the grille. Successful participants were those who used the solution selected by the promoter. Accordingly, competitors were invited to take 'blind shots at a hidden target' (ibid. 426
per Lord Hewart CJ). The fact that some skill may be involved on the part
of a participant will not always prevent a scheme from being a lottery, since
regard must be had to the whole scheme and if it is clear that participants
have little or no control over the outcome of the promotion, it may still be
regarded as a lottery which is primarily dependent on chance. This element
of loss of control is a natural feature of 'chain money' schemes. For example,
in *Re Senator Hanseatische Verwaltungsgesellschaft mbH* [1996] 4 All ER 933
the defendants organised a multi-level snowball scheme under which participants were encouraged to join the Titan Business Club on making a payment,
but stood to make cash gains for each new club member they managed to
recruit. These cash gains would increase with each new member recruited,
but for each recruitment, the organisers were also entitled to a payment.
What was considered to justify the decision that this scheme was an unlawful
lottery was that although those skilled in recruitment of members stood a
better chance than others of making money, that success was nonetheless
dependent upon whether others in the 'chain' performed well or not in
recruiting members and since an individual participant had no control over
those others, the scheme had to be regarded as being dependent on chance.

A further important consideration in these 'snowball' or 'chain money'
schemes is that they are often promoted by a company set up for the specific
purpose of operating the scheme. If this is the case, and the scheme is
declared to be an unlawful lottery, participants in the scheme will be able to
recover all sums paid by them, since the sums paid cannot be regarded as
profits out of which the company may make any form of distribution (*One
Life Ltd* v *Roy* [1996] 2 BCLC 608). If the competition involves a mixture of
luck and skill, much will depend on the extent to which the skill or the chance
determines the outcome. If a contestant is not required to exercise any skill
until he has had the luck to obtain a winning coupon, the competition is more
likely to be regarded as a lottery. For example, in *Director of Public Prosecutions*
v *Bradfute & Associates Ltd* [1967] 2 QB 291 the defendants mounted a
£30,000 bingo game on the tins of cat food produced by them. The labels
on these tins carried a bingo card and a series of numbers. The availability of
a prize depended upon whether the printed numbers completed a line on the
bingo card. Entitlement to the prize then depended upon whether the
winning contestant could solve a puzzle diagram also printed on the labels.
Clearly a game of bingo involves no skill, but solving a problem does.
However, the court considered it necesary to look at the competition as a
whole and since a winning contestant had to have the pure luck of picking up
a winning card before there was any need to exercise the minimal degree of
skill in solving the problem, it could only be concluded that the scheme was
a lottery dependent on the initial chance of buying a tin of cat food which
carried a winning entry.

In *Director of Public Prosecutions* v *Bradfute & Associates Ltd* there was an
illegal lottery because the element of luck preceded the element of skill and

it was necessary to be lucky first before being allowed to participate in that part of the competition which involved the exercise of skill. In contrast in the *Telemillion case* (see (1996) 15 TrL 209) the element of skill comprised in answering a number of questions preceded the element of chance, namely a prize draw. However, the court concluded that because the element of chance involved meant that there was a lottery, this automatically precluded the promotion from being a lawful prize competition under s. 14 of the 1976 Act. This must be regarded as a questionable conclusion, since what allowed entry to the prize draw was surely the exercise of skill in answering the questions. On this basis it is arguable that the Telemillion promotion was neither a lottery nor an unlawful prize competition.

20.3.2 Prize competitions

It has been seen that the exercise of even a minimal degree of skill takes a competition outside the scope of the lottery laws. In particular the view that predicting the outcome of a horse race involves skill on the part of competitors has resulted in the provisions now contained in the Lotteries and Amusements Act 1976, s. 14, in relation to prize competitions.

Under s. 14 it is unlawful for a newspaper or business to promote trade by means of a competition which offers prizes resulting from forecasting (s. 14(1)(a)) or in which success does not depend to a substantial degree on the exercise of skill (s. 14(1)(b)).

While s. 14(1)(a) applies to forecasting the result of a horse race, it also covers other forms of forecasting. Thus predicting the outcome of sporting or other events the result of which is uncertain would also fall within this provision. However, it would appear that a 'spot-the-ball' competition is not covered by s. 14(1)(a) because it involves trying to pinpoint the position of a ball rather than guessing the deliberations of the panel of experts called upon to decide where the ball was positioned. In any case, it might be difficult to regard the position of a football or the predictions of a panel of experts as 'the result of an event' (*News of the World Ltd* v *Friend* [1973] 1 WLR 248).

It may also be argued that pinpointing the position of a football involves the exercise of skill, since those who are more knowledgeable on the matter of the angle at which a ball may move from the head or legs of a professional player may stand a better chance of winning the competition than those who have no knowledge of the game of football at all. However, this is only relevant to cases falling within s. 14(1)(b) since skill is not a relevant factor in s. 14(1)(a).

The main difficulty with s. 14(1)(b) is that 'substantial skill' is required to render the competition lawful, but the requirement of skill has not been the subject of direct judicial scrutiny. It must mean more than just the absence of luck, otherwise s. 14 would not differ from the requirements of the lottery laws. However, in *Witty* v *World Service Ltd* [1936] Ch 303, the court, having decided that a competition which required participants to use their geographical knowledge to identify photographs of parts of the United Kingdom was not a lottery, failed to consider whether the competition required the exercise of substantial skill. But this does not help to decide whether individual research or the use of native wit constitutes the exercise of substantial skill (cf. the *Telemillion case* considered above).

Neither branch of s. 14 mentions an element of payment and it is almost certainly the case that the provisions of s. 14 will apply whether participants have been require to pay for entry or not (*Imperial Tobacco Ltd* v *Attorney-General* [1981] AC 718).

20.4 SALES PROMOTION AND EUROPE

It has been seen already that the European Community has begun to show a distinct interest in consumer affairs and has started to develop a distinct policy in favour of consumers. However, as has also been noted, the consumer interest has to be balanced against other objectives of the EC, such as the desire to eliminate, so far as possible, all unreasonable restrictions upon free trade so as to facilitate the creation of a single market for goods and services across the whole of the Community. In particular, EC rules on quantitative restrictions on trade (see EC Treaty, art. 30) and measures having equivalent effect following the decision of the European Court of Justice in *Rewe-Zentrale AG* v *Bundesmonopolverwaltung für Branntwein* (case 120/78) [1979] ECR 649 (the *Cassis de Dijon case*) are such that some domestic provisions on sales promotion activities may be declared unlawful (see further chapters 2, 14 and 19).

So far as sales promotion matters are concerned, an issue which has arisen for consideration is whether domestic rules on the practice of 'loss-leading' are capable of infringing the EC Treaty, art. 30, in respect of quantitative restrictions on trade. In *Groupement National des Négociants en Pommes de Terre de Belgique* v *ITM Belgium SA* (case C-63/94) [1996] ECR I-2467 it was held that art. 30 had no application to domestic laws which place controls on the practice of loss-leading or sales which generate only a very low level of profit, provided the relevant law applied to all traders operating in the national territory concerned and made no distinction between domestically produced and imported products (*Criminal Proceedings against Keck* (cases C-267 & 268/91) [1993] I-ECR 6097 applied).

Index